나의 토익 목표 달성기

TEST 1을 풀고난 후, 점수에 따라 자신의 수준에 맞는 학습 플랜을 선택하세요.

☐ [800점 이상] 2주 완성 학습 플랜
☐ [600~795점] 3주 완성 학습 플랜
☐ [595점 이하] 4주 완성 학습 플랜

※ 일 단위의 상세 학습 플랜은 p.24~25에 있습니다.

각 TEST를 마친 후, 해당 TEST의 점수를 ・로 표시하여 자신의 점수 변화를 확인하세요.

Listening

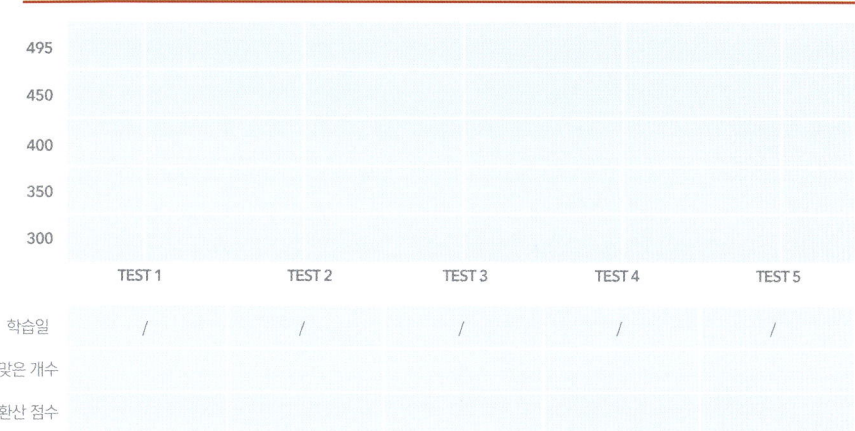

Reading

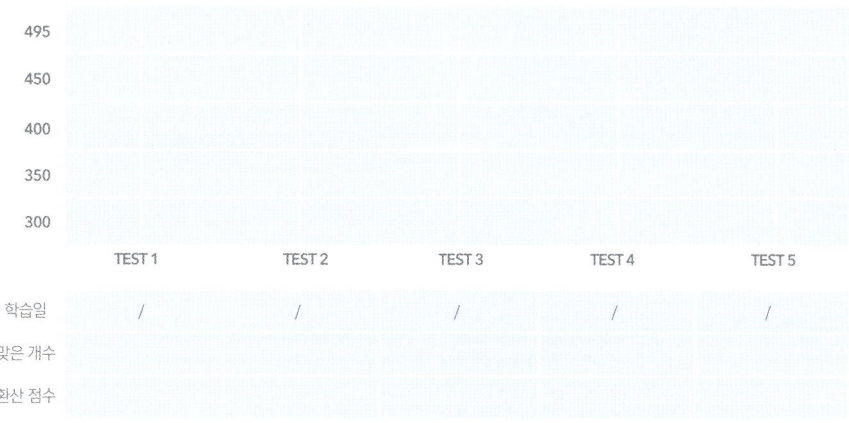

※ 점수 환산표는 p.244~245에 있습니다.

해커스 토익
실전 LC+RC 3
모의고사 + 해설집

해커스 어학연구소

무료 토익·토스·오픽·지텔프 자료
Hackers.co.kr

최신 토익 경향을
완벽하게 반영한 문제로
토익 목표 점수를 달성하세요.

토익 시험을 효과적으로 준비하려면
무엇보다도 최신 경향을 반영한 문제 풀이를 통해
'토익 실전 감각'을 길러야 합니다.

≪해커스 토익 실전 LC+RC 3≫는 2024년 하반기 출제 경향을 완벽 반영했습니다.
실제 시험과 가장 비슷한 문제들을 통해
여러분의 토익 목표 점수 달성에 확실한 해결책이 되기를 소망합니다.

'최신 토익 경향' 코너로
토익 트렌드 파악!

정확한 해석·해설로
정답과 오답의 근거 확실히 이해!

LC·RC 실전 모의고사 5회분으로
실전 감각 UP!

Contents

책의 특징 및 활용 방법	6
토익 소개	10
파트별 출제 유형 및 전략	12
수준별 맞춤 학습 플랜	24
정답	238
점수 환산표	244
Answer Sheet	247

📖 문제집 [본책]

TEST 1
LISTENING TEST	28
READING TEST	40

TEST 2
LISTENING TEST	70
READING TEST	82

TEST 3
LISTENING TEST	112
READING TEST	124

TEST 4
LISTENING TEST	154
READING TEST	166

TEST 5
LISTENING TEST	196
READING TEST	208

해커스 토익 실전 LC+RC 3

해설집 [책 속의 책]

TEST 1
LISTENING TEST 정답·스크립트·해석·해설　　2
READING TEST 정답·해석·해설　　27

TEST 2
LISTENING TEST 정답·스크립트·해석·해설　　49
READING TEST 정답·해석·해설　　73

TEST 3
LISTENING TEST 정답·스크립트·해석·해설　　95
READING TEST 정답·해석·해설　　119

TEST 4
LISTENING TEST 정답·스크립트·해석·해설　　140
READING TEST 정답·해석·해설　　164

TEST 5
LISTENING TEST 정답·스크립트·해석·해설　　185
READING TEST 정답·해석·해설　　209

단어암기자료(HackersIngang.com)

받아쓰기&쉐도잉 워크북(HackersIngang.com)

온라인 실전모의고사(Hackers.co.kr)

책의 특징 및 활용 방법

01 최신 경향을 반영한 모의고사 5회분으로 실전 감각을 높이세요.

토익 실전 감각을 높이기 위해서는 최신 경향이 반영된 문제를 풀어보아야 합니다. ≪해커스 토익 실전 LC+RC 3≫는 2024년 하반기 출제 경향을 반영한 LC와 RC 실전 모의고사를 각 5회분씩 수록하여, 한 권의 교재로 토익 문제 풀이 연습을 끝낼 수 있도록 구성했습니다.

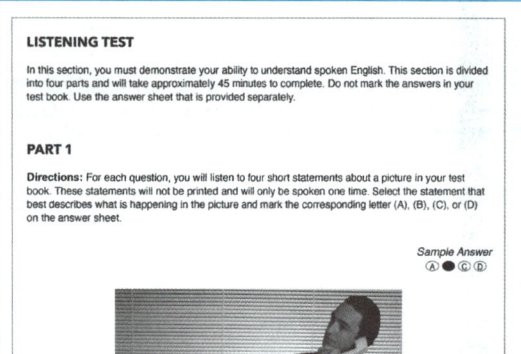

LISTENING TEST

최신 토익 시험의 출제 경향을 완벽하게 반영한 **LC 실전 모의고사 5회분**을 수록하였습니다. 실전과 가장 비슷한 문제들을 풀어보며 빠르게 실전 감각을 쌓을 수 있습니다.

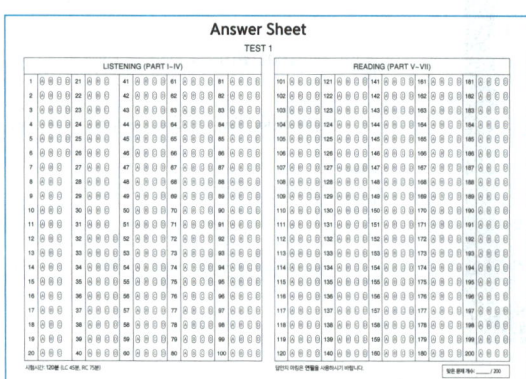

READING TEST

최신 토익 시험의 출제 경향을 완벽하게 반영한 **RC 실전 모의고사 5회분**을 수록하였습니다. 실전과 가장 비슷한 문제들을 풀어보며 빠르게 실전 감각을 쌓을 수 있습니다.

Answer Sheet

교재 뒤에 수록된 Answer Sheet를 활용하여, 답안지 마킹까지 실제 시험처럼 연습해 봄으로써 시간 관리 방법을 익히고, 실전 감각을 보다 극대화할 수 있습니다.

02 정확한 해석·해설로 정답과 오답의 근거를 확실히 파악하세요.

문제 풀이 후, 해석·해설을 확인하며 정답과 오답의 근거를 확실하게 정리하는 것이 중요합니다. ≪해커스 토익 실전 LC+RC 3≫는 모든 문제에 대한 정확한 해석과 해설을 수록하여, 틀린 문제의 원인을 파악하고 보완할 수 있도록 구성했습니다.

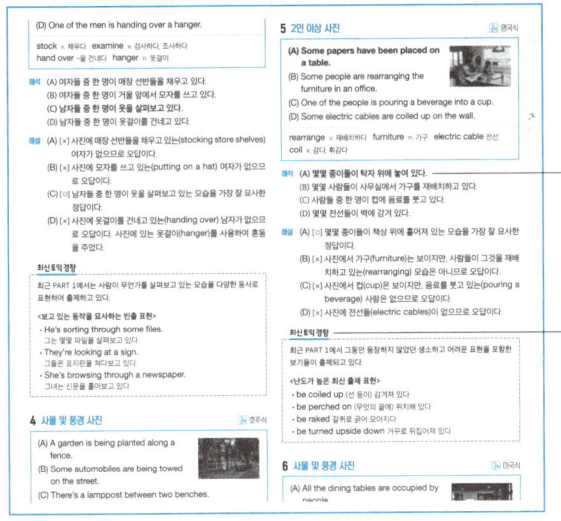

상세한 해석·해설
모든 문제에 대한 해석과 함께, 정답은 물론 오답의 이유까지 상세하게 설명한 해설을 통해 **틀린 문제의 원인을 파악하고 약점을 보완**할 수 있습니다.

최신 토익 경향
최신 토익 경향을 철저히 분석하여 출제 포인트와 함께 알아두면 좋을 빈출 표현들을 제공합니다. 이를 통해 **가장 최신 경향을 파악**하며 복습할 수 있습니다.

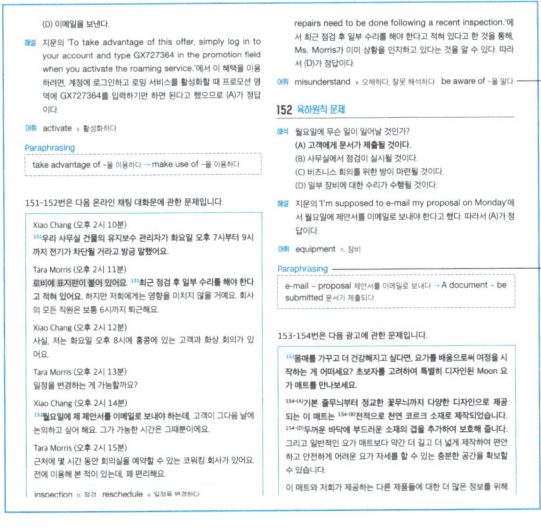

어휘
지문과 문제에서 사용된 **단어와 표현의 의미를 품사와 함께 수록**하여 문제를 복습할 때 사전을 찾는 불편을 덜 수 있습니다.

Paraphrasing
지문의 내용이 문제에서 패러프레이징 된 경우, 이를 정리하여 한눈에 확인할 수 있도록 하였습니다.

03 다양한 부가 학습자료로 약점을 보완하세요.

문제 풀이 후, 자신의 약점이 무엇인지를 파악하고 다양한 학습자료를 이용하여 이를 보완하는 것이 중요합니다. ≪해커스 토익 실전 LC+RC 3≫는 자신의 약점을 보완하여 목표 점수에 좀 더 빠르게 도달할 수 있도록 다양한 부가 학습자료를 제공하고 있습니다.

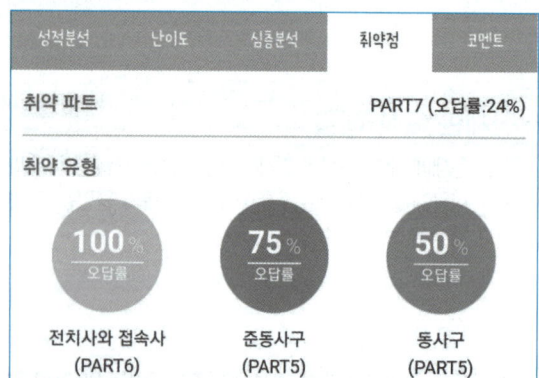

인공지능 1:1 토익어플 '빅플'

교재의 문제를 풀고 답안을 입력하기만 하면, 인공지능 어플 '해커스토익 빅플'이 **자동 채점은 물론 성적분석표와 취약 유형 심층 분석까지 제공**합니다. 이를 통해, 자신이 가장 많이 틀리는 취약 유형이 무엇인지 확인하고, 관련 문제들을 추가로 학습하며 취약 유형을 집중 공략하여 약점을 보완할 수 있습니다.

단어암기자료 (PDF & MP3)

해커스인강(HackersIngang.com) 사이트에서 무료로 제공하는 **단어암기자료(PDF & MP3)**를 활용하여, 교재에 수록된 테스트의 중요 단어와 표현을 복습하고 암기할 수 있습니다.

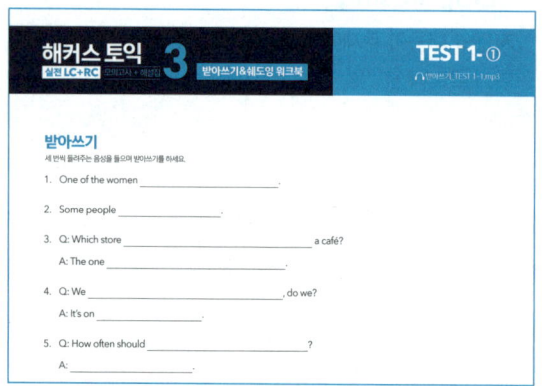

받아쓰기 & 쉐도잉 워크북 (PDF & MP3)

해커스인강(HackersIngang.com) 사이트에서 무료로 제공하는 **받아쓰기 & 쉐도잉 워크북(PDF & MP3)**을 활용하여, 교재에 수록된 핵심 문장을 복습하고 LC 점수를 향상할 수 있는 기본 실력을 갖출 수 있습니다.

해커스 토익 실전 LC+RC 3

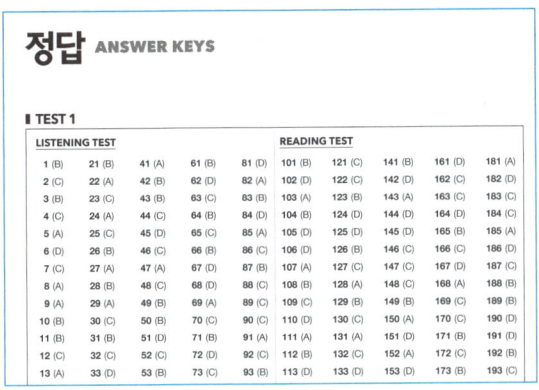

정답녹음 MP3

해커스인강(HackersIngang.com) 사이트에서 무료로 제공하는 **정답녹음 MP3**를 활용하여, 문제 풀이 후 보다 편리하게 채점할 수 있습니다.

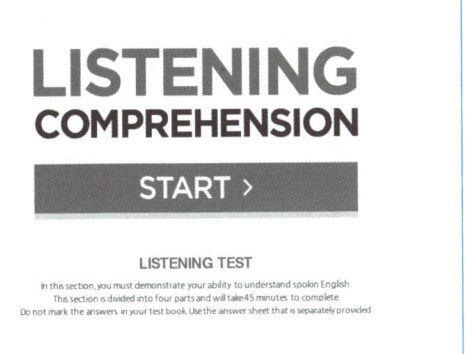

무료 온라인 실전모의고사

해커스토익(Hackers.co.kr) 사이트에서 제공하는 **온라인 실전모의고사**를 추가로 풀어보며 실전 감각을 키울 수 있습니다.

방대한 무료 학습자료

해커스토익(Hackers.co.kr) 사이트에서 토익 적중 예상특강을 비롯한 **방대하고 유용한 토익 학습자료**를 무료로 이용할 수 있습니다.

토익 소개

토익이란 무엇인가?

TOEIC은 Test Of English for International Communication의 약자로 영어가 모국어가 아닌 사람들을 대상으로 언어 본래의 기능인 '커뮤니케이션' 능력에 중점을 두고 일상생활 또는 국제 업무 등에 필요한 실용영어 능력을 평가하는 시험입니다. 토익은 일상 생활 및 비즈니스 현장에서 필요로 하는 내용을 평가하기 위해 개발되었고 다음과 같은 실용적인 주제들을 주로 다룹니다.

- 협력 개발: 연구, 제품 개발
- 재무 회계: 대출, 투자, 세금 회계, 은행 업무
- 일반 업무: 계약, 협상, 마케팅, 판매
- 기술 영역: 전기, 공업 기술, 컴퓨터, 실험실
- 사무 영역: 회의, 서류 업무
- 물품 구입: 쇼핑, 물건 주문, 대금 지불
- 식사: 레스토랑, 회식, 만찬
- 문화: 극장, 스포츠, 피크닉
- 건강: 의료 보험, 병원 진료, 치과
- 제조: 생산 조립 라인, 공장 경영
- 직원: 채용, 은퇴, 급여, 진급, 고용 기회
- 주택: 부동산, 이사, 기업 부지

토익 파트별 구성

구성		내용	문항 수	시간	배점
LISTENING TEST	PART 1	사진 묘사	6문항(1번-6번)	45분	495점
	PART 2	질의응답	25문항(7번-31번)		
	PART 3	짧은 대화	39문항, 13지문(32번-70번)		
	PART 4	짧은 담화	30문항, 10지문(71번-100번)		
READING TEST	PART 5	단문 빈칸 채우기(문법/어휘)	30문항(101번-130번)	75분	495점
	PART 6	장문 빈칸 채우기(문법/어휘/문장 고르기)	16문항, 4지문(131번-146번)		
	PART 7	지문 읽고 문제 풀기(독해)	54문항, 15지문(147번-200번)		
		- 단일 지문(Single Passage)	- 29문항, 10지문(147번-175번)		
		- 이중 지문(Double Passages)	- 10문항, 2지문(176번-185번)		
		- 삼중 지문(Triple Passages)	- 15문항, 3지문(186번-200번)		
TOTAL	7 PARTs		200문항	120분	990점

토익, 접수부터 성적 확인까지

1. 토익 접수

접수 기간 확인	사진(jpg 형식) 준비	인터넷/애플리케이션 접수
· 접수 기간을 TOEIC위원회 인터넷 사이트(www.toeic.co.kr) 혹은 공식 애플리케이션에서 확인합니다.	· 접수 시, jpg 형식의 사진 파일이 필요하므로 미리 준비해둡니다.	· TOEIC위원회 홈페이지 또는 애플리케이션의 시험 접수 창에서 절차에 따라 정보를 입력합니다.

2. 토익 응시

준비물

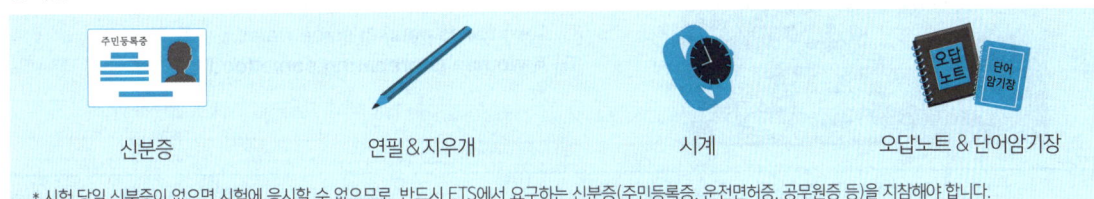

신분증   연필&지우개   시계   오답노트 & 단어암기장

* 시험 당일 신분증이 없으면 시험에 응시할 수 없으므로, 반드시 ETS에서 요구하는 신분증(주민등록증, 운전면허증, 공무원증 등)을 지참해야 합니다. ETS에서 인정하는 신분증 종류는 TOEIC위원회 인터넷 사이트(www.toeic.co.kr)에서 확인 가능합니다.

시험 진행 순서

정기시험/추가시험 (오전)	추가시험 (오후)	진행 내용
AM 09:30 - 09:45	PM 2:30 - 2:45	답안지 작성 및 오리엔테이션
AM 09:45 - 09:50	PM 2:45 - 2:50	쉬는 시간
AM 09:50 - 10:10	PM 2:50 - 3:10	신분 확인 및 문제지 배부
AM 10:10 - 10:55	PM 3:10 - 3:55	듣기 평가 (Listening Test)
AM 10:55 - 12:10	PM 3:55 - 5:10	독해 평가 (Reading Test)

* 추가시험은 토요일 오전 또는 오후에 시행되므로 이 사항도 꼼꼼히 확인합니다.
* 당일 진행 순서에 대한 더 자세한 내용은 해커스토익(Hackers.co.kr) 사이트에서 확인할 수 있습니다.

3. 성적 확인

성적 발표일	시험일로부터 약 10일 이후 낮 12시 (성적 발표 기간은 회차마다 상이함)
성적 확인	TOEIC위원회 인터넷 사이트(www.toeic.co.kr) 혹은 공식 애플리케이션
성적표 수령 방법	우편 수령 또는 온라인 출력(시험 접수 시 선택 가능) *온라인 출력은 성적 발표 즉시 발급 가능하나, 우편 수령은 약 7일가량의 발송 기간이 소요될 수 있음

파트별 출제 유형 및 전략

PART 1 사진 묘사 (6문제)

- PART 1은 주어진 4개의 보기 중에서 사진의 상황을 가장 잘 묘사한 보기를 선택하는 파트입니다.
- 문제지에는 사진만 제시되고 음성에서는 4개의 보기를 들려줍니다.

문제 형태

[문제지]

1.

[음성]

Number 1.

Look at the picture marked number one in your test book.

(A) A woman is serving a meal.
(B) A woman is washing a bowl.
(C) A woman is pouring some water.
(D) A woman is preparing some food.

출제 경향 및 대비 전략

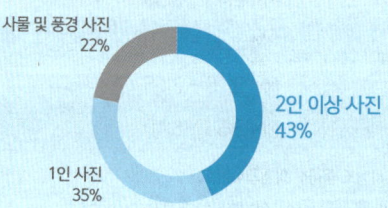

사물 및 풍경 사진 22%
2인 이상 사진 43%
1인 사진 35%

PART 1에서는 사람 중심 사진이 평균 4~5개로 가장 많이 출제됩니다. 사람 중심 사진에서는 2인 이상 사진이 3~4개로 가장 많이 출제되고, 1인 사진이 2~3개 정도 출제됩니다.

핵심 대비 전략

보기를 듣기 전에 사진 유형을 확인하고 관련 표현을 미리 연상합니다.
보기를 듣기 전에 사람의 유무 및 수에 따라 사진 유형을 확인하고, 사람의 동작/상태 또는 사물의 상태/위치와 관련된 표현들을 미리 연상하면 보기를 훨씬 명확하게 들을 수 있어 정답 선택이 쉬워집니다.

사람이 등장하는 사진에 사물을 묘사한 보기가 정답으로 출제될 수 있습니다.
사람이 등장하는 사진이지만, 사물을 묘사한 보기가 정답으로 출제되는 문제가 매회 평균 1문제씩 출제되니, 사진을 꼼꼼히 확인한 후 각 보기를 들어야 합니다.

PART 2 질의응답 (25문제)

- PART 2는 주어진 질문이나 진술에 가장 적절한 응답을 선택하는 파트입니다.
- 문제지에는 질문과 보기가 제시되지 않으며 음성에서는 질문과 3개의 보기를 들려줍니다.

문제 형태

[문제지]

7. Mark your answer on your answer sheet.

[음성]

Number 7.

Where is the nearest park?

(A) There's one on Lincoln Avenue.
(B) No, I don't drive.
(C) I'm nearly finished.

출제 경향 및 대비 전략

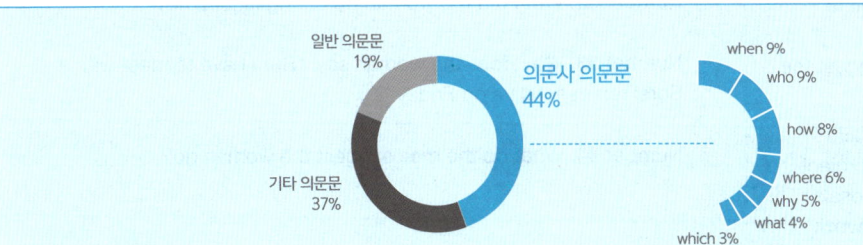

의문사 의문문이 평균 11~12개로 가장 많이 출제됩니다. 다음으로는 기타 의문문(평서문 및 선택/부가/제안·요청 의문문)이 평균 9~10개, 일반 의문문(조동사/Be동사/부정 의문문)이 평균 4~5개 출제됩니다.

핵심 대비 전략

질문의 첫 단어는 절대 놓치지 않고 듣습니다.
PART 2에서 평균 11~12문제 정도 출제되는 의문사 의문문은 첫 단어인 의문사만 들어도 대부분 정답을 선택할 수 있습니다. 단, 부가 의문문은 평서문 뒤에 덧붙여진 'isn't it'이나 'right', 선택 의문문은 질문 중간에 접속사 'or'를 듣고 그 유형을 파악해야 합니다.

질문에 간접적으로 응답하는 문제들이 최근 많이 출제되고 있습니다.
간접적인 응답에는 질문에 대해 되묻는 응답, Yes/No 대신 우회적으로 답하는 응답, 모르겠다는 의도의 모호한 응답이 포함되는데, 질문을 듣고 한 가지의 응답만 예상하기보다는 모든 보기들의 숨은 의도를 정확히 파악하여 가장 적절한 것을 정답으로 골라야 합니다.

파트별 출제 유형 및 전략

PART 3 짧은 대화 (총 13지문, 39문제)

- PART 3는 2~3명의 대화를 듣고 이와 관련된 3개의 문제의 정답을 선택하는 파트입니다.
- 문제지에는 하나의 질문과 4개의 보기로 구성된 39문제가 제시되고, 일부 문제는 시각 자료가 함께 제시됩니다. 음성으로는 하나의 대화와 이에 대한 3개의 문제의 질문을 각각 들려줍니다.

문제 형태

[문제지]

32. What did the woman do during lunchtime?

   (A) Spoke with a supervisor
   (B) Called an important client
   (C) Visited another company
   (D) Finished a report

33. Why does the woman say, "But I have to meet with a Sorel representative on Friday"?

   (A) To confirm an appointment
   (B) To explain a mistake
   (C) To express concern
   (D) To change a deadline

34. What do the men suggest the woman do?

   (A) Deal with a complaint
   (B) Work on another project
   (C) Review their proposals
   (D) Meet them after work

[음성]

Questions 32 through 34 refer to the following conversation with three speakers.

W: George, Jerry . . . I'm sorry I couldn't make it for lunch today. My boss wanted to talk with me about the advertising campaign for Sorel Incorporated. This is a big project, and I'm a little nervous about it.

M1: Don't worry. You're a hard worker. And our clients never complain about your work.

W: But I have to meet with a Sorel representative on Friday. I'm not sure if I'll be able to create a proposal in time.

M2: Why don't we all go to a café after work? We can help you come up with some ideas.

M1: Yeah. We're happy to help.

Number 32. What did the woman do during lunchtime?

Number 33. Why does the woman say, "But I have to meet with a Sorel representative on Friday"?

Number 34. What do the men suggest the woman do?

해커스 토익 실전 LC+RC 3

출제 경향 및 대비 전략

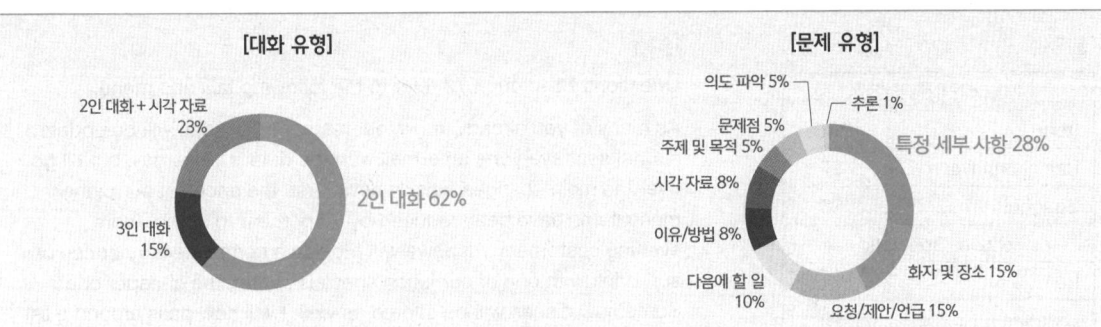

PART 3에서는 3인 대화가 매회 2개, 2인 대화가 매회 8개, 문제와 시각 자료를 함께 확인하면서 푸는 시각 자료 문제가 매회 3개 출제됩니다. 제시된 인용어구에 내포된 의도를 파악하는 의도 파악 문제는 매회 2개 출제됩니다.

핵심 대비 전략

대화를 듣기 전에 반드시 문제를 먼저 읽어야 합니다.
질문의 핵심 어구를 미리 읽으면 대화의 어느 부분을 중점적으로 들어야 할지 전략을 세울 수 있습니다. 시각 자료가 제시된 문제라면, 문제와 시각 자료를 함께 파악합니다. 의도 파악 문제라면, 제시된 인용어구를 먼저 확인하고 해당 인용어구가 사용될 수 있는 문맥을 미리 예측합니다.

대화를 들으면서 동시에 정답을 선택해야 합니다.
문제를 읽을 때 세워놓은 전략에 따라, 대화를 들으면서 3개 문제의 정답을 선택해야 합니다. 즉, 대화를 들려주는 음성이 끝날 때에는 3개 문제의 정답 선택도 완료되어 있어야 합니다.

대화의 초반은 반드시 들어야 합니다.
PART 3에서는 대화의 초반에 언급된 내용 중 80% 이상이 문제로 출제되며, 특히 주제 및 목적 문제나 화자 및 장소 문제처럼 전체 대화 관련 문제에 대한 정답의 단서는 대부분 대화의 초반에 언급됩니다. 대화 초반의 내용을 듣지 못하면 대화 후반에서 언급된 특정 표현을 사용한 오답을 정답으로 선택하는 오류를 범할 수 있으므로 주의해야 합니다.

3인이 등장하는 대화에 유의합니다.
3인 대화에서 같은 성별의 화자 2명은 다른 국적의 발음으로 구분되므로, 미국·영국·호주·캐나다식 발음을 듣고 화자를 구분하여 대화의 문맥을 정확하게 파악하는 연습을 합니다.

파트별 출제 유형 및 전략

PART 4 짧은 담화 (총 10지문, 30문제)

- PART 4는 1명의 담화를 듣고 이와 관련된 3개의 문제의 정답을 선택하는 파트입니다.
- 문제지에는 하나의 질문과 4개의 보기로 구성된 30문제가 제시되고, 일부 문제는 시각 자료가 함께 제시됩니다. 음성으로는 하나의 담화와 이에 대한 3개의 문제의 질문을 각각 들려줍니다.

문제 형태

[문제지]

Lunch Specials	
Item	Price
Panini Sandwich	$7
Spaghetti	$6

Dinner Specials	
Item	Price
Lasagna	$9
Grilled Chicken	$11

71. What did the speaker do yesterday?

    (A) Raised dish prices
    (B) Attended a staff gathering
    (C) Met with customers
    (D) Sent menu information

72. Look at the graphic. Which meal will come with a complimentary beverage?

    (A) Panini Sandwich
    (B) Spaghetti
    (C) Lasagna
    (D) Grilled Chicken

73. What will the speaker probably do next?

    (A) Arrange some tables
    (B) Stock some ingredients
    (C) Hand out a list
    (D) Print a coupon

[음성]

Questions 71 through 73 refer to the following talk and menu.

As many of you already know, our restaurant's menu will be updated soon. I sent everyone an e-mail with the details yesterday, but I'll go over the main changes quickly now. First, the prices of our dinner menu items have been reduced by 10 percent to attract more evening customers. Also, we will provide a complimentary coffee or soft drink with one of our lunch specials . . . uh, the cheaper one. Some new dishes will be offered as well. I will now pass around a list of these dishes and the ingredients they will contain. Please study it so you'll be able to answer diners' questions.

Number 71. What did the speaker do yesterday?

Number 72. Look at the graphic. Which meal will come with a complimentary beverage?

Number 73. What will the speaker probably do next?

출제 경향 및 대비 전략

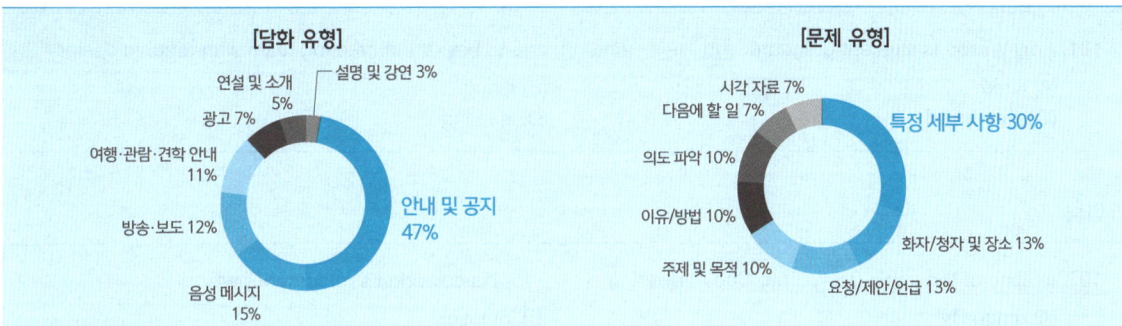

PART 4에서는 안내 및 공지와 음성 메시지가 매회 나오고 있습니다. 뉴스 보도나 팟캐스트 등의 방송·보도, 여행·관람·견학 안내, 광고 등의 담화도 자주 나오는 편입니다. 문제와 시각 자료를 함께 확인하면서 푸는 시각 자료 문제는 매회 2개 출제되고, 제시된 인용어구에 내포된 의도를 파악하는 의도 파악 문제는 매회 3개 출제됩니다.

핵심 대비 전략

담화를 듣기 전에 반드시 문제를 먼저 읽고, 시각 자료의 내용을 파악해야 합니다.
질문의 핵심 어구를 미리 읽으면 담화의 어느 부분을 중점적으로 들어야 할지 전략을 세울 수 있습니다. 시각 자료가 제시된 문제라면, 문제와 시각 자료를 함께 확인하면서 시각 자료의 종류와 내용을 파악합니다. 의도 파악 문제라면, 제시된 인용어구를 먼저 확인하고 해당 인용어구가 사용될 수 있는 문맥을 미리 예측합니다.

담화를 들으면서 동시에 정답을 선택해야 합니다.
문제를 읽을 때 세워놓은 전략에 따라, 담화를 들으면서 3개 문제의 정답을 선택해야 합니다. 즉, 담화를 들려주는 음성이 끝날 때에는 3개 문제의 정답 선택도 완료되어 있어야 합니다.

담화의 초반은 반드시 들어야 합니다.
PART 4에서는 담화의 초반에 언급된 내용 중 80% 이상이 문제로 출제되며, 특히 주제 및 목적 문제나 화자/청자 및 장소 문제처럼 전체 담화 관련 문제에 대한 정답의 단서는 대부분 담화의 초반에 언급됩니다. 담화 초반의 내용을 듣지 못할 경우, 더 이상 문제와 관련된 내용이 언급되지 않아 정답 선택이 어려워질 수 있으므로 주의해야 합니다.

파트별 출제 유형 및 전략

PART 5 단문 빈칸 채우기 (30문제)

- PART 5는 한 문장의 빈칸에 알맞은 문법 사항이나 어휘를 4개의 보기 중에서 골라 채우는 파트입니다.
- PART 7 문제 풀이에 시간이 모자라지 않으려면 각 문제를 20~22초 내로, 총 30문제를 약 11분 내에 끝내야 합니다.

문제 형태

1. 문법

> 101. Amy Wilson is a recent graduate who ------- a month ago to help the marketing team with graphic design.
> (A) hired (B) hiring
> **(C) was hired** (D) is hiring

2. 어휘

> 102. In spite of the traffic delays, Mr. Cho showed up ------- for his coworker's retirement party.
> (A) gradually (B) intensely
> (C) considerably **(D) punctually**

출제 경향 및 대비 전략

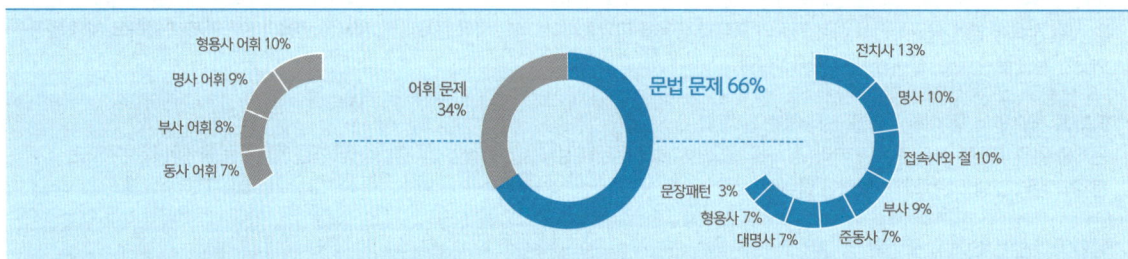

Part 5에서는 문법 문제가 평균 20~21개, 어휘 문제가 평균 9~10개 출제됩니다. 문법 문제에서는 전치사, 접속사 문제가 매회 1~2개씩 꾸준히 출제됩니다. 어휘 문제에서는 문맥에 맞는 동사, 명사, 형용사, 부사 어휘를 고르는 문제가 매회 2~3개씩 골고루 나옵니다.

핵심 대비 전략

보기를 보고 문법 문제인지, 어휘 문제인지를 파악합니다.
보기가 어근은 같지만 형태가 다른 단어들로 구성되어 있다면 문법 문제, 같은 품사의 어휘들로 구성되어 있으면 어휘 문제입니다.

문제 유형에 따라 빈칸 주변이나 문장의 전체적인 구조 및 문맥을 통해 정답을 선택합니다.
문법 문제는 빈칸 주변이나 문장의 전체적인 구조를 통해 빈칸에 적합한 문법적 요소를 정답으로 선택합니다. 만약 구조만으로 풀 수 없는 경우, 문맥을 확인하여 정답을 선택합니다. 어휘 문제는 문맥에 가장 적합한 어휘를 정답으로 선택합니다.

PART 6 장문 빈칸 채우기 (총 4지문, 16문제)

- PART 6는 한 지문 내 4개의 빈칸에 알맞은 문법 사항이나 어휘, 또는 문장을 4개의 보기 중에서 골라 채우는 파트입니다.
- PART 7 문제 풀이에 시간이 모자라지 않으려면 각 문제를 25~30초 내로, 총 16문제를 약 8분 내에 끝내야 합니다.

문제 형태

Questions 131-134 refer to the following e-mail.

-------. As you know, you are in charge of driving our visitor from Fennel Corporation, Mr. Palmer. He will be
131.
here as scheduled from May 16 to 20. However, his arrival time from Dublin has been moved back four hours
because he ------- a quick stop in New York. This means you do not need to be at the airport until 2 P.M. on
132.
the 16th. Also, the factory tour ------- he was supposed to take on Monday morning has been canceled. He'll
133.
have a breakfast meeting with the plant manager instead at the Oberlin Hotel. Attached is a revised -------.
134.

131. (A) Regretfully, Mr. Palmer will no longer be
     needing our services.
   **(B) I'm writing to inform you of a few
     changes concerning our client.**
   (C) The following are some details about the
     new factory manager.
   (D) Finally, I have received the new schedule for
     your flight to Dublin.

132. (A) will be made   **(B) is making**
     (C) had made   (D) has been making

133. (A) this   (B) what
     (C) when   **(D) that**

134. **(A) itinerary**   (B) estimate
     (C) transcript   (D) inventory

출제 경향 및 대비 전략

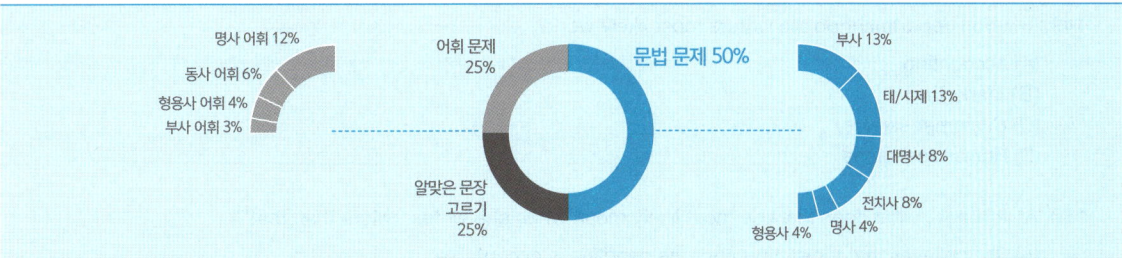

PART 6에서는 빈칸에 알맞은 문장을 고르는 문제가 매회 4개 출제됩니다. 문법 문제는 평균 7~8개, 어휘 문제는 평균 4~5개가 출제됩니다.

핵심 대비 전략

빈칸이 포함된 문장, 또는 앞뒤 문장이나 지문 전체의 문맥을 통해 정답을 선택합니다.
빈칸이 포함된 문장만으로 정답 선택이 어려울 경우, 앞뒤 문장이나 지문 전체의 문맥을 파악하여 가장 적합한 보기를 정답으로 선택해야 합니다.

파트별 출제 유형 및 전략

PART 7 지문 읽고 문제 풀기 (총 15지문, 54문제)

- PART 7은 제시된 지문과 관련된 질문들에 대해 4개의 보기 중에서 가장 적절한 답을 선택하는 파트입니다.
- 독해 지문은 단일 지문(Single Passage), 이중 지문(Double Passages), 삼중 지문(Triple Passages)으로 나뉘며, 단일 지문에서 29문제, 이중 지문에서 10문제, 삼중 지문에서 15문제가 출제됩니다.
- PART 7의 모든 문제를 제한 시간 내에 풀려면 한 문제를 약 1분 내에 풀어야 합니다.

문제 형태

1. 단일 지문(Single Passage)

Questions 149-150 refer to the following text-message chain.

Natasha Lee   4:08 P.M.
Robert, about the sponsorship packages for the Shoreland Music Festival, do you want to go for the Platinum package? It allows us to broadcast commercials during the event.

Robert Brown   4:09 P.M.
That would give us good exposure. Plus, we can put up company banners at the venue.

Natasha Lee   4:10 P.M.
That's right. So, should I go ahead and sign us up? The deadline is this Friday.

Robert Brown   4:10 P.M.
Well, we can't spend any more than $6,000 on this. How much is it?

Natasha Lee   4:12 P.M.
More than that. How about the Gold sponsorship package then? It costs $5,250, and festival announcers will mention our company over the loudspeakers throughout the day.

Robert Brown   4:13 P.M.
That sounds OK to me. Send me all the details once you're done.

---

149. In which department do the writers most likely work?

   (A) Accounting
   (B) Marketing
   (C) Customer service
   (D) Human resources

150. At 4:12 P.M., what does Ms. Lee most likely mean when she writes, "More than that"?

   (A) She believes that registering after the deadline is acceptable.
   (B) She acknowledges that a cost exceeds a budgeted amount.
   (C) She would like to receive some additional sponsorship benefits.
   (D) She doubts that $6,000 is their maximum spending allowance.

2. 이중 지문(Double Passages)

Questions 176-180 refer to the following e-mail and online form.

To	Joshua Ellis <j.ellis@jagmail.com>
From	Travis Whitman <t.whitman@mywebpress.com>
Date	November 1
Subject	Action Needed on Your Account

Dear Ms. Ellis,

Your MyWebPress account is due to renew in 10 days. You have the option to pay for another year at the rate of $29.99, or you may choose the three-year option at $79.99. We also offer a premium version of MyWebPress that enables many more features and design templates. One year of the higher level software costs $49.99 while the three-year package price is $129.99.

These special prices are only available if your renewal form is received by November 10.

Thank you,

Travis Whitman

MyWebPress Subscription Renewal Form   Date: November 8

Please fill out all information to process your renewal request and payment.

Account Name	Joshua Ellis	Account Number	83402839

Please choose your renewal option:

	One Year	Three Years
MyWebPress Standard	☐ $29.99	☐ $79.99
MyWebPress Premium	■ $49.99	☐ $129.99
Pre-made Forms Add-On	☐ $5.99	☐ $8.99
Graphic Design Add-On	☐ $12.99	☐ $18.99

Payment Information:

Credit Card Type	☐ Bankster ■ SureCredit ☐ YPay	Card Number	2934 4992 0041
Expiration Date	November 30	Security Code	557

176. What is indicated about Mr. Ellis?

(A) He is using a new credit card for payment.
(B) He failed to meet a deadline set by MyWebPress.
(C) He chose an upgraded version of his original plan.
(D) He added some security features to his package.

...

파트별 출제 유형 및 전략

3. 삼중 지문(Triple Passages)

Questions 186-190 refer to the following Web page, form, and e-mail.

Laurel Art Center

Upcoming Events

Summer Sounds Fest • Concert featuring local musicians • June 5, from noon to 10 P.M. • Tickets go on sale May 15	**Spectacular Vistas** • Exhibit of watercolor paintings by local landscape artist Samantha Davey • Opens 6 P.M., July 3, at the Campbell Gallery • Refreshments provided by Gordon's Café
Exploring Wood • Seminar conducted by Paula Sue • Thursday July 6 from 10:00 P.M. to 4 P.M. • $25 for eight classes (participants must bring safety glasses and a pair of work gloves)	**Annual Craft Show** • Our biggest event of the year, featuring handicrafts made by talented local artists • August 5, 10 A.M. to 4 P.M. • Admission is $5 for adults and $2 for seniors • Includes a buffet lunch from Kostas Mediterranean Kitchen

To join our mailing list, click here.

Laurel Art Center

Registration Form

Name	Ella Chung	Date	June 12
Telephone	555-3205	Address	108 Spruce Drive Hendersonville, TN 37075
E-mail	e.chung@mymail.net		
Event title	Exploring Wood		

Payment method

☐ Cash (Please pay two weeks in advance to reserve your slot)
■ Credit card: Liberty Bancard 2347-8624-5098-5728

To	Melissa Hamada <m.hamada@laurelart.org>
From	Hector Villa <h.villa@laurelart.org>
Subject	Catering
Date	June 21

Dear Melissa,

As we discussed yesterday afternoon, Kostas Mediterranean Kitchen had to back out of catering our August 5 event due to a scheduling conflict. However, I've received confirmation that Asian Flavors can take their place. Please update our Web site to reflect this change.

Hector Villa
Activities director, Laurel Art Center

186. What is suggested about Ms. Chung?

 (A) She is a member of the Laurel Art Center.
 (B) She will be attending an upcoming exhibit.
 (C) She is expected to bring gear to an activity.
 (D) She will be charged $5 for admission to an event.

187. Which event will Asian Flavors be catering?

 (A) Summer Sounds Fest
 (B) Spectacular Vistas
 (C) Exploring Wood
 (D) Annual Craft Show

 ...

출제 경향 및 대비 전략

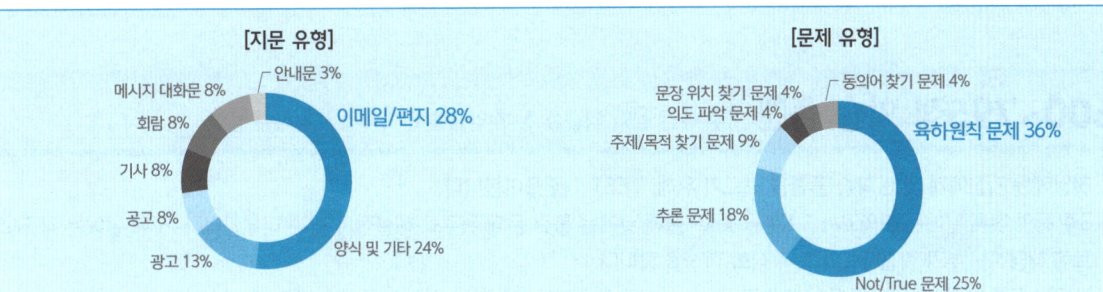

PART 7의 단일 지문에서는 메시지 대화문이 매회 2개 출제되며, 이 지문에서 의도 파악 문제가 각 1문제씩 함께 출제됩니다. 이메일, 편지, 기사도 자주 출제되는 지문 유형입니다. 문장 위치 찾기 문제는 기사, 편지, 공고에서 자주 나오며, 추론 문제는 연계 문제로도 자주 출제됩니다.

핵심 대비 전략

지문의 종류나 글의 제목을 먼저 확인하여 지문의 개괄적인 내용을 추측해야 합니다.
지문 맨 위에 지문을 소개하는 문장을 통해 언급된 지문의 종류를 확인하거나 글의 제목을 읽어서 지문이 어떤 내용을 담고 있을지 추측하며 문제를 풀도록 합니다.

질문을 먼저 읽고, 질문의 핵심 어구와 관련된 정답의 단서를 지문에서 확인해야 합니다.
질문을 읽고 질문의 핵심 어구를 파악한 후, 핵심 어구와 관련된 내용이 언급된 부분을 지문에서 찾아 정답의 단서를 확인합니다. 이중 지문이나 삼중 지문과 같은 연계 지문의 경우, 처음 확인한 단서만으로 정답을 선택할 수 없으면 첫 번째 단서와 관련된 두 번째 단서를 다른 지문에서 찾아야 합니다.

정답의 단서를 그대로 언급했거나 바꾸어 표현한 보기를 정답으로 선택해야 합니다.
정답의 단서를 그대로 언급했거나 바꾸어 표현(Paraphrasing)한 보기를 정답으로 선택해야 합니다. 지문에 나오는 단어를 그대로 이용한 함정 보기가 항상 출제되므로, 지문의 내용과 질문의 의도를 정확하게 파악하여 정답을 고르는 것이 중요합니다.

수준별 맞춤 학습 플랜

TEST 1을 풀어본 뒤, 교재 뒤에 수록된 점수 환산표(p.244~245)에서 자신의 환산 점수를 확인하고 환산 점수에 맞는 학습 플랜을 선택하세요. 매일 박스에 체크하며 공부하고, 해설집과 다양한 부가 학습자료를 활용해 각 테스트를 꼼꼼하게 리뷰하세요.

800점 이상 학습 플랜 2주 동안 문제 풀이와 리뷰를 번갈아 하며 빠르게 실전 감각을 높이는 플랜

- 첫날에는 자신에게 맞는 학습 플랜을 고르기 위해, TEST 1을 풀어봅니다.
- 2주 동안 격일로 하루는 모의고사 1회분을 풀고, 다음 날 리뷰합니다.
- 각 테스트를 마친 후, 테스트 뒤에 수록된 Review 체크리스트를 활용하면 더욱 꼼꼼히 리뷰할 수 있습니다.

	1st Day	2nd Day	3rd Day	4th Day	5th Day
1st week	TEST 1 풀기 ☐	TEST 1 리뷰 ☐	TEST 2 풀기 ☐	TEST 2 리뷰 ☐	TEST 3 풀기 ☐
2nd week	TEST 3 리뷰 ☐	TEST 4 풀기 ☐	TEST 4 리뷰 ☐	TEST 5 풀기 ☐	TEST 5 리뷰 ☐

* 2주 완성의 경우 위의 표를 따르고, 1주 단기 완성을 원할 경우 위의 표에서 이틀 분량을 하루 동안 학습하세요.

600~795점 학습 플랜 3주 동안 심화 학습을 통해 약점을 완벽하게 보완하는 플랜

- 첫날에는 자신에게 맞는 학습 플랜을 고르기 위해, TEST 1을 풀어봅니다.
- 3주 동안 첫째 날에는 모의고사 1회분을 풀고, 둘째 날에는 틀린 문제 위주로 해설집과 함께 리뷰합니다. 셋째 날에는 각 테스트에 해당하는 부가 학습자료와 함께 심화 학습을 합니다.
- 각 테스트를 마친 후, 테스트 뒤에 수록된 Review 체크리스트를 활용하면 더욱 꼼꼼히 리뷰할 수 있습니다.

	1st Day	2nd Day	3rd Day	4th Day	5th Day
1st week	TEST 1 풀기 ☐	TEST 1 리뷰 ☐	TEST 1 심화 학습 ☐	TEST 2 풀기 ☐	TEST 2 리뷰 ☐
2nd week	TEST 2 심화 학습 ☐	TEST 3 풀기 ☐	TEST 3 리뷰 ☐	TEST 3 심화 학습 ☐	TEST 4 풀기 ☐
3rd week	TEST 4 리뷰 ☐	TEST 4 심화 학습 ☐	TEST 5 풀기 ☐	TEST 5 리뷰 ☐	TEST 5 심화 학습 ☐

595점 이하 학습 플랜 4주 동안 각 영역을 꼼꼼하게 리뷰하여 실력을 향상시키는 플랜

- 첫날에는 자신에게 맞는 학습 플랜을 고르기 위해, TEST 1을 풀어봅니다.
- 4주 동안 첫째 날에는 리스닝 모의고사 1회분을 풀고 둘째 날에 리뷰, 셋째 날에는 리딩 모의고사 1회분을 풀고 넷째 날에 리뷰합니다. 학습 플랜의 마지막 날에는 그간 공부한 내용을 총복습합니다.
- 각 테스트를 마친 후, 테스트 뒤에 수록된 Review 체크리스트를 활용하면 더욱 꼼꼼히 리뷰할 수 있습니다.

	1st Day	2nd Day	3rd Day	4th Day	5th Day
1st week	TEST 1 풀기 ☐	TEST 1 LC 리뷰 ☐	TEST 1 RC 리뷰 ☐	TEST 2 LC 풀기 ☐	TEST 2 LC 리뷰 ☐
2nd week	TEST 2 RC 풀기 ☐	TEST 2 RC 리뷰 ☐	TEST 3 LC 풀기 ☐	TEST 3 LC 리뷰 ☐	TEST 3 RC 풀기 ☐
3rd week	TEST 3 RC 리뷰 ☐	TEST 4 LC 풀기 ☐	TEST 4 LC 리뷰 ☐	TEST 4 RC 풀기 ☐	TEST 4 RC 리뷰 ☐
4th week	TEST 5 LC 풀기 ☐	TEST 5 LC 리뷰 ☐	TEST 5 RC 풀기 ☐	TEST 5 RC 리뷰 ☐	총복습 ☐

무료 토익·토스·오픽·지텔프 자료

Hackers.co.kr

해커스 토익 실전 LC+RC 3

TEST 1

LISTENING TEST

PART 1
PART 2
PART 3
PART 4

READING TEST

PART 5
PART 6
PART 7

Review 체크리스트

잠깐! 테스트 전 아래 사항을 꼭 확인하세요.
1. 휴대전화의 전원을 끄셨나요? 예 □
2. Answer Sheet(p.247), 연필, 지우개, 시계를 준비하셨나요? 예 □
3. Listening MP3를 들을 준비가 되셨나요? 예 □

모든 준비가 완료되었으면 목표 점수를 떠올린 후 테스트를 시작합니다.
테스트를 마친 후, Review 체크리스트(p.68)를 보며 자신이 틀린 문제를 반드시 복습합니다.

※ TEST 1을 통해 본인의 실력을 평가해본 후, 본인에게 맞는 학습플랜(p.24~p.25)으로 본 교재를 효율적으로 학습해 보세요.

🎧 TEST 1.mp3
실전용·복습용 문제풀이 MP3 무료 다운로드 및 스트리밍 바로듣기 (HackersIngang.com)
* 실제 시험장의 소음까지 재현해 낸 고사장 소음/매미 버전 MP3, 영국식·호주식 발음 집중 MP3, 고속 버전 MP3까지
  구매하면 실전에 더욱 완벽히 대비할 수 있습니다.

무료MP3 바로듣기

LISTENING TEST

In this section, you must demonstrate your ability to understand spoken English. This section is divided into four parts and will take approximately 45 minutes to complete. Do not mark the answers in your test book. Use the answer sheet that is provided separately.

PART 1

Directions: For each question, you will listen to four short statements about a picture in your test book. These statements will not be printed and will only be spoken one time. Select the statement that best describes what is happening in the picture and mark the corresponding letter (A), (B), (C), or (D) on the answer sheet.

Sample Answer

The statement that best describes the picture is (B), "The man is sitting at the desk." So, you should mark letter (B) on the answer sheet.

1.

2.

3.

4.

5.

6.

PART 2

Directions: For each question, you will listen to a statement or question followed by three possible responses spoken in English. They will not be printed and will only be spoken one time. Select the best response and mark the corresponding letter (A), (B), or (C) on your answer sheet.

7. Mark your answer on your answer sheet.
8. Mark your answer on your answer sheet.
9. Mark your answer on your answer sheet.
10. Mark your answer on your answer sheet.
11. Mark your answer on your answer sheet.
12. Mark your answer on your answer sheet.
13. Mark your answer on your answer sheet.
14. Mark your answer on your answer sheet.
15. Mark your answer on your answer sheet.
16. Mark your answer on your answer sheet.
17. Mark your answer on your answer sheet.
18. Mark your answer on your answer sheet.
19. Mark your answer on your answer sheet.
20. Mark your answer on your answer sheet.
21. Mark your answer on your answer sheet.
22. Mark your answer on your answer sheet.
23. Mark your answer on your answer sheet.
24. Mark your answer on your answer sheet.
25. Mark your answer on your answer sheet.
26. Mark your answer on your answer sheet.
27. Mark your answer on your answer sheet.
28. Mark your answer on your answer sheet.
29. Mark your answer on your answer sheet.
30. Mark your answer on your answer sheet.
31. Mark your answer on your answer sheet.

PART 3

Directions: In this part, you will listen to several conversations between two or more speakers. These conversations will not be printed and will only be spoken one time. For each conversation, you will be asked to answer three questions. Select the best response and mark the corresponding letter (A), (B), (C), or (D) on your answer sheet.

32. Who most likely is the man?
    (A) A technician
    (B) An instructor
    (C) A receptionist
    (D) A doctor

33. What does the woman want to do?
    (A) Place an online order
    (B) Cancel an appointment
    (C) Purchase a gift card
    (D) Lengthen a session

34. How can the woman receive a discount?
    (A) By referring a service to a friend
    (B) By creating a membership
    (C) By signing up for a newsletter
    (D) By writing an online review

35. What is the conversation mainly about?
    (A) A community event
    (B) A maintenance fee
    (C) Some schedule changes
    (D) Some building repairs

36. According to the woman, what was approved this morning?
    (A) An employment offer
    (B) A financial plan
    (C) An event location
    (D) A construction permit

37. What will the speakers do next?
    (A) Talk to an intern
    (B) Update software programs
    (C) Examine some blueprints
    (D) Bring an invoice

38. What does the woman propose doing?
    (A) Making travel arrangements
    (B) Downloading a file
    (C) Writing some articles
    (D) Introducing online classes

39. What is the man concerned about?
    (A) The price of a service
    (B) The size of a venue
    (C) The location of an institution
    (D) The schedule of a program

40. According to the woman, what can be found on a Web site?
    (A) Contact information
    (B) Product reviews
    (C) Discount coupons
    (D) Pricing details

41. What will happen this Friday?
    (A) A fundraiser will be held.
    (B) A business will reopen.
    (C) Volunteer training will take place.
    (D) Some packages will be delivered.

42. What does the woman suggest?
    (A) Using a catering service
    (B) Changing a location
    (C) Replacing some furniture
    (D) Signing a contract

43. What does the man say about the library?
    (A) It was moved to a new location.
    (B) It was recently enlarged.
    (C) It is donating books to schools.
    (D) It is convenient to reach by public transportation.

GO ON TO THE NEXT PAGE

44. What has the woman been hired to do?
    (A) Create an itinerary
    (B) Take photographs
    (C) Lead a program
    (D) Maintain facilities

45. According to the supervisor, what is a goal of the organization?
    (A) To publish scientific information
    (B) To collect charitable donations
    (C) To recruit professional teachers
    (D) To promote environmental awareness

46. What does Gabriel express relief about?
    (A) A trail has reopened.
    (B) Equipment is set up.
    (C) Weather has improved.
    (D) Customer reviews are positive.

47. What are the speakers mainly discussing?
    (A) A tea party
    (B) A food fair
    (C) A hotel buffet
    (D) A company dinner

48. What does the woman say was most impressive?
    (A) The professional staff
    (B) The venue decorations
    (C) The dessert choices
    (D) The musical performance

49. What does the man imply when he says, "there are a lot of other people in those photos"?
    (A) Information should be verified.
    (B) Permission is needed.
    (C) A photographer had to be hired.
    (D) A Web site should be created.

50. What industry do the speakers most likely work in?
    (A) Healthcare
    (B) Law
    (C) Software
    (D) Publishing

51. What does the man say about the Quick-Pay program?
    (A) It is sold in different versions.
    (B) It needs to be updated.
    (C) It is widely used by companies.
    (D) It was recently adopted.

52. Who is Eric Murphy?
    (A) A customer
    (B) A consultant
    (C) A colleague
    (D) An applicant

53. What type of products does the speakers' company produce?
    (A) Vehicles
    (B) Electronics
    (C) Luggage
    (D) Furniture

54. What problem does the man describe?
    (A) Staffing shortages
    (B) Limited warehouse space
    (C) Increased manufacturing costs
    (D) Insufficient inventory

55. What does Caren agree to do?
    (A) Provide the study results
    (B) Conduct an interview
    (C) Request a budget increase
    (D) Check some references

56. What are the speakers discussing?
    (A) An employee orientation
    (B) A grand opening
    (C) A mechanical defect
    (D) A product launch

57. What is the woman worried about?
    (A) Repairing a machine
    (B) Meeting a deadline
    (C) Renovating a workspace
    (D) Issuing a product recall

58. What does the woman ask the man to do?
    (A) Send her a draft
    (B) Negotiate a price
    (C) Prepare a presentation
    (D) Assist her colleague

59. What does the woman's company make?
    (A) Sports drinks
    (B) Frozen meals
    (C) Nutritional supplements
    (D) Exercise clothes

60. Why does the man say, "With our digital billboards, you can display video clips"?
    (A) To ask for some feedback
    (B) To address a concern
    (C) To explain a regulation
    (D) To point out a recent improvement

61. What does the man say about the discount?
    (A) It was recently increased.
    (B) It is offered only for a week.
    (C) It varies depending on the service.
    (D) It is for long-term members.

Lakeville Rental Car		
Car Type	Number of Seats	Price per day
Sports car	2	$90
Sedan	4	$50
Minivan	6	$70
SUV	10	$100

62. Why does the man need to go to San Diego?
    (A) To attend a competition
    (B) To open a new business
    (C) To visit his family
    (D) To participate in a trade show

63. Look at the graphic. Which vehicle will the man select?
    (A) Sports car
    (B) Sedan
    (C) Minivan
    (D) SUV

64. What does the woman ask the man for?
    (A) A credit card
    (B) A driver's license
    (C) Proof of insurance
    (D) A set of keys

GO ON TO THE NEXT PAGE

Jason's Schedule	
Tuesday	Department meeting *All day
Wednesday	Conference call with clients *10 A.M. – 11:30 A.M.
Thursday	Team-building workshop *1:30 P.M. – 3:30 P.M.
Friday	Staff evaluations *9:30 A.M. – 11:30 A.M.

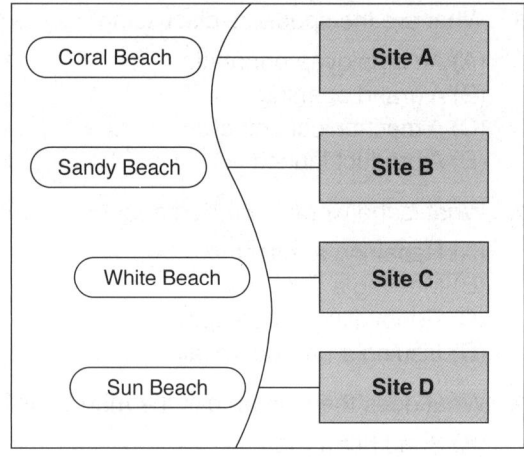

65. Look at the graphic. When will the speakers most likely attend an interview?

(A) On Tuesday
(B) On Wednesday
(C) On Thursday
(D) On Friday

66. What does the woman say she will do this afternoon?

(A) Reserve a conference room
(B) Print a copy of a document
(C) Announce some changes
(D) Order some supplies

67. According to the man, why did Mr. Bennet decide to join the speakers?

(A) A coworker is unavailable.
(B) He has a lot of interview experiences.
(C) His training has not been completed yet.
(D) The applicant applied for his team.

68. Who most likely are the speakers?

(A) Store owners
(B) Media representatives
(C) Property developers
(D) Event organizers

69. Look at the graphic. Which site has picnic tables set up?

(A) Site A
(B) Site B
(C) Site C
(D) Site D

70. What does the man want to change?

(A) Transportation services
(B) Security procedures
(C) Marketing methods
(D) Evaluation standards

PART 4

Directions: In this part, you will listen to several short talks by a single speaker. These talks will not be printed and will only be spoken one time. For each talk, you will be asked to answer three questions. Select the best response and mark the corresponding letter (A), (B), (C), or (D) on your answer sheet.

71. What type of business does the speaker work for?
    (A) A real estate agency
    (B) An Internet service provider
    (C) An online shopping platform
    (D) An office supply store

72. According to the speaker, what has caused a problem?
    (A) A computer virus
    (B) Unclear instructions
    (C) Old equipment
    (D) Bad weather

73. What can the listeners receive by text message?
    (A) A security code
    (B) A delivery notification
    (C) Progress updates
    (D) Feedback forms

74. What did the speaker do yesterday?
    (A) She completed a building plan.
    (B) She attended a meeting.
    (C) She organized a storage area.
    (D) She finalized a budget proposal.

75. What problem does the speaker mention?
    (A) A schedule conflict
    (B) A malfunctioning system
    (C) A lack of construction materials
    (D) A change in building regulations

76. What does the speaker ask the listeners to do?
    (A) Come up with some ideas
    (B) Use a different route
    (C) Review some manuals
    (D) Avoid taking leave days

77. Why is the speaker calling?
    (A) To confirm business hours
    (B) To describe a new policy
    (C) To make a recommendation
    (D) To discuss some charges

78. What is a feature of the card the speaker emphasizes?
    (A) It has no annual fee.
    (B) It can accumulate points.
    (C) It can be customized.
    (D) It has a low interest rate.

79. How can the listener receive a bonus?
    (A) By calling a phone number
    (B) By entering a special drawing
    (C) By applying before a deadline
    (D) By completing a survey

80. Where are the listeners?
    (A) At a theater
    (B) At a swimming pool
    (C) At an amusement park
    (D) At an art museum

81. Why does the speaker say, "You may even discover some you did not know about"?
    (A) To announce a discount
    (B) To promote a new service
    (C) To celebrate a recent achievement
    (D) To suggest trying other attractions

82. According to the speaker, what will happen in a few hours?
    (A) A special show will begin.
    (B) A contest will be held.
    (C) A technician will arrive.
    (D) A safety rule will be explained.

GO ON TO THE NEXT PAGE

83. According to the speaker, what did the company recently do?
    (A) Developed a new product
    (B) Conducted a survey
    (C) Organized a training program
    (D) Hired additional researchers

84. What does the speaker suggest doing?
    (A) Targeting more advertisements to young people
    (B) Including special deals for first-time customers
    (C) Installing rear-view cameras in their cars
    (D) Ensuring all their cars are certified as safe

85. Why does the speaker say, "our vehicles only get 20 miles per gallon"?
    (A) To indicate a weakness
    (B) To compare with a competitor
    (C) To change some incorrect information
    (D) To explain why the vehicles are expensive

86. What does the speaker say is the top priority?
    (A) Securing funding
    (B) Designing the stage
    (C) Selecting the actors
    (D) Promoting the play

87. What does the speaker ask the listeners to do?
    (A) Create some posters
    (B) Share their availability
    (C) Revise a script
    (D) Donate some money

88. Why does the speaker want to use the Dalberg Center?
    (A) It is open all week.
    (B) It gives discounts.
    (C) It has superior facilities.
    (D) It has the largest space.

89. What is being advertised?
    (A) A backpack
    (B) A new bakery
    (C) Some educational sessions
    (D) Some cooking utensils

90. Who is Brandon Ludlow?
    (A) A financial advisor
    (B) A travel agent
    (C) A business owner
    (D) A restaurant critic

91. According to the speaker, what will happen in March?
    (A) A coupon will be posted online.
    (B) A registration process will end.
    (C) A branch will extend its hours.
    (D) A schedule will be updated.

92. What is the speaker mainly discussing?
    (A) An advertising budget
    (B) A site for a new factory
    (C) A new product release
    (D) A meeting with client

93. What does the speaker say about the sales numbers?
    (A) They are at a record low.
    (B) They are affected by preorders.
    (C) They will be revealed soon.
    (D) They are likely to change.

94. What does the speaker mean when she says, "We need to take advantage of this"?
    (A) A staff meeting will be rescheduled.
    (B) A product review will be discussed.
    (C) A game sequel will be planned.
    (D) A marketing campaign will be launched.

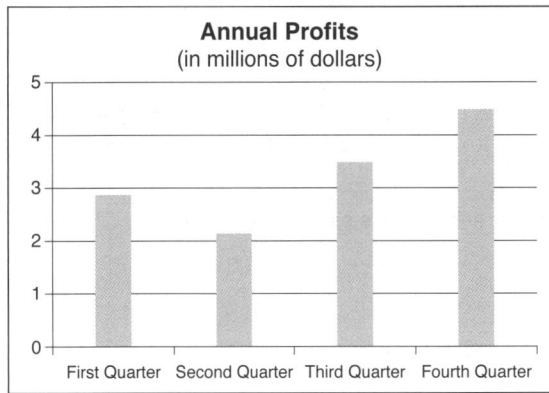

95. What kind of business is the speaker discussing?
(A) A tour company
(B) A car service
(C) A clothing store
(D) An airline

96. Look at the graphic. When did the company make a change?
(A) In the first quarter
(B) In the second quarter
(C) In the third quarter
(D) In the fourth quarter

97. What does the speaker suggest doing?
(A) Contacting a company
(B) Reading a publication
(C) Signing up for a service
(D) Extending a membership

98. Who most likely are the listeners?
(A) Technicians
(B) City officials
(C) Journalists
(D) Volunteers

99. Look at the graphic. Which subway exit will be closed starting May 10?
(A) Exit 1
(B) Exit 2
(C) Exit 3
(D) Exit 4

100. What does the speaker say will be posted online?
(A) Construction plans
(B) Train schedules
(C) Renovation costs
(D) Event details

This is the end of the Listening test. Turn to PART 5 in your test book.

GO ON TO THE NEXT PAGE

READING TEST

In this section, you must demonstrate your ability to read and comprehend English. You will be given a variety of texts and asked to answer questions about these texts. This section is divided into three parts and will take 75 minutes to complete.

Do not mark the answers in your test book. Use the answer sheet that is separately provided.

PART 5

Directions: In each question, you will be asked to review a statement that is missing a word or phrase. Four answer choices will be provided for each statement. Select the best answer and mark the corresponding letter (A), (B), (C), or (D) on the answer sheet.

PART 5 권장 풀이 시간 11분

101. Anna Lin will officially step down from ------- role as chief financial officer when the new fiscal year begins.

    (A) she
    (B) her
    (C) hers
    (D) herself

102. Claymore Inc.'s construction crews worked ------- to meet the deadline for the completion of the new stadium.

    (A) tire
    (B) tired
    (C) tireless
    (D) tirelessly

103. Ms. Wallace is ------- for managing the visitor registration kiosk at this weekend's exposition.

    (A) responsible
    (B) practical
    (C) beneficial
    (D) capable

104. Ms. Finley has ------- called a repairman to fix the broken dishwasher, and he will visit tomorrow.

    (A) overly
    (B) already
    (C) closely
    (D) very

105. ------- he goes on his morning jog, Mr. Ford stretches to avoid any muscle injuries.

    (A) During
    (B) Then
    (C) Around
    (D) Before

106. The Blevins Group marketing team plans to distribute ------- of the product catalog at the upcoming trade show.

    (A) copy
    (B) copied
    (C) copier
    (D) copies

107. The Yomi Bistro offers an extensive ------- of seafood dishes, each prepared with the freshest ingredients available.

    (A) selection
    (B) gift
    (C) cuisine
    (D) system

108. A quarterly review session was held for the ------- staff of Sharpe Beverages to assess progress.

    (A) manage
    (B) managerial
    (C) managers
    (D) manages

109. Mr. Rivera's trip to Rome was one of the most ------- travel experiences of his life.

(A) disappoint
(B) disappointed
(C) disappointing
(D) disappointment

110. The judges noted how ------- he was for solving the problem in seven minutes.

(A) create
(B) creation
(C) creatively
(D) creative

111. Zelway Fashion Outlet updates its inventory on a seasonal ------- to reflect the latest trends.

(A) basis
(B) design
(C) reason
(D) suggestion

112. Customer service ratings remain low for Rosen Telecom, ------- with the recent staff training.

(A) as
(B) even
(C) just
(D) much

113. ------- the initial setbacks, Pontus Apparel successfully launched its tracksuit line within the planned time frame.

(A) Because of
(B) Along
(C) As though
(D) Despite

114. The committee must finalize the budget this week, ------- the marketing campaign for Knox Cosmetics will be postponed.

(A) both
(B) or
(C) unless
(D) soon

115. Mr. Cramer's in-depth experience in international operations will be a ------- addition to our global expansion efforts.

(A) valuable
(B) public
(C) selective
(D) thorough

116. Mr. Hwang submitted his receipt for transportation ------- to receive reimbursement.

(A) branches
(B) materials
(C) expenses
(D) requests

117. Lina Event Planning ------- clients a fee for organizing corporate events based on the type of activities.

(A) undergoes
(B) charges
(C) collects
(D) adjusts

118. The recipe called for an avocado, so the chef looked around the kitchen to find ------- that was ripe.

(A) any other
(B) each
(C) several
(D) one

119. Ms. Eve has felt energetic and motivated to participate in more outdoor activities ------- last month's hiking trip.

(A) until
(B) past
(C) since
(D) in order that

120. Staff from the human resources department will ------- new employees with completing onboarding paperwork.

(A) assist
(B) assists
(C) assisted
(D) assisting

GO ON TO THE NEXT PAGE

121. Attendees of the webinar will receive a follow-up e-mail with a detailed summary ------- the SJ Healthcare Conference concludes.

(A) whereas
(B) toward
(C) when
(D) also

122. Prime Textile uses advanced machinery to replicate colors -------, ensuring consistency across different production batches.

(A) accurate
(B) accuracy
(C) accurately
(D) accurateness

123. ------- closing its unprofitable branch, Westwood Rentals is looking for ways to increase efficiency instead.

(A) Owing to
(B) Rather than
(C) Compared to
(D) In case of

124. During the inventory check, each product's barcode ------- to update the warehouse management system.

(A) scan
(B) scanned
(C) should be scanning
(D) will be scanned

125. The construction of the Greenfield Hospital wing will ------- in March after all necessary permits are obtained.

(A) specify
(B) represent
(C) intervene
(D) commence

126. The Franklin Museum curated a special exhibition, ------- artifacts showcase the cultural heritage of the region.

(A) its
(B) whose
(C) those
(D) that

127. The novel's plot twist was ------- discussed on social media, leading to a dramatic increase in sales.

(A) distantly
(B) extremely
(C) widely
(D) respectively

128. Our article covers eco-friendly ------- by Magana Technologies that are designed to facilitate sustainable living practices.

(A) inventions
(B) invented
(C) to invent
(D) inventor

129. The legal advisor provided ------- advice to the client regarding the potential outcomes of the case.

(A) spacious
(B) impartial
(C) dependent
(D) obedient

130. Ace Systems' latest software tool helps employees collaborate more ------- regardless of their geographic locations.

(A) sternly
(B) frankly
(C) effectively
(D) unexpectedly

PART 6

Directions: In this part, you will be asked to read four English texts. Each text is missing a word, phrase, or sentence. Select the answer choice that correctly completes the text and mark the corresponding letter (A), (B), (C), or (D) on the answer sheet.

PART 6 권장 풀이 시간 8분

Questions 131-134 refer to the following job posting.

Truck Drivers Needed

Currently, Velocity Logistics ------- seeking truck drivers with a commercial license and a clean driving record for full-time positions. Candidates must have a high school diploma and proven truck driving experience. -------. Responsibilities will include transporting goods, planning routes to meet specified deadlines, and performing ------- maintenance checks on your vehicle. -------, candidates must be physically able to load and unload cargo. To apply, please send your résumé to hr@velocitylogistics.com with "Truck Driver Position" in the subject line.

131. (A) is
(B) was
(C) has been
(D) will have been

132. (A) Our headquarters are centrally located to enable easy dispatch.
(B) Industry standards and regulations are subject to change.
(C) At least three years in a similar position is preferable.
(D) All vehicles in our fleet are equipped with safety features.

133. (A) regularize
(B) regularly
(C) regularization
(D) regular

134. (A) Consequently
(B) In addition
(C) For example
(D) Otherwise

GO ON TO THE NEXT PAGE

Questions 135-138 refer to the following article.

STOCKTON (April 5)—Stockton's culinary landscape just got an upgrade with the opening of Savor, ------- specializes in modern British cuisine. Chef and owner Brian Dunn, ------- for winning last year's Diamond Dish Challenge, has designed the menu to appeal to a wide variety of preferences. So far, the response has been positive. -------. Not only has the food been praised extensively, but the ------- has also garnered admiration. The soft lighting and curated artwork make Savor an ideal setting for intimate gatherings.

135. (A) it
 (B) which
 (C) anyone
 (D) where

136. (A) knows
 (B) has known
 (C) known
 (D) to know

137. (A) Customers will submit feedback through its Web site.
 (B) Local residents have reported being thrilled to visit.
 (C) Mr. Dunn won the competition by only three points.
 (D) Private dining rooms are available upon request.

138. (A) atmosphere
 (B) treatment
 (C) voyage
 (D) promotion

Questions 139-142 refer to the following e-mail.

To: Amy Phan <amyp123@silverspoonscafe.com>
From: Charlie Carpenter <c_carpenter@acledadesigns.com>
Date: June 16
Subject: RE: Café Renovation Inquiry

Dear Ms. Phan,

After reviewing your pictures, we have determined that your requested renovation can be completed ------- a two-month time frame. It seems the most significant task will be revamping your seating area. -------. However, rest assured that careful ------- will be given to every detail so that all your specifications are met. In order to view your space and discuss the project with you in person, I would like to arrange a ------- consultation. Please note that even if you decide not to proceed after my visit, you won't be charged for anything. Let me know when you're available.

Regards,

Charlie Carpenter, Acleda Designs

---

139. (A) perhaps
(B) either
(C) within
(D) upon

140. (A) We will have to work with contractors on this.
(B) You should be able to operate the café during this period.
(C) I recommend energy-efficient appliances for your kitchen.
(D) Outdoor seating area is only open when the weather is nice.

141. (A) consider
(B) consideration
(C) considerate
(D) considerately

142. (A) comparable
(B) spontaneous
(C) disruptive
(D) complimentary

Questions 143-146 refer to the following e-mail.

To: All Staff
From: hr@mcconnellyinc.com
Subject: Viviane Hurst's Promotion
Date: February 2

Good afternoon, everyone.

I have news to share. Viviane Hurst has been promoted to the position of marketing manager and will be transferred to our new office in Mumbai. -------, she will be tasked with building new partnerships and increasing our market presence in South Asia. ------- Viviane will be departing at the end of this month, Alexander Novak will be taking over her current assistant manager position as of today. -------. He comes to us from Randolph & Associates, where he was employed as a marketing strategist for over a decade. I will arrange a time for everyone to ------- in the conference room to welcome him.

Linda Evans, HR director

143. (A) Once there
(B) Regardless
(C) Meanwhile
(D) For instance

144. (A) So that
(B) Whether
(C) Afterward
(D) Because

145. (A) A successful expansion into South Asia requires strategic planning.
(B) A farewell party is currently being organized for her.
(C) Hiring a candidate from within the organization will save time.
(D) We are confident that he will bring valuable expertise to the team.

146. (A) notify
(B) instruct
(C) gather
(D) stay

PART 7

Directions: In this part, you will be asked to read several texts, such as advertisements, articles, instant messages, or examples of business correspondence. Each text is followed by several questions. Select the best answer and mark the corresponding letter (A), (B), (C), or (D) on your answer sheet.

Questions 147-148 refer to the following article.

WESTFIELD (June 24)—Town council member Judith Owen offered more details about the plan to repave Wilkinson Drive and build a new exit ramp. The project, which was announced last week, is scheduled to run from August 5 to 20, and the road will be closed to all vehicle traffic during this period. Ms. Owen acknowledged that the timing isn't ideal. Wilkinson Drive is the primary route to Kendra Lake, a popular swimming and picnicking spot for locals in the summer. However, she stressed that the project will not significantly inconvenience anyone looking to cool off since the lake can also be reached by taking Aspen Lane.

By Brett Evans
Westfield Chronicle

147. What is the purpose of the article?

(A) To describe a project to financially support local businesses
(B) To encourage participation in a town council election
(C) To provide information about an upcoming road closure
(D) To announce the construction of new swimming facilities

148. What is true about Kendra Lake?

(A) It will be inaccessible through much of August.
(B) It can be reached using only one route.
(C) It is a popular recreation area for residents.
(D) It was chosen as the site of an official event.

GO ON TO THE NEXT PAGE

Questions 149-150 refer to the following e-mail.

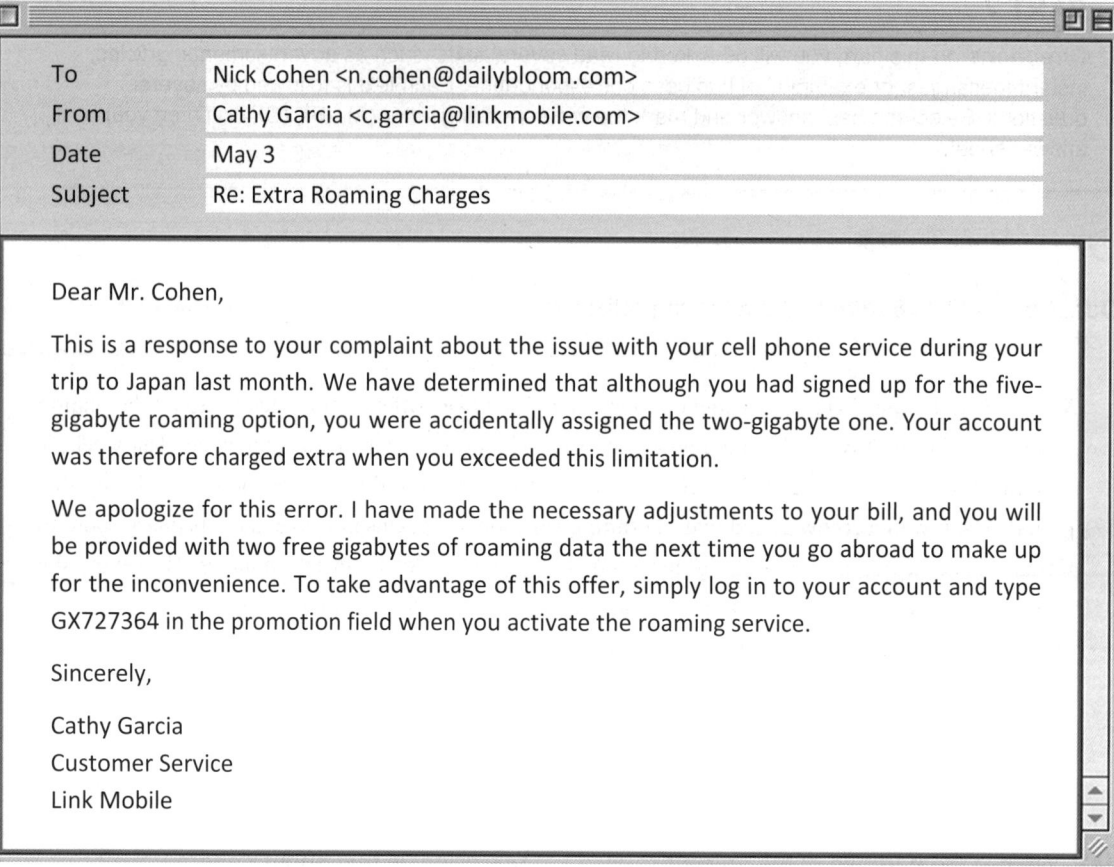

To	Nick Cohen <n.cohen@dailybloom.com>
From	Cathy Garcia <c.garcia@linkmobile.com>
Date	May 3
Subject	Re: Extra Roaming Charges

Dear Mr. Cohen,

This is a response to your complaint about the issue with your cell phone service during your trip to Japan last month. We have determined that although you had signed up for the five-gigabyte roaming option, you were accidentally assigned the two-gigabyte one. Your account was therefore charged extra when you exceeded this limitation.

We apologize for this error. I have made the necessary adjustments to your bill, and you will be provided with two free gigabytes of roaming data the next time you go abroad to make up for the inconvenience. To take advantage of this offer, simply log in to your account and type GX727364 in the promotion field when you activate the roaming service.

Sincerely,

Cathy Garcia
Customer Service
Link Mobile

149. What is suggested about Mr. Cohen?

(A) He bought a cell phone from Ms. Garcia.
(B) He traveled to another country in April.
(C) He upgraded his mobile account last month.
(D) He selected the wrong roaming option.

150. What should Mr. Cohen do to make use of a benefit?

(A) Enter a code
(B) Activate a card
(C) Call a number
(D) Send an e-mail

Questions 151-152 refer to the following online chat discussion.

Xiao Chang	(2:10 P.M.)	Our office building's maintenance manager just told me that the electricity will be shut off from 7 to 9 P.M. on Tuesday.
Tara Morris	(2:11 P.M.)	There is a sign posted in the lobby. It says some repairs need to be done following a recent inspection. It shouldn't affect us, though. Everyone in our company usually leaves by 6.
Xiao Chang	(2:12 P.M.)	Actually, I have a video conference with a client in Hong Kong at 8 P.M. on Tuesday.
Tara Morris	(2:13 P.M.)	Would it be possible to reschedule it?
Xiao Chang	(2:14 P.M.)	I'm supposed to e-mail my proposal on Monday, and the client wants to discuss it the following day. That's the only time he's available.
Tara Morris	(2:15 P.M.)	There is a coworking company nearby where you can book a conference room for a few hours. I've used it before, and it is quite convenient.

151. At 2:11 P.M., what does Ms. Morris most likely mean when she writes, "There is a sign posted in the lobby"?

(A) She feels Mr. Chang has misunderstood a plan.
(B) She was notified in advance about a policy change.
(C) She found a problem that Mr. Chang should be aware of.
(D) She has already been made aware of a situation.

152. What will happen on Monday?

(A) A document will be submitted to a customer.
(B) An inspection will be conducted in an office.
(C) Rooms will be set up for a business conference.
(D) Repairs will be performed on some equipment.

GO ON TO THE NEXT PAGE

Questions 153-154 refer to the following advertisement.

If you are looking to get into shape and become healthier, why not start your journey by taking up yoga? Meet the Moon Yoga Mat—designed specifically with beginners in mind.

Available in a range of designs, from basic stripes to more elaborate floral prints, this mat is made entirely of natural cork. It has a thick base with an additional layer of soft material for your protection. And we have made it slightly longer and wider than a standard yoga mat to ensure that you will have enough room to do difficult yoga positions comfortably and safely.

For more information on this mat and other products we offer, visit www.yogamood.com.

153. Who will most likely use this product?

(A) People who are planning to take a trip
(B) People concerned about an existing health issue
(C) People who are starting a new business
(D) People interested in becoming physically fit

154. What is NOT mentioned as a feature of the product?

(A) Varied patterns
(B) Natural material
(C) Water Resistance
(D) Extra padding

Questions 155-157 refer to the following e-mail.

To: Ahmed Khazim <a.khazim@ezmail.com>
From: Mindy Samson <m.samson@portsidewindows.com>
Date: May 10
Subject: Re: Re: Window Replacement

Dear Mr. Khazim,

Regarding your question about the quote for the window replacement that I e-mailed you yesterday, you are correct that it is slightly higher than what we initially discussed. — [1] —. We were forced to increase the price for two reasons. — [2] —. We will have to make a custom window for you. Another factor is that you informed our technician you would prefer tinted glass to reduce the amount of afternoon sunlight entering your clothing shop. This costs more than the regular glass we first discussed. — [3] —.

I apologize if the higher price caused you any confusion. — [4] —. If you want to discuss the project in person, I would be happy to meet with you. You can reach me at 555-8876 to set up a time.

Sincerely,

Mindy Samson
Portside Windows

---

155. What is the purpose of the e-mail?

(A) To request payment for a product
(B) To demand cancellation of a service
(C) To provide a reason for a delay
(D) To explain a change to an estimate

156. Who most likely is Mr. Khazim?

(A) A property investor
(B) A government official
(C) A business owner
(D) A technical consultant

157. In which of the positions marked [1], [2], [3], and [4] does the following sentence best belong?

"First of all, our technician identified that the window you want replaced is not a standard size."

(A) [1]
(B) [2]
(C) [3]
(D) [4]

Questions 158-160 refer to the following letter.

Amanda Morrison
731 Ward Street
Hartford CT, 06106
August 17

Dear Ms. Morrison,

Thank you for signing up with Coleman Security. You have taken an important first step to safeguard your newly purchased home. The Basic Package you selected includes 24-hour monitoring of the alarm system as well as the rapid dispatch of a response team if it is activated.

I want to inform you that we now have a special offer to encourage customers to upgrade to a Deluxe Package. I have enclosed a brochure with information about it for you to look through. One of the biggest advantages of the Deluxe Package is that our security patrols will check your property in the morning and in the evening. The number of patrol visits can be increased when you are away from your home for an extended period.

The Deluxe Package normally costs $149 per month. However, if you sign up before September 1, you will only be charged $119 per month for the remainder of your current one-year contract. You can do this on our Web site (www.coleman.com/upgrade) or by calling our customer service center at 555-0092.

Sincerely,

Brett Reynolds
Coleman Security

158. What is indicated about Ms. Morrison?

(A) She is the owner of multiple properties.
(B) She met with Mr. Reynolds in early August.
(C) She is a long-term client of Coleman Security.
(D) She bought her current residence recently.

159. Why should Ms. Morrison read a document?

(A) To check the penalties for early cancellation
(B) To make sure she understands a free service
(C) To learn about an option with more features
(D) To compare the prices of different devices

160. How can Ms. Morrison qualify for a discount?

(A) By participating in an online survey
(B) By signing a multiyear contract
(C) By registering before a deadline
(D) By paying a monthly bill in advance

Questions 161-163 refer to the following review.

www.reviews.com/sheffield

Glide LX Review

Rating: ★★☆☆☆ (2 stars)

When my old electric shaver broke, I decided to get Dolman's latest product, the Glide LX. I was very excited about my purchase as I have had positive experiences with this company's products in the past. Unfortunately, the Glide LX did not meet my expectations.

The Glide LX does not give a smooth shave. No matter how careful I am, I still end up with small patches of stubble on my face. Also, it is very inconvenient to clean. You have to disassemble it completely to wash all of its components, which is a time-consuming process. The only positive thing I can say about this device is that it looks very stylish and has a sleek, ergonomic design. But given that the Glide LX costs much more than similar products, this isn't enough to justify purchasing it.

– Michael Warren

---

161. What kind of business is Dolman?

(A) A sporting goods maker
(B) A furniture company
(C) A vehicle manufacturer
(D) An electronics producer

162. Why did Mr. Warren choose the product?

(A) He was offered a price reduction during a promotion.
(B) He read some positive feedback on a consumer Web site.
(C) He was happy with other merchandise from the company.
(D) He received a recommendation from an acquaintance.

163. What aspect of the product is Mr. Warren satisfied with?

(A) Function
(B) Convenience
(C) Appearance
(D) Price

GO ON TO THE NEXT PAGE

Questions 164-167 refer to the following article.

MANCHESTER (15 October)—Continental Rail CEO Tina Nowak officially confirmed that her company has added several new express trains to Budapest and Munich, with plans for more to other central European cities, such as Prague, in the near future. — [1] —. During a press conference at the company's main office in Vienna, Nowak stated that this was a response to the increased demand for convenient yet environmentally friendly travel options in the region. "We are committed to providing travellers with viable alternatives to automobiles," she explained. — [2] —. "By adding more express trains, we intend to ensure that people reach their destinations as fast as possible without having to drive."

At the same media event, Nowak also introduced Continental Rail's new weekly pass for tourists, called Travel Ease. — [3] —. For only €200, visitors can travel anywhere in Europe via Continental Rail for up to seven days all year round. "We are going to launch Travel Ease in the second week of December so that travellers will be able to take advantage of it during the holiday season," Nowak added. Although this plan will likely be a favourite of travellers, there is concern about its impact on revenue. — [4] —. However, Nowak likely had no choice in the matter. Continental Rail's major competitor, Eastern Railways, introduced a similar promotion in August, and it was a success. It remains to be seen whether Continental Rail can match the performance of its rival.

164. Which city is Continental Rail based in?

(A) Budapest
(B) Munich
(C) Prague
(D) Vienna

165. The word "viable" in paragraph 1, line 6, is closest in meaning to

(A) rational
(B) practical
(C) affordable
(D) valuable

166. What will happen in the second week of December?

(A) A company executive will hold a press conference.
(B) A new route will be announced.
(C) A product will become available for purchase.
(D) A seasonal discount will begin to take effect.

167. In which of the positions marked [1], [2], [3], and [4] does the following sentence best belong?

"Some shareholders have even questioned whether the company can make a profit from the passes."

(A) [1]
(B) [2]
(C) [3]
(D) [4]

Questions 168-171 refer to the following information.

There has been a change to the event scheduled for Saturday, August 10 as part of our Summer Kids Program. The magician originally booked for that day is no longer available. However, we have arranged for an educational workshop by Jake Dobson instead. Mr. Dobson is a former wildlife photographer who now devotes himself to spreading knowledge about the animals we share our planet with. He is a funny and informative speaker, and we are lucky to have gotten him on such short notice. During his workshop, Mr. Dobson will not only teach the kids, but as a special treat, he will also let them handle a variety of exotic creatures, including lizards and parrots.

To register your child, visit our Web site at www.madisonlibrary.com/summer. You can also speak to a librarian at the front desk. This event will begin at 10 A.M. and last for approximately two hours. It will be held in our second-floor children's center. Note that although there is no charge for attendance, space is limited. Therefore, only 25 children will be signed up on a first-come, first-served basis. Make sure to register early!

168. What can be inferred about Mr. Dobson?

(A) He has experienced a career change.
(B) He has partnered with another performer.
(C) He is currently employed at a photo studio.
(D) He is an expert on a variety of topics.

169. What is special about the event on August 10?

(A) It will involve a trip to a famous wildlife refuge.
(B) It will have lessons on performing magic tricks.
(C) It will feature an assortment of live animals.
(D) It will include more than one guest speaker.

170. Where will the event take place?

(A) In an elementary school
(B) In a medical center
(C) In a public library
(D) In a science museum

171. What is true about the children's center?

(A) It has been expanded to increase its capacity.
(B) It is located on the second floor of a building.
(C) It will extend its hours of operation in the summer.
(D) It closes for two hours in the morning each day.

GO ON TO THE NEXT PAGE

Questions 172-175 refer to the following text-message chain.

Carla Ewing (9:14 A.M.)
Are you busy, Liam? I have a huge favor to ask of you.

Liam Davis (9:15 A.M.)
Of course. Let me know what you need. I just finished my morning report and have some time.

Carla Ewing (9:16 A.M.)
I'm giving a sales presentation about one of our company's new software applications at Newman Financial this morning. I just arrived here, and I realized I forgot to transfer some important charts from my PC to my laptop. Could you e-mail them to me?

Liam Davis (9:18 A.M.)
Sure. Do I need to enter a password to access your computer?

Carla Ewing (9:19 A.M.)
Yeah. It's "Ewing2024." You'll see a folder on my desktop labeled Newman Financial. There should be three files in there. Send me all of them. I updated those files last night specifically for today's presentation.

Liam Davis (9:21 A.M.)
Got it. I'm on my way to the legal department to drop off some copies of a contract. I'll send your files in about 20 minutes.

Carla Ewing (9:22 A.M.)
The meeting starts at 9:30. Don't worry about it. I'll ask another one of our team members to do this. Sarah Fraser's desk is close to mine.

Liam Davis (9:24 A.M.)
Oh, I didn't realize you were in a rush. I haven't gotten on the elevator yet, so I can do it now. I'll let you know when the files are sent.

172. Why is Ms. Ewing sending the message?

(A) To inquire about the location of an office
(B) To ask for technical assistance with her laptop
(C) To request that several files be sent to her
(D) To confirm that some software was updated

173. What does Mr. Davis ask about?

(A) Why a chart is considered so important
(B) How an electronic device can be accessed
(C) Where a document is located in a workspace
(D) When a presentation is supposed to begin

174. At 9:22 A.M., what does Ms. Ewing most likely mean when she writes, "The meeting starts at 9:30"?

(A) She is worried about her late arrival time.
(B) She hopes to find a parking space nearby.
(C) She needs a task to be completed quickly.
(D) She will return to the office soon.

175. What most likely is the relationship between Ms. Ewing and Ms. Fraser?

(A) Team members
(B) Relatives
(C) Business partners
(D) Former classmates

GO ON TO THE NEXT PAGE

Questions 176-180 refer to the following e-mails.

To: Mike Pollard <mpollard@pollardcatering.com>
From: Aya Mori <a.mori@preston.com>
Subject: Information Request
Date: November 10

Dear Mr. Pollard,

My manager has instructed me to arrange a special lunch for a senior partner at my law firm who is leaving after 15 years of service. I am contacting you because one of my acquaintances recommended your company. You catered her parent's wedding anniversary celebration, and she was more than satisfied with the quality of the food. My company's event will take place at our office, which is located at 345 Braxton Boulevard, and I expect about 30 employees to attend.

We would like sufficient food for everyone, as well as bottled water and juice, and our total budget is $750. If you can accommodate my request, please send me some information about meal options and prices. I would appreciate it if you could reply by Thursday as I will be attending an out-of-town legal conference on Friday.

Sincerely,

Aya Mori
Preston Legal Services

To: Aya Mori <a.mori@preston.com>
From: Mike Pollard <mpollard@pollardcatering.com>
Subject: Re: Information Request
Date: November 12

Dear Ms. Mori,

Thank you for reaching out to me. We regularly cater events similar to the one you are organizing, and we have a range of options available. I have included all of them below for your reference:

Option A: Sushi rolls (tuna and salmon), Miso soup
— *Cost for 30 people: $780 (beverages not included)*

Option B: Individual pizzas, Chicken wings & fries
— *Cost for 30 people: $740 (beverages included)*

Option C: Thai curry, Mango sticky rice
— *Cost for 30 people: $775 (beverages included)*

Option D: Sandwiches (meat and vegetarian), Individual salads
— *Cost for 30 people: $725 (beverages not included)*

Please also note that 50 percent of the total price must be paid at the time of booking. The remainder is due on the day of the event.

Sincerely,

Mike Pollard
Owner, Pollard Catering

176. What type of event has Ms. Mori been asked to organize?

    (A) An anniversary celebration
    (B) A retirement party
    (C) A press conference
    (D) An awards ceremony

177. Which meal option will Ms. Mori most likely select?

    (A) Option A
    (B) Option B
    (C) Option C
    (D) Option D

178. In the first e-mail, the word "accommodate" in paragraph 2, line 2, is closest in meaning to

    (A) verify
    (B) improve
    (C) satisfy
    (D) adapt

179. Why does Ms. Mori want Mr. Pollard to respond before Friday?

    (A) She hopes to receive some sample dishes in advance.
    (B) She must confirm an event schedule with her manager.
    (C) She has an appointment with another catering company.
    (D) She will travel to attend an industry-related event.

180. What is indicated about Pollard Catering?

    (A) It offers complimentary beverages with all orders.
    (B) It provides services primarily to corporate clients.
    (C) It charges extra for preparing vegetarian options.
    (D) It requires payment of a deposit by customers.

GO ON TO THE NEXT PAGE

Questions 181-185 refer to the following advertisement and review.

Perfect for Travelers on a Budget!

The Green Turtle Backpacker's Hostel offers clean yet affordable accommodations. We are conveniently situated in downtown Westport, which is just a short distance from the popular sightseeing destinations of Sheffield and Wiltshire, as well as the transportation hub of Hereford.

We provide a variety of services to guests at no extra charge, including unlimited Wi-Fi, use of our airport shuttle bus, and access to our laundry facilities. We also have on-site parking at very reasonable rates. But the best part of staying here is the fun you will have with the people you meet. We hold regular evening activities to bring everyone together:

- Mondays: Movies (free popcorn included)
- Wednesdays: Board Games
- Thursdays: Karaoke (with prizes for the best singers)
- Saturdays: Arts & Crafts

Check out www.gtbhostel.com for more details about our hostel and to make a booking!

---

www.gtbhostel.com/reviews

My university friend and I wanted to do some hiking during our summer vacation. As the Green Turtle Backpacker's Hostel is close to one of the trails, we decided to stay there for one night. Unfortunately, we had a bad experience because of the racket from the guests singing in the evening. I guess it is a regular event, but nobody told us about it when we checked in. Although I will probably not stay at this facility again, I want to mention that I was very impressed with how helpful the staff members were. The front desk clerk moved us to a dorm room on the upper floor and provided us with complimentary earplugs. And in the morning, one of the employees arranged a taxi and helped us carry our bags out to it. You expect this at a hotel, but it was surprising at a hostel.

Posted by Daryl Roberts on August 25

181. Where is the hostel located?

(A) Westport
(B) Sheffield
(C) Wiltshire
(D) Hereford

182. What is NOT mentioned as something guests can do at no additional charge?

(A) Access the Internet
(B) Travel to the airport
(C) Wash their clothes
(D) Park their vehicles

183. Which night did Mr. Roberts stay at the hostel?

(A) Monday
(B) Wednesday
(C) Thursday
(D) Saturday

184. What was the purpose of Mr. Roberts's trip?

(A) He was applying for a summer job at a company.
(B) He intended to take a tour of a university campus.
(C) He planned to spend time in nature with a friend.
(D) He was attending a special program for students.

185. What does Mr. Roberts mention that he found impressive?

(A) The quality of the customer service
(B) The size of the accommodation facility
(C) The speed of the check-in process
(D) The cleanliness of the dormitory room

GO ON TO THE NEXT PAGE

Questions 186-190 refer to the following e-mails and receipt.

To	Pearson Building Supplies <customerservice@pearson.com>
From	Greg Wallace <g.wallace@aceconstruction.com>
Subject	Follow-Up
Date	May 12

To Whom It May Concern,

I placed an order (#82737) on May 8 for some building supplies I need for a renovation project. The total amount has been charged to my credit card, but I have not received a receipt by e-mail yet. Please send it as soon as possible as I need it for my company records. Also, I was wondering when your store will have Wilson screwdrivers back in stock. I was planning to buy a few, but they are no longer listed on your Web site.

Thanks,

Greg Wallace
Ace Construction

To: Greg Wallace <g.wallace@aceconstruction.com>
From: Pearson Building Supplies <customerservice@pearson.com>
Subject: Re: Follow-Up
Date: May 12

Dear Mr. Wallace,

I just accessed your account, and it appears that our system did not automatically issue you a receipt. I apologize for this error—we installed a new version of the application used to process orders last week, and it would seem that there are some bugs. You should have received an e-mail with the receipt a few minutes ago. Please confirm that you got it.

When I was looking at your account information, I happened to notice that the product on which you spent $60 in total is one that you get almost every week. You may want to consider buying it once a month so that you can qualify for our 10 percent discount on bulk orders. Also, I have asked my manager, Neal Sutter, for the information I need to answer your question. Once I get a response from him, I will let you know.

Sincerely,

Saba Ali
Customer Service Agent
Pearson Building Supplies

Pearson Building Supplies

Date: May 8
Order Number: 82737

Product	Unit Cost	Quantity	Price
Apex Paint	$60 per can	3	$180.00
Millhouse Sandpaper	$20 per roll	3	$60.00
Damien Plaster	$50 per bucket	1	$50.00
Fuller Kitchen Tiles	$20 each	15	$300.00
		Discount	N/A
		Grand Total	$590.00

We encourage you to fill out and submit a customer satisfaction questionnaire to help us improve our service. The form can be accessed on our Web site. To show our appreciation for this helpful feedback, all customers who participate will receive a $25 gift card!

186. Why did Mr. Wallace send the e-mail?

(A) An incorrect amount was charged to his card.
(B) An order was not processed quickly enough.
(C) A shipment was sent to the wrong address.
(D) A transaction record was not received.

187. According to the second e-mail, what recently happened at Pearson Building Supplies?

(A) A mobile application was launched.
(B) A policy was changed.
(C) A software program was updated.
(D) A store branch was renovated.

188. Which item does Ms. Ali suggest ordering on a monthly rather than weekly basis?

(A) Apex Paint
(B) Millhouse Sandpaper
(C) Damien Plaster
(D) Fuller Kitchen Tiles

189. What did Ms. Ali ask Mr. Sutter about?

(A) The name of a tool manufacturer
(B) The availability of a company's products
(C) The accuracy of a financial record
(D) The advantage of a computer system

190. What is indicated about Pearson Building Supplies?

(A) It temporarily reduced the prices of all its products.
(B) It offers a gift card with a minimum purchase.
(C) It only accepts orders through its Web site.
(D) It is conducting a customer survey.

GO ON TO THE NEXT PAGE

Questions 191-195 refer to the following Web page, schedule and testimonial.

---

www.brentwoodcleaning.com/about

| About | Services | Fees | Contact Us |

Brentwood Cleaning has provided excellent service to commercial enterprises located in the greater Portland area for over 30 years. Whatever type of business you run, we can ensure that you offer a clean and sanitary environment for your clients. Our trained staff members will go to great lengths to meet your expectations.

As we take great pride in being a green company, we exclusively use the Greenwash (sustainable packaging and no animal testing) and Ecoclean (100 percent biodegradable and no synthetic ingredients) brands of cleaning supplies. Our goal is to protect the environment while making your workplace spotless!

Whether you have a one-off job, such as getting your business ready for its grand opening, or want to arrange regular janitorial services to keep your premises clean, we are available to assist you. Call 555-0393 to speak with one of our representatives today. Make sure to ask about our reduced fees for clients who schedule daily or weekly visits!

Brentwood Cleaning
Schedule for May 15

Client	Location	Requested Service
Willis Pharmacy	14 Broad Street	Dust shelves and counters
Ruben Graphic Design	23 2nd Avenue	General cleanup after renovations
Kline Publishing	67 Clover Lane	Clean carpets in reception area
Motis Office Supply	56 Sawyer Road	Mop and wax floors in the lobby

- Upon arrival at each location, notify the site contact person and obtain a completion signature after finishing the work.
- Maintain professional conduct and wear company uniform at all locations.

May 16–When the janitorial firm I had been using for years closed down, I decided to give Brentwood Cleaning a chance. I'm glad I did because the company did an excellent job of getting my carpets clean. I can't think of anything I would like to have been done differently. Even the Ecoclean detergent the workers used impressed me because it did not have a strong smell like most other cleaning agents. In addition, the leader of the team of workers was extremely professional. When I told her that I had mistakenly scheduled a client meeting for 2:30 P.M., she made sure the work was completed before that time, even though it was originally supposed to be done at 3 P.M. I definitely plan to make use of Brentwood Cleaning in the future.

– Elena Taylor

191. What is stated about Brentwood Cleaning?

(A) It specializes in cleaning residential properties.
(B) It has increased the costs of some services.
(C) It has opened branches in several cities.
(D) It offers discounts to repeat customers.

192. According to the schedule, which business recently had some remodeling work done?

(A) Willis Pharmacy
(B) Ruben Graphic Design
(C) Kline Publishing
(D) Motis Office Supply

193. Where is Ms. Taylor's business located?

(A) At 14 Broad Street
(B) At 23 2nd Avenue
(C) At 67 Clover Lane
(D) At 56 Sawyer Road

194. What is probably true about the detergent used in Ms. Taylor's workplace?

(A) It costs more than many other brands.
(B) It is made without being tested on animals.
(C) It includes only natural substances.
(D) It is designed to produce a flower scent.

195. What is indicated about the team leader in the testimonial?

(A) She met with a client to explain the cleaning process.
(B) She arrived at a work site much earlier than expected.
(C) She requested additional workers be sent to a business.
(D) She made sure a task was completed ahead of schedule.

GO ON TO THE NEXT PAGE

Questions 196-200 refer to the following advertisement, order form, and e-mail.

Get Ready for the Summer at Zone Sporting Goods

Whether you play a sport professionally or are just looking to get more physically active, Zone Sporting Goods has what you need. With 17 branches in communities across the Pacific Northwest, we have long been the region's most popular supplier of athletic clothing, footwear, and equipment. To celebrate our transition to a nationwide chain with the opening of stores in Chicago, Dallas, and other major cities this summer, we will be offering discounts of up to 40 percent off on many popular brands from July 1 to 15. But that's not all! When you spend at least $250 before tax and shipping fees are applied, we will give you a backpack from First Star Sports. This offer is valid for both in-store and online purchases.

Visit www.zonesport.com/summerpromotion for more information!

---

www.zonesport.com/orders

| HOME | PRODUCTS | **ORDERS** | CONTACT US |

Order number: 029384
Order date: July 2
Deliver to: Beth Kim
Shipping Address: 2834 8th Street, Seattle WA, 98040

Brand	Item Description	Price
Westbrook	Tennis Racket (Extra Long)	$45.00
Brightside	Water Bottle (One Liter)	$15.00
FZ Apparel	Tracksuit (Medium)	$55.00
Zipper	Sneakers (Size 12)	$110.00
	Subtotal	$225.00
	Shipping	$15.00
	Tax	$25.00
	TOTAL	$265.00

Prices above include all applicable discounts. To return an item purchased online, please click **here** to print out a prepaid shipping label. Note that returned items must be received within two weeks of purchase and be in their original packaging for a refund to be issued.

To: Beth Kim <b.kim@realmail.com>
From: Luca Abati <l.abati@zonesports.com>
Subject: Re: Order number 029384
Date: July 17

Dear Ms. Kim,

Thanks for reaching out to the customer service department of Zone Sporting Goods regarding your recent order. In response to your question, there was no error in the assignment of the loyalty points for the items you purchased. Each month, we feature a different company's products and offer double the points to members who purchase them, and our Brand of the Month for July is Zipper. That is why you received 300 points rather than the normal 150 for that item. You can find more information about this program as well as details about the many other benefits of membership on our Web site.

Sincerely,

Luca Abati
Customer Service Agent, Zone Sporting Goods

196. What is the reason Zone Sporting Goods is holding a promotion?

(A) It achieved its sales goal.
(B) It is celebrating its founding.
(C) It was chosen to sponsor an event.
(D) It will expand into other regions.

197. What can be concluded about Ms. Kim?

(A) She did not qualify for a free gift.
(B) She will return a purchased item.
(C) She mistakenly paid a delivery fee.
(D) She did not receive any discounts.

198. What does the order form indicate about Zone Sporting Goods customers?

(A) They can request express delivery.
(B) They cannot print out a receipt.
(C) They do not need to pay for return shipping.
(D) They may only refund damaged items.

199. What is the purpose of the e-mail?

(A) To encourage a customer to apply for a membership
(B) To respond to an inquiry about a possible mistake
(C) To recommend a replacement for an out-of-stock item
(D) To issue an apology after receiving a complaint

200. Which item did Ms. Kim receive extra loyalty points for purchasing?

(A) Tennis racket
(B) Water bottle
(C) Tracksuit
(D) Sneakers

This is the end of the test. You may review Parts 5, 6, and 7 if you finish the test early.

Review 체크리스트

TEST 1을 푼 다음, 아래 체크리스트에 따라 틀린 문제를 리뷰하고 박스에 완료 여부를 표시하세요.
만약 시험까지 얼마 남지 않았다면, [1]번 ~ [3]번 항목이라도 꼭 확인하세요.

☐ [1] 틀린 문제의 경우, 다시 풀어봤다.

☐ [2] 틀린 문제의 경우, 스크립트/해석을 확인하며 지문/문제의 내용을 정확하게 파악했다.

☐ [3] 해설을 통해 각 문제의 정답과 오답의 근거가 무엇인지 정확하게 파악했다.

☐ [4] PART 1과 PART 2에서 틀린 문제의 경우, 선택한 오답의 유형이 무엇이었는지 확인하고 같은 함정에 빠지지 않도록 정리해두었다.

☐ [5] PART 3와 PART 4의 각 문제에서 사용된 패러프레이징을 확인했다.

☐ [6] PART 5와 PART 6의 경우, 틀린 문제에서 사용된 문법 포인트 또는 정답 및 오답 어휘를 정리했다.

☐ [7] PART 6의 알맞은 문장 고르기 문제의 경우, 지문 전체를 정확하게 해석하며 전체 글의 흐름과 빈칸 주변 문맥을 정확하게 파악하는 연습을 했다.

☐ [8] PART 7에서 질문과 보기의 키워드를 찾아 표시하며 지문에서 정답의 근거가 되는 문장이나 구절을 찾아보고, 문제에서 사용된 패러프레이징을 확인했다.

☐ [9] PART 1~PART 4는 받아쓰기 & 쉐도잉 워크북을 활용하여, TEST에 수록된 핵심 문장을 받아쓰고 따라 읽으며 복습했다.

☐ [10] PART 1~PART 7은 단어암기자료를 활용하여, TEST에 수록된 핵심 어휘와 표현을 암기했다.

많은 양의 문제를 푸는 것도 중요하지만, 틀린 문제를 제대로 리뷰하는 것도 중요합니다.
틀린 문제를 한 번 더 꼼꼼히 리뷰한다면, 빠른 시간 내에 효과적으로 목표 점수를 달성할 수 있습니다.

해커스 토익 실전 LC+RC 3

TEST 2

LISTENING TEST

PART 1
PART 2
PART 3
PART 4

READING TEST

PART 5
PART 6
PART 7

Review 체크리스트

> 잠깐! 테스트 전 아래 사항을 꼭 확인하세요.
> 1. 휴대전화의 전원을 끄셨나요? 예 ☐
> 2. Answer Sheet(p.249), 연필, 지우개, 시계를 준비하셨나요? 예 ☐
> 3. Listening MP3를 들을 준비가 되셨나요? 예 ☐
>
> 모든 준비가 완료되었으면 목표 점수를 떠올린 후 테스트를 시작합니다.
> 테스트를 마친 후, Review 체크리스트(p.110)를 보며 자신이 틀린 문제를 반드시 복습합니다.

🎧 TEST 2.mp3
실전용·복습용 문제풀이 MP3 무료 다운로드 및 스트리밍 바로듣기 (HackersIngang.com)
* 실제 시험장의 소음까지 재현해 낸 고사장 소음/매미 버전 MP3, 영국식·호주식 발음 집중 MP3, 고속 버전 MP3까지 구매하면 실전에 더욱 완벽히 대비할 수 있습니다.

무료MP3 바로듣기

LISTENING TEST

In this section, you must demonstrate your ability to understand spoken English. This section is divided into four parts and will take approximately 45 minutes to complete. Do not mark the answers in your test book. Use the answer sheet that is provided separately.

PART 1

Directions: For each question, you will listen to four short statements about a picture in your test book. These statements will not be printed and will only be spoken one time. Select the statement that best describes what is happening in the picture and mark the corresponding letter (A), (B), (C), or (D) on the answer sheet.

Sample Answer

The statement that best describes the picture is (B), "The man is sitting at the desk." So, you should mark letter (B) on the answer sheet.

1.

2.

GO ON TO THE NEXT PAGE

3.

4.

5.

6.

PART 2

Directions: For each question, you will listen to a statement or question followed by three possible responses spoken in English. They will not be printed and will only be spoken one time. Select the best response and mark the corresponding letter (A), (B), or (C) on your answer sheet.

7. Mark your answer on your answer sheet.
8. Mark your answer on your answer sheet.
9. Mark your answer on your answer sheet.
10. Mark your answer on your answer sheet.
11. Mark your answer on your answer sheet.
12. Mark your answer on your answer sheet.
13. Mark your answer on your answer sheet.
14. Mark your answer on your answer sheet.
15. Mark your answer on your answer sheet.
16. Mark your answer on your answer sheet.
17. Mark your answer on your answer sheet.
18. Mark your answer on your answer sheet.
19. Mark your answer on your answer sheet.
20. Mark your answer on your answer sheet.
21. Mark your answer on your answer sheet.
22. Mark your answer on your answer sheet.
23. Mark your answer on your answer sheet.
24. Mark your answer on your answer sheet.
25. Mark your answer on your answer sheet.
26. Mark your answer on your answer sheet.
27. Mark your answer on your answer sheet.
28. Mark your answer on your answer sheet.
29. Mark your answer on your answer sheet.
30. Mark your answer on your answer sheet.
31. Mark your answer on your answer sheet.

PART 3

Directions: In this part, you will listen to several conversations between two or more speakers. These conversations will not be printed and will only be spoken one time. For each conversation, you will be asked to answer three questions. Select the best response and mark the corresponding letter (A), (B), (C), or (D) on your answer sheet.

32. Where is the conversation taking place?
    (A) At a restaurant
    (B) At a factory
    (C) At a car-rental company
    (D) At an apartment complex

33. What problem does the woman mention?
    (A) She reserved the wrong date.
    (B) She chose an unsuitable option.
    (C) She lost her personal item.
    (D) She failed to pay a fee.

34. What does the woman ask about?
    (A) How much a service costs
    (B) When an event will begin
    (C) How to register an extra person
    (D) Where to set up some equipment

35. Who most likely is the man?
    (A) An intern
    (B) A team leader
    (C) A consultant
    (D) A receptionist

36. What industry is the woman involved in?
    (A) Insurance
    (B) Hospitality
    (C) Software
    (D) Publishing

37. What does the woman ask the man to do?
    (A) Sign in at a security desk
    (B) Read an employee manual
    (C) Install a mobile application
    (D) Apply for an access card

38. What are the speakers mainly discussing?
    (A) A product launch
    (B) A branch closure
    (C) A business partnership
    (D) A loan application

39. What does the man suggest doing?
    (A) Contacting a technician
    (B) Transferring some funds
    (C) Printing some documents
    (D) Updating a schedule

40. What does the man say he will do?
    (A) Check a device
    (B) Clean a workspace
    (C) Delete a file
    (D) Sign a contract

41. Why does the man apologize?
    (A) Some tickets cannot be purchased.
    (B) An appointment cannot be kept.
    (C) A store is closed for the weekend.
    (D) Some invitations were sent late.

42. What does the woman say about the tickets?
    (A) They are available at a discount.
    (B) They are for good seats.
    (C) They are only sold online.
    (D) They are nonrefundable.

43. What does the man offer to do?
    (A) Post on social media
    (B) File a complaint
    (C) Send a message
    (D) Change a reservation

GO ON TO THE NEXT PAGE

44. What are the speakers mainly discussing?
    (A) A corporate merger
    (B) A contract revision
    (C) A sales presentation
    (D) A marketing campaign

45. Why is the man impressed with the products?
    (A) They are easy to repair.
    (B) They are highly durable.
    (C) They are simple to use.
    (D) They are affordable.

46. What will Gina most likely do next?
    (A) Perform a staff evaluation
    (B) Discuss a legal agreement
    (C) Explain a business strategy
    (D) Conduct a job interview

47. What are the speakers preparing for?
    (A) A seminar
    (B) A job fair
    (C) A book launch
    (D) A trade show

48. According to the woman, what has Dr. Walker accomplished?
    (A) He won an industry award.
    (B) He established an engineering school.
    (C) He organized a national event.
    (D) He invented an electronic device.

49. What will the man send to the woman?
    (A) A payment record
    (B) A speaker schedule
    (C) A seating chart
    (D) An event pass

50. Why is the man calling?
    (A) To confirm a delivery
    (B) To inquire about availability
    (C) To negotiate a price
    (D) To discuss a business relocation

51. What does the woman say about the apartment unit?
    (A) It is being renovated.
    (B) It has a view of a park.
    (C) It is currently unoccupied.
    (D) It includes a balcony.

52. What does the man ask the woman to do?
    (A) Verify an address
    (B) Provide some images
    (C) Modify an interior design
    (D) Extend a contract

53. Where do the speakers most likely work?
    (A) At an electronics factory
    (B) At a shipping facility
    (C) At a furniture manufacturer
    (D) At a department store

54. Why does the woman say, "The products are put together on the third floor"?
    (A) To show admiration
    (B) To explain a delay
    (C) To request assistance
    (D) To point out a problem

55. What does the man say he will do?
    (A) Share employee feedback
    (B) Train new workers
    (C) Repair some equipment
    (D) Update a Web site

56. Who most likely is the man?
    (A) A news reporter
    (B) A lawyer
    (C) An accountant
    (D) An architect

57. What does the man imply when he says, "the client has requested a lot of changes"?
    (A) A design was not reviewed.
    (B) A deadline cannot be met.
    (C) A complaint was dealt with.
    (D) A company policy will change.

58. What does the woman suggest doing?
    (A) Holding a workshop
    (B) Reassigning a project
    (C) Calling a customer
    (D) Attending a meeting

59. What is the conversation mainly about?
    (A) A relocation plan
    (B) A construction project
    (C) A budget proposal
    (D) An environmental law

60. What is important about Warren Park?
    (A) It includes a sports stadium.
    (B) It attracts many tourists.
    (C) It provides a home to wildlife.
    (D) It hosts community events.

61. What does the man give to Ms. Snyder?
    (A) A report
    (B) A brochure
    (C) A letter
    (D) A book

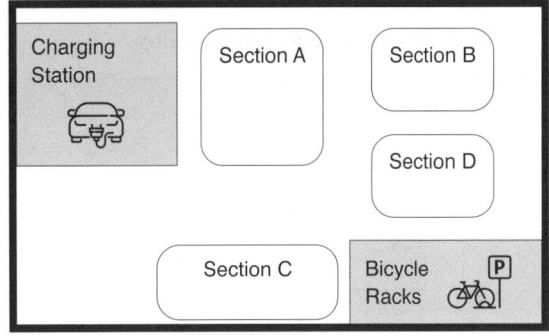

62. What did the man do this morning?
    (A) He performed maintenance.
    (B) He purchased equipment.
    (C) He arranged transportation.
    (D) He requested information.

63. Look at the graphic. Which section of the parking lot will be closed tomorrow?
    (A) Section A
    (B) Section B
    (C) Section C
    (D) Section D

64. How will the woman notify staff members about an issue?
    (A) By holding a meeting
    (B) By texting a message
    (C) By making a post
    (D) By sending an e-mail

GO ON TO THE NEXT PAGE

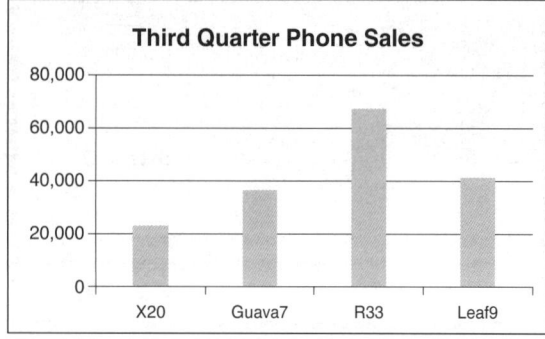

Sauce	Flavor
Apple	Sweet
Tomato	Mild
Pear	Super Sweet
Pepper	Spicy

65. Look at the graphic. Which phone was released in May?
    (A) X20
    (B) Guava7
    (C) R33
    (D) Leaf9

66. What does the man say about some customers?
    (A) They usually purchase the latest model.
    (B) They want to buy what other people own.
    (C) They always look for affordable options.
    (D) They prefer environmentally friendly products.

67. What does the woman ask the man to do?
    (A) Schedule a meeting
    (B) Create an advertisement
    (C) Test a device
    (D) Print a document

68. Where most likely are the speakers?
    (A) At a farmer's market
    (B) At a restaurant
    (C) At an amusement park
    (D) At a food manufacturing plant

69. Look at the graphic. Which sauce does the woman suggest selling online?
    (A) Apple
    (B) Tomato
    (C) Pear
    (D) Pepper

70. What does the man say he will do?
    (A) Revise a recipe
    (B) Expand a product line
    (C) Distribute some flyers
    (D) Speak with a friend

PART 4

Directions: In this part, you will listen to several short talks by a single speaker. These talks will not be printed and will only be spoken one time. For each talk, you will be asked to answer three questions. Select the best response and mark the corresponding letter (A), (B), (C), or (D) on your answer sheet.

71. What is the purpose of a meeting?
    (A) To introduce a staff member
    (B) To explain a policy change
    (C) To confirm a schedule update
    (D) To describe a promotional event

72. What type of business do the listeners most likely work for?
    (A) A furniture store
    (B) A catering company
    (C) A coffee shop
    (D) A photo studio

73. What does the speaker plan to do?
    (A) Set up some refreshments
    (B) Put up a notice
    (C) Contact a customer
    (D) Order some equipment

74. What topic did the listener write an article about?
    (A) Technological risks
    (B) Medical research
    (C) Social programs
    (D) Economic problems

75. What does the speaker like about the article?
    (A) The wording of the title
    (B) The level of difficulty
    (C) The type of evidence
    (D) The point of the argument

76. Where does the speaker want to meet?
    (A) At an office
    (B) At a restaurant
    (C) At a school
    (D) At a city park

77. What does the speaker imply when he says, "I haven't been able to get a reservation yet"?
    (A) An opening has been delayed.
    (B) A menu item was changed.
    (C) An event will be canceled.
    (D) A review will not be shared.

78. What field is Ms. Collins most likely involved in?
    (A) Publishing
    (B) Travel
    (C) Fashion
    (D) Education

79. What does the speaker suggest that the listeners do?
    (A) Visit a Web site
    (B) Purchase an item
    (C) Download an app
    (D) Submit questions

80. What type of event is taking place?
    (A) A parade
    (B) A concert
    (C) A competition
    (D) A charity auction

81. What is mentioned about a route?
    (A) It is blocked off.
    (B) It is clearly marked.
    (C) It will be inspected.
    (D) It will be altered.

82. What will happen at two o'clock?
    (A) A lunch break will be provided.
    (B) A band will perform.
    (C) Awards will be presented.
    (D) Photos will be taken.

GO ON TO THE NEXT PAGE

83. Where does the speaker most likely work?
    (A) At a post office
    (B) At a financial institution
    (C) At a recruitment company
    (D) At a public relations firm

84. Why does the speaker say, "She's one of our most experienced staff members"?
    (A) To encourage an immediate response
    (B) To share a performance evaluation
    (C) To provide a reason for a decision
    (D) To suggest a solution to a problem

85. How can the listener arrange a meeting?
    (A) By sending a group e-mail
    (B) By talking to an assistant
    (C) By calling a client's office
    (D) By visiting on a specific day

86. Where is the talk taking place?
    (A) At an auto repair shop
    (B) At a fitness center
    (C) At an electronics store
    (D) At an equipment rental company

87. What will the speaker probably do later today?
    (A) Finalize a manual
    (B) Bring over a product sample
    (C) Gather some opinions
    (D) Provide temporary laptops

88. What are the listeners reminded to do?
    (A) Update software
    (B) Contact a supplier
    (C) Clean up an area
    (D) Review some instructions

89. What is mentioned about the Lansbury Observatory?
    (A) It is near a public transportation station.
    (B) It will be closed for a month.
    (C) Its facilities were recently renovated.
    (D) It was built using donated funds.

90. What will take place momentarily?
    (A) An experiment will be conducted.
    (B) A presentation will be given.
    (C) A poster will be shown.
    (D) An interview will begin.

91. According to the speaker, what can the listeners do after the tour?
    (A) Make a donation
    (B) Look at photographs
    (C) Purchase souvenirs
    (D) Sign up for another tour

92. Why did the Western Medical Group hold a press conference?
    (A) To introduce a spokesperson
    (B) To address a criticism
    (C) To announce a new service
    (D) To celebrate a financial accomplishment

93. What does the speaker imply when he says, "But there are also new competitors"?
    (A) A difficulty is manageable.
    (B) A cost cannot be determined yet.
    (C) A change will not be immediate.
    (D) A reason is insufficient.

94. What will most likely be discussed next?
    (A) An industry's future
    (B) An investment strategy
    (C) A medical procedure
    (D) A company's expansion

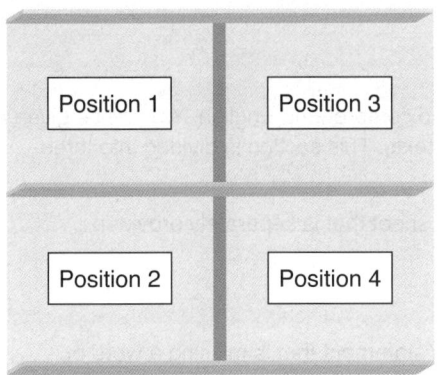

Workshop Topic	Day
E-Mail Phishing	Tuesday
Mobile Device Security	Wednesday
Malware and Viruses	Thursday
Password Protection	Friday

95. What is the theme of the exhibition?
    (A) Modern architecture
    (B) Fashion history
    (C) Geological formations
    (D) Technological innovations

96. Look at the graphic. In which position would the speaker like to place the main photo?
    (A) Position 1
    (B) Position 2
    (C) Position 3
    (D) Position 4

97. According to the speaker, what is causing a delay?
    (A) A printer is malfunctioning.
    (B) Some equipment is being set up.
    (C) Some text is being reviewed.
    (D) A photo shoot is behind schedule.

98. Where does the speaker most likely work?
    (A) At a financial institution
    (B) At an educational facility
    (C) At a security company
    (D) At a software developer

99. Look at the graphic. Which workshop has been canceled?
    (A) E-Mail Phishing
    (B) Mobile Device Security
    (C) Malware and Viruses
    (D) Password Protection

100. What will the speaker most likely do next?
    (A) Meet with an instructor
    (B) Read through a report
    (C) Download an application
    (D) Contact a colleague

This is the end of the Listening test. Turn to PART 5 in your test book.

GO ON TO THE NEXT PAGE

READING TEST

In this section, you must demonstrate your ability to read and comprehend English. You will be given a variety of texts and asked to answer questions about these texts. This section is divided into three parts and will take 75 minutes to complete.

Do not mark the answers in your test book. Use the answer sheet that is separately provided.

PART 5

Directions: In each question, you will be asked to review a statement that is missing a word or phrase. Four answer choices will be provided for each statement. Select the best answer and mark the corresponding letter (A), (B), (C), or (D) on the answer sheet.

PART 5 권장 풀이 시간 11분

101. After the successful product launch, the shareholders' meeting was filled with ------- investors.

(A) satisfy
(B) satisfies
(C) satisfied
(D) satisfaction

102. When Mr. Kumar finished reading the novel *Eternal Spark*, ------- wrote a detailed review.

(A) he
(B) him
(C) his
(D) himself

103. The notification e-mail serves as a ------- to complete the mandatory safety training.

(A) reminds
(B) reminding
(C) reminder
(D) reminded

104. To safely return your product to us, please send it in its ------- package, preferably with the packing slip.

(A) assorted
(B) original
(C) thin
(D) minimal

105. Adams Law Firm has provided legal services for over 20 years, ------- in family law.

(A) special
(B) specializes
(C) specialty
(D) specializing

106. The cost of automobile components is expected to be ------- higher next quarter due to supply chain disruptions.

(A) considerably
(B) adversely
(C) generously
(D) expertly

107. The editorial team outsourced some of its copywriting work to freelancers to meet the -------.

(A) performance
(B) deadline
(C) maintenance
(D) admission

108. During the year-end holiday season, staff at Sutton's Toys may need to take on tasks outside their regular -------.

(A) responses
(B) favors
(C) duties
(D) competitors

109. ------- in to the internship program will depend on academic performance and relevant work experience.

(A) Accept
(B) Accepting
(C) Acceptance
(D) Acceptable

110. Though Mr. Patton and Ms. Liu have different skills, ------- would be a great fit for the project management role.

(A) them
(B) either
(C) more
(D) anyone

111. Mr. Chapman expects it to take ------- three hours to update the software on the company's servers.

(A) rough
(B) roughing
(C) roughly
(D) roughness

112. The product catalog of Scout Apparel includes ------- of all clothing items.

(A) statements
(B) procedures
(C) uncertainties
(D) descriptions

113. Film director Robert Duke ------- shot several scenes of the movie *Outcast* in the dark to create suspense.

(A) intend
(B) intentionally
(C) intention
(D) intending

114. The ------- ingredient in Ms. Belano's dish is fresh basil, which is why it's so flavorful.

(A) diverse
(B) primary
(C) prompt
(D) diligent

115. Workplace safety issues are among the topics that Mr. Lucas will ------- at the meeting on Friday.

(A) appear
(B) activate
(C) complete
(D) address

116. The annual survey lets employees offer Rogers Furniture ------- feedback on its operations.

(A) constructive
(B) construct
(C) constructing
(D) construction

117. Ms. Richardson went ------- with the company's plan, even though she didn't think it was best.

(A) for
(B) to
(C) upon
(D) along

118. To make a warranty claim, be sure ------- the defective product's serial number and the sales receipt.

(A) submitting
(B) submit
(C) to submit
(D) will submit

119. During the conference, Bond Group will cover the cost of a three-day hotel ------- for all attending representatives.

(A) refund
(B) stay
(C) amenity
(D) status

120. The Haynesville Natural History Museum is pleased with the ------- large number of people visiting the butterfly exhibition.

(A) surprising
(B) surprise
(C) surprised
(D) surprisingly

GO ON TO THE NEXT PAGE

121. At Adkins Consulting, job applicants are asked ------- at least two professional references.

    (A) provide
    (B) provides
    (C) to provide
    (D) will provide

122. To finish setting up the tablet, ------- your preferred language and time zone.

    (A) choice
    (B) chose
    (C) chosen
    (D) choose

123. The e-mail Ms. Collins sent to Wrightwell Capital's stakeholders was -------, securing funding for relocation.

    (A) vulnerable
    (B) persuasive
    (C) calculable
    (D) sequential

124. The board of Annika Financial has decided to invest ------- the startup that is focused on AI-driven financial solutions.

    (A) in
    (B) of
    (C) as
    (D) on

125. The lecture on management styles was very long, so it was difficult for Mr. Lee to ------- all the information.

    (A) absorb
    (B) withdraw
    (C) adapt
    (D) surpass

126. Lowery Industries' cybersecurity experts will work on making ------- to systems that are in place to protect company data.

    (A) advance
    (B) advancing
    (C) advanced
    (D) advancements

127. According to the employee handbook, new staff members are eligible for health benefits ------- they complete the 90-day probationary period.

    (A) since
    (B) as if
    (C) once
    (D) unless

128. Solis Education Group's HR department is sorting ------- hundreds of applications to find the best candidates.

    (A) through
    (B) except
    (C) between
    (D) within

129. It is recommended that new technologies be implemented ------- to mitigate any risks that may be associated with them.

    (A) randomly
    (B) gradually
    (C) reluctantly
    (D) interestingly

130. FlexUp Fitness offers various Pilates classes, including ------- for beginners, in order to accommodate different levels.

    (A) which
    (B) those
    (C) one another
    (D) them

PART 6

Directions: In this part, you will be asked to read four English texts. Each text is missing a word, phrase, or sentence. Select the answer choice that correctly completes the text and mark the corresponding letter (A), (B), (C), or (D) on the answer sheet.

Questions 131-134 refer to the following instructions.

One reason for the ------- of banana bread is that it's easy to make. To get started, mash
            131.
some ripe bananas. You can ------- a fork for this. -------, mix butter, sugar, and eggs with the
                              132.   **133.**
bananas before adding flour, baking soda, and salt. Pour the batter into a loaf pan, and

bake it at 180 degrees Celsius. Stick a toothpick into the center of the loaf after an hour.

-------.
134.

131. (A) popularize
     (B) popularity
     (C) popular
     (D) popularly

132. (A) use
     (B) begin
     (C) remove
     (D) connect

133. (A) First
     (B) Instead
     (C) Thus
     (D) Then

134. (A) Many people find that baking reduces their stress.
     (B) If it comes out clean, remove the loaf from the oven.
     (C) Baking soda is great for cleaning pots and pans.
     (D) Store ripe pieces of fruit in the fridge so they last longer.

GO ON TO THE NEXT PAGE

Questions 135-138 refer to the following information.

We are pleased to announce the start of the fifth annual Jabari Prize, a nationwide poetry competition. Submissions for this year's competition ------- due by March 31. They should explore the theme of "Belonging." -------. They must also have not been previously published and be the original work of the author. In addition, there is a ------- of up to three poems per entrant, and a processing fee of $5 will be applied to each submission. Those ------- submit winning poems will receive cash prizes of up to $1,000, and their work will be featured in *The Tinsley Review*.

135. (A) are
 (B) have been
 (C) would be
 (D) were

136. (A) Past winners have published full collections of their work.
 (B) Contestants will be notified of the contest results by this date.
 (C) Both amateur and professional poets should be celebrated.
 (D) Poems should have a title and be no longer than 40 lines.

137. (A) report
 (B) limit
 (C) sign
 (D) program

138. (A) which
 (B) who
 (C) what
 (D) they

Questions 139-142 refer to the following Web page.

Canton Transpo Fares to Increase

The cost of providing transit services is on the rise across the country due to increasing fuel and labor prices. -------, Canton Transpo will be raising fares by 2.5 percent, effective January 1. -------. We understand that ------- increasing prices, we are putting some passengers in a difficult position. Therefore, we will be introducing measures to alleviate the burden, including rewarding ------- riders. Special monthly discounts will be given to anyone who uses our service on a regular basis.

---

139. (A) If not
(B) Nonetheless
(C) Otherwise
(D) Accordingly

140. (A) The standard single-trip fare will increase to $3.75 as a result.
(B) You can load money onto your card at many convenient locations.
(C) Transfers allow you to change vehicles multiple times during your trip.
(D) It is advisable to arrive at your stop a few minutes early.

141. (A) plus
(B) before
(C) by
(D) for

142. (A) previous
(B) frequent
(C) elderly
(D) first-time

Questions 143-146 refer to the following e-mail.

To: Priscilla Murray <pmurray@SchmittCo.com>
From: Damien Parsons <dparsons@SchmittCo.com>
Date: July 7
Subject: RE: Catering

Hi, Priscilla.

With regard to our earlier conversation about switching to a new ------- for catering services,
143.
I have been reviewing the pros and cons of various companies. So far, Lozano Kitchen seems like the best option due to its diverse menu options and commitment to sustainability.

-------. I contacted the owner of the company to arrange for sample dishes to be prepared for
144.
our next weekly meeting so that everyone can have the chance ------- Lozano Kitchen's
145.
offerings and determine if they like them. -------, Lozano Kitchen will become our new official
146.
caterer.

Sincerely,

Damien

143. (A) facility
(B) process
(C) provider
(D) schedule

144. (A) Our current catering company has various vegetarian options.
(B) Fortunately, the meeting will not conflict with anyone's schedule.
(C) Also, it's very affordable for food prepared by professional chefs.
(D) Offering employees lunch in the office increases productivity.

145. (A) tasting
(B) to taste
(C) taste
(D) will taste

146. (A) If so
(B) Until then
(C) However
(D) Conversely

PART 7

Directions: In this part, you will be asked to read several texts, such as advertisements, articles, instant messages, or examples of business correspondence. Each text is followed by several questions. Select the best answer and mark the corresponding letter (A), (B), (C), or (D) on your answer sheet.

Questions 147-148 refer to the following information.

Unfortunately, Melanie Weber won't be performing in tonight's production of *Aeroplane*. Juliette Greer will be replacing her. Juliette is a graduate of the Kirkland Performing Arts Conservatoire and was in the highly acclaimed musical *Spilled Milk*. This will be her first appearance in *Aeroplane*.

We hope you enjoy the show. Please note that there will be a 20-minute interval during the performance. Remember to take your ticket with you if you leave the theatre as it is required for reentry.

147. Where would the information most likely be found?

(A) On a movie poster
(B) In a magazine review
(C) In a confirmation e-mail
(D) In a theater lobby

148. What is indicated about Ms. Greer?

(A) She is attending a performing arts school.
(B) She will replace Ms. Weber permanently.
(C) She had the lead role in *Spilled Milk*.
(D) She is performing in *Aeroplane* for the first time.

GO ON TO THE NEXT PAGE

Questions 149-150 refer to the following announcement.

A temporary water outage will affect households along East Halifax Avenue on Monday, November 12, from 6 A.M. to 2 P.M. This outage will allow workers to perform necessary upgrades to water pipes in the area.

In preparation, residents are advised to set aside water for flushing toilets and brushing teeth. In addition, they are asked to delay any activities that may require significant water consumption, such as watering the garden, washing personal automobiles, or operating washing machines.

For inquiries, please contact Public Works Maintenance Water Superintendent Nancy Dutton at 555-3543.

149. What is the purpose of the announcement?

(A) To notify residents about a meeting
(B) To remind households to pay water bills on time
(C) To provide information about a service interruption
(D) To report a delay in the start of a project

150. What are residents asked to do?

(A) Make appointments with a superintendent
(B) Reschedule some household activities
(C) Permit workers to enter their homes
(D) Temporarily move parked vehicles in affected areas

Questions 151-152 refer to the following brochure.

Built in the late 19th century as the family home of Marcus and Elizabeth Sheppard, the Sheppard Inn & Tea House is the ideal location for memorable getaways and special occasions. As you enter the lobby, you'll be greeted by the breathtaking sight of crystal chandeliers, stained-glass windows, and woodwork restored to its original condition. Yet, despite the historic look, each of the guestrooms is equipped with modern facilities including high-speed Wi-Fi, a state-of-the-art entertainment system, and a whirlpool tub.

Experience our Afternoon High Tea, an exclusive event for guests in the Serenity Room from 3 P.M. to 5 P.M. daily. It features an array of savory foods, all prepared with ingredients from our very own gardens. Take this opportunity to try our new Wu Mei tea, imported from Indonesia.

Call 646-555-4099 to make a booking.

151. What is suggested about the Sheppard Inn & Tea House?

(A) It was renovated less than a year ago.
(B) It is owned and operated by a family.
(C) It features a combination of old and new elements.
(D) It has rooms with garden views.

152. What is indicated about the Afternoon High Tea?

(A) It is provided to guests at no charge.
(B) It offers tea from a different country.
(C) It is served in a garden on the inn's grounds.
(D) It is open to customers who are not guests at the inn.

GO ON TO THE NEXT PAGE

Questions 153-154 refer to the following text-message chain.

Kelly Thompson (10:14 A.M.)
Hey, Michael. This is Kelly from South Side Computer Repairs. We discovered that the source of your computer's freezing problem is a virus, which we've removed.

Michael Gage (10:15 A.M.)
Thank you! I was wondering what the problem was.

Kelly Thompson (10:16 A.M.)
I should also let you know that we found out your hard drive is in poor condition and will likely need to be replaced soon.

Michael Gage (10:17 A.M.)
Oh. How much would that cost?

Kelly Thompson (10:18 A.M.)
Ordinarily it would cost over $100, but we're willing to install a new 500-gigabyte one for just $70. Of course, we would need to have the hard drive shipped here, so we'll have to keep your computer an extra day.

Michael Gage (10:20 A.M.)
I need to work on a report that's due tomorrow. I think I'll pass on that offer and install a new hard drive later.

Kelly Thompson (10:22 A.M.)
Fair enough. In that case, your computer should be ready for pickup by 12:30 P.M. today.

153. Who most likely is Ms. Thompson?

(A) A career counselor
(B) A delivery driver
(C) A Web developer
(D) A repairperson

154. At 10:20 A.M., what does Mr. Gage most likely mean when he writes, "I need to work on a report that's due tomorrow"?

(A) He would like to have some new software installed.
(B) He cannot leave his computer at the shop overnight.
(C) He is too busy with work to complete a new assignment.
(D) He is unable to meet with Ms. Thompson later today.

Questions 155-157 refer to the following Web page.

www.howardnursery.com/about

Welcome to Howard Nursery—the one-stop shop for all your gardening needs!

Share your ideas, photos, and tips for creating and maintaining a beautiful green space. Join fellow gardening enthusiasts on our Web site and get inspired! [Click here]

FAQs

Q1. What kind of houseplants are available?
We have plants of all sizes and species. Choose from hundreds of different succulents, flowering plants, herbs, and more. Use our filtering options to quickly locate a plant that's right for your climate.

Q2. Can I purchase plants for an outside garden?
Howard Nursery offers more than 75 outdoor plants perfect for sprucing up your patio, balcony, or garden. Both ornamental plants and edible plants are available.

Q3. How will items be shipped?
Our shipping service knows how to prevent damage during the shipping process. Most plants are shipped within three to five business days. Overnight shipping and two-day shipping are also available for customers who want their plants right away. Unfortunately, we are not able to ship plants outside the United States.

155. According to the Web page, what can visitors to the Web site do?

(A) Post gardening pictures and advice
(B) Register for plant-care workshops
(C) Subscribe to a monthly newsletter
(D) Schedule home landscaping services

156. What is mentioned about the outdoor plants offered at Howard Nursery?

(A) They come with detailed instructions for their care.
(B) They include both decorative and consumable varieties.
(C) They are sold with a lifetime guarantee.
(D) They are all native to the United States of America.

157. What is true about Howard Nursery's shipping service?

(A) It only offers overnight or two-day shipping.
(B) It allows shipments to be tracked through its app.
(C) It cannot accommodate shipments of large plants.
(D) It is only available for domestic plant delivery.

GO ON TO THE NEXT PAGE

Questions 158-160 refer to the following advertisement.

Sienna Plus Water Filter, Version 2

We are pleased to announce the release of our new Sienna Plus Water Filter, an upgraded version of our original bestselling product. Like the original, the new version can be easily attached to your faucet. It lasts up to four years, twice as long as the original product. In addition, it is even more efficient at filtering out unwanted chemicals. Once attached, the filter will eliminate over 99 percent of the harmful chemicals that are contained in tap water while retaining all the nutritional minerals.

Customers are already raving about the filter, saying that it produces "the freshest water I've ever tasted" and "leaves me feeling better and healthier." To see how our filter works, simply scan the QR code on the packaging and a video will be streamed to your phone. It will only take a few minutes of your time to watch it.

The filter sells for $89.99 on our Web site. It is not currently available in brick-and-mortar stores.

---

158. How is the new Sienna Plus Water Filter better than its predecessor?

(A) It can be used for a longer period of time.
(B) It can accommodate more types of faucets.
(C) It adds a chemical disinfectant to tap water.
(D) It includes a display that shows water purity levels.

159. What can people do by scanning the QR code?

(A) Download a user manual
(B) Access a discount code
(C) Watch an informational video
(D) Read customer reviews

160. How can people purchase the new Sienna Plus Water Filter?

(A) By e-mailing customer service
(B) By placing an online order
(C) By going to a local store
(D) By calling a number

Questions 161-164 refer to the following memo.

MEMO

To: Durant Ltd. Production Staff
From: Jared Skinner
Date: September 30
Subject: New Equipment

Dear Team,

In order to keep pace with advancements within our industry, Durant Ltd. has recently acquired a number of new machines, including some robotic sewing machines and fabric cutters. Since many of you will be using these machines in your daily work going forward, we are organizing a comprehensive training session designed to familiarize you with the correct setup, operation, and shutdown processes associated with each of them. It will take place on-site in our second-floor production facility on October 10 and will span the entire workday.

During the training session, there will be a special focus on the role that the new equipment will play in the production of our line of sustainable fabrics. As these materials are key to the company's strategic goals, mastering the machines is absolutely vital. If you will not be at work on October 10 for any reason, please let me know as soon as possible so we can arrange an alternate time for you to receive this training.

Jared Skinner, Operations Manager

161. What is the purpose of the memo?

(A) To explain changes caused by a relocation
(B) To announce the acquisition of a new facility
(C) To complain about the maintenance of equipment
(D) To inform employees of upcoming training

162. What is suggested about Durant Ltd.?

(A) It is a leader in its field.
(B) It is expanding its operations into new regions.
(C) It is reducing the size of its workforce.
(D) It is involved in textile production.

163. What is true about the production staff?

(A) They will need to complete a certification exam.
(B) They will work on the second floor on October 10.
(C) They will evaluate their peers' mastery of some equipment.
(D) They will have a longer shift on the day of a training session.

164. The word "arrange" in paragraph 2, line 4, is closest in meaning to

(A) schedule
(B) classify
(C) impact
(D) straighten

GO ON TO THE NEXT PAGE

Questions 165-167 refer to the following e-mail.

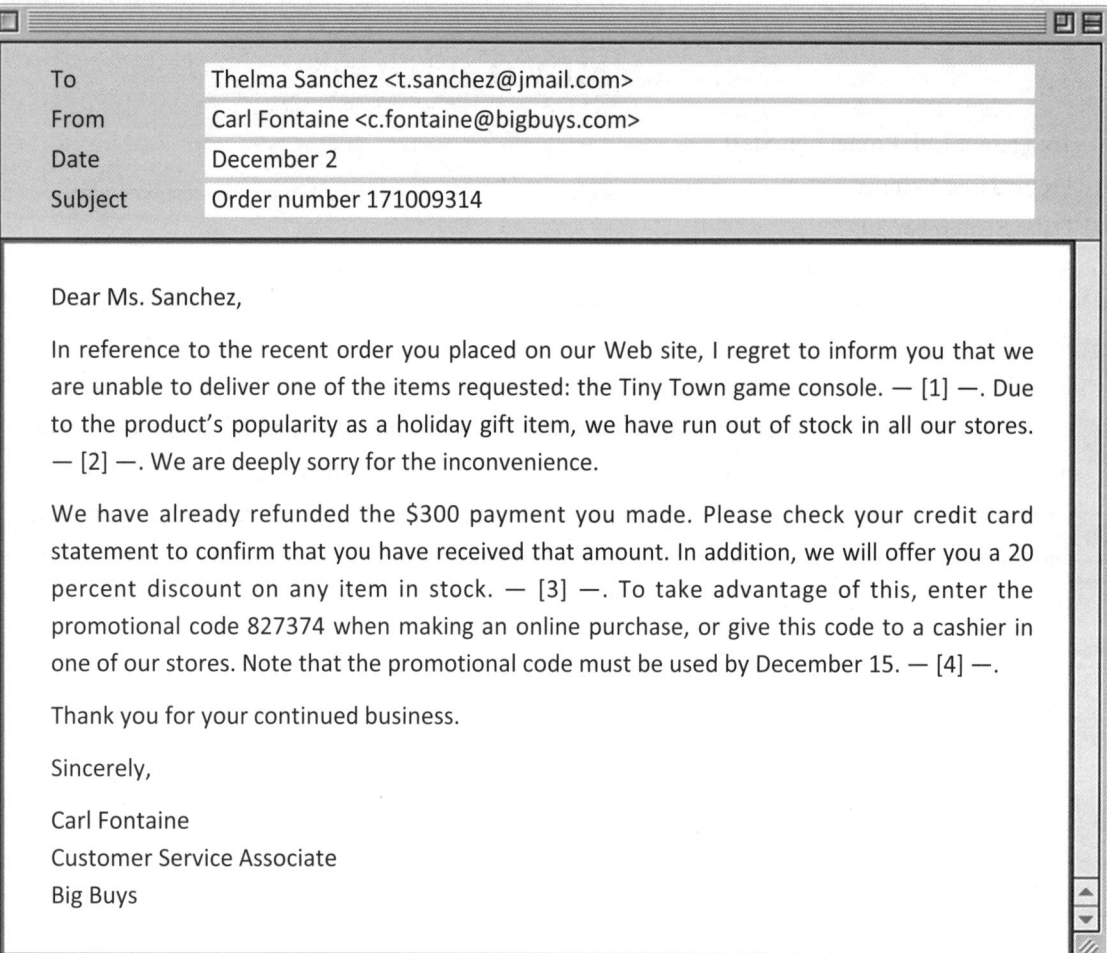

To: Thelma Sanchez <t.sanchez@jmail.com>
From: Carl Fontaine <c.fontaine@bigbuys.com>
Date: December 2
Subject: Order number 171009314

Dear Ms. Sanchez,

In reference to the recent order you placed on our Web site, I regret to inform you that we are unable to deliver one of the items requested: the Tiny Town game console. — [1] —. Due to the product's popularity as a holiday gift item, we have run out of stock in all our stores. — [2] —. We are deeply sorry for the inconvenience.

We have already refunded the $300 payment you made. Please check your credit card statement to confirm that you have received that amount. In addition, we will offer you a 20 percent discount on any item in stock. — [3] —. To take advantage of this, enter the promotional code 827374 when making an online purchase, or give this code to a cashier in one of our stores. Note that the promotional code must be used by December 15. — [4] —.

Thank you for your continued business.

Sincerely,

Carl Fontaine
Customer Service Associate
Big Buys

165. What is mentioned about the Tiny Town game console?

(A) It is unavailable due to high demand.
(B) Its manufacturer recalled the product.
(C) It is not recommended for young children.
(D) Its arrival was delayed by a supplier.

166. What does Mr. Fontaine ask Ms. Sanchez to do?

(A) Visit a physical location
(B) Try another payment option
(C) Change an online account password
(D) Confirm a transaction was processed

167. In which of the positions marked [1], [2], [3], and [4] does the following sentence best belong?

"After this date, it will no longer be valid, and you will miss out on this special offer."

(A) [1]
(B) [2]
(C) [3]
(D) [4]

Questions 168-171 refer to the following article.

LITTLE ROCK (November 19)—Since opening in August, Roll of the Dice has become a hit. Offering everything from classic board games to the latest tabletop role-playing games, this board game store caters to all ages and interests. — [1] —.

The store's co-owners, Noah Lee and Russel McClain, are avid board game enthusiasts who have wanted a store like this in their community for years. When the opportunity came along to fill this gap in the market, the pair took it. Business was slow at first. — [2] —. However, once word got out that there was a game shop in town, it was not long until the store was filled with people.

According to Mr. Lee and Mr. McClain, people also want a space to play the games they love. — [3] —. That's why they've set up a room at the back of the shop that people can use until the store's daily closing time of 8 P.M. — [4] —. In the future, they plan to stay open later to hold tournaments.

168. What is the article mainly about?

(A) A recently established business
(B) A change to a store's opening date
(C) An age restriction placed on a game
(D) A Web site for hard-to-find hobby supplies

169. The word "caters" in paragraph 1, line 5, is closest in meaning to

(A) accepts
(B) provides
(C) serves
(D) applies

170. What is suggested about Roll of the Dice?

(A) It has no employees other than Mr. Lee and Mr. McClain.
(B) It is located on a street with a lot of foot traffic.
(C) It faces a lot of competition from similar businesses.
(D) It will stay open past 8 P.M. for special events.

171. In which of the positions marked [1], [2], [3], and [4] does the following sentence best belong?

"In fact, the pair only made a single sale in their first week in business."

(A) [1]
(B) [2]
(C) [3]
(D) [4]

Questions 172-175 refer to the following online chat discussion.

Ben Pollard	(9:10 A.M.)	I have a quick question, Karen. Ms. Sadi's flight gets in at 9:15 this morning, right? I just want to make sure everything is on schedule.
Karen Chua	(9:11 A.M.)	Actually, I just received a call from her. Her flight landed a bit early, and she's already at the airport.
Ben Pollard	(9:12 A.M.)	That's good to hear. It's about 30 minutes from the airport to our office by taxi, so she should be here soon.
Karen Chua	(9:14 A.M.)	But she's planning to catch a shuttle bus instead of getting a taxi. There is one that leaves at 9:45, which will drop her off nearby about 40 minutes later.
Ben Pollard	(9:15 A.M.)	So she would get here at around 10:25? The meeting starts at 10:30. That's too close for comfort. Can you ask her to reconsider?
Karen Chua	(9:16 A.M.)	OK. I'll mention that our CEO postponed a business trip to meet with her about having her new novel published by our company, so it would look bad if she was late.
Ben Pollard	(9:18 A.M.)	Good idea. By the way, is everything set up in the conference room?
Karen Chua	(9:19 A.M.)	Yeah. And I'll tell one of the interns to go to the bakery across the street to pick up some pastries and coffee.

172. Why did Mr. Pollard send the message?

(A) To make certain of an arrival time
(B) To change some travel arrangements
(C) To request an explanation of a delay
(D) To point out an issue with an itinerary

173. At 9:15 A.M., what does Mr. Pollard most likely mean when he writes, "That's too close for comfort"?

(A) Ms. Sadi must catch an earlier shuttle bus.
(B) Ms. Sadi should take a taxi from the airport.
(C) Ms. Sadi needs to check a meeting agenda.
(D) Ms. Sadi ought to take a morning flight.

174. What is indicated about Ms. Sadi?

(A) She has recently finished writing a new book.
(B) She met with Mr. Pollard on a previous occasion.
(C) She is planning to postpone an upcoming business trip.
(D) She currently works for the publisher.

175. What will Ms. Chua ask an intern to do?

(A) Contact some other workers in the office
(B) Arrange some furniture in the conference room
(C) Buy some refreshments to offer at a meeting
(D) Set up some audiovisual equipment for a presentation

GO ON TO THE NEXT PAGE

Questions 176-180 refer to the following notice and e-mail.

Attention, All Staff

Please be advised that all computers and mobile devices will undergo a security upgrade. This work has been scheduled for Friday, November 22, starting at 4 P.M. Hallington Insurance Group is committed to continuously assessing the company's security system and making necessary adjustments. We have decided to team up with Kellings Tech, a new technology company based in Arizona. During discussions with the lead engineer, we were informed about several weaknesses in our system that place customer accounts and employee information at risk.

Kellings Tech representatives will be on-site the whole day of the planned work. Please bring all the devices you use for remote work. Save all files on the external hard drive that will be provided to you on November 21. Please contact the head of IT, Aaron Beckford, at a.beckford@hallington.com if you have any questions.

From: Martin Clarins <m.clarins@hallington.com>
To: Aaron Beckford <a.beckford@hallington.com>
Date: November 14
Subject: Security upgrade

Hi Aaron,

I was made aware of the upcoming security upgrade. However, as you might know, I am currently working in Singapore and won't be back until the week after the scheduled work. My assistant, Consuelo Cortez, does have access to the computer in my office, so I don't see an issue there.

However, I have my company smartphone and laptop with me. I guess there are a couple of options to deal with this situation. I could just hand these devices over to the technicians once I get back. Or is there a software program I could download and set up myself? I should also mention that I have access to another laptop I can use during my trip in case you want me to mail my work one back right away. The phone needs to remain with me though as it is essential for me to stay in touch with clients and coordinate my calendar.

Please let me know as soon as possible.

Sincerely,

Martin

176. What is the purpose of the notice?

(A) To extend a training session invitation
(B) To describe a company policy change
(C) To announce some computer work
(D) To explain some equipment purchases

177. What is indicated about Hallington Insurance Group?

(A) It has merged with a large corporation.
(B) It has not confirmed the date of a security upgrade.
(C) It has invested in new computer desktops.
(D) It has not worked with Kellings Tech before.

178. Who most likely is Mr. Beckford?

(A) A technical consultant
(B) A department manager
(C) A company president
(D) A personal assistant

179. What does Mr. Clarins suggest about his work?

(A) He will not be in the office until after November 22.
(B) He has been transferred permanently to Singapore.
(C) He has submitted a travel reimbursement form.
(D) He was promoted to a new position one year ago.

180. What is NOT a solution offered by Mr. Clarins?

(A) Waiting until a trip is complete to turn over devices
(B) Installing a software application without assistance
(C) Having a computer delivered to an office branch
(D) Replacing a phone with one issued by the company

GO ON TO THE NEXT PAGE

Questions 181-185 refer to the following Web page and e-mail.

---

www.windowsclearhouston.com

We can clean your windows and do any glass repair work. Windows Clear is a franchise that started in Houston. Other locations are opening in New York, Chicago, and other major cities. The following services are available:

• **Service 1**

Daily window washing. This is recommended for retail locations with a storefront. Our workers will take steps to ensure minimal interruptions to your business. Currently, we are offering an introductory trial week for Houston businesses for $99.

• **Service 2**

Periodical window washing. We also have the equipment for skyscrapers. Sign up for weekly or monthly visits by our workers.

• **Service 3**

One-time job for any specific event or occurrence. We will make the windows of your business or home shine.

• **Service 4**

Window repair. We can repair all types of windows, replacing damaged glass and performing any other related work. This is available for businesses and homes.

If you are interested in any service, one of our representatives will inspect your business or home and provide you with an accurate quote. For Service 4, we recommend sending us photos of the damage. E-mail info@windowsclear.com if you have any questions.

From: Shion Yamada <s.yamada@shionopticalspace.com>
To: Windows Clear <info@windowsclear.com>
Date: June 25
Subject: URGENT

Dear Windows Clear,

I was referred to you by Harry Colton from Starset Pizzeria, which is down the street from us in downtown Houston. He said you visit his business daily and you could help with my problem.

My optical shop was broken into last night, and I need two of the windows repaired. They are the store's front windows, so I cannot open my shop until they are fixed. Therefore, I would like to hire you right away. I will pay myself and then get reimbursed by my insurance company later. Please call me as soon as possible at 555-9493 to arrange a time.

Thanks.

Shion Yamada
Shion Optical Space

181. What is indicated about Windows Clear?

(A) It only serves the downtown area.
(B) It is advertising in a local newspaper.
(C) It is currently expanding into other cities.
(D) It has doubled its sales over the last quarter.

182. According to the Web page, what will happen before a customer is provided with a price estimate?

(A) An online request form will be reviewed.
(B) An inspection of a space will be conducted.
(C) A payment method will be verified.
(D) A photographer will be dispatched.

183. Which service will Ms. Yamada most likely select?

(A) Service 1
(B) Service 2
(C) Service 3
(D) Service 4

184. How did Ms. Yamada hear about Windows Clear?

(A) She met a representative at an industry event.
(B) She visited its Web site while searching online.
(C) She received a referral from a business owner.
(D) She saw a poster advertising its services.

185. What is NOT mentioned about Shion Optical Space?

(A) It is located in downtown Houston.
(B) It will be closed until a repair is made.
(C) It has multiple branches in the same city.
(D) It will be reimbursed by an insurance firm.

GO ON TO THE NEXT PAGE

Questions 186-190 refer to the following memo, advertisement, and review.

MEMO

TO: All Save Smart Staff
FROM: Tony Wilkins
SUBJECT: Clearance Sale
DATE: September 1

Summer is about to end, so we'll be holding a clearance sale next week on all summer clothing and supplies. These include clothing, toys, and other items. I'll post a full list of the products that will be on sale in the break room tomorrow. With luck, these items will sell out within the first week at a 25 percent discount. But if there are a substantial number of products still on the shelves, we'll reduce their prices by 50 percent the following week. Sometime this evening, I'd like some of you to help me hang up posters announcing the sale in our front windows and around the store. It will officially begin on September 7.

Save Smart's Annual SUMMER CLEARANCE SALE!

From September 14 until September 20, all summer items in our store will be 50 percent off. These include:

- T-shirts, swim trunks, sandals, and shorts
- Lawn mowers and sprinklers
- Water slides, water guns, and flotation devices
- Grills and grilling accessories

Be sure to hurry as this sale will only last for another week. Save Smart is open from 9 A.M. to 8 P.M., seven days a week.

*Members of the Save Smart Club will receive an additional 10 percent discount on all of these items.

Homeman Outdoor Grill Reviews

Rating: 5/5

I bought this grill on a whim while wandering through the Save Smart store in Minneapolis. I got it for 60 percent off during the summer clearance sale, so it was a steal. It turns out that this is the best grill I've ever purchased.

During the winter months, which I spend in California, I've used this over 10 times cooking for various guests. It cooks much more efficiently than other grills I've owned. You simply place the meat (or vegetables) inside, choose the right setting, then close the lid and wait. The only problem I had with it occurred when I first changed the propane tank. The new one would not connect. But when I checked the instructions that came with the grill, I was able to quickly figure out what I was doing wrong. I would highly recommend this product.

Arthur Klepper

---

186. According to the memo, what did some employees of Save Smart do on September 1?

(A) They reorganized products on a store's shelves.
(B) They took a detailed inventory of items in stock.
(C) They posted notices about an upcoming promotion.
(D) They set up window displays for new merchandise.

187. What can be concluded about Save Smart's Summer Clearance Sale?

(A) The initial discount amount was reduced.
(B) Many items were unsold in the first week.
(C) The start date was pushed back by one day.
(D) Some customers were unable to make purchases.

188. What is stated about Save Smart in the advertisement?

(A) It manufactures its own products.
(B) It extended its hours in September.
(C) It operates every day of the week.
(D) It recently changed the name of its loyalty club.

189. What is indicated about Mr. Klepper?

(A) He relocated to Minneapolis last month.
(B) He is in the process of returning a product.
(C) He only cooks vegetarian dishes.
(D) He was a Save Smart Club member in September.

190. How did Mr. Klepper resolve an issue he experienced with his grill?

(A) By visiting a Web site
(B) By checking a user manual
(C) By speaking to a store employee
(D) By calling a service center

Questions 191-195 refer to the following e-mails and text-message chain.

To: All Staff <group@leonfinancial.com>
From: Brenda Carver <b.carver@leonfinancial.com>
Subject: Workshop
Date: January 15

Hi Everyone,

As announced last week, the use of Core Tech's EZFile software program was approved by our CEO, Logan Morales. This application will automate many of the routine tasks involved in filing our clients' tax returns.

I have arranged for a representative from Core Tech to conduct a workshop at our office next month. Tina Williams is highly knowledgeable about this program and has worked closely with the lead designer, Brock Desai, so I am sure you will learn a lot from her. The workshop will take place in Room 201 on February 17. It will start at 10 A.M. and end at 3 P.M., with a 30-minute break for lunch. The EZFile training is mandatory for all accountants. Staff members in other roles at our company do not have to participate.

Thanks.

Brenda Carver
Human Resources, Leon Financial

Chad Ellis [February 17, 2:10 P.M.]
Could you do me a favor, Diya? As you know, I have the afternoon off because I need to get a wisdom tooth pulled out. I was on the way to see my dentist when I realized I'd forgotten to do something before leaving the office.

Diya Patel [February 17, 2:11 P.M.]
Sure. I've got some time now. It's been a slow afternoon, actually. There were not many tech support requests from the other staff here.

Chad Ellis [February 17, 2:12 P.M.]
There should be a green folder containing receipts for computer parts on my desk. Some of the accountants' computers had to be upgraded before the EZFile software was installed. Could you give it to our department head before you go home today?

Diya Patel [February 17, 2:14 P.M.]
Of course. I'll take care of that.

To	All Staff <group@leonfinancial.com>
From	Brenda Carver <b.carver@leonfinancial.com>
Subject	Request
Date	February 18
Attachment	Questionnaire

Hi,

I'd like to gather some feedback from those of you who attended the EZFile workshop yesterday morning in Room 301. If you did take part, please fill out the attached questionnaire and send it back to me by February 21. There are several questions focusing on the instructor and how well the topic was explained. I am also interested in knowing whether the scheduled 30-minute break was sufficient.

Thank you in advance for taking the time to fill this out.

Brenda Carver
Human Resources, Leon Financial

191. According to the first e-mail, who will lead the training session?

(A) Brenda Carver
(B) Logan Morales
(C) Tina Williams
(D) Brock Desai

192. What was Mr. Ellis doing when he contacted Ms. Patel?

(A) Going to a clinic
(B) Cleaning his office
(C) Calling a technician
(D) Returning to his home

193. What can be concluded about Ms. Patel?

(A) She was not informed about Mr. Ellis's plan to leave early.
(B) She is a member of Leon Financial's human resources department.
(C) She was asked to purchase some components for a device.
(D) She is not required to learn how to use the EZFile software.

194. What does Mr. Ellis request that Ms. Patel do?

(A) Attend a departmental meeting
(B) Follow up on a leave request
(C) Print out some financial records
(D) Bring an item to a manager

195. What did Ms. Carver change to her original plan?

(A) The location of an event
(B) The length of a break
(C) The subject of a lesson
(D) The date of a workshop

Questions 196-200 refer to the following Web page, job posting, and online review.

www.herman.com/about

Herman Solutions

We get your goods where they need to go!

Offering customers the option of making online purchases has become necessary for even the smallest brick-and-mortar stores, but the cost of providing fast deliveries can be prohibitive. That's where Herman Solutions comes in. We handle all of the shipping logistics so that you can focus on meeting your customers' needs.

Here's how our system works:

- Our shipment-processing software is integrated into your Web site and mobile application.
- When a customer selects the delivery option, the address is automatically entered into our system.
- Every Friday, one of our drivers will visit your shop to pick up and deliver any outstanding orders.
- You will be billed monthly for completed deliveries.

For information about our rates, please click here. And if you sign up by November 15, you will not be charged for your first 10 deliveries.

Herman Solutions is hiring delivery drivers!

Join the fastest-growing delivery company in the country. We offer competitive compensation as well as a range of benefits, including health insurance, flexible hours, and generous annual leave.

Qualifications
- Minimum of two years' relevant experience
- Valid commercial-class driver's license
- Ability to lift heavy objects (up to 60 kilograms)
- High school diploma

To apply, visit www.herman.com/join and complete the electronic application form. All successful applicants will be required to undergo seven days of instruction with an experienced driver before beginning their regular duties.

www.herman.com/feedback

Review by David Wilkins

I registered for Herman Solutions on November 10, and I have been quite impressed overall. As a store specializing in sports memorabilia and collectibles, we have customers around the country. Herman Solutions has made it possible to ship them our products quickly and affordably. In addition, I have been very happy with the professionalism of the Herman staff members. Our regular driver Sharon, for example, always arrives on time and takes great care to ensure that our packages are not damaged or lost. I strongly recommend Herman Solutions to other small business owners who are looking to simplify the delivery process.

196. What is the purpose of the Web page?

(A) To announce a retailer's partnership with a business
(B) To explain a recent increase in the cost of deliveries
(C) To describe improvements to an existing system
(D) To provide an overview of a company's service

197. What is true about Herman Solutions?

(A) It requires clients to use its own mobile application.
(B) It requests delivery addresses through e-mail.
(C) It picks up packages from stores once a week.
(D) It demands payment in advance for shipments.

198. What did Mr. Wilkins qualify for?

(A) Access to a customer database
(B) A complimentary product upgrade
(C) A special rate on express deliveries
(D) Use of service at no charge

199. What is mentioned as a requirement for the delivery driver position?

(A) A year spent working in a similar role
(B) Completion of a government safety program
(C) Ability to lift objects over 60 kilograms
(D) A certificate of graduation from high school

200. What can be concluded about Sharon?

(A) She received training for a period of one week.
(B) She dropped off an application form in person.
(C) She will request additional annual leave.
(D) She will replace another driver for a month.

This is the end of the test. You may review Parts 5, 6, and 7 if you finish the test early.

Review 체크리스트

TEST 2를 푼 다음, 아래 체크리스트에 따라 틀린 문제를 리뷰하고 박스에 완료 여부를 표시하세요.
만약 시험까지 얼마 남지 않았다면, [1]번 ~ [3]번 항목이라도 꼭 확인하세요.

☐ [1] 틀린 문제의 경우, 다시 풀어봤다.

☐ [2] 틀린 문제의 경우, 스크립트/해석을 확인하며 지문/문제의 내용을 정확하게 파악했다.

☐ [3] 해설을 통해 각 문제의 정답과 오답의 근거가 무엇인지 정확하게 파악했다.

☐ [4] PART 1과 PART 2에서 틀린 문제의 경우, 선택한 오답의 유형이 무엇이었는지 확인하고 같은 함정에 빠지지 않도록 정리해두었다.

☐ [5] PART 3와 PART 4의 각 문제에서 사용된 패러프레이징을 확인했다.

☐ [6] PART 5와 PART 6의 경우, 틀린 문제에서 사용된 문법 포인트 또는 정답 및 오답 어휘를 정리했다.

☐ [7] PART 6의 알맞은 문장 고르기 문제의 경우, 지문 전체를 정확하게 해석하며 전체 글의 흐름과 빈칸 주변 문맥을 정확하게 파악하는 연습을 했다.

☐ [8] PART 7에서 질문과 보기의 키워드를 찾아 표시하며 지문에서 정답의 근거가 되는 문장이나 구절을 찾아보고, 문제에서 사용된 패러프레이징을 확인했다.

☐ [9] PART 1~PART 4는 받아쓰기 & 쉐도잉 워크북을 활용하여, TEST에 수록된 핵심 문장을 받아쓰고 따라 읽으며 복습했다.

☐ [10] PART 1~PART 7은 단어암기자료를 활용하여, TEST에 수록된 핵심 어휘와 표현을 암기했다.

많은 양의 문제를 푸는 것도 중요하지만, 틀린 문제를 제대로 리뷰하는 것도 중요합니다.
틀린 문제를 한 번 더 꼼꼼히 리뷰한다면, 빠른 시간 내에 효과적으로 목표 점수를 달성할 수 있습니다.

해커스 토익 실전 LC+RC 3

TEST 3

LISTENING TEST

PART 1
PART 2
PART 3
PART 4

READING TEST

PART 5
PART 6
PART 7

Review 체크리스트

잠깐! 테스트 전 아래 사항을 꼭 확인하세요.
1. 휴대전화의 전원을 끄셨나요? 예 □
2. Answer Sheet(p.251), 연필, 지우개, 시계를 준비하셨나요? 예 □
3. Listening MP3를 들을 준비가 되셨나요? 예 □

모든 준비가 완료되었으면 목표 점수를 떠올린 후 테스트를 시작합니다.
테스트를 마친 후, Review 체크리스트(p.152)를 보며 자신이 틀린 문제를 반드시 복습합니다.

🎧 TEST 3.mp3
실전용·복습용 문제풀이 MP3 무료 다운로드 및 스트리밍 바로듣기 (HackersIngang.com)
* 실제 시험장의 소음까지 재현해 낸 고사장 소음/매미 버전 MP3, 영국식·호주식 발음 집중 MP3, 고속 버전 MP3까지 구매하면 실전에 더욱 완벽히 대비할 수 있습니다.

무료MP3 바로듣기

LISTENING TEST

In this section, you must demonstrate your ability to understand spoken English. This section is divided into four parts and will take approximately 45 minutes to complete. Do not mark the answers in your test book. Use the answer sheet that is provided separately.

PART 1

Directions: For each question, you will listen to four short statements about a picture in your test book. These statements will not be printed and will only be spoken one time. Select the statement that best describes what is happening in the picture and mark the corresponding letter (A), (B), (C), or (D) on the answer sheet.

Sample Answer

The statement that best describes the picture is (B), "The man is sitting at the desk." So, you should mark letter (B) on the answer sheet.

1.

2.

3.

4.

5.

6.

PART 2

Directions: For each question, you will listen to a statement or question followed by three possible responses spoken in English. They will not be printed and will only be spoken one time. Select the best response and mark the corresponding letter (A), (B), or (C) on your answer sheet.

7. Mark your answer on your answer sheet.
8. Mark your answer on your answer sheet.
9. Mark your answer on your answer sheet.
10. Mark your answer on your answer sheet.
11. Mark your answer on your answer sheet.
12. Mark your answer on your answer sheet.
13. Mark your answer on your answer sheet.
14. Mark your answer on your answer sheet.
15. Mark your answer on your answer sheet.
16. Mark your answer on your answer sheet.
17. Mark your answer on your answer sheet.
18. Mark your answer on your answer sheet.
19. Mark your answer on your answer sheet.
20. Mark your answer on your answer sheet.
21. Mark your answer on your answer sheet.
22. Mark your answer on your answer sheet.
23. Mark your answer on your answer sheet.
24. Mark your answer on your answer sheet.
25. Mark your answer on your answer sheet.
26. Mark your answer on your answer sheet.
27. Mark your answer on your answer sheet.
28. Mark your answer on your answer sheet.
29. Mark your answer on your answer sheet.
30. Mark your answer on your answer sheet.
31. Mark your answer on your answer sheet.

PART 3

Directions: In this part, you will listen to several conversations between two or more speakers. These conversations will not be printed and will only be spoken one time. For each conversation, you will be asked to answer three questions. Select the best response and mark the corresponding letter (A), (B), (C), or (D) on your answer sheet.

32. Why does the woman ask for help?
    (A) She is unfamiliar with a task.
    (B) She cannot find a file.
    (C) She is unable to attend a meeting.
    (D) She cannot locate a business.

33. What will happen next month?
    (A) An executive will retire.
    (B) Some technology will be updated.
    (C) A company will expand a facility.
    (D) Some new employees will be trained.

34. What does the man give to the woman?
    (A) A corrected chart
    (B) An attendance list
    (C) Contact information
    (D) Customer reviews

35. Where most likely are the speakers?
    (A) At a zoo
    (B) At a theater
    (C) At a community center
    (D) At a history museum

36. What was the woman surprised about?
    (A) The schedule of events
    (B) The price of parking
    (C) The reviews of attendees
    (D) The availability of tickets

37. What does the man suggest doing?
    (A) Changing seats
    (B) Buying souvenirs
    (C) Taking pictures
    (D) Wearing headphones

38. Where does the conversation most likely take place?
    (A) At a hotel
    (B) At a grocery store
    (C) At an organic farm
    (D) At an electronics store

39. What does Sebastian ask about?
    (A) How much an item costs
    (B) How long a task will take
    (C) When a store will open
    (D) Where to plug in an appliance

40. What does the woman recommend?
    (A) Beginning at an earlier time
    (B) Developing new flavors
    (C) Offering samples
    (D) Ordering some equipment

41. What did the man review yesterday?
    (A) A budget
    (B) A list of supplies
    (C) An employee evaluation
    (D) An attendance report

42. According to the woman, what do some visitors want to do?
    (A) Make donations
    (B) Receive a newsletter
    (C) Purchase diverse paintings
    (D) Interact with exhibits

43. What will the woman send by e-mail?
    (A) A survey form
    (B) A gift catalog
    (C) Some receipts
    (D) Some articles

GO ON TO THE NEXT PAGE

44. Where do the speakers most likely work?

(A) At a national park
(B) At an advertising firm
(C) At a media company
(D) At a photography studio

45. According to the man, why does the woman need to get a pass?

(A) To follow a new security regulation
(B) To meet the organizers of an event
(C) To gain access to all areas of a site
(D) To avoid paying an entrance fee

46. What will happen next Monday?

(A) A festival will end.
(B) A facility will be closed.
(C) An article will be released.
(D) A space will be redesigned.

47. Why is the woman visiting?

(A) To provide business advice
(B) To negotiate a contract
(C) To attend a convention
(D) To speak at a corporate event

48. What does the woman ask about?

(A) The name of a department head
(B) The cause of increased investments
(C) The location of overseas branches
(D) The date of a company event

49. What will Mr. Klein most likely do next?

(A) Book a flight ticket
(B) Contact another staff
(C) Order new office furniture
(D) Bring financial data

50. What are the speakers mainly discussing?

(A) Organizing a health fair
(B) Addressing a safety issue
(C) Arranging a building tour
(D) Attracting more clients

51. Why does the woman say, "It's also better for the environment"?

(A) To explain a policy
(B) To confirm an error
(C) To compliment a colleague
(D) To support a suggestion

52. What does the man volunteer to do?

(A) Print an invoice
(B) Visit a factory
(C) Research a product
(D) Check the weather

53. What does the man want to improve?

(A) Employee benefits
(B) Customer service
(C) Team member collaboration
(D) Future sales revenue

54. Why does the woman recommend Mike Williams?

(A) He majored in a related field.
(B) He won an employee award.
(C) He has a lot of experience.
(D) He transferred from another department.

55. What does the woman say she will do later?

(A) Copy some documents
(B) Give information to staff
(C) Meet with a supervisor
(D) Clean a break room

56. What event is taking place?
(A) A career fair
(B) An awards ceremony
(C) A fundraising dinner
(D) An academic seminar

57. What does the man say about his company?
(A) It is planning an internship program.
(B) It has merged with foreign business.
(C) It will expand to another country.
(D) It will provide a free service.

58. What does the woman mean when she says, "I'll be working at my family's business then"?
(A) She will not be available.
(B) She will start her own business.
(C) She needs some help with a project.
(D) She thinks a deadline should be extended.

59. What did the speakers recently do?
(A) They purchased some items.
(B) They attended a meeting.
(C) They trained a new employee.
(D) They had lunch together.

60. What problem does the man mention?
(A) An item has been damaged.
(B) A Web site is not functioning properly.
(C) A client is not happy with a company's work.
(D) An important document has been misplaced.

61. What will the man do in the afternoon?
(A) Revise the drafts
(B) Make a phone call
(C) Go to a dentist
(D) Check a Web site

Instructor	Room
Sam Hurley	103
Mitch Marks	104
Claire Newson	105
Betty Walz	106

62. What task has the man just completed?
(A) Placing an order
(B) Editing a video
(C) Renting some equipment
(D) Organizing some materials

63. Look at the graphic. Which room has the projector that needs to be replaced?
(A) Room 103
(B) Room 104
(C) Room 105
(D) Room 106

64. What does the woman inquire about?
(A) Where to park her car
(B) Whether an office is open
(C) How many items are needed
(D) When a device was used

GO ON TO THE NEXT PAGE

Office Supplies Order Form	
Item	Quantity
Ink Cartridges (Color)	4
Printer Paper (Pack)	8
Manila Envelopes (box)	2
Staplers (Large)	3

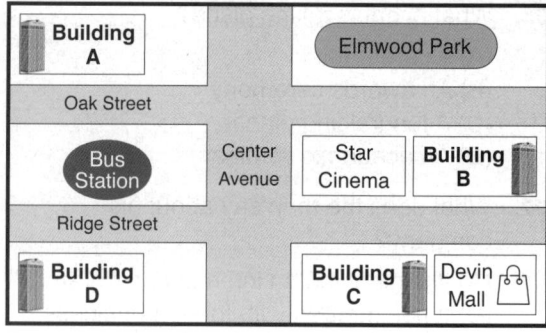

65. Which industry do the speakers most likely work in?
    (A) Health care
    (B) Marketing
    (C) Accounting
    (D) Technology

66. Look at the graphic. Which quantity does the woman ask to be increased?
    (A) 4
    (B) 8
    (C) 2
    (D) 3

67. What will the man do next?
    (A) Contact a supplier
    (B) Confirm a price
    (C) Speak with a coworker
    (D) Visit a storage area

68. Who most likely is the man?
    (A) A realtor
    (B) A photographer
    (C) A movie director
    (D) An accountant

69. What information did the woman notice on the Web site?
    (A) A tracking number
    (B) A schedule change
    (C) A list of options
    (D) A discount offer

70. Look at the graphic. Where will the speakers meet?
    (A) At Building A
    (B) At Building B
    (C) At Building C
    (D) At Building D

PART 4

Directions: In this part, you will listen to several short talks by a single speaker. These talks will not be printed and will only be spoken one time. For each talk, you will be asked to answer three questions. Select the best response and mark the corresponding letter (A), (B), (C), or (D) on your answer sheet.

71. What is being advertised?
    (A) A community college
    (B) A used bookstore
    (C) A stationery store
    (D) A publishing company

72. What change does the speaker mention?
    (A) An app has been developed.
    (B) More employees have been hired.
    (C) Operating hours have been extended.
    (D) An additional branch has opened.

73. What can visitors receive for free today?
    (A) A fabric bag
    (B) A book stand
    (C) A desk lamp
    (D) A logo T-shirt

74. Where does the speaker most likely work?
    (A) At a marketing agency
    (B) At a consulting firm
    (C) At a financial institution
    (D) At a pharmaceutical company

75. According to the speaker, what will happen later this morning?
    (A) An experiment will begin.
    (B) Clients will visit.
    (C) Workers will get new assignments.
    (D) A parking lot will be temporarily closed.

76. What should the listeners do by Friday?
    (A) Participate in a poll
    (B) Submit a product idea
    (C) Pick up a badge
    (D) Have a picture taken

77. Why is the speaker calling?
    (A) To confirm an order
    (B) To cancel an appointment
    (C) To inform about an employee's leave
    (D) To check a preference

78. Why does the speaker say, "He has been with us for over 10 years"?
    (A) To give an update
    (B) To justify a cost
    (C) To provide reassurance
    (D) To deny responsibility

79. How can the listener request a schedule change?
    (A) By clicking on a link
    (B) By returning a phone call
    (C) By using a mobile application
    (D) By visiting in person

80. What is the speaker mainly discussing?
    (A) A design conference
    (B) A product presentation
    (C) A branch opening
    (D) A training workshop

81. According to the speaker, why will Steven be replaced?
    (A) A venue cannot be changed.
    (B) A project was canceled.
    (C) An audience has complained.
    (D) An event cannot be delayed.

82. What does the speaker expect the listeners to do?
    (A) Complete an order form
    (B) Provide some feedback
    (C) Choose a candidate
    (D) Make some presentation slides

GO ON TO THE NEXT PAGE

83. Who most likely is the speaker?
    (A) A tour guide
    (B) A sales associate
    (C) A security guard
    (D) A hotel manager

84. What does the speaker imply when she says, "It's always full of locals"?
    (A) A community restricts access to a location.
    (B) A store is not big enough for everyone.
    (C) A service is only available for residents.
    (D) A business has a good reputation.

85. What will the listeners most likely do next?
    (A) Board a bus
    (B) Leave a review
    (C) Purchase some clothes
    (D) Unpack some luggage

86. According to the speaker, why are traffic delays expected?
    (A) A bridge is being repaired.
    (B) A pipe was damaged.
    (C) A parade will take place.
    (D) A tunnel is being constructed.

87. Who is Paul Reeves?
    (A) A business owner
    (B) A construction worker
    (C) A government official
    (D) A company spokesperson

88. What will the listeners hear after a commercial break?
    (A) Some sports scores
    (B) Some election results
    (C) A newly released song
    (D) A celebrity interview

89. What type of event is most likely taking place?
    (A) A retirement banquet
    (B) A food festival
    (C) A company retreat
    (D) A cooking contest

90. What is going to be shown on a screen?
    (A) A special advertisement
    (B) A sponsor's message
    (C) A documentary film
    (D) A cooking presentation

91. What does the speaker advise the listeners to do?
    (A) Read a set of directions
    (B) Sit close to the main stage
    (C) Applaud the winner
    (D) Pay attention to announcements

92. What is the speaker mainly discussing?
    (A) Hiring more employees
    (B) Working from home
    (C) Training new staff
    (D) Purchasing some tools

93. What does the speaker mean when he says, "we are just one of the departments"?
    (A) A decision needs to be made soon.
    (B) An urgent meeting will be scheduled.
    (C) A request cannot be fulfilled.
    (D) A solution was not satisfied.

94. According to the speaker, what factor influences job satisfaction the most?
    (A) Annual bonuses
    (B) Vacation policies
    (C) Health benefits
    (D) Employee connections

Trek Master Hiking Boots	
* Discount applied to the price	
Product	**Price**
Action Walk	$90.70
Slope Ultra	$65.00
Trail Runner	$85.50
Route Plus	$70.00

95. What is the reason for the sale?
    (A) To mark a company anniversary
    (B) To celebrate the start of summer
    (C) To promote a new store branch
    (D) To make room for new stock

96. Look at the graphic. Which product is made of recycled materials?
    (A) Action Walk
    (B) Slope Ultra
    (C) Trail Runner
    (D) Route Plus

97. What does the speaker encourage the listeners to do?
    (A) Create an account
    (B) Download coupons
    (C) Compare prices
    (D) Check a warranty

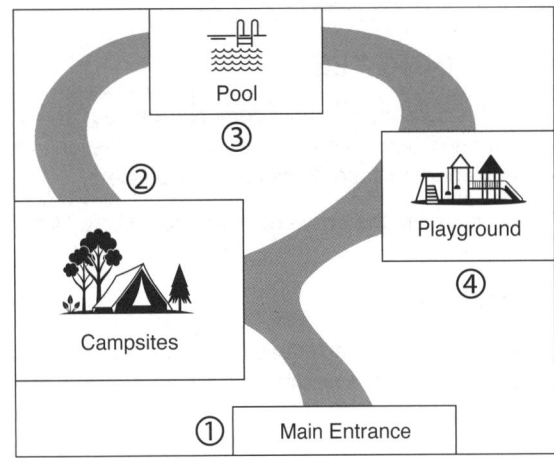

98. According to the speaker, what was recently completed?
    (A) A worker orientation
    (B) A safety inspection
    (C) A delivery order
    (D) A site expansion

99. Look at the graphic. Where will the listeners meet the assistant manager?
    (A) At Location 1
    (B) At Location 2
    (C) At Location 3
    (D) At Location 4

100. What are the listeners instructed to do?
    (A) Bring a floor plan
    (B) Wear a name badge
    (C) Repair some equipment
    (D) Use a different driving route

This is the end of the Listening test. Turn to PART 5 in your test book.

GO ON TO THE NEXT PAGE

READING TEST

In this section, you must demonstrate your ability to read and comprehend English. You will be given a variety of texts and asked to answer questions about these texts. This section is divided into three parts and will take 75 minutes to complete.

Do not mark the answers in your test book. Use the answer sheet that is separately provided.

PART 5

Directions: In each question, you will be asked to review a statement that is missing a word or phrase. Four answer choices will be provided for each statement. Select the best answer and mark the corresponding letter (A), (B), (C), or (D) on the answer sheet.

101. The sign is positioned ------- the café entrance, so everyone who enters will see it.
    (A) down
    (B) beside
    (C) prior to
    (D) aside from

102. Your subscription to *Mod Magazine* will ------- renew unless you contact us to cancel it.
    (A) automatic
    (B) automation
    (C) automatically
    (D) automate

103. In addition to older pieces, the Sprockwell Museum regularly ------- contemporary works.
    (A) tolerates
    (B) instructs
    (C) showcases
    (D) operates

104. Customers are encouraged to arrive at the ------- time to pick up their orders.
    (A) designates
    (B) designated
    (C) designating
    (D) designation

105. Mr. Kline's conference call with the financial advisor of Henner Industrial will begin ------- at 9:30 A.M.
    (A) precisely
    (B) hourly
    (C) spaciously
    (D) simultaneously

106. The head of the legal team was one of the ------- speakers during the business negotiations.
    (A) persuasiveness
    (B) persuasively
    (C) more persuasively
    (D) most persuasive

107. Trett Electronics offers a ------- discount on all electronic devices during the annual clearance sale.
    (A) reputable
    (B) disposable
    (C) redundant
    (D) significant

108. The show *Gallegos Manor* is ------- based on historical events, with some of the characters and events being fictional.
    (A) loose
    (B) loosed
    (C) loosely
    (D) loosens

109. ------- the help of a local volunteer group, the community arranged a successful neighborhood cleanup event.

    (A) In
    (B) With
    (C) Only
    (D) For

110. As the deadline for submission approached, the pressure within the design team became -------.

    (A) intense
    (B) intensifies
    (C) intensely
    (D) intenseness

111. Milestone Construction is ------- seeking a wide variety of skilled workers for its upcoming projects.

    (A) deceptively
    (B) actively
    (C) infinitely
    (D) loyally

112. ------- in the housing market has led to a decline in property values.

    (A) Weak
    (B) Weaken
    (C) Weakened
    (D) Weakness

113. Joseph Tanner was ------- the applicants who were chosen to return for a second interview.

    (A) from
    (B) except
    (C) onto
    (D) among

114. Printers include a ------- for adjusting the alignment of paper to prevent jams.

    (A) mechanic
    (B) mechanize
    (C) mechanism
    (D) mechanistic

115. With the team's star player on the bench, no one ------- that the Paulsburg Pumas would win the game so decisively.

    (A) issued
    (B) approved
    (C) expected
    (D) revealed

116. Harper Manufacturing is encouraging ------- staff to propose themes for next month's company workshop.

    (A) them
    (B) its
    (C) itself
    (D) theirs

117. The lease for the office space has several ------- that must be considered, including one about premature termination.

    (A) qualities
    (B) provisions
    (C) appointments
    (D) capabilities

118. After conducting a thorough risk assessment, Connel Insurance ------- agreed to fund the technology start-up.

    (A) final
    (B) finalized
    (C) finally
    (D) finalization

119. ------- hard she tried, Ms. Jin could not keep up with the rest of her indoor cycling class.

    (A) However
    (B) Fairly
    (C) Even if
    (D) Somehow

120. At Acuo Clothing, sales associates ------- a 15 percent commission on each sale they make.

    (A) receiving
    (B) receives
    (C) receive
    (D) receipt

GO ON TO THE NEXT PAGE

121. The employee training program was updated after ------- complaints related to customer service began coming in.

(A) responsible
(B) numerous
(C) average
(D) tolerant

122. The collaboration ------- the marketing team and the research department resulted in a successful product launch.

(A) between
(B) over
(C) toward
(D) behind

123. The orientation session ensures that all new employees are ------- about the policies at Pittman Financial.

(A) acquainted
(B) effective
(C) knowledgeable
(D) convenient

124. Additional staff members were hired ------- Murillo Department Store could extend its operating hours during the holiday season.

(A) in effect
(B) so that
(C) or else
(D) only if

125. Tickets purchased for all Western Airline flights are not ------- to another person.

(A) transfer
(B) transferring
(C) transferable
(D) transferability

126. The CEO's ------- at the charity gala demonstrated Daugherty Corporation's dedication to giving back to the community.

(A) appear
(B) appeared
(C) to appear
(D) appearance

127. Meltonville is committed to ------- the wetlands and forests that serve as the natural habitats of local wildlife.

(A) preserving
(B) devoting
(C) donating
(D) enclosing

128. After reviewing ------- of the proposals for the advertising campaign, the committee selected the most cost-effective option.

(A) others
(B) many
(C) anyone
(D) whom

129. Ms. Buckley ------- with her fabric supplier before she confirmed the terms and conditions for the bulk purchase.

(A) is meeting
(B) had met
(C) to meet
(D) has to meet

130. With an ------- cooking style, the hotel's chefs successfully tailored their dishes to suit various international guests' tastes.

(A) overall
(B) adaptable
(C) incomplete
(D) identical

PART 6

Directions: In this part, you will be asked to read four English texts. Each text is missing a word, phrase, or sentence. Select the answer choice that correctly completes the text and mark the corresponding letter (A), (B), (C), or (D) on the answer sheet.

Questions 131-134 refer to the following notice.

Attention All Staff

I am pleased to inform you that Henderson Grocers ------- self-service kiosks. The
                                                    131.
installation is scheduled to begin next Monday and should be completed within the same

week. These kiosks are designed to allow customers to check out their purchases -------.
                                                                              132.
This should result in enhanced customer satisfaction.

-------, the introduction of these kiosks does not diminish the importance of our cashiers. All
133.
cashiers will receive training on how to use the kiosks so they can assist customers when

necessary. -------.
         134.

131. (A) has installed
     (B) installed
     (C) installs
     (D) will install

132. (A) independent
     (B) independence
     (C) independency
     (D) independently

133. (A) Alternatively
     (B) Of course
     (C) On the other hand
     (D) In that case

134. (A) Kiosk screens will display advertisements for in-store promotions.
     (B) A training schedule has been posted in the break room.
     (C) Customers favor products that offer good value for their money.
     (D) We encourage customers to provide feedback regarding these machines.

GO ON TO THE NEXT PAGE

Questions 135-138 refer to the following advertisement.

We're thrilled to announce the opening of Quentin Furniture Warehouse! -------. From April 2 to 16, join us for exclusive offers and unbeatable discounts.
    135.

------- your home! No matter what you're looking for, we promise we can help you turn your space into the home you want. Plus, for every purchase over $500, you'll receive a
136.

complimentary item. These gifts can be selected from our ------- range of home décor products. ------- you've been thinking about refreshing your home's interior, now is the
                                                                137.
138.

perfect time. Visit us at 437 Hemlock Road today!

135. (A) Book a consultation with one of our design experts.
(B) A lifetime warranty comes with all bed frames.
(C) To celebrate, we're having a sale you won't want to miss.
(D) The grand opening event was an outstanding success.

136. (A) Appreciate
(B) Transform
(C) Maintain
(D) Rent

137. (A) extensive
(B) defective
(C) compatible
(D) dominant

138. (A) When
(B) Although
(C) While
(D) If

Questions 139-142 refer to the following press release.

FOR IMMEDIATE RELEASE

LOUISVILLE (March 14)—In a press statement made earlier today, Archer Books owner Rob Foley revealed ------- plans for the Louisville bookshop, stating that the popular store is set to open a new location in Lexington this July.
139.

During his statement, Mr. Foley said, "We are excited about the ------- growth of Archer Books. -------. The city's recent economic boom and its reputation for innovation made it the obvious choice."
140. **141.**

Being an independent bookstore, Archer Books has an inventory of publications that reflects the interests of the local community. It listens to its customers and ------- books in response to their requests.
142.

139. (A) expansion
    (B) expand
    (C) to expand
    (D) expanding

140. (A) loud
    (B) brief
    (C) rapid
    (D) single

141. (A) Our stores will each feature a small coffee shop.
    (B) The science fiction and fantasy genres are experiencing a boom.
    (C) We have chosen Lexington for various important reasons.
    (D) Customers can earn points whenever they make purchases.

142. (A) orders
    (B) writes
    (C) borrows
    (D) organizes

Questions 143-146 refer to the following Web page information.

At Stan Office Essentials, we are not just dedicated to providing high-quality workplace equipment but are also concerned with -------. Because we are striving for a greener future,
                                                                                    143.
we offer a recycling service for old printers, computers, and other devices. Since we started this program, our stores ------- over one million pounds of devices that would have otherwise
                                          144.
ended up in landfills. To participate, simply bring your devices to the drop-off desk in any Stan Office Essentials. You'll be eligible to join our Recycling Rewards Program ------- your
                                                                                                                                                          145.
devices are assessed by a Stan Office Essentials associate. For each device you recycle, you'll earn points. -------.
                              146.

143. (A) affordability
     (B) sustainability
     (C) diversity
     (D) profitability

144. (A) are going to recycle
     (B) recycle
     (C) have recycled
     (D) will have recycled

145. (A) further
     (B) whether
     (C) unless
     (D) once

146. (A) These can be redeemed for discounts on anything in the store.
     (B) Switching to paperless billing conserves natural resources.
     (C) Stan Office Essentials now offers shipping and print services.
     (D) We sell a wide selection of eco-friendly products.

PART 7

Directions: In this part, you will be asked to read several texts, such as advertisements, articles, instant messages, or examples of business correspondence. Each text is followed by several questions. Select the best answer and mark the corresponding letter (A), (B), (C), or (D) on your answer sheet.

Questions 147-148 refer to the following notice.

NOTICE

On July 7, as part of our efforts to eliminate pests, we will spray pesticide in all areas of the building, including individual units. Please refer to the following schedule:

Floors 1–3: 8:00 A.M. to 10:00 A.M.
Floors 4–6: 10:30 A.M. to 12:30 P.M.
Floors 7–9: 1:00 P.M. to 3:00 P.M.
Floors 10–12: 3:30 P.M. to 5:30 P.M.

Please ensure pets are secured or removed when your apartment is being sprayed.

147. For whom is the notice most likely intended?

(A) Home inspectors
(B) Building residents
(C) Professional chefs
(D) Sanitation workers

148. By what time will the pesticide spraying be over on Floor 8?

(A) 12:30 P.M.
(B) 1:00 P.M.
(C) 3:00 P.M.
(D) 5:30 P.M.

GO ON TO THE NEXT PAGE

Questions 149-150 refer to the following e-mail.

To: w_schaefer@sportsplaza.com
From: d_conway@conwaysonslandscaping.com
Subject: Landscaping Proposal
Date: May 14

Dear Ms. Schaefer,

I hope this e-mail finds you well. My name is Daniel Conway, and I represent Conway & Sons Landscaping, a family-owned business with over a decade of experience creating beautiful outdoor spaces. I am writing to offer our services to your sports complex on 45th Street and would like to arrange a meeting to discuss your requirements. I am available from Tuesday to Friday after 2 P.M.

If my proposal is of interest to you, could you please provide me with a rough estimate of your budget? I'll go over it and let you know what services we can provide. Thank you, and I look forward to hearing from you.

Sincerely,

Daniel Conway
Conway & Sons

149. What is the purpose of the e-mail?

(A) To request a meeting
(B) To finalize a contract
(C) To demand payment
(D) To collect feedback

150. What information does Mr. Conway request from Ms. Schaefer?

(A) A street address
(B) An approximate budget
(C) A project timeline
(D) A site blueprint

Questions 151-152 refer to the following advertisement.

Chenille Hotel: A Getaway You'll Remember

Located just 50 kilometers from the Davenport International Airport, the Chenille Hotel is the ideal place to escape from the hustle and bustle of the big city. Enjoy a variety of activities, from kayaking on beautiful Lake Mendi to cycling the bicycle paths that stretch across the 35-acre hotel grounds. If you enjoy spending time in nature, this is the place for you.

All of our rooms include a balcony overlooking Lake Mendi and a comfortable bed. And if you are looking for something special, consider one of our deluxe rooms, which feature a whirlpool tub, a full kitchen, and a separate office area to catch up on work. Call 555-8245 to make your reservation today!

151. For whom is the advertisement most likely intended?

(A) People who enjoy outdoor activities
(B) Tourists looking to see historic attractions
(C) Business travelers attending a conference
(D) Families requiring child-friendly facilities

152. What is NOT mentioned about the deluxe rooms?

(A) They provide a view of a lake.
(B) They have an area to prepare food.
(C) They feature a separate bedroom.
(D) They include a space to do work.

GO ON TO THE NEXT PAGE

Questions 153-154 refer to the following text-message chain.

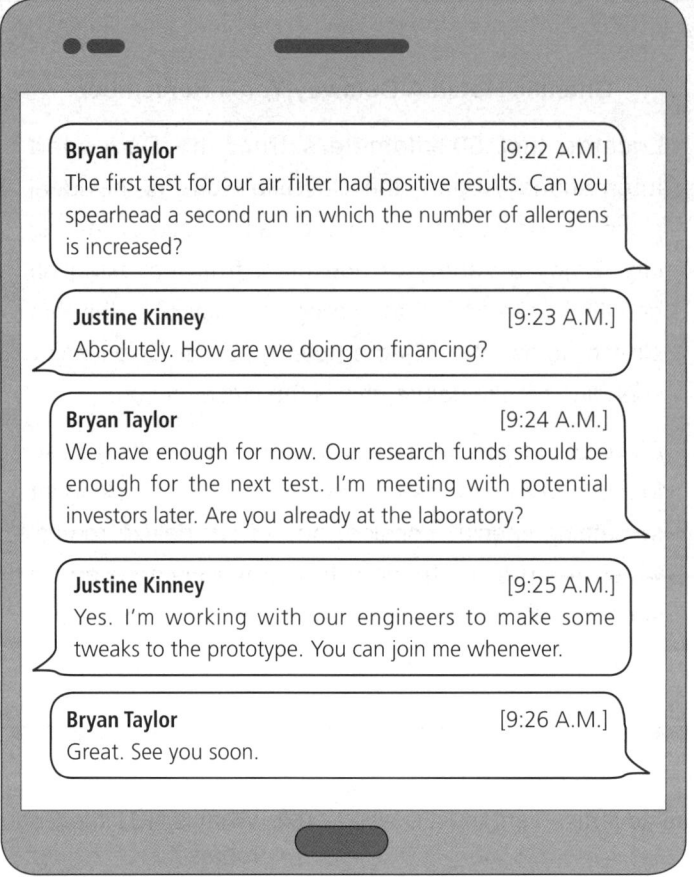

Bryan Taylor [9:22 A.M.]
The first test for our air filter had positive results. Can you spearhead a second run in which the number of allergens is increased?

Justine Kinney [9:23 A.M.]
Absolutely. How are we doing on financing?

Bryan Taylor [9:24 A.M.]
We have enough for now. Our research funds should be enough for the next test. I'm meeting with potential investors later. Are you already at the laboratory?

Justine Kinney [9:25 A.M.]
Yes. I'm working with our engineers to make some tweaks to the prototype. You can join me whenever.

Bryan Taylor [9:26 A.M.]
Great. See you soon.

153. What is indicated about the air filter?

(A) It is being marketed to health practitioners.
(B) It is waiting to be shipped to stores.
(C) It will undergo another test phase.
(D) It is being inspected by an official organization.

154. At 9:24 A.M., what does Mr. Taylor most likely mean when he writes, "We have enough for now"?

(A) A laboratory space is large enough.
(B) Supplies have already been ordered.
(C) The number of staff is sufficient.
(D) Funds will cover a project.

Questions 155-157 refer to the following article.

VANCOUVER (October 11)—The online food delivery service Doorbell Diners, headquartered in Edmonton, has announced the layoff of approximately 800 employees nationwide. The measure aims to cut costs in response to rising inflation and interest rates.

With the announcement coming just months after Cartwright Foods took similar action, concern is mounting that an even greater shift toward the gig economy is taking place within the industry. Carolyn Hudson, who assumed the role of CEO following Edward Reed's resignation in September, denied that the layoffs reflect a preference for gig workers.

"This was not a simple decision, and I appreciate that people are struggling right now," Ms. Hudson said. "However, the measure we took was driven by necessity. Looking ahead, we expect to rehire some laid-off employees as market conditions improve."

155. What is the purpose of the article?
 (A) To promote a company's new services
 (B) To report on personnel changes within an organization
 (C) To announce the relocation of a corporate headquarters
 (D) To analyze the growth of the food delivery market

156. What is suggested about Doorbell Diners?
 (A) It recently experienced a change in leadership.
 (B) It has partnered with Cartwright Foods.
 (C) It will be hiring more delivery drivers.
 (D) It plans to increase spending on employee training.

157. The word "appreciate" in paragraph 3, line 1, is closest in meaning to
 (A) value
 (B) understand
 (C) admire
 (D) represent

GO ON TO THE NEXT PAGE

Questions 158-160 refer to the following Web page.

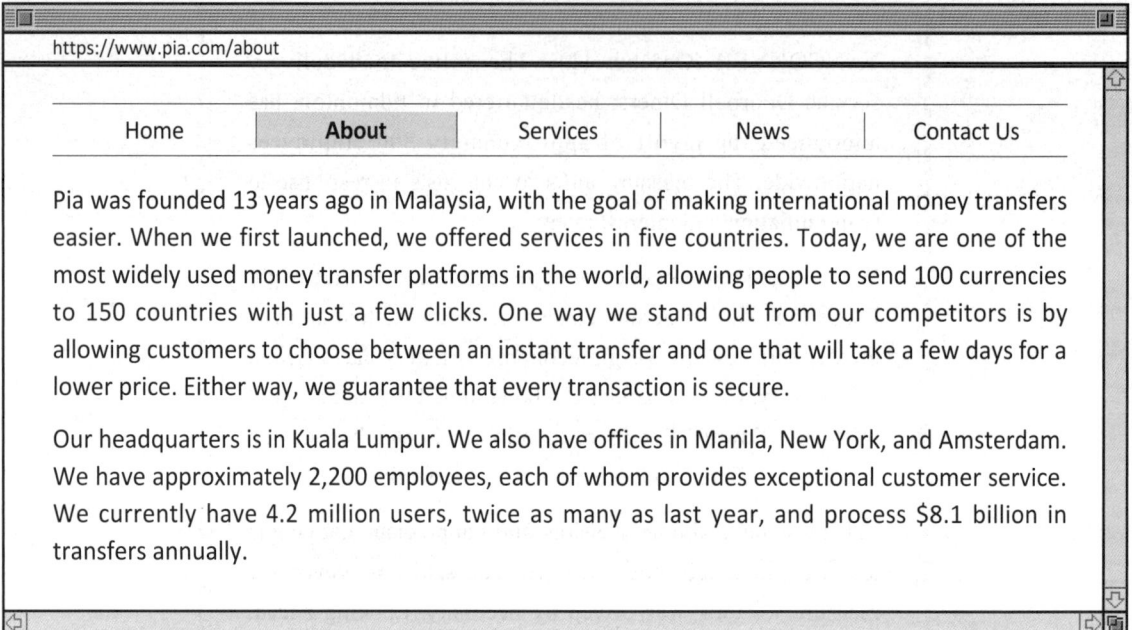

158. What information is included in the Web page?

(A) Testimonials by satisfied customers
(B) Details about upcoming changes
(C) Instructions on how to sign up for the service
(D) Information about the company's early days

159. According to the Web page, what does Pia offer that distinguishes it from its rivals?

(A) The ability to make free transactions
(B) Around-the-clock customer service
(C) Multiple options for transfer speed
(D) Rewards for frequent use

160. What is NOT stated about Pia?

(A) It has offices in several cities.
(B) It employs over 2,000 people.
(C) It doubled its total number of users.
(D) It has merged with another company.

Questions 161-163 refer to the following article.

Chicago Is Ready

February 14—The Chicago International Airport has added three de-icing facilities. The facilities are close to the runways and can each service two planes at once. This system is highly efficient, as evidenced by a test conducted at the Calgary Airport, which showed that similar facilities decreased delays by 80 percent during cold months.

In Chicago, airlines paid for the $100 million project and will pay maintenance fees. Formerly, airlines had to individually defrost equipment at the gates by spraying it with de-icing liquids, which was often a time-consuming process. The facilities also improve safety since planes can take off shortly after being de-iced, minimizing the chance of ice re-forming on critical surfaces.

Having the largest plane fleet at the Chicago International Airport, Virviana Airlines has been granted priority access to the new de-icing facilities and is already using them. So far, a 95 percent success rate has been reported.

161. What is the article mainly about?

(A) A terminal remodeling project
(B) An airline shareholders' meeting
(C) A change to a flight route
(D) A new airport feature

162. What is indicated about airlines in Chicago?

(A) They had to cancel numerous winter flights.
(B) They will fund the upkeep of the facilities.
(C) They will continue using de-icing liquids.
(D) They received government subsidies for a project.

163. According to the article, why does Virviana Airlines have priority access?

(A) It submitted an advanced payment.
(B) It helped develop a new technology.
(C) It has the largest number of aircraft at the airport.
(D) It has added more flights during winter.

GO ON TO THE NEXT PAGE

Questions 164-167 refer to the following e-mail.

To: Beth Hong <b.hong@speedymail.com>
From: Jeffrey Anderson <j.anderson@fenn.com>
Date: March 10
Subject: Fenn Mart

Dear Ms. Hong,

Congratulations. You did well during the interview, and we have decided to offer you a position. We would like you to participate in a training session at our location on 249 Clark Street. — [1] —. It is our biggest location, so we train all of our new hires there. You will work closely with several of our experienced staff members. We do not expect perfection, but we do look for a willingness to take the initiative. — [2] —.

After your training is complete, you will be assigned to a different location. — [3] —. Please mention if you have any specific requests. We prefer to have our employees work at branches close to their homes.

The training session is scheduled for March 17, from 8 A.M. until 12 P.M., and you will be assigned a uniform. Lunch will be provided immediately after the training concludes. Please confirm your attendance. — [4] —.

Sincerely,

Jeffrey Anderson
Fenn Mart

---

164. What is the purpose of the e-mail?

(A) To explain a company's hiring process
(B) To request some banking information
(C) To confirm a schedule change
(D) To provide an update about an application

165. What is true about Fenn Mart?

(A) It has more than one location.
(B) It is looking to replace a regional manager.
(C) It holds monthly training sessions.
(D) It has banned single-use plastic food containers.

166. What will happen in the afternoon of March 17?

(A) Job interviews will be conducted.
(B) A meal will be served to trainees.
(C) A list of store branches will be posted online.
(D) Worker photographs will be taken.

167. In which of the positions marked [1], [2], [3], and [4] does the following sentence best belong?

"I would appreciate it if you could do this no later than March 15."

(A) [1]
(B) [2]
(C) [3]
(D) [4]

Questions 168-171 refer to the following article.

GEORGETOWN (May 17)—In recent months, Georgetown has seen an influx of new businesses opening across town. Among them is The Whodunit, a specialty shop dedicated to mystery novels, run by business partners Natasha Baker and Eric Pope. — [1] —. Although The Whodunit initially struggled to attract customers, Ms. Baker and Mr. Pope began hosting weekly mystery-themed party events back in February. — [2] —. Since then, business has picked up considerably. "We couldn't be more pleased with how things are going now," Ms. Baker stated. The store's monthly sales have tripled since launching these mystery events, with an average of 45 participants attending each weekly gathering.

Another recent addition to Georgetown's business landscape is Suds, a dry cleaner owned by local entrepreneur Norman Nash. — [3] —. Judging by the number of vehicles parked outside the establishment, it's difficult to imagine that Mr. Nash was in trouble just a few months ago. "I could barely turn a profit at first. Not enough people knew I was even open for business," Mr. Nash said. — [4] —. However, once he increased Suds' presence on social media, residents began to take notice. Now with a loyal customer base and steady revenue, Mr. Nash is planning to expand his services next month to include same-day dry cleaning options. The expansion will feature a mobile app that allows customers to schedule contactless pickup and delivery services.

168. What kind of business do Ms. Baker and Mr. Pope run?

(A) A bookstore
(B) A party supply store
(C) A dry cleaner
(D) A car wash

169. What do The Whodunit and Suds have in common?

(A) They both host weekly events for customers.
(B) They both have their own parking lot.
(C) They both have a strong online presence.
(D) They both struggled when they were first opened.

170. What will Mr. Nash most likely do in June?

(A) Launch an advertising campaign
(B) Hold a special promotion
(C) Renovate a commercial property
(D) Introduce a new service option

171. In which of the positions marked [1], [2], [3], and [4] does the following sentence best belong?

"People can participate in solving fictional crimes every Saturday night while browsing the latest releases."

(A) [1]
(B) [2]
(C) [3]
(D) [4]

GO ON TO THE NEXT PAGE

Questions 172-175 refer to the following online chat discussion.

Jordan Mitchell (2:38 P.M.)		As of today, *Hidden Jungle: Escape* has been out for two months. How have sales been?
Alice Turner (2:39 P.M.)		They're not quite as good as the first game. So far, we've only sold about 500,000 units.
Jordan Mitchell (2:40 P.M.)		That's about 200,000 less than the first one during the same time frame. It seems we need to identify the key factors behind this.
George Parker (2:41 P.M.)		It probably has something to do with the mediocre reviews it has gotten. Most game critics objected to the fact that you can finish the levels within just 10 hours.
Jordan Mitchell (2:42 P.M.)		How about the response from gamers themselves?
Alice Turner (2:43 P.M.)		Well, judging by customer reviews on our sales page, the reception has been generally positive. They do point out some technical flaws, though.
Jordan Mitchell (2:44 P.M.)		Those are being addressed. George, please provide an update on the progress of the patch.
George Parker (2:45 P.M.)		We've fixed the occasional freezes on level three, as well as some of the graphics resolution issues. The patch should be available for download by September 1.
Jordan Mitchell (2:46 P.M.)		Excellent. Hopefully, that'll draw more people to the game.

172. What is indicated about *Hidden Jungle: Escape*?

(A) It was created using new game design software.
(B) It is a sequel to a previous game.
(C) It was delayed for months before its release.
(D) It features 10 challenging levels.

173. What problem do critics have with *Hidden Jungle: Escape*?

(A) It can be completed relatively quickly.
(B) It does not meet visual expectations.
(C) It does not work well with controllers.
(D) It has a storyline that is hard to follow.

174. At 2:44 P.M., what does Mr. Mitchell most likely mean when he writes, "Those are being addressed"?

(A) New levels are in the process of being developed.
(B) Budget concerns are being resolved.
(C) Some technological glitches are being fixed.
(D) A lack of staff members will be dealt with.

175. What will most likely happen in September?

(A) A new game will begin production.
(B) An update will be released.
(C) A company retreat will take place.
(D) A gaming competition will be held.

GO ON TO THE NEXT PAGE

Questions 176-180 refer to the following invitation and schedule.

Friday, 28 July
from 8 P.M. to Midnight
The Grand Centre, Dublin

The Dublin Jazz Showcase has become a popular attraction each summer, and this year's event won't disappoint. We moved to a more sizeable venue this time and switched things up a bit. Instead of a regular concert format, we have decided to hold several concerts at once. At the centre, several performance spaces are booked. You can stay in one or visit all of them. In each space, unique dishes will be served. Pairing the delicious food with the wonderful music will surely delight your senses.

Tickets will go on sale on 24 June at 10 A.M. at our box office or online at www.dublinjazzshowcase.ie. Tickets are €50 per programme. Discounts are available for seniors and students. Valid identification must be shown upon entry. The ticket price includes the cost of the food served in most cases. However, the dishes available on the terrace must be paid for separately.

Members of the Dublin Jazz Association will have access to tickets starting on 22 June at 10 A.M. Please have your membership identification number ready before booking.

Dublin Jazz Showcase

Space	Programme	Food & Drinks
Room 210	Jazz trio Tre will delight with traditional jazz.	Try some gourmet popcorn flavoured with truffle oil and other seasonings. Pair it with sparkling wine from the Finglas Winery.
Auditorium 105	Listen to singer Roberta Woods, along with the contemporary jazz quartet Lubion.	Enjoy fresh seafood and a wide assortment of local beers from the Gilmore Brewery.
Terrace	Group CTjazz specializes in Latin jazz. Relax in the lounge, or have fun on the dance floor.	Have a cocktail, and choose from several traditional Irish dishes prepared by master chef Mary Mallet of the Burnside Eatery.
Room 310	Smooth jazz is performed by James Danton and his band, with supporting vocals by Marvin Hammer.	Drink coffee from the Harborview Café, and try some delicious pastries from the Coleman Bakery.

176. What does the invitation suggest about the event?

(A) It will last for a period of two days.
(B) It has been held in previous years.
(C) It is scheduled to end in the afternoon.
(D) It was funded by a government program.

177. In the invitation, the word "regular" in paragraph 1, line 3, is closest in meaning to

(A) decent
(B) orderly
(C) steady
(D) conventional

178. Why are some individuals eligible for early ticket booking?

(A) They have purchased some event merchandise.
(B) They are staff members of the Dublin Jazz Showcase.
(C) They have a membership with a local organization.
(D) They have made generous donations to an organization.

179. What can be concluded about Mary Mallet?

(A) She will be singing with a famous music group.
(B) Her restaurant is located close to a venue.
(C) She has catered for the Dublin Jazz Association before.
(D) Her dishes must be purchased separately.

180. What kind of music will attendees be able to enjoy while drinking a beverage from the Gilmore Brewery?

(A) Traditional jazz
(B) Contemporary jazz
(C) Latin jazz
(D) Smooth jazz

GO ON TO THE NEXT PAGE

Questions 181-185 refer to the following e-mails.

TO: Cathy Wang <cathy.w@wmail.com>
FROM: Jim Ricci <jim28@clarksonpublishing.com>
SUBJECT: Illustrations
DATE: October 29
ATTACHMENT: Chapter 1

Dear Ms. Wang,

My name is Jim Ricci, and I'm from Clarkson Publishing. We've never worked together directly, but I made some edits to the *Marine Line* book we put out last year, which you helped illustrate. I was really impressed with your illustrations, so I'm pleased to hear you'll be working with us again on our new book, *Dinosaurs: A Prehistoric Journey*.

Our writer for the book is Mike Hernandez, a well-known reporter for *Science Weekly* magazine. He has completed the first chapter, which is attached to this e-mail. I was thinking of including the following drawings:

- Page 3: An illustration of a prehistoric landscape (color)
- Page 7: A picture of a Tyrannosaurs rex (black and white)
- Page 12: A picture of the plant life found in prehistoric times (black and white)
- Page 14: A picture of a Stegosaurus (black and white)

Let me know what you think of these illustration ideas. If they sound good to you, please send in your drawings by November 10.

Best Regards,

Jim Ricci
Clarkson Publishing

TO: Jim Ricci <jim28@clarksonpublishing.com>
FROM: Cathy Wang <cathy.w@wmail.com>
SUBJECT: Re: Illustrations
DATE: November 10
ATTACHMENT: Illustrations_Ch1

Dear Mr. Ricci,

Attached are illustrations for the first chapter. Note that the color illustration is going to take a little more time to complete, but I will submit that within two days. If there's anything wrong with these in your estimation, please notify me promptly.

Although I was able to complete these illustrations using the text itself and some outside sources, I still struggled a bit to find all the necessary information to create these pictures. What are the best outside sources I can use to learn about dinosaurs? I'm not an expert myself, so I'll need to conduct some research in order to create accurate images.

I appreciate all the help you've given me so far. I look forward to hearing from you.

Sincerely,

Cathy Wang

181. What does the first e-mail indicate about Mr. Ricci?

(A) He established a highly successful publishing company.
(B) He authored a publication about prehistoric creatures.
(C) He provided Ms. Wang with some sample illustrations.
(D) He made some changes to a book released last year.

182. Who most likely is Mike Hernandez?

(A) A print journalist
(B) A book editor
(C) A research scientist
(D) A magazine illustrator

183. Which illustration did Ms. Wang not submit on time?

(A) The Page 3 illustration
(B) The Page 7 illustration
(C) The Page 12 illustration
(D) The Page 14 illustration

184. In the second e-mail, the word "estimation" in paragraph 1, line 3, is closest in meaning to

(A) matter
(B) capacity
(C) method
(D) opinion

185. What information does Ms. Wang request from Mr. Ricci?

(A) The deadline for some pictures
(B) The layout of a text
(C) The best references for a subject
(D) The contact information for Mr. Ricci

GO ON TO THE NEXT PAGE

Questions 186-190 refer to the following article, e-mail and memo.

SINGAPORE (July 11)—Appliance maker Soltano, which began operations 25 years ago, is recalling nearly 10,000 electric grills sold before May 1 of this year. The product, which sells as the Firelight EZ1 in the United States and as the Fireside Grill in Canada, contains a defect that causes it to overheat if it is used for an extended period. According to Tom Morgan, the head of product safety at Soltano, no serious incidents have been reported, but the recall is being issued out of a concern for customer safety.

Mr. Morgan specified that the product defect was discovered by the company and that it occurred due to lapses in the quality assurance procedures at one of the company's factories. All further sales of the product have been halted, and customers who have already purchased the product have the option to return it for a refund or have the faulty part replaced at no added cost.

To: Lauren Galloway <l.galloway@megatronic.com>
From: Justin Hammond <j.hammond@megatronic.com>
Subject: Soltano recall
Date: July 15

Hello Lauren,

Soltano, one of the companies that supply our stores with products, recently issued a recall of the Fireside Grill. Below is a list of the stores in our region and the inventory count of those grills. Could you verify that the quantity of your store inventory matches our count and identify how many were sold to customers? You will also need to follow our standard procedure for recalls to ensure that our customers are adequately informed. Please prepare the items for return shipment.

Store Name	Inventory count
Bergland	237
Harrison	844
McGinnis	911
Stratton	612

Thank you,

Justin Hammond
Regional Manager
Megatronic Appliances

MEMO

To: All Staff
From: Lauren Galloway, Store Manager
Date: July 16
Subject: Product Recall

I've been informed by the regional manager about a recall of a Soltano product. In line with our standard policies, I posted information about the recall next to the store's main door this morning. If you receive inquiries about the product or the recall from customers, please direct them to the customer service department. Moreover, notify them that Megatronic has posted information about the recall on its Web site and mobile app.

Because we have the highest number of products that need to be returned to Soltano out of all Megatronic's stores, I will be looking for several volunteers to help out with preparing the items for shipment. Please let me know your availability so that I can create a schedule.

---

186. What is indicated about Soltano?

(A) It was notified about a problem by a customer.
(B) It experienced a small fire at one of its factories.
(C) It has been in business for over two decades.
(D) It will continue selling a newer model of its electric grill.

187. What problem is mentioned in the article?

(A) A fake copy of a real product was sold.
(B) A supplier delivered an incorrect part.
(C) A plant did not follow a process correctly.
(D) A piece of factory equipment broke down.

188. What is suggested about Mr. Hammond?

(A) He was recently appointed as a manager.
(B) He supervises store locations in Canada.
(C) He sold the highest number of Soltano grills.
(D) He personally purchased a Soltano grill.

189. What did Ms. Galloway do on July 16?

(A) She posted some information online.
(B) She helped a shopper fill out a form.
(C) She met with customer service staff.
(D) She put up a notice near an entrance.

190. In which store does Ms. Galloway most likely work?

(A) Bergland
(B) Harrison
(C) McGinnis
(D) Stratton

GO ON TO THE NEXT PAGE

Questions 191-195 refer to the following e-mail, invoice, and coupon.

To: Rossy Beverages Corporation <sales@rossybeverages.net>
From: Patricia Reyes <patricia@sipplecoffeshops.com>
Subject: Inquiry
Date: June 15

To Whom It May Concern:

My name is Patricia Reyes, and I am the owner of Sipple Coffee, which includes 10 locations in the greater San Francisco area. We roast our own beans that we get from Ethiopia and sell them to other cafés. We also supply several stores, including the Organico health food chain. We would like to bottle our coffee and sell it in grocery stores. Since our cold-brew coffee is widely popular, we feel confident that we can achieve success without resorting to discounts or other special offers. That is why I am reaching out to you. Your company has worked with other small-scale operations, so I believe you can help us get the project off the ground. I have a budget of $5,000 in mind overall. I look forward to hearing from you.

Sincerely,

Patricia Reyes
Owner, Sipple Coffee

Rossy Beverages Corporation Invoice

Bill to: Patricia Reyes
Company: Sipple Coffee
Account: 5285
Sent: July 2

Details of the Order

Item	Item description	Price
Item 1	New Beverage Development	$2,000
Item 2	Recipe Ownership & Trademark	$500
Item 3	Design and Packaging	$2,000
Item 4	200 Glass Bottles	$400
Item 5	Storage	$200
Item 6	Shipping	$100
Item 7	Retail Operation Management	$500
	Subtotal	$5,700
	Tax	$570
	Total	$6,270

Please send payment within 10 days of receiving this invoice. A 10 percent penalty fee will be charged if payment is made after this. Thank you for your business.

Cawston Groceries Coupon

Your favorite local coffee shop, Sipple Coffee, has created a special drink. It consists of the original cold-brew coffee and some agave nectar, along with milk and vanilla flavoring. This makes for a delicious and energizing beverage. And thanks to an exclusive deal with Sipple Coffee, if you buy one, you will get a second one for free. This offer is only valid at Cawston Groceries locations in San Francisco.

191. What is mentioned about Sipple Coffee?
(A) It operates multiple branches in one city.
(B) It sells beverage products in other countries.
(C) It purchases beans from another café chain.
(D) It offers customers healthy food items.

192. According to the e-mail, why has Ms. Reyes selected Rossy Beverages Corporation?
(A) It charges lower fees than its competitors.
(B) It is in close proximity to a café location.
(C) It has worked with small companies.
(D) It is in charge of a large distribution network.

193. What is indicated about the order?
(A) It will ship within 10 business days.
(B) It consists of several beverage flavors.
(C) It exceeded the original budget.
(D) It includes some advertising expenses.

194. What will happen if Ms. Reyes waits longer than 10 days to pay an invoice?
(A) An order will be canceled.
(B) A charge will be applied.
(C) A complaint will be submitted.
(D) An account will be closed.

195. What did Ms. Reyes most likely change for Cawston Groceries?
(A) A marketing budget
(B) An order quantity
(C) A promotion strategy
(D) A delivery address

GO ON TO THE NEXT PAGE

Questions 196-200 refer to the following article, advertisement, and e-mail.

SEATTLE (April 18)—The Seattle government has announced a plan to provide free access to bicycles. The program will be exclusive to the Coleridge neighborhood, which includes many popular tourist attractions. Docking stations are being installed, and they will be operational by May 1. As of now, 30 stations are planned for popular tourist attractions.

The bike program is called Seattle Path, and it uses an online application designed and operated by the Seattle Bureau of Tourism. According to government insiders, a deal with Tapco, the leader in bike rentals could not be reached. Tapco focuses on commuter rentals whereas Seattle Path is targeted at tourists. Each ride on a Seattle Path bike will be limited to two hours. Otherwise, a charge will occur.

Tapco
Choose a bike, tap, and go

Tapco is the leader in bike rentals. With hundreds of available bikes all over Seattle, we make it possible to simply skip the traffic and ride around one of the most bike-friendly cities in the country. The Tapco application is easy to use, and we have a number of special promotions in May.

- New members get a first-time $20 credit. Try our bikes, and see for yourself.
- Members enjoy 20 percent off on all rides.
- Members who book a bike for a minimum of 12 hours will receive a 50 percent discount.
- Any ride that is tapped in and out within 20 minutes is completely free, allowing for complimentary commutes over short distances.

We require that each rider wear a helmet to reduce the risk of injury if an accident occurs.

To: Lucy Kimpton <l.kimpton@tapcobikes.com>
From: Jackson Hoover <j.hoover@tapcobikes.com>
Subject: Update
Date: May 21
Attachment: Performance Review

Lucy,

Attached, please find our performance numbers for the Seattle market. We saw an overall increase of 5 percent in bike usage. This is similar to other markets on the West Coast like Fresno and Sacramento.

However, as you know, we heavily discounted our services in Seattle. There were almost no new users that registered. Our research shows that within only a couple of weeks, Seattle Path has taken 15 percent of our ridership. Their stations in the Queen Ann and Ballard neighborhoods are particularly popular.

We might have to consider partnering with other cities in the future. Let's meet today or tomorrow to discuss strategies to regain some customers. What is your schedule?

Regards,

Jackson Hoover

---

196. What is the article mainly about?

(A) A political election campaign
(B) An upcoming citywide celebration
(C) A review of a new technology gadget
(D) An announcement of a public program

197. What does Tapco require that its customers do?

(A) Update their location using an app
(B) Put on safety equipment before riding
(C) Limit each cycling session to 20 minutes
(D) Report any accidents to the authorities

198. Which Tapco promotion was not successful?

(A) $20 credit
(B) 20 percent discount
(C) 50 percent discount
(D) Free commutes

199. What is suggested about Seattle Path?

(A) It is financed by a local increase in the sales tax.
(B) It expanded from its original target neighborhood.
(C) It has received numerous complaints from local residents.
(D) It commissioned a local technology firm to create an application.

200. What does Mr. Hoover think a company might have to do?

(A) Hire more technical workers
(B) Lower an hourly fee permanently
(C) Form partnerships with other cities
(D) Replace some older equipment

This is the end of the test. You may review Parts 5, 6, and 7 if you finish the test early.

Review 체크리스트

TEST 3를 푼 다음, 아래 체크리스트에 따라 틀린 문제를 리뷰하고 박스에 완료 여부를 표시하세요.
만약 시험까지 얼마 남지 않았다면, [1]번 ~ [3]번 항목이라도 꼭 확인하세요.

☐ [1] 틀린 문제의 경우, 다시 풀어봤다.

☐ [2] 틀린 문제의 경우, 스크립트/해석을 확인하며 지문/문제의 내용을 정확하게 파악했다.

☐ [3] 해설을 통해 각 문제의 정답과 오답의 근거가 무엇인지 정확하게 파악했다.

☐ [4] PART 1과 PART 2에서 틀린 문제의 경우, 선택한 오답의 유형이 무엇이었는지 확인하고 같은 함정에 빠지지 않도록 정리해두었다.

☐ [5] PART 3와 PART 4의 각 문제에서 사용된 패러프레이징을 확인했다.

☐ [6] PART 5와 PART 6의 경우, 틀린 문제에서 사용된 문법 포인트 또는 정답 및 오답 어휘를 정리했다.

☐ [7] PART 6의 알맞은 문장 고르기 문제의 경우, 지문 전체를 정확하게 해석하며 전체 글의 흐름과 빈칸 주변 문맥을 정확하게 파악하는 연습을 했다.

☐ [8] PART 7에서 질문과 보기의 키워드를 찾아 표시하며 지문에서 정답의 근거가 되는 문장이나 구절을 찾아보고, 문제에서 사용된 패러프레이징을 확인했다.

☐ [9] PART 1~PART 4는 받아쓰기 & 쉐도잉 워크북을 활용하여, TEST에 수록된 핵심 문장을 받아쓰고 따라 읽으며 복습했다.

☐ [10] PART 1~PART 7은 단어암기자료를 활용하여, TEST에 수록된 핵심 어휘와 표현을 암기했다.

많은 양의 문제를 푸는 것도 중요하지만, 틀린 문제를 제대로 리뷰하는 것도 중요합니다.
틀린 문제를 한 번 더 꼼꼼히 리뷰한다면, 빠른 시간 내에 효과적으로 목표 점수를 달성할 수 있습니다.

해커스 토익 실전 LC+RC 3

TEST 4

LISTENING TEST

PART 1
PART 2
PART 3
PART 4

READING TEST

PART 5
PART 6
PART 7

Review 체크리스트

잠깐! 테스트 전 아래 사항을 꼭 확인하세요.
1. 휴대전화의 전원을 끄셨나요? 예 □
2. Answer Sheet(p.253), 연필, 지우개, 시계를 준비하셨나요? 예 □
3. Listening MP3를 들을 준비가 되셨나요? 예 □

모든 준비가 완료되었으면 목표 점수를 떠올린 후 테스트를 시작합니다.
테스트를 마친 후, Review 체크리스트(p.194)를 보며 자신이 틀린 문제를 반드시 복습합니다.

🎧 TEST 4.mp3
실전용·복습용 문제풀이 MP3 무료 다운로드 및 스트리밍 바로듣기 (HackersIngang.com)
* 실제 시험장의 소음까지 재현해 낸 고사장 소음/매미 버전 MP3, 영국식·호주식 발음 집중 MP3, 고속 버전 MP3까지 구매하면 실전에 더욱 완벽히 대비할 수 있습니다.

무료MP3 바로듣기

LISTENING TEST

In this section, you must demonstrate your ability to understand spoken English. This section is divided into four parts and will take approximately 45 minutes to complete. Do not mark the answers in your test book. Use the answer sheet that is provided separately.

PART 1

Directions: For each question, you will listen to four short statements about a picture in your test book. These statements will not be printed and will only be spoken one time. Select the statement that best describes what is happening in the picture and mark the corresponding letter (A), (B), (C), or (D) on the answer sheet.

Sample Answer

The statement that best describes the picture is (B), "The man is sitting at the desk." So, you should mark letter (B) on the answer sheet.

1.

2.

3.

4.

5.

6.

GO ON TO THE NEXT PAGE

PART 2

Directions: For each question, you will listen to a statement or question followed by three possible responses spoken in English. They will not be printed and will only be spoken one time. Select the best response and mark the corresponding letter (A), (B), or (C) on your answer sheet.

7. Mark your answer on your answer sheet.
8. Mark your answer on your answer sheet.
9. Mark your answer on your answer sheet.
10. Mark your answer on your answer sheet.
11. Mark your answer on your answer sheet.
12. Mark your answer on your answer sheet.
13. Mark your answer on your answer sheet.
14. Mark your answer on your answer sheet.
15. Mark your answer on your answer sheet.
16. Mark your answer on your answer sheet.
17. Mark your answer on your answer sheet.
18. Mark your answer on your answer sheet.
19. Mark your answer on your answer sheet.
20. Mark your answer on your answer sheet.
21. Mark your answer on your answer sheet.
22. Mark your answer on your answer sheet.
23. Mark your answer on your answer sheet.
24. Mark your answer on your answer sheet.
25. Mark your answer on your answer sheet.
26. Mark your answer on your answer sheet.
27. Mark your answer on your answer sheet.
28. Mark your answer on your answer sheet.
29. Mark your answer on your answer sheet.
30. Mark your answer on your answer sheet.
31. Mark your answer on your answer sheet.

PART 3

Directions: In this part, you will listen to several conversations between two or more speakers. These conversations will not be printed and will only be spoken one time. For each conversation, you will be asked to answer three questions. Select the best response and mark the corresponding letter (A), (B), (C), or (D) on your answer sheet.

32. Why does the man want to make a reservation?
    (A) To spend time with colleagues
    (B) To celebrate a birthday
    (C) To meet with a client
    (D) To host a retirement party

33. What does the woman say about the restaurant?
    (A) It is typically busy on weekends.
    (B) It offers private rooms for groups.
    (C) It accepts bookings by e-mail.
    (D) It is introducing new menu items.

34. What information will the man most likely provide next?
    (A) A delivery address
    (B) A payment method
    (C) Some social media links
    (D) Some contact information

35. What industry do the speakers most likely work in?
    (A) Accounting
    (B) Software
    (C) Transportation
    (D) Entertainment

36. What did the man do this morning?
    (A) He downloaded an application.
    (B) He attended an interview.
    (C) He visited a Web site.
    (D) He conducted an inspection.

37. What does the woman offer to do?
    (A) Post a safety notice
    (B) Send an e-mail
    (C) Arrange a video call
    (D) Create a job advertisement

38. What kind of work does Mr. Jennings do?
    (A) Plumbing
    (B) Carpentry
    (C) Gardening
    (D) Auto repair

39. What does the man imply when he says, "we're on a tight budget"?
    (A) He thinks a budget plan should be reviewed.
    (B) He wants to cancel a costly order.
    (C) He is planning to request a discount.
    (D) He prefers an inexpensive material.

40. What will the woman show to the man?
    (A) Some images
    (B) Some tools
    (C) A product sample
    (D) A building permit

41. What is the topic of the conversation?
    (A) A city's celebrity
    (B) A region's culture
    (C) An area's cuisine
    (D) A community's history

42. What does Ms. Reyes say recently happened?
    (A) An organization was formed.
    (B) A document was found.
    (C) An institution was opened.
    (D) A publication was released.

43. What will the man do next?
    (A) Write a letter
    (B) Check a record
    (C) Confirm a date
    (D) Take a picture

GO ON TO THE NEXT PAGE

44. Why is the man calling?

    (A) To describe a store promotion
    (B) To apologize for a cancellation
    (C) To discuss an order issue
    (D) To request an online payment

45. What problem does the man mention?

    (A) Some equipment was damaged.
    (B) There were technical problems.
    (C) A business is understaffed.
    (D) Some guidelines were unclear.

46. What does the woman inquire about?

    (A) The price of a product
    (B) The color of an item
    (C) A delivery date
    (D) A return policy

47. What are the speakers mainly discussing?

    (A) Opening an office in another location
    (B) Promoting a skilled worker
    (C) Developing a sales strategy
    (D) Filling an open position

48. Why does the woman say, "We have a busy schedule this winter"?

    (A) To explain a delay
    (B) To reject an option
    (C) To justify a decision
    (D) To correct some errors

49. What will the man do next?

    (A) Provide some feedback
    (B) Create customer surveys
    (C) Reschedule the meeting
    (D) Contact a candidate

50. What type of industry do the speakers most likely work in?

    (A) Tourism
    (B) Medical research
    (C) Food production
    (D) Information technology

51. What are the men planning to do?

    (A) Review a contract
    (B) Move a display
    (C) Revise an event schedule
    (D) Share some ideas

52. What does the woman say she will take care of?

    (A) Scheduling an alternative date
    (B) Managing advertising strategies
    (C) Researching online activities
    (D) Obtaining new vendors

53. Who most likely is the man?

    (A) A newspaper reporter
    (B) A podcast host
    (C) A restaurant owner
    (D) A food critic

54. What does the woman say is special about a dish?

    (A) It includes a rare ingredient.
    (B) It creates a delicious smell.
    (C) It possesses strong flavors.
    (D) It has a long history.

55. What will happen next month?

    (A) A business will open.
    (B) A contest will take place.
    (C) A festival will be held.
    (D) A tour will be conducted.

56. What is the conversation mainly about?
    (A) Organizing an activity
    (B) Extending a class
    (C) Redesigning a Web site
    (D) Giving a presentation

57. What does the man say about the Marlow Aquarium?
    (A) It will be relocated.
    (B) It will host a private event.
    (C) It requires a reservation.
    (D) It will raise the entrance fee.

58. Why does the woman suggest deciding soon?
    (A) A special rate is offered.
    (B) A booking is nonrefundable.
    (C) A venue will be changed.
    (D) A site gets many visitors.

59. What problem does the woman mention?
    (A) Some customers have complained about pricing.
    (B) Some reactions to a product are negative.
    (C) A facility failed an inspection.
    (D) An item has not sold well in certain stores.

60. What did the speakers' company recently do?
    (A) Built a warehouse
    (B) Launched a store promotion
    (C) Used a different ingredient
    (D) Invested in a new plant

61. What information will the man most likely emphasize?
    (A) Large portions
    (B) Health benefits
    (C) Structural improvements
    (D) Affordable prices

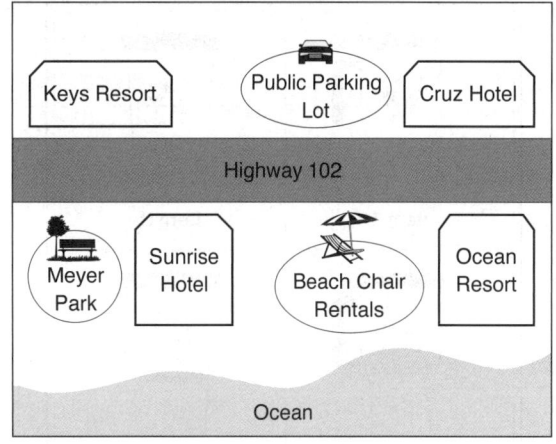

62. Why does the man apologize?
    (A) He arrived late.
    (B) He missed a meeting.
    (C) He deleted a message.
    (D) He lost a ticket.

63. Look at the graphic. Which accommodation facility was built last year?
    (A) Keys Resort
    (B) Cruz Hotel
    (C) Sunrise Hotel
    (D) Ocean Resort

64. What solution does the man propose?
    (A) Hiring more employees
    (B) Relocating a business
    (C) Reducing some room rates
    (D) Offering a free service

GO ON TO THE NEXT PAGE

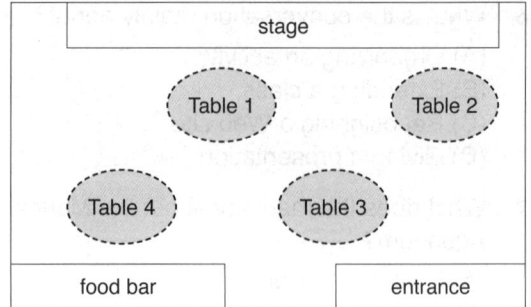

65. Who is the woman planning to give a gift to?
    (A) A coworker
    (B) A friend
    (C) A client
    (D) A family member

66. What kind of item does the woman want?
    (A) Something useful
    (B) Something fun
    (C) Something affordable
    (D) Something unique

67. Look at the graphic. Which item will the woman most likely buy?
    (A) Item 1
    (B) Item 2
    (C) Item 3
    (D) Item 4

68. What type of event is being hosted?
    (A) An awards ceremony
    (B) A fundraising banquet
    (C) A music festival
    (D) A cooking demonstration

69. What problem does the man mention?
    (A) Some equipment has malfunctioned.
    (B) Some chairs cannot be found.
    (C) A delivery has been delayed.
    (D) A technician has not yet arrived.

70. Look at the graphic. Where will Ms. Stein sit?
    (A) At Table 1
    (B) At Table 2
    (C) At Table 3
    (D) At Table 4

PART 4

Directions: In this part, you will listen to several short talks by a single speaker. These talks will not be printed and will only be spoken one time. For each talk, you will be asked to answer three questions. Select the best response and mark the corresponding letter (A), (B), (C), or (D) on your answer sheet.

71. What will the listeners receive?
    (A) Meal coupons
    (B) Light refreshments
    (C) Informational brochures
    (D) Admission passes

72. Where will the tour end?
    (A) At a transit station
    (B) At a national museum
    (C) At a restaurant
    (D) At a nearby park

73. What are the listeners reminded to do?
    (A) Mind their belongings
    (B) Watch out for wildlife
    (C) Avoid flash photography
    (D) Stay close at all times

74. Where is the announcement most likely being made?
    (A) At an apartment complex
    (B) At a supermarket
    (C) At a bank
    (D) At a phone repair shop

75. What has caused a problem?
    (A) An overdue payment
    (B) A personnel problem
    (C) A change in a policy
    (D) An Internet connection

76. What does the speaker ask the listeners to do?
    (A) Delay a grand opening
    (B) Conduct a survey
    (C) Check an assignment sheet
    (D) Notify customers

77. Where is the meeting taking place?
    (A) At a hospital
    (B) At a hotel
    (C) At a real estate agency
    (D) At a hardware store

78. What does the speaker imply when he says, "I want to say it's about time"?
    (A) Some results were unexpected.
    (B) Some items needed to be replaced.
    (C) Some staff should come in early.
    (D) Some tasks must be done urgently.

79. What will most likely be discussed next?
    (A) Departmental duties
    (B) Food service menus
    (C) Maintenance costs
    (D) Financial reports

80. What is the broadcast mainly about?
    (A) A political event
    (B) A construction project
    (C) A transportation issue
    (D) A housing problem

81. What does the speaker say about Mr. Rosen?
    (A) He rejected a plan.
    (B) He is an engineer.
    (C) He will sign a contract.
    (D) He is retiring next year.

82. According to the speaker, what will open next year?
    (A) A stadium
    (B) A metro station
    (C) A science museum
    (D) A retail facility

GO ON TO THE NEXT PAGE

83. Who are the listeners?
    (A) Applicants
    (B) Students
    (C) Instructors
    (D) Interns

84. What does the speaker imply when he says "I've spent over 20 years working in the advertising industry"?
    (A) He is considering retirement.
    (B) He has received good advice.
    (C) He hopes to make a career change.
    (D) He will provide useful information.

85. Why should the listeners raise their hand?
    (A) To provide an example
    (B) To ask a question
    (C) To explain a concept
    (D) To correct a mistake

86. Why does the speaker want to purchase air purifiers?
    (A) To donate to a hospital
    (B) To give to her sister as a gift
    (C) To address staff complaints
    (D) To comply with a new regulation

87. What does the speaker say is a requirement for the air purifier?
    (A) It must be quiet.
    (B) It must be inexpensive.
    (C) It must have a warranty.
    (D) It must be compact.

88. What does the speaker ask about?
    (A) A billing error
    (B) Minimum order quantity
    (C) A possibility of discount
    (D) A type of delivery service

89. What is the purpose of the talk?
    (A) To discuss a schedule
    (B) To suggest changing suppliers
    (C) To train employees
    (D) To develop an inventory system

90. Where are the listeners?
    (A) At a restaurant
    (B) At a bicycle shop
    (C) At a manufacturer
    (D) At a publishing company

91. What does the speaker say she will do?
    (A) Create a Web page
    (B) Give a list of products
    (C) Evaluate some workers
    (D) Update a manual

92. What industry does Ms. Lockwood most likely work in?
    (A) Science
    (B) Education
    (C) Film
    (D) Publishing

93. What does the speaker mean when he says, "And stick around"?
    (A) A popular program will begin after a commercial break.
    (B) Ms. Lockwood has made a special request.
    (C) Listeners will be able to call in with questions.
    (D) Listeners will want to hear a guest's remarks.

94. What will happen at 6 P.M.?
    (A) A movie trailer will be shown.
    (B) A social media page will be updated.
    (C) A schedule will be announced.
    (D) A promotional offer will be revealed.

Quarterly Sales Report	
Age Range	Sales (millions of dollars)
18-25	10
26-35	8
36-45	8.5
46-55	6

Berkshire Office Tower
Floor 4 Western Legal Services
Floor 3 Coleman Publishing
Floor 2 Macro Technologies
Floor 1 Larsen Software

95. What type of product is being discussed?
(A) Convenience food
(B) Wholemeal bread
(C) Instant soups
(D) Bottled sauces

96. According to the speaker, what will be the focus of the advertisement?
(A) A user-friendly Web site
(B) A reduction in price
(C) Freshness of ingredients
(D) Sustainable packaging

97. Look at the graphic. What is the age range of the fastest-growing customer group?
(A) 18-25
(B) 26-35
(C) 36-45
(D) 46-55

98. Who most likely is the speaker?
(A) A writer
(B) An architect
(C) A lawyer
(D) A landscaper

99. According to the speaker, what will some workers enjoy?
(A) Free breakfast
(B) Ample parking space
(C) State-of-the-art facilities
(D) Access to an outdoor area

100. Look at the graphic. Which floor was the last to be rented out?
(A) Floor 1
(B) Floor 2
(C) Floor 3
(D) Floor 4

This is the end of the Listening test. Turn to PART 5 in your test book.

GO ON TO THE NEXT PAGE

READING TEST

In this section, you must demonstrate your ability to read and comprehend English. You will be given a variety of texts and asked to answer questions about these texts. This section is divided into three parts and will take 75 minutes to complete.

Do not mark the answers in your test book. Use the answer sheet that is separately provided.

PART 5

Directions: In each question, you will be asked to review a statement that is missing a word or phrase. Four answer choices will be provided for each statement. Select the best answer and mark the corresponding letter (A), (B), (C), or (D) on the answer sheet.

101. Joseph Sykes was hired to manage Calhoun Design's ------- with important clients in Shanghai.
    (A) relative
    (B) related
    (C) relate
    (D) relationship

102. The contest will give amateur photographers the ------- to demonstrate their talent.
    (A) reservation
    (B) preference
    (C) expression
    (D) opportunity

103. To prevent accidents, all employees must follow the safety ------- when operating heavy machinery.
    (A) regulate
    (B) regulations
    (C) regulating
    (D) to regulate

104. Hannah Stevens has been producing her ------- personal finance podcast for two years.
    (A) popular
    (B) expandable
    (C) immediate
    (D) equivalent

105. Westover Road will not be passable to vehicles ------- workers clear all the snow that fell overnight.
    (A) of
    (B) until
    (C) which
    (D) beside

106. Mr. Cavendish forgot to bring ------- phone charger when he went to Cancun on vacation.
    (A) him
    (B) his
    (C) he
    (D) himself

107. Updates to company policies can ------- at any time on our intranet page.
    (A) view
    (B) viewed
    (C) viewable
    (D) be viewed

108. As we move into the next ------- of development, our focus will shift to improving product functionality and the user experience.
    (A) phase
    (B) root
    (C) certainty
    (D) statement

109. Baxter Group is now ------- skilled social media marketing managers to enhance its online presence.

    (A) composing
    (B) servicing
    (C) recruiting
    (D) analyzing

110. The Witwave Comedy Festival will be held in the city of Edmonton this year, ------- comedy fans from around the world.

    (A) attraction
    (B) has attracted
    (C) attracting
    (D) attractive

111. After reading all the online reviews, we decided which company ------- with for promoting our restaurant.

    (A) contracting
    (B) contracts
    (C) to contract
    (D) contract

112. The business expo was so highly anticipated that the hotel rooms nearby were ------- booked for weeks.

    (A) completely
    (B) occasionally
    (C) instinctively
    (D) structurally

113. The logo ------- was selected to represent Air Tech's overseas subsidiary will be revealed next week.

    (A) what
    (B) those
    (C) whom
    (D) that

114. A recent article in *Economic Eye Magazine* ------- that mortgage rates will stabilize soon.

    (A) writes
    (B) issues
    (C) predicts
    (D) complies

115. An artist's brilliant ------- paintings do not guarantee that future creations will be as widely praised.

    (A) yet
    (B) along
    (C) fully
    (D) past

116. To get a refund, please bring back your purchase to the store ------- 30 days of the date on the receipt.

    (A) upon
    (B) toward
    (C) within
    (D) during

117. The Estes Valley Community Center's training program will ------- participants on how to administer first aid.

    (A) educating
    (B) educated
    (C) educate
    (D) had educated

118. The results of the customer survey indicate that East Airlines has ------- improved its customer satisfaction.

    (A) consistently
    (B) emotionally
    (C) commonly
    (D) resistantly

119. Our team of ------- insurance specialists is equipped to help you choose the plan most suitable for your needs.

    (A) experience
    (B) experienced
    (C) experiencing
    (D) experiences

120. As the account manager, Ms. Abara ------- as the main point of contact for all client communication.

    (A) drives
    (B) holds
    (C) serves
    (D) employs

GO ON TO THE NEXT PAGE

121. Jewelry items created by Barron Jewelers are distributed ------- via secured vehicles.

    (A) domesticate
    (B) domestic
    (C) domestically
    (D) domestication

122. At the press conference, both firms presented ------- stories about the cause of the merger failure.

    (A) restful
    (B) premature
    (C) payable
    (D) conflicting

123. Archway Cinema offers a 15 percent discount on all adult tickets ------- Tuesday evening.

    (A) other
    (B) every
    (C) either
    (D) some

124. Ms. Knapp intended to buy a new car this year, but ------- the increased prices, she postponed her purchase.

    (A) because of
    (B) in spite of
    (C) such as
    (D) provided that

125. Burch Furniture needed to find a new ------- of materials after its previous supplier went out of business.

    (A) license
    (B) host
    (C) format
    (D) source

126. The new team leader will need strong ------- skills to effectively manage the project and ensure team productivity.

    (A) supervised
    (B) supervise
    (C) supervisory
    (D) supervises

127. Allowing employees to work from home continues to be a topic of ------- for Winn Enterprise's management team.

    (A) debatably
    (B) debated
    (C) debate
    (D) debatable

128. The service contract was signed by ------- Mr. Lim and Mast Telecom at yesterday's meeting.

    (A) all
    (B) both
    (C) neither
    (D) such

129. Zimmerman Beverages has been receiving ------- more online orders since redesigning its mobile application.

    (A) consideration
    (B) considerably
    (C) considering
    (D) considerable

130. Belton Tours' main server freezes -------, which leads to a temporary loss of access to crucial business documents.

    (A) intermittently
    (B) hesitantly
    (C) correctly
    (D) indirectly

PART 6

Directions: In this part, you will be asked to read four English texts. Each text is missing a word, phrase, or sentence. Select the answer choice that correctly completes the text and mark the corresponding letter (A), (B), (C), or (D) on the answer sheet.

Questions 131-134 refer to the following e-mail.

To: wesley_j_moore@kruegerinc.ca
From: contact@gilmorefamilydental.ca
Subject: AUTOMATIC REPLY: Inquiry
Date: 7 September

Thank you for contacting Gilmore Family Dental. Our office is currently closed, but your inquiry has been forwarded ------- a member of our staff. An employee will ------- during our
   131.   132.
regular business hours of 9 A.M. to 5 P.M., Monday through Saturday. If the situation is -------,
                                                                                        133.
please contact our after-hours hotline at 555-9283. A dental professional will always be available to take your call. -------.
                                          134.

Best,

The Gilmore Family Dental Team

131. (A) to
     (B) as
     (C) at
     (D) on

132. (A) move
     (B) agree
     (C) participate
     (D) reply

133. (A) urgent
     (B) urgently
     (C) urgency
     (D) urge

134. (A) Our clinic is fully booked until the end of next week.
     (B) We've recently opened a new location in Vancouver.
     (C) You will receive immediate assistance with any pressing concerns.
     (D) Two dental checkups per year are recommended.

GO ON TO THE NEXT PAGE

Questions 135-138 refer to the following Web page.

The Cadabra Sponge, Spencer & Sutton's top-performing product for over a decade, ------- **135.** to handle even the toughest kitchen and bathroom cleanup jobs. It allows you to remove stubborn stains with ------- effort. Just a light swipe is enough to tackle even the grimiest **136.** spots. The grooves on the sides match your finger placement. -------. The secure grip design **137.** prevents slipping, eliminating the need for excessive force and reducing hand fatigue. -------, **138.** the Cadabra Sponge works without the need for chemicals, making it safe to use around kids and pets.

135. (A) has designed
 (B) designed
 (C) is designing
 (D) has been designed

136. (A) mutual
 (B) minimal
 (C) continuous
 (D) extra

137. (A) It is advisable to replace your kitchen sponge every two weeks.
 (B) The Cadabra Sponge is typically sold in packs of five.
 (C) It will therefore fit perfectly in the palm of your hand.
 (D) Using it with the specific detergent doubled its effectiveness.

138. (A) However
 (B) In comparison
 (C) Best of all
 (D) In other words

Questions 139-142 refer to the following announcement.

Attention, Rockford Apartment Residents

Effective May 1, a city ordinance ------- parking on Robson Street from 8 A.M. to 7 P.M. on
                                    139.
weekdays will take effect. Individuals who park on any part of the street during these hours

will be subject to fines. -------.
                         140.

As Robson Street is directly in front of our apartment building, people commonly leave their

cars there while visiting -------. You should make sure to advise guests of the new rule so
                          141.

that they do not park at this location. -------, they can use 2nd Avenue behind our building.
                                        142.

Parking is permitted there throughout the day.

If you have any questions, please feel free to contact the building management office.

---

139. (A) introducing
(B) guaranteeing
(C) scheduling
(D) prohibiting

140. (A) Check the schedule on the city's Web site.
(B) Their vehicle may even be towed away.
(C) These must be paid by May 10 at the latest.
(D) The street will be blocked off in the morning.

141. (A) occupants
(B) pedestrians
(C) employees
(D) drivers

142. (A) Furthermore
(B) Likewise
(C) Unfortunately
(D) Instead

Questions 143-146 refer to the following advertisement.

Crystal Clear Pool Maintenance
121 Carter Road, Sunnyvale, Ohio

With summer on the way, it's time to get the pool ready! Sign a contract with us, and we will send a professional to your home every week to ensure the cleanliness and proper ------- of your pool. We will remove any debris and make the necessary adjustments to the water's chemical balance. -------, we will check the pump and other equipment for technical issues that can negatively affect their operation.

-------. Each has been employed in the field for a period of at least five years. ------- a free consultation, call us at 555-0292 today. You will be provided with a detailed cost estimate to review before making a final decision.

143. (A) functionally
(B) functional
(C) function
(D) functioned

144. (A) In response
(B) In contrast
(C) Nevertheless
(D) Moreover

145. (A) All of our staff members have extensive experience.
(B) We have a wide range of pool accessories for purchase.
(C) Remember to put a cover on your pool when it's not in use.
(D) Your pool will need to be replaced if it has been damaged.

146. (A) Arranges
(B) To arrange
(C) Having been arranged
(D) Being arranged

PART 7

Directions: In this part, you will be asked to read several texts, such as advertisements, articles, instant messages, or examples of business correspondence. Each text is followed by several questions. Select the best answer and mark the corresponding letter (A), (B), (C), or (D) on your answer sheet.

Questions 147-148 refer to the following advertisement.

Spark's Party Depot

89 Hamilton Avenue, Watertown, CT 06795
www.sparkspartydepot.com

Are you planning an event? Look no further than Spark's Party Depot. This month, we're offering our members deals on a variety of products! Not a member yet? Sign up now to enjoy discounts on:

- Balloons and decorations
- Tableware and utensils
- Party favors
- Custom banners
- Themed party kits

Returns are accepted within 30 days of purchase for a full refund. Items must be unused and undamaged. You will be asked to fill out a form that specifies why you are returning them.

147. What is one purpose of the advertisement?

(A) To offer party planning services
(B) To encourage customers to become members
(C) To promote an event venue
(D) To announce the opening of a new branch

148. What is indicated about returned items?

(A) They will be inspected by a store manager.
(B) They must be shipped at the sender's expense.
(C) They can only be exchanged for store credit.
(D) They have to be submitted with a form.

GO ON TO THE NEXT PAGE

Questions 149-150 refer to the following letter.

Dear Editor,

I read the article titled "Vanishing North American Wildlife" in your latest issue. It was very informative for the most part, but I must correct an error that was made about the American marten. The article states that this species of animal is now extinct in Newfoundland. It is true that it was endangered here for many decades and on the verge of becoming extinct. However, conservation efforts that I have been involved in professionally have resulted in the American marten making a significant comeback within the province. If you need more information to revise the article, please feel free to contact me.

Regards,

Sonya Lee

149. Why did Ms. Lee write the letter?

(A) To cancel a subscription
(B) To request clarification
(C) To correct a mistake
(D) To inquire about a source

150. What is most likely true about Ms. Lee?

(A) She has contributed articles to the magazine.
(B) She is a long-time reader of the publication.
(C) She works to protect wildlife in a region.
(D) She studies environmental science at university.

Questions 151-152 refer to the following online chat discussion.

Amy Hong [8:41 A.M.]
Takeshi just called to let me know he's sick and can't make it in today. We are fully booked for his 12 P.M. boat tour. Is anyone else available to lead it?

Connor Morris [8:41 A.M.]
Unfortunately, the other guides all have tours of their own scheduled for 12 P.M.

Amy Hong [8:43 A.M.]
That's too bad. We may have to cancel the tour.

Connor Morris [8:44 A.M.]
I'd prefer not to do that. Let me call Duncan River Tours and see if they can send over one of their guides.

Amy Hong [8:45 A.M.]
OK, great. Please let me know what you find out.

Connor Morris [8:46 A.M.]
I'll get back to you in a few minutes.

151. At 8:43 A.M., what does Ms. Hong most likely mean when she writes, "That's too bad"?

(A) She may need to hire some new employees.
(B) She thinks a client behaved unreasonably.
(C) She is disappointed about the lack of available staff.
(D) She plans to give customers a full refund.

152. What will Mr. Morris do next?

(A) Send clients an e-mail
(B) Book a new river tour
(C) Alter a posted schedule
(D) Make a telephone call

Questions 153-154 refer to the following announcement.

Attention, Dayton Community Center Visitors

Every year on December 31, we decorate the community center with lights to celebrate the advent of the new year. At this year's event, there will be vendors selling cookies and hot chocolate, as well as scarves and knit caps. At 11:59 P.M., we will hold a countdown in the auditorium and then release confetti the moment the new year arrives. Following that, a concert by local band Lake Lovers will take place. Photographers will take pictures of visitors and post them on our Web site, www.daytoncenter.com.

153. What is the occasion for the celebration?

(A) The anniversary of a center's founding
(B) The completion of a new facility
(C) The change to a new year
(D) The success of a community program

154. What is NOT listed as a feature of the celebration?

(A) Sales of sweets
(B) A musical performance
(C) Professional photographs
(D) A lottery with prizes

Questions 155-157 refer to the following article.

VDF Industries Makes Changes

MICHIGAN (June 5)—As global demand for sustainable transportation continues to rise, vehicle manufacturers are shifting their focus to environmentally friendly products. — [1] —. A number of automobile makers have already begun phasing out gasoline-powered cars, which has created challenges for companies that manufacture parts specifically for these vehicles. — [2] —.

VDF Industries, one of the leading suppliers of parts for gasoline-powered vehicles, is among the companies feeling the impact of this shift. — [3] —. To remain competitive, it has announced its decision to begin producing electric vehicle parts. — [4] —.

According to VDF Industries CEO Drew Soto, manufacturing electric vehicle parts should help the company meet the evolving needs of customers. "I don't think the demand for gasoline-powered vehicle parts will disappear entirely due to the strong hybrid market. We're still going to make them, but diversifying will help us stay versatile."

155. What does VDF Industries most likely sell?

(A) Electric vehicles
(B) Automobile parts
(C) Navigation devices
(D) Manufacturing equipment

156. Why does VDF Industries want to diversify its product offerings?

(A) To take advantage of new technologies
(B) To enhance brand reputation
(C) To sell products overseas
(D) To meet changing consumer demand

157. In which of the positions marked [1], [2], [3], and [4] does the following sentence best belong?

"The new components will be available starting early next year."

(A) [1]
(B) [2]
(C) [3]
(D) [4]

Questions 158-160 refer to the following e-mail.

TO	All Employees, Cincinnati Branch <cincinnati.staff@mixologystores.com>
FROM	Brandon Flannigan <b.flannigan@mixologystores.com>
SUBJECT	Canada
DATE	September 4

Dear Staff,

I am looking to form a team capable of taking on a special assignment. As you already know, our company is set to open its very first location in Canada next month. Our branch was selected to help launch the new Mixology store in Toronto. This will include training the store employees from October 3 to October 18.

If you are interested in this exciting challenge, please contact me directly via e-mail. I am only looking for individuals who can commit to a full-time schedule for the entire period. All expenses will be paid. The company will provide flights, a room at the Toronto Mirage Hotel, local transportation costs, and a daily food allowance. Furthermore, your current hourly wage will be temporarily increased by 20 percent. You will also receive an additional five vacation days.

Sincerely,

Brandon Flannigan
Branch Manager, Mixology

158. What is the purpose of the e-mail?

(A) To inform employees of an expansion
(B) To announce a benefit program
(C) To recruit some employees
(D) To introduce a new store policy

159. According to the e-mail, what will happen in October?

(A) A new store location will open.
(B) A limited-edition product line will be launched.
(C) A company-wide celebration will take place.
(D) A funding request will be approved.

160. What is NOT mentioned as a benefit of working in Toronto?

(A) Free hotel accommodations
(B) A temporary wage increase
(C) A project completion bonus
(D) Additional vacation days

Questions 161-164 refer to the following article.

BEDFORD (May 15)—The City of Bedford is embarking on an ambitious public art project in partnership with the local art group Up Studios. The project, which is expected to last three months and has been allocated a budget of $250,000 by the city, will involve the painting of a number of large murals, which residents may contribute their ideas for until May 31.

According to Art Commissioner Loretta Weiss, several sites have already been selected for the murals, including a number of blank walls in the commercial district as well as the underpass near Bautisa Station. All sites chosen for the murals will remain accessible to the public.

"Keep in mind that we're looking for mural concepts that reflect the city's history and culture," said Ms. Weiss. "We've posted the criteria online, so be sure to check that information before submitting your ideas." Residents who would like to volunteer to assist with the painting of the murals can contact Up Studios at www.upstudios.org. For more information about the initiative and to contribute ideas, visit the city's official Web site.

161. What is the purpose of the article?

(A) To promote an art gallery
(B) To describe a city's plan
(C) To announce a painting contest
(D) To praise some recent improvements

162. What is mentioned about the project?

(A) It is being paid for with municipal funds.
(B) It will eventually lead to several road closures.
(C) It is intended to promote tourism in the area.
(D) It was postponed more than once before.

163. What does Ms. Weiss advise people to do?

(A) Become a member of Up Studios
(B) Participate in a vote on mural designs
(C) Check some guidelines online
(D) Take pictures of some sites

164. The word "accessible" in paragraph 2, line 7, is closest in meaning to

(A) satisfactory
(B) open
(C) feasible
(D) clear

Questions 165-168 refer to the following job description.

Citadel Construction is seeking an experienced construction site supervisor to oversee a number of ongoing residential housing development projects in Jackson County. As multiple sites will need to be accessed, a work vehicle will be provided in addition to a competitive salary and comprehensive health benefits. — [1] —.

Responsibilities for this position include performing regular inspections of construction sites, delegating tasks to construction personnel, and ensuring that the materials being used are appropriate. The construction site supervisor will also be responsible for identifying and addressing potential safety hazards, which involves making sure that all personnel are wearing the required protective gear and using equipment properly. — [2] —.

Moreover, the successful candidate will work closely with project managers. — [3] —. Applicants should be ready to adapt to varying weather conditions as outdoor work is frequent. Occasional weekend availability may be necessary depending on project timelines. — [4] —. To apply, please submit a résumé and cover letter to careers@citadelconstruction.com by May 7.

165. What is suggested about Jackson County?

(A) It offers tax incentives for new construction projects.
(B) It has more affordable housing than other areas.
(C) It is undergoing growth in its housing sector.
(D) It is a popular destination for tourists.

166. What will the work vehicle provided to the construction site supervisor most likely be used for?

(A) Commuting to the company's headquarters
(B) Transporting construction materials
(C) Traveling between various worksites
(D) Conducting site tours for investors

167. What is NOT mentioned as a responsibility of the construction site supervisor?

(A) Sourcing building materials
(B) Inspecting worksites periodically
(C) Assigning tasks to workers
(D) Handling safety concerns

168. In which of the positions marked [1], [2], [3], and [4] does the following sentence best belong?

"This will involve providing progress updates and discussing any changes that may arise."

(A) [1]
(B) [2]
(C) [3]
(D) [4]

Questions 169-171 refer to the following memo.

MEMO

To: All department heads
From: Elina Poole, HR manager
Subject: Remote work trial
Date: 20 August

As you are aware, Wellington Ltd. is planning to move to a smaller office next year due to the recent increase in the cost of renting our current space. As we are not reducing the size of our staff, we need to explore alternative work arrangements. To this end, I would like to initiate a pilot programme to assess how viable it would be for staff to work outside of the office for part of the week. I therefore ask that you each select two members of your team to take part in this trial.

Participants will work remotely on Mondays, Wednesdays, and Fridays for a period of two months, during which time they will utilise work-from-home technologies such as virtual meeting software. You will be responsible for assessing the quality and regularity of the work they produce. Please e-mail me the names of suitable employees by the end of the week. Once approved, participants will be briefed on the technical aspects of the programme before beginning.

Thanks.

Elina Poole

---

169. What is mentioned about Wellington Ltd.?

(A) It has recently moved into a new office space.
(B) Its productivity is suffering due to low morale.
(C) It will begin laying off employees early next year.
(D) Its rental costs for a workspace increased.

170. What is each department head asked to do?

(A) Recommend work-from-home technologies
(B) Work remotely for three days of the week
(C) Choose a staff member to participate in a trial
(D) Train employees to use virtual meeting software

171. The word "aspects" in paragraph 2, line 5, is closest in meaning to

(A) difficulties
(B) elements
(C) outlooks
(D) requirements

Questions 172-175 refer to the following online chat discussion.

Jeffrey Kwon [10:59 A.M.]
Hi, Eric. I was wondering when I would receive my payment for the article I submitted for publication.

Eric Michaels [11:00 A.M.]
Which one was that? I'm sorry, but it's been really busy here for the past few days.

Jeffrey Kwon [11:02 A.M.]
Oh, it's the one about online travel companies using AI to plan people's vacations.

Eric Michaels [11:02 A.M.]
Ah, yes. I believe our content editor, Ms. Beecham, has read it, and she may have some feedback. Let me check with her.

Jeffrey Kwon [11:04 A.M.]
Thanks, and I'm sorry to bother you with this. I realize you're busy, but I wasn't sure who else to ask about payment.

Eric Michaels [11:05 A.M.]
No worries! We need to wait a few minutes for Ms. Beecham. She's talking to a client.

Sandy Beecham [11:10 A.M.]
Mr. Kwon, I saw what you wrote. I think it's great! I'd like to use it in our upcoming issue as is. Eric, please go ahead and start processing Mr. Kwon's payment. I'll note the approval in our computer system shortly.

Jeffrey Kwon [11:11 A.M.]
That's good to know. Thank you, Ms. Beecham.

Eric Michaels [11:12 A.M.]
Is a check OK with you, Mr. Kwon? Ms. Summers can prepare it now for you to pick up.

Jeffrey Kwon [11:13 A.M.]
That's fine. Thanks for your help.

Send

172. Who most likely is Mr. Kwon?

(A) A magazine subscriber
(B) A content developer
(C) A recent job applicant
(D) A computer programmer

173. What does Mr. Kwon apologize for?

(A) Submitting an assignment late
(B) Missing an important meeting
(C) Interrupting an employee's workday
(D) Forgetting to fill out a form

174. In which department does Ms. Summers probably work?

(A) Legal
(B) Accounting
(C) Transportation
(D) Information technology

175. At 11:11 A.M., what does Mr. Kwon most likely mean when he writes, "That's good to know"?

(A) He is eligible to apply for a position.
(B) He does not need to revise any work.
(C) He will receive more money than he expected.
(D) He found the contact details he was looking for.

GO ON TO THE NEXT PAGE

Questions 176-180 refer to the following Web pages.

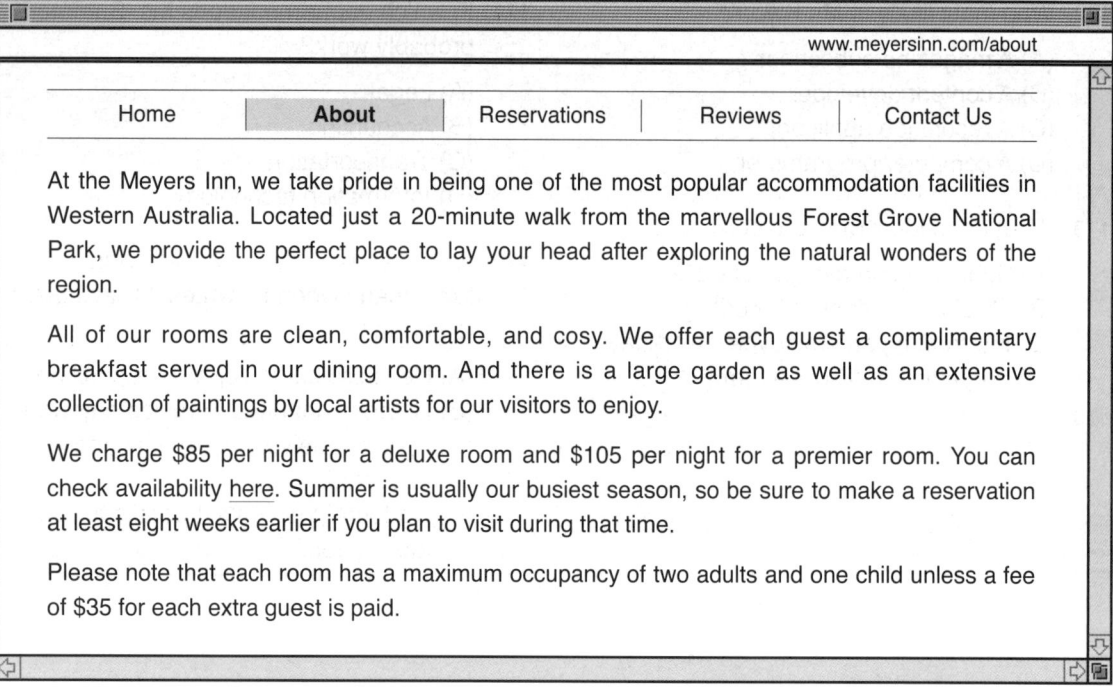

www.meyersinn.com/about

| Home | **About** | Reservations | Reviews | Contact Us |

At the Meyers Inn, we take pride in being one of the most popular accommodation facilities in Western Australia. Located just a 20-minute walk from the marvellous Forest Grove National Park, we provide the perfect place to lay your head after exploring the natural wonders of the region.

All of our rooms are clean, comfortable, and cosy. We offer each guest a complimentary breakfast served in our dining room. And there is a large garden as well as an extensive collection of paintings by local artists for our visitors to enjoy.

We charge $85 per night for a deluxe room and $105 per night for a premier room. You can check availability here. Summer is usually our busiest season, so be sure to make a reservation at least eight weeks earlier if you plan to visit during that time.

Please note that each room has a maximum occupancy of two adults and one child unless a fee of $35 for each extra guest is paid.

www.meyersinn.com/reviews

| Home | About | Reservations | **Reviews** | Contact Us |

Guest: Tim Blackwell
Rating: 4/5

I visited the Meyers Inn with my wife and two children. I was very impressed with how well this place was managed. The check-in process went smoothly, and the room was very spacious and modern. We also really enjoyed the complimentary breakfast that was served each morning. And the owner, Gunnar Meyers, was incredibly kind. He even gave us a ride to a hospital in a neighbouring town when one of my children came down with the flu. I suppose the only problem I had with this place was that the room was either too hot or too cold, no matter how often I adjusted the thermostat. Overall, though, I'd highly recommend this hotel.

176. What does the first Web page indicate about the Meyers Inn?

(A) It is equipped with a large indoor pool.
(B) It is located close to a recreational area.
(C) It serves free meals three times a day.
(D) It offers discounted rates to families.

177. What are guests advised to do if they plan to visit during the summer?

(A) Make a booking two months in advance
(B) Arrange a tour of a nearby garden
(C) Confirm room availability by phone
(D) Check for a seasonal increase in price

178. What can be concluded about Mr. Blackwell?

(A) He purchased a book about a national park.
(B) He visited the inn during the quietest month.
(C) He paid an additional fee for his room.
(D) He travels to Australia frequently.

179. What did Mr. Meyers do for Mr. Blackwell's family?

(A) He provided them with a room upgrade.
(B) He transported them to a medical facility.
(C) He allowed them to check out later than usual.
(D) He gave them information about weather conditions.

180. What problem did Mr. Blackwell have with his room?

(A) The bathroom was not cleaned properly.
(B) The size was not sufficient for a family.
(C) The furniture was not in good condition.
(D) The temperature was not comfortable.

GO ON TO THE NEXT PAGE

Questions 181-185 refer to the following notice and e-mail.

NOTICE

Dear Motorist,

We are hereby informing you that your car, with the license plate number X09123, is parked in a restricted area. The 1800 block of Coleman Street is reserved for people with parking permits. If you do not move your car by 10 A.M., the city will be forced to tow it at your expense.

If your car does get towed, you may retrieve it at one of the city's towing lots. Go to www.sanjosecity.com/towedvehicles, and search for your license plate number to find it. The costs of towing are $150 for vehicles under 7,500 pounds and $250 for vehicles over that weight.

If you have questions or concerns, e-mail us at towing@sanjosecity.com.

Thank you,

City of San Jose

TO: towing@sanjosecity.com
FROM: Alison Pierce <a.pierce@fastmail.com>
SUBJECT: Towing
DATE: May 8

To Whom It May Concern:

My name is Alison Pierce, and I am the owner of a red sedan with the license plate number X09123. I parked my car on Coleman Street earlier today for about an hour, as I was having coffee with a client. When I returned, my car had been towed.

The problem is that my car should not have been towed. I frequently park on this street and have a permit that's located on the bottom left corner of my windshield. It's possible that it was obscured by a fallen leaf or something. Still, if you examine my car, you should find it. If there is a database of people permitted to park on this street, I encourage you to search for my name.

Provided that you're able to verify this information, I would like to pick up my car without paying the fee.

Sincerely,

Alison Pierce

181. What information is listed in the notice?

(A) The name of a motorist
(B) The towing rates for cars
(C) The location of a facility
(D) The parking fees for residents

182. How can people find out where their cars have been towed?

(A) By calling a special toll-free number
(B) By using an online search engine
(C) By e-mailing a city official
(D) By going to a government office

183. What is indicated about Ms. Pierce?

(A) She lives in an apartment building on Coleman Street.
(B) She recently decided to purchase a new vehicle.
(C) She departed from the coffee shop after 10 A.M.
(D) She has had her car towed by the city before.

184. What does Ms. Pierce ask the city to do?

(A) Look for her name in a directory
(B) Issue a new parking permit
(C) Return her car to a location
(D) Look up a municipal policy

185. Why does Ms. Pierce believe a towing fee should be waived?

(A) She was visiting a resident of the area.
(B) She has a valid parking permit.
(C) Her car was damaged during the towing process.
(D) A city official told her the towing was done in error.

GO ON TO THE NEXT PAGE

Questions 186-190 refer to the following advertisement, form, and e-mail.

Ready for photos – Space Photoland

Space Photoland can meet all your photography needs. The following studios are available to rent at our complex at 384 South Grand Avenue.

Studio 1	Small Studio (45 square meters): With the dark walls and the absence of natural light, this studio allows for greater control of lighting conditions. It is perfect for simple photo shoots.
Studio 2	Medium Studio (75 square meters): It has light walls and includes various furniture pieces. Natural light is blocked to make it easier to create specific effects with lighting equipment.
Studio 3	Large Studio (100 square meters): Designed to appear as a luxury apartment, this studio includes a kitchen, living room, and bedroom. Each has windows to allow in natural light.
Studio 4	Extra-Large Studio (150 square meters): Equipped with all of the apartment facilities of the large studio, it also features an outdoor area with a pool that overlooks the city.

Visit www.photoland.com for more information and to make a booking.

If needed, lighting and photography equipment from ImageSource is available to rent at reasonable rates.

---

www.photoland.com

Space Photoland Booking Request Form

Name: Albert Compton
Company: Sanas Investments
Address: 3801 Quebec St, Denver, CO 80207
Phone: 555-4884
E-mail: a.compton@sanasinvestments.com

> I am interested in booking one of your studios for a two-day period. My company will be creating a series of advertisements to appear in magazines. June 23 and 24 would work best for us, but we are willing to consider other dates if necessary. We would prefer to use the studio that includes a luxurious living space as well as a pool.

To: Connie Orwell <connie@spacephotoland.com>
From: Albert Compton <a.compton@sanasinvestments.com>
Subject: Shoot
Date: June 29

Dear Ms. Orwell,

I want to thank you again for your assistance during our campaign shoot. I am surprised we were able to get all the content we needed in one day and evening. Everything went well, and the ImageSource camera provided by your company was exactly what we needed. Our in-house photographer was very impressed with it. So I'd love to book one of your studios again for our upcoming marketing campaign. We are currently in the planning stages, and I will reach out to you once we are ready for another booking.

Sincerely,

Albert Compton
Sanas Investments

186. What is indicated about Space Photoland?
   (A) It can also be rented for social events.
   (B) It has several studios at one address.
   (C) It has been featured in a recent magazine article.
   (D) It may shut down temporarily for renovations.

187. What do Studio 1 and Studio 2 have in common?
   (A) Each is decorated with various furniture items.
   (B) Each is greater than 50 square meters in size.
   (C) Each includes walls that have a dark color.
   (D) Each requires the use of artificial light sources.

188. Which studio is Mr. Compton most interested in booking?
   (A) Studio 1
   (B) Studio 2
   (C) Studio 3
   (D) Studio 4

189. What can be inferred about Mr. Compton?
   (A) He purchased some ImageSource gear online.
   (B) He paid an equipment rental fee to Space Photoland.
   (C) He ended a photo session early due to a lighting issue.
   (D) He made a booking one month before a photo shoot.

190. According to the e-mail, what is Mr. Compton's company currently doing?
   (A) Reviewing an invoice prior to payment
   (B) Conceptualizing an advertising campaign
   (C) Choosing from a selection of photos
   (D) Ordering some camera accessories

GO ON TO THE NEXT PAGE

Questions 191-195 refer to the following e-mail, schedule, and text-message chain.

TO: Pam Headly <p.headly@brownhigh.com>, Nathan Michaels<n.michaels@brownhigh.com>
FROM: Samantha Bowman <s.bowman@brownhigh.com>
SUBJECT: Conference
DATE: March 11

Dear Ms. Headly and Mr. Michaels,

As the most experienced teachers here at Brown High School, you each play a vital role in ensuring our students receive a quality education. That's why I'd like to invite both of you to join me at the upcoming Florida Educators Conference in Orlando, which takes place on May 1.

At this conference, teachers and administrators from Florida's public high schools will share their teaching strategies and discuss the latest developments in the field of education. I'm going to be giving an hour-long talk about the use of tablets in the classroom, and I was hoping you two could join me for a subsequent panel discussion. Given that our school has won several government awards for its innovative education programs, I'm sure many participants will be interested in hearing from you. Please let me know soon if you can make it.

Best regards,

Samantha Bowman
Principal, Brown High School

FLORIDA EDUCATORS' CONFERENCE

May 1
Cody Convention Center
Orlando, FL

Join us for the largest annual gathering of teachers and administrators in Florida. Registration costs $40 for attendees and is free for all speakers. Below is this year's schedule.

10:00 A.M.	Nick D'Annunzio: Effective Learning Games
11:30 A.M.	Samantha Bowman: Educational Technology — Generative AI
12:00 P.M.	Lunch
1:30 P.M.	Samantha Bowman, Pam Headly, and Nathan Michaels: Panel Discussion
3:00 P.M.	Robert Sash: Designing the Perfect Field Trip
5:00 P.M.	Carmen Hernandez: Rethinking Bilingual Education

Visit www.floridaeducators.com to sign up. A pass will then be sent to you.

Pam Headly [May 1, 12:40 P.M.]
Hi, Samantha. I ran into a bit of a problem. I'm at the entrance to the convention center, but I just realized I left my pass at the hotel.

Samantha Bowman [May 1, 12:42 P.M.]
Oh, no. Can't you just show your ID to the person at the entrance? You're registered, so your name must be on a list.

Pam Headly [May 1, 12:43 P.M.]
I tried but was told I need my pass to get into the building. So I'm going to head to the hotel now to get it. Given that the hotel is about 30 minutes from here by taxi, I won't return until about 1:45.

Samantha Bowman [May 1, 12:44 P.M.]
That's unfortunate. Please hurry and join us when you get back.

191. Why was the e-mail written?

   (A) To plan a talk at a conference
   (B) To praise two teachers' abilities
   (C) To invite the recipients to a convention
   (D) To list some instructors to invite

192. What is stated about Brown High School?

   (A) It will launch a new program to increase enrollment.
   (B) It only admits students with good academic records.
   (C) It is funded by donations from individuals and companies.
   (D) It has received formal recognition from the government.

193. What is a requirement to attend the conference?

   (A) Sending personal information by mail
   (B) Receiving an invitation from a school official
   (C) Calling a convention center employee
   (D) Completing an online registration process

194. What is indicated about Ms. Bowman?

   (A) She traveled with three teachers to Orlando.
   (B) She decided to change the subject of a talk.
   (C) She was asked to postpone her presentation.
   (D) She was required to purchase an event ticket.

195. What can be inferred about Ms. Headly?

   (A) She forgot her conference pass in a taxi.
   (B) She will be unable to join Ms. Bowman.
   (C) She has gone to the wrong entrance.
   (D) She will miss the start of a discussion.

GO ON TO THE NEXT PAGE

Questions 196-200 refer to the following e-mails and memo.

To: Saul Samson <s.samson@pfg.com>
From: Luanne Mendez <l.mendez@coral.com>
Subject: Your work
Date: May 25

Dear Mr. Samson,

Thank you for the effort you put into creating the supplementary materials for the textbook we will be publishing next month. As usual, your work was excellent. In fact, you have proven to be one of the most reliable freelancers our company works with. That's why I'd like you to consider joining our firm. We have an opening for a full-time writer, and I think you would be perfect.

I'll be out of the office all day tomorrow attending a book fair, but please feel free to contact me the following day if you have any questions.

Sincerely,

Luanne Mendez
Coral Publishing

To: Anjay Khan <a.khan@coral.com>
From: Luanne Mendez <l.mendez@coral.com>
Subject: Follow-up
Date: May 28

Dear Mr. Khan,

We will need to post an advertisement for the writer position. As we discussed, I asked one of our freelancers if he would be interested. However, he has enrolled in a two-year graduate program at a university in London and will be moving to the UK later this month.

The advertisement will be posted by the end of the week, and I'll conduct the interviews myself. Applicants will be required to submit three academic writing samples, which will be reviewed by our head editor, Clara Dover. I expect to find a suitable candidate by July 10, and I'll keep you updated throughout the process.

Thanks,

Luanne Mendez

MEMO

To: All Coral Publishing Staff
From: Luanne Mendez
Subject: Next Week
Date: July 15

We have finally hired a new member of the writing team. Based on the quality of the writing samples Tanya Murray submitted with her application, I expect she will perform well in this role.

Ms. Murray will begin working here on Monday at 9 A.M., and I'll go over the employee manual with her and handle her orientation. However, I have an important meeting until 10 A.M. that morning, so I'd like one of you to volunteer to give Ms. Murray a tour of our office first. Please let me know if you are willing to do this.

196. Why was the first e-mail written?
    (A) To discuss changes to a publication
    (B) To make an offer of employment
    (C) To confirm receipt of a payment
    (D) To describe a freelance project

197. What will Ms. Mendez do on May 26?
    (A) Participate in an industry event
    (B) Attend a leadership workshop
    (C) Conduct an interview of a candidate
    (D) Register for a course on writing

198. What is indicated about Mr. Samson?
    (A) He met Ms. Mendez at a local book fair.
    (B) He is currently seeking a new position.
    (C) He completed a university program recently.
    (D) He plans to relocate to another country.

199. What is suggested about Ms. Murray's writing samples?
    (A) They included nonacademic content.
    (B) They were evaluated by Ms. Dover.
    (C) They were submitted after a deadline.
    (D) They received feedback from Mr. Khan.

200. Why does Ms. Mendez need a volunteer?
    (A) To perform an inspection of an office
    (B) To print out a copy of an employee manual
    (C) To train a new employee for a project
    (D) To show a recent hire around a workspace

This is the end of the test. You may review Parts 5, 6, and 7 if you finish the test early.

Review 체크리스트

TEST 4를 푼 다음, 아래 체크리스트에 따라 틀린 문제를 리뷰하고 박스에 완료 여부를 표시하세요.
만약 시험까지 얼마 남지 않았다면, [1]번 ~ [3]번 항목이라도 꼭 확인하세요.

☐ [1] 틀린 문제의 경우, 다시 풀어봤다.

☐ [2] 틀린 문제의 경우, 스크립트/해석을 확인하며 지문/문제의 내용을 정확하게 파악했다.

☐ [3] 해설을 통해 각 문제의 정답과 오답의 근거가 무엇인지 정확하게 파악했다.

☐ [4] PART 1과 PART 2에서 틀린 문제의 경우, 선택한 오답의 유형이 무엇이었는지 확인하고 같은 함정에 빠지지 않도록 정리해두었다.

☐ [5] PART 3와 PART 4의 각 문제에서 사용된 패러프레이징을 확인했다.

☐ [6] PART 5와 PART 6의 경우, 틀린 문제에서 사용된 문법 포인트 또는 정답 및 오답 어휘를 정리했다.

☐ [7] PART 6의 알맞은 문장 고르기 문제의 경우, 지문 전체를 정확하게 해석하며 전체 글의 흐름과 빈칸 주변 문맥을 정확하게 파악하는 연습을 했다.

☐ [8] PART 7에서 질문과 보기의 키워드를 찾아 표시하며 지문에서 정답의 근거가 되는 문장이나 구절을 찾아보고, 문제에서 사용된 패러프레이징을 확인했다.

☐ [9] PART 1~PART 4는 받아쓰기 & 쉐도잉 워크북을 활용하여, TEST에 수록된 핵심 문장을 받아쓰고 따라 읽으며 복습했다.

☐ [10] PART 1~PART 7은 단어암기자료를 활용하여, TEST에 수록된 핵심 어휘와 표현을 암기했다.

많은 양의 문제를 푸는 것도 중요하지만, 틀린 문제를 제대로 리뷰하는 것도 중요합니다.
틀린 문제를 한 번 더 꼼꼼히 리뷰한다면, 빠른 시간 내에 효과적으로 목표 점수를 달성할 수 있습니다.

해커스 토익 실전 LC+RC 3

TEST 5

LISTENING TEST
PART 1
PART 2
PART 3
PART 4

READING TEST
PART 5
PART 6
PART 7

Review 체크리스트

잠깐! 테스트 전 아래 사항을 꼭 확인하세요.
1. 휴대전화의 전원을 끄셨나요? 예 □
2. Answer Sheet(p.255), 연필, 지우개, 시계를 준비하셨나요? 예 □
3. Listening MP3를 들을 준비가 되셨나요? 예 □

모든 준비가 완료되었으면 목표 점수를 떠올린 후 테스트를 시작합니다.
테스트를 마친 후, Review 체크리스트(p.236)를 보며 자신이 틀린 문제를 반드시 복습합니다.

🎧 TEST 5.mp3
실전용·복습용 문제풀이 MP3 무료 다운로드 및 스트리밍 바로듣기 (HackersIngang.com)
* 실제 시험장의 소음까지 재현해 낸 고사장 소음/매미 버전 MP3, 영국식·호주식 발음 집중 MP3, 고속 버전 MP3까지 구매하면 실전에 더욱 완벽히 대비할 수 있습니다.

무료MP3 바로듣기

LISTENING TEST

In this section, you must demonstrate your ability to understand spoken English. This section is divided into four parts and will take approximately 45 minutes to complete. Do not mark the answers in your test book. Use the answer sheet that is provided separately.

PART 1

Directions: For each question, you will listen to four short statements about a picture in your test book. These statements will not be printed and will only be spoken one time. Select the statement that best describes what is happening in the picture and mark the corresponding letter (A), (B), (C), or (D) on the answer sheet.

Sample Answer

The statement that best describes the picture is (B), "The man is sitting at the desk." So, you should mark letter (B) on the answer sheet.

1.

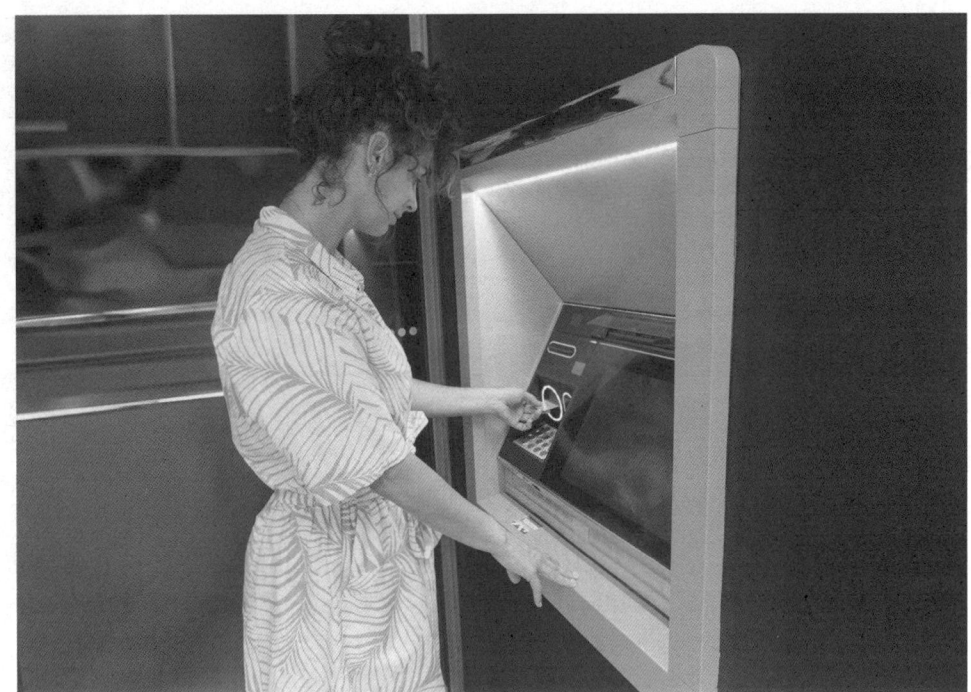

2.

3.

4.

5.

6.

PART 2

Directions: For each question, you will listen to a statement or question followed by three possible responses spoken in English. They will not be printed and will only be spoken one time. Select the best response and mark the corresponding letter (A), (B), or (C) on your answer sheet.

7. Mark your answer on your answer sheet.
8. Mark your answer on your answer sheet.
9. Mark your answer on your answer sheet.
10. Mark your answer on your answer sheet.
11. Mark your answer on your answer sheet.
12. Mark your answer on your answer sheet.
13. Mark your answer on your answer sheet.
14. Mark your answer on your answer sheet.
15. Mark your answer on your answer sheet.
16. Mark your answer on your answer sheet.
17. Mark your answer on your answer sheet.
18. Mark your answer on your answer sheet.
19. Mark your answer on your answer sheet.
20. Mark your answer on your answer sheet.
21. Mark your answer on your answer sheet.
22. Mark your answer on your answer sheet.
23. Mark your answer on your answer sheet.
24. Mark your answer on your answer sheet.
25. Mark your answer on your answer sheet.
26. Mark your answer on your answer sheet.
27. Mark your answer on your answer sheet.
28. Mark your answer on your answer sheet.
29. Mark your answer on your answer sheet.
30. Mark your answer on your answer sheet.
31. Mark your answer on your answer sheet.

PART 3

Directions: In this part, you will listen to several conversations between two or more speakers. These conversations will not be printed and will only be spoken one time. For each conversation, you will be asked to answer three questions. Select the best response and mark the corresponding letter (A), (B), (C), or (D) on your answer sheet.

32. Where is the conversation most likely taking place?

    (A) At a clothing boutique
    (B) At a pharmacy
    (C) At a hardware shop
    (D) At an art supply store

33. What does the woman offer to help with?

    (A) Locating some items
    (B) Processing a refund
    (C) Carrying some supplies
    (D) Assembling some equipment

34. What does the man say he will do?

    (A) Return to a business later
    (B) Switch to another product type
    (C) Read through a user manual
    (D) Check for information online

35. What is the conversation mainly about?

    (A) A teambuilding exercise
    (B) An office relocation
    (C) A management transition
    (D) A workspace reconfiguration

36. What is Erik concerned about?

    (A) Increased distractions
    (B) Additional expenses
    (C) Reduced benefits
    (D) Negative reviews

37. What does the woman suggest doing?

    (A) Verifying information
    (B) Collecting feedback
    (C) Organizing a meeting
    (D) Raising an issue

38. Why was the man late for the appointment?

    (A) A road was congested.
    (B) A parking lot was full.
    (C) A schedule was changed.
    (D) A building was inaccessible.

39. Who most likely is the woman?

    (A) A realtor
    (B) A tour guide
    (C) A receptionist
    (D) An architect

40. What does the woman mean when she says, "The owner wants someone new right away"?

    (A) The man should avoid any delays.
    (B) The man met the owner before.
    (C) The man can get a good deal.
    (D) The man made the right decision.

41. Why does the man need the woman's help?

    (A) To record some audio files
    (B) To proofread some documents
    (C) To access a download link
    (D) To obtain some records

42. What task has the man been assigned?

    (A) Updating a system
    (B) Preparing a report
    (C) Giving a presentation
    (D) Summarizing meeting notes

43. What will the man most likely do next?

    (A) Speak with a customer
    (B) Print a summary
    (C) Contact a supervisor
    (D) Adjust delivery schedule

GO ON TO THE NEXT PAGE

44. Where do the speakers most likely work?

(A) At an art museum
(B) At a furniture manufacturer
(C) At a post office
(D) At an interior company

45. What does the man say about a shipping company?

(A) It has a good reputation.
(B) It made a mistake before.
(C) It has an office downtown.
(D) It launched a new service.

46. What will the woman send to the man?

(A) Some photographs
(B) Some invoices
(C) Some design drafts
(D) Some magazine articles

47. Why is the woman calling?

(A) To apply for a membership
(B) To check a timetable
(C) To ask about a purchase
(D) To cancel a reservation

48. What does the woman request?

(A) A receipt
(B) A refund
(C) A brochure
(D) An upgrade

49. What does the man offer to do?

(A) E-mail a ticket
(B) Confirm a price
(C) Change a schedule
(D) Provide a coupon

50. What are the speakers mainly discussing?

(A) A financial problem
(B) A production process
(C) A design change
(D) A promotion strategy

51. Why does the man say, "It'll take a lot of effort to implement that feedback"?

(A) To ask for another option
(B) To correct a misunderstanding
(C) To give more details
(D) To express some doubts

52. What will the speakers probably do next?

(A) Sign a document
(B) Revise a budget
(C) Read a publication
(D) Hold a meeting

53. What happened last week?

(A) A program was updated.
(B) A delivery was received.
(C) A laptop was returned.
(D) An order was canceled.

54. What does Markus say he can do?

(A) Replace a machine
(B) Offer a discount
(C) Repair a device
(D) Find a product

55. What does the woman inquire about?

(A) A model's availability
(B) A service's cost
(C) An employee's name
(D) A store's hours

56. Where do the speakers most likely work?
(A) At an advertising agency
(B) At a fitness center
(C) At a language school
(D) At a medical clinic

57. What does the woman say about a machine?
(A) It needs to be set up soon.
(B) It has received positive reviews.
(C) It was delivered by mistake.
(D) It includes new features.

58. What will the man most likely do next?
(A) Edit some videos
(B) Share some feedback
(C) Clean out an area
(D) Unpack some equipment

59. What recently happened at the business?
(A) A workshop was rescheduled.
(B) A safety policy was changed.
(C) A business merger was finalized.
(D) An inspection was conducted.

60. What is the man concerned about?
(A) A production disruption
(B) A materials shortage
(C) A building closure
(D) A security breach

61. Why is the woman going to contact Safe Sprinkler?
(A) To complain about a service
(B) To correct some figures
(C) To change a reservation
(D) To make an appointment

Weather Forecast			
	Conditions	Chance of Rain	Temperature High
Tuesday	☁️///	80%	18°C
Wednesday	⛅	0%	20°C
Thursday	☁️	20%	19°C
Friday	☀️	0%	21°C

62. What does the man suggest doing?
(A) Finishing up a work task
(B) Trying a new restaurant
(C) Visiting a city park
(D) Talking with a client

63. Look at the graphic. When will the speakers probably meet?
(A) On Tuesday
(B) On Wednesday
(C) On Thursday
(D) On Friday

64. What does the man give to the woman?
(A) A ticket
(B) A map
(C) A report
(D) A menu

GO ON TO THE NEXT PAGE

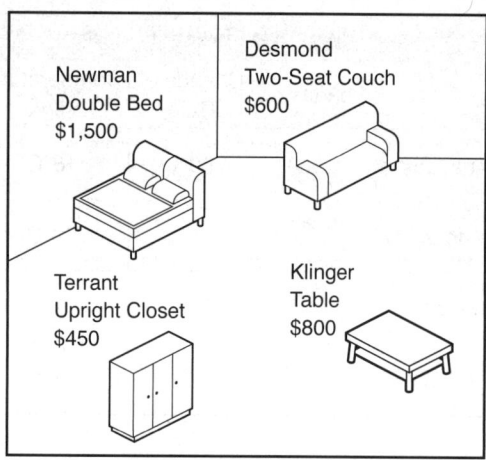

Sandalwood Bistro
Lunch Specials
Personal Pizza $6
Caesar Salad $9
Classic Hamburger $10
Chicken Pasta $12

65. Look at the graphic. Which company's item is the man interested in buying?
    (A) Newman
    (B) Terrant
    (C) Desmond
    (D) Klinger

66. What information does the woman share with the man?
    (A) The cost of a product
    (B) The origin of a brand
    (C) The policies of a business
    (D) The benefits of a material

67. How did the man learn about the store?
    (A) From a Web site
    (B) From a coworker
    (C) From a TV commercial
    (D) From a neighbor

68. Why has the woman's presentation been postponed?
    (A) A meeting agenda was updated.
    (B) A technical issue has occurred.
    (C) A special guest will be absent.
    (D) A conference room is occupied.

69. What will the woman do after lunch?
    (A) Compare product prices
    (B) Revise marketing strategies
    (C) Go over survey results
    (D) Leave a review

70. Look at the graphic. How much will the man's lunch cost?
    (A) $6
    (B) $9
    (C) $10
    (D) $12

PART 4

Directions: In this part, you will listen to several short talks by a single speaker. These talks will not be printed and will only be spoken one time. For each talk, you will be asked to answer three questions. Select the best response and mark the corresponding letter (A), (B), (C), or (D) on your answer sheet.

71. What type of business does the speaker work for?
    (A) A landscaping service
    (B) An Internet service provider
    (C) An electronics store
    (D) A social media platform

72. What problem does the speaker mention?
    (A) A shipment arrived late.
    (B) A payment was not processed.
    (C) An item is no longer in stock.
    (D) An area is closed to the public.

73. What is available on the Web site?
    (A) A special offer
    (B) A store directory
    (C) Tracking information
    (D) Business hours

74. What is the purpose of the advertisement?
    (A) To advertise camping gear
    (B) To sell tickets for an outdoor event
    (C) To promote a recreational facility
    (D) To introduce a new travel agency

75. How is the speaker's company different from its competitors?
    (A) It supplies equipment for free.
    (B) It allows telephone bookings.
    (C) It offers family discounts.
    (D) It provides transportation.

76. Why should the listeners visit a Web site?
    (A) To make a reservation
    (B) To post a review
    (C) To purchase a ticket
    (D) To download a coupon

77. What is the focus of the training?
    (A) Creating advertisements
    (B) Using some software
    (C) Understanding a company policy
    (D) Processing customer complaints

78. According to the speaker, what is a characteristic of the new version?
    (A) It is easy to install.
    (B) It is available in many languages.
    (C) It produces high-quality graphics.
    (D) It speeds up work processes.

79. What are the listeners asked to do?
    (A) Change passwords
    (B) Submit updates
    (C) Activate devices
    (D) Wear identification badges

80. Who most likely is the speaker?
    (A) A government official
    (B) A consultant
    (C) A researcher
    (D) A sales associate

81. What did the listeners receive earlier?
    (A) Protective equipment
    (B) Building maps
    (C) Employee manuals
    (D) Security passes

82. Why does the speaker say, "we've also got some lockers"?
    (A) To assign some tasks
    (B) To give assurance
    (C) To explain a policy change
    (D) To present an alternative

GO ON TO THE NEXT PAGE

83. What type of event is most likely taking place?
    (A) A food festival
    (B) An awards ceremony
    (C) A press conference
    (D) A trade show

84. What does the speaker ask the listeners to do?
    (A) Install a device
    (B) Open a door
    (C) Inspect a booth
    (D) Test an outlet

85. According to the speaker, how can the listeners request help?
    (A) By talking to an employee
    (B) By visiting a help counter
    (C) By completing a form
    (D) By using a mobile application

86. What is the broadcast mainly about?
    (A) A change in an event schedule
    (B) A radio host's retirement
    (C) A music festival lineup
    (D) A rehearsal for a performance

87. What does the speaker imply when she says, "nobody raised any issues"?
    (A) Feedback was not requested.
    (B) A decision was supported.
    (C) A meeting was rescheduled.
    (D) Information was not available.

88. What will the listeners hear next?
    (A) A weather forecast
    (B) An advertisement
    (C) Traffic updates
    (D) New songs

89. What is the speaker mainly discussing?
    (A) A maintenance report
    (B) A new team member
    (C) A branch closure
    (D) A customer complaint

90. Where do the listeners most likely work?
    (A) At a car dealership
    (B) At a financial institution
    (C) At a construction firm
    (D) At a real estate agency

91. What does the speaker hope will happen?
    (A) An amount will become much greater.
    (B) An application will be carefully reviewed.
    (C) A process will become more efficient.
    (D) A transfer will be quickly approved.

92. Who is the speaker presenting to?
    (A) Construction workers
    (B) Council members
    (C) Sales representatives
    (D) Local journalists

93. What does the speaker say about some existing structures?
    (A) They are under construction.
    (B) They are not frequently used.
    (C) They are in disrepair.
    (D) They are expensive to maintain.

94. Why does the speaker say, "each includes a digital display for advertisements"?
    (A) To correct some information
    (B) To justify a cost
    (C) To state a problem
    (D) To explain a service delay

CONSUMER ELECTRONICS
Market Share

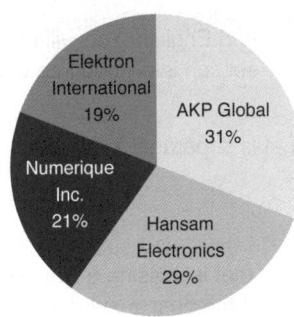

Train Number	Departure Time
11	1:10 P.M.
81	2:35 P.M.
25	3:20 P.M.
20	4:45 P.M.

95. Look at the graphic. In which company does the speaker work?

(A) AKP Global
(B) Hansam Electronics
(C) Numerique Inc.
(D) Elektron International

96. What does the speaker want to do?

(A) Increase company advertising
(B) Add new job positions
(C) Acquire new clients
(D) Hire a marketing firm

97. What will Ms. Keith do next?

(A) Demonstrate a product
(B) Present survey results
(C) Hand out questionnaires
(D) Give a financial report

98. Why has the schedule changed?

(A) A group of workers went on strike.
(B) A station experienced a power outage.
(C) A signal failure occurred on a train line.
(D) A train will need some repairs.

99. What is being offered to some passengers?

(A) A free monthly pass
(B) A shuttle service
(C) A ticket refund
(D) A complimentary drink

100. Look at the graphic. Which train is today's last train to Midland?

(A) 11
(B) 81
(C) 25
(D) 20

This is the end of the Listening test. Turn to PART 5 in your test book.

GO ON TO THE NEXT PAGE

READING TEST

In this section, you must demonstrate your ability to read and comprehend English. You will be given a variety of texts and asked to answer questions about these texts. This section is divided into three parts and will take 75 minutes to complete.

Do not mark the answers in your test book. Use the answer sheet that is separately provided.

PART 5

Directions: In each question, you will be asked to review a statement that is missing a word or phrase. Four answer choices will be provided for each statement. Select the best answer and mark the corresponding letter (A), (B), (C), or (D) on the answer sheet.

PART 5 권장 풀이 시간 **11분**

101. Ms. Tate bought ------- a comfortable chair to improve her home office setup.

(A) she
(B) her
(C) hers
(D) herself

102. Please make sure to return all library books ------- the due date, or else further borrowing will be restricted.

(A) for
(B) once
(C) next
(D) by

103. The manager's e-mail summary is ------- than the full report, but it still covers all the key points.

(A) brief
(B) briefly
(C) briefest
(D) briefer

104. Innova Communications is introducing a new service ------- to capture a larger market share.

(A) categorize
(B) category
(C) categories
(D) categorical

105. Mr. Arnold received a ------- evaluation on his annual performance review, so he was offered a raise.

(A) detailed
(B) convenient
(C) positive
(D) mandatory

106. The film tells the ------- story of a 19th-century Chinese family that overcomes many challenges to survive.

(A) movingly
(B) moving
(C) mover
(D) movement

107. Draper Foods' stock price dropped after its chief financial officer publicly announced his -------.

(A) resigned
(B) resign
(C) resignation
(D) to resign

108. The production schedule has been adjusted due to delays in receiving components ------- from Germany.

(A) maintained
(B) imported
(C) reflected
(D) preserved

109. Staff should use the designated access points while the main entrance ------- .
    (A) paints
    (B) painting
    (C) is painting
    (D) is being painted

110. Barrera Apparel's products must be ------- priced for the Vietnamese market, or they will not sell.
    (A) competitively
    (B) competition
    (C) competitive
    (D) competitor

111. The marketing team at Baldwin Media conducted extensive research ------- better understand customers' needs.
    (A) because
    (B) even though
    (C) as a result
    (D) in order to

112. The dress code at Pollard Mobile is business casual, but an ------- to this rule is made on Fridays.
    (A) except
    (B) exception
    (C) exceptional
    (D) exceptionally

113. Hurst Designs made noticeable modifications to the building's interior ------- left the outside of it mostly unchanged.
    (A) not
    (B) or
    (C) so
    (D) but

114. Because of the high demand for orders, machine ------- at Bowers Manufacturing may have to work overtime this month.
    (A) operates
    (B) operators
    (C) operations
    (D) operating

115. Event volunteers are asked to fold the brochures ------- before placing them in the envelopes.
    (A) neatly
    (B) honestly
    (C) deeply
    (D) occasionally

116. To succeed as Garner Group's chief technology officer, Mr. Wilson must ------- innovation and system security.
    (A) overwhelm
    (B) balance
    (C) gather
    (D) deposit

117. The tent should be secured ------- the ground with stakes to prevent it from blowing away.
    (A) beside
    (B) to
    (C) of
    (D) down

118. Mr. Bain's analysis of the ------- of brand loyalty shows the importance of customer retention strategies.
    (A) reason
    (B) decision
    (C) project
    (D) value

119. The bridge across the Coldwater River was closed to traffic ------- heavy rains caused flooding in the area.
    (A) during
    (B) beyond
    (C) following
    (D) after

120. ------- working at the library, Mr. Choi tutors kids at the local community center.
    (A) Becoming
    (B) Likewise
    (C) Besides
    (D) Otherwise

GO ON TO THE NEXT PAGE

121. To ------- appreciation for your leadership during the launch, we're nominating you for Employee of the Month.

(A) revoke
(B) express
(C) enlist
(D) conclude

122. Not only has Mr. Shin worked ------- on BeilCo's expansion plan, but he has also increased the company's profitability.

(A) completely
(B) accessibly
(C) functionally
(D) diligently

123. Customers of Streaming Sphere may turn off the ------- renewal option by logging in to their accounts and clicking on "Manage My Subscription."

(A) automation
(B) automate
(C) automatic
(D) automatically

124. According to Amaryllis Hotel's -------, guests are responsible for any damage they cause to hotel property.

(A) addition
(B) policy
(C) distribution
(D) industry

125. If the financial data is -------, the accounting department will use it to prepare the report.

(A) accurate
(B) intellectual
(C) deliberate
(D) flexible

126. Manos Furniture recorded strong sales ------- the year, with the final quarter being the strongest.

(A) about
(B) near
(C) throughout
(D) among

127. ------- the employees of Koch Cosmetics are aware of the upcoming merger, many are raising concerns about layoffs.

(A) Now that
(B) As long as
(C) In case
(D) In order that

128. The cereal manufacturer's recent survey shows that consumers prefer ------- with nuts in it.

(A) almost
(B) anything
(C) which
(D) somebody

129. ------- tenants plan to leave their rooms vacant for more than five days, they should notify the building administrator.

(A) Simply
(B) So that
(C) Whenever
(D) Owing to

130. While we understand ------- circumstances affected production, we still expect the supplier to meet the shipment date.

(A) favorable
(B) approximate
(C) reputable
(D) unforeseen

PART 6

Directions: In this part, you will be asked to read four English texts. Each text is missing a word, phrase, or sentence. Select the answer choice that correctly completes the text and mark the corresponding letter (A), (B), (C), or (D) on the answer sheet.

Questions 131-134 refer to the following voucher.

Gladstone Bistro Voucher

This voucher allows the holder to receive one free appetizer or dessert at any Gladstone Bistro location ------- the order of an entrée valued at $15 or more. Until its expiration date, it
131.
may be used on ------- weekdays or weekends during our regular hours of operation. -------.
132. **133.**
Only one voucher will be accepted per dining party, and it may not be combined with any other special offer. Please notify your server that you intend to use this voucher before you place your order. The server will then check to ensure it hasn't expired. Once its ------- is
134.
confirmed, you may make your selections.

Expires August 15

131. (A) over
(B) as
(C) with
(D) at

132. (A) both
(B) either
(C) neither
(D) each

133. (A) All branches are open from 11 A.M. to 10 P.M.
(B) The voucher is only valid on the specified days.
(C) We offer a variety of entrées for $10 or less.
(D) Make sure to ask about our daily lunch specials.

134. (A) quality
(B) validity
(C) location
(D) ownership

Questions 135-138 refer to the following article.

Surge Solutions Releases the FT3

SEATTLE (June 1)—Surge Solutions just announced the release of the FT3. This smartwatch ------- its predecessor, the FT2, which was released last year and whose primary feature was basic activity tracking. -------, the newer version is equipped with extensive health-monitoring systems, including advanced heart-rate sensors and sleep-analysis capabilities. -------. So you won't have to worry about charging it often. If ------- you are looking for is a device with the ability to comprehensively monitor your health, the FT3 is the ideal choice.

135. (A) interests
(B) benefits
(C) enhances
(D) follows

136. (A) In other words
(B) For instance
(C) In contrast
(D) Otherwise

137. (A) The device comes with a two-year warranty.
(B) Its battery life is also much longer.
(C) This makes it an affordable alternative.
(D) Issues with the device heating up have been reported.

138. (A) what
(B) some
(C) that
(D) most

Questions 139-142 refer to the following e-mail.

To: Laura Buchanan <l_buchanan@tierra.com>
From: Dominic Hubert <domhubert@homebasics.com>
Subject: Your handcrafted candles
Date: November 3

Dear Ms. Buchanan,

I am writing with regard to our customers' ------- to your handcrafted candles. For the most
                                         139.
part, the feedback has been very positive. -------.
                                            140.
Because they are in high demand, I would like to order twice the number of candles as we did last time. Would you be able to ------- such a large order?
                                        141.
I do not want to compromise the quality of your product, so if increasing production is a challenge right now, perhaps we could discuss entering into a longer-term contract instead. I believe such an arrangement could serve ------- both very well. Please let me know your
                                              142.
thoughts on this.

Sincerely,

Dominic Hubert
Home Basics

---

139. (A) access
(B) sensitivity
(C) response
(D) objection

140. (A) Selling your goods to other buyers is a breach of contract.
(B) We are considering starting a customer loyalty program.
(C) Many have commented on how good they smell.
(D) We've done this to make them more visible in our store.

141. (A) modify
(B) purchase
(C) delay
(D) fulfill

142. (A) you
(B) us
(C) them
(D) these

Questions 143-146 refer to the following e-mail.

To: All Staff, research department
From: mina_vo@armstronginc.com
Subject: Malfunctioning office printer
Date: October 17

Hello, everyone.

The office printer has been malfunctioning and needs to be replaced -------. I understand that it is challenging for some members of staff to do their work ------- a functional printer. Therefore, I have ordered a new one, and it should arrive by early next week.

-------, if you need to print out any documents, please use the one in the marketing team's office. Note that it requires a four-digit access code (1928). -------. Thank you for understanding.

Mina Vo, Office Manager

143. (A) prompt
 (B) prompts
 (C) promptly
 (D) promptness

144. (A) outside
 (B) against
 (C) beyond
 (D) without

145. (A) In the meantime
 (B) To this end
 (C) On the other hand
 (D) In particular

146. (A) The company newsletter will be distributed via e-mail today.
 (B) We will be holding a team-building event next Thursday afternoon.
 (C) I realize this is less convenient than having a printer in our workspace.
 (D) The new printer has several new features including wireless printing.

PART 7

Directions: In this part, you will be asked to read several texts, such as advertisements, articles, instant messages, or examples of business correspondence. Each text is followed by several questions. Select the best answer and mark the corresponding letter (A), (B), (C), or (D) on your answer sheet.

Questions 147-148 refer to the following report.

Verona Appliances
Company Hotline Report for February

ITEM	FIGURE
Total number of received calls	811
Average call waiting time (in minutes)	7
Average call length (in minutes)	4
Number of resolved calls	349
Number of unresolved calls	462
Average customer satisfaction score out of 5	2

For Internal Use Only

147. Which department's activities are most likely covered by the report?

(A) Marketing
(B) Accounting
(C) Customer service
(D) Human resources

148. What is indicated in the report?

(A) Calls took under five minutes on average to answer.
(B) Some customers called back more than once.
(C) Most customers were satisfied with a service.
(D) More calls were unresolved than resolved.

GO ON TO THE NEXT PAGE

Questions 149-150 refer to the following announcement.

This year, Cleveland Restaurant Week will run from August 24 to August 30, with 50 amazing dining establishments ranging from cozy cafés to upscale steak houses participating. Discounts of as much as 25 percent off selected lunch and dinner menu items will be offered. Throughout the week, parking along Main Street will be free of charge, making it easier for food enthusiasts to explore the city's diverse culinary options. They'll also be able to enjoy the open-air entertainment provided by street performers at no cost and will receive complimentary T-shirts and hats to mark the occasion.

Visit Cleveland City Hall's official Web site for a list of participating establishments.

149. What is mentioned about Cleveland Restaurant Week?
   (A) It will be held at a different time of year than normal.
   (B) It will feature a large number of participating businesses.
   (C) It will conclude with a ceremony on Main Street.
   (D) It has been organized to celebrate a national holiday.

150. What will NOT be free during Cleveland Restaurant Week?
   (A) Parking
   (B) Meals
   (C) Entertainment
   (D) Souvenirs

Questions 151-152 refer to the following information.

Welcome to Lanai Botanical Gardens!

To ensure your safety and comfort, please observe the following rules:

- Place all garbage in the blue trash cans located throughout the facility. Do not litter.
- Do not pick any flowers. Visitors are welcome to take photographs, but please don't touch any of the plants.
- If you are in a large group, make sure not to block the walkways.
- Pets are not permitted within Lanai Botanical Gardens. Please leave your pet within the designated pet play area next to the picnic grounds.

151. What is indicated about Lanai Botanical Gardens?

(A) It is open seven days a week.
(B) It offers self-guided tours.
(C) It allows plants to be photographed.
(D) It charges seniors a reduced admission fee.

152. According to the information, what are all visitors with a pet expected to do?

(A) Provide proof that their pet is vaccinated
(B) Keep their pet leashed at all times
(C) Drop their pet off at a specified location
(D) Dispose of their pet's waste in the blue bins

GO ON TO THE NEXT PAGE

Questions 153-154 refer to the following text-message chain.

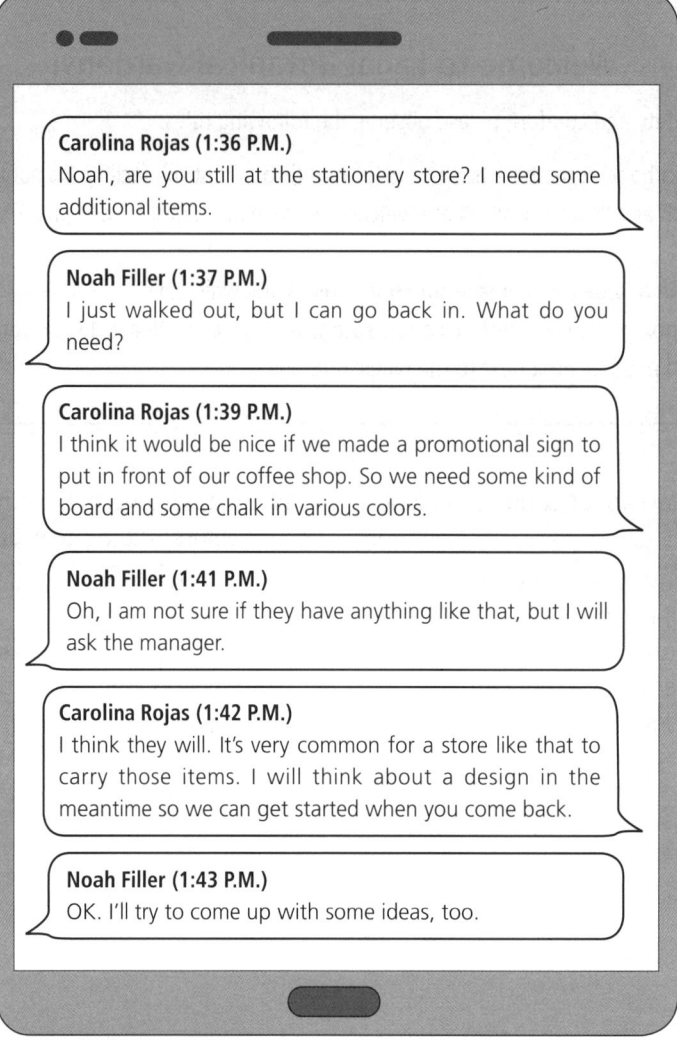

Carolina Rojas (1:36 P.M.)
Noah, are you still at the stationery store? I need some additional items.

Noah Filler (1:37 P.M.)
I just walked out, but I can go back in. What do you need?

Carolina Rojas (1:39 P.M.)
I think it would be nice if we made a promotional sign to put in front of our coffee shop. So we need some kind of board and some chalk in various colors.

Noah Filler (1:41 P.M.)
Oh, I am not sure if they have anything like that, but I will ask the manager.

Carolina Rojas (1:42 P.M.)
I think they will. It's very common for a store like that to carry those items. I will think about a design in the meantime so we can get started when you come back.

Noah Filler (1:43 P.M.)
OK. I'll try to come up with some ideas, too.

153. Why did Ms. Rojas contact Mr. Filler?

(A) To ask him to purchase more items
(B) To request his assistance with a design
(C) To inform him of an issue at their coffee shop
(D) To complain that he has been gone too long

154. At 1:42 P.M., what does Ms. Rojas most likely mean when she writes, "I think they will"?

(A) She believes a manager is aware of a request.
(B) She feels that customers will appreciate a promotion.
(C) She is confident a store carries some items.
(D) She expects a discount to be available.

Questions 155-157 refer to the following letter.

June 5

Calista Parker
769 River Place Drive, Unit 321
Detroit, MI 48207

Dear Ms. Parker,

We hereby accept your application to volunteer at the Detroit Food Center. Volunteers like you are critical to our goal of serving hundreds of people a daily healthy meal that might not be available to them otherwise. As you are a chef, we will have you work in the kitchen. Mostly, we serve simple American classics, but we are always open to new ideas.

You are scheduled to volunteer for six hours per week. Since you said you prefer the weekend, we would like to assign you to the first shift on Saturdays. It starts at 7 A.M. and ends at 1 P.M. Please call me directly at 555-4985 to let me know if this time suits you.

Thank you again for your help.

Sincerely,

Jonathan Dempsey
Detroit Food Center
Program Coordinator

---

155. What is indicated about Ms. Parker?

(A) She has recently retired from her job as a chef.
(B) She is unavailable to work on Saturday afternoons.
(C) She is expected to create a new menu.
(D) She will prepare meals on a voluntary basis.

156. The word "critical" in paragraph 1, line 2, is closest in meaning to

(A) superior
(B) judgmental
(C) essential
(D) consistent

157. Why would Ms. Parker most likely call Mr. Dempsey?

(A) To change a volunteering location
(B) To confirm a work schedule
(C) To finalize a donation payment
(D) To discuss her qualifications

Questions 158-160 refer to the following invitation.

You are cordially invited to an exclusive performance of *Three Colours* organised by the Edinburgh Opera Theatre. The event will take place on 22 October, three nights before the production's official debut on 25 October. The entire cast, including acclaimed tenor Sandra Walker and alto Patrick Fern, will be performing.

Only those who are members of the Edinburg Opera Theatre can access tickets to this event, and each attendee will be given a seat close to the front of the stage, in the first 12 rows. If you are interested in taking advantage of this unique opportunity, please contact Claire Keith at tickets@edinburghopera.scot. You may bring one guest.

Edinburgh Opera Theatre

158. What event is the invitation for?

(A) An opera fundraiser
(B) A preview of a show
(C) A celebration of the theater's anniversary
(D) A photo session with the cast and crew

159. What is indicated about the members of the Edinburgh Opera Theatre?

(A) They will be seated close to the performance space.
(B) They will be expected to adhere to a dress code.
(C) They will get priority access to an autograph-signing event.
(D) They will receive a discount on their guest's ticket.

160. Who most likely is Ms. Keith?

(A) An art critic
(B) An opera singer
(C) A performance's director
(D) A theater employee

Questions 161-163 refer to the following notice.

Jefferson Financial has partnered with the Abrams Foundation to provide volunteering opportunities for our staff. — [1] —. At Jefferson Financial, we encourage active community engagement and giving back to the organizations we believe in. Abrams Foundation is an Evanston-based nongovernmental organization matching volunteers with young children for tutoring services. — [2] —. It plays an important role, as public schools often lack the funds for tutoring services and parents have a hard time finding the right person. We would like to have you help children in a variety of subjects. — [3] —.

We are confident each one of you has valuable skills that extend beyond your financial expertise. Anyone interested should e-mail Kathy Winfrey at k.winfrey@jeffersonfinancial.com. Please include your area of knowledge and your preferred time commitment. We encourage weekly volunteering sessions with the same child. — [4] —. Anyone participating will get a half-day off from work when a tutoring session is scheduled.

161. What is the purpose of the notice?

(A) To announce a corporate merger
(B) To recruit some part-time employees
(C) To inform staff about a social engagement opportunity
(D) To share some budget calculations

162. What is suggested about the Abrams Foundation?

(A) It has not reached a quarterly donation goal.
(B) It is opening a language school.
(C) It is not managed by government officials.
(D) It offers financial help to private schools.

163. In which of the positions marked [1], [2], [3], and [4] does the following sentence best belong?

"This is because consistency helps build stronger relationships."

(A) [1]
(B) [2]
(C) [3]
(D) [4]

Questions 164-167 refer to the following text-message chain.

Beth Lawrence (1:25 P.M.)
What time are you going to Westborough Accounting's office today, Chuck? I'm curious to find out what they think of the print advertisement our firm created for them.

Chuck Jancovik (1:26 P.M.)
I was originally supposed to be there at 2, but the CEO of that company pushed the meeting back to 4. He has an overseas conference call to make earlier this afternoon, so he won't be free until then.

Beth Lawrence (1:27 P.M.)
Got it. Let me know how it goes. By the way, did you hear that our building's parking garage will be closed next week? I guess the walls will be repainted. I'm a little annoyed because that means I'll have to pay for parking somewhere else.

Chuck Jancovik (1:28 P.M.)
Actually, there was a memo from management this morning saying that staff can use the pay lot on Oakley Street for free. We just need to apply for a temporary parking pass at the HR office.

Beth Lawrence (1:29 P.M.)
I can't believe I missed that. I'm heading there now.

Chuck Jancovik (1:32 P.M.)
Good plan. The process for requesting one is pretty simple. And I was told that I'd receive mine before the end of the week.

164. In what type of business do the writers most likely work?

(A) A publishing company
(B) An accounting firm
(C) A law office
(D) A marketing agency

165. Why was a meeting with a client delayed?

(A) An office building will be temporarily closed down.
(B) A foreign branch will not be open on time.
(C) A business conference will start later than planned.
(D) A corporate executive will not be available.

166. At 1:29 P.M., what does Ms. Lawrence most likely mean when she writes, "I'm heading there now"?

(A) She has to pay a parking ticket.
(B) She will attend a meeting.
(C) She will apply what she learned.
(D) She is going to submit a complaint.

167. What can be inferred about Mr. Jancovik?

(A) He will meet with Ms. Lawrence at 2 P.M.
(B) He specializes in online advertising.
(C) He has requested a temporary parking pass.
(D) He is a member of the human resources team.

Questions 168-171 refer to the following e-mail.

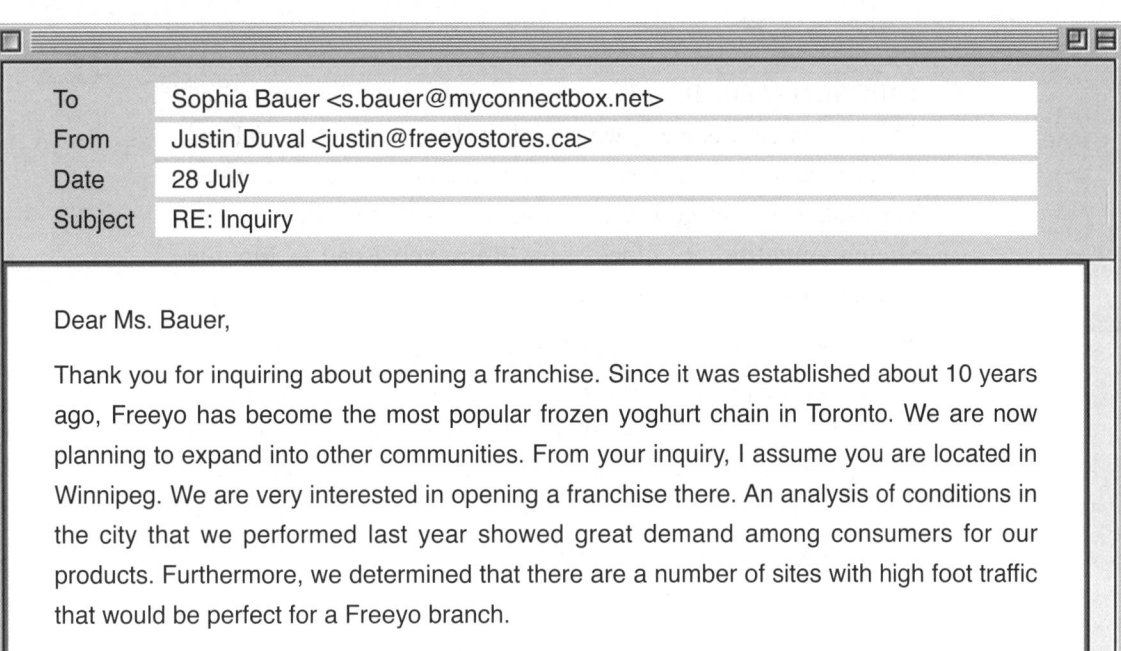

To: Sophia Bauer <s.bauer@myconnectbox.net>
From: Justin Duval <justin@freeyostores.ca>
Date: 28 July
Subject: RE: Inquiry

Dear Ms. Bauer,

Thank you for inquiring about opening a franchise. Since it was established about 10 years ago, Freeyo has become the most popular frozen yoghurt chain in Toronto. We are now planning to expand into other communities. From your inquiry, I assume you are located in Winnipeg. We are very interested in opening a franchise there. An analysis of conditions in the city that we performed last year showed great demand among consumers for our products. Furthermore, we determined that there are a number of sites with high foot traffic that would be perfect for a Freeyo branch.

One of our senior representatives, Jessica Rodriguez, is handling the initial stages of the franchising process. I have passed your inquiry on to her, and she will contact you shortly to set up a meeting. Please note that you will be asked to sign a confidentiality agreement. She will go over it when you meet with her.

Sincerely,

Justin Duval, Freeyo

---

168. What is indicated about Freeyo?
(A) It was founded over 15 years ago.
(B) It is now planning to expand into the Toronto area.
(C) It formed a partnership with another chain.
(D) It is currently operating branches in only one city.

169. According to Mr. Duval, what happened last year?
(A) A sales consultant was hired.
(B) Research on market conditions was conducted.
(C) A new product was developed.
(D) Data about a branch's performance was obtained.

170. The word "determined" in paragraph 1, line 6, is closest in meaning to
(A) discovered
(B) confirmed
(C) predicted
(D) influenced

171. What can be concluded about Ms. Rodriguez?
(A) She represented Freeyo in a legal dispute.
(B) She was unable to contact Ms. Bauer.
(C) She will explain the terms of a contract.
(D) She has made an investment in a franchise.

Questions 172-175 refer to the following article.

CHICAGO (April 10)—The company behind the long-promised Miller Yard development, which will include both residential and commercial units, has finally broken ground. — [1] —. Located alongside the Chicago River's southern branch, the structure will stretch an entire city block, from Roosevelt Road to Monroe Avenue, and will cost an estimated $85 million to build.

One of Mayor Marlene Carter's passion projects, it faced many hurdles in the planning phase. — [2] —. There was criticism of Mayor Carter's decision to partially fund the development through city tax revenues, as well as concern about the environmental impact on the river. However, the project is now underway, and it will include a new cinema and a library. There will be several major retail outlets in the building as well. — [3] —.

The construction started this week and is expected to last until the middle of next year, with a tentative opening scheduled for July 1. "This project is a major step forward for Chicago, not only in terms of revitalizing this part of the city but also in addressing the urgent need for affordable housing," Mayor Carter remarked. "We've included provisions for 20 percent of the residential units within this development to be offered to individuals in need of housing at significantly lower than market rates. — [4] —. What's more, Miller Yard will create hundreds of jobs, which will strengthen the local economy."

172. What is the article mainly about?

(A) A municipal election
(B) A government policy
(C) A multi-use structure
(D) A fundraising event

173. What is NOT mentioned about Miller Yard?

(A) It encountered difficulties during planning.
(B) It is partially funded by local taxes.
(C) It will be connected to a public transit station.
(D) It will be located next to a water body.

174. What does Ms. Carter indicate about Miller Yard's residential units?

(A) Some will be available at reduced prices.
(B) They will take up 20 percent of the total space.
(C) Some will be managed directly by the city.
(D) They will come with fully furnished interiors.

175. In which of the positions marked [1], [2], [3], and [4] does the following sentence best belong?

"For example, the supermarket chain Wellmax has already announced its plans to open a branch."

(A) [1]
(B) [2]
(C) [3]
(D) [4]

Questions 176-180 refer to the following e-mail and booking confirmation.

To: Allen Sanders <a.sanders@spluravisions.uk>
From: Carol Mason <c.mason@spluravisions.uk>
Date: 19 April
Subject: Request

Hi Allen,

As you might have heard, a delegation from our production team has been invited to present some designs in Beijing. I have created a preliminary list of individuals who need to go there. Please book both the hotel and flights for the group. The meeting takes place on 2 May, so I would suggest an arrival on 1 May and a departure on 3 May. For the two nights, I would like the delegation to stay at the Bravo International Hotel as we have a corporate membership in that chain's loyalty programme. The following people are tentatively planned for the trip:

- Benjamin Aiden
- Ken Izaki
- Tyler Lowe
- Paulina Jansen
- Su-min Chung

Before making the bookings, please double-check that each person is available for the trip so that there are no last-minute complications. If a problem does arise, let me know and I will find someone else to join the delegation.

I appreciate you taking care of the bookings.

Sincerely,

Carol Mason

---

www.bivoairlines.com/booking

Booking Confirmation

Date of Booking: 22 April
Company Name: Splura Visions
Total Amount Charged: £2,530

Booking Reference: 5YUT32
Account Number: 233-9112-2345
Credit Card Number: 300-994-XXX-XXX

Flight Summary

From	To	Departure	Flight
London	Beijing	30 April, 10 A.M.	B323

Booking Details

Traveller Name	Ticket Number	Seat Number	Class	Dinner Preference
Su-min Chung	440231	5F	Business	Chicken
Benjamin Aiden	440232	5E	Business	Seafood
Sandra Morton	440233	23B	Economy	Chicken
Ken Izaki	440234	25C	Economy	Chicken
Paulina Jansen	440245	36B	Economy	Beef

All bookings are non-refundable. A service fee of £50 will be charged for any change to a booking.

176. In the e-mail, the word "present" in paragraph 1, line 1, is closest in meaning to

(A) offer
(B) designate
(C) show
(D) prepare

177. Why did Ms. Mason write Mr. Sanders the e-mail?

(A) To provide confirmation of a shipment
(B) To make an appointment with a client
(C) To request information about a project
(D) To give an assignment related to a trip

178. What is suggested about the Bravo International Hotel chain?

(A) It has hosted Splura Visions employees before.
(B) It is known for its convenient location.
(C) It has launched a spa brand in Beijing.
(D) It is planning to renovate some of its properties.

179. What can be concluded about Ms. Mason?

(A) She will appraise various designs prior to a meeting.
(B) She has contacted an airline for an inquiry.
(C) She decided to accompany her employees to Beijing.
(D) She had to change the composition of a delegation.

180. What is indicated in the booking confirmation about some travelers?

(A) They have all paid with separate credit cards.
(B) Some have requested the same meal option.
(C) They will all be sitting close to each other.
(D) Some will depart on a later date than others.

GO ON TO THE NEXT PAGE

Questions 181-185 refer to the following job advertisement and e-mail.

Job Opportunities at VegLite

VegLite is a fast-growing vegetarian restaurant chain that will be taking over the Los Angeles area. First established in San Francisco, VegLite has been adding branches in states like Washington and New York. VegLite believes in a healthy, plant-based diet. However, we do not require our team members to be vegetarian. Here are the positions we are currently looking to fill:

- **Cooks:** A minimum of two years of relevant experience is required. You must be familiar with vegetarian dishes. Only full-time positions are available.
- **Restaurant Managers:** A minimum of three years of relevant experience and a degree in business administration is required. Only full-time positions are available.
- **Assistant Managers:** A minimum of five years of relevant experience is required. A degree in business administration is preferred but not required. Both full- and part-time positions are available.
- **Servers:** A minimum of one year of relevant experience is required. Must have excellent customer service skills. Both full- and part-time positions are available.

Apply today at www.veglite.com/careers. Pick the position you are interested in, and then upload your résumé and a letter of recommendation from a former employer.

To: Martin Cunningham <m.cunningham@veglite.com>
From: Fumiko Yamamoto <f.yamamoto@veglite.com>
Subject: Downtown Location
Date: April 29

Dear Mr. Cunningham,

I would like to personally recommend a cook for the downtown location. Brandon Soloway is a certified chef who has worked in similar establishments. We actually attended the same culinary school together several years ago. We need to staff this position quickly as it's the only one that has not been filled yet.

On another note, I think it would be a great idea to add a small outdoor patio at that branch. However, I am not familiar with the city permit regulations. Do you know anything about these?

Regards,

Fumiko Yamamoto

181. What is stated about VegLite?

(A) It was founded by a resident of Los Angeles.
(B) It has been opening branches in several regions.
(C) It requires all employees to be vegetarian.
(D) It will be expanding into other countries.

182. What is a requirement of the assistant manager position?

(A) Familiarity with how meatless dishes are prepared
(B) A college degree related to managing a business
(C) At least five years of experience in a similar role
(D) The ability to provide good service to customers

183. What must all applicants include with an application?

(A) An educational record
(B) A professional reference
(C) A cover letter
(D) A government certificate

184. What can be inferred about Mr. Soloway?

(A) He is a former coworker of Mr. Cunningham.
(B) He has been recommended for a full-time role.
(C) He has managed a fast food restaurant.
(D) He specializes in European cuisines.

185. Why does Ms. Yamamoto ask about some city regulations?

(A) She is interested in hiring workers from another country.
(B) She was unable to schedule a government inspection.
(C) She would like to build an outdoor seating area.
(D) She wants to keep the restaurant open 24 hours a day.

GO ON TO THE NEXT PAGE

Questions 186-190 refer to the following order form, e-mail, and online review.

www.brightelectronics.com

Bright Electronics

| Home | **Orders** | Product Reviews | Contact us |

Order Number: LK8272   **Customer:** Alita Adams
Order Date: May 15   **Delivery Address:** 456 Oak Lane, Portland OR, 97035

Item	Quantity	Price per Unit	Total Price
Delta Tech 43-inch Smart TV Model number: 72736009	1	$850.00	$850.00
Westgate Wireless Headset Model number: 94857847	2	$120.00	$240.00
		Discount	-
		Subtotal	**$1,090.00**
		Tax	$144.00
		Delivery Fee	$25.00
		Total	**$1,259.00**

- Returns are accepted up to one month from the date of purchase.
- Regular shipping takes four to seven business days, while express shipping takes two to three business days (additional $15 fee).
- All Bright Electronics products come with a two-year warranty.
- Purchases over $500 qualify for free installation. Old devices can be brought to the store for recycling.

Get a Bright Membership Card to receive 10 percent off on all purchases.

To: Bright Electronics <cs@brightelectronics.com>
From: Alita Adams <a.adams@starmail.com>
Subject: Order LK8272
Date: May 16

To Whom It May Concern:

After placing my online order, I noticed that I had mistakenly requested two headsets rather than one as intended. However, I cannot find an option to change a processed order on your Web site. Please make the necessary adjustment and refund the cost of one headset. While you are doing this, please also note that I have a Bright Membership Card (account number: 4448373). This should be reflected on my order as well.

If you need to speak with me, I can be reached at 555-3938.

Thank you.

Alita Adams

www.brightelectronics.com

Bright Electronics

| Home | Orders | **Product Reviews** | Contact us |

Product: Delta Tech 43-inch Smart TV
Customer: Alita Adams
Posted on June 2

I am the owner of a small company called Data Solutions, and I recently decided to redecorate the reception area of my office. When this sleek, modern TV was delivered, I could tell right away that it would fit right in with the furnishings I purchased. Also, the picture and sound quality are excellent. The only issue I feel the need to point out is that the remote-control buttons are too small, so it is kind of hard to change the channels or access the settings menus. In fact, it took me almost 15 minutes just to log in to my Wi-Fi.

Product Rating: 4/5

---

186. What is indicated about Bright Electronics?

(A) It permits returns for an eight-week period.
(B) It offers expedited shipping for an extra fee.
(C) It includes a one-year warranty with its items.
(D) It charges all customers for installation.

187. What is the purpose of the e-mail?

(A) To request access to an online service
(B) To complain about a product defect
(C) To remove an item from an order
(D) To change a method of payment

188. What is suggested about Ms. Adams?

(A) She selected the wrong product while ordering.
(B) She is required to pay for a device to be set up.
(C) She is eligible to get a discount on a purchase.
(D) She provided the incorrect address for a delivery.

189. What can be concluded about Data Solutions?

(A) It is closing for renovations in June.
(B) Its ownership recently underwent a change.
(C) It sent a TV to Bright Electronics for recycling.
(D) Its office is located in the city of Portland.

190. According to the online review, what is a drawback of the Delta Tech Smart TV?

(A) An accessory is difficult to use.
(B) The image quality is inadequate.
(C) A menu is hard to understand.
(D) It is incompatible with other devices.

GO ON TO THE NEXT PAGE

Questions 191-195 refer to the following Web page, list, and e-mail.

---

www.desmondrealestate.com/about

| Home | About | Agents | Contact Us |

For over 50 years, Desmond Real Estate has helped small business owners in Seattle find the perfect locations for their enterprises. Our agents have a reputation for being highly knowledgeable about the city and ensuring that our clients find what they need at a price they can afford.

Unlike many of our competitors, we view tenants rather than property owners as our clients. This is reflected in the extra services our agents provide. Once you have found a space that meets your specifications, the agent will act as your go-between with the owner to request any changes to the lease agreement that you require.

Properties in North Seattle are handled by Peter Walker, while those in Central Seattle are managed by Judith Harris. For all other districts, William Lee and Deanna Lewis will take the lead.

Desmond Real Estate
List of Available Properties

Location	Availability	Size	Cost
Unit 101, 234 Bailey Street (North Seattle)	July 1	220 square meters	$1,800 per month
4736 Center Avenue (East Seattle)	June 1	410 square meters	$2,400 per month
Unit 202, 324 Pine Street (Central Seattle)	August 1	260 square meters	$1,950 per month
3445 Harborview Avenue (West Seattle)	July 1	520 square meters	$2,900 per month

Viewings can be scheduled on weekdays from 9 A.M. to 7 P.M. and on weekends from 9 A.M. to noon.

To: Desmond Real Estate <information@desmondrealestate.com>
From: Liam Morris <l.morris@seattleflowers.com>
Subject: Inquiry
Date: May 17

To Whom It May Concern,

The building in which I currently operate my flower shop was recently sold, and the new owner plans to use the space for her own business. So I need to find a new location by July 1. I recently saw an advertisement for your company, so I decided to give your services a try.

From looking at your list of available properties, I see that you have two that would work with my deadline. Could I arrange viewings of each of them this Sunday? I am not available on any other day because I am too busy at my shop. Thank you.

Sincerely,

Liam Morris
Seattle Flowers

---

191. What is true about Desmond Real Estate?

(A) It employs over a dozen real estate agents.
(B) It provides services in a variety of cities.
(C) It focuses primarily on commercial spaces.
(D) It offers reduced rates to local residents.

192. According to the Web page, what will an agent do for a client?

(A) Check the financial history of an owner
(B) Conduct an inspection of a property
(C) Provide a comparison of rental fees
(D) Negotiate the terms of a contract

193. Who is in charge of renting out the property on Pine Street?

(A) Peter Walker
(B) Judith Harris
(C) William Lee
(D) Deanna Lewis

194. What is suggested about Mr. Morris?

(A) He plans to purchase a building in Seattle.
(B) He has been forced to relocate his business.
(C) He will open a second branch of his flower shop.
(D) He used Desmond Real Estate's services before.

195. What can be concluded about the viewings Mr. Morris wants to arrange?

(A) They will require more than one day to complete.
(B) They will be scheduled to occur in early July.
(C) They will involve properties in the same area.
(D) They will have to take place in the morning.

GO ON TO THE NEXT PAGE

Questions 196-200 refer to the following flyer, e-mail and schedule.

Dearborn Block Party
Saturday, August 4 – Sunday, August 5
9 A.M. to 11:30 P.M.
Free Entry

The Dearborn Block Party is in its third year, and we have expanded. The festivities will take place on Dearborn Street, between where it intersects with Pollock Avenue and Indiana Avenue. The street will be closed to regular traffic. Visit the crafts tents, and enjoy hundreds of different food options from local vendors. The main stage near Pollock Avenue will host a variety of musical guests including superstar group The Callers, acclaimed violinist Jessica Diaz, singer Justin Woo, and the jazz quartet Midnight Clue, among others. We are still looking for volunteers. Reach out to brianna@dearbornblockparty.com if you are able to help out.

To: Stanis Hemsworth <stanis.hemsworth@dearbornblockparty.com>
From: Carissa Walder <c.walder@upstartmusicagency.com>
Date: July 19
Subject: Justin Woo

Dear Mr. Hemsworth,

I'd like to inform you that my client, Justin Woo, has a scheduling conflict. Unfortunately, he will not be able to perform at your event on August 4. He is already scheduled for a show at another venue on Saturday, so I would like to push his set at the block party to the next day.

To make up for the inconvenience, I will have one of my aspiring stars perform with Justin as a special guest. However, you will have to set aside an extra 30 minutes to ensure that there is enough time for this performance.

Mr. Woo will not be available for a sound check, so please make sure everything is set up according to his requirements. If you want, I can have Justin pose for some photos afterwards. Related to this, could you let me know if any news organizations will be covering the event?

Sincerely,

Carissa Walder
Upstart Music Agency

Dearborn Block Party

Sunday, August 5
Pollock Stage

9:30 A.M. – 10:30 A.M.	An aerobics class led by local instructor Patrick Yellen.
11:00 A.M. – 12:30 P.M.	Cooking demonstrations by chefs from the following restaurants: The Light Duck, Pizzeria Quatro, Loop Dumplings, and The Taco Bowl.
2:00 P.M. – 3:30 P.M.	Entertainment for kids provided by The River North Theater Group
4:00 P.M. – 5:00 P.M.	Open mic so that locals can sing, dance, read poetry, etc.
6:00 P.M. – 7:00 P.M.	Jessica Diaz
8:00 P.M. – 9:30 P.M.	Justin Woo (with special guest Celeste Perry)
10:00 P.M. – closing	Midnight Clue

Follow Dearborn Block Party on social media to get updates.

196. What information is included in the flyer?

(A) The number of volunteers
(B) The duration of a celebration
(C) The availability of parking
(D) The names of food vendors

197. What did Ms. Walder ask about?

(A) Whether an event will receive media coverage
(B) Where she can book a rehearsal space
(C) How much some rental equipment costs
(D) When a sound check can commence

198. What is implied about Ms. Walder?

(A) She is the assistant of a well-known photographer.
(B) She is the booking coordinator for a music festival.
(C) She will attend both days of a block party.
(D) She represents Celeste Perry in her agency.

199. According to the schedule, what type of event has been arranged specifically for children?

(A) An exercise class
(B) A cooking demonstration
(C) A theater performance
(D) An open mic

200. What is indicated about a jazz group?

(A) They will close out a two-day event.
(B) They will play songs by other artists.
(C) They are on tour with Justin Woo.
(D) They have signed a recording contract.

This is the end of the test. You may review Parts 5, 6, and 7 if you finish the test early.

Review 체크리스트

TEST 5를 푼 다음, 아래 체크리스트에 따라 틀린 문제를 리뷰하고 박스에 완료 여부를 표시하세요.
만약 시험까지 얼마 남지 않았다면, [1]번 ~ [3]번 항목이라도 꼭 확인하세요.

☐ [1] 틀린 문제의 경우, 다시 풀어봤다.

☐ [2] 틀린 문제의 경우, 스크립트/해석을 확인하며 지문/문제의 내용을 정확하게 파악했다.

☐ [3] 해설을 통해 각 문제의 정답과 오답의 근거가 무엇인지 정확하게 파악했다.

☐ [4] PART 1과 PART 2에서 틀린 문제의 경우, 선택한 오답의 유형이 무엇이었는지 확인하고 같은 함정에 빠지지 않도록 정리해두었다.

☐ [5] PART 3와 PART 4의 각 문제에서 사용된 패러프레이징을 확인했다.

☐ [6] PART 5와 PART 6의 경우, 틀린 문제에서 사용된 문법 포인트 또는 정답 및 오답 어휘를 정리했다.

☐ [7] PART 6의 알맞은 문장 고르기 문제의 경우, 지문 전체를 정확하게 해석하며 전체 글의 흐름과 빈칸 주변 문맥을 정확하게 파악하는 연습을 했다.

☐ [8] PART 7에서 질문과 보기의 키워드를 찾아 표시하며 지문에서 정답의 근거가 되는 문장이나 구절을 찾아보고, 문제에서 사용된 패러프레이징을 확인했다.

☐ [9] PART 1~PART 4는 받아쓰기 & 쉐도잉 워크북을 활용하여, TEST에 수록된 핵심 문장을 받아쓰고 따라 읽으며 복습했다.

☐ [10] PART 1~PART 7은 단어암기자료를 활용하여, TEST에 수록된 핵심 어휘와 표현을 암기했다.

많은 양의 문제를 푸는 것도 중요하지만, 틀린 문제를 제대로 리뷰하는 것도 중요합니다.
틀린 문제를 한 번 더 꼼꼼히 리뷰한다면, 빠른 시간 내에 효과적으로 목표 점수를 달성할 수 있습니다.

해커스 토익 실전 LC+RC 3

정답
점수 환산표
ANSWER SHEET

정답 ANSWER KEYS

TEST 1

LISTENING TEST

1 (B)	21 (B)	41 (A)	61 (B)	81 (D)
2 (C)	22 (A)	42 (B)	62 (D)	82 (A)
3 (B)	23 (C)	43 (B)	63 (C)	83 (B)
4 (C)	24 (A)	44 (C)	64 (B)	84 (D)
5 (A)	25 (C)	45 (D)	65 (C)	85 (A)
6 (D)	26 (B)	46 (C)	66 (B)	86 (C)
7 (C)	27 (A)	47 (A)	67 (D)	87 (B)
8 (A)	28 (B)	48 (C)	68 (D)	88 (C)
9 (A)	29 (A)	49 (B)	69 (A)	89 (C)
10 (B)	30 (C)	50 (B)	70 (C)	90 (C)
11 (B)	31 (B)	51 (D)	71 (B)	91 (A)
12 (C)	32 (C)	52 (C)	72 (D)	92 (C)
13 (A)	33 (D)	53 (B)	73 (C)	93 (B)
14 (C)	34 (B)	54 (C)	74 (B)	94 (D)
15 (B)	35 (D)	55 (A)	75 (A)	95 (D)
16 (A)	36 (B)	56 (D)	76 (D)	96 (C)
17 (B)	37 (C)	57 (B)	77 (C)	97 (B)
18 (A)	38 (D)	58 (A)	78 (B)	98 (C)
19 (A)	39 (A)	59 (D)	79 (C)	99 (B)
20 (C)	40 (D)	60 (B)	80 (C)	100 (D)

READING TEST

101 (B)	121 (C)	141 (B)	161 (D)	181 (A)
102 (D)	122 (C)	142 (D)	162 (C)	182 (D)
103 (A)	123 (B)	143 (A)	163 (C)	183 (C)
104 (B)	124 (D)	144 (D)	164 (C)	184 (C)
105 (D)	125 (D)	145 (D)	165 (B)	185 (A)
106 (D)	126 (B)	146 (C)	166 (C)	186 (D)
107 (A)	127 (C)	147 (C)	167 (D)	187 (C)
108 (B)	128 (A)	148 (C)	168 (A)	188 (B)
109 (C)	129 (B)	149 (B)	169 (C)	189 (B)
110 (D)	130 (C)	150 (A)	170 (C)	190 (D)
111 (A)	131 (A)	151 (D)	171 (B)	191 (D)
112 (B)	132 (C)	152 (A)	172 (C)	192 (B)
113 (D)	133 (D)	153 (D)	173 (B)	193 (C)
114 (B)	134 (B)	154 (C)	174 (C)	194 (C)
115 (A)	135 (B)	155 (D)	175 (A)	195 (D)
116 (C)	136 (C)	156 (C)	176 (B)	196 (D)
117 (B)	137 (B)	157 (B)	177 (B)	197 (A)
118 (C)	138 (A)	158 (D)	178 (C)	198 (C)
119 (C)	139 (C)	159 (C)	179 (D)	199 (B)
120 (A)	140 (A)	160 (C)	180 (D)	200 (D)

TEST 2

LISTENING TEST

1 (B)	21 (C)	41 (B)	61 (A)	81 (B)
2 (C)	22 (A)	42 (D)	62 (D)	82 (C)
3 (C)	23 (C)	43 (C)	63 (A)	83 (D)
4 (D)	24 (C)	44 (D)	64 (C)	84 (C)
5 (A)	25 (B)	45 (B)	65 (C)	85 (B)
6 (B)	26 (A)	46 (B)	66 (B)	86 (A)
7 (B)	27 (C)	47 (A)	67 (D)	87 (C)
8 (A)	28 (A)	48 (A)	68 (A)	88 (A)
9 (A)	29 (B)	49 (C)	69 (B)	89 (D)
10 (C)	30 (A)	50 (B)	70 (D)	90 (B)
11 (B)	31 (C)	51 (C)	71 (B)	91 (C)
12 (C)	32 (C)	52 (B)	72 (C)	92 (B)
13 (A)	33 (B)	53 (C)	73 (B)	93 (D)
14 (C)	34 (C)	54 (D)	74 (A)	94 (A)
15 (C)	35 (A)	55 (A)	75 (C)	95 (B)
16 (B)	36 (C)	56 (D)	76 (B)	96 (C)
17 (B)	37 (B)	57 (B)	77 (D)	97 (C)
18 (A)	38 (D)	58 (D)	78 (C)	98 (A)
19 (A)	39 (C)	59 (B)	79 (A)	99 (D)
20 (B)	40 (A)	60 (C)	80 (C)	100 (D)

READING TEST

101 (C)	121 (C)	141 (C)	161 (D)	181 (C)
102 (A)	122 (D)	142 (B)	162 (D)	182 (B)
103 (C)	123 (B)	143 (C)	163 (B)	183 (D)
104 (B)	124 (A)	144 (C)	164 (A)	184 (C)
105 (D)	125 (A)	145 (B)	165 (A)	185 (C)
106 (A)	126 (D)	146 (A)	166 (D)	186 (C)
107 (B)	127 (C)	147 (D)	167 (D)	187 (B)
108 (C)	128 (A)	148 (D)	168 (A)	188 (C)
109 (C)	129 (B)	149 (C)	169 (C)	189 (D)
110 (B)	130 (B)	150 (B)	170 (D)	190 (B)
111 (C)	131 (B)	151 (C)	171 (B)	191 (C)
112 (D)	132 (A)	152 (B)	172 (A)	192 (A)
113 (B)	133 (D)	153 (D)	173 (B)	193 (D)
114 (B)	134 (B)	154 (B)	174 (A)	194 (D)
115 (D)	135 (A)	155 (A)	175 (C)	195 (A)
116 (A)	136 (D)	156 (B)	176 (C)	196 (D)
117 (D)	137 (B)	157 (D)	177 (D)	197 (C)
118 (C)	138 (B)	158 (A)	178 (B)	198 (D)
119 (B)	139 (D)	159 (C)	179 (A)	199 (D)
120 (D)	140 (A)	160 (B)	180 (D)	200 (A)

정답 ANSWER KEYS

TEST 3

LISTENING TEST

1 (C)	21 (B)	41 (D)	61 (C)	81 (D)
2 (A)	22 (C)	42 (D)	62 (D)	82 (C)
3 (C)	23 (C)	43 (A)	63 (C)	83 (A)
4 (D)	24 (A)	44 (C)	64 (D)	84 (D)
5 (C)	25 (C)	45 (C)	65 (A)	85 (A)
6 (A)	26 (B)	46 (C)	66 (B)	86 (B)
7 (B)	27 (A)	47 (A)	67 (D)	87 (C)
8 (C)	28 (C)	48 (B)	68 (B)	88 (A)
9 (B)	29 (B)	49 (D)	69 (D)	89 (B)
10 (A)	30 (C)	50 (B)	70 (B)	90 (D)
11 (C)	31 (B)	51 (D)	71 (B)	91 (D)
12 (A)	32 (A)	52 (C)	72 (A)	92 (B)
13 (C)	33 (C)	53 (B)	73 (A)	93 (C)
14 (C)	34 (C)	54 (C)	74 (D)	94 (D)
15 (A)	35 (B)	55 (B)	75 (C)	95 (A)
16 (B)	36 (D)	56 (A)	76 (D)	96 (D)
17 (A)	37 (B)	57 (C)	77 (C)	97 (C)
18 (B)	38 (B)	58 (A)	78 (C)	98 (D)
19 (C)	39 (D)	59 (B)	79 (B)	99 (D)
20 (A)	40 (C)	60 (C)	80 (B)	100 (B)

READING TEST

101 (B)	121 (B)	141 (C)	161 (D)	181 (D)
102 (C)	122 (A)	142 (A)	162 (B)	182 (A)
103 (C)	123 (C)	143 (B)	163 (C)	183 (A)
104 (B)	124 (B)	144 (C)	164 (D)	184 (D)
105 (A)	125 (C)	145 (D)	165 (A)	185 (C)
106 (D)	126 (D)	146 (A)	166 (B)	186 (C)
107 (D)	127 (A)	147 (B)	167 (D)	187 (C)
108 (C)	128 (B)	148 (C)	168 (A)	188 (B)
109 (B)	129 (B)	149 (A)	169 (D)	189 (D)
110 (A)	130 (B)	150 (B)	170 (D)	190 (C)
111 (B)	131 (D)	151 (A)	171 (B)	191 (A)
112 (D)	132 (D)	152 (C)	172 (B)	192 (C)
113 (D)	133 (B)	153 (C)	173 (A)	193 (C)
114 (C)	134 (B)	154 (D)	174 (C)	194 (B)
115 (C)	135 (C)	155 (B)	175 (B)	195 (C)
116 (B)	136 (B)	156 (A)	176 (B)	196 (D)
117 (B)	137 (A)	157 (B)	177 (D)	197 (B)
118 (C)	138 (D)	158 (D)	178 (C)	198 (A)
119 (A)	139 (A)	159 (C)	179 (D)	199 (B)
120 (C)	140 (C)	160 (D)	180 (B)	200 (C)

TEST 4

LISTENING TEST

1 (A)	21 (B)	41 (D)	61 (B)	81 (B)
2 (C)	22 (A)	42 (B)	62 (A)	82 (D)
3 (B)	23 (C)	43 (D)	63 (C)	83 (B)
4 (B)	24 (A)	44 (C)	64 (D)	84 (D)
5 (D)	25 (C)	45 (B)	65 (C)	85 (C)
6 (A)	26 (A)	46 (A)	66 (A)	86 (D)
7 (C)	27 (B)	47 (D)	67 (C)	87 (A)
8 (B)	28 (C)	48 (B)	68 (B)	88 (C)
9 (B)	29 (B)	49 (D)	69 (A)	89 (C)
10 (A)	30 (A)	50 (C)	70 (D)	90 (A)
11 (C)	31 (C)	51 (D)	71 (B)	91 (B)
12 (C)	32 (B)	52 (B)	72 (A)	92 (C)
13 (B)	33 (A)	53 (B)	73 (D)	93 (D)
14 (A)	34 (D)	54 (C)	74 (B)	94 (B)
15 (A)	35 (B)	55 (C)	75 (D)	95 (A)
16 (C)	36 (C)	56 (A)	76 (D)	96 (D)
17 (A)	37 (D)	57 (B)	77 (B)	97 (B)
18 (B)	38 (A)	58 (D)	78 (B)	98 (B)
19 (C)	39 (D)	59 (B)	79 (A)	99 (D)
20 (A)	40 (A)	60 (C)	80 (B)	100 (B)

READING TEST

101 (D)	121 (C)	141 (A)	161 (B)	181 (B)
102 (D)	122 (D)	142 (D)	162 (A)	182 (B)
103 (B)	123 (B)	143 (C)	163 (C)	183 (C)
104 (A)	124 (A)	144 (D)	164 (B)	184 (A)
105 (B)	125 (D)	145 (A)	165 (C)	185 (B)
106 (B)	126 (C)	146 (B)	166 (C)	186 (B)
107 (D)	127 (C)	147 (B)	167 (A)	187 (D)
108 (A)	128 (B)	148 (D)	168 (C)	188 (D)
109 (C)	129 (B)	149 (C)	169 (D)	189 (B)
110 (C)	130 (A)	150 (C)	170 (C)	190 (B)
111 (C)	131 (A)	151 (C)	171 (B)	191 (C)
112 (A)	132 (D)	152 (D)	172 (B)	192 (D)
113 (D)	133 (A)	153 (C)	173 (C)	193 (D)
114 (C)	134 (C)	154 (C)	174 (B)	194 (B)
115 (D)	135 (D)	155 (B)	175 (B)	195 (D)
116 (C)	136 (B)	156 (D)	176 (B)	196 (B)
117 (C)	137 (C)	157 (D)	177 (A)	197 (A)
118 (A)	138 (C)	158 (C)	178 (C)	198 (D)
119 (B)	139 (D)	159 (A)	179 (B)	199 (B)
120 (C)	140 (B)	160 (C)	180 (D)	200 (D)

정답 ANSWER KEYS

TEST 5

LISTENING TEST

1 (C)	21 (B)	41 (D)	61 (D)	81 (A)
2 (D)	22 (A)	42 (B)	62 (C)	82 (D)
3 (B)	23 (A)	43 (C)	63 (D)	83 (D)
4 (C)	24 (C)	44 (A)	64 (B)	84 (C)
5 (B)	25 (B)	45 (B)	65 (B)	85 (A)
6 (C)	26 (B)	46 (A)	66 (D)	86 (A)
7 (A)	27 (C)	47 (C)	67 (B)	87 (B)
8 (C)	28 (A)	48 (B)	68 (A)	88 (A)
9 (C)	29 (C)	49 (D)	69 (C)	89 (B)
10 (B)	30 (A)	50 (C)	70 (C)	90 (B)
11 (A)	31 (B)	51 (D)	71 (C)	91 (C)
12 (B)	32 (C)	52 (D)	72 (B)	92 (B)
13 (A)	33 (A)	53 (A)	73 (C)	93 (C)
14 (B)	34 (B)	54 (C)	74 (C)	94 (B)
15 (C)	35 (D)	55 (B)	75 (D)	95 (D)
16 (C)	36 (A)	56 (B)	76 (A)	96 (C)
17 (B)	37 (D)	57 (C)	77 (B)	97 (B)
18 (A)	38 (A)	58 (B)	78 (D)	98 (D)
19 (C)	39 (A)	59 (D)	79 (C)	99 (B)
20 (C)	40 (C)	60 (A)	80 (C)	100 (C)

READING TEST

101 (D)	121 (B)	141 (D)	161 (C)	181 (B)
102 (D)	122 (D)	142 (B)	162 (C)	182 (C)
103 (D)	123 (C)	143 (C)	163 (D)	183 (B)
104 (B)	124 (B)	144 (D)	164 (D)	184 (B)
105 (C)	125 (A)	145 (A)	165 (D)	185 (C)
106 (B)	126 (C)	146 (C)	166 (C)	186 (B)
107 (C)	127 (A)	147 (C)	167 (C)	187 (C)
108 (B)	128 (B)	148 (D)	168 (D)	188 (C)
109 (D)	129 (C)	149 (B)	169 (B)	189 (D)
110 (A)	130 (D)	150 (B)	170 (A)	190 (A)
111 (D)	131 (C)	151 (C)	171 (C)	191 (C)
112 (B)	132 (B)	152 (C)	172 (C)	192 (D)
113 (D)	133 (A)	153 (A)	173 (C)	193 (B)
114 (B)	134 (B)	154 (C)	174 (A)	194 (B)
115 (A)	135 (D)	155 (D)	175 (C)	195 (D)
116 (B)	136 (C)	156 (C)	176 (C)	196 (B)
117 (B)	137 (B)	157 (B)	177 (D)	197 (A)
118 (D)	138 (A)	158 (B)	178 (A)	198 (D)
119 (D)	139 (C)	159 (A)	179 (D)	199 (C)
120 (C)	140 (C)	160 (D)	180 (B)	200 (A)

무료 토익·토스·오픽·지텔프 자료
Hackers.co.kr

 점수 환산표

※ 점수 환산표는 해커스토익 사이트 유저 데이터를 근거로 제작되었으며, 주기적으로 업데이트되고 있습니다. 해커스토익(Hackers.co.kr) 사이트에서 최신 경향을 반영하여 업데이트된 점수환산기를 이용하실 수 있습니다. (토익 > 토익게시판 > 토익점수환산기)

LISTENING

아래 점수 환산표로 자신의 토익 리스닝 점수를 예상해 봅니다.

정답수	예상 점수	정답수	예상 점수	정답수	예상 점수
100	495	66	305	32	135
99	495	65	300	31	130
98	495	64	295	30	125
97	495	63	290	29	120
96	490	62	285	28	115
95	485	61	280	27	110
94	480	60	275	26	105
93	475	59	270	25	100
92	470	58	265	24	95
91	465	57	260	23	90
90	460	56	255	22	85
89	455	55	250	21	80
88	450	54	245	20	75
87	445	53	240	19	70
86	435	52	235	18	65
85	430	51	230	17	60
84	425	50	225	16	55
83	415	49	220	15	50
82	410	48	215	14	45
81	400	47	210	13	40
80	395	46	205	12	35
79	390	45	200	11	30
78	385	44	195	10	25
77	375	43	190	9	20
76	370	42	185	8	15
75	365	41	180	7	10
74	355	40	175	6	5
73	350	39	170	5	5
72	340	38	165	4	5
71	335	37	160	3	5
70	330	36	155	2	5
69	325	35	150	1	5
68	315	34	145	0	5
67	310	33	140		

READING

아래 점수 환산표로 자신의 토익 리딩 점수를 예상해 봅니다.

정답수	예상 점수	정답수	예상 점수	정답수	예상 점수
100	495	66	305	32	125
99	495	65	300	31	120
98	495	64	295	30	115
97	485	63	290	29	110
96	480	62	280	28	105
95	475	61	275	27	100
94	470	60	270	26	95
93	465	59	265	25	90
92	460	58	260	24	85
91	450	57	255	23	80
90	445	56	250	22	75
89	440	55	245	21	70
88	435	54	240	20	70
87	430	53	235	19	65
86	420	52	230	18	60
85	415	51	220	17	60
84	410	50	215	16	55
83	405	49	210	15	50
82	400	48	205	14	45
81	390	47	200	13	40
80	385	46	195	12	35
79	380	45	190	11	30
78	375	44	185	10	30
77	370	43	180	9	25
76	360	42	175	8	20
75	355	41	170	7	20
74	350	40	165	6	15
73	345	39	160	5	15
72	340	38	155	4	10
71	335	37	150	3	5
70	330	36	145	2	5
69	320	35	140	1	5
68	315	34	135	0	5
67	310	33	130		

무료 토익·토스·오픽·지텔프 자료

Hackers.co.kr

자르는 선

Answer Sheet

TEST 1

LISTENING (PART I~IV)

1	A B C D	21	A B C	41	A B C D	61	A B C D	81	A B C D
2	A B C D	22	A B C	42	A B C D	62	A B C D	82	A B C D
3	A B C D	23	A B C	43	A B C D	63	A B C D	83	A B C D
4	A B C D	24	A B C	44	A B C D	64	A B C D	84	A B C D
5	A B C D	25	A B C	45	A B C D	65	A B C D	85	A B C D
6	A B C D	26	A B C	46	A B C D	66	A B C D	86	A B C D
7	A B C	27	A B C	47	A B C D	67	A B C D	87	A B C D
8	A B C	28	A B C	48	A B C D	68	A B C D	88	A B C D
9	A B C	29	A B C	49	A B C D	69	A B C D	89	A B C D
10	A B C	30	A B C	50	A B C D	70	A B C D	90	A B C D
11	A B C	31	A B C	51	A B C D	71	A B C D	91	A B C D
12	A B C	32	A B C D	52	A B C D	72	A B C D	92	A B C D
13	A B C	33	A B C D	53	A B C D	73	A B C D	93	A B C D
14	A B C	34	A B C D	54	A B C D	74	A B C D	94	A B C D
15	A B C	35	A B C D	55	A B C D	75	A B C D	95	A B C D
16	A B C	36	A B C D	56	A B C D	76	A B C D	96	A B C D
17	A B C	37	A B C D	57	A B C D	77	A B C D	97	A B C D
18	A B C	38	A B C D	58	A B C D	78	A B C D	98	A B C D
19	A B C	39	A B C D	59	A B C D	79	A B C D	99	A B C D
20	A B C	40	A B C D	60	A B C D	80	A B C D	100	A B C D

시험시간: **120분** (LC 45분, RC 75분)

READING (PART V~VII)

101	A B C D	121	A B C D	141	A B C D	161	A B C D	181	A B C D
102	A B C D	122	A B C D	142	A B C D	162	A B C D	182	A B C D
103	A B C D	123	A B C D	143	A B C D	163	A B C D	183	A B C D
104	A B C D	124	A B C D	144	A B C D	164	A B C D	184	A B C D
105	A B C D	125	A B C D	145	A B C D	165	A B C D	185	A B C D
106	A B C D	126	A B C D	146	A B C D	166	A B C D	186	A B C D
107	A B C D	127	A B C D	147	A B C D	167	A B C D	187	A B C D
108	A B C D	128	A B C D	148	A B C D	168	A B C D	188	A B C D
109	A B C D	129	A B C D	149	A B C D	169	A B C D	189	A B C D
110	A B C D	130	A B C D	150	A B C D	170	A B C D	190	A B C D
111	A B C D	131	A B C D	151	A B C D	171	A B C D	191	A B C D
112	A B C D	132	A B C D	152	A B C D	172	A B C D	192	A B C D
113	A B C D	133	A B C D	153	A B C D	173	A B C D	193	A B C D
114	A B C D	134	A B C D	154	A B C D	174	A B C D	194	A B C D
115	A B C D	135	A B C D	155	A B C D	175	A B C D	195	A B C D
116	A B C D	136	A B C D	156	A B C D	176	A B C D	196	A B C D
117	A B C D	137	A B C D	157	A B C D	177	A B C D	197	A B C D
118	A B C D	138	A B C D	158	A B C D	178	A B C D	198	A B C D
119	A B C D	139	A B C D	159	A B C D	179	A B C D	199	A B C D
120	A B C D	140	A B C D	160	A B C D	180	A B C D	200	A B C D

답안지 마킹은 **연필**을 사용하시기 바랍니다.

맞은 문제 개수: _____ / 200

무료 토익·토스·오픽·지텔프 자료

Hackers.co.kr

Answer Sheet

TEST 2

무료 토익·토스·오픽·지텔프 자료
Hackers.co.kr

✂ 자르는 선

Answer Sheet

TEST 3

LISTENING (PART I~IV)

1	A B C D	21	A B C	41	A B C D	61	A B C D	81	A B C D
2	A B C D	22	A B C	42	A B C D	62	A B C D	82	A B C D
3	A B C D	23	A B C	43	A B C D	63	A B C D	83	A B C D
4	A B C D	24	A B C	44	A B C D	64	A B C D	84	A B C D
5	A B C D	25	A B C	45	A B C D	65	A B C D	85	A B C D
6	A B C D	26	A B C	46	A B C D	66	A B C D	86	A B C D
7	A B C	27	A B C	47	A B C D	67	A B C D	87	A B C D
8	A B C	28	A B C	48	A B C D	68	A B C D	88	A B C D
9	A B C	29	A B C	49	A B C D	69	A B C D	89	A B C D
10	A B C	30	A B C	50	A B C D	70	A B C D	90	A B C D
11	A B C	31	A B C	51	A B C D	71	A B C D	91	A B C D
12	A B C	32	A B C D	52	A B C D	72	A B C D	92	A B C D
13	A B C	33	A B C D	53	A B C D	73	A B C D	93	A B C D
14	A B C	34	A B C D	54	A B C D	74	A B C D	94	A B C D
15	A B C	35	A B C D	55	A B C D	75	A B C D	95	A B C D
16	A B C	36	A B C D	56	A B C D	76	A B C D	96	A B C D
17	A B C	37	A B C D	57	A B C D	77	A B C D	97	A B C D
18	A B C	38	A B C D	58	A B C D	78	A B C D	98	A B C D
19	A B C	39	A B C D	59	A B C D	79	A B C D	99	A B C D
20	A B C	40	A B C D	60	A B C D	80	A B C D	100	A B C D

시험시간: **120분** (LC 45분, RC 75분)

READING (PART V~VII)

101	A B C D	121	A B C D	141	A B C D	161	A B C D	181	A B C D
102	A B C D	122	A B C D	142	A B C D	162	A B C D	182	A B C D
103	A B C D	123	A B C D	143	A B C D	163	A B C D	183	A B C D
104	A B C D	124	A B C D	144	A B C D	164	A B C D	184	A B C D
105	A B C D	125	A B C D	145	A B C D	165	A B C D	185	A B C D
106	A B C D	126	A B C D	146	A B C D	166	A B C D	186	A B C D
107	A B C D	127	A B C D	147	A B C D	167	A B C D	187	A B C D
108	A B C D	128	A B C D	148	A B C D	168	A B C D	188	A B C D
109	A B C D	129	A B C D	149	A B C D	169	A B C D	189	A B C D
110	A B C D	130	A B C D	150	A B C D	170	A B C D	190	A B C D
111	A B C D	131	A B C D	151	A B C D	171	A B C D	191	A B C D
112	A B C D	132	A B C D	152	A B C D	172	A B C D	192	A B C D
113	A B C D	133	A B C D	153	A B C D	173	A B C D	193	A B C D
114	A B C D	134	A B C D	154	A B C D	174	A B C D	194	A B C D
115	A B C D	135	A B C D	155	A B C D	175	A B C D	195	A B C D
116	A B C D	136	A B C D	156	A B C D	176	A B C D	196	A B C D
117	A B C D	137	A B C D	157	A B C D	177	A B C D	197	A B C D
118	A B C D	138	A B C D	158	A B C D	178	A B C D	198	A B C D
119	A B C D	139	A B C D	159	A B C D	179	A B C D	199	A B C D
120	A B C D	140	A B C D	160	A B C D	180	A B C D	200	A B C D

답안지 마킹은 **연필**을 사용하시기 바랍니다.

맞은 문제 개수: _____ / 200

무료 토익·토스·오픽·지텔프 자료
Hackers.co.kr

Answer Sheet
TEST 4

무료 토익·토스·오픽·지텔프 자료
Hackers.co.kr

자르는 선

Answer Sheet

TEST 5

LISTENING (PART I~IV)

1	A B C D	21	A B C	41	A B C D	61	A B C D	81	A B C D
2	A B C D	22	A B C	42	A B C D	62	A B C D	82	A B C D
3	A B C D	23	A B C	43	A B C D	63	A B C D	83	A B C D
4	A B C D	24	A B C	44	A B C D	64	A B C D	84	A B C D
5	A B C D	25	A B C	45	A B C D	65	A B C D	85	A B C D
6	A B C D	26	A B C	46	A B C D	66	A B C D	86	A B C D
7	A B C	27	A B C	47	A B C D	67	A B C D	87	A B C D
8	A B C	28	A B C	48	A B C D	68	A B C D	88	A B C D
9	A B C	29	A B C	49	A B C D	69	A B C D	89	A B C D
10	A B C	30	A B C	50	A B C D	70	A B C D	90	A B C D
11	A B C	31	A B C	51	A B C D	71	A B C D	91	A B C D
12	A B C	32	A B C D	52	A B C D	72	A B C D	92	A B C D
13	A B C	33	A B C D	53	A B C D	73	A B C D	93	A B C D
14	A B C	34	A B C D	54	A B C D	74	A B C D	94	A B C D
15	A B C	35	A B C D	55	A B C D	75	A B C D	95	A B C D
16	A B C	36	A B C D	56	A B C D	76	A B C D	96	A B C D
17	A B C	37	A B C D	57	A B C D	77	A B C D	97	A B C D
18	A B C	38	A B C D	58	A B C D	78	A B C D	98	A B C D
19	A B C	39	A B C D	59	A B C D	79	A B C D	99	A B C D
20	A B C	40	A B C D	60	A B C D	80	A B C D	100	A B C D

시험시간: **120분** (LC 45분, RC 75분)

READING (PART V~VII)

101	A B C D	121	A B C D	141	A B C D	161	A B C D	181	A B C D
102	A B C D	122	A B C D	142	A B C D	162	A B C D	182	A B C D
103	A B C D	123	A B C D	143	A B C D	163	A B C D	183	A B C D
104	A B C D	124	A B C D	144	A B C D	164	A B C D	184	A B C D
105	A B C D	125	A B C D	145	A B C D	165	A B C D	185	A B C D
106	A B C D	126	A B C D	146	A B C D	166	A B C D	186	A B C D
107	A B C D	127	A B C D	147	A B C D	167	A B C D	187	A B C D
108	A B C D	128	A B C D	148	A B C D	168	A B C D	188	A B C D
109	A B C D	129	A B C D	149	A B C D	169	A B C D	189	A B C D
110	A B C D	130	A B C D	150	A B C D	170	A B C D	190	A B C D
111	A B C D	131	A B C D	151	A B C D	171	A B C D	191	A B C D
112	A B C D	132	A B C D	152	A B C D	172	A B C D	192	A B C D
113	A B C D	133	A B C D	153	A B C D	173	A B C D	193	A B C D
114	A B C D	134	A B C D	154	A B C D	174	A B C D	194	A B C D
115	A B C D	135	A B C D	155	A B C D	175	A B C D	195	A B C D
116	A B C D	136	A B C D	156	A B C D	176	A B C D	196	A B C D
117	A B C D	137	A B C D	157	A B C D	177	A B C D	197	A B C D
118	A B C D	138	A B C D	158	A B C D	178	A B C D	198	A B C D
119	A B C D	139	A B C D	159	A B C D	179	A B C D	199	A B C D
120	A B C D	140	A B C D	160	A B C D	180	A B C D	200	A B C D

답안지 마킹은 **연필**을 사용하시기 바랍니다.

맞은 문제 개수: ______ / 200

무료 토익·토스·오픽·지텔프 자료

Hackers.co.kr

최신 토익 기출경향 완벽 반영

해커스 토익
실전 LC+RC 3
모의고사 + 해설집

초판 6쇄 발행 2025년 12월 1일
초판 1쇄 발행 2025년 1월 2일

지은이	해커스 어학연구소
펴낸곳	㈜해커스 어학연구소
펴낸이	해커스 어학연구소 출판팀
주소	서울특별시 서초구 강남대로61길 23 ㈜해커스 어학연구소
고객센터	02-537-5000
교재 관련 문의	publishing@hackers.com
동영상강의	HackersIngang.com
ISBN	978-89-6542-748-3 (13740)
Serial Number	01-06-01

저작권자 ⓒ 2025, 해커스 어학연구소
이 책 및 음성파일의 모든 내용, 이미지, 디자인, 편집 형태에 대한 저작권은 저자에게 있습니다.
서면에 의한 저자와 출판사의 허락 없이 내용의 일부 혹은 전부를 인용, 발췌하거나 복제, 배포할 수 없습니다.

외국어인강 1위, 해커스인강
HackersIngang.com
해커스인강

· 해커스 토익 스타강사의 **본 교재 인강**
· 단기 리스닝 점수 향상을 위한 **받아쓰기&쉐도잉 워크북**
· 들으면서 외우는 **단어암기장 및 단어암기 MP3**
· 빠르고 편리하게 채점하는 **정답녹음 MP3**

영어 전문 포털, 해커스토익
Hackers.co.kr
해커스 토익

· 최신 출제경향이 반영된 **온라인 실전모의고사**
· 매월 **적중예상특강** 및 실시간 **토익시험 정답확인/해설강의**
· 매일 실전 LC/RC 문제 및 **토익 기출보카 TEST**, 정기토익 기출단어 등 다양한 무료 학습 콘텐츠

헤럴드 선정 2018 대학생 선호브랜드 대상 '대학생이 선정한 외국어인강' 부문 1위

토익 시험일 실검 1위 해커스토익!

14만 토익커가 해커스토익으로 몰리는 이유는?

시험 당일!

1
시험 종료 직후 공개!
**토익 정답
실시간 확인 서비스**

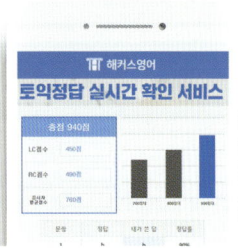

· 정답/응시자 평균점수 즉시 공개
· 빅데이터 기반 가채점+성적 분석
· 개인별 취약 유형 약점보완문제 무료

2
실시간 시험 후기 확인!
**해커스토익
자유게시판**

· 토익시험 난이도 & 논란문제 종결
· 생생한 시험후기 공유
· 고득점 비법/무료 자료 공유

3
오늘 시험에서는요!
**스타강사의
해커스토익 총평강의**

· 스타강사의 파트별 총평강의
· 토익시험 정답 & 난이도 분석
· 취약 파트별 전략 공개

4

토익에 대한 모든 정보가
모여있는 곳!
**토익 전문 커뮤니티
해커스토익**

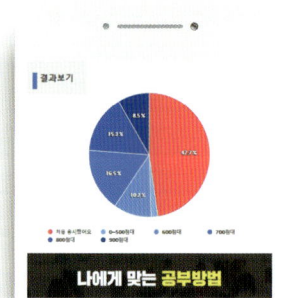

· 토익 고득점 수기, 비법자료 및 스타강사 비법강의 100% 무료!
· 전국 토익 고사장 스피커/시설/평점 공개
· 물토익 VS 불토익 시험당일 난이도 투표부터 나에게 맞는 공부법 추천까지!

[실검 1위] N사 실시간 급상승 검색어 20대 1위(2018.10.14. 13:00 기준)
[14만] 해커스토익(Hackers.co.kr) 일일 방문자 수(2021.02.07. PC+모바일/중복 방문자 포함)

시험당일, 토익 정답을 바로 확인하고 싶다면 [해커스토익] [검색]

해커스토익
바로가기▶

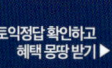

토익정답 확인하고
혜택 몽땅 받기▶

해커스 토익 실전 LC+RC 3

해설집

해커스 어학연구소

저작권자 ⓒ 2025, 해커스 어학연구소 이 책 및 음성파일의 모든 내용, 이미지, 디자인, 편집 형태에 대한 저작권은 저자에게 있습니다.
서면에 의한 저자와 출판사의 허락 없이 내용의 일부 혹은 전부를 인용, 발췌하거나 복제, 배포할 수 없습니다.

TEST 1

LISTENING TEST p.28

1 (B)	21 (B)	41 (A)	61 (B)	81 (D)
2 (C)	22 (A)	42 (B)	62 (D)	82 (A)
3 (B)	23 (C)	43 (B)	63 (C)	83 (B)
4 (C)	24 (A)	44 (C)	64 (B)	84 (D)
5 (A)	25 (C)	45 (D)	65 (C)	85 (A)
6 (D)	26 (B)	46 (C)	66 (D)	86 (C)
7 (C)	27 (A)	47 (A)	67 (D)	87 (B)
8 (A)	28 (B)	48 (C)	68 (D)	88 (C)
9 (A)	29 (C)	49 (B)	69 (A)	89 (C)
10 (B)	30 (C)	50 (B)	70 (C)	90 (C)
11 (B)	31 (B)	51 (D)	71 (B)	91 (A)
12 (C)	32 (C)	52 (C)	72 (D)	92 (C)
13 (A)	33 (D)	53 (B)	73 (C)	93 (B)
14 (C)	34 (B)	54 (C)	74 (B)	94 (D)
15 (B)	35 (D)	55 (A)	75 (A)	95 (D)
16 (A)	36 (B)	56 (D)	76 (D)	96 (C)
17 (B)	37 (C)	57 (B)	77 (C)	97 (B)
18 (A)	38 (D)	58 (A)	78 (B)	98 (C)
19 (A)	39 (A)	59 (D)	79 (C)	99 (B)
20 (C)	40 (D)	60 (B)	80 (C)	100 (D)

READING TEST p.40

101 (B)	121 (C)	141 (B)	161 (D)	181 (A)
102 (D)	122 (C)	142 (D)	162 (C)	182 (D)
103 (A)	123 (B)	143 (A)	163 (D)	183 (C)
104 (B)	124 (D)	144 (D)	164 (D)	184 (C)
105 (D)	125 (D)	145 (D)	165 (B)	185 (A)
106 (D)	126 (B)	146 (C)	166 (C)	186 (D)
107 (A)	127 (C)	147 (C)	167 (D)	187 (C)
108 (B)	128 (A)	148 (C)	168 (A)	188 (B)
109 (C)	129 (B)	149 (B)	169 (C)	189 (B)
110 (D)	130 (C)	150 (A)	170 (C)	190 (D)
111 (A)	131 (A)	151 (D)	171 (B)	191 (D)
112 (B)	132 (C)	152 (A)	172 (C)	192 (B)
113 (D)	133 (D)	153 (D)	173 (B)	193 (C)
114 (B)	134 (B)	154 (C)	174 (C)	194 (C)
115 (A)	135 (B)	155 (D)	175 (A)	195 (D)
116 (C)	136 (C)	156 (C)	176 (B)	196 (C)
117 (B)	137 (B)	157 (B)	177 (B)	197 (A)
118 (D)	138 (A)	158 (D)	178 (C)	198 (C)
119 (C)	139 (C)	159 (C)	179 (D)	199 (B)
120 (A)	140 (A)	160 (C)	180 (D)	200 (D)

PART 1

1 1인 사진   호주식

(A) He's spraying cleaning liquid onto tiles.
(B) He's wiping down a kitchen appliance.
(C) He's mopping the floor of a lobby.
(D) He's operating a laundry machine.

cleaning liquid 세척제, 세정액   appliance n. 기기, 기구
mop v. 대걸레로 닦다   operate v. 작동시키다
laundry machine 세탁기

해석 (A) 그는 타일에 세척제를 뿌리고 있다.
(B) 그는 주방 기기를 닦고 있다.
(C) 그는 로비 바닥을 대걸레로 닦고 있다.
(D) 그는 세탁기를 작동시키고 있다.

해설 (A) [x] 사진에 있는 세척제(cleaning liquid)를 사용하여 혼동을 준 오답이다.
(B) [o] 남자가 주방 기기를 닦고 있는 모습을 가장 잘 묘사한 정답이다.
(C) [x] mopping the floor(바닥을 대걸레로 닦고 있다)는 남자의 동작과 무관하므로 오답이다.
(D) [x] 사진에 세탁기(a laundry machine)가 없으므로 오답이다.

최신토익경향

사람이 무언가를 닦거나 치우는 등의 청소하는 동작을 묘사하는 표현들은 PART 1에서 정답으로 자주 출제된다.

<청소하는 동작을 묘사하는 빈출 표현>
• He's cleaning up some debris.
  그는 쓰레기를 치우고 있다.
• The man is sweeping the floor.
  남자는 바닥을 쓸고 있다.
• She's using a vacuum to clean out a car.
  그녀는 진공청소기를 사용하여 자동차를 청소하고 있다.

2 2인 이상 사진   캐나다식

(A) They're sitting in front of a computer monitor.
(B) They're distributing some books.
(C) They're walking side by side near a shelf.
(D) They're looking in the same direction.

distribute v. 나누어 주다   side by side 나란히
shelf n. 책꽂이, 선반   direction n. 방향

해석 (A) 그들은 컴퓨터 화면 앞에 앉아 있다.

(B) 그들은 몇 권의 책들을 나누어 주고 있다.
(C) **그들은 책꽂이 근처에서 나란히 걷고 있다.**
(D) 그들은 같은 방향을 바라보고 있다.

해설 (A) [x] sitting(앉아 있다)은 사람들의 동작과 무관하므로 오답이다.
(B) [x] 두 사람이 책을 나누어 주고 있다(distributing)고 잘못 묘사한 오답이다. 사진에 있는 책(books)을 사용하여 혼동을 주었다.
(C) [o] 두 사람이 책꽂이 근처에서 나란히 걷고 있는 모습을 가장 잘 묘사한 정답이다.
(D) [x] 두 사람이 서로 다른 방향을 바라보고 있으므로 오답이다. They're looking(그들이 바라보고 있다)까지만 듣고 정답으로 고르지 않도록 주의한다.

3 2인 이상 사진

 미국식

(A) The men are raising some window blinds.
(B) **One of the women is giving a presentation.**
(C) Some notes have been pinned to a wall.
(D) Some chairs are stacked along the windows.

raise v. 올리다, 들어 올리다   presentation n. 발표   note n. 메모
pin v. (핀으로) 고정하다, 꽂다

해설 (A) 남자들이 몇몇 블라인드를 올리고 있다.
(B) **여자들 중 한 명이 발표를 하고 있다.**
(C) 몇몇 메모들이 벽에 고정되어 있다.
(D) 몇몇 의자들이 창문을 따라 쌓여 있다.

해설 (A) [x] 사진에 있는 블라인드(window blinds)를 사용하여 혼동을 준 오답이다.
(B) [o] 여자들 중 한 명이 발표를 하고 있는 모습을 가장 잘 묘사한 정답이다.
(C) [x] 사진에 메모들(notes)이 없으므로 오답이다.
(D) [x] 사진에서 의자(chairs)와 창문(windows)은 보이지만 의자들이 쌓여 있는(stacked) 모습은 아니므로 오답이다.

최신토익경향

최근 PART 1에서는 동작의 의도를 설명하는 표현이 정답으로 자주 출제되고 있다. 따라서 사진에 보이는 상황과 그 동작을 왜 하고 있는지 생각하며 들어야 한다.

<사진 상황에 따른 동작의 의도가 포함된 표현>

A. 한 사람이 칠판 앞에서 말하고 있고, 그 모습을 다른 사람들이 보고 있는 사진에 가능한 정답
• One of the women is speaking into a microphone.
  여자들 중 한 명이 마이크에 대고 말하고 있다.
• Some people are attending a presentation.
  몇몇 사람들이 발표에 참여하고 있다.

B. 상점에서 한 사람이 카운터 뒤에 있는 사람에게 카드 또는 돈을 건네고 있는 사진에 가능한 정답
• A woman is standing behind a counter.
  여자는 계산대 뒤에 서 있다.
• A man is purchasing some fruit from a vendor.
  남자는 상인에게서 과일을 구매하고 있다.
• A woman is paying a cashier for groceries.
  여자는 계산원에게 식료품값을 지불하고 있다.

4 사물 및 풍경 사진

 호주식

(A) Some umbrellas have been closed in an outdoor dining area.
(B) A balcony has been decorated with some banners.
(C) **There is a path running through the lawn.**
(D) Potted plants are being watered in the garden.

dining area 식사 공간   decorate v. 장식하다
banner n. 현수막, 플래카드   path n. 길   potted adj. 화분에 심은

해설 (A) 몇몇 파라솔들이 야외 식사 공간에서 접혀 있다.
(B) 발코니가 몇몇 현수막들로 장식되어 있다.
(C) **잔디밭을 가로지르는 길이 있다.**
(D) 정원에서 화분에 심은 식물들에 물이 뿌려지고 있다.

해설 (A) [x] 사진에 파라솔들(umbrellas)이 보이지만 접혀 있는(have been closed) 모습은 아니므로 오답이다.
(B) [x] 사진에 현수막들(banners)이 없으므로 오답이다.
(C) [o] 잔디밭을 가로지르는 길이 있는 모습을 가장 잘 묘사한 정답이다.
(D) [x] 사진에 화분에 심은 식물들(Potted plants)은 보이지만 물이 뿌려지고 있는(are being watered) 모습은 아니므로 오답이다.

최신토익경향

최근 PART 1에서 작은 길이나 도로가 길게 뻗어 있는 상태를 동사 run을 이용하여 주로 표현한다.

<길이 뻗어 있는 모습을 묘사하는 빈출 표현>
• A path runs through the woods.
  길이 숲을 관통하여 길게 뻗어 있다.
• A road runs along the shoreline.
  도로가 해안가를 따라 길게 뻗어 있다.
• A walkway runs along the body of water.
  보도가 강을 따라 길게 뻗어 있다.

5 2인 이상 사진

 영국식

(A) **Some people are standing behind a checkout counter.**
(B) One of the women is picking up her purse.
(C) One of the men is scrubbing a display case with a cloth.
(D) Some people are walking down a store aisle.

purse n. 지갑   scrub v. 문질러 닦다   display case 진열장
cloth n. 천, 옷감   aisle n. 통로

해설 (A) **몇몇 사람들이 계산대 뒤에 서 있다.**
(B) 여자들 중 한 명이 지갑을 집어 올리고 있다.
(C) 남자들 중 한 명이 천으로 진열장을 문질러 닦고 있다.
(D) 몇몇 사람들이 상점 통로를 걸어가고 있다.

해설 (A) [o] 몇몇 사람들이 계산대 뒤에 서 있는 모습을 가장 잘 묘사한 정답이다.
(B) [x] 사진에 지갑을 집어 올리고 있는(picking up her purse) 여자가 없으므로 오답이다.

(C) [×] 사진에 진열장을 문질러 닦고 있는(scrubbing a display case) 남자가 없으므로 오답이다.
(D) [×] 사진에 걸어가고 있는(walking down) 사람들이 없으므로 오답이다.

6 1인 사진 　　　　　　　　　　　　　　　🔊 미국식

(A) The woman is locking a bicycle to a rack.
(B) The woman is hiking through the snow.
(C) There's a water bottle hanging from one of the handles.
(D) There are some bags attached to a bicycle.

lock　v. (자물쇠로) 걸어 잠그다　　rack　n. 고정대, 받침대
attach　v. 부착하다, 붙이다

해석　(A) 여자가 자전거를 고정대에 걸어 잠그고 있다.
　　(B) 여자가 눈 속을 하이킹하고 있다.
　　(C) 손잡이 중 하나에 매달려 있는 물병이 있다.
　　(D) 자전거에 부착되어 있는 몇몇 가방들이 있다.

해설　(A) [×] 사진에 있는 자전거(a bicycle)를 사용하여 혼동을 준 오답이다.
　　(B) [×] hiking(하이킹하다)은 여자의 동작과 무관하므로 오답이다.
　　(C) [×] 사진에 물병(a water bottle)이 없으므로 오답이다. 사진에 있는 자전거의 손잡이(handles)를 사용하여 혼동을 주었다.
　　(D) [o] 몇몇 가방들이 자전거에 부착되어 있는 모습을 가장 잘 묘사한 정답이다.

PART 2

7 조동사 의문문 　　　　　　　　　　　　🔊 캐나다식 → 미국식

Have you been to the Thai restaurant on Pine Street?
(A) That's enough, thanks.
(B) I'll pay for your lunch.
(C) Yes. Many times.

enough　adj. 충분한　　pay for　계산하다, 돈을 지불하다

해석　Pine가에 있는 태국 음식점에 가본 적 있나요?
　　(A) 충분해요, 감사합니다.
　　(B) 제가 당신의 점심을 계산할게요.
　　(C) 네, 여러 번이요.

해설　(A) [×] Pine가의 태국 음식점에 가본 적이 있는지를 물었는데, 이와 관련이 없는 충분하다는 말로 응답했으므로 오답이다.
　　(B) [×] 질문의 restaurant(음식점)에서 연상할 수 있는 식사와 관련된 lunch(점심)를 사용하여 혼동을 준 오답이다.
　　(C) [o] Yes로 그 음식점에 가본 적이 있음을 전달한 후, 여러 번 갔다고 부연 설명을 했으므로 정답이다.

8 평서문 　　　　　　　　　　　　　　　🔊 영국식 → 호주식

Don't forget to review the sales report before posting it.
(A) I'll make sure to do that.
(B) With a 20 percent discount.
(C) I'm sorry. I can't give you a ride.

sales　n. 매출(량), 판매　　review　v. 검토하다　　post　v. 게시하다
ride　n. 태우고 가기

해석　매출 보고서를 게시하기 전에 검토하는 것을 잊지 마세요.
　　(A) 반드시 그렇게 하도록 할게요.
　　(B) 20퍼센트 할인과 함께요.
　　(C) 죄송해요. 당신을 태워다 줄 수 없어요.

해설　(A) [o] 반드시 그렇게 하도록 할 것이라는 말로, 매출 보고서를 게시하기 전에 검토하겠다고 응답했으므로 정답이다.
　　(B) [×] 질문의 sales(매출, 판매)에서 연상할 수 있는 discount(할인)를 사용하여 혼동을 준 오답이다.
　　(C) [×] 매출 보고서를 게시하기 전에 검토하는 것을 잊지 말라고 했는데, 이와 관련이 없는 태워다 줄 수 없다는 내용으로 응답했으므로 오답이다.

9 Who 의문문 　　　　　　　　　　　　🔊 캐나다식 → 영국식

Who is going to the medical technology fair tomorrow?
(A) Clara is.
(B) Here is the prescription.
(C) The taxi fare was expensive.

medical technology　의학 기술　　fair　n. 박람회
prescription　n. 처방전　　fare　n. 요금

해석　누가 내일 의학 기술 박람회에 가나요?
　　(A) Clara가요.
　　(B) 여기 처방전이 있어요.
　　(C) 택시 요금은 비쌌어요.

해설　(A) [o] Clara라는 말로, 내일 의료 기술 박람회에 가는 사람을 언급했으므로 정답이다.
　　(B) [×] 질문의 medical(의학의)에서 연상할 수 있는 prescription(처방전)을 사용하여 혼동을 준 오답이다.
　　(C) [×] fair - fare의 유사 발음 어휘를 사용하여 혼동을 준 오답이다.

10 Why 의문문 　　　　　　　　　　　　🔊 미국식 → 캐나다식

Why is the West Wing of the Boston Art Center closed off?
(A) It is a great way to close the ceremony.
(B) Because it is undergoing renovation.
(C) From nine o'clock until twelve.

wing　n. (건물의) 동, 부속 건물　　undergo　v. 진행하다, 겪다
renovation　n. 보수 공사, 개조 작업

해석　Boston 예술 회관의 서쪽 부속 건물은 왜 문이 닫혔나요?
　　(A) 그것은 식을 마무리하기에 좋은 방법이에요.
　　(B) 그곳은 보수 공사를 진행하고 있기 때문이에요.
　　(C) 9시부터 12시까지요.

해설 (A) [x] closed - close의 유사 발음 어휘를 사용하여 혼동을 준 오답이다.
(B) [o] 보수 공사를 진행하고 있기 때문이라는 말로, Boston 예술 회관의 서쪽 부속 건물이 문을 닫은 이유를 언급했으므로 정답이다.
(C) [x] Boston 예술 회관의 서쪽 부속 건물이 왜 문이 닫혔는지 이유를 물었는데, 이와 관련이 없는 시간으로 응답했으므로 오답이다.

11 When 의문문
🔊 호주식 → 영국식

When are your building plans due?
(A) In parking area B.
(B) Next Monday at the latest.
(C) Yes, it's a 10-story building.

due adj. ~하기로 되어 있는, 예정인 at the latest 늦어도 story n. 층

해설 당신의 건설 계획안은 언제까지 하기로 되어 있나요?
(A) B 주차장에서요.
(B) 늦어도 다음 주 월요일이요.
(C) 네, 그것은 10층으로 된 건물이에요.

해설 (A) [x] 건설 계획안이 언제까지 하기로 되어 있는지를 물었는데, 이와 관련이 없는 장소로 응답했으므로 오답이다. 질문의 When을 Where로 혼동하여 이를 정답으로 선택하지 않도록 주의한다.
(B) [o] 늦어도 다음 주 월요일이라는 말로, 예정된 기한을 언급했으므로 정답이다.
(C) [x] 의문사 의문문에 Yes로 응답했으므로 오답이다. 질문의 building을 반복 사용하여 혼동을 주었다.

12 부정 의문문
🔊 캐나다식 → 호주식

Isn't our packaging supposed to be redesigned?
(A) No, it's a packaging machine.
(B) An interior design course.
(C) Yes. Without the company name.

packaging n. 포장지 redesign v. 다시 디자인하다 course n. 강의, 과정

해설 우리의 포장지가 다시 디자인되기로 되어 있지 않나요?
(A) 아니요, 그것은 포장 기계예요.
(B) 인테리어 디자인 강의요.
(C) 네. 회사 이름을 제외한 채로요.

해설 (A) [x] 질문의 packaging을 반복 사용하여 혼동을 준 오답이다. No까지만 듣고 정답으로 고르지 않도록 주의한다.
(B) [x] redesigned - design의 유사 발음 어휘를 사용하여 혼동을 준 오답이다.
(C) [o] Yes로 포장지가 다시 디자인되기로 되어 있음을 전달한 후, 회사 이름을 제외한 채로 디자인된다는 부연 설명을 했으므로 정답이다.

13 Which 의문문
🔊 영국식 → 호주식

Which store is set to be converted into a café?
(A) The one next to the central train station.
(B) Yes, it's the converted version.
(C) To sample a new fruit beverage.

convert v. 개조하다, 전환시키다, 변환하다 central adj. 중앙의 sample v. 시음하다, 시식하다 beverage n. 음료

해설 어떤 가게가 카페로 개조될 예정인가요?
(A) 중앙 기차역 옆에 있는 것이요.
(B) 네, 그것은 변환된 버전이에요.
(C) 새로운 과일 음료를 시음하기 위해서요.

해설 (A) [o] 중앙 기차역 옆에 있는 것이라는 말로, 카페로 개조될 예정인 가게를 언급했으므로 정답이다.
(B) [x] 의문사 의문문에 Yes로 응답했으므로 오답이다. 질문의 converted를 반복 사용하여 혼동을 주었다.
(C) [x] 질문의 café(카페)에서 연상할 수 있는 메뉴와 관련된 fruit beverage(과일 음료)를 사용하여 혼동을 준 오답이다.

14 How 의문문
🔊 미국식 → 캐나다식

How did you find out about the fundraising event?
(A) Attendance is limited.
(B) For the upcoming fundraiser.
(C) My colleague told me about it.

fundraising n. 모금 attendance n. 참석자 수, 참석 upcoming adj. 곧 있을, 다가오는 colleague n. 동료

해설 모금 행사에 대해 어떻게 알게 되었나요?
(A) 참석자 수가 제한되어 있어요.
(B) 곧 있을 모금 행사를 위해서요.
(C) 제 동료가 저에게 그것에 대해 말해줬어요.

해설 (A) [x] 질문의 fundraising event(모금 행사)와 관련 있는 Attendance(참석자 수)를 사용하여 혼동을 준 오답이다.
(B) [x] fundraising - fundraiser의 유사 발음 어휘를 사용하여 혼동을 준 오답이다.
(C) [o] 동료가 말해줬다는 말로, 모금 행사에 대해 알게 된 경로를 언급했으므로 정답이다.

15 Where 의문문
🔊 호주식 → 영국식

Where can I drop off my dry cleaning around here?
(A) Within a few days.
(B) There's a shop on Ferguson Avenue.
(C) You dropped your pen.

drop off 맡기다, 두고 오다 drop v. 떨어뜨리다

해설 이 근처에서 제 드라이클리닝 세탁물을 어디에 맡길 수 있을까요?
(A) 며칠 이내로요.
(B) Ferguson가에 가게가 있어요.
(C) 당신이 펜을 떨어뜨렸어요.

해설 (A) [×] 이 근처에서 자신의 드라이클리닝 세탁물을 어디에 맡길 수 있는지 장소를 물었는데, 이와 관련이 없는 기간으로 응답했으므로 오답이다. 질문의 Where를 When으로 혼동하여 이를 정답으로 선택하지 않도록 주의한다.
(B) [○] Ferguson가에 가게가 있다는 말로, 근처에 세탁물을 맡길 수 있는 장소를 언급했으므로 정답이다.
(C) [×] 질문의 drop을 반복 사용하여 혼동을 준 오답이다.

16 평서문
🔊 캐나다식 → 미국식

We're taking the representatives from the Shanghai branch to the factory after the presentation.
(A) Then I'll reserve a van.
(B) One of our sales representatives.
(C) The machines on the factory floor.

representative n. 직원, 대표자   branch n. 지점, 지사
reserve v. 예약하다   van n. 승합차, 밴

해설 우리는 발표 후에 상하이 지점에서 온 직원들을 공장으로 데리고 갈 거예요.
(A) 그러면 제가 승합차를 예약할게요.
(B) 저희 영업 직원들 중 한 명이요.
(C) 공장 작업장의 기계들이요.

해설 (A) [○] 상하이 지점의 직원들을 공장으로 데리고 갈 것이라는 말에 그러면 자신이 승합차를 예약하겠다고 제안했으므로 정답이다.
(B) [×] 질문의 representatives를 반복 사용하여 혼동을 준 오답이다.
(C) [×] 질문의 factory를 반복 사용하여 혼동을 준 오답이다.

17 선택 의문문
🔊 영국식 → 캐나다식

Should we take a short break or continue with the meeting?
(A) No, I'm certain about that.
(B) Let's wrap up the meeting first.
(C) Thanks for providing a solution.

break n. 휴식   wrap up ~을 마무리하다   provide v. 제공하다
solution n. 해결책

해설 우리 잠깐 휴식을 취해야 할까요, 아니면 회의를 계속 진행해야 할까요?
(A) 아니요, 저는 그것에 대해 확신해요.
(B) 먼저 회의를 마무리합시다.
(C) 해결책을 제공해 주셔서 감사해요.

해설 (A) [×] 선택 의문문에 No로 응답했으므로 오답이다.
(B) [○] 먼저 회의를 마무리하자는 말로, 회의를 계속 진행할 것임을 간접적으로 선택했으므로 정답이다.
(C) [×] 질문의 meeting(회의)에서 연상할 수 있는 solution(해결책)을 사용하여 혼동을 주었다.

18 평서문
🔊 호주식 → 영국식

I'm interested in purchasing a custom computer desk.
(A) What price range do you have in mind?
(B) Here's the list of regular customers.
(C) With high specifications.

custom adj. 맞춤형의   price range 가격대
regular customer 단골 손님   specification n. 사양, 설계 구조

해설 저는 맞춤형 컴퓨터 책상을 구매하는 것에 관심이 있어요.
(A) 생각하신 가격대는 무엇인가요?
(B) 여기 단골 손님들의 목록이요.
(C) 높은 사양으로요.

해설 (A) [○] 생각하고 있는 가격대가 무엇인지 되물어, 맞춤형 컴퓨터 책상 구매에 대한 추가 정보를 요구한 정답이다.
(B) [×] custom - customers의 유사 발음 어휘를 사용하여 혼동을 준 오답이다.
(C) [×] 질문의 computer(컴퓨터)와 관련 있는 specifications(사양)을 사용하여 혼동을 준 오답이다.

19 Who 의문문
🔊 영국식 → 호주식

Who can help me with the illustrations for this book?
(A) Alberto is a skilled artist.
(B) The colors are unique.
(C) A vacancy for an illustrator.

illustration n. 삽화   skilled adj. 숙련된   vacancy n. 공석, 빈자리

해설 누가 이 책의 삽화들에 대해 도와줄 수 있나요?
(A) Alberto가 숙련된 화가예요.
(B) 색이 독특하네요.
(C) 삽화가의 공석이요.

해설 (A) [○] Alberto가 숙련된 화가라는 말로, 그가 이 책의 삽화 작업들을 도와줄 수 있음을 간접적으로 전달했으므로 정답이다.
(B) [×] 질문의 illustrations(삽화들)와 관련 있는 colors(색)를 사용하여 혼동을 준 오답이다.
(C) [×] illustrations - illustrator의 유사 발음 어휘를 사용하여 혼동을 준 오답이다.

20 부가 의문문
🔊 호주식 → 영국식

We don't need to book a table in advance, do we?
(A) The booking number for verification.
(B) A table for six, please.
(C) It's on a first-come, first-served basis.

book v. 예약하다   verification n. 확인, 입증

해설 우리가 미리 자리를 예약할 필요는 없어요, 그렇죠?
(A) 확인을 위한 예약 번호요.
(B) 여섯 명을 위한 자리로 부탁해요.
(C) 선착순이에요.

해설 (A) [×] book - booking의 유사 발음 어휘를 사용하여 혼동을 준 오답이다.

(B) [×] 질문의 table을 반복 사용하여 혼동을 준 오답이다.
(C) [○] 선착순이라는 말로, 미리 자리를 예약할 필요가 없음을 간접적으로 전달했으므로 정답이다.

최신토익경향

PART 2에서 평균 2문제씩 출제되는 부가 의문문은 Yes/No로 답변할 수도 있지만, Yes/No가 생략된 응답이 주로 정답으로 출제된다. Yes/No가 생략될 경우 그 의도를 파악하기가 어려우니 다양한 예문에 익숙해져 보자.

<부가 의문문에 Yes/No를 생략하고 답하는 응답>
The shelves we ordered are two meters wide, right?
우리가 주문한 선반의 폭이 2미터죠, 그렇죠?
[답변] That's what the Web site said.
웹사이트에 그렇게 나와 있었어요.
* 주문한 선반의 폭이 2미터인 것이 맞는지 확인하는 부가 의문문에 웹사이트에 그렇게 나와 있었다며 선반의 폭이 2미터 맞을 것임을 전달한 응답

The PR team will go to Hong Kong to give a presentation, right?
홍보팀이 발표를 하기 위해 홍콩에 갈 거예요, 그렇죠?
[답변] The budget for business trips has been cut.
출장비가 삭감됐어요.
* 홍보팀이 발표를 하기 위해 홍콩에 가는 것이 맞는지 확인하는 부가 의문문에 출장비가 삭감됐다며 홍보팀이 홍콩에 가지 않을 것임을 전달한 응답

21 평서문   미국식 → 캐나다식

The response to the last job fair was better than expected.
(A) At the Chicago Business Center.
(B) That's good to hear.
(C) Let me look over the job posting.

response n. 반응 job fair 취업 박람회 look over ~을 살펴보다 job posting 구인 공고

해석 지난번 취업 박람회의 반응이 예상보다 더 좋았어요.
(A) 시카고 비즈니스 센터에서요.
(B) 좋은 소식이네요.
(C) 제가 구인 공고를 살펴볼게요.

해설 (A) [×] 질문의 job fair(취업 박람회)에서 연상할 수 있는 장소와 관련된 Business Center를 사용하여 혼동을 준 오답이다.
(B) [○] 좋은 소식이라는 말로, 취업 박람회의 반응이 예상보다 좋았다는 말에 대한 의견을 제시했으므로 정답이다.
(C) [×] 질문의 job을 반복 사용하여 혼동을 준 오답이다.

22 How 의문문   영국식 → 호주식

How often should the air purifier filter be replaced?
(A) Every three months.
(B) Yes, I got one.
(C) She's done it for years.

air purifier 공기 청정기 replace v. 교체하다

해석 공기 청정기의 필터는 얼마나 자주 교체되어야 하나요?
(A) 3개월마다요.
(B) 네, 제가 하나 샀어요.
(C) 그녀는 그것을 수년 동안 해오고 있어요.

해설 (A) [○] 3개월마다라는 말로, 공기 청정기 필터의 교체 주기를 언급했으므로 정답이다.
(B) [×] 의문사 의문문에 Yes로 응답했으므로 오답이다. the air purifier filter(공기 청정기 필터)를 가리킬 수 있는 one(하나)을 사용하여 혼동을 주었다.
(C) [×] 공기 청정기의 필터가 얼마나 자주 교체되어야 하는지를 물었는데, 기간으로 응답했으므로 오답이다. 기간은 How long(얼마나 오래)의 질문에 대한 응답으로 주로 쓰인다는 것을 알아둔다.

최신토익경향

정도를 묻는 How 의문문은 How 뒤에 나오는 often, much, many, long 등을 정확하게 듣지 못하면 오답을 고를 수 있으니 주의해야 한다.

<정도를 묻는 How 의문문과 응답>
How often does the bus stop at this location?
이 장소에 버스는 얼마나 자주 멈추나요?
[답변] Every 10 minutes.
10분마다요.
How long has the manager been with us?
그 매니저는 우리와 얼마나 오래 함께했죠?
[답변] For about two years.
약 2년 동안이요.

23 Why 의문문   캐나다식 → 미국식

Why hasn't the projector been turned off in the conference room yet?
(A) No, on the third floor.
(B) To meet the project deadline.
(C) Because the presentation will resume soon.

projector n. 영사기 deadline n. 기한, 마감 일자 resume v. 다시 시작하다

해석 회의실 안에 있는 영사기는 왜 아직 꺼지지 않았나요?
(A) 아니요, 3층에서요.
(B) 프로젝트 기한을 맞추기 위해서요.
(C) 발표가 곧 다시 시작될 것이기 때문이에요.

해설 (A) [×] 의문사 의문문에 No로 응답했으므로 오답이다. 질문의 conference room(회의실)에서 연상할 수 있는 위치와 관련된 third floor(3층)를 사용하여 혼동을 주었다.
(B) [×] projector - project의 유사 발음 어휘를 사용하여 혼동을 준 오답이다.
(C) [○] 발표가 곧 다시 시작될 것이기 때문이라는 말로, 회의실의 영사기가 아직 꺼지지 않은 이유를 응답했으므로 정답이다.

24 What 의문문   미국식 → 영국식

What was the total cost of repairing the elevator?
(A) More than 600 dollars.
(B) Only a few times.
(C) It is across from the reception desk.

total adj. 총, 전체의 repair v. 수리하다 reception desk 접수처

해석   엘리베이터의 총 수리 비용은 얼마였나요?
(A) 600달러가 넘었어요.
(B) 단지 몇 번만요.
(C) 접수처 맞은편이에요.

해설   (A) [o] 600달러가 넘었다는 말로, 엘리베이터의 총 수리 비용을 언급했으므로 정답이다.
(B) [x] 엘리베이터의 총 수리 비용이 얼마인지를 물었는데, 이와 관련이 없는 단지 몇 번만이라는 내용으로 응답했으므로 오답이다.
(C) [x] 질문의 elevator(엘리베이터)에서 연상할 수 있는 위치와 관련된 across from the reception desk(접수처의 맞은편)를 사용하여 혼동을 준 오답이다.

25 제안 의문문
🔊 미국식 → 호주식

Would you like to take this electric bicycle for a test ride?
(A) Bicycle lanes are clearly marked.
(B) Near the service center.
(C) Sure. But can I try this one first?

electric   adj. 전기의   bicycle lane 자전거 전용 도로
service center 정비소

해석   이 전기 자전거를 시승해 보시겠어요?
(A) 자전거 전용 도로가 또렷하게 표시되어 있어요.
(B) 정비소 근처에요.
(C) 물론이죠. 그런데 이거 먼저 타봐도 될까요?

해설   (A) [x] 질문의 bicycle을 반복 사용하여 혼동을 준 오답이다.
(B) [x] 질문의 electric bicycle(전기 자전거)에서 연상할 수 있는 service center(정비소)를 사용하여 혼동을 준 오답이다.
(C) [o] Sure로 제안을 수락한 후, 이거 먼저 타봐도 될지 되물어 나중에 시승하겠다고 전달했으므로 정답이다.

26 Be동사 의문문
🔊 캐나다식 → 미국식

Is the new online ordering process more efficient?
(A) Yes, she is new here.
(B) It only took me 10 minutes.
(C) To process the payment.

process   n. 절차; v. 처리하다   efficient   adj. 효율적인
payment   n. 결제, 지불금

해석   새로운 온라인 주문 절차가 더 효율적인가요?
(A) 네, 그녀는 여기가 처음이에요.
(B) 저는 10분밖에 걸리지 않았어요.
(C) 결제를 처리하기 위해서요.

해설   (A) [x] 질문의 new를 반복 사용하여 혼동을 준 오답이다. Yes까지만 듣고 정답으로 고르지 않도록 주의한다.
(B) [o] 10분밖에 걸리지 않았다는 말로, 새로운 온라인 주문 절차가 더 효율적임을 간접적으로 전달했으므로 정답이다.
(C) [x] 질문의 ordering process(주문 절차)와 관련 있는 payment(결제)를 사용하여 혼동을 준 오답이다.

27 부가 의문문
🔊 미국식 → 캐나다식

The subscription fee for our magazine will be increased, right?
(A) Just a little bit.
(B) Most of the young subscribers.
(C) The top publishing firm.

subscription fee 구독료   increase v. 인상되다, 증가하다
subscriber n. 구독자   publishing firm 출판사

해석   우리의 잡지 구독료는 인상될 거예요, 그렇죠?
(A) 조금만요.
(B) 젊은 구독자들의 대부분이요.
(C) 최고의 출판사요.

해설   (A) [o] 조금만이라는 말로, 잡지 구독료가 인상될 것임을 간접적으로 전달했으므로 정답이다.
(B) [x] subscription - subscribers의 유사 발음 어휘를 사용하여 혼동을 준 오답이다.
(C) [x] 질문의 magazine(잡지)에서 연상할 수 있는 publishing firm(출판사)을 사용하여 혼동을 준 오답이다.

28 부정 의문문
🔊 호주식 → 미국식

Don't you think we should change the location of the movie premiere?
(A) Where is the pickup location?
(B) The invitations have already been sent.
(C) With a famous movie director.

premiere n. 시사회, 초연   invitation n. 초대장
movie director 영화감독

해석   우리가 영화 시사회의 장소를 바꿔야 한다고 생각하지 않나요?
(A) 수령 장소가 어디인가요?
(B) 초대장들을 이미 보냈어요.
(C) 유명한 영화감독과 함께요.

해설   (A) [x] 질문의 location을 반복 사용하여 혼동을 준 오답이다.
(B) [o] 초대장들을 이미 보냈다는 말로, 영화 시사회 장소를 바꾸면 안 된다고 생각하고 있음을 간접적으로 전달했으므로 정답이다.
(C) [x] 질문의 movie premiere(영화 시사회)에서 연상할 수 있는 movie director(영화감독)를 사용하여 혼동을 준 오답이다.

29 How 의문문
🔊 호주식 → 캐나다식

How is the construction work going at the hotel downtown?
(A) I haven't been there recently.
(B) Room 402 is prepared for you.
(C) We hired them to fix the roof.

recently   adv. 최근에

해석   시내 호텔의 건설 작업은 어떻게 진행되고 있나요?
(A) 저는 최근에 그곳에 가본 적이 없어요.
(B) 402호 방이 당신을 위해 준비되어 있어요.

(C) 우리는 지붕을 고치기 위해 그들을 고용했어요.

해설 (A) [○] 최근에 그곳에 가본 적이 없다는 말로, 시내 호텔의 건설 작업이 어떻게 진행되고 있는지 모른다는 것을 간접적으로 전달했으므로 정답이다.
(B) [×] 질문의 hotel(호텔)과 관련 있는 Room 402(402호)를 사용하여 혼동을 준 오답이다.
(C) [×] 질문의 construction work(건설 작업)에서 연상할 수 있는 fix the roof(지붕을 고치다)를 사용하여 혼동을 준 오답이다.

30 선택 의문문
영국식 → 미국식

Should I bring some flowers or some cake to the office party?
(A) That was a live performance.
(B) For the new interns.
(C) Don't you live near a bakery?

performance n. 공연   intern n. 인턴

해설 회사 파티에 꽃을 가져가야 할까요, 아니면 케이크를 가져가야 할까요?
(A) 그것은 라이브 공연이었어요.
(B) 신입 인턴들을 위해서요.
(C) 당신은 빵집 근처에 살지 않나요?

해설 (A) [×] 질문의 party(파티)에서 연상할 수 있는 live performance(라이브 공연)를 사용하여 혼동을 준 오답이다.
(B) [×] 질문의 office(회사)와 관련 있는 new interns(신입 인턴들)를 사용하여 혼동을 준 오답이다.
(C) [○] 빵집 근처에 살지 않냐고 되물어, 회사 파티에 케이크를 들고 올 것을 간접적으로 선택했으므로 정답이다.

31 제안 의문문
호주식 → 미국식

Why don't we move the discount item section closer to the entrance?
(A) The market closes on Wednesdays.
(B) The space must be kept clear for emergencies.
(C) The final clearance sale in winter.

section n. 구역, 부분   entrance n. 입구   emergency n. 응급상황

해설 할인 품목 구역을 입구에 더 가깝게 옮기는 게 어때요?
(A) 시장은 수요일마다 문을 닫아요.
(B) 그 공간은 응급상황을 대비하여 비워 두어야 해요.
(C) 겨울철 최종 재고 정리 세일이요.

해설 (A) [×] closer - closes의 유사 발음 어휘를 사용하여 혼동을 준 오답이다.
(B) [○] 그 공간은 응급상황을 대비하여 비워 두어야 한다는 말로, 할인 품목 구역을 입구에 더 가깝게 옮기자는 제안을 간접적으로 거절했으므로 정답이다.
(C) [×] 질문의 discount(할인)와 관련 있는 clearance sale(재고 정리 세일)을 사용하여 혼동을 준 오답이다.

PART 3

[32-34]
캐나다식 → 미국식

Questions 32-34 refer to the following conversation.

M: ³²Welcome to Solace Spa. Do you have an appointment for today?
W: Yes. My name is Bianca Wallace. My friend made the reservation for me.
M: Let me check . . . It looks like you have been scheduled for a 60-minute Swedish massage.
W: Right. ³³But can I extend it to 90 minutes?
M: It won't be a problem. It will just be an extra 30 dollars. ³⁴You can get a 10 percent discount if you become a member of our Solace Spa Loyalty Club.

appointment n. 예약, 약속   reservation n. 예약
extend v. 늘리다, 연장하다

해설 32-34번은 다음 대화에 관한 문제입니다.

남: ³²Solace 스파에 오신 것을 환영합니다. 오늘 예약이 되어 있으신가요?
여: 네. 제 이름은 Bianca Wallace예요. 제 친구가 저를 위해 예약을 해주었어요.
남: 확인해보겠습니다... 손님께서는 60분짜리 스웨덴 마사지로 일정이 잡혀 있으신 것 같네요.
여: 맞아요. ³³하지만 제가 그것을 90분으로 늘릴 수 있을까요?
남: 그건 문제가 되지 않습니다. 30달러의 추가금이 들어갈 뿐이죠. ³⁴손님께서 만약 저희 Solace 스파 로열티 클럽의 회원이 되신다면 10퍼센트 할인을 받으실 수 있습니다.

32 화자 문제

해설 남자는 누구인 것 같은가?
(A) 기술자
(B) 강사
(C) 접수원
(D) 의사

해설 대화에서 신분 및 직업과 관련된 표현을 놓치지 않고 듣는다. 남자가 "Welcome to Solace Spa. Do you have an appointment for today?"라며 Solace 스파에 온 것을 환영하고 오늘 예약이 되어 있는지 묻는 것을 통해 남자가 접수원임을 알 수 있다. 따라서 (C)가 정답이다.

33 특정 세부 사항 문제

해설 여자는 무엇을 하기를 원하는가?
(A) 온라인 주문하기
(B) 예약 취소하기
(C) 기프트 카드 구매하기
(D) 시간 연장하기

해설 대화에서 여자의 말을 주의 깊게 듣는다. 여자가 "But can I extend it to 90 minutes?"라며, 60분짜리 스웨덴 마사지를 90분으로 늘릴 수 있는지 묻는 것을 통해 여자가 시간을 연장하기를 원한다는 것

을 알 수 있다. 따라서 (D)가 정답이다.

어휘 lengthen v. 연장하다, 늘이다

34 방법 문제

해석 여자는 어떻게 할인을 받을 수 있는가?
(A) 친구에게 서비스를 언급함으로써
(B) 회원권을 만듦으로써
(C) 소식지를 신청함으로써
(D) 온라인 후기를 작성함으로써

해설 질문의 핵심 어구(discount)가 언급된 주변을 주의 깊게 듣는다. 남자가 "You can get a 10 percent discount if you become a member of our Solace Spa Loyalty Club."이라며 만약 Solace 스파 로열티 클럽의 회원이 된다면 10퍼센트 할인을 받을 수 있다고 하였다. 따라서 (B)가 정답이다.

어휘 refer v. 언급하다, 지칭하다   newsletter n. 소식지

[35-37]   🎧 호주식 → 영국식

Questions 35-37 refer to the following conversation.

M: Hey, Yun? ³⁵Are the plans for the electrical repairs to the community center going well?
W: ³⁶The budget proposal was approved this morning, so we can proceed as planned. I also confirmed the schedule for the electricians to visit tomorrow.
M: Great. Then, ³⁷why don't we look at the building plans now? We can figure out which areas the electricians should start on.
W: Sure. ³⁷I'll bring them over.

electrical adj. 전기의   budget proposal 예산안
approve v. 승인하다, 찬성하다   proceed v. 진행하다
confirm v. 확정하다, 확인하다   figure out 파악하다, 이해하다

해석
35-37번은 다음 대화에 관한 문제입니다.
남: 저기요, Yun? ³⁵지역 문화 회관의 전기 수리를 위한 계획은 잘 진행되고 있나요?
여: ³⁶예산안이 오늘 오전에 승인돼서 계획대로 진행할 수 있어요. 저는 또한 전기 기술자들이 내일 방문하는 일정을 확정해 두었어요.
남: 좋네요. 그럼, ³⁷지금 건물 도면을 살펴보는 것이 어떨까요? 우리가 전기 기술자들이 어느 구역들부터 시작해야 하는지 파악할 수 있을 거예요.
여: 좋아요. ³⁷제가 그것들을 가지고 올게요.

35 주제 문제

해석 대화는 주로 무엇에 대한 것인가?
(A) 지역사회 행사
(B) 유지 비용
(C) 일정 변경
(D) 건물 수리

해설 대화의 주제를 묻는 문제이므로, 지문의 초반을 반드시 듣는다. 남자가 "Are the plans for the electrical repairs to the community center going well?"이라며 지역 문화 회관의 전기

수리를 위한 계획이 잘 진행되고 있는지 물은 후, 건물 수리에 대한 내용으로 대화가 이어지고 있다. 따라서 (D)가 정답이다.

어휘 maintenance n. 유지, 보수 관리

36 특정 세부 사항 문제

해석 여자에 따르면, 오늘 오전에 무엇이 승인되었는가?
(A) 채용 제안
(B) 재정 계획
(C) 행사 장소
(D) 건설 허가

해설 여자의 말에서 질문의 핵심 어구(approved this morning)가 언급된 주변을 주의 깊게 듣는다. 여자가 "The budget proposal was approved this morning"이라며 예산안이 오늘 오전에 승인되었다고 하였다. 따라서 (B)가 정답이다.

어휘 employment n. 채용, 취업   financial adj. 재정의, 재무의
construction n. 건설, 공사

Paraphrasing

The budget proposal 예산안 → A financial plan 재정 계획

37 다음에 할 일 문제

해석 화자들은 다음에 무엇을 할 것인가?
(A) 인턴과 이야기한다.
(B) 소프트웨어 프로그램을 업데이트한다.
(C) 설계도를 검토한다.
(D) 송장을 가져온다.

해설 대화의 마지막 부분을 주의 깊게 듣는다. 남자가 "why don't we look at the building plans now?"라며 지금 건물 도면을 살펴보자고 제안하자, 여자가 "I'll bring them over."라며 자신이 설계도를 가지고 오겠다고 하였다. 따라서 (C)가 정답이다.

어휘 blueprint n. 설계도, 청사진   invoice n. 송장, 청구서

Paraphrasing

look at ~을 살펴보다 → Examine 검토하다
the building plans 건물 도면 → blueprints 설계도

[38-40]   🎧 미국식 → 호주식

Questions 38-40 refer to the following conversation.

W: I feel that our staff could enhance their work productivity. ³⁸What about offering online training courses? I found a company called EduSphere. They have courses in database management, proposal writing, and even marketing.
M: I've heard of that company as well. ³⁹But aren't those courses expensive?
W: Actually, they're free during the first month. We also get additional discounts if we subscribe for over a year. ⁴⁰The company's Web site provides detailed information about the cost of the various classes for each program.

enhance v. 높이다, 향상시키다 productivity n. 생산성
proposal n. 제안서, 제의 additional adj. 추가의, 가외의
subscribe v. 구독하다, 가입하다 detailed adj. 상세한

해석
38-40번은 다음 대화에 관한 문제입니다.

여: 저는 우리 직원들이 그들의 업무 생산성을 높일 수 있을 것 같다고 생각해요. ³⁸온라인 교육 과정을 제공해 보는 것은 어떨까요? 제가 EduSphere라는 회사를 찾았어요. 그들은 데이터베이스 관리, 제안서 작성, 심지어는 마케팅에 관한 강좌도 갖추고 있어요.
남: 저 또한 그 회사에 대해 들어봤어요. ³⁹하지만 그 강좌들은 비싸지 않나요?
여: 사실, 그것들이 첫 달에는 무료예요. 우리가 만약 1년 이상 구독한다면 추가 할인도 받을 수 있고요. ⁴⁰그 회사의 웹사이트는 각 프로그램에 맞는 다양한 수업들의 비용에 대한 상세한 정보를 제공하고 있어요.

38 제안 문제

해석 여자는 무엇을 하라고 제안하는가?
(A) 여행 준비하기
(B) 파일 다운로드하기
(C) 기사 작성하기
(D) 온라인 수업 도입하기

해설 여자의 말에서 제안과 관련된 표현이 언급된 내용을 주의 깊게 듣는다. 여자가 "What about offering online training courses?"라며 온라인 교육 과정을 제공해 보는 것이 어떨지 묻고 있다. 따라서 (D)가 정답이다.

어휘 arrangement n. 준비, 마련 introduce v. 도입하다, 소개하다

Paraphrasing
offering online training courses 온라인 교육 과정을 제공하는 것
→ Introducing online classes 온라인 수업 도입하기

39 문제점 문제

해석 남자는 무엇에 대해 걱정하는가?
(A) 서비스의 비용
(B) 장소의 크기
(C) 기관의 위치
(D) 프로그램의 일정

해설 남자의 말에서 부정적인 표현이 언급된 주변을 주의 깊게 듣는다. 남자가 "But aren't those courses expensive?"라며 그 강좌들은 비싸지 않은지 묻는 것을 통해 남자가 서비스 비용에 대해 걱정하고 있음을 알 수 있다. 따라서 (A)가 정답이다.

어휘 venue n. 장소 institution n. 기관

40 특정 세부 사항 문제

해석 여자에 따르면, 웹사이트에서 무엇을 찾을 수 있는가?
(A) 연락처
(B) 제품 후기
(C) 할인 쿠폰
(D) 가격 세부 정보

해설 질문의 핵심 어구(Web site)가 언급된 주변을 주의 깊게 듣는다. 여자가 "The company's Web site provides detailed information about the cost of the various classes for each program."이라며 그 회사의 웹사이트는 각 프로그램에 맞는 다양한 수업들의 비용에 대한 상세한 정보를 제공하고 있다고 하였다. 따라서 (D)가 정답이다.

Paraphrasing
detailed information about the cost 비용에 대한 상세한 정보
→ Pricing details 가격 세부 정보

[41-43] 영국식 → 캐나다식

Questions 41-43 refer to the following conversation.

W: Tyler, could you please give me a hand moving the boxes out of the lecture hall? ⁴¹**The guests will visit here during the fundraising event this Friday.**
M: I'm not sure if we will have enough space for the guests. I heard that the event is getting a great response from Cranbury residents.
W: Hmm . . . ⁴²**Why don't we move the event to the Cranbury Public Library?**
M: ⁴³**It has recently expanded its auditorium**, so it should be large enough to fit everyone.

lecture n. 강의 fundraising n. 모금 response n. 호응, 반응 expand v. 확장하다, 확대되다 auditorium n. 강당, 객석

해석
41-43번은 다음 대화에 관한 문제입니다.

여: Tyler, 강의실 밖으로 상자를 옮기는 것 좀 도와주시겠어요? ⁴¹이번 주 금요일 모금 행사 동안 손님들이 이곳을 방문할 예정이에요.
남: 손님들을 위한 충분한 공간이 있을지 잘 모르겠어요. 저는 Cranbury 주민들로부터 그 행사가 큰 호응을 얻고 있다고 들었어요.
여: 흠… ⁴²행사를 Cranbury 공공 도서관으로 옮기는 게 어떨까요?
남: ⁴³최근 그곳의 강당을 확장했으니 모두가 들어갈 수 있을 만큼 넓을 거예요.

41 다음에 할 일 문제

해석 이번 주 금요일에 무슨 일이 일어날 것인가?
(A) 모금 행사가 열릴 것이다.
(B) 사업체가 다시 문을 열 것이다.
(C) 자원봉사자 교육이 열릴 것이다.
(D) 몇몇 소포가 배달될 것이다.

해설 질문의 핵심 어구(this Friday)가 언급된 주변을 주의 깊게 듣는다. 여자가 "The guests will visit here during the fundraising event this Friday."라며 이번 주 금요일 모금 행사 동안 손님들이 강의실을 방문할 예정이라고 한 것을 통해 이번 주 금요일에 모금 행사가 열릴 것임을 알 수 있다. 따라서 (A)가 정답이다.

어휘 fundraiser n. 모금 행사 volunteer n. 자원봉사자 package n. 소포, 포장물

42 제안 문제

해석 여자는 무엇을 제안하는가?
(A) 출장 연회 서비스 이용하기
(B) 장소 바꾸기
(C) 몇몇 가구 교체하기
(D) 계약서에 서명하기

해설 여자의 말에서 제안과 관련된 표현이 언급된 다음을 주의 깊게 듣는다. 여자가 남자에게 "Why don't we move the event to the Cranbury Public Library?"라며 행사를 Cranbury 공공 도서관으로 옮기는 게 어떠냐고 하였다. 따라서 (B)가 정답이다.

어휘 catering n. 출장 연회, 요식 조달업 replace v. 교체하다, 대신하다
furniture n. 가구 contract n. 계약서, 계약

43 언급 문제

해석 남자는 도서관에 대해 무엇을 말하는가?
(A) 새 장소로 이전했다.
(B) 최근 확장됐다.
(C) 학교에 책을 기부하고 있다.
(D) 대중교통으로 접근하기 용이하다.

해설 남자의 말에서 질문의 핵심 어구(library)가 언급된 주변을 주의 깊게 듣는다. 남자가 "It[the library] has recently expanded its auditorium"이라며 도서관이 최근에 강당을 확장했다고 하였다. 따라서 (B)가 정답이다.

어휘 enlarge v. 확장하다 donate v. 기부하다
convenient adj. 용이한, 편리한

Paraphrasing

expanded its auditorium 강당을 확장했다
→ was ~ enlarged 확장됐다

[44-46]

🎧 캐나다식 → 영국식 → 호주식

Questions 44-46 refer to the following conversation with three speakers.

> M1: Hello, Marta. [44]**Are you ready to begin your first day of work here at Pine Crest State Park? Leading the Junior Park Ranger Program is a big responsibility.**
> W: Yes. And I'm really excited to be here.
> M1: Great. [45]**As a supervisor, I'd like to say that one of our organization's goals is to make young people more environmentally responsible.** Oh, [46]**here comes Gabriel.** He's another ranger here.
> M2: Hi. I just want to remind you about the stargazing activity this evening. [46]**We've postponed it for several days due to the heavy clouds, but I'm relieved to say the stars will be visible tonight.**

ranger n. 경비원, 공원 관리원 responsibility n. 임무, 책임
supervisor n. 관리자, 감독관 organization n. 조직, 구성
remind v. 상기시키다, 기억나게 하다 postpone v. 연기하다, 미루다
visible adj. 볼 수 있는, 보이는

해석 44-46번은 다음 세 명의 대화에 관한 문제입니다.
남1: 안녕하세요, Marta. [44]이곳 Pine Crest 주립공원에서 첫날 근무를 시작할 준비가 되었나요? 청소년 공원 경비원 프로그램을 이끄는 것은 큰 임무입니다.
여: 네. 그리고 여기 오게 되어 정말 기쁩니다.
남1: 좋아요. [45]관리자로서, 저는 우리 조직의 목표 중 하나가 젊은이들이 환경에 더 책임감을 갖도록 만드는 것이라고 말하고 싶어요. 아, [46]Gabriel이 오네요. 그는 이곳의 또 다른 경비원입니다.
남2: 안녕하세요. 저는 단지 오늘 저녁 별 관측 활동에 대해 상기시키고 싶어요. [46]구름이 많아 며칠 동안 그것을 연기했지만, 오늘 밤에는 별을 볼 수 있게 되어 안심돼요.

44 특정 세부 사항 문제

해석 여자는 무엇을 하기 위해 고용되었는가?
(A) 일정표 만들기
(B) 사진 찍기
(C) 프로그램 이끌기
(D) 시설 관리하기

해설 대화에서 질문의 핵심 어구(woman ~ hired to do)와 관련된 내용을 주의 깊게 듣는다. 남자1이 여자에게 "Are you ready to begin your first day of work here at Pine Crest State Park? Leading the Junior Park Ranger Program is a big responsibility."라며 이곳 주립공원에서 첫날 근무를 시작할 준비가 되었는지 물은 후, 청소년 공원 경비원 프로그램을 이끄는 것은 큰 임무라고 한 것을 통해 여자가 공원에서 프로그램을 이끌기 위해 고용되었음을 알 수 있다. 따라서 (C)가 정답이다.

어휘 itinerary n. 일정표, 여정 maintain v. 관리하다, 유지하다
facility n. 시설, 기능

45 특정 세부 사항 문제

해석 관리자에 따르면, 조직의 목표는 무엇인가?
(A) 과학 정보지 발행하기
(B) 자선 기부금 모으기
(C) 전문 교사 채용하기
(D) 환경적 인식 증진하기

해설 관리자의 말에서 질문의 핵심 어구(goal of the organization)와 관련된 내용을 주의 깊게 듣는다. 남자1이 "As a supervisor, I'd like to say that one of our organization's goals is to make young people more environmentally responsible."이라며 관리자로서 조직의 목표 중 하나가 젊은이들이 환경에 더 책임감을 갖도록 만드는 것이라고 말하고 싶다고 하였다. 따라서 (D)가 정답이다.

어휘 charitable adj. 자선의 recruit v. 채용하다, 모집하다
promote v. 증진하다, 고취시키다 awareness n. 인식, 관심

46 특정 세부 사항 문제

해석 Gabriel은 무엇에 대해 안도감을 표하는가?
(A) 산길이 다시 개방되었다.
(B) 기구가 설치되었다.
(C) 날씨가 나아졌다.

(D) 고객 후기가 긍정적이다.

해설 Gabriel의 말에서 질문의 핵심 어구(express relief)와 관련된 내용을 주의 깊게 듣는다. 남자1이 "here comes Gabriel"이라며 Gabriel을 소개하는 말을 통해 남자2가 Gabriel이라는 것을 알 수 있고, 남자2가 "We've postponed it for several days due to the heavy clouds, but I'm relieved to say the stars will be visible tonight."이라며 구름이 많아 별 관측 활동을 며칠 연기했지만, 오늘 밤에는 별을 볼 수 있게 되어 안심된다고 하였다. 따라서 (C)가 정답이다.

어휘 equipment n. 기구, 장비 set up ~을 설치하다, 세우다
improve v. 나아지다, 개선되다

[47-49]

🎧 캐나다식 → 미국식

Questions 47-49 refer to the following conversation.

M: Tanya. ⁴⁷**You attended the tea party hosted by the Shell Hotel last weekend, right? How was it?**
W: ⁴⁷**It was great.** ⁴⁸**The dessert selection was most impressive.** It paired well with the various teas served.
M: Did you take lots of pictures?
W: Take a look. ⁴⁹**I'm thinking of uploading these photos to my social media page.**
M: But there are a lot of other people in those photos. ⁴⁹**They wouldn't like it if they were on someone's social media page without knowing it.**

attend v. 참석하다 host v. 주최하다, 개최하다
selection n. 선정, 선택 impressive adj. 인상적인
various adj. 다양한, 여러 가지의 serve v. 제공하다

해석
47-49번은 다음 대화에 관한 문제입니다.
남: Tanya. ⁴⁷지난 주말 Shell 호텔에서 주최한 티 파티에 참석하셨죠, 그렇죠? 어땠나요?
여: ⁴⁷정말 좋았어요. ⁴⁸디저트 선정이 가장 인상적이었어요. 제공되는 다양한 차와 잘 어울렸어요.
남: 사진은 많이 찍었나요?
여: 보세요. ⁴⁹이 사진들을 제 소셜 미디어 페이지에 업로드하는 것을 생각 중이에요.
남: 하지만 그 사진들에는 다른 사람들이 많이 있어요. ⁴⁹그들이 자신도 모르게 누군가의 소셜 미디어 페이지에 있다면 좋아하지 않을 거예요.

47 주제 문제

해석 화자들은 주로 무엇에 대해 이야기하고 있는가?
(A) 티 파티
(B) 음식 박람회
(C) 호텔 뷔페
(D) 회사 만찬

해설 대화의 주제를 묻는 문제이므로, 대화의 초반을 반드시 듣는다. 남자가 여자에게 "You attended the tea party hosted by the Shell Hotel last weekend, right? How was it?"이라며 지난 주말 Shell 호텔에서 주최한 티 파티는 어땠는지 묻자 여자가 "It was great."이라며 정말 좋았다고 한 후, 티 파티에 대한 내용으로 대화가 이어지고 있다. 따라서 (A)가 정답이다.

어휘 fair n. 박람회

48 특정 세부 사항 문제

해석 여자는 무엇이 가장 인상적이었다고 말하는가?
(A) 전문적인 직원들
(B) 장소 장식
(C) 디저트 선정
(D) 음악 공연

해설 여자의 말에서 질문의 핵심 어구(most impressive)가 언급된 주변을 주의 깊게 듣는다. 여자가 "The dessert selection was most impressive."라며 디저트 선정이 가장 인상적이었다고 하였다. 따라서 (C)가 정답이다.

어휘 professional adj. 전문적인 decoration n. 장식
performance n. 공연

Paraphrasing
selection 선정 → choices 선정

49 의도 파악 문제

해석 남자는 "그 사진들에는 다른 사람들이 많이 있어요"라고 말할 때 무엇을 의도하는가?
(A) 정보가 확인되어야 한다.
(B) 허가가 필요하다.
(C) 사진사가 고용되어야 했다.
(D) 웹사이트가 만들어져야 한다.

해설 질문의 인용어구(there are a lot of other people in those photos)가 언급된 주변을 주의 깊게 듣는다. 여자가 "I'm thinking of uploading these photos to my social media page."라며 사진들을 소셜 미디어 페이지에 업로드하는 것을 생각 중이라고 하자, 남자가 "They wouldn't like it if they were on someone's social media page without knowing it."이라며 그들이 자신도 모르게 누군가의 소셜 미디어 페이지에 있다면 좋아하지 않을 거라고 한 것을 통해 남자는 사진을 업로드하는 것에 대해 허가가 필요하다고 의도한 것임을 알 수 있다. 따라서 (B)가 정답이다.

어휘 verify v. 확인하다, 입증하다 permission n. 허가, 승인
hire v. 고용하다

[50-52]

🎧 호주식 → 영국식

Questions 50-52 refer to the following conversation.

M: Hi Sandra. It's Jin-Woo. ⁵⁰**There have been mistakes in a few of the recent invoices issued by our law firm.** Several clients were overcharged for their consultations. ⁵¹**It looks like the problem is due to the Quick-Pay automatic payment software that we began using this month.**
W: Do you know how many invoices were affected?
M: Five clients have contacted me so far. But I'm afraid that there might be some others.

W: Hmm . . . We need to review all our client accounts and correct any remaining errors. ⁵²**Eric Murphy in the finance department could help.**

invoice n. 청구서, 송장   issue v. 발급하다, 교부하다
overcharge v. 과다 청구하다   consultation n. 상담, 협의
automatic adj. 자동의   affect v. 영향을 미치다   contact v. 연락하다
account n. 계정, 계좌   correct v. 수정하다, 바로잡다
finance n. 재무

해석 50-52번은 다음 대화에 관한 문제입니다.

남: 안녕하세요, Sandra. 저는 Jin-Woo예요. ⁵⁰최근 우리 법률 사무소에서 발급한 몇몇 청구서에 실수가 있었어요. 여러 고객들에게 상담 비용이 과다 청구되었어요. ⁵¹그 문제는 우리가 이번 달에 사용하기 시작한 Quick-Pay 자동 결제 소프트웨어 때문인 것 같아요.

여: 얼마나 많은 송장들이 영향을 받았는지 아시나요?

남: 지금까지 5명의 고객이 제게 연락해 왔어요. 하지만 다른 고객이 몇 분 계실까 봐 걱정돼요.

여: 흠... 우리는 모든 고객 계정을 검토하고 남은 오류를 수정해야 겠어요. ⁵²재무 부서의 Eric Murphy가 도와줄 수 있을 거예요.

50 화자 문제

해석 화자들은 어떤 산업에서 일하는 것 같은가?
(A) 의료
(B) 법률
(C) 소프트웨어
(D) 출판

해설 대화에서 신분 및 직업과 관련된 표현을 놓치지 않고 듣는다. 남자가 "There have been mistakes in a few of the recent invoices issued by our law firm."이라며 최근 우리 법률 사무소에서 발급한 몇몇 청구서에 실수가 있었다고 한 것을 통해 화자들이 법률 업계에서 일한다는 것을 알 수 있다. 따라서 (B)가 정답이다.

51 언급 문제

해석 남자는 Quick-Pay 프로그램에 대해 무엇을 말하는가?
(A) 다양한 버전들로 판매된다.
(B) 업데이트되어야 한다.
(C) 회사들에 의해 널리 사용된다.
(D) 최근에 채택되었다.

해설 남자의 말에서 질문의 핵심 어구(Quick-Pay program)와 관련된 내용을 주의 깊게 듣는다. 남자가 "It looks like the problem is due to the Quick-Pay automatic payment software that we began using this month."라며 이번 달에 사용하기 시작한 Quick-Pay 자동 결제 소프트웨어 때문에 문제가 발생한 것 같다고 하였다. 따라서 (D)가 정답이다.

어휘 widely adv. 널리, 폭넓게   adopt v. 채택하다, 쓰다

Paraphrasing

began using this month 이번 달에 사용하기 시작했다 → recently adopted 최근에 채택된

52 특정 세부 사항 문제

해석 Eric Murphy는 누구인가?
(A) 고객
(B) 상담가
(C) 동료
(D) 지원자

해설 질문의 대상(Eric Murphy)의 신분 및 직업과 관련된 표현을 놓치지 않고 듣는다. 여자가 "Eric Murphy in the finance department could help."라며 재무 부서의 Eric Murphy가 도와줄 수 있을 것이라고 한 것을 통해 화자들의 동료임을 알 수 있다. 따라서 (C)가 정답이다.

[53-55] ③ 영국식 → 호주식 → 미국식

Questions 53-55 refer to the following conversation with three speakers.

W1: Hi, everybody. ⁵³**The increase in sales of our tablets for businesses this summer has been significant.**

M: Well, the overall trend for businesses is to go paperless. ⁵⁴**However, the issue we're facing now is the rising cost of the materials and equipment required to make batteries for the tablets.**

W2: That's right. We'll have no choice but to raise the price of the product.

M: But what would be a fair price to charge our customers for these tablets?

W2: ⁵⁵**Our marketing team recently conducted a study on that.**

W1: ⁵⁵**Caren, could you share the results when you get them?**

W2: ⁵⁵**Sure, I'll do that.**

increase n. 증가, 상승   significant adj. 상당한, 중요한
overall adj. 전반적인, 종합적인   trend n. 추세, 경향
issue n. 문제, 쟁점   face v. 직면하다   material n. 재료, 원료
raise v. 인상하다, 올리다   fair adj. 타당한, 공정한   charge v. 부과하다
conduct v. 실시하다, (특정 활동을) 하다

해석 53-55번은 다음 세 명의 대화에 관한 문제입니다.

여1: 안녕하세요, 여러분. ⁵³올여름 우리의 기업용 태블릿 판매량 증가가 상당했어요.

남: 음, 기업의 전반적인 추세는 종이를 쓰지 않는 것입니다. 하지만, ⁵⁴현재 우리가 직면하고 있는 문제는 태블릿용 배터리를 만드는 데 필요한 재료와 장비의 비용 상승이에요.

여2: 맞아요. 제품 가격을 인상할 수밖에 없을 것 같아요.

남: 하지만 이 태블릿에 대해 고객에게 부과하는 타당한 가격은 얼마일까요?

여2: ⁵⁵우리 마케팅팀이 최근에 그것에 대한 조사를 실시했어요.

여1: ⁵⁵Caren, 결과를 받으면 공유해 주시겠어요?

여2: ⁵⁵물론이죠, 그렇게 할게요.

53 특정 세부 사항 문제

해석 화자들의 회사는 어떤 종류의 제품들을 생산하는가?
(A) 차량
(B) 전자제품
(C) 여행 가방
(D) 가구

해설 대화에서 질문의 핵심 어구(speakers' company produce)와 관련된 내용을 주의 깊게 듣는다. 여자1이 "The increase in sales of our tablets for businesses this summer has been significant."라며 올여름 우리의 기업용 태블릿 판매량 증가가 상당했다고 한 것을 통해 화자들의 회사가 전자제품을 생산한다는 것을 알 수 있다. 따라서 (B)가 정답이다.

54 문제점 문제

해석 남자는 어떤 문제점을 말하는가?
(A) 인력 부족
(B) 제한된 창고 공간
(C) 인상된 제조 비용
(D) 부족한 재고

해설 남자의 말에서 부정적인 표현이 언급된 주변을 주의 깊게 듣는다. 남자가 "However, the issue we're facing now is the rising cost of the materials and equipment required to make batteries for the tablets."라며 현재 우리가 직면하고 있는 문제는 태블릿용 배터리를 만드는 데 필요한 재료와 장비의 비용 상승이라고 하였다. 따라서 (C)가 정답이다.

어휘 shortage n. 부족, 결핍   warehouse n. 창고
manufacturing n. 제조, 제조업   insufficient adj. 부족한, 불충분한
inventory n. 재고

Paraphrasing

the rising cost of the materials and equipment 재료와 장비의 비용 상승 → Increased manufacturing costs 인상된 제조 비용

55 특정 세부 사항 문제

해석 Caren은 무엇을 하는 데 동의하는가?
(A) 연구 결과 제공하기
(B) 면접 시행하기
(C) 예산 증가 요청하기
(D) 몇몇 참고 문헌 확인하기

해설 Caren의 말에서 질문의 핵심 어구(agree to do)와 관련된 내용을 주의 깊게 듣는다. 여자2[Caren]가 "Our marketing team recently conducted a study on that."이라며 마케팅팀이 관련 조사를 실시했다고 하자, 여자1이 "Caren, could you share the results when you get them?"이라며 연구 결과를 받으면 공유해 주겠냐고 물었고 이에 대해 여자2[Caren]가 "Sure, I'll do that."이라며 그렇게 하겠다고 하였다. 따라서 (A)가 정답이다.

어휘 request v. 요청하다   budget n. 예산
reference n. 참고 문헌, 참조

[56-58]

미국식 → 호주식

Questions 56-58 refer to the following conversation.

W: ⁵⁶The launch of our new Dazzler toy is two weeks away. How have the preparations been coming along?

M: ⁵⁶It's been challenging. There were comments from the CEO that the packaging design is outdated, so it needs to be changed.

W: ⁵⁷I'm worried about whether we'll be able to complete everything on schedule. Have you decided on what design to use?

M: Not yet. ⁵⁸The design team will submit a draft of the new package design by this Wednesday.

W: Then, ⁵⁸please forward it to me when you receive it.

launch n. 출시, 개시   preparation n. 준비
comment n. 의견, 논평   outdated adj. 구식인   submit v. 제출하다
draft n. 초안, 원고   forward v. 전달하다, 보내다   receive v. 받다

해석
56-58번은 다음 대화에 관한 문제입니다.
여: ⁵⁶우리의 새로운 Dazzler 장난감의 출시가 2주 앞으로 다가왔습니다. 준비는 어떻게 진행되고 있나요?
남: ⁵⁶녹록지 않아요. 포장 디자인이 구식이라 바꿔야 한다는 대표이사의 의견이 있었습니다.
여: ⁵⁷일정대로 모든 것을 완료할 수 있을지 걱정되네요. 어떤 디자인을 사용할지 결정했나요?
남: 아직 못했어요. ⁵⁸디자인 팀이 이번 주 수요일까지 새로운 포장 디자인 초안을 제출할 거예요.
여: 그렇다면, ⁵⁸그것을 받으면 저에게 전달해 주세요.

56 주제 문제

해석 화자들은 무엇에 대해 논의하는가?
(A) 직원 오리엔테이션
(B) 대규모 개점
(C) 기계적 결함
(D) 제품 출시

해설 대화의 주제를 묻는 문제이므로, 대화의 초반을 반드시 듣는다. 여자가 "The launch of our new Dazzler toy is two weeks away. How have the preparations been coming along?"이라며 장난감의 출시가 2주 앞으로 다가왔는데 준비가 어떻게 진행되고 있냐고 묻자, 남자가 "It's been challenging."이라며 녹록지 않다고 답한 후 장난감 출시에 대한 내용으로 대화가 이어지고 있다. 따라서 (D)가 정답이다.

어휘 mechanical adj. 기계적인   defect n. 결함

57 문제점 문제

해석 여자는 무엇에 대해 걱정하는가?
(A) 기계를 수리하는 것
(B) 마감일을 맞추는 것
(C) 작업 공간을 개조하는 것

(D) 제품 회수를 실시하는 것

해설 여자의 말에서 부정적인 표현이 언급된 주변을 주의 깊게 듣는다. 여자가 "I'm worried about whether we'll be able to complete everything on schedule."이라며 일정대로 모든 것을 완료할 수 있을지 걱정된다고 하였다. 따라서 (B)가 정답이다.

어휘 repair v. 수리하다 renovate v. 개조하다 recall n. 회수

Paraphrasing

whether we'll be able to complete everything on schedule 일정대로 모든 것을 완료할 수 있을지 → Meeting a deadline 마감일을 맞추는 것

58 요청 문제

해석 여자는 남자에게 무엇을 하라고 요청하는가?
(A) 그녀에게 초안을 보낸다.
(B) 비용을 협상한다.
(C) 발표를 준비한다.
(D) 그녀의 동료를 돕는다.

해설 여자의 말에서 요청과 관련된 표현이 언급된 주변을 주의 깊게 듣는다. 남자가 "The design team will submit a draft of the new package design by this Wednesday."라며 디자인 팀이 이번 주 수요일까지 새로운 포장 디자인 초안을 제출할 것이라고 하자, 여자가 "please forward it to me when you receive it"이라며 디자인 초안을 받으면 본인에게 전달해 달라고 하였다. 따라서 (A)가 정답이다.

어휘 negotiate v. 협상하다 assist v. 돕다 colleague n. 동료

Paraphrasing

forward 보내다 → send 보내다

[59-61]

🔊 캐나다식 → 미국식

Questions 59-61 refer to the following conversation.

> M: Hello. I'm Michael Choi from the Vision Ad company. I'm calling to follow up on your e-mail inquiry.
> W: Thank you for calling. We are interested in promoting our products to a larger audience. One concern is that ⁵⁹we specialize in producing sportswear, so ⁶⁰we need our ads to showcase dynamic movement.
> M: With our digital billboards, you can display video clips. ⁶⁰They can show the movement your company wants to emphasize.
> W: Then, we would like to try your digital billboards for two months.
> M: All right. ⁶¹Just for this week, we're giving a 50 percent discount to those who sign up for our service.

follow up on ~에 대한 후속 조치를 하다 inquiry n. 문의, 연구
specialize v. 전문적으로 하다 showcase v. 보여주다
dynamic adj. 역동적인 billboard n. 광고판, 게시판
display v. 내보이다, 전시하다 emphasize v. 강조하다
sign up for ~에 가입하다, 신청하다

해석
59-61번은 다음 대화에 관한 문제입니다.
남: 안녕하세요. 저는 Vision 광고 회사의 Michael Choi입니다. 이메일 문의에 대한 후속 조치를 하기 위해 전화드렸습니다.
여: 전화 주셔서 감사해요. 저희는 더 많은 고객들에게 저희의 제품을 홍보하는 데 관심이 있습니다. 한 가지 우려되는 점은 ⁵⁹저희가 스포츠 의류를 전문적으로 생산하고 있어서 ⁶⁰저희의 광고들이 역동적인 움직임을 보여줄 필요가 있다는 것입니다.
남: 저희의 디지털 광고판을 사용하면 비디오 클립을 내보일 수 있습니다. ⁶⁰그것들은 당신의 회사가 강조하고자 하는 움직임을 보여줄 수 있어요.
여: 그렇다면, 두 달 동안 디지털 광고판을 사용해 보고 싶어요.
남: 알겠습니다. ⁶¹저희는 이번 주 동안에만 서비스에 가입하는 분들에게 50퍼센트 할인을 제공하고 있어요.

59 특정 세부 사항 문제

해석 여자의 회사는 무엇을 만드는가?
(A) 스포츠 음료
(B) 냉동 음식
(C) 영양 보조제
(D) 운동복

해설 질문의 핵심 어구(woman's company make)와 관련된 내용이 언급된 부분을 주의 깊게 듣는다. 여자가 "we specialize in producing sportswear"라며 우리는 스포츠 의류를 전문적으로 생산한다고 하였다. 따라서 (D)가 정답이다.

어휘 nutritional adj. 영양의 supplement n. 보조제, 보충물

Paraphrasing

sportswear 스포츠 의류 → Exercise clothes 운동복

60 의도 파악 문제

해석 남자는 왜 "저희의 디지털 광고판을 사용하면 비디오 클립을 내보일 수 있습니다"라고 말하는가?
(A) 의견을 요청하기 위해
(B) 우려를 해결하기 위해
(C) 규정을 설명하기 위해
(D) 최근의 개선점을 언급하기 위해

해설 질문의 인용어구(With our digital billboards, you can display video clips)가 언급된 주변을 주의 깊게 듣는다. 여자가 "we need our ads to showcase dynamic movement"라며 광고들이 역동적인 움직임을 보여줄 필요가 있다고 하자, 남자가 "They can show the movement your company wants to emphasize."라며 자신들의 광고판은 회사가 강조하고자 하는 움직임을 보여줄 수 있다고 한 것을 통해 여자가 우려하는 점을 해결하기 위함임을 알 수 있다. 따라서 (B)가 정답이다.

어휘 address v. 해결하다, 연설하다 regulation n. 규정, 규제
point out 언급하다, 지적하다

61 언급 문제

해석 남자는 할인에 대해 무엇을 말하는가?

(A) 최근에 인상되었다.
(B) 일주일 동안만 제공된다.
(C) 서비스에 따라 달라진다.
(D) 장기 회원들을 위한 것이다.

해설 남자의 말에서 질문의 핵심 어구(discount)가 언급된 부분을 주의 깊게 듣는다. 남자가 "Just for this week, we're giving a 50 percent discount to those who sign up for our service."라며 이번 주 동안에만 서비스에 가입하면 50퍼센트 할인이 제공된다고 하였다. 따라서 (B)가 정답이다.

어휘 vary v. 달라지다, 다르다   depending on ~에 따라
long-term adj. 장기적인

[62-64]
영국식 → 호주식

Questions 62-64 refer to the following conversation and list.

W: Welcome to Lakeville Rental Car. How may I help you today?
M: ⁶²I'm going to San Diego to attend a trade show today. Is there a vehicle I can rent for three days?
W: Is there anything you are looking for in particular?
M: Actually, ⁶³I was hoping for something with at least five seats. I would also like to keep the total cost under 80 dollars per day.
W: We do have one option. I'll prepare the rental agreement for you to fill out. ⁶⁴May I have your driver's license, please?

trade show 무역 박람회   vehicle n. 차량   rent v. 대여하다, 빌리다
in particular 특별히, 특히   seat n. 좌석, 자리   total adj. 총, 전체의
prepare v. 준비하다   agreement n. 계약서, 합의
driver's license 운전면허증

해석
62-64번은 다음 대화와 목록에 관한 문제입니다.

여: Lakeville 렌터카에 오신 것을 환영합니다. 오늘 무엇을 도와드릴까요?
남: ⁶²저는 오늘 무역 박람회에 참석하기 위해 샌디에이고에 갑니다. 3일 동안 빌릴 수 있는 차량이 있나요?
여: 특별히 찾고 계신 것이 있으신가요?
남: 사실, ⁶³저는 최소 5개의 좌석이 있는 것을 바라고 있었어요. 또한 총비용을 하루 80달러 아래로 유지하고 싶습니다.
여: 한 개의 선택권이 있네요. 렌트 계약서를 작성하시도록 준비할게요. ⁶⁴운전면허증을 주시겠어요?

Lakeville 렌터카		
차량 종류	좌석 수	하루 비용
스포츠카	2	90달러
세단	4	50달러
⁶³미니밴	6	70달러
SUV	10	100달러

62 이유 문제

해석 남자는 왜 샌디에이고에 가야 하는가?

(A) 대회에 참가하기 위해
(B) 새로운 사업체를 열기 위해
(C) 그의 가족을 방문하기 위해
(D) 무역 박람회에 참석하기 위해

해설 남자의 말에서 질문의 핵심 어구(San Diego)가 언급된 주변을 주의 깊게 듣는다. 남자가 "I'm going to San Diego to attend a trade show today."라며 오늘 무역 박람회에 참석하기 위해 샌디에이고에 간다고 하였다. 따라서 (D)가 정답이다.

어휘 competition n. 대회, 경쟁   participate in ~에 참석하다

63 시각 자료 문제

해석 시각 자료를 보아라. 남자는 어떤 차량을 선택할 것인가?
(A) 스포츠카
(B) 세단
(C) 미니밴
(D) SUV

해설 제시된 목록의 정보를 확인한 후 질문의 핵심 어구(vehicle ~ man select)와 관련된 내용을 주의 깊게 듣는다. 남자가 "I was hoping for something with at least five seats. I would also like to keep the total cost under 80 dollars per day."라며 최소 5개의 좌석이 있고 하루 총비용이 80달러 아래인 차량을 찾고 있다고 했고, 이 조건에 맞는 차량은 미니밴임을 목록에서 알 수 있다. 따라서 (C)가 정답이다.

64 요청 문제

해석 여자는 남자에게 무엇을 요청하는가?
(A) 신용카드
(B) 운전면허증
(C) 보험 증명서
(D) 열쇠 꾸러미

해설 여자의 말에서 요청과 관련된 표현이 언급된 다음을 주의 깊게 듣는다. 여자가 "May I have your driver's license, please?"라며 운전면허증을 달라고 요청했다. 따라서 (B)가 정답이다.

어휘 proof n. 증명서, 증거   insurance n. 보험

[65-67]
영국식 → 캐나다식

Questions 65-67 refer to the following conversation and schedule.

W: Jason, don't forget that ⁶⁵we need to interview a job candidate this week. Pauleen Marks will be coming to our office on the day we have the team-building workshop.
M: Oh, right. Thanks for reminding me.
W: ⁶⁶I'll print out a copy of the interview questions for you this afternoon. If you have any questions you'd like to add, please let me know.
M: Thanks. ⁶⁷Can you give a copy to Mr. Bennet too? Since the candidate applied to his department, he decided to join us for the interview.

candidate n. 지원자 apply v. 지원하다 department n. 부서
decide v. 결정하다

해석

65-67번은 다음 대화와 일정표에 관한 문제입니다.

여: Jason, ⁶⁵우리가 이번 주에 입사 지원자를 면접해야 한다는 사실을 잊지 마세요. 팀워크 워크숍이 있는 날에 Pauleen Marks가 우리 사무실에 올 거예요.

남: 오, 맞네요. 상기시켜 주셔서 감사해요.

여: ⁶⁶오늘 오후에 면접 질문 사본을 인쇄해 드릴게요. 추가하고 싶은 질문이 있으면 제게 알려주세요.

남: 감사합니다. ⁶⁷Mr. Bennet에게도 사본을 주실 수 있나요? 지원자가 그의 부서에 지원했기 때문에 그도 면접에 우리와 함께 하기로 결정했어요.

	Jason의 일정표
화요일	부서 회의 *하루 종일
수요일	고객들과 화상 전화 *오전 10시 - 오전11:30
⁶⁵목요일	팀워크 워크숍 *오후 1:30 - 오후 3:30
금요일	직원 평가 *오전 9:30 - 오전 11:30

65 시각 자료 문제

해석 시각 자료를 보아라. 화자들은 언제 면접에 참석할 것 같은가?
(A) 화요일에
(B) 수요일에
(C) 목요일에
(D) 금요일에

해설 제시된 일정표의 정보를 확인한 후 질문의 핵심 어구(attend an interview)와 관련된 내용을 주의 깊게 듣는다. 여자가 "we need to interview a job candidate this week. Pauleen Marks will be coming to our office on the day we have the team-building workshop."이라며 우리가 이번 주에 입사 지원자를 면접해야 하는데 팀워크 워크숍이 있는 날에 Pauleen Marks가 사무실에 올 것이라고 했고, 팀워크 워크숍이 있는 날은 목요일임을 일정표에서 알 수 있다. 따라서 (C)가 정답이다.

66 다음에 할 일 문제

해석 여자는 오늘 오후에 무엇을 할 것이라고 말하는가?
(A) 회의실을 예약한다.
(B) 문서의 사본을 인쇄한다.
(C) 몇 가지 변경 사항을 알린다.
(D) 몇몇 용품을 주문한다.

해설 여자의 말에서 질문의 핵심 어구(this afternoon)가 언급된 주변을 주의 깊게 듣는다. 여자가 "I'll print out a copy of the interview questions for you this afternoon."이라며 오늘 오후에 면접 질문 사본을 인쇄할 것이라고 하였다. 따라서 (B)가 정답이다.

어휘 reserve v. 예약하다 conference n. 회의 document n. 서류
announce v. 알리다

67 이유 문제

해석 남자에 따르면, 왜 Mr. Bennet은 화자들과 함께 하기로 결정했는가?
(A) 동료가 시간이 안 된다.
(B) 그는 면접 경험이 많다.
(C) 그의 교육이 아직 완료되지 않았다.
(D) 지원자가 그의 팀에 지원했다.

해설 남자의 말에서 질문의 핵심 어구(Mr. Bennet)가 언급된 주변을 주의 깊게 듣는다. 남자가 "Can you give a copy to Mr. Bennet too? Since the candidate applied to his department, he decided to join us for the interview."라며 지원자가 Mr. Bennet의 부서에 지원했기 때문에 면접에 우리와 함께 하기로 했으니 Mr. Bennet에게도 면접 질문 사본을 주라고 하였다. 따라서 (D)가 정답이다.

어휘 coworker n. 동료 unavailable adj. 시간이 안 되는
experience n. 경험 applicant n. 지원자

Paraphrasing

candidate 지원자 → applicant 지원자
department 부서 → team 팀

[68-70]

🎧 캐나다식 → 미국식

Questions 68-70 refer to the following conversation and map.

M: ⁶⁸We still have a lot to do for the upcoming fireworks festival.

W: Well, ⁶⁸our first priority is to pick a site. We have four spots to choose from.

M: I think parking availability is an important factor to consider.

W: ⁶⁹The site at Coral Beach has the most parking spaces. It's also the only place with picnic tables.

M: That choice works for me. ⁷⁰We should reconsider how to advertise the festival. We've stuck to posters and flyers in the past, but I want to use social media this time.

firework festival 불꽃축제 priority n. 우선순위
availability n. 가능 여부, 이용 가능성 factor n. 요소, 요인
consider v. 고려하다, 여기다 advertise v. 홍보하다, 광고하다
stick to ~을 고수하다, ~을 지키다 flyer n. 전단지

해석

68-70번은 다음 대화와 지도에 관한 문제입니다.

남: ⁶⁸곧 있을 불꽃축제를 위해 우리가 해야 할 일이 여전히 많아요.

여: 음, ⁶⁸우리의 최우선순위는 장소를 선정하는 것이에요. 선택할 수 있는 곳이 네 곳이 있어요.

남: 저는 주차 가능 여부가 고려해야 할 중요한 요소라고 생각해요.

여: ⁶⁹Coral 해변에 있는 곳에 가장 많은 주차 공간이 있습니다. 피크닉 테이블이 있는 유일한 장소이기도 해요.

남: 그 선택지는 저도 좋아요. ⁷⁰우리는 축제를 홍보하는 방법을 다시 고려해 봐야 해요. 과거에는 포스터와 전단지를 고수했지만, 이번에 저는 소셜 미디어를 사용하고 싶어요.

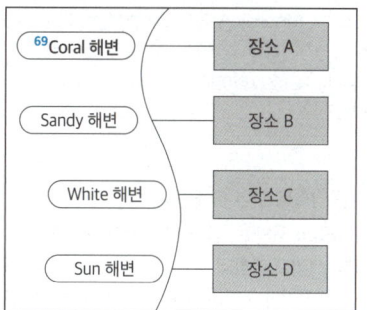

하는 방법을 다시 고려해 봐야 하는데 과거에는 포스터와 전단지를 고수했지만, 이번에는 소셜 미디어를 사용하고 싶다고 하였다. 따라서 (C)가 정답이다.

어휘 security n. 보안 procedure n. 절차, 수술 method n. 방법
evaluation n. 평가 standard n. 기준, 표준

Paraphrasing

how to advertise 홍보하는 방법 → Marketing methods 마케팅 방법

68 화자 문제

해석 화자들은 누구인 것 같은가?
(A) 가게 주인들
(B) 언론사 직원들
(C) 부동산 개발업자들
(D) 행사 주최자들

해설 대화에서 신분 및 직업과 관련된 표현을 놓치지 않고 듣는다. 남자가 "We still have a lot to do for the upcoming fireworks festival."이라며 곧 있을 불꽃축제를 위해 우리가 해야 할 것들이 여전히 많다고 하자, 여자가 "our first priority is to pick a site"라며 최우선 순위는 장소를 선정하는 것이라고 한 말을 통해 화자들은 축제 주최자들임을 알 수 있다. 따라서 (D)가 정답이다.

어휘 representative n. 직원, 대리인 property n. 부동산, 건물
organizer n. 주최자, 조직자

69 시각 자료 문제

해석 시각 자료를 보아라. 어떤 장소에 피크닉 테이블이 설치되어 있는가?
(A) 장소 A
(B) 장소 B
(C) 장소 C
(D) 장소 D

해설 제시된 지도의 정보를 확인한 후 질문의 핵심 어구(picnic tables)와 관련된 내용을 주의 깊게 듣는다. 여자가 "The site at Coral Beach has the most parking spaces. It's also the only place with picnic tables."라며 Coral 해변에 있는 곳이 가장 많은 주차 공간이 있고, 피크닉 테이블이 있는 유일한 장소이기도 하다고 했고, Coral 해변에 있는 장소는 장소 A임을 지도에서 알 수 있다. 따라서 (A)가 정답이다.

70 특정 세부 사항 문제

해석 남자는 무엇을 변경하고 싶어 하는가?
(A) 교통 서비스
(B) 보안 절차
(C) 마케팅 방법
(D) 평가 기준

해설 남자의 말에서 질문의 핵심 어구(change)와 관련된 내용을 주의 깊게 듣는다. 남자가 "We should reconsider how to advertise the festival. We've stuck to posters and flyers in the past, but I want to use social media this time."이라며 축제를 홍보

PART 4

[71-73]

Questions 71-73 refer to the following telephone message.

> [71]You have reached Ballard Communications. If you are calling about the recent interruption to your Internet service, please note that we are aware of the problem and are taking the necessary steps to address it. [72]The severe storm that occurred over the weekend damaged some of our equipment and cables. We expect the repairs to be completed within the next 24 to 48 hours. [73]If you leave your name and phone number, we will send you updates on our progress through text message. Thank you for your patience.

reach v. 연락하다, 도달하다 interruption n. 중단, 가로막음
be aware of ~을 인지하고 있다, ~을 알고 있다
necessary adj. 필요한, 필연적인 address v. 해결하다, 다루다
severe adj. 심각한, 극심한 occur v. 발생하다, 일어나다
damage v. 손상을 주다, 훼손하다 expect v. 예상하다
repair n. 수리 complete v. 완료하다, 작성하다
leave v. 남기다, 두고 가다 patience n. 인내

해석
71-73번은 다음 전화 메시지에 관한 문제입니다.
[71]귀하는 Ballard 커뮤니케이션사에 연락하셨습니다. 최근 인터넷 서비스가 중단된 것에 대해 전화하신 거라면, 저희가 문제를 인지하고 있으며 이를 해결하기 위해 필요한 조치를 취하고 있다는 점을 알아주시기 바랍니다. [72]주말 동안 발생한 심각한 폭풍이 일부 장비와 케이블에 손상을 주었습니다. 저희는 향후 24시간에서 48시간 이내에 수리가 완료될 것으로 예상됩니다. [73]성함과 전화번호를 남기시면, 저희가 문자 메시지를 통해 진행 상황에 대한 업데이트를 보내드리겠습니다. 고객님의 인내에 감사드립니다.

71 화자 문제

해석 화자는 어떤 종류의 업체에서 일하는가?
(A) 부동산 중개업
(B) 인터넷 서비스 제공업체
(C) 온라인 쇼핑 플랫폼
(D) 사무용품 판매점

해설 지문에서 신분 및 직업과 관련된 표현을 놓치지 않고 듣는다. "You have reached Ballard Communications. If you are calling about the recent interruption to your Internet service, please note that we are aware of the problem and are taking the necessary steps to address it."이라며 최근 인터넷 서비스가 중단된 것에 대해 Ballard 커뮤니케이션사에 전화한 거라면, 문제를 인지하고 있으며 이를 해결하기 위해 필요한 조치를 취하고 있다는 점을 알아달라고 한 것을 통해 화자는 인터넷 서비스 제공업체에서 일하고 있음을 알 수 있다. 따라서 (B)가 정답이다.

어휘 real estate 부동산　office supply 사무용품

72 특정 세부 사항 문제

해석 화자에 따르면, 무엇이 문제를 야기했는가?
(A) 컴퓨터 바이러스
(B) 명확하지 않은 지침
(C) 오래된 장비
(D) 안 좋은 날씨

해설 질문의 핵심 어구(caused a problem)와 관련된 내용을 주의 깊게 듣는다. "The severe storm that occurred over the weekend damaged some of our equipment and cables."라며 주말 동안 발생한 심각한 폭풍이 일부 장비와 케이블에 손상을 주었다고 하였다. 따라서 (D)가 정답이다.

어휘 instruction n. 지침, 설명　equipment n. 장비

Paraphrasing
severe storm 심각한 폭풍 → Bad weather 안 좋은 날씨

73 특정 세부 사항 문제

해석 청자들은 문자 메시지로 무엇을 받을 수 있는가?
(A) 보안 코드
(B) 배달 알림
(C) 진행 상황 업데이트
(D) 피드백 양식

해설 질문의 핵심 어구(text message)와 관련된 내용을 주의 깊게 듣는다. "If you leave your name and phone number, we will send you updates on our progress through text message."라며 성함과 전화번호를 남기면 문자 메시지를 통해 진행 상황에 대한 업데이트를 보내주겠다고 하였다. 따라서 (C)가 정답이다.

어휘 notification n. 알림　form n. 양식

[74-76]
영국식

Questions 74-76 refer to the following talk.

⁷⁴Yesterday, I had a meeting with members of Dewford City Council regarding the bike path extension project. And they finally asked us to lead the project. ⁷⁵But the problem is that the schedule overlaps with that of the River's Bend housing development project. The city council has requested that we complete the bike-path project by June 15, which is the deadline for the housing project. So ⁷⁶I'm asking every one of you to refrain from using vacation days during this period to ensure that both projects are completed on time.

council n. 의회　regarding prep. ~에 관한　path n. 도로
extension n. 연장　lead v. 이끌다, 주도하다　overlap v. 겹치다
development n. 개발　refrain v. 자제하다, 삼가다
on time 제때, 정각에

해석
74-76번은 다음 담화에 관한 문제입니다.
⁷⁴어제 저는 Dewford 시의회 의원들과 자전거 도로 연장 프로젝트에 관한 회의를 했습니다. 그리고 마침내 그들이 우리에게 프로젝트를 이끌어 달라고 요청했습니다. ⁷⁵하지만 문제는 River's Bend 주택 개발 프로젝트의 일정과 일정이 겹친다는 것입니다. 시의회는 주택 프로젝트 마감일인 6월 15일까지 자전거 도로 프로젝트를 완료해 달라고 요청했습니다. 따라서 두 프로젝트가 제때 완료될 수 있도록 ⁷⁶이 기간 동안 휴가를 사용하는 것을 자제해 주시길 모두에게 부탁드립니다.

74 특정 세부 사항 문제

해석 화자는 어제 무엇을 했는가?
(A) 건물 도면을 완성했다.
(B) 회의에 참석했다.
(C) 보관 공간을 정리했다.
(D) 예산안을 마무리했다.

해설 질문의 핵심 어구(yesterday)가 언급된 주변을 주의 깊게 듣는다. "Yesterday, I had a meeting with members of Dewford City Council regarding the bike path extension project."라며 어제 Dewford 시의회 의원들과 자전거 도로 연장 프로젝트에 관한 회의를 했다고 하였다. 따라서 (B)가 정답이다.

어휘 storage n. 보관, 저장　finalize v. 마무리하다, 완결하다
budget proposal 예산안, 예산 제안서

75 특정 세부 사항 문제

해석 화자는 무슨 문제를 언급하는가?
(A) 일정의 겹침
(B) 오작동하는 시스템
(C) 건설 자재의 부족
(D) 건축 규정의 변경

해설 질문의 핵심 어구(problem)가 언급된 주변을 주의 깊게 듣는다. "But the problem is that the schedule overlaps with that of the River's Bend housing development project."라며 문제는 River's Bend 주택 개발 프로젝트의 일정과 일정이 겹친다는 것이라고 하였다. 따라서 (A)가 정답이다.

어휘 schedule conflict 일정의 겹침　malfunction v. 오작동하다
lack n. 부족, 결핍　construction n. 건설　material n. 자재
regulation n. 규정, 규제

Paraphrasing
the schedule overlaps 일정이 겹친다 → A schedule conflict 일정의 겹침

76 요청 문제

해석 화자는 청자들에게 무엇을 하라고 요청하는가?

(A) 아이디어를 제안한다.
(B) 다른 경로를 이용한다.
(C) 매뉴얼을 검토한다.
(D) 휴가를 사용하는 것을 피한다.

해설 지문에서 요청과 관련된 표현이 언급된 주변을 주의 깊게 듣는다. "I'm asking every one of you to refrain from using vacation days during this period"라며 이 기간 동안 휴가를 사용하는 것을 자제할 것을 모두에게 부탁한다고 하였다. 따라서 (D)가 정답이다.

어휘 come up with ~을 제안하다, 제시하다   route n. 경로, 길
manual n. 매뉴얼, 설명서   avoid v. 피하다, 방지하다

Paraphrasing

refrain from 자제하다 → Avoid 피하다
vacation days 휴가 → leave days 휴가

[77-79]

3 캐나다식

Questions 77-79 refer to the following telephone message.

Ms. Beyer, this is Tucker Pearson calling from Floyd Bank. [77]**I checked your post on our Web site inquiring about our credit cards. I'm calling to suggest the best option for you.** As you take lots of business trips overseas, I think the Turbo card would suit you. [78]**I'd like to highlight that this card accumulates points that can be converted into airline miles.** As part of a special summer promotional event, [79]**you'll also receive a sign-up bonus of 100 dollars if you complete the application by tomorrow.**

inquire v. 문의하다, 조사하다   overseas adv. 해외로, 해외에
suit v. 적합하다, 맞다   highlight v. 강조하다
accumulate v. 적립하다, 모으다   convert v. 전환시키다
application n. 신청

해석 77-79번은 다음 전화 메시지에 관한 문제입니다.
Ms. Bayer, 저는 Floyd 은행의 Tucker Pearson입니다. [77]저희 웹사이트에서 신용카드에 대해 문의하신 게시글을 확인했습니다. 귀하에게 가장 적합한 옵션을 제안해 드리기 위해 전화드렸습니다. 귀하는 해외로 출장을 많이 다니시기 때문에 Turbo 카드가 적합할 것 같습니다. [78]이 카드에는 항공사 마일리지로 전환될 수 있는 포인트가 적립된다는 것을 강조하고 싶습니다. 특별한 여름 프로모션 이벤트의 일환으로, [79]내일까지 신청을 완료하시면 가입 보너스 100달러도 받으실 수 있습니다.

77 목적 문제

해설 화자는 왜 전화하고 있는가?
(A) 영업시간을 확인하기 위해
(B) 새로운 정책을 설명하기 위해
(C) 추천을 해주기 위해
(D) 청구 비용을 논의하기 위해

해설 전화 메시지의 목적을 묻는 문제이므로, 지문의 초반을 주의 깊게 듣는다. "I checked your post on our Web site inquiring about our credit cards. I'm calling to suggest the best option for you."라며 청자가 웹사이트에 남겨 놓은 신용카드 관련 문의 글을 확

인했고 가장 적합한 옵션을 제안하기 위해 전화했다고 하였다. 따라서 (C)가 정답이다.

어휘 confirm v. 확인하다, 확정하다   describe v. 설명하다, 묘사하다
recommendation n. 추천

Paraphrasing

suggest 제안하다 → make a recommendation 추천을 해주다

78 특정 세부 사항 문제

해설 화자가 강조하는 카드의 특징은 무엇인가?
(A) 연회비가 없다.
(B) 포인트를 쌓을 수 있다.
(C) 개인 맞춤화될 수 있다.
(D) 이자율이 낮다.

해설 질문의 핵심 어구(feature of the card)와 관련된 내용이 언급된 주변을 주의 깊게 듣는다. "I'd like to highlight that this card accumulates points that can be converted into airline miles."라며 이 카드에는 항공사 마일리지로 전환될 수 있는 포인트가 적립된다는 것을 강조하고 싶다고 하였다. 따라서 (B)가 정답이다.

어휘 annual fee 연회비   customize v. 개인 맞춤화하다, 주문 제작하다
interest rate 이자율

Paraphrasing

highlight 강조하다 → emphasize 강조하다

79 방법 문제

해설 청자는 어떻게 보너스를 받을 수 있는가?
(A) 전화번호로 전화함으로써
(B) 특별 추첨에 응모함으로써
(C) 마감일 전에 신청함으로써
(D) 설문조사를 완료함으로써

해설 질문의 핵심 어구(receive a bonus)와 관련된 내용을 주의 깊게 듣는다. "you'll also receive a sign-up bonus of 100 dollars if you complete the application by tomorrow"라며 내일까지 신청을 완료하면 가입 보너스 100달러도 받을 수 있다고 하였다. 따라서 (C)가 정답이다.

어휘 drawing n. 추첨, 뽑기   apply v. 신청하다

Paraphrasing

complete the application by tomorrow 내일까지 신청을 완료하다 → applying before a deadline 마감일 전에 신청함

[80-82]

3 미국식

Questions 80-82 refer to the following announcement.

May I have your attention, please? [80]**Our most popular ride, the Meteor Roller Coaster, will not be in operation today due to a safety inspection.** We sincerely apologize for any inconvenience. But [81]**there are still plenty of other exciting attractions available.** Please pick up a park map at one of our information kiosks to find out where they are located. You may even discover some you did not know about. ⁸²The Latin dance performance will proceed as planned. It starts in a few hours, so don't miss it.

ride n. 놀이기구 operation n. 운행, 활동 inspection n. 점검, 검사
sincerely adv. 진심으로 apologize v. 사과하다
inconvenience n. 불편 plenty of 많은
attraction n. 놀이기구, 명소 discover v. 발견하다
performance n. 공연 proceed v. 진행되다, 계속해서 ~을 하다
miss v. 놓치다

해석
80-82번은 다음 공지에 관한 문제입니다.
주목해 주시겠어요? ⁸⁰저희의 가장 인기 있는 놀이기구인 유성 롤러코스터는 안전 점검으로 인해 오늘 운행되지 않을 것입니다. 불편을 끼쳐 드려 진심으로 죄송합니다. 하지만 ⁸¹다른 흥미로운 놀이기구들이 여전히 많이 있습니다. 안내 키오스크 중 한 곳에서 공원 지도를 찾아 그것들이 어디에 있는지를 알아보세요. 심지어 몰랐던 것들도 발견할 수 있습니다. ⁸²라틴 댄스 공연은 계획대로 진행될 예정입니다. 몇 시간 후에 시작되니 놓치지 마세요.

80 장소 문제

해석 청자들은 어디에 있는가?
(A) 극장에
(B) 수영장에
(C) 놀이공원에
(D) 미술관에

해설 지문에서 장소와 관련된 표현을 놓치지 않고 듣는다. "Our most popular ride, the Meteor Roller Coaster, will not be in operation today due to a safety inspection."이라며 가장 인기 있는 놀이기구인 유성 롤러코스터가 안전 점검으로 인해 오늘 운행되지 않을 것이라고 한 것을 통해 공지가 이뤄지고 있는 장소는 놀이공원임을 알 수 있다. 따라서 (C)가 정답이다.

81 의도 파악 문제

해석 화자는 왜 "심지어 몰랐던 것들도 발견할 수 있습니다"라고 말하는가?
(A) 할인을 알리기 위해
(B) 새로운 서비스를 홍보하기 위해
(C) 최근의 성과를 축하하기 위해
(D) 다른 놀이기구를 타볼 것을 제안하기 위해

해설 질문의 인용어구(You may even discover some you did not know about)가 언급된 주변을 주의 깊게 듣는다. "there are still plenty of other exciting attractions available"이라며 롤러코스터는 운행하지 않지만 다른 흥미로운 놀이기구들이 여전히 많다고 하였다. 따라서 (D)가 정답이다.

어휘 celebrate v. 축하하다, 기념하다 achievement n. 성과, 업적

82 다음에 할 일 문제

해석 화자에 따르면, 몇 시간 후에 무슨 일이 일어날 것인가?
(A) 특별한 행사가 시작될 것이다.
(B) 대회가 열릴 것이다.
(C) 기술자가 도착할 것이다.
(D) 안전 규칙이 설명될 것이다.

해설 질문의 핵심 어구(in a few hours)가 언급된 주변을 주의 깊게 듣는다. "The Latin dance performance will proceed as planned. It starts in a few hours, so don't miss it."이라며 라틴 댄스 공연이 계획대로 진행될 예정이며, 몇 시간 후에 시작할 것이라고 하였다. 따라서 (A)가 정답이다.

어휘 contest n. 대회, 시합 technician n. 기술자 explain v. 설명하다

Paraphrasing
The Latin dance performance 라틴 댄스 공연 → A special show 특별한 행사

[83-85] 호주식

Questions 83-85 refer to the following talk.

⁸³Last month, our research team surveyed over 5,000 people between the ages of 20 and 60 to discover what they're seeking in a car. The responses varied among the different demographic groups. However, regardless of age, everyone prioritized safety above everything else. Going forward, ⁸⁴we should design our cars in such a way that they all receive five-star safety ratings and showcase this fact in our advertisements. ⁸⁵Another major concern among those surveyed was fuel efficiency. Unfortunately, our vehicles only get 20 miles per gallon.

survey v. 설문 조사하다 demographic adj. 인구의, 인구 통계학적인
prioritize v. 우선시하다, 우선순위를 매기다 rating n. 등급, 순위
showcase v. 보여주다 concern n. 관심사, 걱정
fuel efficiency 연비, 연료 효율 unfortunately adv. 안타깝게도
vehicle n. 차량

해석
83-85번은 다음 담화에 관한 문제입니다.
⁸³지난달에, 우리 연구팀은 20세에서 60세 사이의 5,000명이 넘는 사람들을 대상으로 자동차에서 무엇을 추구하는지 설문 조사했습니다. 응답은 서로 다른 인구 집단들 사이에서 다양했습니다. 하지만, 연령과 관계없이 모든 사람이 안전을 무엇보다도 우선시했습니다. 앞으로, 우리는 ⁸⁴우리의 모든 차량들이 별 다섯 개의 안전 등급을 받도록 자동차를 설계하고 이 사실을 광고에 보여줘야 합니다. ⁸⁵설문 조사 대상자들 사이에서 또 다른 주요 관심사는 연비였습니다. 안타깝게도, 우리의 차량들은 갤런당 20마일에 불과합니다.

83 특정 세부 사항 문제

해석 화자에 따르면, 회사는 최근에 무엇을 했는가?
(A) 신제품을 개발했다.
(B) 설문 조사를 실시했다.
(C) 교육 프로그램을 기획했다.
(D) 추가 연구원들을 고용했다.

해설 질문의 핵심 어구(recently do)와 관련된 내용을 주의 깊게 듣는다. "Last month, our research team surveyed over 5,000 people ~ to discover what they're seeking in a car."라며 지난달에 5,000명이 넘는 사람들을 대상으로 자동차에서 무엇을 추구하는지 설문 조사를 했다고 하였다. 따라서 (B)가 정답이다.

어휘 develop v. 개발하다　additional adj. 추가의

84 제안 문제

해석 화자는 무엇을 할 것을 제안하는가?
(A) 더 많은 광고를 젊은 사람들에게 타겟팅하기
(B) 첫 구매자들을 위한 특별 할인 포함하기
(C) 그들의 차량에 후방 카메라 설치하기
(D) 그들의 모든 차량이 반드시 안전한 것으로 증명되게 하기

해설 지문의 중후반에서 제안과 관련된 표현이 언급된 다음을 주의 깊게 듣는다. "we should design our cars in such a way that they all receive five-star safety ratings"라며 우리의 모든 차량들이 별 다섯 개의 안전 등급을 받도록 설계해야 한다고 하였다. 따라서 (D)가 정답이다.

어휘 include v. 포함하다　install v. 설치하다
ensure v. 반드시 ~하게 하다, 보장하다
certify v. 증명하다, 자격증을 교부하다

Paraphrasing
receive five-star safety ratings 별 다섯 개의 안전 등급을 받다
→ are certified as safe 안전한 것으로 증명되다

85 의도 파악 문제

해석 화자는 왜 "우리의 차량들은 갤런당 20마일에 불과합니다"라고 말하는가?
(A) 약점을 나타내기 위해
(B) 경쟁사와 비교를 하기 위해
(C) 부정확한 정보를 수정하기 위해
(D) 차량들이 왜 비싼지 설명하기 위해

해설 질문의 인용어구(our vehicles only get 20 miles per gallon)가 언급된 주변을 주의 깊게 듣는다. "Another major concern among those surveyed was fuel efficiency."라며 설문조사에 참여한 사람들의 또 다른 관심사는 연비였다고 했다. 그런데 화자의 회사의 차량들은 갤런당 20마일에 불과하다고 했으므로 연비가 좋지 않다는 약점을 나타내기 위함임을 알 수 있다. 따라서 (A)가 정답이다.

어휘 indicate v. 나타내다, 시사하다　compare v. 비교하다
competitor n. 경쟁사, 경쟁자　incorrect adj. 부정확한
expensive adj. 비싼

[86-88]
🎧 캐나다식

Questions 86-88 refer to the following excerpt from a meeting.

Now that we've finally secured funding for our play, *Willow Tree*, ⁸⁶**the top priority for this production should be casting.** I'll be putting out a casting call for auditions in local newspapers and on Web sites. ⁸⁷**Please e-mail me a list of times when you're free from your usual duties to assist with the audition process.** ⁸⁸**The best space to hold these auditions is probably the Dalberg Center since it has professional sound and lighting equipment.** I'll reach out to them after this meeting.

secure v. 확보하다, 획득하다　funding n. 자금, 재원

priority n. 우선순위　production n. 제작, 생산　usual adj. 평소의
duty n. 업무, 의무　assist v. 돕다, 도움이 되다　process n. 과정, 절차
probably adv. 아마도　professional adj. 전문의, 전문적인
reach out ~에게 연락하다

해석
86-88번은 다음 회의 발췌록에 관한 문제입니다.

이제 우리가 마침내 연극 *Willow Tree*를 위한 자금을 확보했으니, ⁸⁶이번 제작의 최우선순위는 캐스팅이 될 것입니다. 제가 지역 신문과 웹사이트에 오디션을 위한 캐스팅 콜을 발표할 예정입니다. ⁸⁷오디션 과정을 돕기 위해 여러분들이 평소의 업무에서 여유가 있는 시간대의 목록을 제게 이메일로 보내주세요. ⁸⁸전문 음향 및 조명 장비를 갖추고 있기 때문에 오디션을 개최하기에 가장 좋은 장소는 아마도 Dalberg 센터일 것입니다. 이 회의가 끝난 후에 제가 그들에게 연락할게요.

86 특정 세부 사항 문제

해석 화자는 무엇이 최우선순위라고 말하는가?
(A) 자금을 확보하는 것
(B) 무대를 디자인하는 것
(C) 배우들을 선정하는 것
(D) 연극을 홍보하는 것

해설 질문의 핵심 어구(top priority)가 언급된 주변을 깊게 듣는다. "the top priority for this production should be casting"이라며 이번 제작의 최우선순위는 캐스팅이 될 것이라고 하였다. 따라서 (C)가 정답이다.

어휘 select v. 선정하다, 선택하다　promote v. 홍보하다

Paraphrasing
casting 캐스팅 → Selecting the actors 배우들을 선정하는 것

87 요청 문제

해석 화자는 청자들에게 무엇을 하라고 요청하는가?
(A) 포스터를 제작한다.
(B) 업무 가능성을 공유한다.
(C) 대본을 수정한다.
(D) 돈을 기부한다.

해설 지문의 중후반에서 요청과 관련된 표현이 포함된 문장을 주의 깊게 듣는다. "Please e-mail me a list of times when you're free from your usual duties to assist with the audition process."라며 오디션 과정을 돕기 위해 평소의 업무에서 여유가 있는 시간대의 목록을 이메일로 보내달라고 하였다. 따라서 (B)가 정답이다.

어휘 share v. 공유하다　revise v. 수정하다　script n. 대본, 각본
donate v. 기부하다

88 이유 문제

해석 화자는 왜 Dalberg 센터를 이용하길 원하는가?
(A) 일주일 내내 연다.
(B) 할인을 제공한다.
(C) 우수한 설비가 있다.

(D) 가장 큰 공간을 가지고 있다.

해설 질문의 핵심 어구(Dalberg Center)가 언급된 주변을 주의 깊게 듣는다. "The best space to hold these auditions is probably the Dalberg Center since it has professional sound and lighting equipment."라며 Dalberg 센터가 전문 음향 및 조명 장비를 갖추고 있어서 오디션을 개최하기에 가장 좋은 장소일 거라고 하였다. 따라서 (C)가 정답이다.

어휘 superior adj. 우수한 facility n. 설비, 시설

Paraphrasing

professional sound and lighting equipment 전문 음향 및 조명 장비 → superior facilities 우수한 설비

[89-91]   🔊 미국식

Questions 89-91 refer to the following advertisement.

> Do you want to make baking a hobby? Or is it your dream to open your own bakery? Then, [89]**consider taking our weekly baking lessons.** [90]**Ludlow Bakeshop owner Brandon Ludlow** leads the sessions and shares some of his baking tips. Fresh, locally sourced ingredients will be provided to students during the classes. [91]**And for the month of March, we have a very special promotion. Everyone registering for our classes will be able to download a 20 percent off coupon for the Ludlow Bakeshop on our Web site.**

hobby n. 취미 consider v. 고려하다, 생각하다
session n. 수업, 시간 locally adv. 현지에서, 지방적으로
source v. 조달하다, 얻다 ingredient n. 재료, 원료
register for ~에 등록하다

해설 89-91번은 다음 광고에 관한 문제입니다.

제빵을 취미로 삼고 싶나요? 아니면 자신만의 제과점을 여는 것이 꿈인가요? 그렇다면, [89]매주 저희의 제빵 수업을 받는 것을 고려해 보세요. [90]Ludlow 제과점 주인인 Brandon Ludlow가 수업을 이끌고 제빵 팁들을 공유합니다. 수업 중에는 현지에서 조달된 신선한 재료가 학생들에게 제공될 예정입니다. [91]그리고 3월 한 달 동안 매우 특별한 프로모션이 진행됩니다. 수업에 등록하는 모든 사람은 웹사이트에서 Ludlow 제과점의 20퍼센트 할인 쿠폰을 다운로드할 수 있습니다.

89 주제 문제

해설 무엇이 광고되고 있는가?
(A) 배낭
(B) 새로운 제과점
(C) 교육 강좌
(D) 요리 도구

해설 광고의 주제를 묻는 문제이므로, 지문의 초반을 반드시 듣는다. "consider taking our weekly baking lessons"라며 매주 저희의 제빵 수업을 받는 것을 고려해 보라고 한 후, 제빵 수업에 대한 내용으로 이어지고 있다. 따라서 (C)가 정답이다.

어휘 educational adj. 교육의 utensil n. 도구, 기구

Paraphrasing

lessons 수업 → educational sessions 교육 강좌

90 특정 세부 사항 문제

해설 Brandon Ludlow는 누구인가?
(A) 재정 고문
(B) 여행사 직원
(C) 업체 소유주
(D) 레스토랑 비평가

해설 질문 대상(Brandon Ludlow)의 신분 및 직업과 관련된 표현을 놓치지 않고 듣는다. "Ludlow Bakeshop owner Brandon Ludlow"라며 Brandon Ludlow가 Ludlow 제과점의 주인이라고 하였다. 따라서 (C)가 정답이다.

어휘 financial adj. 재정의 advisor n. 고문, 조언자 critic n. 비평가

91 특정 세부 사항 문제

해설 화자에 따르면, 3월에 무슨 일이 있을 것인가?
(A) 쿠폰이 온라인에 게재될 것이다.
(B) 등록 절차가 끝날 것이다.
(C) 지점이 영업시간을 연장할 것이다.
(D) 일정이 업데이트될 것이다.

해설 질문의 핵심 어구(March)가 언급된 주변을 주의 깊게 듣는다. "And for the month of March, we have a very special promotion. Everyone registering for our classes will be able to download a 20 percent off coupon ~ on our Web site."라며 3월에는 특별한 프로모션이 진행되는데, 수업에 등록한 모든 사람은 웹사이트에서 할인 쿠폰을 다운로드할 수 있다고 하였다. 따라서 (A)가 정답이다.

어휘 registration n. 등록 extend v. 연장하다, 확대하다

[92-94]   🔊 영국식

Questions 92-94 refer to the following excerpt from a meeting.

> [92]**We're just one day out from the release of our latest video game, Velcrom.** I'd like to thank each of you for all the hard work you have put into this project. [93]**We're expecting to see high sales figures due to the record number of preorders.** We need to take advantage of this. [94]**So for the remainder of this meeting, I would like you to look at these three advertising plans and share your opinions about which we should put into action.**

release n. 출시, 개봉 latest adj. 최신의, 최근의 figure n. 수치
record adj. 기록적인 preorder n. 선주문
take advantage of ~을 활용하다 remainder n. 남은 것, 나머지
put into action 실행에 옮기다

해설
92-94번은 다음 회의 발췌록에 관한 문제입니다.

[92]우리의 최신 비디오 게임인 Velcrom의 출시가 하루 앞으로 다가왔습니다. 이 프로젝트에 투입해 주신 여러분의 모든 노고에 감사드립니다. [93]기록적인 선주문 건수로 인해 높은 매출 수치를 기록할 것으로 예상됩니다. 우리

는 이를 활용해야 합니다. **94**따라서 이번 회의의 남은 시간 동안 이 세 가지 광고 계획을 살펴보고 어떤 것을 실행에 옮겨야 할지에 대한 의견을 공유해 주셨으면 합니다.

92 주제 문제

해석 화자는 주로 무엇에 대해 이야기하는가?
(A) 광고 예산
(B) 새로운 공장을 위한 부지
(C) 신제품 출시
(D) 고객과의 회의

해설 회의의 주제를 묻는 문제이므로, 지문의 초반을 반드시 듣는다. "We're just one day out from the release of our latest video game, Velcrom."이라며 최신 비디오 게임의 출시가 하루 앞으로 다가왔다고 한 후, 비디오 게임 출시에 대한 내용으로 이어지고 있다. 따라서 (C)가 정답이다.

어휘 budget n. 예산 site n. 부지, 장소 factory n. 공장

93 언급 문제

해석 화자는 매출 수치에 대해 무엇을 말하는가?
(A) 사상 최저치이다.
(B) 사전 주문의 영향을 받는다.
(C) 곧 공개될 예정이다.
(D) 변경될 가능성이 있다.

해설 질문의 핵심 어구(sales numbers)가 언급된 주변을 주의 깊게 듣는다. "We're expecting to see high sales figures due to the record number of preorders."라며 기록적인 선주문 건수로 인해 높은 매출 수치를 기록할 것으로 예상된다고 하였다. 따라서 (B)가 정답이다.

어휘 affect v. 영향을 미치다 reveal v. 공개하다, 드러내다

94 의도 파악 문제

해석 화자는 "우리는 이를 활용해야 합니다"라고 말할 때 무엇을 의도하는가?
(A) 직원회의 일정이 변경될 것이다.
(B) 제품 후기가 논의될 것이다.
(C) 게임 후속편이 계획될 것이다.
(D) 마케팅 캠페인이 시작될 것이다.

해설 질문의 인용어구(We need to take advantage of this)가 언급된 주변을 주의 깊게 듣는다. "So for the remainder of this meeting, I would like you to look at these three advertising plans and share your opinions about which we should put into action."이라며 남은 회의 시간 동안 광고 계획을 살펴보고 어떤 것을 실행에 옮겨야 할지에 대한 의견을 공유해달라고 한 것을 통해 마케팅 캠페인이 시작될 것임을 알 수 있다. 따라서 (D)가 정답이다.

어휘 reschedule v. 일정을 변경하다 sequel n. 후속편, 결과 launch v. 시작하다, 착수하다

[95-97]

미국식

Questions 95-97 refer to the following news report and graph.

You're listening to *Business Today* with Beth Colbert. **95**Plateau Air, which first began operations in January, has surprised everyone by becoming the most popular regional airline. CEO Benedict Evans attributes the company's rapid success to **96**the decision to eliminate baggage fees, which was implemented in the quarter following the one with the lowest earnings. For anyone wanting to learn more about Plateau Air, there is an interview with Mr. Evans in this month's issue of *Finance Magazine*. **97**It's an interesting article, so I suggest you check it out.

operation n. 운항, 운영 surprise v. 놀라게 하다
regional adj. 지역의 attribute v. ~의 덕분으로 보다
rapid adj. 빠른 decision n. 결정 eliminate v. 없애다, 제거하다
baggage n. 수하물, 짐 implement v. 시행하다 quarter n. 분기

해석
95-97번은 다음 뉴스 보도와 그래프에 관한 문제입니다.
여러분들은 Beth Colbert와 함께하는 *Business Today*를 듣고 계십니다. **95**1월에 처음 운항을 시작한 Plateau 항공사는 가장 인기 있는 지역 항공사가 되어 모두를 놀라게 했습니다. 대표이사인 Benedict Evans는 회사의 빠른 성공을 **96**수하물 수수료를 없애기로 한 결정 덕분이라고 보는데, 이는 가장 낮은 실적을 기록한 분기의 다음 분기에 시행된 것입니다. Plateau 항공사에 대해 더 알고 싶은 분들을 위해, *Finance Magazine*의 이번 달 호에 Mr. Evans와의 인터뷰가 실려있습니다. **97**그것은 흥미로운 기사이니, 확인해 보실 것을 제안합니다.

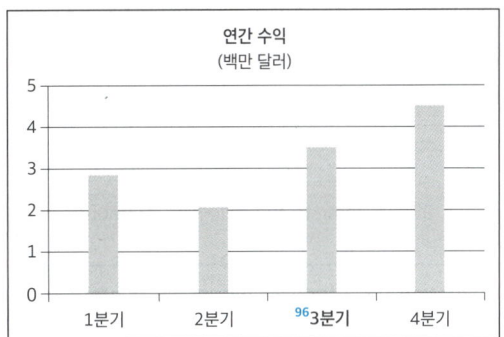

95 주제 문제

해석 화자는 어떤 종류의 사업에 대해 이야기하고 있는가?
(A) 여행 회사
(B) 차량 서비스
(C) 의류 회사
(D) 항공사

해설 뉴스 보도의 주제를 묻는 문제이므로, 지문의 초반을 반드시 듣는다. "Plateau Air, which first began operations in January, has surprised everyone by becoming the most popular regional airline."이라며 1월에 처음 운항을 시작한 Plateau 항공사는 가장 인기 있는 지역 항공사가 되어 모두를 놀라게 했다고 한 후, 해당 항공사에 대한 내용으로 이어지고 있다. 따라서 (D)가 정답이다.

96 시각 자료 문제

해석 시각 자료를 보아라. 회사는 언제 변화를 시행했는가?
(A) 1분기에
(B) 2분기에
(C) 3분기에
(D) 4분기에

해설 제시된 그래프의 정보를 확인한 후 질문의 핵심 어구(make a change)와 관련된 내용을 주의 깊게 듣는다. "the decision to eliminate baggage fees, which was implemented in the quarter following the one with the lowest earnings"라며 수하물 수수료를 없애기로 한 결정은 가장 낮은 실적을 기록한 다음 분기에 시행되었다고 했다. 그래프에서 가장 낮은 실적을 기록했을 때는 2분기이므로 그다음 분기인 3분기에 정책 변화가 시행되었음을 알 수 있다. 따라서 (C)가 정답이다.

97 제안 문제

해석 화자는 무엇을 하기를 제안하는가?
(A) 회사에 연락하기
(B) 출간물을 읽기
(C) 서비스를 신청하기
(D) 멤버십을 연장하기

해설 지문의 중후반에서 제안과 관련된 표현이 포함된 문장을 주의 깊게 듣는다. "It's an interesting article, so I suggest you check it out."이라며 흥미로운 기사이니 확인해 볼 것을 제안한다고 하였다. 따라서 (B)가 정답이다.

어휘 publication n. 출간물, 출판 sign up for ~를 신청하다

Paraphrasing

article 기사 → publication 출간물

[98-100]

🇨🇦 캐나다식

Questions 98-100 refer to the following announcement and map.

> [96]**Thank you for attending this press conference.** I'm Dennis Nolan, the director of the public transportation department, and I'll be making a few announcements about the renovation of the Portside Subway Station. First, the start date has been pushed back to May 8, the day after the national holiday. Second, [99]**the subway exit leading to the Oakridge Apartments will be closed from May 10 to 12 while workers install new escalators**. I would also like to mention that there will be a ceremony to celebrate the completion of the project on May 20. [100]**More information about the ceremony will be posted on the city's Web site.**

press conference 기자회견 director n. 국장, 관리자
department n. 부서 renovation n. 보수, 개조
push back 미루다, 밀치다 exit n. 출구 mention v. 언급하다, 말하다
ceremony n. 기념식 celebrate v. 축하하다, 기념하다
completion n. 완료

해석 98-100번은 다음 공지와 지도에 관한 문제입니다.

[98]이 기자회견에 참석해 주셔서 감사합니다. 저는 대중교통 부서의 Dennis Nolan 국장이며, Portside 지하철역 보수 공사에 대해 몇 가지 발표할 예정입니다. 첫째, 시작일은 공휴일 다음 날인 5월 8일로 미뤄졌습니다. 둘째, [99]Oakridge 아파트로 이어지는 지하철 출구는 직원들이 새 에스컬레이터를 설치할 동안 5월 10일부터 12일까지 폐쇄될 것입니다. 또한 5월 20일에 프로젝트 완료를 축하하는 기념식이 있을 예정이라는 점도 언급하고 싶습니다. [100]기념식에 대한 더 많은 정보는 시 웹사이트에 게시될 것입니다.

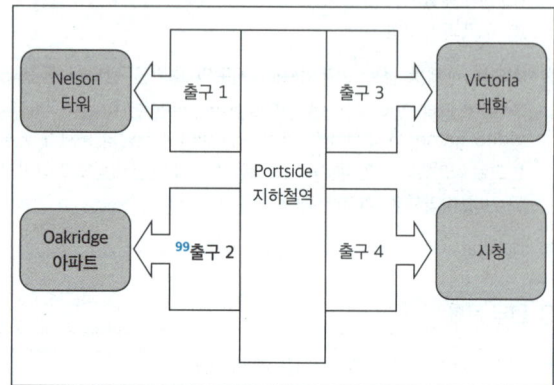

98 청자 문제

해석 청자들은 누구인 것 같은가?
(A) 기술자들
(B) 공무원들
(C) 기자들
(D) 자원봉사자들

해설 지문에서 신분 및 직업과 관련된 표현을 놓치지 않고 듣는다. "Thank you for attending this press conference."라며 이 기자회견에 참석해 주어 고맙다고 한 것을 통해 청자들은 기자들임을 알 수 있다. 따라서 (C)가 정답이다.

99 시각 자료 문제

해석 시각 자료를 보아라. 어떤 지하철 출구가 5월 10일부터 폐쇄될 것인가?
(A) 출구 1
(B) 출구 2
(C) 출구 3
(D) 출구 4

해설 제시된 지도의 정보를 확인한 후 질문의 핵심 어구(closed starting May 10)와 관련된 내용을 주의 깊게 듣는다. "the subway exit leading to the Oakridge Apartments will be closed from May 10 to 12 while workers install new escalators"라며 Oakridge 아파트로 이어지는 지하철 출구는 5월 10일부터 12일까지 폐쇄될 것이라고 했고, Oakridge 아파트로 이어지는 출구는 출구 2임을 지도에서 알 수 있다. 따라서 (B)가 정답이다.

100 특정 세부 사항 문제

해석 화자는 온라인에 무엇이 게시될 것이라고 말하는가?
(A) 건설 계획

(B) 열차 일정
(C) 보수공사 비용
(D) 행사 세부 사항

해설 질문의 핵심 어구(posted online)와 관련된 내용을 주의 깊게 듣는다. "More information about the ceremony will be posted on the city's Web site."라며 기념식에 대한 더 많은 정보는 시 웹사이트에 게시될 것이라고 하였다. 따라서 (D)가 정답이다.

어휘 construction n. 건설 detail n. 세부 사항

Paraphrasing

more information about the ceremony 기념식에 대한 더 많은 정보 → event details 행사 세부 사항

PART 5

101 격에 맞는 인칭대명사 채우기

해설 명사(role) 앞에서 형용사처럼 쓰일 수 있는 인칭대명사는 소유격이므로 (B) her가 정답이다. 주격 인칭대명사 (A), 소유대명사 (C), 재귀대명사 (D)는 명사를 꾸밀 수 없다.

해설 Anna Lin은 새 회계연도가 시작되면 최고 재무 책임자로서의 그녀의 역할에서 공식적으로 물러날 것이다.

어휘 step down ~에서 물러나다, 사직하다 financial adj. 재무의, 금융의
fiscal year 회계연도

102 부사 자리 채우기

해설 동사(worked)를 꾸밀 수 있는 것은 부사이므로 부사 (D) tirelessly (지칠 줄 모르고)가 정답이다. 동사 (A), 동사 또는 과거분사 (B), 형용사 (C)는 동사를 꾸밀 수 없다.

해설 Claymore사의 건설 인부들은 새 경기장의 완공 기한을 맞추기 위해 지칠 줄 모르고 일했다.

어휘 construction n. 건설 completion n. 완공, 완료
stadium n. 경기장

최신 토익 경향

부사 자리 문제는 PART 5에서 매회 2~3문제씩 출제되는 빈출 유형이다. 부사는 명사를 제외한 모든 품사를 꾸며줄 수 있으므로 문장 내에서 들어갈 수 있는 자리가 다양하다.

<부사가 들어갈 수 있는 자리> *빈칸이 부사 자리이다.

A. 부사가 동사를 수식하는 경우
(1) 주어 + ____ + 동사
(2) 자동사 + ____
(3) 자동사 + 전치사 + 목적어 + ____
(4) 타동사 + 목적어 + ____

B. 부사가 형용사 및 분사를 수식하는 경우
(1) be + ____ + 형용사
(2) be + ____ + 형용사 + 명사
(3) be + ____ + 숫자 + 명사
(4) be + ____ + 한정사(관사/소유격/지시형용사/수량형용사) + 명사
(5) be + ____ + p.p./-ing
(6) have/has/had + ____ + p.p./-ing

103 형용사 관련 어구 완성하기

해설 '방문자 등록 키오스크를 관리하는 것에 대한 책임이 있다'라는 문맥이므로 빈칸 앞의 be동사 is와 뒤의 전치사 for와 함께 '~에 대한 책임이 있다'라는 의미의 어구 be responsible for를 만드는 형용사 (A) responsible이 정답이다. (B) practical과 (C) beneficial도 전치사 for와 함께 쓰일 수 있지만, 각각 '~에 실용적인', '~에게 이로운'이라는 의미로 어색한 문맥이 되므로 답이 될 수 없다. (D) capable 은 '~을 할 수 있는'이라는 의미로 전치사 of와 함께 쓰인다.

해설 Ms. Wallace는 이번 주말의 박람회에서 방문자 등록 키오스크를 관리하는 것에 대한 책임이 있다.

어휘 manage v. 관리하다 registration n. 등록
exposition n. 박람회, 전시

104 부사 어휘 고르기

해설 '이미 수리공을 불렀고, 그는 내일 방문할 것이다'라는 문맥이므로 (B) already(이미)가 정답이다. (A) overly는 '너무, 몹시', (C) closely는 '가까이, 면밀히', (D) very는 '매우, 아주'라는 의미이다.

해설 Ms. Finley는 고장 난 식기세척기를 수리하기 위해 이미 수리공을 불렀고, 그는 내일 방문할 것이다.

어휘 repairman n. 수리공 dishwasher n. 식기세척기

105 부사절 접속사 채우기

해설 이 문장은 주어(Mr. Ford)와 동사(stretches)를 갖춘 완전한 절이므로 ____ ~ his morning jog는 수식어 거품으로 보아야 한다. 이 수식어 거품은 동사(goes)가 있는 거품절이므로, 거품절을 이끌 수 있는 부사절 접속사 (D) Before(~하기 전에)가 정답이다. 전치사 (A) During(~ 동안), 부사 (B) Then(그때, 그러고 나서), 전치사 또는 부사 (C) Around(~ 주위에; 약, 사방에)는 거품절을 이끌 수 없다.

해설 아침 조깅을 하러 가기 전에, Mr. Ford는 어떠한 근육 부상이라도 방지하기 위해 스트레칭을 한다.

어휘 avoid v. 방지하다, 피하다 injury n. 부상, 상처

106 명사 자리 채우기

해설 동사(distribute)의 목적어 역할을 할 수 있는 것은 명사이므로 명사 (A), (C), (D)가 정답의 후보이다. '카탈로그의 사본들을 배부할 계획이다'라는 문맥이고 빈칸 앞에 부정관사(a/an)가 없으므로 복수 명사 (D) copies가 정답이다. 동사 또는 과거분사 (B)는 명사 자리에 올 수 없다.

해설 Blevins 그룹 마케팅팀은 다가오는 무역 박람회에서 제품 카탈로그의 사본들을 배부할 계획이다.

어휘 distribute v. 배부하다, 나누어 주다
upcoming adj. 다가오는, 곧 있을

107 명사 어휘 고르기

해설 '다양한 해산물 요리를 제공하다'라는 문맥이므로 '다양한'이라는 의미의 'an extensive selection of'를 완성하는 (A) selection(선택된 것)이 정답이다. 참고로, 'a wide/diverse selection of'도 '다양한'의 의미로 자주 출제된다. (C) cuisine(요리법)도 의미상 그럴듯해 보이지만 cuisine은 특정 지역이나 문화의 요리법을 나타내어 local cuisine, French cuisine 등과 같은 형태로 주로 쓰인다. (B) gift는 '선물', (D) system은 '체계, 제도'라는 의미이다.

해석 Yomi 비스트로는 다양한 해산물 요리를 제공하며, 각 요리는 구할 수 있는 가장 신선한 재료들로 준비된다.

어휘 ingredient n. 재료, 구성 요소
available adj. 구할 수 있는, 여유가 있는

108 형용사 자리 채우기

해설 빈칸 앞에 정관사(the), 빈칸 뒤에 명사(staff)가 있으므로 명사를 꾸미는 형용사 (B) managerial(관리의, 경영자의)이 정답이다. 명사 manager(관리자)의 복수형인 (C) managers는 staff와 복합 명사를 이루지 못하므로 답이 될 수 없다. 동사 (A)와 (D)는 명사를 꾸밀 수 없다.

해석 진행 상황을 평가하기 위해 Sharpe 음료사의 관리 직원들을 대상으로 분기별 검토 세션이 개최되었다.

어휘 quarterly adj. 분기별의   assess v. 평가하다

109 현재분사와 과거분사 구별하여 채우기

해설 빈칸 뒤의 명사(travel experiences)를 꾸며줄 수 있는 것은 형용사이므로 형용사 역할을 하는 과거분사 (B)와 현재분사 (C)가 정답의 후보이다. 꾸밈을 받는 명사와 분사가 '실망을 주는 여행'이라는 의미의 능동 관계이므로 현재분사 (C) disappointing(실망스러운)이 정답이다. 과거분사 (B) disappointed를 쓸 경우 여행이 감정을 느낀다는 의미가 되어 '실망을 느끼는 여행'이라는 어색한 문맥이 되므로 답이 될 수 없다.

해석 Mr. Rivera의 로마로의 여행은 그의 인생에서 가장 실망스러운 여행 경험 중 하나였다.

어휘 experience n. 경험   disappoint v. 실망시키다

110 형용사 자리 채우기

해설 이 문장은 동사 noted의 목적어 자리에 'how ___ he was'의 간접 의문문이 온 구조이다. how는 형용사나 부사를 수식할 수 있으므로 (C)와 (D)가 정답의 후보이다. 간접 의문문의 끝에 be 동사(was)가 있으므로 be동사의 보어 역할을 할 수 있는 형용사가 들어가야 한다. 따라서 (D) creative(창의적인)가 정답이다. 참고로 'how(얼마나)+형용사+주어+be 동사', 'how(얼마나)+부사+주어+일반동사'의 구조를 구분하여 알아두자.

해석 심사위원들은 7분 만에 문제를 해결하는 것에 대해 얼마나 그가 창의적인지를 알아차렸다.

어휘 judge n. 심사위원   solve v. 해결하다, 풀다

111 명사 관련 어구 완성하기

해설 '트렌드를 반영하기 위해 계절별로 물품 목록을 업데이트하다'라는 문맥이므로 '계절별로, 계절에 기반하여'라는 의미의 표현인 'on a seasonal basis'를 완성하는 (A) basis(기반)가 정답이다. (B) design은 '디자인, 설계', (C) reason은 '이유', (D) suggestion은 '제안'이라는 의미이다. 참고로 'on a ~ basis' 표현을 관용 표현으로 알아둔다. (on a regular basis: 정기적으로, on a weekly basis: 주 단위로)

해석 Zelway 패션 아웃렛은 최신 트렌드를 반영하기 위해 계절별로 물품 목록을 업데이트한다.

어휘 inventory n. 물품 목록, 재고   reflect v. 반영하다, 비추다
latest adj. 최신의, 최근의

112 강조 부사 채우기

해설 '심지어 최근의 직원 교육에도 고객 서비스 등급이 낮다'라는 의미가 되어야 하므로 단어나 구를 앞에서 강조하는 강조 부사 (B) even(심지어, ~ 조차도)이 정답이다. 부사, 전치사, 또는 부사절 접속사 (A) as는 부사로 쓰일 경우 '~ 만큼 ~한'의 의미로 형용사 또는 부사를 꾸미고, 전치사로 쓰일 경우 '~로서'의 의미로 자격이나 신분을 나타내며, 부사절 접속사로 쓰일 경우 '~함에 따라, ~하는 대로'라는 의미로 완전한 절을 이끈다. 부사 (C) just는 '딱, 꼭, 방금', 형용사 또는 부사 (D) much는 형용사일 경우 '많은', 부사일 경우 '매우, 훨씬'이라는 의미이다.

해석 심지어 최근의 직원 교육에도, Rosen Telecom의 고객 서비스 등급은 여전히 낮다.

어휘 rating n. 등급, 순위   staff training 직원 교육

113 전치사 채우기

해설 이 문장은 주어(Pontus Apparel), 동사(launched), 목적어(its tracksuit line)를 모두 갖춘 완전한 절이므로 ___ ~ setbacks는 수식어 거품으로 보아야 한다. 이 수식어 거품은 동사가 없는 거품구이므로 거품구를 이끌 수 있는 전치사 (A), (B), (D)가 정답의 후보이다. '초기의 난관에도 불구하고 운동복 라인을 성공적으로 출시했다'라는 의미가 되어야 하므로 전치사 (D) Despite(~에도 불구하고)가 정답이다. (A) Because of는 '~때문에'라는 의미로 이유를 나타내고, (B) Along은 '~을 따라서'라는 의미로 방향을 나타낸다. (C) As though는 '마치 ~인 것처럼'이라는 의미의 부사절 접속사로 거품구가 아닌 거품절을 이끈다.

해석 초기의 난관에도 불구하고, Pontus 의류는 계획된 기간 내에 운동복 라인을 성공적으로 출시했다.

어휘 initial adj. 초기의, 처음의   setback n. 난관, 차질
launch v. 출시하다, 시작하다   tracksuit n. 운동복

최신토익경향

전치사 문제에서 양보의 의미를 나타내는 despite(~에도 불구하고)이 정답으로 자주 출제되고 있다. 같은 의미의 부사절 접속사 although(비록 ~이지만)가 보기에 함께 제시되어, 전치사와 접속사를 구분할 수 있는지 묻는 경우도 있다.

<의미가 유사하여 혼동되는 전치사와 부사절 접속사>

의미	전치사	부사절 접속사
조건	without ~이 없다면, ~없이	unless 만약 ~이 아니라면
양보	despite, in spite of ~에도 불구하고	although, even though 비록 ~이지만
기타	like ~처럼	as if, as though 마치 ~인 것처럼

<최근 출제된 명사 관련 어구>
- product line 제품군
- travel arrangement 여행 준비
- conservation practice 보존(을 위한) 실천

114 등위접속사 채우기

해설 절(The committee ~ this week)과 절(the marketing campaign ~ be postponed)을 연결할 수 있는 등위접속사 (B)와 부사절 접속사 (C)가 정답의 후보이다. '이번 주에 예산을 확정해야 하고, 그렇지 않으면 마케팅 캠페인은 연기될 것이다'라는 의미가 되어야 하므로 등위접속사 (B) or(그렇지 않으면, 또는)가 정답이다. 부사절 접속사 (C) unless(~하지 않는 한)는 조건을 나타낼 경우, 미래 시제 대신 현재 시제를 쓴다. 대명사 또는 형용사 (A) both(둘 다; 둘 다의)와 부사 (D) soon(곧)은 절과 절을 연결할 수 없다.

해석 위원회는 이번 주에 예산을 확정해야 하고, 그렇지 않으면 Knox 화장품사를 위한 마케팅 캠페인은 연기될 것이다.

어휘 committee n. 위원회   finalize v. 확정하다, 마무리 짓다
budget n. 예산   postpone v. 연기하다, 미루다

115 형용사 어휘 고르기

해설 '해외 사업에 대한 심도 있는 경험은 글로벌 확장 노력에 귀중한 보탬이 될 것이다'라는 문맥이므로 (A) valuable(귀중한, 값진)이 정답이다. (D) thorough(철저한, 완전한)도 해석상 그럴듯해 보이지만 thorough는 특정 행위가 철저한 것을 나타낼 때 사용하므로 이 문장에는 적절하지 않다. (thorough investigation: 철저한 조사) (B) public은 '공공의', (C) selective는 '선택적인, 선별적인'이라는 의미이다.

해석 Mr. Cramer의 해외 사업에 대한 심도 있는 경험은 우리의 글로벌 확장 노력에 귀중한 보탬이 될 것이다.

어휘 in-depth adj. 심도 있는, 면밀한   effort n. 노력

116 명사 관련 어구 완성하기

해설 '환급을 받기 위해 교통비 영수증을 제출하다'라는 문맥이므로 빈칸 앞의 명사(transportation)와 함께 '교통비'라는 의미의 어구 transportation expense를 만드는 명사 expense(비용, 경비)의 복수형 (C) expenses가 정답이다. (A)의 branch는 '지사, 분점', (B)의 material은 '재료, 자료', (D)의 request는 '요청'이라는 의미이다.

해석 Mr. Hwang은 환급을 받기 위해 교통비 영수증을 제출했다.

어휘 submit v. 제출하다   receipt n. 영수증
reimbursement n. 환급, 상환

최신 토익 경향
명사 관련 어구 문제는 PART 5에서 꾸준히 출제되고 있다. 하나의 단어로 알아두지 않으면 오답을 고르기 쉬우므로 덩어리로 암기해두자.

117 동사 어휘 고르기

해설 '기업 행사를 준비하는 것에 대한 수수료를 고객에게 청구하다'라는 문맥이므로 2개의 목적어, 즉 간접 목적어(clients)와 직접 목적어(a fee)를 갖는 4형식 동사로 쓰이는 charge(청구하다)의 3인칭 단수형 (B) charges가 정답이다. (C)의 collect(모으다, 징수하다)도 해석상 그럴듯해 보이지만 collect는 3형식 동사로 뒤에 1개의 목적어가 나와 collects a fee의 어순으로 써야 하므로 답이 될 수 없다. (A)의 undergo는 '겪다, 경험하다', (D)의 adjust는 '조정하다'라는 의미이다.

해석 Lina 이벤트 기획사는 활동의 유형에 기반하여 기업 행사를 준비하는 것에 대한 수수료를 고객에게 청구한다.

어휘 organize v. 준비하다, 정리하다   based on ~에 기반하여

118 부정대명사 채우기

해설 '아보카도를 필요로 해서 잘 익은 하나를 찾기 위해 주방을 둘러보다'라는 의미가 되어야 하므로, 정해지지 않은 단수 가산 명사를 대신하는 부정대명사 (D) one(하나)이 정답이다. 참고로, one은 앞에 있는 avocado(아보카도)를 지칭하고 있음을 알아둔다. (A) any other(어떤 다른)는 이미 언급한 것 이외의 어떤 다른 것을 의미하는 형용사로 쓰이며, 대명사일 경우에는 any others의 형태로 쓰여 '(이미 언급한 것 이외의) 어떤 다른 것들'을 의미한다. (B) each는 '각각'이라는 의미이므로 문맥상 어색하다. (C) several(몇 개)은 복수 취급하므로 뒤에 나온 관계절의 단수 동사(was)와 함께 쓰일 수 없다.

해석 그 조리법은 아보카도를 필요로 해서 요리사는 잘 익은 하나를 찾기 위해 주방을 둘러보았다.

어휘 recipe n. 조리법, 방안   look around 둘러보다
ripe adj. 잘 익은, 여문

119 전치사 채우기

해설 이 문장은 필수성분(Ms. Eve has felt ~ outdoor activities)을 갖춘 완전한 절이므로, ___ ~ hiking trip은 수식어 거품으로 보아야 한다. 이 수식어 거품은 동사가 없는 거품구이므로, 거품구를 이끌 수 있는 전치사 (A), (B), (C)가 정답의 후보이다. '지난달의 하이킹 여행 이후 더 활기차게 느끼고 더 많은 야외 활동에 참여하도록 동기가 부여되다'라는 의미가 되어야 하므로 시점을 나타내는 전치사 (C) since(~ 이후, ~ 이래로)가 정답이다. 참고로, 전치사 since는 현재완료 시제(has/have p.p.)와 함께 자주 쓰임을 알아둔다. (A) until은 '~(때)까지', (B) past는 '(시간이) ~을 지나서, (정도를) 넘어서'라는 의미이다. 부사절 접속사 (D) in order that(~하기 위해, ~할 수 있도록)은 동사가 있는 거품절을 이끈다.

해석 Ms. Eve는 지난달의 하이킹 여행 이후 더 활기차게 느꼈고 더 많은 야외 활동에 참여하도록 동기가 부여되었다.

어휘 energetic adj. 활기찬, 활동적인
motivate v. 동기를 부여하다, 이유가 되다

120 조동사 다음에 동사원형 채우기

해설 조동사(will) 다음에는 동사원형이 와야 하므로 (A) assist(돕다)가 정답이다. 3인칭 단수형 동사 (B), 과거형 동사 또는 과거분사 (C), 동명사 또는 현재분사 (D)는 조동사 다음에 올 수 없다.

해석 인사 부서의 직원이 신입 사원들의 온보딩 서류를 작성하는 것을 도울 것이다.

어휘 onboarding n. 온보딩(신입 사원을 교육하는 과정)
paperwork n. 서류 (작업), 문서 업무

121 부사절 접속사 채우기

해설 이 문장은 주어(Attendees), 동사(will receive), 목적어(a follow-up e-mail)를 갖춘 완전한 절이므로, ___ ~ concludes는 수식어 거품으로 보아야 한다. 이 수식어 거품은 동사(concludes)가 있는 거품절이므로, 부사절 접속사인 (A)와 (C)가 정답의 후보이다. '학회가 끝나면 세부 요약서가 포함된 후속 이메일을 받을 것이다'라는 의미가 되어야 하므로 (C) when(~하면, ~한 때)이 정답이다. (A) whereas는 '~한 반면에'라는 의미이므로 어색한 문맥을 만든다. 전치사 (B) toward(~ 쪽으로)는 거품절이 아닌 거품구를 이끌고, 부사 (D) also (또한)는 거품절을 이끌 수 없다.

해석 웨비나의 참석자들은 SJ 의료 학회가 끝나면 세부 요약서가 포함된 후속 이메일을 받을 것이다.

어휘 attendee n. 참석자 follow-up adj. 후속의, 잇따른; n. 후속 조치
summary n. 요약(서), 개요 conclude v. 끝나다, 결론을 내리다

122 부사 자리 채우기

해설 to 부정사(to replicate)를 꾸밀 수 있는 것은 부사이므로 부사 (C) accurately(정확하게)가 정답이다. 형용사 (A), 명사 (B)와 (D)는 동사를 꾸밀 수 없다.

해석 Prime 직물사는 색상을 정확하게 모사하기 위해 고급 기계를 사용하는데, 이는 서로 다른 생산분에 걸쳐 일관성을 보장한다.

어휘 advanced adj. 고급의, 선진의 machinery n. 기계(류), 장치
replicate v. 모사하다, 복제하다 consistency n. 일관성, 한결같음
batch n. (한 회)분, 한 묶음

123 전치사 채우기

해설 '수익성이 낮은 지점을 폐쇄하는 것보다는, 대신에 효율성을 높일 수 있는 방법을 모색하다'라는 의미가 되어야 하므로 '~보다는, ~ 대신에'의 의미를 갖는 전치사 (B) Rather than이 정답이다. (A) Owing to는 '~ 때문에', (C) Compared to는 '~과 비교하여', (D) In case of는 '~의 경우에'라는 의미이다.

해석 수익을 못 내는 지점을 폐쇄하는 것보다는, Westwood 대여사는 대신에 효율성을 높일 수 있는 방법을 모색하고 있다.

어휘 unprofitable adj. 수익을 못 내는 instead adv. 대신에

124 태에 맞는 동사 채우기

해설 문장에 동사가 없으므로 동사인 모든 보기가 정답의 후보이다. 주어(each product's barcode)와 동사(scan)가 '각 제품의 바코드가 스캔되어지다'라는 수동의 의미가 되어야 하므로 수동태 동사 (D) will be scanned가 정답이다.

해석 재고 확인 중에는, 창고 관리 시스템을 업데이트하기 위해 각 제품의 바코드가 스캔될 것이다.

어휘 warehouse n. 창고 management n. 관리

125 동사 어휘 고르기

해설 '부속 건물의 건설은 3월에 시작될 것이다'라는 문맥이므로 (D) commence(시작되다, 시작하다)가 정답이다. (A) specify는 '명시하다', (B) represent는 '나타내다', (C) intervene은 '개입하다'라는 의미이다.

해석 Greenfield 병원의 부속 건물의 건설은 필요한 모든 허가를 받은 후 3월에 시작될 것이다.

어휘 permit n. 허가(증), 면허 obtain v. 받다, 얻다

126 관계대명사 채우기

해설 이 문장은 주어(The Franklin Museum), 동사(curated), 목적어(a special exhibition)를 갖춘 완전한 절이므로, ___ ~ of the region은 수식어 거품으로 보아야 한다. 이 수식어 거품은 빈칸 앞의 명사(a special exhibition)를 선행사로 갖는 관계절이므로 관계대명사 (B)와 (D)가 정답의 후보이다. 빈칸 뒤의 명사(artifacts)를 꾸며주는 소유격 역할을 하는 것은 소유격 관계대명사이므로 (B) whose가 정답이다. (D) that은 주격 관계대명사 또는 목적격 관계대명사로, 뒤에 나오는 명사를 꾸밀 수 없고 콤마(,) 바로 뒤에 올 수 없다. 소유격 대명사 (A) its와 지시대명사 또는 지시형용사 (C) those는 관계절을 이끌 수 없다.

해석 Franklin 박물관은 특별 전시회를 기획했는데, 그것의 유물들은 그 지역의 문화유산을 보여준다.

어휘 exhibition n. 전시회, 진열 artifact n. 유물, 인공물
showcase v. 보여주다, 전시하다 heritage n. 유산

127 부사 어휘 고르기

해설 '소설의 줄거리 반전이 소셜 미디어에서 널리 논의되다'라는 문맥이므로 (C) widely(널리)가 정답이다. (A) distantly는 '멀리, 떨어져서', (B) extremely는 '극도로, 극히', (D) respectively는 '각자, 각각'이라는 의미이다.

해석 그 소설의 줄거리 반전은 소셜 미디어에서 널리 논의되었는데, 이는 매출의 극적인 상승으로 이어졌다.

어휘 plot n. 줄거리, 구성 twist n. 반전, 비틀기 dramatic adj. 극적인

128 사람명사와 사물/추상명사 구별하여 채우기

해설 빈칸은 형용사(eco-friendly)의 수식을 받는 명사 자리이므로 명사인 (A)와 (D)가 정답의 후보이다. 'Magana 기술사에 의한 친환경적인 발명품들'이라는 의미가 되어야 하므로 명사 invention(발명품)의 복수형 (A) inventions가 정답이다. (D) inventor(발명가)를 쓰면 'Magana 기술사에 의한 친환경적인 발명가'라는 어색한 의미를 만들기 때문에 답이 될 수 없다. 동사 또는 과거분사 (B)와 to 부정사 (C)는 형용사의 수식을 받는 명사 자리에 올 수 없다.

해석 우리의 기사는 지속 가능한 생활 습관을 촉진하도록 고안된 Magana 기술사에 의한 친환경적인 발명품들을 다룬다.

어휘 cover v. 다루다 eco-friendly adj. 친환경적인, 환경친화적인
facilitate v. 촉진하다 sustainable adj. 지속 가능한
practice n. 습관, 관행

129 형용사 어휘 고르기

해설 '소송의 잠재적 결과에 대한 편견 없는 조언을 하다'라는 문맥이므로 (B) impartial(편견 없는)이 정답이다. (A) spacious는 '넓찍한', (C) dependent는 '의존적인', (D) obedient는 '말을 잘 듣는'이라는 의미이다.

해석 법률 고문은 고객에게 소송의 잠재적 결과에 대한 편견 없는 조언을 했다.

어휘 legal adj. 법률의, 법률과 관련된 advisor n. 고문, 조언자
potential adj. 잠재적인, 가능성이 있는 outcome n. 결과
case n. 소송, 사례

130 부사 어휘 고르기

해설 '최신 소프트웨어 도구가 더 효과적으로 협업하도록 돕다'라는 문맥이므로 (C) effectively(효과적으로)가 정답이다. (A) sternly는 '엄격하게', (B) frankly는 '솔직히', (D) unexpectedly는 '예기치 못하게'라는 의미이다.

해석 Ace 시스템사의 최신 소프트웨어 도구는 직원들이 그들의 지리적인 위치에 상관없이 더 효과적으로 협업하도록 돕는다.

어휘 collaborate v. 협업하다, 협력하다 regardless of ~에 상관없이
geographic adj. 지리적인, 지리학의

PART 6

131-134번은 다음 구인 공고에 관한 문제입니다.

트럭 운전자들이 필요합니다

131현재, Velocity 물류사에서 상업용 면허와 깨끗한 운전 기록을 가진 정규직 트럭 운전자들을 찾고 있습니다. 지원자들은 고등학교 졸업장과 입증된 트럭 운전 경력을 가지고 있어야 합니다. 132비슷한 직책에서 최소 3년의 경력이 선호됩니다. 133담당할 일은 상품을 수송하고, 명시된 기한을 맞추기 위한 경로를 구상하고, 귀하의 차량에 대한 정기적인 정비 점검을 수행하는 것을 포함할 것입니다. 134또한, 지원자들은 화물을 싣고 내리는 것이 신체적으로 가능해야 합니다. 지원하시려면, 귀하의 이력서를 제목란에 "트럭 운전자 직책"이라고 기재하여 hr@velocitylogistics.com으로 보내주세요.

commercial adj. 상업용의, 상업적인 license n. 면허, 인가
diploma n. 졸업장, 수료증 specified adj. 명시된
maintenance n. 정비, 유지 physically adv. 신체적으로, 물리적으로
cargo n. 화물 apply v. 지원하다

131 올바른 시제의 동사 채우기

해설 현재를 나타내는 시간 표현(Currently)이 있으므로, 빈칸 뒤의 현재분사 seeking과 함께 현재진행 시제를 완성하는 (A) is가 정답이다.

132 알맞은 문장 고르기

해석 (A) 저희의 본사는 수월한 발송을 가능하게 하기 위해 중심부에 위치하고 있습니다.
(B) 산업 기준 및 규제는 변경될 수 있습니다.
(C) 비슷한 직책에서 최소 3년의 경력이 선호됩니다.
(D) 저희가 보유한 차량들의 모든 자동차들은 안전 기능을 갖추고 있습니다.

해설 앞 문장 'Candidates must have a high school diploma and proven truck driving experience.'에서 지원자들은 고등학교 졸업장과 입증된 트럭 운전 경력을 가지고 있어야 한다고 했으므로, 빈칸에는 지원자들의 자격 요건과 관련된 내용이 들어가야 함을 알 수 있다. 따라서 (C)가 정답이다.

어휘 headquarters n. 본사 enable v. 가능하게 하다
dispatch n. 발송, 파견 subject adj. ~될 수 있는
preferable adj. 선호되는, 더 좋은
fleet n. (한 기관이 소유한 비행기·버스 등의) 무리

133 형용사 자리 채우기

해설 빈칸 뒤의 복합 명사(maintenance checks)를 꾸밀 수 있는 것은 형용사이므로 형용사 (D) regular(정기적인)가 정답이다. 동사 (A), 부사 (B)는 명사를 꾸밀 수 없고, 명사 (C)는 복합 명사(maintenance checks)를 꾸밀 수 없다.

어휘 regularly adv. 정기적으로

134 접속부사 채우기 주변 문맥 파악

해설 빈칸이 콤마와 함께 문장의 맨 앞에 온 접속부사 자리이므로, 앞 문장과 빈칸이 있는 문장의 의미 관계를 파악하여 정답을 선택한다. 앞 문장에서 담당할 일은 상품을 수송하고, 명시된 기한을 맞추기 위한 경로를 구상하고, 차량에 대한 정비 점검을 수행하는 것을 포함한다고 했고, 빈칸이 있는 문장에서는 지원자들이 화물을 싣고 내리는 것이 신체적으로 가능해야 한다고 했으므로 앞에서 언급된 내용에 추가 정보를 덧붙일 때 사용되는 접속부사 (B) In addition(또한, 게다가)이 정답이다.

어휘 consequently adv. 그 결과, 따라서
otherwise adv. 그렇지 않으면, 달리

135-138번은 다음 기사에 관한 문제입니다.

스톡턴 (4월 5일) ― 135스톡턴의 요리 업계는 현대 영국 요리를 전문으로 하는 Savor의 개점과 함께 향상되었다. 136지난해 Diamond 요리 챌린지에서 우승한 것으로 잘 알려진, 요리사이자 소유주 Brian Dunn은 다양한 선호에 맞춘 메뉴를 고안해 왔다. 지금까지, 반응은 긍정적이다. 137현지 거주민들은 방문하게 되어 매우 기쁘다고 전해왔다. 138음식이 광범위하게 칭찬받았을 뿐만 아니라, 분위기 또한 찬사를 받고 있다. 부드러운 조명과 엄선된 미술품은 Savor를 친목

모임들을 위한 이상적인 장소로 만들고 있다.

culinary adj. 요리의, 음식의 specialize v. 전문으로 하다
cuisine n. 요리, 요리법 preference n. 선호, 기호
praise v. 칭찬하다 extensively adv. 광범위하게, 널리
admiration n. 찬사, 감탄 ideal adj. 이상적인 gathering n. 모임

135 관계대명사 채우기

해설 이 문장은 주어(Stockton's culinary landscape), 동사(got), 목적어(an upgrade)를 갖춘 완전한 절이므로, ____ ~ modern British cuisine은 수식어 거품으로 보아야 한다. 이 수식어 거품은 빈칸 앞의 명사(Savor)를 선행사로 갖는 관계절이므로 (B)와 (D)가 정답의 후보이다. 관계절에 주어가 없으므로 주격 관계대명사 (B) which가 정답이다. 관계부사 (D) where는 뒤에 완전한 절이 와야 하므로 답이 될 수 없다. 대명사 (A) it과 (C) anyone은 접속사 없이 두 개의 문장을 연결할 수 없다.

136 분사구문 채우기

해설 이 문장은 주어(Chef and owner Brian Dunn), 동사(has designed), 목적어(the menu)를 갖춘 완전한 절이므로, ____ ~ last year's Diamond Dish Challenge는 수식어 거품으로 보아야 한다. 보기 중 수식어 거품이 될 수 있는 것은 과거분사 (C)와 to 부정사 (D)이고, 빈칸 앞의 명사(Brian Dunn)를 '요리 챌린지에서 우승한 것으로 잘 알려진 Brian Dunn'이라는 수동의 의미로 수식하고 있으므로 과거분사 (C) known이 정답이다. 동사 (A)와 (B)는 수식어 거품을 이끌 수 없다.

137 알맞은 문장 고르기

해석 (A) 고객들은 웹사이트를 통해 피드백을 제출할 것이다.
(B) 현지 거주민들은 방문하게 되어 매우 기쁘다고 전해왔다.
(C) Mr. Dunn은 단 3점 차이로 대회에서 우승했다.
(D) 사적인 식사 공간은 요청에 따라 이용 가능하다.

해설 앞 문장 'So far, the response has been positive.'에서 지금까지 반응이 긍정적이라고 했으므로, 빈칸에는 긍정적인 반응과 관련된 내용이 들어가야 함을 알 수 있다. 따라서 (B)가 정답이다.

어휘 resident n. 거주민, 주민 thrilled adj. 매우 기쁜, 황홀한
competition n. (경연) 대회, 경쟁 private adj. 사적인, 사유의

138 명사 어휘 고르기 주변 문맥 파악

해설 '____ 또한 찬사를 받고 있다'라는 문맥이므로 모든 보기가 정답의 후보이다. 빈칸이 있는 문장만으로 정답을 고를 수 없으므로 주변 문맥이나 전체 문맥을 파악한다. 뒤 문장에서 '부드러운 조명과 엄선된 미술품은 Savor를 친목 모임들을 위한 이상적인 장소로 만들고 있다(The soft lighting and curated artwork make Savor an ideal setting for intimate gatherings).'고 했으므로 분위기가 찬사를 받고 있음을 알 수 있다. 따라서 (A) atmosphere(분위기)가 정답이다. (B) treatment는 '대우', (C) voyage는 '여행, 항해', (D) promotion은 '홍보 (활동)'라는 의미이다.

139-142번은 다음 이메일에 관한 문제입니다.

수신: Amy Phan <amyp123@silverspoonscafe.com>
발신: Charlie Carpenter <c_carpenter@acledadesigns.com>
날짜: 6월 16일
주제: 회신: 카페 보수 문의

Ms. Phan께,

[139]귀하의 사진들을 검토해 본 결과, 저희는 귀하가 요청하신 보수가 두 달의 시간 내에 완료될 수 있다고 결정했습니다. 가장 중요한 작업은 귀하의 좌석 공간을 개조하는 것으로 보입니다. [140]저희는 이를 위해 도급업자들과 함께 일을 해야 합니다. [141]그러나, 귀하의 규격이 모두 충족될 수 있도록 모든 세부 사항에 대해 세심한 배려가 기울여질 것이니 안심하세요. [142]공간을 확인하고 귀하를 직접 만나 프로젝트를 논의하기 위해, 저는 무료 상담을 마련하고 싶습니다. 제 방문 이후에 진행하지 않기로 결정하신다 할지라도, 귀하에게 어떤 비용도 청구되지 않을 것이라는 점을 알아주시기를 바랍니다. 귀하께서 언제 시간이 있는지 알려주세요.

Charlie Carpenter 드림, Acleda 설계사

renovation n. 보수, 개조 significant adj. 중요한, 의미 있는
revamp v. 개조하다 specification n. 규격, 사양
consultation n. 상담 proceed v. 진행하다 charge v. 청구하다

139 전치사 채우기

해설 명사절 접속사 that 뒤에 주어(your requested renovation)와 동사(can be completed)를 갖춘 완전한 절이 왔으므로, ____ a two-month time frame은 수식어 거품으로 보아야 한다. 이 수식어 거품은 동사가 없는 거품구이므로, 거품구를 이끌 수 있는 전치사 (C)와 (D)가 정답의 후보이다. '보수가 두 달의 시간 내에 완료될 수 있다'라는 의미가 되어야 하므로 '~이내에'라는 의미의 전치사 (C) within이 정답이다. (D) upon은 '~하는 즉시'라는 의미로 특정 시점을 나타내는 명사와 함께 쓰인다. 부사 (A) perhaps(아마도)와 대명사 또는 부사 (B) either(어느 하나; ~도 역시)는 수식어 거품구를 이끌 수 없다.

140 알맞은 문장 고르기

해석 (A) 저희는 이를 위해 도급업자들과 함께 일을 해야 할 것입니다.
(B) 귀하께서는 이 기간 동안 카페를 운영하실 수 있을 것입니다.
(C) 저는 귀하의 주방에 에너지 효율적인 가전제품들을 추천합니다.
(D) 실외 좌석 공간은 오직 날씨가 좋을 때만 개방됩니다.

해설 앞 문장 'It seems the most significant task will be revamping your seating area.'에서 가장 중요한 작업은 좌석 공간을 개조하는 것이라고 했으므로, 빈칸에는 공간을 개조하는 작업과 관련된 내용이 들어가야 함을 알 수 있다. 따라서 (A)가 정답이다. 참고로, (A)의 this가 revamping your seating area(좌석 공간을 개조하는 것)를 가리킨다.

어휘 contractor n. 도급업자, 계약자 operate v. 운영하다
energy-efficient adj. 에너지 효율적인, 연료 효율이 좋은

141 명사 자리 채우기

해설 동사(will be given) 앞 주어 자리에 올 수 있고, 형용사(careful)의 꾸밈을 받을 수 있는 것은 명사이므로 명사 (B) consideration(배려)이 정답이다. 동사 (A), 형용사 (C), 부사 (D)는 명사 자리에 올 수 없다.

142 형용사 어휘 고르기 주변 문맥 파악

해설 '____ 상담을 마련하고 싶다'라는 문맥이므로 (A), (B), (D)가 정답의 후보이다. 빈칸이 있는 문장만으로 정답을 고를 수 없으므로 주변 문맥이나 전체 문맥을 파악한다. 뒤 문장에서 '제 방문 이후에 진행하지 않기로 결정하신다 할지라도, 귀하에게 어떤 비용도 청구되지 않을 것이라는 점을 알아주시기를 바랍니다(Please note that even if you decide not to proceed after my visit, you won't be charged for anything).'라고 했으므로, 무료 상담을 마련하고 싶다는 것임을 알 수 있다. 따라서 (D) complimentary(무료의)가 정답이다. (A) comparable은 '비슷한, 비교할 만한', (B) spontaneous는 '즉흥의, 자발적인', (C) disruptive는 '지장을 주는'이라는 의미이다.

143-146번은 다음 이메일에 관한 문제입니다.

수신: 전 직원
발신: hr@mcconnellyinc.com
주제: Viviane Hurst의 승진
날짜: 2월 2일

여러분, 좋은 오후입니다.

저는 공유할 소식이 있습니다. Viviane Hurst가 마케팅 책임자 직책으로 승진하였고 뭄바이에 있는 우리의 새로운 사무실로 전근 갈 것입니다. ¹⁴³일단 그곳에 가면, 그녀는 새로운 동업자 관계를 구축하고 남아시아에서 우리의 시장 영향력을 높이는 업무를 맡게 될 것입니다. ¹⁴⁴Viviane이 이번 달 말에 떠날 것이기 때문에, Alexander Novak이 오늘부로 그녀의 현재 부책임자 직책을 인계받을 것입니다. ¹⁴⁵우리는 그가 팀에 귀중한 전문 지식을 제공해 줄 것이라고 확신합니다. 그는 Randolph & Associates에서 우리에게 오는 것인데, 그곳에서 그는 10년 이상 마케팅 전략가로 고용되어 있었습니다. ¹⁴⁶그를 환영하기 위해 모두가 회의실에서 모일 시간을 마련하겠습니다.

Linda Evans, 인사부 이사

share v. 공유하다, 함께 쓰다 **promote** v. 승진시키다, 홍보하다
task v. 업무를 맡기다 **presence** n. 영향력, 존재 **depart** v. 떠나다
take over ~을 인계받다 **current** adj. 현재의
employ v. 고용하다, 쓰다 **strategist** n. 전략가

143 접속부사 채우기 주변 문맥 파악

해설 빈칸이 콤마와 함께 문장의 맨 앞에 온 접속부사 자리이므로, 앞 문장과 빈칸이 있는 문장의 의미 관계를 파악하여 정답을 선택한다. 앞 문장에서 Viviane Hurst가 마케팅 책임자 직책으로 승진하여 뭄바이의 새로운 사무실로 전근 갈 것이라고 했고, 빈칸이 있는 문장에서는 그녀가 새로운 동업자 관계를 구축하고 남아시아에서 우리의 시장 영향력을 높이는 업무를 맡게 될 것이라고 했으므로, (A) Once there (일단 그곳에 가면)가 정답이다. 참고로, 여기서 Once there는 부사절 접속사 once 뒤에 부사 there가 있는 형태로, 시간을 나타내는 부사구이다. 부사구가 문장의 맨 앞에 위치하여 접속부사처럼 앞뒤 절의 의미를 연결할 수도 있다는 것을 알아두자.

어휘 **regardless** adv. 개의치 않고, 상관하지 않고
meanwhile adv. 그동안에, 한편

144 부사절 접속사 채우기

해설 이 문장은 필수성분(Alexander Novak will be ~ as of today)을 갖춘 완전한 절이므로 ____ ~ this month는 수식어 거품으로 보아야 한다. 이 수식어 거품은 동사(will be departing)가 있는 거품절이므로, 거품절을 이끌 수 있는 부사절 접속사 (A), (B), (D)가 정답의 후보이다. 'Viviane이 이번 달 말에 떠날 것이기 때문에, Alexander Novak이 오늘부로 그녀의 현재 부책임자 직책을 인계받을 것이다'라는 의미가 되어야 하므로, '~ 때문에'라는 의미의 부사절 접속사 (D) Because가 정답이다. (A) So that은 '~하기 위해서', (B) Whether는 '~이든 아니든'이라는 의미이다. 부사 (C) Afterward(나중에)는 거품절을 이끌 수 없다.

145 알맞은 문장 고르기

해석 (A) 남아시아로의 성공적인 확장은 전략적인 계획을 필요로 합니다.
(B) 송별 파티가 현재 그녀를 위해 준비되고 있습니다.
(C) 조직 내에서 지원자를 채용하는 것이 시간을 아낄 것입니다.
(D) 우리는 그가 팀에 귀중한 전문 지식을 제공해 줄 것이라고 확신합니다.

해설 뒤 문장 'He comes to us from Randolph & Associates, where he was employed as a marketing strategist for over a decade.'에서 그는 Randolph & Associates에서 오는데, 그곳에서 10년 이상 마케팅 전략가로 고용되어 있었다고 했으므로, 빈칸에는 Alexander Novak이 Viviane의 직책을 인계받게 된 이유와 관련된 내용이 들어가야 함을 알 수 있다. 따라서 (D)가 정답이다.

어휘 **valuable** adj. 귀중한, 가치가 큰 **expertise** n. 전문 지식

146 동사 어휘 고르기 주변 문맥 파악

해설 '모두가 회의실에서 ____ 할 시간을 마련하겠다'라는 문맥이므로 (C)와 (D)가 정답의 후보이다. 빈칸이 있는 문장만으로 정답을 고를 수 없으므로 주변 문맥이나 전체 문맥을 파악한다. 앞 문장에서 '그는 Randolph & Associates에서 우리에게 오는 것인데, 그곳에서 그는 10년 이상 마케팅 전략가로 고용되어 있었습니다(He comes to us from Randolph & Associates, where he was employed as a marketing strategist for over a decade).'라고 했으므로, 새로운 직원을 환영하기 위해 모두가 회의실에서 모일 시간을 마련하겠다는 문맥임을 알 수 있다. 따라서 (C) gather(모이다)가 정답이다. (A) notify는 '통지하다, 알리다', (B) instruct는 '지시하다', (D) stay는 '머무르다, 남다'라는 의미이다.

PART 7

147-148번은 다음 기사에 관한 문제입니다.

웨스트필드 (6월 24일) — 시의회 의원 Judith Owen은 Wilkinson로를 다시 포장하고 새로운 출구 경사로를 건설하는 계획에 대한 더 많은 세부 사항들을 제공했다. [147]지난주에 발표된 그 프로젝트는 8월 5일부터 20일까지 진행될 예정이며, 이 기간 동안 그 도로는 모든 차량 통행이 금지될 예정이다. Ms. Owen은 시기가 이상적이지 않다는 점을 인정했다. [148-(C)]Wilkinson로는 여름철 지역 주민들이 수영과 소풍을 즐기는 인기 있는 장소인 Kendra 호수로 가는 주요 경로이다. 그러나, 그녀는 [148-(B)]Aspen로를 이용해서도 호수에 도착할 수 있기 때문에 프로젝트가 더위를 식히려는 누구라도 크게 불편하지 않을 것이라고 강조했다.

Brett Evans 작성
Westfield Chronicle

council n. 의회   repave v. 다시 포장하다   ramp n. 경사로
traffic n. 통행, 교통   acknowledge v. 인정하다   ideal adj. 이상적인
primary adj. 주요한, 주된   inconvenience v. 불편하게 하다; n. 불편

147 목적 찾기 문제

해설   기사의 목적은 무엇인가?
(A) 지역 기업을 재정적으로 지원하는 프로젝트를 설명하기 위해
(B) 시의회 선거에의 참여를 장려하기 위해
(C) 다가오는 도로 폐쇄에 대한 정보를 제공하기 위해
(D) 새로운 수영 시설의 건설을 알리기 위해

해설   지문의 'The project ~ is scheduled to run from August 5 to 20, and the road will be closed to all vehicle traffic during this period.'에서 그 프로젝트(도로를 다시 포장하고 새로운 출구 경사로를 건설하는 것)는 8월 5일부터 20일까지 진행될 예정이며 이 기간 동안 도로는 모든 차량 통행이 금지될 예정이라고 했으므로 (C)가 정답이다.

어휘   financially adv. 재정적으로   participation n. 참여
election n. 선거   closure n. 폐쇄

Paraphrasing

the road will be closed to all vehicle traffic 도로는 모든 차량 통행이 금지될 예정이다 → an upcoming road closure 다가오는 도로 폐쇄

148 Not/True 문제

해설   Kendra 호수에 대해 사실인 것은?
(A) 8월 대부분 기간 동안 접근할 수 없을 것이다.
(B) 하나의 경로만 이용하여 접근될 수 있다.
(C) 주민들에게 인기 있는 휴양지이다.
(D) 공식 행사 장소로 선정되었다.

해설   지문의 'Wilkinson Drive is the primary route to Kendra Lake, a popular swimming and picnicking spot for locals in the summer.'에서 Kendra 호수가 여름철 지역 주민들이 수영과 소풍을 즐기는 인기 있는 장소라고 했으므로 (C)가 지문의 내용과 일치한다. 따라서 (C)가 정답이다. (A)와 (D)는 지문에 언급되지 않은 내용이다. (B)는 'the lake can also be reached by taking Aspen Lane'에서 Aspen로를 이용해서도 호수에 도착할 수 있다고 했으므로 지문의 내용과 일치하지 않는다.

어휘   inaccessible adj. 접근할 수 없는   recreation area 휴양지, 휴식처

149-150번은 다음 이메일에 관한 문제입니다.

수신: Nick Cohen <n.cohen@dailybloom.com>
발신: Cathy Garcia <c.garcia@linkmobile.com>
[149]날짜: 5월 3일
제목: 회신: 추가 로밍 요금

Mr. Cohen께,

[149]지난달 귀하의 일본 여행 동안 휴대폰 서비스 문제에 대한 귀하의 불만 사항에 대한 답변입니다. 귀하께서 5기가바이트 로밍 옵션에 가입하셨지만, 잘못하여 2기가바이트 로밍 옵션을 할당받으신 것으로 확인되었습니다. 그로 인해 이 한도를 초과했을 때 귀하의 계정에 추가 요금이 부과되었습니다.

이 오류에 대해 사과드립니다. 귀하의 청구서에 필요한 사항을 조정했으며, 불편에 대한 보상으로 다음에 해외에 가실 때 무료로 2기가바이트의 로밍 데이터를 제공받으실 것입니다. [150]이 혜택을 이용하시려면, 귀하의 계정에 로그인하고 로밍 서비스를 활성화할 때 프로모션 영역에 GX727364를 입력하시기만 하면 됩니다.

Cathy Garcia 드림
고객 서비스
Link 모바일사

charge n. 요금   complaint n. 불만
accidentally adv. 잘못하여, 뜻하지 않게   assign v. 할당하다
exceed v. 초과하다   limitation n. 한도, 제한
adjustment n. 조정, 수정   take advantage of ~을 이용하다
activate v. 활성화하다

149 추론 문제

해설   Mr. Cohen에 대해 암시되는 것은?
(A) Ms. Garcia로부터 휴대폰을 구입했다.
(B) 4월에 다른 나라로 여행을 갔다.
(C) 지난달에 휴대폰 계정을 업그레이드했다.
(D) 잘못된 로밍 옵션을 선택했다.

해설   지문의 'Date: May 3', 'This is a response to your complaint about the issue with your cell phone service during your trip to Japan last month.'에서 이메일을 쓴 날짜가 5월 3일이고, 지난달(4월) 귀하의 일본 여행 중 휴대폰 서비스 문제에 대한 불만 사항에 대한 답변이라고 했으므로 Mr. Cohen이 4월에 다른 나라로 여행을 갔다는 것을 추론할 수 있다. 따라서 (B)가 정답이다.

150 육하원칙 문제

해설   Mr. Cohen은 혜택을 이용하기 위해 무엇을 해야 하는가?
(A) 코드를 입력한다.
(B) 카드를 활성화한다.
(C) 번호로 전화한다.

(D) 이메일을 보낸다.

해설 지문의 'To take advantage of this offer, simply log in to your account and type GX727364 in the promotion field when you activate the roaming service.'에서 이 혜택을 이용하려면, 계정에 로그인하고 로밍 서비스를 활성화할 때 프로모션 영역에 GX727364를 입력하기만 하면 된다고 했으므로 (A)가 정답이다.

어휘 activate v. 활성화하다

Paraphrasing
take advantage of ~을 이용하다 → make use of ~을 이용하다

151-152번은 다음 온라인 채팅 대화문에 관한 문제입니다.

> Xiao Chang (오후 2시 10분)
> [151]우리 사무실 건물의 유지보수 관리자가 화요일 오후 7시부터 9시까지 전기가 차단될 거라고 방금 말했어요.
>
> Tara Morris (오후 2시 11분)
> 로비에 표지판이 붙어 있어요. [151]최근 점검 후 일부 수리를 해야 한다고 적혀 있어요. 하지만 저희에게는 영향을 미치지 않을 거예요. 회사의 모든 직원은 보통 6시까지 퇴근해요.
>
> Xiao Chang (오후 2시 12분)
> 사실, 저는 화요일 오후 8시에 홍콩에 있는 고객과 화상 회의가 있어요.
>
> Tara Morris (오후 2시 13분)
> 일정을 변경하는 게 가능할까요?
>
> Xiao Chang (오후 2시 14분)
> [152]월요일에 제 제안서를 이메일로 보내야 하는데, 고객이 그다음 날에 논의하고 싶어 해요. 그가 가능한 시간은 그때뿐이에요.
>
> Tara Morris (오후 2시 15분)
> 근처에 몇 시간 동안 회의실을 예약할 수 있는 코워킹 회사가 있어요. 전에 이용해 본 적이 있는데, 꽤 편리해요.

inspection n. 점검   reschedule v. 일정을 변경하다
coworking n. 코워킹(사무실을 공유하면서 독립적인 작업을 하는 형태)
convenient adj. 편리한

151 의도 파악 문제

해설 오후 2시 11분에, Ms. Morris가 "There is a sign posted in the lobby"라고 썼을 때, 그녀가 의도한 것은?
(A) Mr. Chang이 계획을 오해했다고 생각한다.
(B) 정책 변경에 대해 사전에 통지를 받았다.
(C) Mr. Chang이 알아야 할 문제를 발견했다.
(D) 이미 상황을 인지하고 있다.

해설 지문의 'Our office building's maintenance manager just told me that the electricity will be shut off from 7 to 9 P.M. on Tuesday.'에서 Xiao Chang이 우리 사무실 건물의 유지보수 관리자가 화요일 오후 7시부터 9시까지 전기가 차단될 거라고 방금 말했다고 하자, Ms. Morris가 'There is a sign posted in the lobby'(로비에 표지판이 붙어 있어요)라고 한 후, 'It says some repairs need to be done following a recent inspection.'에서 최근 점검 후 일부 수리를 해야 한다고 적혀 있다고 한 것을 통해, Ms. Morris가 이미 상황을 인지하고 있다는 것을 알 수 있다. 따라서 (D)가 정답이다.

어휘 misunderstand v. 오해하다, 잘못 해석하다   be aware of ~을 알다

152 육하원칙 문제

해설 월요일에 무슨 일이 일어날 것인가?
(A) 고객에게 문서가 제출될 것이다.
(B) 사무실에서 점검이 실시될 것이다.
(C) 비즈니스 회의를 위한 방이 마련될 것이다.
(D) 일부 장비에 대한 수리가 수행될 것이다.

해설 지문의 'I'm supposed to e-mail my proposal on Monday'에서 월요일에 제안서를 이메일로 보내야 한다고 했다. 따라서 (A)가 정답이다.

어휘 equipment n. 장비

Paraphrasing
e-mail ~ proposal 제안서를 이메일로 보내다 → A document ~ be submitted 문서가 제출되다

153-154번은 다음 광고에 관한 문제입니다.

> [153]몸매를 가꾸고 더 건강해지고 싶다면, 요가를 배움으로써 여정을 시작하는 게 어떠세요? 초보자를 고려하여 특별히 디자인된 Moon 요가 매트를 만나보세요.
>
> [154-(A)]기본 줄무늬부터 정교한 꽃무늬까지 다양한 디자인으로 제공되는 이 매트는 [154-(B)]전적으로 천연 코르크 소재로 제작되었습니다. [154-(D)]두꺼운 바닥에 부드러운 소재의 겹을 추가하여 보호해 줍니다. 그리고 일반적인 요가 매트보다 약간 더 길고 더 넓게 제작하여 편안하고 안전하게 어려운 요가 자세를 취할 수 있는 충분한 공간을 확보할 수 있습니다.
>
> 이 매트와 저희가 제공하는 다른 제품들에 대한 더 많은 정보를 위해서는 www.yogamood.com을 방문하세요.

get into shape 몸매를 가꾸다   take up ~을 배우다, ~을 시작하다
specifically adv. 특별히, 구체적으로
with ~ in mind ~을 고려하여, ~을 염두에 두고   elaborate adj. 정교한
floral adj. 꽃무늬의   entirely adv. 전적으로, 전부   protection n. 보호
slightly adv. 약간   comfortably adv. 편안하게

153 추론 문제

해설 누가 이 제품을 사용할 것 같은가?
(A) 여행 가는 것을 계획하고 있는 사람들
(B) 기존 건강 문제에 대해 우려하는 사람들
(C) 새로운 사업을 시작하는 사람들
(D) 신체적으로 건강해지는 것에 관심이 있는 사람들

해설 지문의 'If you are looking to get into shape and become healthier, why not start your journey by taking up yoga? Meet the Moon Yoga Mat—designed specifically with beginners in mind.'에서 몸매를 가꾸고 더 건강해지고 싶다면, 요가를 시작해 보라며, 초보자를 고려하여 특별히 디자인된 Moon 요가 매트를 만나보라고 했으므로 신체적으로 건강해지는 것에 관심이 있는 사람들이 이 제품을 사용할 것임을 추론할 수 있다. 따라서 (D)가 정답이다.

어휘 physically adv. 신체적으로

Paraphrasing
get into shape and become healthier 몸매를 가꾸고 더 건강해지다 → becoming physically fit 신체적으로 건강해지는 것

154 Not/True 문제

해석 제품의 특징으로 언급되지 않은 것은?
(A) 다양한 무늬
(B) 천연 재료
(C) 물이 스며들지 않음
(D) 추가 충전재

해설 (A)는 지문의 'Available in a range of designs, from basic stripes to more elaborate floral prints'에서 기본 줄무늬부터 정교한 꽃무늬까지 다양한 디자인으로 제공된다고 했으므로 지문의 내용과 일치한다. (B)는 'this mat is made entirely of natural cork'에서 이 매트가 전적으로 천연 코르크 소재로 제작되었다고 했으므로 지문의 내용과 일치한다. (D)는 'It has a thick base with an additional layer of soft material for your protection.'에서 두꺼운 바닥에 부드러운 소재의 겹을 추가하여 보호해 준다고 했으므로 지문의 내용과 일치한다. (C)는 지문에 언급되지 않은 내용이다. 따라서 (C)가 정답이다.

어휘 resistance n. 내성, 저항력 padding n. 충전재

Paraphrasing
a range of designs, from basic stripes to more elaborate floral prints 기본 줄무늬부터 정교한 꽃무늬까지 다양한 디자인 → Varied patterns 다양한 무늬
natural cork 천연 코르크 → Natural material 천연 재료
a thick base with an additional layer of soft material 부드러운 소재의 겹을 추가한 두꺼운 바닥 → Extra padding 추가 충전재

155-157번은 다음 이메일에 관한 문제입니다.

수신: Ahmed Khazim <a.khazim@ezmail.com>
발신: Mindy Samson <m.samson@portsidewindows.com>
날짜: 5월 10일
제목: 회신: 회신: 창문 교체

Mr. Khazim께,

[155]어제 귀하께 이메일로 보내드린 창문 교체 견적에 대한 귀하의 질문과 관련하여, 처음에 논의했던 것보다 약간 더 높은 것이 맞습니다. — [1] —. 두 가지 이유로 인해 가격을 인상할 수밖에 없었습니다. — [2] —. [157]저희는 귀하를 위한 맞춤형 창문을 만들어야 할 것입니다. 또 다른 요인은 [156]기술자에게 귀하의 의류 매장에 들어오는 오후 햇빛의 양을 줄이기 위해 색이 들어간 유리를 선호한다고 알려 주셨다는 것입니다. 이는 처음에 논의했던 일반 유리보다 비용이

더 많이 듭니다. — [3] —.

인상된 비용으로 인해 혼란스러우셨다면 사과드립니다. — [4] —. 프로젝트에 대해 직접 논의하고 싶으시다면, 기꺼이 만나 뵙겠습니다. 저에게 555-8876으로 연락하시면 시간을 정할 수 있습니다.

Mindy Samson 드림
Portside 창문 회사

replacement n. 교체 initially adv. 처음에
custom adj. 맞춤의, 주문된 tinted adj. 색이 들어간
confusion n. 혼란, 혼동 in person 직접

155 목적 찾기 문제

해석 이메일의 목적은 무엇인가?
(A) 제품에 대한 결제를 요청하기 위해
(B) 서비스 취소를 요구하기 위해
(C) 지연 이유를 제공하기 위해
(D) 견적 변경을 설명하기 위해

해설 지문의 'Regarding your question about the quote for the window replacement that I e-mailed you yesterday, you are correct that it is slightly higher than what we initially discussed. We were forced to increase the price for two reasons.'에서 어제 이메일로 보낸 창문 교체 견적에 대한 질문과 관련하여, 처음에 논의했던 것보다 약간 더 높은 것이 맞으며 두 가지 이유로 인해 가격을 인상할 수밖에 없었다고 했으므로 (D)가 정답이다.

어휘 demand v. 요구하다 cancellation n. 취소 estimate n. 견적

156 추론 문제

해석 Mr. Khazim은 누구일 것 같은가?
(A) 부동산 투자자
(B) 공무원
(C) 사업주
(D) 기술 자문 위원

해설 지문의 'you informed our technician you would prefer tinted glass to reduce the amount of afternoon sunlight entering your clothing shop'에서 Mr. Khazim이 기술자에게 자신의 의류 매장에 들어오는 오후 햇빛의 양을 줄이기 위해 색이 들어간 유리를 선호한다고 알려 주었다고 했으므로 Mr. Khazim이 의류 매장의 사업주임을 추론할 수 있다. 따라서 (C)가 정답이다.

어휘 property n. 부동산 investor n. 투자자

157 문장 위치 찾기 문제

해석 [1], [2], [3], [4]로 표시된 위치 중, 다음 문장이 들어갈 곳으로 가장 적절한 것은?

"우선, 저희 기술자는 귀하께서 교체하려는 창문이 표준 크기가 아니라는 것을 확인했습니다."

(A) [1]
(B) [2]
(C) [3]
(D) [4]

해설 주어진 문장은 교체하려는 창문의 크기와 관련된 내용 주변에 나올 것임을 예상할 수 있다. [2]의 뒤 문장인 'We will have to make a custom window for you.'에서 Mr. Khazim을 위한 맞춤형 창문을 만들어야 할 것이라고 했으므로, [2]에 주어진 문장이 들어가면 교체하려는 창문의 크기가 표준 크기가 아니기 때문에 Mr. Khazim을 위한 맞춤형 창문을 만들어야 할 것이라는 자연스러운 문맥이 된다는 것을 알 수 있다. 따라서 (B)가 정답이다.

어휘 identify v. 확인하다, 알아보다

158-160번은 다음 편지에 관한 문제입니다.

Amanda Morrison
731번지 Ward가
하트퍼드, 코네티컷주, 06106

8월 17일

Ms. Morrison께,

158-(C)Coleman 보안 회사에 가입해 주셔서 감사합니다. 158-(D)귀하의 새로 구입하신 주택을 보호하기 위한 중요한 첫걸음을 내디디셨습니다. 선택하신 베이직 패키지는 경보 시스템이 활성화될 경우 대응팀의 신속한 파견뿐만 아니라 24시간 경보 시스템 모니터링을 포함합니다. 159고객분들이 디럭스 패키지로 업그레이드하도록 권장하기 위한 특별한 할인 제공이 현재 있다는 것을 알려드리고 싶습니다. 귀하께서 살펴보실 수 있게 이에 대한 정보가 있는 브로슈어를 동봉하였습니다. 디럭스 패키지의 가장 큰 장점 중 하나는 보안 순찰대가 아침과 저녁에 귀하의 건물을 확인할 것이라는 점입니다. 장기간 집을 비우실 때는 순찰 방문 횟수를 늘릴 수 있습니다. 160디럭스 패키지는 일반적으로 한 달에 149달러입니다. 그러나, 9월 1일 이전에 가입하신다면, 현재 귀하의 1년 계약의 나머지 기간 동안 한 달에 119달러만 청구될 것입니다. 웹사이트(www.coleman.com/upgrade) 또는 555-0092로 저희의 고객 서비스 센터에 전화하여 신청하실 수 있습니다.

Brett Reynolds 드림
Coleman 보안 회사

safeguard v. 보호하다   dispatch n. 파견   enclose v. 동봉하다
patrol n. 순찰대   extended adj. 장기간에 걸친   period n. 기간
remainder n. 나머지

158 Not/True 문제

해석 Ms. Morrison에 대해 명시된 것은?
(A) 여러 부동산의 소유자이다.
(B) 8월 초에 Mr. Reynolds와 만났다.
(C) Coleman 보안 회사의 장기 고객이다.
(D) 최근에 현재 거주지를 구입했다.

해설 지문의 'You have taken an important first step to safeguard your newly purchased home.'에서 Ms. Morrison이 최근에 주택을 새로 구입했다는 것을 알 수 있으므로 (D)가 정답이다. (A)와 (B)는 지문에 언급되지 않은 내용이다. (C)는 'Thank you for signing up with Coleman Security.'에서 Coleman 보안 회사에 가입해 주어서 감사하다고 했으므로 지문의 내용과 일치하지 않는다.

어휘 residence n. 거주지, 주택

Paraphrasing

home 집, 주택 → residence 거주지

159 육하원칙 문제

해석 Ms. Morrison은 왜 문서를 읽어야 하는가?
(A) 조기 취소에 대한 위약금을 확인하기 위해
(B) 무료 서비스를 이해하는지 확인하기 위해
(C) 더 많은 특징이 있는 옵션에 대해 알아보기 위해
(D) 서로 다른 장치의 가격을 비교하기 위해

해설 지문의 'I want to inform you that we now have a special offer to encourage customers to upgrade to a Deluxe Package. I have enclosed a brochure with information about it for you to look through.'에서 고객들이 디럭스 패키지로 업그레이드하도록 권장하기 위한 특별한 할인 제공이 있고, 이에 대한 정보가 있는 브로슈어를 동봉하였다고 했으므로 (C)가 정답이다.

어휘 additional adj. 추가의   penalty n. 위약금, 벌금

Paraphrasing

brochure 브로슈어 → document 문서

160 육하원칙 문제

해석 Ms. Morrison은 어떻게 할인받을 자격을 갖출 수 있는가?
(A) 온라인 설문조사에 참여함으로써
(B) 다년간의 계약을 맺음으로써
(C) 마감일 전에 신청함으로써
(D) 월별 청구서를 미리 납부함으로써

해설 지문의 'The Deluxe Package normally costs $149 per month. However, if you sign up before September 1, you will only be charged $119 per month for the remainder of your current one-year contract.'에서 디럭스 패키지는 일반적으로 한 달에 149달러지만, 9월 1일 이전에 가입하면, 현재 1년 계약의 나머지 기간 동안 한 달에 119달러만 청구될 것이라고 했으므로 (C)가 정답이다.

어휘 multiyear adj. 다년간의   bill n. 청구서, 고지서

161-163번은 다음 후기에 관한 문제입니다.

Glide LX 후기
평가: ★★☆☆☆ (별 2개)

161저의 오래된 전기면도기가 고장 났을 때, 저는 Dolman사의 최신 제품인 Glide LX를 구입하기로 결정했습니다. 162저는 과거에 이 회사 제품에 대해 긍정적인 경험을 한 적이 있었기 때문에 구매에 대해 매우 신나 있었습니다. 안타깝게도, Glide LX는 제 기대에 미치지 못했습니다.

Glide LX는 면도가 매끄럽게 되지 않습니다. 제가 아무리 조심해도, 얼굴에 짧은 수염이 작게 남습니다. 또한, 세척하기가 매우

불편합니다. 모든 부품을 세척하려면 완전히 분해해야 하는데, 이것은 시간이 걸리는 과정입니다. ¹⁶³이 기기에 대해 제가 말할 수 있는 유일한 긍정적인 점은 매우 스타일리시해 보이고, 세련된 인체 공학적인 디자인을 가지고 있다는 것입니다. 하지만 Glide LX가 유사한 제품들보다 가격이 훨씬 더 비싸다는 점을 고려하면, 구매를 정당화하기에는 충분하지 않습니다.

— Michael Warren

electric shaver 전기면도기 expectation n. 기대
patch n. 부분, 얼룩 stubble n. 짧은 수염
disassemble v. 분해하다, 해체하다 component n. 부품
time-consuming adj. 시간이 걸리는 sleek adj. 세련된
ergonomic adj. 인체 공학적인 justify v. 정당화하다

161 육하원칙 문제

해석 Dolman은 어떤 종류의 회사인가?
(A) 스포츠용품 제조업체
(B) 가구 회사
(C) 차량 제조업체
(D) 전자제품 생산업체

해설 지문의 'When my old electric shaver broke, I decided to get Dolman's latest product, the Glide LX.'에서 오래된 전기면도기가 고장 났을 때, Dolman사의 최신 제품인 Glide LX를 구입하기로 결정했다고 했으므로 (D)가 정답이다.

Paraphrasing
electric shaver 전기면도기 → An electronics 전자제품

162 육하원칙 문제

해석 Mr. Warren은 왜 그 제품을 선택했는가?
(A) 프로모션 기간 동안 가격 할인을 제공받았다.
(B) 소비자 웹사이트에서 몇몇 긍정적인 피드백을 읽었다.
(C) 그 회사의 다른 상품에 만족했다.
(D) 지인의 추천을 받았다.

해설 지문의 'I was very excited about my purchase as I have had positive experiences with this company's products in the past.'에서 과거에 이 회사 제품에 대해 긍정적인 경험을 한 적이 있었기 때문에 구매에 대해 매우 신나 있었다고 했으므로 Mr. Warren이 회사의 다른 상품에 만족해서 그 제품(Glide LX 면도기)을 구매했다는 것을 알 수 있다. 따라서 (C)가 정답이다.

어휘 reduction n. 할인, 인하 consumer n. 소비자
merchandise n. 상품, 제품 acquaintance n. 지인

Paraphrasing
have had positive experiences with ~ ~에 대해 긍정적인 경험을 한 적이 있다 → was happy with ~ ~에 만족했다
company's products 회사 제품들 → merchandise from the company 회사의 상품

163 육하원칙 문제

해석 Mr. Warren은 제품의 어떤 측면에 만족하는가?
(A) 기능
(B) 편리함
(C) 외관
(D) 가격

해설 지문의 'The only positive thing I can say about this device is that it looks very stylish and has a sleek, ergonomic design.'에서 이 기기에 대해 말할 수 있는 유일한 긍정적인 점은 매우 스타일리시해 보이고, 세련된 인체 공학적인 디자인을 가지고 있다는 것이라고 했으므로 (C)가 정답이다.

어휘 function n. 기능 appearance n. 외관, 겉모습

164-167번은 다음 기사에 관한 문제입니다.

맨체스터 (10월 15일) — Continental 철도사의 대표 이사 Tina Nowak은 부다페스트와 뮌헨으로 가는 여러 편의 새로운 급행열차를 추가했으며 가까운 시일 내에 프라하와 같은 다른 중부 유럽 도시로 가는 것들도 추가할 계획이라고 공식적으로 확인해 주었다. — [1] —. ¹⁶⁴빈에 위치한 회사 본사에서 열린 기자 회견에서, Nowak은 이것이 이 지역에서 편리하면서도 환경친화적인 여행 옵션에 대한 수요의 증가에 대한 대응이라고 말했다. "¹⁶⁵저희는 여행객들에게 자동차에 대한 실행 가능한 대안을 제공하기 위해 최선을 다하고 있습니다."라고 그녀는 설명했다. — [2] —. "급행열차를 더 추가함으로써, 사람들이 운전할 필요 없이 가능한 한 빨리 목적지에 도착할 수 있도록 할 계획입니다."

같은 미디어 행사에서, Nowak은 여행객을 위한 Continental 철도사의 새로운 주간 패스권인 Travel Ease를 소개했다. — [3] —. 단 200유로에 방문객들은 연중 최대 7일 동안 Continental 철도를 통해 유럽 어디든 여행할 수 있다. ¹⁶⁶"12월 둘째 주에 Travel Ease를 출시하여 여행객들이 연휴에 이것을 이용할 수 있게 할 것입니다."라고 Nowak은 덧붙였다. 이 계획은 여행객들이 가장 좋아할 것이 되겠지만, ¹⁶⁷수익에 미칠 영향에 대한 우려가 있다. — [4] —. 그러나, Nowak은 이 사안에 대해 선택의 여지가 없었을 것이다. Continental Rail의 주요 경쟁사인 Eastern Railways가 8월에 비슷한 프로모션을 도입했고, 성공을 거두었다. Continental 철도사가 경쟁사의 성과에 필적할 수 있을지는 아직 미지수이다.

officially adv. 공식적으로 press conference 기자 회견
environmentally friendly 환경친화적인 alternative n. 대안
destination n. 목적지 via prep. ~을 통해 impact n. 영향
revenue n. 수익 matter n. 사안

164 육하원칙 문제

해석 Continental Rail은 어느 도시에 기반을 두고 있는가?
(A) 부다페스트
(B) 뮌헨
(C) 프라하
(D) 빈

해설 지문의 'During a press conference at the company's main office in Vienna'에서 빈에 위치한 회사 본사에서 기자 회견이 열렸

165 동의어 찾기 문제

해석 1문단 여섯 번째 줄의 단어 "viable"은 의미상 -와 가장 가깝다.
(A) 합리적인
(B) 실현 가능한
(C) 가격이 알맞은
(D) 귀중한

해설 viable을 포함한 구절 '"We are committed to providing travellers with viable alternatives to automobiles,"'에서 viable은 '실행 가능한'이라는 뜻으로 사용되었다. 따라서 (B)가 정답이다.

166 육하원칙 문제

해설 12월 둘째 주에 무슨 일이 일어날 것인가?
(A) 회사 임원이 기자 회견을 열 것이다.
(B) 새로운 노선이 발표될 것이다.
(C) 제품을 구매할 수 있게 될 것이다.
(D) 계절 할인이 적용되기 시작할 것이다.

해설 지문의 '"We are going to launch Travel Ease in the second week of December so that travellers will be able to take advantage of it during the holiday season,"'에서 12월 둘째 주에 Travel Ease를 출시하여 여행객들이 연휴에 이것을 이용할 수 있게 할 것이라고 했다. 따라서 (C)가 정답이다.

어휘 executive n. 임원, 이사 take effect 적용되다, 시행되다

Paraphrasing

launch 출시하다 → will become available for purchase 구매할 수 있게 될 것이다

167 문장 위치 찾기 문제

해설 [1], [2], [3], [4]로 표시된 위치 중, 다음 문장이 들어갈 곳으로 가장 적절한 것은?

"일부 주주들은 회사가 패스권을 통해 수익을 올릴 수 있을지에 대해 의문을 제기하기도 했다."

(A) [1]
(B) [2]
(C) [3]
(D) [4]

해설 주어진 문장은 회사의 수익에 대한 의견과 관련된 내용 주변에 나와야 함을 예상할 수 있다. [4]의 앞 문장인 'there is concern about its impact on revenue'에서 수익에 미칠 영향에 대한 우려가 있다고 했으므로, [4]에 주어진 문장이 들어가면 수익이 미칠 영향에 대해 우려가 있는데, 일부 주주들은 회사가 패스권을 통해 수익을 올릴 수 있을지에 대해 의문을 제기하기도 했다는 자연스러운 문맥이 된다는 것을 알 수 있다. 따라서 (D)가 정답이다.

어휘 shareholder n. 주주 question v. 의문을 제기하다

168-171번은 다음 안내문에 관한 문제입니다.

Summer Kids 프로그램의 일환으로 [169]8월 10일 토요일로 예정된 행사에 변경 사항이 있습니다. 원래 그날로 예약됐던 마술사가 더 이상 오실 수 없게 되었습니다. 하지만, 대신 [169]Jake Dobson의 교육 워크숍을 마련했습니다. [168]Mr. Dobson은 전직 야생동물 사진작가로 현재는 우리의 행성을 함께 공유하는 동물에 대한 지식을 전파하는 데 전념하고 있습니다. 그는 재미있고 유익한 연사이며, 갑작스러운 연락에도 그를 모시게 되어 행운입니다. [169]워크숍 동안, Mr. Dobson은 아이들을 가르칠 뿐만 아니라, [169]특별 선물로 그는 아이들이 도마뱀과 앵무새를 포함한 다양한 이국적인 동물을 만져볼 수 있게 할 것입니다.

[170]귀하의 자녀를 등록하시려면, 저희 웹사이트 www.madisonlibrary.com/summer를 방문하세요. 안내 데스크의 사서에게 이야기하셔도 됩니다. 이 행사는 오전 10시에 시작하여 약 2시간 동안 지속될 것입니다. [171-(B)]행사는 2층 어린이 센터에서 열릴 것입니다. 참가비는 없지만, 공간이 제한되어 있습니다. 따라서, 선착순 25명의 어린이만 등록될 것입니다. 빨리 등록하세요!

educational adj. 교육의 former adj. 이전의, 과거의
devote v. 전념하다 informative adj. 유익한 treat n. 선물, 특별한 것
handle v. 만지다, 다루다 exotic adj. 이국적인, 외래의
creature n. 동물 lizard n. 도마뱀 parrot n. 앵무새
librarian n. 사서 attendance n. 참가, 참석
first-come, first-served basis 선착순

168 추론 문제

해설 Mr. Dobson에 대해 추론될 수 있는 것은?
(A) 경력 전환을 경험했다.
(B) 다른 공연자와 협력했다.
(C) 현재 사진 스튜디오에 고용되어 있다.
(D) 다양한 주제에 대한 전문가이다.

해설 지문의 'Mr. Dobson is a former wildlife photographer who now devotes himself to spreading knowledge about the animals we share our planet with.'에서 Mr. Dobson은 전직 야생동물 사진작가로 현재는 우리의 행성을 함께 공유하는 동물에 대한 지식을 전파하는 데 전념하고 있다고 했으므로 Mr. Dobson이 경력 전환을 경험했다는 것을 추론할 수 있다. 따라서 (A)가 정답이다.

어휘 currently adv. 현재 expert n. 전문가

169 육하원칙 문제

해설 8월 10일에 열리는 행사의 특별한 점은 무엇인가?
(A) 유명한 야생동물 보호소로의 여행을 포함할 것이다.
(B) 마술 속임수를 수행하는 방법에 대한 교육이 있을 것이다.
(C) 여러 가지 살아있는 동물을 특별히 포함할 것이다.
(D) 한 명 이상의 초청 연사를 포함할 것이다.

해설 지문의 'for Saturday, August 10', 'we have arranged for an educational workshop by Jake Dobson', 'During his workshop, Mr. Dobson ~ as a special treat, he will also let them handle a variety of exotic creatures, including lizards and parrots'에서 8월 10일 토요일에 Jake Dobson의 워크숍을 준비했고, 워크숍 동안에 그는 특별 선물로 아이들이 도마뱀과 앵무

새를 포함한 다양한 이국적인 동물을 만져볼 수 있게 할 예정이라고 했으므로 (C)가 정답이다.

어휘 refuge n. 보호소, 피난처   an assortment of 여러 가지의

Paraphrasing

a variety of exotic creatures, including lizards and parrots
도마뱀과 앵무새를 포함한 다양한 이국적인 동물 → an assortment of live animals 여러 가지 살아있는 동물

170 육하원칙 문제

해석 행사는 어디에서 열릴 것인가?
(A) 초등학교에서
(B) 의료 센터에서
(C) 공립 도서관에서
(D) 과학 박물관에서

해설 지문의 'To register your child, visit our Web site at www.madisonlibrary.com/summer. You can also speak to a librarian at the front desk.'에서 자녀를 등록하려면 웹사이트를 방문하거나, 안내 데스크의 사서에게 이야기해도 된다고 했으므로 (C)가 정답이다.

171 Not/True 문제

해석 어린이 센터에 대해 사실인 것은?
(A) 수용 인원을 늘리기 위해 확장되었다.
(B) 건물의 2층에 위치해 있다.
(C) 여름에 운영 시간을 연장할 것이다.
(D) 매일 아침 2시간 동안 문을 닫는다.

해설 지문의 'It will be held in our second-floor children's center.'에서 행사는 2층 어린이 센터에서 열릴 것이고 했으므로 (B)는 지문의 내용과 일치한다. 따라서 (B)가 정답이다.

어휘 capacity n. 수용 인원, 용량   operation n. 운영

172-175번은 다음 문자 메시지 대화문에 관한 문제입니다.

> Carla Ewing [오전 9시 14분]
> 바쁘신가요, Liam? 한 가지 큰 부탁이 있어서요.
>
> Liam Davis [오전 9시 15분]
> 물론이죠. 필요한 것을 알려주세요. 저는 지금 막 아침 보고서를 끝냈고 시간이 조금 있어요.
>
> Carla Ewing [오전 9시 16분]
> 제가 오늘 아침에 Newman 금융사에서 저희 회사의 새로운 소프트웨어 애플리케이션 중 하나에 대해 영업 프레젠테이션을 할 예정이에요. ¹⁷²방금 이곳에 도착했는데, 몇 가지 중요한 도표를 PC에서 노트북으로 옮기는 것을 깜박한 것을 깨달았어요. 그것들을 제게 이메일로 보내주실 수 있나요?
>
> Liam Davis [오전 9시 18분]
> 물론이죠. ¹⁷³컴퓨터에 접속하려면 비밀번호를 입력해야 하나요?
>
> Carla Ewing [오전 9시 19분]
> 네. "Ewing2024"예요. 제 데스크톱에 Newman 금융사로 분류된

폴더가 보이실 거예요. 그 안에는 세 개의 파일이 있을 거예요. 그것들을 모두 보내주세요. 제가 특별히 오늘 발표를 위해 어젯밤에 그 파일들을 업데이트했거든요.

> Liam Davis [오전 9시 21분]
> 알겠어요. 제가 계약서 사본을 제출하기 위해 법무팀에 가는 중이어서요. ¹⁷⁴약 20분 후에 파일을 보내드릴게요.
>
> Carla Ewing [오전 9시 22분]
> 회의가 9시 30분에 시작돼요. 걱정하지 마세요. ¹⁷⁴/¹⁷⁵우리 팀원 중 다른 한 명에게 이것을 해 달라고 부탁할게요. ¹⁷⁵Sarah Fraser의 책상이 제 책상과 가까워요.
>
> Liam Davis [오전 9시 24분]
> 아, 서두르고 있는 줄 몰랐어요. 아직 엘리베이터를 타지 않아서, 제가 지금 할 수 있어요. 파일이 전송되면 알려드릴게요.

어휘 favor n. 부탁, 호의   transfer v. 옮기다   access v. 접속하다
label v. 분류하다   be in a rush 서두르다

172 목적 찾기 문제

해석 Ms. Ewing은 왜 메시지를 보내고 있는가?
(A) 사무실 위치에 대해 문의하기 위해
(B) 그녀의 노트북에 대한 기술 지원을 요청하기 위해
(C) 파일 몇 개를 그녀에게 보내 달라고 요청하기 위해
(D) 일부 소프트웨어가 업데이트된 것을 확인하기 위해

해설 지문의 'I just arrived here, and I realized I forgot to transfer some important charts from my PC to my laptop. Could you e-mail them to me?'에서 Ms. Ewing이 방금 프레젠테이션을 하는 장소에 도착했는데, 몇 가지 중요한 도표를 PC에서 노트북으로 옮기는 것을 깜박한 것을 깨달았다며, 그것들을 이메일로 보내 줄 수 있는지 묻고 있으므로 (C)가 정답이다.

어휘 technical adj. 기술의   assistance n. 지원

173 육하원칙 문제

해석 Mr. Davis는 무엇에 대해 묻는가?
(A) 도표가 왜 그렇게 중요하다고 여겨지는지
(B) 전자 기기에 어떻게 접속하는지
(C) 문서가 작업 공간 어디에 있는지
(D) 프레젠테이션이 언제 시작하기로 되어있는지

해설 지문의 'Do I need to enter a password to access your computer?'에서 Mr. Davis가 Ms. Ewing의 컴퓨터에 접속하려면 비밀번호를 입력해야 하는지 묻고 있으므로 (B)가 정답이다.

어휘 workspace n. 작업 공간

174 의도 파악 문제

해석 오전 9시 22분에, Ms. Ewing이 "The meeting starts at 9:30"라고 썼을 때, 그녀가 의도한 것 같은 것은?
(A) 늦은 도착 시간에 대해 걱정하고 있다.
(B) 근처에 주차 공간을 찾기를 바란다.
(C) 작업이 빨리 완료되어야 한다.
(D) 곧 사무실로 복귀할 것이다.

해설 지문의 'I'll send your files in about 20 minutes.'에서 Mr. Davis가 약 20분 후에 파일을 보내주겠다고 하자, Ms. Ewing이 'The meeting starts at 9:30'(회의가 9시 30분에 시작돼요)라고 한 후, 'I'll ask another one of our team members to do this.'에서 우리 팀원 중 다른 한 명에게 이것을 해 달라고 부탁하겠다는 것을 통해, Ms. Ewing의 작업이 빨리 완료되어야 한다는 것을 알 수 있다. 따라서 (C)가 정답이다.

175 추론 문제

해석 Ms. Ewing과 Ms. Fraser는 무슨 관계일 것 같은가?
(A) 팀원
(B) 친척
(C) 동업자
(D) 동창

해설 지문의 'I'll ask another one of our team members to do this. Sarah Fraser's desk is close to mine.'에서 팀원 중 한 명에게 이것을 해 달라고 부탁하겠다며, Sarah Fraser의 책상이 자신의 책상과 가깝다고 했으므로 Ms. Ewing과 Ms. Fraser는 팀원 사이임을 추론할 수 있다. 따라서 (A)가 정답이다.

어휘 relative n. 친척

176-180번은 다음 두 이메일에 관한 문제입니다.

수신: Mike Pollard <mpollard@pollardcatering.com>
발신: Aya Mori <a.mori@preston.com>
제목: 정보 요청
날짜: 11월 10일

Mr. Pollard께,

[176]저의 관리자가 15년의 근무를 마치고 그만두는 저희 법률 사무소의 선임 파트너를 위한 특별 점심 식사를 준비해 달라고 지시했습니다. 저의 지인 중 한 명이 귀사를 추천해서 연락드립니다. 귀사는 그녀의 부모님의 결혼 기념일 축하 행사에 음식을 제공해 주었고, 그녀는 음식의 우수함에 매우 만족해했습니다. 저희 회사의 행사는 Braxton 대로 345번지에 위치한 저희 사무실에서 열릴 것이며, 약 30명의 직원들이 참석할 것으로 예상합니다.

[177]병에 든 생수와 주스뿐만 아니라 모두를 위한 충분한 음식도 필요하며, 총예산은 750달러입니다. [178]제 요청 사항에 부응해 주실 수 있다면, 식사 선택지와 가격에 대한 정보를 보내주세요. [179]제가 금요일에 교외의 법률 콘퍼런스에 참석할 예정이어서 목요일까지 답변해 주시면 감사하겠습니다.

Aya Mori 드림
Preston 법률 서비스

senior adj. 선임의   cater v. 음식을 제공하다
acquaintance n. 지인, 아는 사람   sufficient adj. 충분한
budget n. 예산   out-of-town adj. 교외의, 도시 외곽의

수신: Aya Mori <a.mori@preston.com>
발신: Mike Pollard <mpollard@pollardcatering.com>
제목: 회신: 정보 요청
날짜: 11월 12일

Ms. Mori께,

제게 연락해 주셔서 감사합니다. 저희는 귀사가 준비하고 있는 것과 유사한 행사들에 정기적으로 음식을 제공하며 이용 가능한 다양한 선택지가 있습니다. 참고하실 수 있게 아래에 모든 선택지를 포함하였습니다:

선택지 A: 스시 롤(참치와 연어), 된장국
— 30인분 비용: 780달러(음료 미포함)

[177]선택지 B: 개별 피자, 치킨 윙 & 감자튀김
— [177]30인분 비용: 740달러(음료 포함)

선택지 C: 태국식 카레, 망고 찹쌀밥
— 30인분 비용: 775달러(음료 포함)

선택지 D: 샌드위치(고기 및 채식), 개별 샐러드
— 30인분 비용: 725달러(음료 미포함)

[180]또한 예약할 때 총가격의 50퍼센트를 지불해야 한다는 점에 유의하시기 바랍니다. 나머지는 행사 당일에 지불해야 합니다.

Mike Pollard 드림
소유주, Pollard 케이터링 회사

similar adj. 유사한, 비슷한   for one's reference 참고를 위하여
beverage n. 음료   remainder n. 나머지

176 육하원칙 문제

해석 Ms. Mori는 어떤 종류의 행사를 준비해 달라는 요청을 받는가?
(A) 기념일 축하 행사
(B) 퇴직 파티
(C) 기자 회견
(D) 시상식

해설 지문의 'My manager has instructed me to arrange a special lunch for a senior partner at my law firm who is leaving after 15 years of service.'에서 관리자가 15년의 근무를 마치고 그만두는 법률 사무소의 선임 파트너를 위한 특별 점심 식사를 준비해 달라고 부탁했다고 했으므로 (B)가 정답이다.

어휘 retirement n. 퇴직, 은퇴

177 추론 문제 연계

해석 Ms. Mori가 고를 것 같은 식사 선택지는 어떤 것인가?
(A) 선택지 A
(B) 선택지 B
(C) 선택지 C
(D) 선택지 D

해설 Ms. Mori가 작성한 첫 번째 이메일을 먼저 확인한다.
단서 1 첫 번째 이메일의 'We would like sufficient food for everyone, as well as bottled water and juice, and our total budget is $750.'에서 Ms. Mori가 병에 든 생수와 주스뿐만 아니라 모두를 위한 충분한 음식도 필요하며, 총예산은 750달러라고 했다. 그런데 식사 선택지가 어떤 것인지 제시되지 않았으므로 두 번째 이메일에서 관련 내용을 확인한다.
단서 2 두 번째 이메일의 'Option B', 'Cost for 30 people:

$740 (beverages included)'에서 선택지 B의 30인분 비용은 음료를 포함하여 740달러인 것을 확인할 수 있다.
두 단서를 종합할 때, Ms. Mori가 고를 것 같은 식사 선택지는 '선택지 B'임을 추론할 수 있다. 따라서 (B)가 정답이다.

178 동의어 찾기 문제

해석 첫 번째 이메일에서, 2문단 두 번째 줄의 단어 "accommodate"은 의미상 -와 가장 가깝다.
(A) 확인하다
(B) 개선하다
(C) 충족시키다
(D) 적응하다

해설 accommodate을 포함한 구절 'If you can accommodate my request, please send me some information about meal options and prices.'에서 accommodate은 '부응하다'의 뜻으로 사용되었다. 따라서 (C)가 정답이다.

179 육하원칙 문제

해석 Ms. Mori는 왜 금요일 전에 Mr. Pollard가 답변해 주기를 원하는가?
(A) 미리 샘플 음식을 받기를 바란다.
(B) 그녀의 관리자와 행사 일정을 확정해야 한다.
(C) 다른 케이터링 회사와 예약이 있다.
(D) 업계 관련 행사에 참석하기 위해 출장을 갈 것이다.

해설 첫 번째 이메일의 'I would appreciate it if you could reply by Thursday as I will be attending an out-of-town legal conference on Friday.'에서 Ms. Mori가 금요일에 교외의 법률 콘퍼런스에 참석할 예정이어서 목요일까지 답변해 주면 감사하겠다고 했으므로 (D)가 정답이다.

어휘 appointment n. 예약, 약속

Paraphrasing

an ~ legal conference 법률 콘퍼런스 → an industry-related event 업계 관련 행사

180 추론 문제

해석 Pollard 케이터링 회사에 대해 암시되는 것은?
(A) 모든 주문에 대해 무료 음료를 제공한다.
(B) 주로 기업 고객에게 서비스를 제공한다.
(C) 채식 선택지를 준비하는 데 추가 요금을 부과한다.
(D) 고객에게 착수금 지불을 요구한다.

해설 두 번째 이메일의 'Please also note that 50 percent of the total price must be paid at the time of booking. The remainder is due on the day of the event.'에서 예약할 때 총 가격의 50퍼센트를 지불해야 한다는 점에 유의하라며, 나머지는 행사 당일에 지불해야 한다고 했으므로 Pollard 케이터링 회사는 고객에게 착수금 지불을 요구한다는 것을 추론할 수 있다. 따라서 (D)가 정답이다.

어휘 complimentary adj. 무료의 corporate adj. 기업의
deposit n. 착수금, 보증금

181-185번은 다음 광고와 후기에 관한 문제입니다.

한정된 예산의 여행객들에게 안성맞춤!

Green Turtle Backpacker's 호스텔은 깨끗하지만 저렴한 숙박시설을 제공합니다. 저희는 Hereford의 교통 중심지에서 가까운 거리에 있을 뿐만 아니라 인기 관광지인 Sheffield와 Wiltshire와 가까운 [181]Westport 시내에 편리하게 위치해 있습니다.

[182-(A)/(B)/(C)]저희는 무제한 와이파이, 공항 셔틀버스 이용, 그리고 세탁시설 이용을 포함하여 다양한 서비스를 추가 비용 없이 숙박객들에게 제공합니다. [182-(D)]또한 매우 합리적인 요금으로 현장 주차가 가능합니다. 하지만 이곳에 머무는 것의 가장 좋은 점은 만나는 사람들과 즐거운 시간을 보내는 것입니다. 저희는 모두를 친밀하게 만들기 위해 정기적인 저녁 활동을 진행합니다:

- 월요일: 영화 (무료 팝콘 포함)
- 수요일: 보드게임
- [183]목요일: 노래방 (최고의 가수에게 주어지는 상품 포함)
- 토요일: 예술 및 공예

호스텔에 대한 더 많은 세부 사항과 예약을 하기 위해서는 www.gtbhostel.com을 확인하세요!

on a budget 한정된 예산으로 accommodation n. 숙박 시설
sightseeing n. 관광 laundry n. 세탁 on-site adj. 현장의
reasonable adj. 합리적인 rate n. 요금 craft n. 공예

[184]대학 친구와 저는 여름 방학 동안 하이킹을 하고 싶었습니다. Green Turtle Backpacker's 호스텔이 등산로 중 한 곳과 가까워서, 하룻밤 동안 거기에 머물기로 결정했습니다. [183]안타깝게도, 저녁에 노래하는 투숙객들의 시끄러운 소리 때문에 좋지 않은 경험을 했습니다. 정기적인 행사인 것 같은데, 체크인할 때 아무도 이것에 대해 알려주지 않았습니다. 다시는 이 시설에 머물지는 않겠지만, [185]직원들이 얼마나 도움이 되었는지 매우 감명받았다는 점을 말씀드리고 싶습니다. 안내 데스크 직원이 저희를 위층에 있는 기숙사 방으로 옮겨 주었고 무료 귀마개를 제공해 주었습니다. 그리고 아침에 직원 중 한 명이 택시를 예약해 주고 저희가 가방을 밖으로 나르는 것을 도와주었습니다. 호텔에서는 이런 일을 예상하겠지만, 호스텔에서는 뜻밖의 일이었습니다.

8월 25일에 Daryl Roberts 작성

trail n. 등산로, 둘레길 racket n. 시끄러운 소리, 소음
clerk n. 직원, 점원 dorm n. 기숙사

181 육하원칙 문제

해석 호스텔은 어디에 위치해 있는가?
(A) Westport
(B) Sheffield
(C) Wiltshire
(D) Hereford

해설 광고의 'We are conveniently situated in downtown Westport'에서 Westport 시내에 편리하게 위치해 있다고 했으므로 (A)가 정답이다.

182 Not/True 문제

해석 투숙객들이 추가 요금 없이 할 수 있는 것으로 언급되지 않은 것은?
(A) 인터넷에 접속한다.
(B) 공항까지 이동한다.
(C) 옷을 세탁한다.
(D) 차량을 주차한다.

해설 (A), (B), (C)는 광고의 'We provide a variety of services to guests at no extra charge, including unlimited Wi-Fi, use of our airport shuttle bus, and access to our laundry facilities.'에서 무료한 와이파이, 공항 셔틀버스 이용, 그리고 세탁 시설 이용을 포함하여 다양한 서비스를 추가 비용 없이 투숙객들에게 제공한다고 언급되어 있다. (D)는 'We also have on-site parking at very reasonable rates.'에서 매우 합리적인 요금으로 현장 주차가 가능하다고 했으므로 차량을 주차하기 위해서는 추가 요금을 내야 한다는 것을 알 수 있다. 따라서 (D)가 정답이다.

183 육하원칙 문제 연계

해석 Mr. Roberts는 어느 날 밤에 호스텔에 머물렀는가?
(A) 월요일
(B) 수요일
(C) 목요일
(D) 토요일

해설 Mr. Roberts가 작성한 후기를 먼저 확인한다.
단서 1 후기의 'Unfortunately, we had a bad experience because of the racket from the guests singing in the evening. I guess it is a regular event, but nobody told us about it when we checked in.'에서 저녁에 노래하는 투숙객들의 시끄러운 소리 때문에 좋지 않은 경험을 했다고 하면서, 정기적인 행사인 것 같은데 체크인할 때 아무도 이것에 대해 알려주지 않았다고 했다. 그런데 노래하는 행사가 어떤 요일에 진행되는지 제시되지 않았으므로 광고에서 관련 내용을 확인한다.
단서 2 광고의 'Thursdays: Karaoke (with prizes for the best singers)'에서 목요일에 노래방 행사가 있다는 것을 확인할 수 있다.
두 단서를 종합할 때, Mr. Roberts는 목요일 밤에 호스텔에 머물렀음을 알 수 있다. 따라서 (C)가 정답이다.

184 육하원칙 문제

해석 Mr. Roberts의 여행 목적은 무엇이었는가?
(A) 한 회사에 여름 일자리에 지원하고 있었다.
(B) 대학 캠퍼스를 둘러보려고 했었다.
(C) 친구와 함께 자연에서 시간을 보낼 계획이었다.
(D) 학생들을 위한 특별 프로그램에 참석하고 있었다.

해설 후기의 'My university friend and I wanted to do some hiking during our summer vacation. As the Green Turtle Backpacker's Hostel is close to one of the trails'에서 Mr. Roberts가 대학 친구와 여름 방학 동안 하이킹을 하고 싶었고 Green Turtle Backpacker's 호스텔이 등산로 중 한 곳과 가까웠다고 했으므로 (C)가 정답이다.

185 육하원칙 문제

해석 Mr. Roberts가 감명받았다고 언급한 것은 무엇인가?
(A) 고객 서비스의 품질
(B) 숙박 시설의 크기
(C) 체크인 절차의 속도
(D) 기숙사 방의 깨끗함

해설 후기의 'I want to mention that I was very impressed with how helpful the staff members were'에서 Mr. Roberts가 직원들이 얼마나 도움이 되었는지 매우 감명받았다는 점을 말하고 싶다고 했으므로 (A)가 정답이다.

어휘 cleanliness n. 깨끗함

Paraphrasing

how helpful the staff members were 직원들이 얼마나 도움이 되었는지 → The quality of the customer service 고객 서비스의 품질

186-190번은 다음 두 이메일과 영수증에 관한 문제입니다.

수신: Pearson Building Supplies <customerservice@pearson.com>
발신: Greg Wallace <g.wallace@aceconstruction.com>
제목: 후속 조치
날짜: 5월 12일

관계자분께,

저는 보수 프로젝트에 필요한 몇 가지 건축 자재를 5월 8일에 주문했습니다(#82737). ¹⁸⁶총 금액이 신용카드로 청구되었지만, 아직 이메일로 영수증을 받지 못했습니다. 회사 기록용으로 필요하니 최대한 빨리 보내주세요. 또한, ¹⁸⁹귀사의 매장에 Wilson 드라이버 재고가 언제 다시 입고되는지 궁금합니다. 몇 개를 구매하려고 했는데, 더 이상 귀사의 웹사이트에 기재되어 있지 않습니다.

감사합니다.

Greg Wallace 드림
Ace 건설사

follow-up n. 후속 조치 building supplies 건축 자재
screwdriver n. 드라이버 stock n. 재고

수신: Greg Wallace <g.wallace@aceconstruction.com>
발신: Pearson Building Supplies <customerservice@pearson.com>
제목: 회신: 후속 조치
날짜: 5월 12일

Mr. Wallace께,

제가 방금 귀하의 계정에 접속했는데, 시스템에서 자동으로 영수증을 발급하지 않은 것 같습니다. 이 오류에 대해 사과드립니다. ¹⁸⁷저희는 주문을 처리하는 데 사용되는 애플리케이션의 새 버전을 지난주에 설치했는데, 몇몇 버그가 있는 것 같습니다. 몇 분 전에 영수증이 포함된 이메일을 받으셨어야 합니다. 받으셨는지 확인해 주세요.

¹⁸⁸귀하의 계정 정보를 살펴보던 중, 총 60달러를 지출하신 제품이 거의 매주 받으시는 제품이라는 것을 우연히 알게 되었습니다. 대량 주문에 대한 10퍼센트 할인을 받을 수 있도록 한 달에 한 번

구매하는 것을 고려해 보실 수 있습니다. 또한, [189]귀하의 질문에 답변하기 위해 필요한 정보를 제 관리자인 Neal Sutter에게 요청했습니다. 그에게 답변을 받으면 알려드리겠습니다.

Saba Ali 드림
고객 서비스 직원
Pearson 건설용품사

automatically adv. 자동으로 happen to 우연히 ~하다
bulk order 대량 주문

Pearson 건설용품사

날짜: 5월 8일
주문 번호: 82737

제품	단가	수량	가격
Apex 페인트	캔당 60달러	3	180달러
[188]Millhouse 사포	롤당 20달러	3	[188]60달러
Damien 석고	버킷당 50달러	1	50달러
Fuller 주방 타일	각 20달러	15	300달러
		할인	해당 없음
		총액	590달러

[190-(D)]저희가 서비스를 개선하는 데 도움이 될 수 있도록 고객 만족도 설문지를 작성하여 제출해 주시기 바랍니다. 양식은 웹사이트에서 이용하실 수 있습니다. 이 유용한 피드백에 감사를 표하기 위해, 참여하시는 모든 고객님들은 25달러 기프트 카드를 받으실 것입니다!

unit cost 단가 sandpaper n. 사포 plaster n. 석고, 회반죽
fill out ~을 작성하다 satisfaction n. 만족 appreciation n. 감사

186 목적 찾기 문제

해석 Mr. Wallace는 왜 이메일을 보냈는가?
(A) 카드에 잘못된 금액이 청구되었다.
(B) 주문이 충분하게 신속하게 처리되지 않았다.
(C) 배송이 잘못된 주소로 보내졌다.
(D) 거래 기록을 받지 못했다.

해설 Mr. Wallace가 작성한 첫 번째 이메일의 'The total amount has been charged to my credit card, but I have not received a receipt by e-mail yet. Please send it as soon as possible as I need it for my company records.'에서 Mr. Wallace가 총 금액이 신용카드로 청구되었지만 아직 이메일로 영수증을 받지 못했으며 회사 기록용으로 필요하니 최대한 빨리 보내달라고 했으므로 (D)가 정답이다.

어휘 transaction n. 거래

Paraphrasing
receipt 영수증 → transaction record 거래 기록

187 육하원칙 문제

해석 두 번째 이메일에 따르면, 최근 Pearson 건설용품사에서 무슨 일이 있었는가?
(A) 모바일 애플리케이션이 출시되었다.
(B) 정책이 변경되었다.
(C) 소프트웨어 프로그램이 업데이트되었다.
(D) 매장 지점이 개조되었다.

해설 두 번째 이메일의 'we[Pearson Building Supplies] installed a new version of the application used to process orders last week, and it would seem that there are some bugs'에서 주문을 처리하는 데 사용되는 애플리케이션의 새 버전을 지난주에 설치했는데 몇몇 버그가 있는 것 같다고 했으므로 (C)가 정답이다.

어휘 launch v. 출시하다, 시작하다

Paraphrasing
installed a new version of the application 애플리케이션의 새 버전을 설치했다 → A software program was updated. 소프트웨어 프로그램이 업데이트되었다.

188 육하원칙 문제 연계

해석 Ms. Ali는 어떤 품목을 주 단위가 아닌 월 단위로 주문할 것을 제안하는가?
(A) Apex 페인트
(B) Millhouse 사포
(C) Damien 석고
(D) Fuller 주방 타일

해설 Ms. Ali가 작성한 두 번째 이메일을 먼저 확인한다.
단서 1 두 번째 이메일의 'When I was looking at your[Mr. Wallace] account information, I happened to notice that the product on which you spent $60 in total is one that you get almost every week. You may want to consider buying it once a month so that you can qualify for our 10 percent discount on bulk orders.'에서 Mr. Wallace의 계정 정보를 살펴보던 중 총 60달러를 지출한 제품이 거의 매주 받는 제품이라는 것을 우연히 알게 되었는데, 대량 주문에 대한 10퍼센트 할인을 받을 수 있도록 한 달에 한 번 구매하는 것을 고려해 볼 수 있다고 했다. 그런데 Mr. Wallace가 총 60달러를 지출한 제품이 무엇인지 제시되지 않았으므로 영수증에서 관련 내용을 확인한다.
단서 2 영수증의 'Millhouse Sandpaper', '$60.00'에서 총 60달러를 지출한 제품이 Millhouse 사포인 것을 알 수 있다.
두 단서를 종합할 때, Ms. Ali가 월 단위로 주문할 것을 제안하는 품목은 Millhouse 사포임을 알 수 있다. 따라서 (B)가 정답이다.

189 육하원칙 문제 연계

해석 Ms. Ali는 Mr. Sutter에게 무엇에 대해 물었는가?
(A) 도구 제조업체의 이름
(B) 회사 제품의 이용 가능성
(C) 재무 기록의 정확성
(D) 컴퓨터 시스템의 장점

해설 Ms. Ali가 작성한 두 번째 이메일을 먼저 확인한다.
단서 1 두 번째 이메일의 'I have asked my manager, Neal Sutter, for the information I need to answer your [Mr. Wallace] question.'에서 Mr. Wallace의 질문에 답변하기 위해 필요한 정보를 관리자인 Neal Sutter에게 요청했다고 했다. 그런데 Mr. Wallace의 질문이 무엇인지 제시되지 않았으므로 첫 번째

이메일에서 관련 내용을 확인한다.

단서 2 첫 번째 이메일의 'I was wondering when your store will have Wilson screwdrivers back in stock'에서 Mr. Wallace는 매장에 Wilson 드라이버 재고가 언제 다시 입고되는지 묻고 있다.

두 단서를 종합할 때, Ms. Ali가 Mr. Sutter에게 회사 제품의 이용 가능성에 대해 물었음을 알 수 있다. 따라서 (B)가 정답이다.

어휘 manufacturer n. 제조업체 availability n. 이용 가능성 accuracy n. 정확(성)

190 Not/True 문제

해석 Pearson 건설용품사에 대해 명시된 것은?
(A) 일시적으로 모든 제품의 가격을 인하했다.
(B) 최소 구매 시 기프트 카드를 제공한다.
(C) 웹사이트를 통해서만 주문을 받는다.
(D) 고객 설문조사를 진행 중이다.

해설 영수증의 'We encourage you to fill out and submit a customer satisfaction questionnaire to help us improve our service.'에서 서비스를 개선하는 데 도움이 될 수 있도록 고객 만족도 설문지를 작성하여 제출해 달라고 했으므로 (D)는 지문의 내용과 일치한다. 따라서 (D)가 정답이다. (A), (B), (C)는 지문에 언급되지 않은 내용이다.

어휘 temporarily adv. 일시적으로, 임시로

191-195번은 다음 웹페이지, 일정, 추천 글에 관한 문제입니다.

| 소개 | 서비스 | 비용 | 연락처 |

Brentwood 클리닝사는 포틀랜드 대도시 지역에 위치한 상업 기업들에 30년 이상 훌륭한 서비스를 제공해 왔습니다. 당신이 어떤 유형의 사업체를 운영하든, 저희는 당신이 당신의 고객에게 깨끗하고 위생적인 환경을 제공할 수 있도록 보장합니다. 저희의 숙련된 직원들은 당신의 기대에 부응하기 위해 많은 노력을 기울일 것입니다.

저희는 친환경 기업이라는 자부심이 큰 만큼 오직 Greenwash(지속 가능한 포장 및 동물 실험을 하지 않음)와 ¹⁹⁴Ecoclean(100퍼센트 자연분해성이고 인조 성분 없음) 브랜드의 청소용품만 사용합니다. 저희의 목표는 당신의 직장을 티끌 하나 없이 만드는 동시에 환경을 보호하는 것입니다!

당신의 사업체의 개점을 위해 준비하는 것과 같은 일회성 업무가 있거나, 건물을 깨끗하게 유지하기 위해 정기적인 청소 서비스를 예약하고 싶으시다면 저희가 도와드릴 수 있습니다. 오늘 555-0393으로 전화하여 저희의 담당자 중 한 명과 상담하세요. ¹⁹¹⁻⁽ᴰ⁾매일 또는 매주 방문을 잡으시는 고객을 위한 할인된 수수료에 대해 꼭 문의하세요!

commercial adj. 상업의 enterprise n. 기업 run v. 운영하다
sanitary adj. 위생적인 exclusively adv. 오로지 ~만
spotless adj. 티끌 하나 없는 premises n. 건물, 토지

Brentwood 클리닝사
5월 15일 일정

고객	위치	요청된 서비스
Willis 약국	Broad가 14번지	선반과 카운터 먼지 털기
¹⁹²Ruben 그래픽 디자인사	2번가 23번지	¹⁹²보수 공사 후 일반 청소
Kline 출판사	¹⁹³Clover로 67번지	¹⁹³접수 구역 카펫 청소
Motis 사무용품점	Sawyer로 56번지	로비 바닥 대걸레질 및 왁스 칠

- 각 장소에 도착하면, 현장 연락 담당자에게 알리고 작업을 완료한 후에는 완료 서명을 받으세요.
- 전문적인 행동을 유지하고 모든 장소에서 회사 유니폼을 착용하세요.

pharmacy n. 약국 dust v. 먼지를 털다 mop v. 대걸레로 닦다

5월 16일-제가 수년간 이용해 온 청소업체가 문을 닫으면서 Brentwood 클리닝사에 기회를 주기로 결심했습니다. ¹⁹³그 회사에서 저희의 카펫을 훌륭하게 청소해 주었기 때문에 제가 그 선택을 한 것이 기쁩니다. 다르게 했으면 싶었던 일은 생각나지 않습니다. ¹⁹⁴심지어 직원들이 사용했던 Ecoclean 세제도 다른 대부분의 세제 같은 강한 냄새가 나지 않아 인상적이었습니다. 게다가 ¹⁹⁵⁻⁽ᴰ⁾직원들의 팀장은 매우 전문적이었습니다. 제가 오후 2시 30분에 고객 미팅 일정을 실수로 잡았다고 말하자, 원래 오후 3시에 완료하기로 되어 있었는데도 불구하고 그 전에 작업이 확실히 완료되도록 했습니다. 저는 앞으로 Brentwood 클리닝사를 꼭 이용할 계획입니다.

- Elena Taylor

janitorial adj. 청소의 detergent n. 세제

191 Not/True 문제

해석 Brentwood 클리닝사에 대해 명시된 것은?
(A) 주거용 건물들을 청소하는 것을 전문으로 한다.
(B) 몇몇 서비스의 비용을 인상했다.
(C) 여러 도시에 지점을 열었다.
(D) 다시 찾는 고객들을 위한 할인을 제공한다.

해설 웹페이지의 'Make sure to ask about our reduced fees for clients who schedule daily or weekly visits!'에서 매일 또는 매주 방문을 잡는 고객을 위한 할인된 수수료에 대해 꼭 문의하라고 했으므로 다시 방문을 잡는 고객들에게 할인이 제공된다는 것을 알 수 있다. 따라서 (D)가 정답이다.

어휘 residential adj. 주거의 repeat customer 다시 찾는 고객

Paraphrasing

clients who schedule daily or weekly visits 매일 또는 매주 방문을 잡는 고객 → repeat customer 다시 찾는 고객

192 육하원칙 문제

해석 일정표에 따르면, 어떤 사업체가 최근에 개조를 했는가?

(A) Willis 약국
(B) Ruben 그래픽 디자인사
(C) Kline 출판사
(D) Motis 사무용품점

해설 일정표의 'Requested Service'에서 Ruben 그래픽 디자인사가 요청한 서비스가 'General cleanup after renovations'로, 보수 공사 후 일반 청소를 요청했음을 알 수 있다. 따라서 (B)가 정답이다.

Paraphrasing

renovations 보수 공사 → remodeling 개조

193 육하원칙 문제 연계

해설 Ms. Taylor의 사업체는 어디에 위치해 있는가?
(A) Broad가 14번지에
(B) 2번가 23번지에
(C) Clover로 67번지에
(D) Sawyer로 56번지에

해설 Ms. Taylor가 작성한 추천 글을 먼저 확인한다.
단서 1 추천 글의 'I'm glad I did because the company did an excellent job of getting my carpets clean.'에서 우리 회사의 카펫을 청소해 주었다고 했다. 그런데 카펫 청소를 요청한 업체가 제시되지 않았으므로 일정표에서 관련 내용을 확인한다.
단서 2 일정표의 'Requested Service'의 'Clean carpets in reception area'에서 접수 구역의 카펫을 청소해 달라고 요청한 업체는 Kline 출판사임을 알 수 있다.
두 단서를 종합할 때, 카펫 청소를 요청한 Kline 출판사가 위치한 곳은 Clover로 67번지임을 알 수 있으므로 (C)가 정답이다.

194 추론 문제 연계

해설 Ms. Taylor의 직장에 사용된 세제에 대해 사실일 것 같은 것은?
(A) 다른 많은 브랜드들보다 더 비싸다.
(B) 동물에게 실험을 하지 않고 만들어진다.
(C) 천연 물질만 포함한다.
(D) 꽃향기를 발생시키도록 고안되었다.

해설 Ms. Taylor가 작성한 추천 글을 먼저 확인한다.
단서 1 추천 글의 'Even the Ecoclean detergent the workers used impressed me because it did not have a strong smell like most other cleaning agents.'에서 심지어 직원들이 사용한 Ecoclean 세제도 다른 대부분의 세제 같은 강한 냄새가 나지 않아 인상적이었다고 했다. 그런데 이 세제의 특징이 제시되지 않았으므로 웹페이지에서 Ecoclean 세제 관련 내용을 확인한다.
단서 2 웹페이지의 'Ecoclean (100 percent biodegradable and no synthetic ingredients)'에서 Ecoclean 청소용품은 100 퍼센트 자연분해성이고 인조 성분이 없다고 했다.
두 단서를 종합할 때, Ms. Taylor의 직장에 사용된 세제인 Ecoclean은 천연 물질만 포함하고 있음을 추론할 수 있다. 따라서 (C)가 정답이다.

어휘 substance n. 물질 scent n. 향

195 Not/True 문제

해설 추천 글에서 팀장에 대해 명시된 것은?
(A) 청소 과정을 설명하기 위해 고객과 만났다.
(B) 예상보다 훨씬 더 일찍 업무 현장에 도착했다.
(C) 사업체에 추가 직원들이 보내지도록 요청했다.
(D) 일정보다 앞서 업무가 완료되도록 확실히 했다.

해설 추천 글의 'the leader of the team of workers was extremely professional. ~ she made sure the work was completed before that time, even though it was originally supposed to be done at 3 P.M.'에서 직원들의 팀장은 매우 전문적이었다고 했고, 원래 오후 3시에 완료하기로 되어 있었는데도 불구하고 오후 2시 30분 전에 작업이 확실히 완료되도록 했다고 했다. 따라서 (D)가 정답이다.

어휘 site n. 현장 additional adj. 추가의

196-200번은 다음 광고, 주문서, 이메일에 관한 문제입니다.

Zone 스포츠용품점에서 여름을 준비하세요

당신이 전문적으로 스포츠를 즐기든, 신체적으로 더 활발하게 활동하고 싶든, Zone 스포츠용품점은 필요한 모든 것을 갖추고 있습니다. 태평양 연안 북서부 전역에 17개 지점을 두고 있는 저희는 오랫동안 이 지역에서 가장 인기 있는 운동복, 신발 및 장비 공급업체입니다. [196]올 여름 시카고, 댈러스 및 다른 주요 도시들에 매장을 오픈하면서 전국적인 체인점으로 전환한 것을 기념하여, [197]7월 1일부터 15일까지 많은 인기 브랜드에 대해 최대 40퍼센트 할인을 제공할 예정입니다. 하지만 그게 전부는 아닙니다! [197]세금과 배송비가 적용되기 전 최소 250 달러를 지출하시면, First Star Sports의 배낭을 드립니다. 이 혜택은 매장 및 온라인 구매 모두에 유효합니다.

더 많은 정보를 위해 www.zonesport.com/summerpromotion을 방문하세요!

professionally adv. 전문적으로 physically adv. 신체적으로
region n. 지역 athletic adj. 운동의 footwear n. 신발
equipment n. 장비 celebrate v. 기념하다 transition n. 전환
nationwide adj. 전국적인 in-store adj. 매장 내의

| 홈 | 제품 | 주문 | 연락처 |

주문 번호: 029384
[197]주문 날짜: 7월 2일
배송 받는 사람: Beth Kim
배송 주소: 2834번지 8번가, 시애틀, 워싱턴주, 98040

브랜드	품목 설명	가격
Westbrook	테니스 라켓(매우 긴 것)	45달러
Brightside	물병(1리터)	15달러
FZ Apparel	운동복(중간 사이즈)	55달러
[200]Zipper	운동화(사이즈 12)	110달러
	[197]소계	225달러
	[197]배송비	15달러
	[197]세금	25달러
	[197]총액	265달러

위 가격에는 해당되는 모든 할인이 포함되어 있습니다.

198-(C) 온라인으로 구매하신 상품을 반품하시려면, 여기를 클릭하여 선불된 배송 라벨을 인쇄하세요. 반품된 품목은 구매 후 2주 이내에 저희가 받아야 하며 환불이 되기 위해서는 원래의 포장 상태여야 합니다.

tracksuit n. 운동복   applicable adj. 해당되는
prepaid adj. 선불된, 선납된

수신: Beth Kim <b.kim@realmail.com>
발신: Luca Abati <l.abati@zonesports.com>
제목: 회신: 주문 029384
날짜: 7월 17일

Ms. Kim께,

귀하의 최근 주문과 관련하여 Zone 스포츠용품점의 고객 서비스 부서에 연락해 주셔서 감사합니다. **199**귀하의 질문에 답변드리자면, 구매하신 품목의 로열티 포인트 부여에는 오류가 없었습니다. **200**매달, 저희는 다른 회사의 제품을 선보이고 구매 회원분들께 두 배의 포인트를 제공하고 있으며, 7월 이달의 브랜드는 Zipper입니다. 그렇기 때문에 귀하께서 해당 품목에 대해 일반적인 150포인트가 아닌 300포인트를 받으신 것입니다. 이 프로그램에 대한 자세한 정보 및 멤버십의 다른 많은 혜택에 대한 자세한 내용은 웹사이트에서 확인하실 수 있습니다.

Luca Abati 드림
고객 서비스 직원, Zone 스포츠용품점

department n. 부서   assignment n. 부여, 할당

---

196 육하원칙 문제

해석 Zone 스포츠용품점이 판촉 행사를 여는 이유는 무엇인가?
(A) 매출 목표를 달성했다.
(B) 창립을 기념하고 있다.
(C) 행사를 후원하기로 선정되었다.
(D) 다른 지역들로 확장할 예정이다.

해설 광고의 'To celebrate our transition to a nationwide chain with the opening of stores in Chicago, Dallas, and other major cities this summer, we will be offering discounts of up to 40 percent off on many popular brands from July 1 to 15.'에서 올 여름 시카고, 댈러스 및 다른 주요 도시들에 매장을 오픈하면서 전국적인 체인점으로 전환한 것을 기념하여, 7월 1일부터 15일까지 많은 인기 브랜드에 대해 최대 40퍼센트 할인을 제공할 예정이라고 했으므로 (D)가 정답이다.

어휘 anniversary n. 기념일

Paraphrasing

transition to a nationwide chain with the opening of stores in Chicago, Dallas, and other major cities 시카고, 댈러스 및 다른 주요 도시들에 매장을 오픈하면서 전국적인 체인점으로의 전환
→ expand into other regions 다른 지역들로 확장하다

---

197 추론 문제 연계

해석 Ms. Kim에 대해 결론지을 수 있는 것은?
(A) 경품을 받을 자격이 없었다.

(B) 구매한 품목을 반품할 것이다.
(C) 실수로 배송비를 지불했다.
(D) 할인 혜택을 받지 못했다.

해설 Ms. Kim의 주문서를 먼저 확인한다.
단서 1 주문서의 'Order date: July 2', 'Subtotal', '$225.00', 'Shipping', '$15.00', 'Tax', '$25.00', 'Total', '$265.00'에서 7월 2일에 주문한 금액이 배송비와 세금이 포함되기 전에 225달러임을 알 수 있다.
단서 2 광고의 'from July 1 to 15', When you spend at least $250 before tax and shipping fees are applied, we will give you a backpack from First Star Sports.'에서 7월 1일부터 15일까지 세금과 배송비가 적용되기 전 최소 250달러를 지출하면 First Star Sports의 배낭을 준다는 것을 알 수 있다.
두 단서를 종합할 때, Ms. Kim은 경품을 받을 자격이 없었음을 추론할 수 있다. 따라서 (A)가 정답이다.

어휘 mistakenly adv. 실수로

---

198 Not/True 문제

해석 주문서가 Zone 스포츠용품점의 고객들에 대해 명시하는 것은?
(A) 빠른 배송을 요청할 수 있다.
(B) 영수증을 출력할 수 없다.
(C) 반품 배송비를 지불할 필요가 없다.
(D) 손상된 제품만 환불할 수 있다.

해설 주문서의 'To return an item purchased online, please click here to print out a prepaid shipping label.'에서 온라인으로 구매한 상품을 반품하려면, 여기를 클릭하여 선불된 배송 라벨을 인쇄하라고 했으므로 구입품을 반품할 때 배송비를 지불할 필요가 없다는 것을 알 수 있다. 따라서 (C)가 정답이다. (A), (B), (D)는 지문에 명시되지 않은 내용이다.

---

199 목적 찾기 문제

해석 이메일의 목적은 무엇인가?
(A) 고객에게 멤버십을 신청하도록 권장하기 위해
(B) 있을 수 있는 실수에 대한 문의에 답변하기 위해
(C) 품절된 품목의 대체품을 추천하기 위해
(D) 불만 사항을 접수한 후 사과문을 발행하기 위해

해설 이메일의 'In response to your question, there was no error in the assignment of the loyalty points for the items you purchased.'에서 Ms. Kim의 질문에 답변하자면 구매한 품목의 로열티 포인트 부여에는 오류가 없었다고 했으므로 (B)가 정답이다.

어휘 replacement n. 대체품   out-of-stock adj. 품절된, 재고가 떨어진

Paraphrasing

response to your question 질문에 대한 답변 → respond to an inquiry 문의에 대한 답변

---

200 육하원칙 문제 연계

해석 Ms. Kim이 구매에 대해 추가 로열티 포인트를 받은 품목은 무엇인가?
(A) 테니스 라켓

(B) 물병
(C) 운동복
(D) 운동화

해설 Ms. Kim에게 보내진 이메일을 먼저 확인한다.

단서 1 이메일의 'Each month, we[Zone Sporting Goods] feature a different company's products and offer double the points to members who purchase them, and our Brand of the Month for July is Zipper. That is why you received 300 points rather than the normal 150 for that item.'에서 Zone 스포츠용품점은 매달 다른 회사의 제품을 선보이고 구매 회원들에게 두 배의 포인트를 제공하고 있으며, 7월 이달의 브랜드가 Zipper여서 Ms. Kim이 해당 품목에 대해 일반적인 150 포인트가 아닌 300포인트를 받은 것이라고 했다. 그런데 Ms. Kim이 Zipper 브랜드의 무엇을 구매했는지 제시되지 않았으므로 주문서에서 관련 내용을 확인한다.

단서 2 주문서의 'Zipper', 'Sneakers'에서 Ms. Kim이 구매한 것이 운동화임을 알 수 있다.

두 단서를 종합할 때, Ms. Kim이 구매에 대해 추가 로열티 포인트를 받은 품목이 운동화인 것을 알 수 있다. 따라서 (D)가 정답이다.

TEST 2

LISTENING TEST
p.70

1 (B)	21 (C)	41 (B)	61 (A)	81 (B)
2 (C)	22 (A)	42 (D)	62 (D)	82 (C)
3 (C)	23 (C)	43 (C)	63 (A)	83 (D)
4 (D)	24 (C)	44 (D)	64 (C)	84 (C)
5 (A)	25 (B)	45 (B)	65 (C)	85 (B)
6 (B)	26 (A)	46 (B)	66 (B)	86 (A)
7 (B)	27 (C)	47 (A)	67 (D)	87 (C)
8 (A)	28 (A)	48 (A)	68 (A)	88 (C)
9 (A)	29 (B)	49 (C)	69 (B)	89 (D)
10 (C)	30 (A)	50 (B)	70 (D)	90 (B)
11 (B)	31 (C)	51 (C)	71 (B)	91 (C)
12 (C)	32 (C)	52 (B)	72 (C)	92 (B)
13 (A)	33 (C)	53 (C)	73 (B)	93 (D)
14 (C)	34 (C)	54 (D)	74 (A)	94 (A)
15 (C)	35 (A)	55 (A)	75 (C)	95 (B)
16 (B)	36 (C)	56 (D)	76 (B)	96 (C)
17 (B)	37 (B)	57 (B)	77 (D)	97 (C)
18 (A)	38 (D)	58 (D)	78 (C)	98 (A)
19 (A)	39 (C)	59 (B)	79 (A)	99 (D)
20 (B)	40 (A)	60 (C)	80 (C)	100 (D)

READING TEST
p.82

101 (C)	121 (C)	141 (C)	161 (D)	181 (C)
102 (A)	122 (D)	142 (B)	162 (D)	182 (B)
103 (C)	123 (B)	143 (C)	163 (B)	183 (D)
104 (B)	124 (A)	144 (C)	164 (A)	184 (B)
105 (D)	125 (A)	145 (B)	165 (A)	185 (C)
106 (A)	126 (D)	146 (A)	166 (D)	186 (B)
107 (C)	127 (C)	147 (D)	167 (D)	187 (B)
108 (C)	128 (A)	148 (D)	168 (A)	188 (C)
109 (C)	129 (B)	149 (C)	169 (C)	189 (D)
110 (B)	130 (B)	150 (B)	170 (D)	190 (B)
111 (C)	131 (B)	151 (C)	171 (B)	191 (C)
112 (D)	132 (A)	152 (B)	172 (A)	192 (A)
113 (B)	133 (C)	153 (D)	173 (B)	193 (D)
114 (B)	134 (B)	154 (D)	174 (A)	194 (B)
115 (D)	135 (A)	155 (A)	175 (C)	195 (B)
116 (A)	136 (C)	156 (B)	176 (C)	196 (C)
117 (D)	137 (B)	157 (D)	177 (D)	197 (C)
118 (C)	138 (B)	158 (A)	178 (B)	198 (C)
119 (B)	139 (D)	159 (C)	179 (A)	199 (D)
120 (D)	140 (A)	160 (B)	180 (D)	200 (A)

PART 1

1 1인 사진
 호주식

(A) He's climbing up some stairs.
(B) He's grasping walking sticks with both hands.
(C) He's looking into his backpack.
(D) He's kneeling down to tie his shoelaces.

grasp v. 쥐다, 붙잡다　walking stick 지팡이
kneel down 무릎을 꿇다, 꿇어앉다　shoelace n. 신발 끈

해석　(A) 그는 몇몇 계단들을 오르고 있다.
　　(B) 그는 양손으로 지팡이들을 쥐고 있다.
　　(C) 그는 배낭 속을 들여다보고 있다.
　　(D) 그는 신발 끈을 묶기 위해 무릎을 꿇고 있다.

해설　(A) [×] 사진에 계단(stairs)이 없으므로 오답이다. He's climbing up(그가 오르고 있다)까지만 듣고 정답으로 선택하지 않도록 주의한다.
　　(B) [○] 남자가 양손으로 지팡이들을 쥐고 있는 모습을 가장 잘 묘사한 정답이다.
　　(C) [×] 남자가 배낭 속을 들여다보고(looking into) 있지 않으므로 오답이다.
　　(D) [×] kneeling down to tie(묶기 위해 무릎을 꿇고 있다)는 남자의 동작과 무관하므로 오답이다.

2 1인 사진
 영국식

(A) The woman is wearing a set of headphones.
(B) The woman is measuring the height.
(C) The woman is closing a box with tape.
(D) The woman is dipping a brush into a can.

measure v. 측정하다　height n. 높이　dip v. 살짝 담그다

해석　(A) 여자가 한 짝의 헤드폰을 착용하고 있다.
　　(B) 여자가 높이를 측정하고 있다.
　　(C) 여자가 테이프로 상자를 밀봉하고 있다.
　　(D) 여자가 붓을 깡통에 살짝 담그고 있다.

해설　(A) [×] 사진에 헤드폰(headphones)이 없으므로 오답이다.
　　(B) [×] measuring the height(높이를 측정하고 있다)은 여자의 동작과 무관하므로 오답이다.
　　(C) [○] 여자가 테이프로 상자를 밀봉하고 있는 모습을 가장 잘 묘사한 정답이다.
　　(D) [×] dipping(살짝 담그고 있다)은 여자의 동작과 무관하고, 사진에 붓(brush)과 깡통(can)도 없으므로 오답이다.

3 2인 이상 사진 〖3회〗 캐나다식

(A) One of the women is stocking store shelves.
(B) One of the women is putting on a hat in front of a mirror.
(C) One of the men is examining a clothing item.
(D) One of the men is handing over a hanger.

stock v. 채우다   examine v. 검사하다, 조사하다
hand over ~을 건네다   hanger n. 옷걸이

해석 (A) 여자들 중 한 명이 매장 선반들을 채우고 있다.
(B) 여자들 중 한 명이 거울 앞에서 모자를 쓰고 있다.
(C) 남자들 중 한 명이 옷을 살펴보고 있다.
(D) 남자들 중 한 명이 옷걸이를 건네고 있다.

해설 (A) [×] 사진에 매장 선반들을 채우고 있는(stocking store shelves) 여자가 없으므로 오답이다.
(B) [×] 사진에 모자를 쓰고 있는(putting on a hat) 여자가 없으므로 오답이다.
(C) [○] 남자들 중 한 명이 옷을 살펴보고 있는 모습을 가장 잘 묘사한 정답이다.
(D) [×] 사진에 옷걸이를 건네고 있는(handing over) 남자가 없으므로 오답이다. 사진에 있는 옷걸이(hanger)를 사용하여 혼동을 주었다.

최신토익 경향

최근 PART 1에서는 사람이 무언가를 살펴보고 있는 모습을 다양한 동사로 표현하여 출제하고 있다.

<보고 있는 동작을 묘사하는 빈출 표현>
• He's sorting through some files.
  그는 몇몇 파일을 살펴보고 있다.
• They're looking at a sign.
  그들은 표지판을 쳐다보고 있다.
• She's browsing through a newspaper.
  그녀는 신문을 훑어보고 있다.

4 사물 및 풍경 사진 〖3회〗 호주식

(A) A garden is being planted along a fence.
(B) Some automobiles are being towed on the street.
(C) There's a lamppost between two benches.
(D) Brick buildings are built in a row.

fence n. 울타리   automobile n. 자동차   tow v. 견인하다, 끌다
lamppost n. 가로등 기둥   in a row 일렬로, 잇달아

해석 (A) 울타리를 따라 정원에 식물이 심어지고 있다.
(B) 몇몇 자동차들이 거리에서 견인되고 있다.
(C) 두 벤치 사이에 가로등 기둥이 있다.
(D) 벽돌로 된 건물들이 일렬로 지어져 있다.

해설 (A) [×] 사진에서 울타리(fence)는 보이지만, 정원에 식물이 심어지고 있는(A garden is being planted) 것은 아니므로 오답이다.
(B) [×] 자동차들이 견인되고 있는(being towed) 모습은 아니므로 오답이다.
(C) [×] 사진에 벤치(benches)가 없으므로 오답이다. 사진에 있는 가로등 기둥(lamppost)을 사용하여 혼동을 주었다.
(D) [○] 벽돌로 된 건물들이 일렬로 지어져 있는 모습을 가장 잘 묘사한 정답이다.

5 2인 이상 사진 〖3회〗 영국식

(A) Some papers have been placed on a table.
(B) Some people are rearranging the furniture in an office.
(C) One of the people is pouring a beverage into a cup.
(D) Some electric cables are coiled up on the wall.

rearrange v. 재배치하다   furniture n. 가구   electric cable 전선
coil v. 감다, 휘감다

해석 **(A) 몇몇 종이들이 탁자 위에 놓여 있다.**
(B) 몇몇 사람들이 사무실에서 가구를 재배치하고 있다.
(C) 사람들 중 한 명이 컵에 음료를 붓고 있다.
(D) 몇몇 전선들이 벽에 감겨 있다.

해설 (A) [○] 몇몇 종이들이 책상 위에 흩어져 있는 모습을 가장 잘 묘사한 정답이다.
(B) [×] 사진에서 가구(furniture)는 보이지만, 사람들이 그것을 재배치하고 있는(rearranging) 모습은 아니므로 오답이다.
(C) [×] 사진에서 컵(cup)은 보이지만, 음료를 붓고 있는(pouring a beverage) 사람은 없으므로 오답이다.
(D) [×] 사진에 전선들(electric cables)이 없으므로 오답이다.

최신토익 경향

최근 PART 1에서 그동안 등장하지 않았던 생소하고 어려운 표현을 포함한 보기들이 출제되고 있다.

<난도가 높은 최신 출제 표현>
• be coiled up (선 등이) 감겨져 있다
• be perched on (무엇의 끝에) 위치해 있다
• be raked 갈퀴로 긁어 모아지다
• be turned upside down 거꾸로 뒤집어져 있다

6 사물 및 풍경 사진 〖3회〗 미국식

(A) All the dining tables are occupied by people.
(B) Some plants have been hung from a ceiling.
(C) Some overhead lights are being installed.
(D) There's a vase of flowers displayed on the table.

dining table 식탁   occupy v. (자리를) 차지하다
hang v. 매달다   overhead adj. 머리 위의

해석 (A) 모든 식탁이 사람들로 자리가 차 있다.
(B) 몇몇 식물들이 천장에 매달려 있다.
(C) 몇몇 머리 위 조명들이 설치되고 있다.

해설 (D) 탁자 위에 진열된 꽃병이 있다.

해설 (A) [×] 사진에서 식탁(dining tables)은 보이지만, 사람들로 자리가 채워져(occupied) 있지 않으므로 오답이다.
(B) [○] 몇몇 식물들이 천장에 매달려 있는 모습을 가장 잘 묘사한 정답이다.
(C) [×] 사진에 머리 위 조명들(overhead lights)은 보이지만, 설치되고 있는(being installed) 모습은 아니므로 오답이다.
(D) [×] 사진에 꽃병(vase of flowers)이 없으므로 오답이다.

최신토익경향

최근 PART 1에서 동사 hang(걸다, 매달다)을 이용하여 사물의 상태를 묘사하는 보기들이 자주 출제되고 있다.

<hang을 이용한 빈출 표현>
- A menu board has been hung on the wall.
  메뉴판이 벽에 걸려 있다.
- Some lights have been hung from a ceiling.
  조명들이 천장에 매달려 있다.
- A jacket has been hung on a hanger.
  재킷이 옷걸이에 걸려 있다.
- Some aprons are hanging from hooks.
  앞치마들이 고리에 걸려 있다.

PART 2

7 요청 의문문 캐나다식 → 미국식

Could you help me move this couch?
(A) It can seat up to four people.
(B) I'd be happy to.
(C) One bedroom.

couch n. 소파, 긴 의자   be happy to 기꺼이 ~하다

해설 이 소파를 옮기는 것을 도와주실 수 있나요?
(A) 그것은 최대 네 명까지 앉을 수 있어요.
(B) 기꺼이요.
(C) 침실 하나요.

해설 (A) [×] 질문의 couch(소파)에서 연상할 수 있는 seat(앉히다)을 사용하여 혼동을 준 오답이다.
(B) [○] 기꺼이 도울 수 있다는 말로, 소파를 옮기는 것을 도와 달라는 요청을 수락한 정답이다.
(C) [×] 질문의 couch(소파)에서 연상할 수 있는 공간과 관련된 bedroom(침실)을 사용하여 혼동을 준 오답이다.

8 선택 의문문 영국식 → 호주식

Is the client visiting our office later today or tomorrow?
(A) She'll be here this afternoon.
(B) With some prospective clients.
(C) There is a room for visitors.

client n. 고객   prospective adj. 잠재의, 장래의   room n. 공간, 방

해설 고객이 우리 사무실을 오늘 늦게 방문하나요, 아니면 내일 방문하나요?
(A) 그녀는 오늘 오후에 여기로 올 거예요.
(B) 몇몇 잠재 고객들과 함께요.
(C) 방문객들을 위한 공간이 있어요.

해설 (A) [○] 고객이 오늘 오후에 방문할 것이라며, 오늘 늦게 방문할 것임을 선택했으므로 정답이다.
(B) [×] 질문의 client를 clients로 반복 사용하여 혼동을 준 오답이다.
(C) [×] visiting - visitors의 유사 발음 어휘를 사용하여 혼동을 준 오답이다.

9 When 의문문 캐나다식 → 영국식

When was the furnace replaced?
(A) Just last Wednesday.
(B) I've never heard of that place.
(C) Yes, it takes place every morning.

furnace n. 보일러, 화로   replace v. 교체하다, 대신하다
take place 발생하다, 일어나다

해설 언제 보일러가 교체됐나요?
(A) 바로 지난주 수요일이에요.
(B) 저는 그 장소에 대해 들어본 적이 없어요.
(C) 네, 매일 아침 발생해요.

해설 (A) [○] 지난주 수요일이라는 말로, 보일러를 교체한 시점을 전달했으므로 정답이다.
(B) [×] replaced - place의 유사 발음 어휘를 사용하여 혼동을 준 오답이다.
(C) [×] 의문사 의문문에 Yes로 응답했으므로 오답이다. When 의문문에 답할 수 있는 every morning(매일 아침)을 듣고 이를 정답으로 선택하지 않도록 주의한다.

10 How 의문문 미국식 → 캐나다식

How many applicants are we going to interview today?
(A) Download the application form.
(B) The interview was great.
(C) There will be more than five.

applicant n. 지원자   interview v. 면접을 보다
application form 지원서, 신청서

해설 오늘 우리가 얼마나 많은 지원자들을 면접 볼 예정인가요?
(A) 지원서를 다운로드 받으세요.
(B) 그 면접은 훌륭했어요.
(C) 다섯 명 넘게 있을 거예요.

해설 (A) [×] 질문의 applicants(지원자들)에서 연상할 수 있는 application form(지원서)을 사용하여 혼동을 준 오답이다.
(B) [×] 질문의 interview를 '면접'이라는 의미의 명사로 반복 사용하여 혼동을 준 오답이다.
(C) [○] 다섯 명 넘게 있을 거라는 말로, 면접을 볼 지원자들의 수를 전달했으므로 정답이다.

11 부가 의문문

🔊 영국식 → 호주식

We're holding the press conference this Friday, aren't we?
(A) Twenty people attended.
(B) No. It's next week.
(C) A reporter from the *Meyerville News*.

hold v. 열다, 개최하다   press conference 기자 회견
reporter n. 기자

해석 우리는 이번 주 금요일에 기자 회견을 열 예정이죠, 그렇지 않나요?
(A) 스무 명이 참석했어요.
(B) 아니요. 다음 주예요.
(C) *Meyerville News*의 기자요.

해설 (A) [×] 질문의 press conference(기자 회견)에서 연상할 수 있는 참석자 수와 관련된 attended(참석했다)를 사용하여 혼동을 준 오답이다.
(B) [○] No로 기자 회견이 이번 주 금요일에 열리지 않을 거라고 전달한 후, 다음 주라는 부연 설명을 했으므로 정답이다.
(C) [×] 질문의 press conference(기자 회견)와 관련 있는 reporter(기자)를 사용하여 혼동을 준 오답이다.

12 평서문

🔊 캐나다식 → 영국식

Our company is known for offering custom-made furniture pieces.
(A) A cupboard will be shipped today.
(B) Only for loyal customers.
(C) Are they durable?

custom-made adj. 주문 제작한   ship v. 운송하다, 수송하다
loyal customer 단골 고객   durable adj. 내구성이 있는, 오래가는

해석 우리 회사는 주문 제작 가구를 제공하는 것으로 유명해요.
(A) 찬장이 오늘 배송될 거예요.
(B) 단골 고객들을 위해서만요.
(C) 그것들은 내구성이 있나요?

해설 (A) [×] 질문의 furniture(가구)에서 연상할 수 있는 cupboard(찬장)를 사용하여 혼동을 준 오답이다.
(B) [×] custom - customers의 유사 발음 어휘를 사용하여 혼동을 준 오답이다.
(C) [○] 그것들이 내구성이 있는지를 되물어, 주문 제작 가구에 대한 추가 정보를 요구한 정답이다.

13 부정 의문문

🔊 호주식 → 영국식

Isn't Jeremy supposed to arrange floral decorations for the party?
(A) Yes. Let me call him.
(B) It was a long gardening class.
(C) A party of three.

arrange v. 준비하다, 마련하다   decoration n. 장식, 장식품
gardening n. 원예   party n. 일행, 단체

해석 Jeremy가 파티를 위해 꽃장식들을 준비하기로 되어 있지 않나요?
(A) 네. 제가 그에게 전화할게요.
(B) 긴 원예 수업이었어요.
(C) 일행 세 명이요.

해설 (A) [○] Yes로 Jeremy가 파티를 위해 꽃장식들을 준비하기로 되어 있다고 전달한 후, 자신이 그에게 전화하겠다고 제안한 정답이다.
(B) [×] 질문의 floral decorations(꽃장식들)에서 연상할 수 있는 gardening class(원예 수업)를 사용하여 혼동을 준 오답이다.
(C) [×] 질문의 party를 '일행'이라는 의미의 명사로 반복 사용하여 혼동을 준 오답이다.

14 선택 의문문

🔊 미국식 → 호주식

Will you use the same travel agency for this vacation or a different one?
(A) Accommodation costs are included.
(B) That flight departs soon.
(C) The same one as before.

travel agency 여행사   accommodation n. 숙박, 숙소
include v. 포함하다   depart v. 출발하다

해석 당신은 이번 휴가에 같은 여행사를 이용할 건가요, 아니면 다른 곳을 이용할 건가요?
(A) 숙박비가 포함되어 있어요.
(B) 그 항공기는 곧 출발할 거예요.
(C) 지난번과 같은 곳이요.

해설 (A) [×] 질문의 travel agency(여행사)와 관련 있는 Accommodation costs(숙박비)를 사용하여 혼동을 준 오답이다.
(B) [×] 질문의 vacation(휴가)에서 연상할 수 있는 flight(항공기)를 사용하여 혼동을 준 오답이다.
(C) [○] 지난번과 같은 곳이라는 말로, 이번 휴가에 같은 여행사를 이용할 것을 선택했으므로 정답이다.

15 What 의문문

🔊 호주식 → 캐나다식

What type of promotions did you work on at your previous company?
(A) For promotional purposes.
(B) She worked an afternoon shift.
(C) Mostly social media advertisements.

promotion n. 홍보   previous adj. 이전의   purpose n. 목적

해석 당신은 이전 회사에서 어떤 유형의 홍보 활동을 담당했었나요?
(A) 홍보 목적을 위해서요.
(B) 그녀는 오후 근무를 했어요.
(C) 주로 소셜 미디어 광고요.

해설 (A) [×] promotions - promotional의 유사 발음 어휘를 사용하여 혼동을 준 오답이다.
(B) [×] 질문의 work를 반복 사용하여 혼동을 준 오답이다.
(C) [○] 주로 소셜 미디어 광고라는 말로, 이전 회사에서 담당했던 홍보 활동 유형을 언급했으므로 정답이다.

16 조동사 의문문
🔊 캐나다식 → 미국식

Have you completed the seating layout for Mr. Hwang's retirement luncheon?
(A) It was delicious, thank you.
(B) It's on your desk.
(C) Right down the hallway.

complete v. 완성하다, 완료하다　seating layout 좌석 배치도
retirement n. 은퇴　luncheon n. 오찬, 점심 만찬

해석　Mr. Hwang의 은퇴 오찬을 위한 좌석 배치도를 완성했나요?
(A) 그것은 맛있었어요. 감사합니다.
(B) 그것은 당신의 책상 위에 있어요.
(C) 복도를 따라 곧장 내려가면 있어요.

해설　(A) [×] 질문의 luncheon(오찬)에서 연상할 수 있는 delicious(맛있는)를 사용하여 혼동을 준 오답이다.
(B) [○] 그것은 당신의 책상 위에 있다는 말로, 은퇴 오찬을 위한 좌석 배치도를 완성했음을 간접적으로 전달했으므로 정답이다.
(C) [×] 좌석 배치도를 완성했는지를 물었는데, 이와 관련이 없는 복도를 따라 곧장 내려가면 있다고 응답했으므로 오답이다.

17 Where 의문문
🔊 영국식 → 캐나다식

Where did the package on the reception desk come from?
(A) A stylish package design.
(B) It has the sender's name on it.
(C) In June this year.

package n. 소포　reception desk 접수처
sender n. 발송자, 보내는 사람

해석　접수처에 있는 소포는 어디에서 왔나요?
(A) 유행을 따른 포장 디자인이요.
(B) 발송자 이름이 그 위에 있어요.
(C) 올해 6월에요.

해설　(A) [×] 질문의 package를 반복 사용하여 혼동을 준 오답이다.
(B) [○] 그 위에 발송자 이름이 있다는 말로, 접수처에 있는 소포가 어디에서 왔는지 모른다는 것을 간접적으로 전달했으므로 정답이다.
(C) [×] 접수처에 있는 소포의 출처를 물었는데, 날짜로 응답했으므로 오답이다. 질문의 Where를 When으로 혼동하여 이를 정답으로 선택하지 않도록 주의한다.

18 부가 의문문
🔊 미국식 → 영국식

The product demonstration can be viewed online, right?
(A) No. You must attend the event.
(B) One sample per person.
(C) Your demonstration was helpful.

demonstration n. 시연, 설명　view v. 보다

해석　제품 시연은 온라인에서 볼 수 있어요, 그렇죠?
(A) 아니요. 행사에 참석하셔야 해요.
(B) 한 사람당 샘플 하나예요.
(C) 당신의 시연은 도움이 되었어요.

해설　(A) [○] No로 제품 시연은 온라인에서 볼 수 없음을 전달한 후, 행사에 참석해야 한다는 부연 설명을 했으므로 정답이다.
(B) [×] 질문의 product demonstration(제품 시연)에서 연상할 수 있는 sample(샘플)을 사용하여 혼동을 준 오답이다.
(C) [×] 질문의 demonstration을 반복 사용하여 혼동을 준 오답이다.

19 요청 의문문
🔊 영국식 → 호주식

Could you please print the document I just sent you by e-mail?
(A) I'll do it right away.
(B) OK, I'll just follow them.
(C) In the file cabinet.

document n. 문서, 서류　file cabinet 서류함

해석　제가 당신에게 방금 이메일로 보낸 문서를 인쇄해 주시겠어요?
(A) 바로 할게요.
(B) 좋아요, 그냥 그들을 따라갈게요.
(C) 서류함 안에요.

해설　(A) [○] 바로 할 것이라는 말로, 이메일로 보낸 문서를 인쇄해 달라는 요청을 수락한 정답이다.
(B) [×] 이메일로 보낸 문서를 인쇄해 줄 수 있는지를 물었는데, 이와 관련이 없는 그들을 따라가겠다고 응답했으므로 오답이다. OK, I'까지만 듣고 정답으로 고르지 않도록 주의한다.
(C) [×] 질문의 document(문서)에서 연상할 수 있는 file cabinet(서류함)을 사용하여 혼동을 준 오답이다.

20 Who 의문문
🔊 호주식 → 영국식

Who remodeled your kitchen?
(A) The sink is blocked.
(B) We did it ourselves.
(C) About three days ago.

remodel v. 개조하다　sink n. 싱크대, 개수대　block v. 막다, 차단하다

해석　누가 당신의 주방을 개조했나요?
(A) 싱크대가 막혔어요.
(B) 우리가 직접 했어요.
(C) 3일 전쯤이요.

해설　(A) [×] 질문의 kitchen(주방)에서 연상할 수 있는 sink(싱크대)를 사용하여 혼동을 준 오답이다.
(B) [○] 우리가 직접 했다는 말로, 누가 주방을 개조했는지를 언급했으므로 정답이다.
(C) [×] 누가 주방을 개조했는지를 물었는데, 이와 관련이 없는 시점으로 응답했으므로 오답이다.

21 선택 의문문
🔊 미국식 → 영국식

Should we take the bus or the subway to the museum?
(A) Please park close to the museum.
(B) Yes, I heard it was impressive.
(C) Let's ask Yuki first.

close adv. 가까이   impressive adj. 인상적인

해석 우리는 박물관까지 버스를 타야 할까요, 지하철을 타야 할까요?
(A) 박물관 가까이에 주차해 주세요.
(B) 네, 그것이 인상적이었다고 들었어요.
(C) Yuki에게 먼저 물어봅시다.

해설 (A) [x] 질문의 museum을 반복 사용하여 혼동을 준 오답이다.
(B) [x] 선택 의문문에 Yes로 응답했으므로 오답이다. museum(박물관)에서 연상할 수 있는 관람 후기와 관련된 impressive(인상적인)를 사용하여 혼동을 주었다.
(C) [○] Yuki에게 먼저 물어보자는 말로, 버스와 지하철 둘 다 간접적으로 선택하지 않은 정답이다.

22 Which 의문문
🔊 미국식 → 호주식

Which section are you compiling for the annual report?
(A) The one with quarterly sales figures.
(B) To finish the budget report.
(C) Can I copy this?

compile v. 편집하다, 엮다   quarterly adj. 분기별의   budget n. 예산

해석 당신은 연례 보고서의 어느 부분을 편집하고 있나요?
(A) 분기별 매출 수치가 있는 부분이요.
(B) 예산 보고서를 마무리하기 위해서요.
(C) 이것을 복사해도 될까요?

해설 (A) [○] 분기별 매출 수치가 있는 부분이라는 말로, 편집하고 있는 연례 보고서의 부분을 언급했으므로 정답이다.
(B) [x] 질문의 report를 반복 사용하여 혼동을 준 오답이다.
(C) [x] 질문의 report(보고서)에서 연상할 수 있는 copy(복사하다)를 사용하여 혼동을 준 오답이다.

23 평서문
🔊 캐나다식 → 호주식

The grocery store was completely out of pumpkins.
(A) Yes, the farm is located by the river.
(B) A traditional local market.
(C) Sweet potatoes can be an alternative for the pie.

grocery store 식료품점   farm n. 농장   traditional adj. 전통적인
alternative n. 대체제

해석 식료품점에 호박들이 모두 품절됐어요.
(A) 네, 그 농장은 강 옆에 있어요.
(B) 전통적인 현지 시장이요.
(C) 고구마가 파이를 위한 대체제가 될 수 있어요.

해설 (A) [x] 질문의 pumpkins(호박들)에서 연상할 수 있는 장소와 관련된 farm(농장)을 사용하여 혼동을 준 오답이다.
(B) [x] 질문의 grocery store(식료품점)와 관련 있는 local market(현지 시장)을 사용하여 혼동을 준 오답이다.
(C) [○] 고구마가 파이를 위한 대체제가 될 수 있다는 말로, 문제점에 대한 해결책을 제시했으므로 정답이다.

최신토익경향

Part 2에서 평균 3문제씩 출제되는 평서문은 객관적인 사실을 전달하기도 하지만, 문제 상황을 전달하기도 한다. 특히 최근에는 문제 상황을 언급하는 평서문에 대한 해결책을 제시하는 응답이 정답으로 자주 출제되고 있다.

<평서문에 해결책을 제시하는 응답>
The coffee machine is malfunctioning again.
커피 머신이 또 제대로 작동하지 않고 있어요.
<답변> I'll call the service technician.
        제가 서비스 기술자를 부를게요.
* 커피 머신이 또 제대로 작동하지 않고 있다고 문제 상황을 전달하는 평서문에 자신이 서비스 기술자를 부르겠다고 해결책을 제시한 응답

24 선택 의문문
🔊 호주식 → 미국식

Do you prefer scheduling the appointment with Dr. Murad for the morning or afternoon?
(A) Oh, that's a good point.
(B) It's a new hospital.
(C) Before lunch is better for me.

prefer v. 선호하다, 더 좋아하다   appointment n. 예약, 약속

해석 Dr. Murad와의 예약을 오전에 잡는 것을 선호하시나요, 아니면 오후에 잡는 것을 선호하시나요?
(A) 오, 그거 좋은 요점이네요.
(B) 새 병원이에요.
(C) 점심 전이 저에게는 더 좋아요.

해설 (A) [x] appointment - point의 유사 발음 어휘를 사용하여 혼동을 준 오답이다.
(B) [x] 질문의 Dr. Murad의 doctor에서 연상할 수 있는 장소와 관련된 hospital(병원)을 사용하여 혼동을 준 오답이다.
(C) [○] 점심 전이 더 좋다는 말로, 오전을 간접적으로 선택했으므로 정답이다.

25 평서문
🔊 영국식 → 미국식

The microphone needs to be repaired by two o'clock.
(A) The equipment rental company.
(B) I'm almost done.
(C) Sorry, but it can't be refunded.

microphone n. 마이크   rental n. 대여, 임대   refund v. 환불하다

해석 2시까지 마이크가 수리돼야 해요.
(A) 장비 대여 회사요.
(B) 거의 다 됐어요.
(C) 죄송하지만, 그것은 환불이 될 수 없습니다.

해설 (A) [x] 질문의 microphone(마이크)과 관련 있는 equipment(장비)를 사용하여 혼동을 준 오답이다.
(B) [○] 거의 다 됐다는 말로, 2시까지 마이크가 수리될 것임을 간접

적으로 전달했으므로 정답이다.
(C) [x] 마이크가 수리돼야 한다고 했는데, 이와 관련이 없는 환불이 될 수 없다는 내용으로 응답했으므로 오답이다.

26 Why 의문문
영국식 → 캐나다식

Why are all the interns gathered in the auditorium?
(A) I heard there will be an orientation.
(B) The contract expired last month.
(C) No, we have 10 people in total.

gather v. 모으다, 모이다   auditorium n. 강당   expire v. 만료되다

해석 왜 모든 인턴들이 강당에 모여 있나요?
(A) 그곳에서 예비 교육이 있을 것이라고 들었어요.
(B) 그 계약은 지난달에 만료됐어요.
(C) 아니요, 우리는 총 10명이에요.

해설 (A) [o] 그곳에서 예비 교육이 있을 것이라고 들었다는 말로, 모든 인턴들이 강당에 모인 이유를 언급했으므로 정답이다.
(B) [x] 강당에 인턴들이 모인 이유를 물었는데, 이와 관련이 없는 지난달에 계약이 만료됐다는 내용으로 응답했으므로 오답이다.
(C) [x] 의문사 의문문에 No로 응답했으므로 오답이다. 질문의 gathered(모여 있다)에서 연상할 수 있는 사람 수와 관련된 10 people in total(총 10명)을 사용하여 혼동을 주었다.

27 Be동사 의문문
호주식 → 캐나다식

Are you going to register at the gym that recently opened across the street?
(A) A personal trainer and gym owner.
(B) Yes, the elevator is broken.
(C) Discounts are no longer offered.

register v. 등록하다   recently adv. 최근에   owner n. 소유주, 주인   offer v. 제공하다

해석 길 건너에 최근 문을 연 체육관에 등록할 건가요?
(A) 개인 트레이너이자 체육관 소유주예요.
(B) 네, 엘리베이터가 고장 났어요.
(C) 할인이 더 이상 제공되지 않아요.

해설 (A) [x] 질문의 gym을 반복 사용하여 혼동을 준 오답이다.
(B) [x] 체육관에 등록할 것인지를 물었는데, 이와 관련이 없는 엘리베이터가 고장 났다고 응답했으므로 오답이다. Yes까지만 듣고 정답으로 고르지 않도록 주의한다.
(C) [o] 할인이 더 이상 제공되지 않는다는 말로, 체육관에 등록하지 않을 것임을 간접적으로 전달했으므로 정답이다.

최신토익경향

최근 출제되는 Be동사 의문문에는 Yes/No가 생략된 간접 응답이 자주 출제되고 있는데, 이 경우 그 의도를 파악하기 어려울 수 있다. 아래 예문을 통해 실전에 대비하자.

<Be동사 의문문에 Yes/No를 생략한 응답>
Are you going to buy a house near a train station?
기차역 근처에 집을 구매하실 건가요?

<답변> I don't want to move.
이사하고 싶지 않아요.
* 기차역 근처에 집을 구매할 것인지를 묻는 Be동사 의문문에 이사하고 싶지 않다는 말로 집을 구매하지 않을 것임을 간접적으로 전달한 응답

28 부정 의문문
미국식 → 캐나다식

Didn't we hire too many temporary employees?
(A) This is the busiest month of the year.
(B) Under a long-term agreement.
(C) I'll send you a temporary password.

temporary adj. 임시의   long-term adj. 장기의, 장기적인   agreement n. 계약, 합의

해석 우리가 임시 직원들을 너무 많이 채용하지 않았나요?
(A) 이번 달이 올해 가장 바쁜 달이에요.
(B) 장기 계약에 따라서요.
(C) 제가 임시 비밀번호를 보내드릴게요.

해설 (A) [o] 이번 달이 올해 가장 바쁜 달이라는 말로, 임시 직원들을 너무 많이 채용한 것은 아니라는 의견을 간접적으로 전달했으므로 정답이다.
(B) [x] 질문의 hire(채용하다)에서 연상할 수 있는 채용 과정과 관련된 long-term agreement(장기 계약)를 사용하여 혼동을 준 오답이다.
(C) [x] 질문의 temporary를 반복 사용하여 혼동을 준 오답이다.

29 Who 의문문
호주식 → 미국식

Who's interested in designing our team uniform?
(A) It was an interesting movie.
(B) Here is the list of companies.
(C) One more paintbrush, please.

interesting adj. 흥미로운   paintbrush n. 페인트 붓, 그림 그리는 붓

해석 누가 우리 팀 유니폼을 디자인하는 것에 관심이 있나요?
(A) 그것은 흥미로운 영화였어요.
(B) 여기 회사 목록이에요.
(C) 페인트 붓을 하나 더 주세요.

해설 (A) [x] interested - interesting의 유사 발음 어휘를 사용하여 혼동을 준 오답이다.
(B) [o] 여기 회사 목록이 있다는 말로, 팀 유니폼을 디자인하는 것에 관심이 있는 여러 회사들이 있다고 응답했으므로 정답이다.
(C) [x] 질문의 designing(디자인하다)에서 연상할 수 있는 도구와 관련된 paintbrush(페인트 붓)를 사용하여 혼동을 준 오답이다.

30 조동사 의문문
영국식 → 캐나다식

Has Patrick come into the office today?
(A) His briefcase is on his desk.
(B) My office is only two blocks away.
(C) Sure. It will only take a few minutes.

briefcase n. 서류 가방   block n. 블록, 구역

해석 Patrick이 오늘 사무실로 출근했나요?
(A) 그의 서류 가방이 그의 책상 위에 있어요.
(B) 제 사무실은 단지 두 블록 떨어져 있어요.
(C) 물론이죠. 몇 분밖에 걸리지 않을 거예요.

해설 (A) [○] 그의 서류 가방이 그의 책상 위에 있다는 말로, Patrick이 오늘 사무실로 출근했음을 간접적으로 전달했으므로 정답이다.
(B) [×] 질문의 office를 반복 사용하여 혼동을 준 오답이다.
(C) [×] Patrick이 오늘 사무실로 출근했는지를 물었는데, 이와 관련이 없는 몇 분밖에 걸리지 않을 것이라는 내용으로 응답했으므로 오답이다.

31 When 의문문

호주식 → 미국식

When will the pizza we ordered on the mobile app arrive?
(A) I saw a vending machine in the lobby.
(B) Please leave it in the break room.
(C) The roads are quite congested now.

order v. 주문하다　leave v. 놓고 가다　congested adj. 혼잡한

해석 우리가 모바일 앱에서 주문한 피자는 언제 도착하나요?
(A) 저는 로비에서 자판기를 봤어요.
(B) 휴게실에 놓고 가세요.
(C) 도로가 지금 꽤 혼잡해요.

해설 (A) [×] 주문한 피자가 언제 도착하는지를 물었는데, 이와 관련이 없는 자판기를 로비에서 봤다고 응답했으므로 오답이다.
(B) [×] 질문의 pizza we ordered(우리가 주문한 피자)에서 연상할 수 있는 배달 상황과 관련된 leave it in the break room(휴게실에 놓고 가다)을 사용하여 혼동을 준 오답이다.
(C) [○] 도로가 지금 꽤 혼잡하다는 말로, 주문한 피자가 언제 도착할지 모른다는 것을 간접적으로 전달했으므로 정답이다.

PART 3

[32-34]

호주식 → 미국식

Questions 32-34 refer to the following conversation.

M: ³²**Welcome to Aberdeen Auto Rental.** Do you have a reservation?
W: Yes. My booking number is 28837. ³³**However, I just realized that I selected a car that seats only four people, but there are six of us.**
M: Let me check . . . Oh, another customer canceled his reservation. The vehicle he booked is available, and it's big enough for you. The price is the same, so you won't have to pay extra.
W: Thank you. One more thing . . . ³⁴**How can I add an additional driver?**

reservation n. 예약　additional adj. 추가의

해석
32-34번은 다음 대화에 관한 문제입니다.

남: ³²Aberdeen 자동차 대여소에 오신 것을 환영합니다. 예약을 하셨나요?
여: 네. 제 예약 번호는 28837입니다. 그런데 ³³저는 4인승 차량을 선택했는데, 저희가 여섯 명이라는 사실을 방금 깨달았어요.
남: 제가 확인해 볼게요... 오, 다른 고객이 예약을 취소하셨네요. 그가 예약했던 차량이 대여 가능하고, 고객님에게 충분히 클 거예요. 가격이 동일해서, 추가 금액을 지불할 필요는 없습니다.
여: 감사해요. 한 가지 더요... ³⁴제가 어떻게 추가 운전자를 추가할 수 있나요?

32 장소 문제

해석 대화는 어디에서 일어나고 있는가?
(A) 식당에서
(B) 공장에서
(C) 자동차 대여 회사에서
(D) 아파트 단지에서

해설 대화에서 장소와 관련된 표현을 놓치지 않고 듣는다. 남자가 "Welcome to Aberdeen Auto Rental."이라며 Aberdeen 자동차 대여소에 오신 것을 환영한다고 하였다. 이를 통해 자동차 대여소에서 대화가 일어나고 있음을 알 수 있다. 따라서 (C)가 정답이다.

33 문제점 문제

해석 여자는 무슨 문제를 언급하는가?
(A) 잘못된 날짜를 예약했다.
(B) 적합하지 않은 옵션을 골랐다.
(C) 개인 물품을 잃어버렸다.
(D) 요금을 지급하지 못했다.

해설 여자의 말에서 부정적인 표현이 언급된 다음을 주의 깊게 듣는다. 여자가 "However, I just realized that I selected a car that seats only four people, but there are six of us."라며 4인승 차량을 선택했는데, 인원이 여섯 명이라는 사실을 방금 깨달았다고 하였다. 따라서 (B)가 정답이다.

어휘 unsuitable adj. 적합하지 않은　fee n. 요금, 수수료

34 특정 세부 사항 문제

해석 여자는 무엇에 관해 묻는가?
(A) 서비스 비용이 얼마인지
(B) 행사가 언제 시작하는지
(C) 추가 인원을 어떻게 등록하는지
(D) 몇몇 장비들을 어디에 설치할지

해설 여자의 말에서 질문의 핵심 어구(ask about)와 관련된 내용을 주의 깊게 듣는다. 여자가 "How can I add an additional driver?"라며 추가 운전자를 어떻게 추가할 수 있는지를 물었다. 따라서 (C)가 정답이다.

어휘 register v. 등록하다　set up ~을 설치하다　equipment n. 장비

Paraphrasing

add an additional driver 추가 운전자를 추가하다 → register an extra person 추가 인원을 등록하다

[35-37]

Questions 35-37 refer to the following conversation.

🎧 영국식 → 호주식

W: Hi. I'm Esra Boz, and I'm leading a team you will be assigned to during ³⁵your internship here.
M: Nice to meet you, Ms. Boz. I'm very excited about spending my summer working here. ³⁶The mobile banking and messaging applications you have developed are quite impressive. I'm sure I'll learn a lot.
W: That's good to hear. ³⁷Please look through this employee manual first. I'll be back with your staff ID.

assign v. 배정하다   develop v. 개발하다   quite adv. 꽤
impressive adj. 인상 깊은

해석 35-37번은 다음 대화에 관한 문제입니다.
여: 안녕하세요. 저는 Esra Boz이고, 저는 여기에서 ³⁵당신의 인턴십 동안 당신이 배정받을 팀을 이끌고 있어요.
남: Ms. Boz, 만나서 반갑습니다. 저는 여름을 여기서 일하면서 보내게 되어 굉장히 기뻐요. ³⁶당신이 개발한 모바일 뱅킹 및 메시지 애플리케이션들은 꽤 인상 깊었어요. 저는 제가 많은 것을 배울 것이라 확신합니다.
여: 듣기 좋은 말이네요. ³⁷먼저 이 직원 매뉴얼을 봐주세요. 제가 당신의 사원증을 가지고 올게요.

35 화자 문제

해설 남자는 누구인 것 같은가?
(A) 인턴
(B) 팀장
(C) 자문 위원
(D) 접수 담당자

해설 대화에서 신분 및 직업과 관련된 표현을 놓치지 않고 듣는다. 여자가 남자에게 "your internship"이라고 한 말을 통해 남자는 인턴임을 알 수 있다. 따라서 (A)가 정답이다.

36 특정 세부 사항 문제

해설 여자는 어떤 산업에 종사하고 있는가?
(A) 보험
(B) 접객
(C) 소프트웨어
(D) 출판

해설 질문의 핵심 어구(industry ~ involved in)와 관련된 내용을 주의 깊게 듣는다. 남자가 "The mobile banking and messaging applications you have developed are quite impressive."라며 여자가 개발한 모바일 뱅킹 및 메시지 애플리케이션들이 꽤 인상 깊었다고 하였다. 따라서 (C)가 정답이다.

37 요청 문제

해설 여자는 남자에게 무엇을 하도록 요청하는가?
(A) 보안 데스크에서 서명하고 들어간다.
(B) 직원 매뉴얼을 읽는다.
(C) 모바일 애플리케이션을 설치한다.
(D) 출입증을 신청한다.

해설 여자의 말에서 요청과 관련된 표현이 언급된 다음을 주의 깊게 듣는다. 여자가 남자에게 "Please look through this employee manual first."라며 먼저 직원 매뉴얼을 봐달라고 요청하였다. 따라서 (B)가 정답이다.

어휘 sign in 서명하고 들어가다   install v. 설치하다
access card 출입증

[38-40]

🎧 캐나다식 → 미국식

Questions 38-40 refer to the following conversation.

M: Sarah, ³⁸are you ready for our meeting with the representative of Western Bank?
W: Yes. ³⁸I really hope our request to borrow money is approved. We need those funds to open up a second branch of our bakery.
M: You have the copies of our sales records from the past three years, right?
W: I transferred them to this USB stick.
M: ³⁹Maybe you should print them out.
W: OK. Give me a few minutes . . . Oh, the printer doesn't seem to be working.
M: ⁴⁰Let me see what's wrong.

representative n. 담당자, 대표자   approve v. 승인하다
branch n. 분점   sales records 판매 기록   transfer v. 옮기다

해석
38-40번은 다음 대화에 관한 문제입니다.
남: Sarah, ³⁸Western 은행 담당자와 회의할 준비가 되었나요?
여: 네. ³⁸우리의 대출 요청이 승인되길 정말로 바라요. 우리 제과점의 두 번째 분점을 내는 데 그 자금이 필요하잖아요.
남: 우리의 지난 3년간의 판매 기록 사본을 가지고 있죠, 그렇죠?
여: 제가 그것들을 이 USB에 옮겼어요.
남: ³⁹아마도 그것들을 출력해야 할 것 같아요.
여: 알겠어요. 몇 분만 주세요... 아, 프린터가 작동하지 않는 것 같아요.
남: ⁴⁰제가 무엇이 문제인지 살펴볼게요.

38 주제 문제

해설 화자들이 주로 논의하고 있는 것은 무엇인가?
(A) 제품 출시
(B) 지점 폐점
(C) 사업 협력
(D) 대출 신청

해설 대화의 주제를 묻는 문제이므로, 대화의 초반을 반드시 듣는다. 남자가 "are you ready for our meeting with the representative of Western Bank?"라며 Western 은행 담당자와 회의할 준비가 되었냐고 묻자 여자가 "I really hope our request to borrow money is approved."라며 대출 요청이 승인되길 정말로 바란다고 한 후, 대출 신청에 대한 내용으로 대화가 이어지고 있다. 따라서 (D)가 정답이다.

어휘 launch n. 출시   loan application 대출 신청

Paraphrasing

request to borrow money 대출 요청 → loan application 대출 신청

39 제안 문제

해석 남자는 무엇을 하라고 제안하는가?
(A) 기술자에게 연락하기
(B) 자금을 이체하기
(C) 문서들을 인쇄하기
(D) 일정을 업데이트하기

해설 남자의 말에서 제안과 관련된 표현 다음을 주의 깊게 듣는다. 남자가 "Maybe you should print them out."이라며 여자에게 판매 기록 사본들을 출력할 것을 제안하였다. 따라서 (C)가 정답이다.

어휘 transfer v. 이체하다, 이동하다

40 다음에 할 일 문제

해석 남자는 무엇을 할 것이라고 말하는가?
(A) 기기를 점검한다.
(B) 작업 공간을 청소한다.
(C) 파일을 삭제한다.
(D) 계약서에 서명한다.

해설 대화의 마지막 부분을 주의 깊게 듣는다. 남자가 "Let me see what's wrong."이라며 무엇이 문제인지 살펴보겠다고 한 것을 통해 남자가 프린터를 점검할 것임을 알 수 있다. 따라서 (A)가 정답이다.

어휘 workspace n. 작업 공간   contract n. 계약서

Paraphrasing

printer 프린터 → device 기기

[41-43]

Questions 41-43 refer to the following conversation.   호주식 → 미국식

M: Hey, Amanda. ⁴¹**I'm sorry, but I won't be able to go to the concert with you this Friday.** My company is participating in an exposition that starts next Monday, so I'll be busy preparing for it on Friday.

W: ⁴²**It was difficult to get the tickets for us, and they can't be refunded.** Do you know anyone who might be interested in going with me?

M: Hector said he really wanted to go to that concert. ⁴³**I can send him a text to see if he is available.**

participate v. 참가하다   exposition n. 박람회   refund v. 환불하다
available adj. 시간이 되는, 시간이 있는

해석
41-43번은 다음 대화에 관한 문제입니다.
남: 안녕하세요, Amanda. ⁴¹**죄송하지만, 제가 이번 주 금요일에 당신과 함께 콘서트에 가지 못할 것 같아요.** 제 회사가 다음 주 월요일에 시작하는 박람회에 참가할 것이라서, 저는 금요일에 그것을 준비하느라 바쁠 거예요.

여: ⁴²**우리 티켓들을 구하기가 어려웠고, 그것들은 환불이 안 되는걸요.** 저와 함께 가고 싶어 할 만한 사람을 알고 있나요?
남: Hector가 그 콘서트에 정말 가기를 원했다고 말했어요. ⁴³**그가 시간이 되는지 알아보기 위해서 제가 그에게 문자 메시지를 보낼 수 있어요.**

41 이유 문제

해석 남자는 왜 사과하는가?
(A) 몇몇 티켓들을 구매할 수 없다.
(B) 약속이 지켜질 수 없다.
(C) 매장이 주말 동안 문을 닫는다.
(D) 몇몇 초대장들이 늦게 발송되었다.

해설 질문의 핵심 어구(apologize)와 관련된 내용을 주의 깊게 듣는다. 남자가 "I'm sorry, but I won't be able to go to the concert with you this Friday."라며 이번 주 금요일에 여자와 함께 콘서트에 가지 못할 것 같아 미안하다고 하였다. 따라서 (B)가 정답이다.

어휘 purchase v. 구매하다   invitation n. 초대장

42 언급 문제

해석 여자는 티켓들에 대해 무엇을 말하는가?
(A) 할인된 가격에 이용할 수 있다.
(B) 좋은 좌석용이다.
(C) 온라인에서만 판매된다.
(D) 환불이 불가능하다.

해설 여자의 말에서 질문의 핵심 어구(tickets)가 언급된 주변을 주의 깊게 듣는다. 여자가 "It was difficult to get the tickets for us, and they can't be refunded."라며 티켓들을 구하기가 어려웠고, 그것들은 환불도 안 된다고 하였다. 따라서 (D)가 정답이다.

어휘 nonrefundable adj. 환불이 불가능한

Paraphrasing

can't be refunded 환불이 안 된다 → nonrefundable 환불이 불가능한

43 제안 문제

해석 남자는 무엇을 해주겠다고 제안하는가?
(A) 소셜 미디어에 게시한다.
(B) 불만을 제기한다.
(C) 메시지를 보낸다.
(D) 예약을 변경한다.

해설 남자의 말에서 여자를 위해 해주겠다고 언급한 내용을 주의 깊게 듣는다. 남자가 "I can send him[Hector] a text to see if he is available."이라며 Hector가 시간이 되는지 알아보기 위해 문자 메시지를 보낼 수 있다고 하였다. 따라서 (C)가 정답이다.

어휘 file v. 제기하다   complaint n. 불만

[44-46]

🎧 영국식 → 캐나다식 → 미국식

Questions 44-46 refer to the following conversation with three speakers.

> W1: Daniel, ⁴⁴**I'm happy that you've agreed to appear in the new TV commercials for our line of tennis rackets**. Having a famous player like you promote our products is sure to boost sales.
>
> M: ⁴⁵**I've always been impressed by how well-made they are compared to those of other brands. In fact, they almost never break.**
>
> W1: Great. ⁴⁶**Gina from the legal team should arrive any minute . . . Oh, here she is now.**
>
> W2: Good morning. ⁴⁶**Here's a copy of your contract. I'll go through and explain each section.**

appear v. 나오다, 출연하다   commercial n. 광고
promote v. 홍보하다   boost v. 끌어 올리다, 북돋우다
compared to ~와 비교하여

해석

44-46번은 다음 세 명의 대화에 관한 문제입니다.

여1: Daniel, ⁴⁴당신이 우리 테니스 라켓 라인을 위한 신규 텔레비전 광고에 나오는 것을 동의했다니 기뻐요. 당신처럼 유명한 선수가 우리의 제품을 홍보하는 것은 확실히 판매를 끌어 올릴 거예요.

남: ⁴⁵저는 항상 다른 브랜드들의 라켓들에 비해 그것들이 얼마나 잘 만들어졌는지에 감명을 받았어요. 사실, 그것들은 거의 망가지지 않아요.

여1: 좋아요. ⁴⁶법무팀의 Gina가 곧 도착할 거예요... 아, 그녀가 지금 오네요.

여2: 안녕하세요. ⁴⁶여기 당신의 계약서 사본이 있어요. 제가 각 부분을 보면서 설명해 드릴게요.

44 주제 문제

해석 화자들이 주로 논의하고 있는 것은 무엇인가?

(A) 기업 합병
(B) 계약 변경
(C) 매출액 발표
(D) 마케팅 캠페인

해설
대화의 주제를 묻는 문제이므로, 대화의 초반을 반드시 듣는다. 여자1이 남자에게 "I'm happy that you've agreed to appear in the new TV commercials for our line of tennis rackets"라며 테니스 라켓 라인을 위한 신규 텔레비전 광고에 남자가 나오는 것이 기쁘다고 한 뒤, 회사 광고에 대한 내용으로 대화를 이어가고 있다. 따라서 (D)가 정답이다.

어휘 merger n. 합병

Paraphrasing

TV commercials 텔레비전 광고 → marketing campaign 마케팅 캠페인

45 이유 문제

해석 남자는 왜 제품들에 감명을 받았는가?

(A) 수리하기 쉽다.
(B) 내구성이 매우 좋다.
(C) 사용하기에 간편하다.
(D) 저렴하다.

해설
질문의 핵심 어구(impressed with the products)와 관련된 내용을 주의 깊게 듣는다. 남자가 "I've always been impressed by how well-made they are compared to those of other brands. In fact, they almost never break."라며 다른 브랜드들의 라켓들에 비해 여자의 회사의 테니스 라켓이 얼마나 잘 만들어졌는지 감명을 받았고, 그것들은 거의 망가지지 않는다고 하였다. 따라서 (B)가 정답이다.

어휘 repair v. 수리하다   durable adj. 내구성이 있는
affordable adj. 저렴한, 가격이 알맞은

Paraphrasing

almost never break 거의 망가지지 않는다 → highly durable 내구성이 매우 좋은

46 다음에 할 일 문제

해설 Gina는 다음에 무엇을 할 것 같은가?

(A) 직원 평가를 실시한다.
(B) 법적 계약을 논의한다.
(C) 사업 전략을 설명한다.
(D) 채용 면접을 실시한다.

해설
질문의 핵심 어구(Gina ~ do next)와 관련된 내용을 주의 깊게 듣는다. 여자1이 "Gina from the legal team should arrive any minute . . . Oh, here she is now."라며 법무팀의 Gina가 곧 도착할 것이라며 그녀가 지금 온다고 한 말을 통해 여자2가 Gina라는 것을 알 수 있다. 여자2[Gina]가 "Here's a copy of your contract. I'll go through and explain each section."이라며 여기 계약서 사본이 있으며, 각 부분을 보면서 설명해 주겠다고 한 것을 통해 Gina가 법적 계약에 대해 논의할 것임을 알 수 있다. 따라서 (B)가 정답이다.

어휘 evaluation n. 평가   strategy n. 전략   conduct v. 실시하다, 하다

Paraphrasing

contract 계약서 → legal agreement 법적 계약

[47-49]

🎧 미국식 → 캐나다식

Questions 47-49 refer to the following conversation.

> W: Craig, ⁴⁷**how are the preparations for the upcoming seminar going**? Did you find a suitable location for it?
>
> M: I need to know the number of attendees before making a final decision.
>
> W: We're expecting about 100 people. Our keynote speaker, ⁴⁸**Dr. Walker, was the winner of last year's National Engineering Award**. So the event has attracted many professionals in his field.
>
> M: In that case, the auditorium at the Doyle Convention Center seems best.
>
> W: Got it. Do you know how the seats are arranged in the auditorium?

M: ⁴⁹I just downloaded a graphic showing the layout of the auditorium from the center's Web site. I'll e-mail it to you now.

preparation n. 준비   suitable adj. 적합한   attendee n. 참석자
make a decision 결정하다   keynote speaker 기조연설자
professional n. 전문가   field n. 분야

해석
47-49번은 다음 대화에 관한 문제입니다.
여: Craig, ⁴⁷곧 있을 세미나 준비는 어떻게 되어가고 있나요? 그것을 위한 적합한 장소를 찾았나요?
남: 저는 최종 결정을 하기 전에 참석자들의 수를 알아야 해요.
여: 우리는 약 100명으로 예상하고 있어요. 우리의 기조연설자인 ⁴⁸Dr. Walker가 작년 국가 공학상의 수상자였어요. 그래서 행사가 그의 분야에서 많은 전문가들의 관심을 불러일으켰어요.
남: 그렇다면, Doyle 컨벤션 센터의 강당이 최선인 것 같아요.
여: 알겠어요. 강당에 좌석들이 어떻게 배치되어 있는지 아시나요?
남: ⁴⁹제가 지금 막 센터의 웹사이트에서 그 강당의 배치를 보여주는 그래픽을 다운로드했어요. 지금 당신에게 그것을 이메일로 보낼게요.

47 특정 세부 사항 문제

해석 화자들은 무엇을 준비하고 있는가?
(A) 세미나
(B) 채용 박람회
(C) 도서 출간 행사
(D) 무역 박람회

해설 질문의 핵심 어구(preparing for)와 관련된 내용을 주의 깊게 듣는다. 여자가 "how are the preparations for the upcoming seminar going"이라며 곧 있을 세미나 준비는 어떻게 되어가고 있는지를 물었다. 따라서 (A)가 정답이다.

어휘 fair n. 박람회

48 특정 세부 사항 문제

해석 여자에 따르면, Dr. Walker가 이룬 것은 무엇인가?
(A) 업계의 상을 받았다.
(B) 공학 학교를 설립했다.
(C) 국가적 행사를 조직했다.
(D) 전자 기기를 발명했다.

해설 여자의 말에서 질문의 핵심 어구(Dr. Walker accomplished)와 관련된 내용을 주의 깊게 듣는다. 여자가 "Dr. Walker, was the winner of last year's National Engineering Award"라며 Dr. Walker가 작년 국가 공학상의 수상자였다고 하였다. 따라서 (A)가 정답이다.

어휘 accomplish v. 이루다, 성취하다   establish v. 설립하다
organize v. 조직하다   invent v. 발명하다

Paraphrasing

the winner of last year's National Engineering Award 작년 국가 공학상의 수상자 → won an industry award 업계의 상을 받았다

49 특정 세부 사항 문제

해석 남자는 여자에게 무엇을 보낼 것인가?
(A) 지불 기록
(B) 연설자 일정
(C) 좌석 배치도
(D) 행사 출입증

해설 질문의 핵심 어구(the man send to the woman)와 관련된 내용을 주의 깊게 듣는다. 강당에 좌석들이 어떻게 배치되어 있는지 아냐고 묻는 여자의 말에 남자가 "I just downloaded a graphic showing the layout of the auditorium from the center's Web site. I'll e-mail it to you now."라며 지금 막 센터의 웹사이트에서 그 강당의 배치를 보여주는 그래픽을 다운로드했고, 그것을 여자에게 이메일로 보내겠다고 하였다. 따라서 (C)가 정답이다.

어휘 seating chart 좌석 배치도

Paraphrasing

a graphic showing the layout of the auditorium 강당의 배치를 보여주는 그래픽 → A seating chart 좌석 배치도

[50-52]   🎧 캐나다식 → 영국식

Questions 50-52 refer to the following conversation.

M: Hi. ⁵⁰I'm calling about the two-bedroom apartment on your agency's Web site. Is it still available?
W: Yes. ⁵¹The previous tenant moved out last week, so the owner is hoping to find a new one as soon as possible.
M: Great. Would I be able to view it this afternoon?
W: Actually, my schedule is full until 8 P.M. today. What about stopping by tomorrow morning?
M: That works for me. ⁵²Could you send me some pictures of the interior?
W: Of course. I'll text them right away.

tenant n. 세입자   move out 이사를 나가다   stop by ~에 들르다
interior n. 내부

해석
50-52번은 다음 대화에 관한 문제입니다.
남: 안녕하세요. ⁵⁰저는 귀사의 웹사이트에 있는 두 개의 침실이 딸린 아파트 관련해서 전화드려요. 여전히 이용 가능한가요?
여: 네. ⁵¹이전 세입자가 지난주에 이사를 나가서, 집주인이 가능한 한 빨리 새 세입자를 찾고 싶어 합니다.
남: 잘됐네요. 오늘 오후에 그곳을 볼 수 있을까요?
여: 사실, 제 일정이 오늘 오후 8시까지 꽉 찼어요. 내일 아침에 들르시는 것은 어떠실까요?
남: 가능합니다. ⁵²제게 몇몇 실내 사진들을 보내주실 수 있나요?
여: 그럼요. 제가 바로 그것들을 문자로 보낼게요.

50 목적 문제

해석 남자는 왜 전화하고 있는가?
(A) 배송을 확정하기 위해

(B) 가능성에 대해 문의하기 위해
(C) 가격을 협상하기 위해
(D) 사업 이전을 논의하기 위해

해설 전화의 목적을 묻는 문제이므로, 대화의 초반을 반드시 듣는다. 남자가 "I'm calling about the two-bedroom apartment on your agency's Web site. Is it still available?"이라며 웹사이트에 있는 두 개의 침실이 딸린 아파트 관련해서 전화했다고 한 후, 여전히 이용 가능한지를 묻고 있다. 따라서 (B)가 정답이다.

어휘 confirm v. 확정하다 inquire v. 문의하다 negotiate v. 협상하다
relocation n. 이전

51 언급 문제

해설 여자는 아파트 가구에 대해 무엇이라 말하는가?
(A) 보수되는 중이다.
(B) 공원 전망이다.
(C) 현재 비어 있다.
(D) 발코니를 포함한다.

해설 여자의 말에서 질문의 핵심 어구(apartment unit)와 관련된 내용을 주의 깊게 듣는다. 여자가 "The previous tenant moved out last week"이라며 이전 세입자가 지난주에 이사를 나갔다고 했으므로 그 아파트 가구는 현재 비어 있음을 알 수 있다. 따라서 (C)가 정답이다.

어휘 renovate v. 보수하다 unoccupied adj. 비어 있는

52 요청 문제

해설 남자는 여자에게 무엇을 하라고 요청하는가?
(A) 주소를 확인한다.
(B) 몇몇 이미지를 제공한다.
(C) 실내 디자인을 수정한다.
(D) 계약을 연장한다.

해설 남자의 말에서 요청과 관련된 표현이 언급된 다음을 주의 깊게 듣는다. 남자가 여자에게 "Could you send me some pictures of the interior?"라며 몇몇 실내 사진들을 보내줄 수 있는지를 물었다. 따라서 (B)가 정답이다.

어휘 verify v. 확인하다 address n. 주소 modify v. 수정하다
extend v. 연장하다

Paraphrasing

send ~ some pictures 몇몇 사진들을 보내다 → Provide some images 몇몇 이미지들을 제공하다

[53-55]

3인 영국식 → 호주식

Questions 53-55 refer to the following conversation.

W: Marvin, I've got an idea for ⁵³**the factory where we produce our chairs and sofas**.

M: Is this to address the efficiency issue we've been talking about?

W: Right. ⁵⁴**Think about how we currently do things . . . The products are put together on the third floor.** ⁵⁴**This is quite far from where the components are made on the first floor.** Both areas should be on the same floor.

M: Hmm . . . ⁵⁵**Why don't I meet with some of the workers to get their opinions? I'll let you know what they say.**

address v. 다루다, 처리하다 efficiency n. 효율성, 능률
put together 조립하다, 합하다 component n. 부품, 요소

해석
53-55번은 다음 대화에 관한 문제입니다.
여: Marvin, ⁵³우리가 의자들과 소파들을 생산하는 공장에 관한 생각이 있어요.
남: 이것은 우리가 이야기해 왔던 효율성 문제를 다루기 위함인가요?
여: 맞아요. ⁵⁴우리가 현재 어떻게 일을 하는지 생각해 봐요... 제품들은 3층에서 조립돼요. ⁵⁴이곳은 1층에서 부품들이 만들어지는 곳과 꽤 멀어요. 두 공간들은 같은 층에 있어야 해요.
남: 흠... ⁵⁵제가 몇몇 직원들을 만나서 그들의 의견들을 구해보는 것은 어때요? 제가 그들이 무엇이라고 말하는지 당신에게 알려줄게요.

53 화자 문제

해설 화자들은 어디에서 일하는 것 같은가?
(A) 전자제품 공장에서
(B) 운송 시설에서
(C) 가구 제조업체에서
(D) 백화점에서

해설 대화에서 신분 및 직업과 관련된 표현을 놓치지 않고 듣는다. 여자가 남자에게 "the factory where we produce our chairs and sofas"라며 우리가 의자들과 소파들을 생산하는 공장이라고 한 말을 통해 화자들이 가구 제조업체에서 일한다는 것을 알 수 있다. 따라서 (C)가 정답이다.

어휘 facility n. 시설 manufacturer n. 제조업체
department store 백화점

54 의도 파악 문제

해설 여자는 왜 "제품들은 3층에서 조립돼요"라고 말하는가?
(A) 감탄을 나타내기 위해
(B) 지연을 설명하기 위해
(C) 도움을 요청하기 위해
(D) 문제점을 지적하기 위해

해설 질문의 인용어구(The products are put together on the third floor)가 언급된 주변을 주의 깊게 듣는다. 여자가 "Think about how we currently do things"라며 현재 어떻게 일을 하는지 생각해 보라고 한 후, "This is quite far from where the components are made on the first floor."라며 이곳은 1층에서 부품들이 만들어지는 곳과 꽤 멀다고 한 것을 통해 문제점을 지적하고 있음을 알 수 있다. 따라서 (D)가 정답이다.

어휘 admiration n. 감탄, 존경 delay n. 지연 assistance n. 도움

55 다음에 할 일 문제

해설 남자는 무엇을 할 것이라고 말하는가?
(A) 직원 의견을 공유한다.
(B) 신입 근로자들을 교육한다.

(C) 몇몇 장비를 수리한다.
(D) 웹사이트를 업데이트한다.

해설 대화의 마지막 부분을 주의 깊게 듣는다. 남자가 "Why don't I meet with some of the workers to get their opinions? I'll let you know what they say."라며 자신이 직원들을 만나 의견을 구한 후 그 의견들을 여자에게 알려주겠다고 하였다. 따라서 (A)가 정답이다.

어휘 feedback n. 의견 train v. 교육하다

Paraphrasing

opinions 의견 → feedback 의견

[56-58]

🎧 호주식 → 미국식

Questions 56-58 refer to the following conversation.

M: Do you have a few minutes, Ms. Reynolds?
W: Of course, Marik. ⁵⁶You're working on the new office building, right? The one our firm is designing for Croft Accounting.
M: ⁵⁶That's right. ⁵⁷I'm supposed to submit the blueprints to you by June 15. But, well . . . the client has requested a lot of changes.
W: I see. How much more time do you need?
M: Another week should be sufficient. Do you think this delay will cause any issues with upcoming projects?
W: I'm not sure. But ⁵⁸I'm scheduled to meet with our department head this afternoon. Why don't you accompany me to explain this situation to him?

firm n. 회사 be supposed to ~하기로 되어 있다
submit v. 제출하다 blueprint n. 청사진, 설계도
request v. 요청하다 sufficient adj. 충분한
accompany v. 함께 가다, 동반하다

해석
56-58번은 다음 대화에 관한 문제입니다.

남: Ms. Reynolds, 몇 분 정도 시간 있으실까요?
여: 그럼요, Marik. ⁵⁶당신은 새 사무실 건물을 작업하고 있죠, 그렇죠? 우리 회사가 Croft 회계 법인을 위해 설계 중인 건물이요.
남: ⁵⁶맞아요. ⁵⁷제가 당신에게 6월 15일까지 청사진들을 제출하기로 되어 있어요. 하지만, 음... 고객이 많은 수정을 요청했어요.
여: 그렇군요. 얼마나 시간이 더 필요한가요?
남: 일주일이면 충분해요. 이 지연으로 앞으로의 프로젝트에 문제가 생길 것으로 생각하시나요?
여: 잘 모르겠어요. 하지만 ⁵⁸저는 오늘 오후에 우리의 부서장과 회의를 하기로 예정되어 있어요. 저와 함께 가서 이 상황을 그에게 설명하는 게 어때요?

56 화자 문제

해설 남자는 누구인 것 같은가?
(A) 뉴스 기자
(B) 변호사
(C) 회계사
(D) 건축가

해설 대화에서 신분 및 직업과 관련된 표현을 놓치지 않고 듣는다. 여자가 남자에게 "You're working on the new office building, right? The one our firm is designing for Croft Accounting."이라며 Croft 회계 법인을 위한 건물 설계를 남자가 작업하고 있는지 묻자 남자가 "That's right."이라며 맞다고 한 것을 통해 남자가 건축가라는 것을 알 수 있다. 따라서 (D)가 정답이다.

57 의도 파악 문제

해설 남자는 "고객이 많은 수정을 요청했어요"라고 말할 때 무엇을 의도하는가?
(A) 디자인이 검토되지 않았다.
(B) 마감일을 맞출 수 없다.
(C) 불만이 처리되었다.
(D) 회사 정책이 변경될 것이다.

해설 질문의 인용어구(the client has requested a lot of changes)가 언급된 주변을 주의 깊게 듣는다. 남자가 "I'm supposed to submit the blueprints to you by June 15."이라며 청사진들의 제출이 6월 15일까지라고 한 것을 통해 남자가 마감일을 맞출 수 없음을 알 수 있다. 따라서 (B)가 정답이다.

어휘 review v. 검토하다, 다시 조사하다 deal with ~을 처리하다, 다루다
policy n. 정책

58 제안 문제

해설 여자는 무엇을 하라고 제안하는가?
(A) 워크숍 열기
(B) 프로젝트 다시 지정하기
(C) 고객에게 전화하기
(D) 회의 참석하기

해설 여자의 말에서 제안과 관련된 표현이 언급된 내용을 주의 깊게 듣는다. 여자가 "I'm scheduled to meet with our department head this afternoon."이라며 오늘 오후에 부서장과 회의를 하기로 예정되어 있다고 한 후, "Why don't you accompany me to explain this situation to him?"이라며 남자에게 함께 가서 이 상황을 부서장에게 설명하는 게 어떠냐고 제안하였다. 따라서 (D)가 정답이다.

어휘 reassign v. 다시 지정하다

[59-61]

🎧 미국식 → 영국식 → 캐나다식

Questions 59-61 refer to the following conversation with three speakers.

W1: Thanks for meeting with us. As a city council member, you're probably very busy.
W2: It's not a problem. ⁵⁹Your civic group is concerned about the proposal to build a new sports stadium in our community, right?
M: Yes. We're worried about the environmental impact. ⁶⁰The site is right next to Warren Park, which is important because it's a habitat for many types of birds.
W1: Exactly. The main problem is excessive noise and light from the stadium. These can be harmful to birds.

M: ⁶¹We prepared a document with some data about this. Here's a copy, Ms. Snyder.
W2: Thanks. I'll read through it to better understand this issue.

council n. 의회 probably adv. 아마도 civic group 시민 단체
proposal n. 제안 habitat n. 서식지 excessive adj. 심한, 과도한
harmful adj. 해로운

해석
59-61번은 다음 세 명의 대화에 관한 문제입니다.
여1: 저희를 만나주셔서 감사합니다. 시의원으로서, 당신은 아마 매우 바쁘시겠어요.
여2: 괜찮아요. ⁵⁹당신의 시민 단체는 우리 지역 사회에 새 스포츠 경기장을 짓는다는 제안에 우려를 표하고 있어요, 그렇죠?
남: 네, 저희는 환경에 미치는 영향에 대해 걱정하고 있어요. ⁶⁰그 부지는 Warren 공원 바로 옆이고, 그곳은 많은 종류의 새들의 서식지이기 때문에 중요합니다.
여1: 맞아요. 주요 문제는 경기장에서 나오는 심한 소음과 빛이에요. 이것들은 새들에게 해로울 수 있어요.
남: ⁶¹저희는 이와 관련된 몇몇 자료를 포함하고 있는 문서를 준비했어요. 여기 사본이 있어요, Ms. Snyder.
여2: 감사합니다. 제가 이 문제를 더 잘 이해하기 위해 그것을 꼼꼼히 읽어 볼게요.

59 주제 문제

해석 대화는 주로 무엇에 대한 것인가?
(A) 이전 계획
(B) 건설 프로젝트
(C) 예산 제안
(D) 환경법

해설 대화의 주제를 묻는 문제이므로, 대화의 초반을 반드시 듣는다. 여자2가 "Your civic group is concerned about the proposal to build a new sports stadium in our community"라며 시민 단체가 지역 사회에 새 스포츠 경기장을 짓는다는 제안에 우려를 표하고 있다고 말하며, 새 스포츠 경기장 건설에 대한 내용으로 대화가 이어지고 있다. 따라서 (B)가 정답이다.

어휘 relocation n. 이전

60 특정 세부 사항 문제

해석 Warren 공원과 관련하여 중요한 것은 무엇인가?
(A) 스포츠 경기장을 포함한다.
(B) 많은 관광객을 끌어들인다.
(C) 야생 동물에게 서식지를 제공한다.
(D) 지역 사회 행사를 주최한다.

해설 질문의 핵심 어구(Warren Park)가 언급된 주변을 주의 깊게 듣는다. 남자가 "The site is right next to Warren Park, which is important because it's a habitat for many types of birds."라며 새 경기장 부지가 Warren 공원 바로 옆이고, 그곳은 많은 종류의 새들의 서식지이기 때문에 중요하다고 하였다. 따라서 (C)가 정답이다.

어휘 attract v. 끌어들이다 wildlife n. 야생 동물

Paraphrasing
is a habitat for many types of birds 많은 종류의 새들의 서식지이다
→ provides a home to wildlife 야생 동물에게 서식지를 제공한다

61 특정 세부 사항 문제

해석 남자는 Ms. Snyder에게 무엇을 주는가?
(A) 보고서
(B) 책자
(C) 편지
(D) 책

해설 질문의 핵심 어구(man give to Ms. Snyder)와 관련된 내용을 주의 깊게 듣는다. 남자가 "We prepared a document with some data about this. Here's a copy, Ms. Snyder."라며 새들에게 미칠 환경적 악영향에 대한 자료를 포함하고 있는 문서를 Ms. Snyder에게 건넸다. 따라서 (A)가 정답이다.

[62-64]
캐나다식 → 영국식

Questions 62-64 refer to the following conversation and parking map.

M: I saw a sign about the waterproofing work planned for our building's parking lot, so ⁶²I stopped by the maintenance office this morning to ask for more details.
W: Did you find out which spaces will be inaccessible?
M: ⁶³The section next to the charging station for electric vehicles will be closed tomorrow. The other sections, as well as the bicycle racks, will remain open.
W: ⁶⁴That's going to be inconvenient. The parking lot usually fills up pretty fast. I'll put a notice up on our intranet board.
M: Don't forget to indicate that this is an urgent notice.

waterproofing n. 방수 처리, 방수제 maintenance n. 관리
inaccessible adj. 접근할 수 없는 charging station 충전소
rack n. 거치대, 받침대 inconvenient adj. 불편한
indicate v. 표시하다, 나타내다 urgent adj. 긴급한, 다급한

해석
62-64번은 다음 대화와 주차장 지도에 관한 문제입니다.
남: 제가 우리 건물 주차장에 예정된 방수 처리 작업에 대한 표지판을 봐서, ⁶²오늘 아침에 관리 사무실에 들러서 자세한 내용을 물어봤어요.
여: 어느 공간들이 접근할 수 없는 건지 알아냈나요?
남: ⁶³내일 전기 자동차 충전소 옆의 구역이 폐쇄될 거예요. 자전거 거치대뿐만 아니라, 다른 구역들은 계속 열려 있을 거예요.
여: ⁶⁴그것은 불편할 거예요. 주차장은 보통 꽤 빠르게 꽉 차는걸요. 제가 인트라넷 게시판에 공지를 올릴게요.
남: 이것이 긴급 공지임을 표시하는 것을 잊지 마세요.

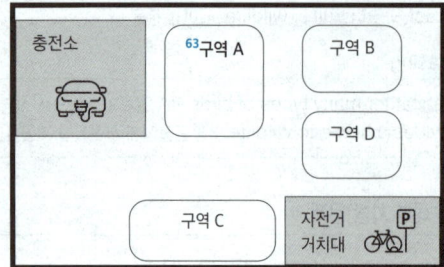

62 특정 세부 사항 문제

해석 남자는 오늘 아침에 무엇을 했는가?
(A) 정비 작업을 수행했다.
(B) 장비를 구매했다.
(C) 운송수단을 마련했다.
(D) 정보를 요청했다.

해설 질문의 핵심 어구(this morning)가 언급된 주변을 주의 깊게 듣는다. 남자가 "I stopped by the maintenance office this morning to ask for more details."라며 오늘 아침에 관리 사무실에 들러서 자세한 내용을 물어봤다고 하였다. 따라서 (D)가 정답이다.

어휘 arrange v. 마련하다, 정리하다 transportation n. 운송수단, 운송

Paraphrasing

ask for more details 자세한 내용을 물어보다 → requested information 정보를 요청했다

63 시각 자료 문제

해석 시각 자료를 보아라. 주차장의 어느 구역이 내일 폐쇄될 것인가?
(A) 구역 A
(B) 구역 B
(C) 구역 C
(D) 구역 D

해설 제시된 주차장 지도의 정보를 확인한 후 질문의 핵심 어구(be closed tomorrow)와 관련된 내용을 주의 깊게 듣는다. 남자가 "The section next to the charging station for electric vehicles will be closed tomorrow."라며 전기 자동차 충전소 옆의 구역이 폐쇄될 것이라고 했고, 전기 자동차 충전소 옆의 구역은 구역 A임을 지도에서 알 수 있다. 따라서 (A)가 정답이다.

64 방법 문제

해석 여자는 직원들에게 어떻게 문제에 대해 알릴 것인가?
(A) 회의를 함으로써
(B) 메시지를 보냄으로써
(C) 게시글을 작성함으로써
(D) 이메일을 보냄으로써

해설 질문의 핵심 어구(notify ~ about an issue)와 관련된 내용을 주의 깊게 듣는다. 여자가 "That's going to be inconvenient. The parking lot usually fills up pretty fast. I'll put a notice up on our intranet board."라며 주차장이 빨리 차서 불편할 거라며 자신이 인트라넷 게시판에 공지를 올리겠다고 하였다. 따라서 (C)가 정답이다.

어휘 notify v. 알리다 post n. 게시글

[65-67]

영국식 → 호주식

Questions 65-67 refer to the following conversation and graph.

W: Ralph, ⁶⁵**did you check the sales report from the third quarter? The phone we launched in May has become our top seller.**
M: I was expecting it to do well, but that's very impressive.
W: We should brainstorm some ideas to keep this trend going.
M: I agree. ⁶⁶**Some consumers prefer to buy what lots of other people have purchased.** So why don't we promote the phone by making these sales figures public?
W: Great idea. Let's organize a meeting with the marketing team. ⁶⁷**Could you please print the sales report for the meeting?**

quarter n. 분기   launch v. 출시하다, 시작하다
impressive adj. 인상적인   brainstorm v. 브레인스토밍하다
trend n. 추세, 경향   figure n. 수치

해설
65-67번은 다음 대화와 그래프에 관한 문제입니다.
여: Ralph, ⁶⁵3분기 판매 보고서를 확인했나요? 5월에 우리가 출시한 휴대전화가 최고 판매품이 되었어요.
남: 그것이 잘될 것이라 기대했지만, 정말 인상적이네요.
여: 우리가 이 추세를 유지하기 위해 몇몇 아이디어들을 브레인스토밍해야겠어요.
남: 동의해요. ⁶⁶몇몇 소비자들은 많은 다른 사람들이 구매한 것을 사는 것을 선호해요. 그러니까 우리가 이 판매 수치를 공개해서 그 휴대전화를 홍보하는 것은 어때요?
여: 좋은 생각이네요. 마케팅팀과 회의를 주선해 봅시다. ⁶⁷회의를 위해 판매 보고서를 인쇄해 주시겠어요?

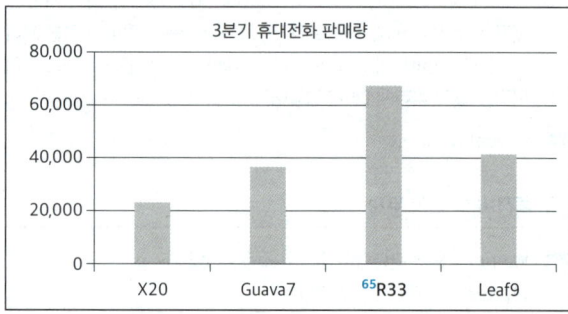

65 시각 자료 문제

해석 시각 자료를 보아라. 어떤 휴대전화가 5월에 출시되었는가?
(A) X20
(B) Guava7
(C) R33
(D) Leaf9

해설 제시된 그래프의 정보를 확인한 후 질문의 핵심 어구(released in

May)와 관련된 내용을 주의 깊게 듣는다. 여자가 "did you check the sales report from the third quarter? The phone we launched in May has become our top seller."라며 3분기 판매 보고서를 확인했냐고 물었고, 5월에 출시한 휴대전화가 최고 판매품이 되었다고 하였다. 그래프에서 최고 판매량을 가진 휴대전화는 R33임을 알 수 있다. 따라서 (C)가 정답이다.

66 언급 문제

해석 남자는 몇몇 소비자들에 대해 무엇을 말하는가?
(A) 보통 최신 모델을 구매한다.
(B) 다른 사람들이 소유한 것을 사고 싶어 한다.
(C) 항상 가격이 적절한 선택지들을 찾는다.
(D) 환경친화적인 제품들을 선호한다.

해설 남자의 말에서 질문의 핵심 어구(some customers)가 언급된 주변을 주의 깊게 듣는다. 남자가 "Some consumers prefer to buy what lots of other people have purchased."라며 몇몇 소비자들은 많은 다른 사람들이 구매한 것을 사는 것을 선호한다고 하였다. 따라서 (B)가 정답이다.

어휘 latest adj. 최신의, 최근의
affordable adj. (가격이) 적절한, 감당할 수 있는
environmentally friendly 환경친화적인

Paraphrasing

what lots of other people have purchased 많은 다른 사람들이 구매한 것 → what other people own 다른 사람들이 소유한 것

67 요청 문제

해석 여자는 남자에게 무엇을 하라고 요청하는가?
(A) 회의 일정을 잡는다.
(B) 광고를 만든다.
(C) 장치를 테스트한다.
(D) 문서를 인쇄한다.

해설 여자의 말에서 요청과 관련된 표현이 언급된 다음을 주의 깊게 듣는다. 여자가 남자에게 "Could you please print the sales report for the meeting?"이라며 회의를 위해 판매 보고서를 인쇄해 줄 수 있는지 물었다. 따라서 (D)가 정답이다.

Paraphrasing

sales report 판매 보고서 → document 문서

[68-70]

호주식 → 미국식

Questions 68-70 refer to the following conversation and product list.

M: [68]**I'm glad we decided to set up a booth at this farmer's market.** The sauces we made seem to be very popular with shoppers.
W: I guess so. Our apple and pear sauces are doing really well, but [69]**nobody seems interested in the mild one. Maybe we should consider selling it online.**
M: That's a good idea. There are several Web sites that feature homemade, organic food products like ours.
W: We'll need to come up with an eye-catching container label and a logo.
M: [70]**I have a friend who is a graphic designer. I'll reach out to him this afternoon.**

set up ~을 설치하다   mild adj. 순한, 가벼운
consider v. 고려하다, 여기다   feature v. 특징으로 하다
organic adj. 유기농의, 생물의   come up with 생각해 내다, 떠올리다
eye-catching adj. 눈길을 끄는   container n. 용기, 그릇
field n. 분야, 범위   reach out ~에게 연락하다

해석
68-70번은 다음 대화와 제품 목록에 관한 문제입니다.
남: [68]우리가 이 농산물 시장에서 부스를 설치하기로 해서 기뻐요. 우리가 만든 소스는 쇼핑객들에게 매우 인기 있는 것 같아요.
여: 그러게요. 우리의 사과와 배 소스는 정말 잘 팔리고 있지만, [69]아무도 순한 소스에는 관심이 없어 보여요. 아마도 우리는 그것을 온라인으로 판매하는 것을 고려해야 할 것 같아요.
남: 좋은 생각이네요. 우리의 것들처럼 수제의, 유기농 식품을 특징으로 하는 여러 웹사이트들이 있어요.
여: 우리는 눈길을 끄는 용기 라벨과 로고를 생각해 내야 할 필요가 있어요.
남: [70]저는 그래픽 디자이너인 친구가 있어요. 제가 오늘 오후에 그에게 연락할게요.

소스	맛
사과	단 맛
[69]토마토	순한 맛
배	매우 단 맛
고추	매운맛

68 장소 문제

해석 화자들은 어디에 있는 것 같은가?
(A) 농산물 시장에
(B) 식당에
(C) 놀이공원에
(D) 식품 제조 공장에

해설 대화에서 장소와 관련된 표현을 놓치지 않고 듣는다. 남자가 "I'm glad we decided to set up a booth at this farmer's market."이라며 이 농산물 시장에서 부스를 설치하기로 해서 기쁘다고 한 것을 통해 화자들은 농산물 시장에 있음을 알 수 있다. 따라서 (A)가 정답이다.

어휘 amusement park 놀이공원   manufacturing n. 제조
plant n. 공장

69 시각 자료 문제

해석 시각 자료를 보아라. 여자는 어떤 소스를 온라인으로 판매할 것을 제안하는가?
(A) 사과
(B) 토마토
(C) 배
(D) 고추

해설 제시된 제품 목록의 정보를 확인한 후 질문의 핵심 어구(selling online)가 언급된 주변을 주의 깊게 듣는다. 여자가 "nobody seems interested in the mild one. Maybe we should consider selling it online."이라며 아무도 순한 소스에는 관심이 없어 보인다고 한 후, 아마도 그것을 온라인으로 판매하는 것을 고려해야 할 것이라고 했고, 순한 맛의 소스는 토마토임을 제품 목록에서 확인할 수 있다. 따라서 (B)가 정답이다.

70 다음에 할 일 문제

해설 남자는 무엇을 할 것이라고 말하는가?
(A) 레시피를 수정한다.
(B) 제품군을 확장한다.
(C) 전단을 나눠 준다.
(D) 친구와 이야기한다.

해설 대화의 마지막 부분을 주의 깊게 듣는다. 남자가 "I have a friend who is a graphic designer. I'll reach out to him this afternoon."이라며 그래픽 디자이너인 친구에게 오늘 오후에 연락하겠다고 한 것을 통해 남자가 친구와 이야기할 것임을 알 수 있다. 따라서 (D)가 정답이다.

어휘 expand v. 확장하다 distribute v. 나눠 주다 flyer n. 전단

PART 4

[71-73]
🔊 호주식

Questions 71-73 refer to the following excerpt from a meeting.

> ⁷¹**I'd like to take a few minutes to go over the new rule that will take effect next Monday.** We've decided to reduce waste to protect the environment. ⁷²**So customers will no longer be permitted to drink beverages in take-out cups if they stay in our café.** Only people who intend to take their orders outside should be given take-out containers. ⁷³**I'll put up the poster with this information at the end of the day.**

take effect 시행되다, 효과가 나타나다 reduce v. 줄이다
waste n. 쓰레기, 낭비 permit v. 허용하다, 허가하다
beverage n. 음료 container n. 용기, 그릇

해설
71-73번은 다음 회의 발췌록에 관한 문제입니다.

⁷¹저는 다음 주 월요일부터 시행될 새로운 규칙을 몇 분간 점검하려고 합니다. 우리는 환경을 보호하기 위해 쓰레기를 줄이기로 했습니다. ⁷²그래서 만약 손님들이 우리 카페 안에 머무른다면 테이크아웃 컵에 음료를 마시는 것은 더 이상 허용되지 않을 것입니다. 주문한 것을 밖으로 가지고 나가려는 사람들만 테이크아웃 용기를 제공받을 것입니다. ⁷³저는 오늘 하루가 끝날 때쯤 이 안내 사항을 다룬 포스터를 게시하겠습니다.

71 목적 문제

해설 회의의 목적은 무엇인가?
(A) 직원을 소개하기 위해
(B) 방침 변경을 설명하기 위해
(C) 일정 업데이트를 확인하기 위해
(D) 판촉 행사를 설명하기 위해

해설 회의의 목적을 묻는 문제이므로, 지문의 초반을 반드시 듣는다. "I'd like to take a few minutes to go over the new rule that will take effect next Monday."라며 다음 주 월요일부터 시행될 새로운 규칙을 몇 분간 점검하려고 한다고 한 후, 새로운 규칙에 대한 내용으로 지문이 이어지고 있다. 따라서 (B)가 정답이다.

어휘 introduce v. 소개하다, 도입하다 describe v. 설명하다
promotional adj. 판촉의

Paraphrasing

rule 규칙 → policy 방침

72 청자 문제

해설 청자들은 어떤 유형의 사업체에서 일하는 것 같은가?
(A) 가구 매장
(B) 출장 음식 업체
(C) 커피 가게
(D) 사진 스튜디오

해설 지문에서 신분 및 직업과 관련된 표현을 놓치지 않고 듣는다. "So customers are no longer permitted to drink beverages in take-out cups if they stay in our café."라며 손님들이 우리 카페 안에 머무른다면 테이크아웃 컵에 음료를 마시는 것은 더 이상 허용되지 않을 것이라고 한 것을 통해 청자들이 커피 가게에서 일한다는 것을 알 수 있다. 따라서 (C)가 정답이다.

73 다음에 할 일 문제

해설 화자는 무엇을 할 계획인가?
(A) 다과를 준비한다.
(B) 공지를 게시한다.
(C) 고객에게 연락한다.
(D) 몇몇 장비를 주문한다.

해설 지문의 마지막 부분을 주의 깊게 듣는다. "I'll put up the poster with this information at the end of the day."라며 오늘 하루가 끝날 때쯤 이 안내 사항을 다룬 포스터를 게시하겠다고 한 것을 통해 공지를 게시할 계획임을 알 수 있다. 따라서 (B)가 정답이다.

어휘 refreshment n. 다과

[74-76]
🔊 영국식

Questions 74-76 refer to the following telephone message.

> Good morning, Derek. This is Brenda Fuller from *New Horizons Magazine*. ⁷⁴**I read your article about the dangers of artificial intelligence.** My concern is that the language is too technical. ⁷⁵**I appreciate that you included scientific evidence to support your argument**, but you need to simplify the wording. ⁷⁶**Why don't we meet and discuss this? There is a great Italian place across the street from my office.** We could have lunch together, and I could share my ideas. I'm free any time next week, so let me know your availability.

article n. 기사 technical adj. 기술적인, 전문적인
appreciate v. 높이 평가하다 evidence n. 증거
argument n. 주장, 논거 simplify v. 단순하게 하다, 간소화하다
discuss v. 논의하다 share v. 공유하다

해석
74-76번은 다음 전화 메시지에 관한 문제입니다.

안녕하세요, Derek. *New Horizons* 잡지사의 Brenda Fuller입니다. ⁷⁴저는 인공 지능의 위험성에 대한 당신의 기사를 읽었습니다. 제가 우려하는 점은 용어가 너무 기술적이라는 것이에요. ⁷⁵당신의 주장을 뒷받침하기 위해 과학적 증거를 포함했다는 점은 높이 평가하지만, 당신은 표현을 단순하게 해야 할 필요가 있습니다. ⁷⁶저희가 만나서 이에 대해 논의해 보는 것은 어떨까요? 제 사무실 건너편에 훌륭한 이탈리안 음식점이 있습니다. 같이 점심을 먹으면서, 제 생각을 공유해드릴 수 있습니다. 저는 다음 주에 언제든 시간이 있으니, 가능한 시간을 알려주세요.

74 특정 세부 사항 문제

해석 청자는 무슨 주제에 대한 기사를 썼는가?
(A) 기술적 위험
(B) 의학 연구
(C) 사회 프로그램
(D) 경제 문제

해석 질문의 핵심 어구(topic ~ an article)와 관련된 내용을 주의 깊게 듣는다. "I read your article about the dangers of artificial intelligence."라며 인공 지능의 위험성에 대한 당신의 기사를 읽었다고 했으므로, 청자가 쓴 기사의 주제가 인공 지능의 위험성임을 알 수 있다. 따라서 (A)가 정답이다.

어휘 risk n. 위험 medical adj. 의학의 economic adj. 경제의

Paraphrasing
dangers of artificial intelligence 인공 지능의 위험성
→ Technological risks 기술적 위험

75 특정 세부 사항 문제

해석 화자는 기사의 어떤 점을 마음에 들어 하는가?
(A) 제목의 표현
(B) 난이도
(C) 증거 유형
(D) 주장의 요점

해석 질문의 핵심 어구(like about the article)와 관련된 내용을 주의 깊게 듣는다. "I appreciate that you included scientific evidence to support your argument"라며 주장을 뒷받침하기 위해 과학적 증거를 포함했다는 점은 높이 평가한다고 한 것을 통해, 기사에 포함된 과학적 증거를 마음에 들어 함을 알 수 있다. 따라서 (C)가 정답이다.

어휘 title n. 제목 level of difficulty 난이도

76 특정 세부 사항 문제

해석 화자는 어디에서 만나고 싶어 하는가?
(A) 사무실에서
(B) 식당에서
(C) 학교에서
(D) 도시공원에서

해석 지문에서 질문의 핵심 어구(want to meet)와 관련된 표현을 놓치지 않고 듣는다. "Why don't we meet and discuss this? There is a great Italian place across the street from my office."라며 만나서 이에 대해 논의해 보는 것은 어떤지 제안한 후, 자신의 사무실 건너편에 훌륭한 이탈리안 음식점이 있다고 한 것을 통해 화자가 식당에서 만나고 싶어 함을 알 수 있다. 따라서 (B)가 정답이다.

[77-79] 캐나다식

Questions 77-79 refer to the following podcast.

Welcome to today's episode of the *San Francisco Stories* podcast. ⁷⁷I promised to share my thoughts about the Coast Sushi restaurant that opened last month, but, well . . . I haven't been able to get a reservation yet. It's just too popular right now. But to make up for this, I have a special guest today. ⁷⁸Deborah Collins has been designing women's formalwear for over a decade, and her work has been featured in prestigious boutiques around the city. ⁷⁹You can see pictures of her pieces if you go to www.deborahcollins.com. I encourage you to check them out. Welcome to the show, Ms. Collins.

promise v. 약속하다 thought n. 생각, 사고 reservation n. 예약
formalwear n. 정장, 예복 decade n. 10년
prestigious adj. 유명한, 명망 있는 encourage v. 권장하다

해석
77-79번은 다음 팟캐스트에 관한 문제입니다.

샌프란시스코 이야기 팟캐스트의 오늘의 에피소드에 오신 것을 환영합니다. ⁷⁷제가 지난달에 문을 연 Coast 초밥 레스토랑에 대한 제 생각을 공유하겠다고 약속했지만, 음... 아직 예약을 하지 못했습니다. 지금 너무 인기가 많아요. 하지만 이를 보상해 드리기 위해 오늘 특별한 게스트를 모셨습니다. ⁷⁸Deborah Collins는 10년 넘게 여성 정장을 디자인해 왔으며, 그녀의 옷은 시의 유명 부티크에서 소개되어 왔습니다. ⁷⁹www.deborahcollins.com에 가시면 그녀의 옷 사진을 볼 수 있습니다. 꼭 그것들을 확인해 보실 것을 권장해요. 방송에 오신 것을 환영합니다, Ms. Collins.

77 의도 파악 문제

해석 화자는 "아직 예약을 하지 못했습니다"라고 말할 때 무엇을 의도하는가?
(A) 개업이 연기되었다.
(B) 메뉴 항목이 변경되었다.
(C) 행사가 취소될 것이다.
(D) 후기가 공유되지 않을 것이다.

해석 질문의 인용어구(I haven't been able to get a reservation yet)가 언급된 주변을 주의 깊게 듣는다. "I promised to share my thoughts about the Coast Sushi restaurant that opened last month"라며 지난달에 문을 연 Coast 초밥 레스토랑에 대한 화자의 생각을 오늘의 팟캐스트에서 공유하겠다고 약속했다고 한 것을 통해, 후기를 공유할 수 없을 것임을 알 수 있다. 따라서 (D)가 정답이다.

Paraphrasing

share ~ thoughts 생각을 공유하다 → review ~ be shared 후기가 공유되다

78 특정 세부 사항 문제

해석 Ms. Collins는 어떤 분야에 종사할 것 같은가?
(A) 출판
(B) 여행
(C) 패션
(D) 교육

해설 질문의 대상(Ms. Collins)의 신분 및 직업과 관련된 표현을 놓치지 않고 듣는다. "Deborah Collins has been designing women's formalwear for over a decade"라며 Deborah Collins가 10년 넘게 여성 정장을 디자인해 왔다고 하였다. 따라서 (C)가 정답이다.

79 제안 문제

해석 화자는 청자들에게 무엇을 하라고 제안하는가?
(A) 웹사이트를 방문한다.
(B) 제품을 구입한다.
(C) 앱을 다운로드한다.
(D) 질문을 제출한다.

해설 지문의 중후반에서 제안과 관련된 표현이 포함된 문장을 주의 깊게 듣는다. "You can see pictures of her pieces if you go to www.deborahcollins.com. I encourage you to check them out."이라며 www.deborahcollins.com에 가면 Deborah Collins의 옷 사진을 볼 수 있는데 꼭 확인해 볼 것을 권장한다고 하였다. 따라서 (A)가 정답이다.

어휘 purchase v. 구입하다, 구매하다 submit v. 제출하다

[80-82] 🔊 미국식

Questions 80-82 refer to the following announcement.

> Attention, please. ⁸⁰The marathon will begin in 10 minutes, so all runners should proceed to the starting line. Make sure you are wearing the number you have been assigned to identify you. ⁸¹The route the runners will follow is lined with highly visible red flags, and water stations are set up every two kilometers along the route. ⁸²At two o'clock, there will be an official ceremony, during which medals and cash prizes will be given by our sponsor.
>
> proceed v. 이동하다, 나아가다 assign v. 지정하다, 할당하다
> identify v. 식별하다, 확인하다 route n. 경로 follow v. 따라가다
> visible adj. 눈에 띄는 flag n. 깃발 official adj. 공식적인, 공무상의
> sponsor n. 후원자, 후원자

해석 80-82번은 다음 공지에 관한 문제입니다.

주목해 주십시오. ⁸⁰마라톤은 10분 후에 시작될 것이므로 모든 주자들은 출발선으로 이동해야 합니다. 본인을 식별하기 위해 지정된 번호를 착용하고 있는지 확인하세요. ⁸¹주자들이 따라갈 경로에는 눈에 잘 띄는 빨간색 깃발이 줄지어 있으며, 경로를 따라 2킬로미터마다 물을 마실 수 있는 장소가 설치되어 있습니다. ⁸²2시에는 공식적인 시상식이 열릴 것이며, 시상식 동안 우리의 후원사가 메달과 상금을 수여할 것입니다.

80 주제 문제

해석 어떤 종류의 행사가 열리고 있는가?
(A) 퍼레이드
(B) 콘서트
(C) 대회
(D) 자선 경매

해설 공지의 주제를 묻는 문제이므로, 지문의 초반을 반드시 듣는다. "The marathon will begin in 10 minutes, so all runners should proceed to the starting line."이라며 마라톤이 10분 후에 시작되니 모든 주자는 출발선으로 이동하라고 한 것을 통해 마라톤 대회가 열리고 있음을 알 수 있다. 따라서 (C)가 정답이다.

81 언급 문제

해석 경로에 대해 무엇이 언급되는가?
(A) 막혀 있다.
(B) 명확히 표시되어 있다.
(C) 점검될 것이다.
(D) 변경될 것이다.

해설 질문의 핵심 어구(route)가 언급된 주변을 주의 깊게 듣는다. "The route the runners will follow is lined with highly visible red flags"라며 주자들이 따라갈 경로에는 눈에 잘 띄는 빨간색 깃발이 줄지어 있다고 하였다. 따라서 (B)가 정답이다.

어휘 block off ~을 막다, 차단하다 mark v. 표시하다
inspect v. 점검하다 alter v. 변경하다

Paraphrasing

lined with highly visible red flags 눈에 잘 띄는 빨간색 깃발이 줄지어 있는 → clearly marked 명확히 표시되어 있는

82 다음에 할 일 문제

해석 2시에 무슨 일이 일어날 것인가?
(A) 점심 휴식이 제공될 것이다.
(B) 밴드가 공연할 것이다.
(C) 상이 수여될 것이다.
(D) 사진이 찍힐 것이다.

해설 질문의 핵심 어구(two o'clock)와 관련된 내용을 주의 깊게 듣는다. "At two o'clock, there will be an official ceremony, during which medals and cash prizes will be given by our sponsor."라며 2시에는 공식적인 시상식이 열릴 것이며, 시상식 동안 후원사가 메달과 상금을 수여할 것이라고 하였다. 따라서 (C)가 정답이다.

어휘 perform v. 공연하다, 수행하다 award n. 상, 상금
present v. 수여하다, 주다

Paraphrasing

medals and cash prizes will be given 메달과 상금이 수여될 것이다 → Awards will be presented 상이 수여될 것이다

[83-85]

Questions 83-85 refer to the following telephone message.

> Hello, Bianca. I heard back from the representative of Sten Investment. **83He was very impressed with your presentation and wants our company to handle all of their press releases and other public communications.** Obviously, you'll be closely involved in developing Sten Investment's communications strategy. But **84I'm putting Saskia Lee in charge of the project**. She's one of our most experienced staff members. I'll be out of the office today and tomorrow, but we can talk about this in person next week if you want. **85Just call my secretary to set up a time.**

representative n. 담당자, 대표
impressed adj. 깊은 인상을 받은, 감명을 받은
handle v. 다루다, 처리하다 press release 보도 자료
public communication 홍보 활동 involve v. 관여하다
strategy n. 전략 experienced adj. 경험이 많은 secretary n. 비서

해석
83-85번은 다음 전화 메시지에 관한 문제입니다.
안녕하세요, Bianca. 저는 Sten 투자사의 담당자로부터 답변을 들었습니다. 83그는 당신의 프레젠테이션에 매우 깊은 인상을 받았으며 우리 회사가 그들의 모든 보도 자료와 다른 홍보 활동을 다루길 원합니다. 당연히 당신은 Sten 투자사의 커뮤니케이션 전략을 발전시키는 데 밀접하게 관여할 것입니다. 하지만 84저는 Saskia Lee에게 그 프로젝트를 맡길 것입니다. 그녀는 가장 경험이 많은 직원 중 한 명입니다. 제가 오늘과 내일은 사무실을 비울 예정이지만, 원한다면 다음 주에 직접 만나서 이것에 대해 이야기해도 됩니다. 85제 비서에게 전화를 걸어 시간을 정하세요.

83 화자 문제

해설 화자는 어디에서 일하는 것 같은가?
(A) 우체국에서
(B) 금융 기관에서
(C) 채용 회사에서
(D) 홍보 회사에서

해설 지문에서 신분 및 직업과 관련된 표현을 놓치지 않고 듣는다. "He was very impressed with your presentation and wants our company to handle all of their press releases and other public communications."라며 우리 회사가 모든 보도 자료와 다른 홍보 활동을 다루길 원한다고 한 것을 통해 홍보 회사에서 일하는 것임을 알 수 있다. 따라서 (D)가 정답이다.

어휘 financial adj. 금융의, 재무의 institution n. 기관
recruitment n. 채용 public relations 홍보

84 의도 파악 문제

해설 화자는 왜 "그녀는 가장 경험이 많은 직원 중 한 명입니다"라고 말하는가?
(A) 즉각적인 대응을 장려하기 위해
(B) 업무 평가를 공유하기 위해
(C) 결정에 대한 이유를 제공하기 위해
(D) 문제에 대한 해결책을 제안하기 위해

해설 질문의 인용어구(She's one of our most experienced staff members)가 언급된 주변을 주의 깊게 듣는다. "I'm putting Saskia Lee in charge of the project"라며 Saskia Lee에게 그 프로젝트를 맡길 것이라고 했으므로 담당자를 정한 결정에 대한 이유를 제공하기 위해 그녀가 가장 경험이 많은 직원 중 한 명이라고 말했음을 알 수 있다. 따라서 (C)가 정답이다.

어휘 immediate adj. 즉각적인 evaluation n. 평가 reason n. 이유

85 방법 문제

해설 청자는 어떻게 회의를 잡을 수 있는가?
(A) 그룹 메일을 보냄으로써
(B) 보조원에게 말함으로써
(C) 고객의 사무실에 전화함으로써
(D) 특정 요일에 방문함으로써

해설 질문의 핵심 어구(arrange a meeting)와 관련된 내용을 주의 깊게 듣는다. "Just call my secretary to set up a time."이라며 화자의 비서에게 전화를 걸어 시간을 잡으라고 했으므로 (B)가 정답이다.

어휘 specific adj. 특정한, 구체적인

Paraphrasing

secretary 비서 → assistant 보조원

[86-88]

Questions 86-88 refer to the following talk.

> **86Starting today, all mechanics should use the Autocheck Diagnostic Tablet. This tablet will help you accurately determine what's wrong with a car.** Just connect it to the vehicle and select the "Scan" option. The tablet will then provide you with a list of steps you can take to confirm the problem. **87Later today, I'll follow up with each of you to find out what you think about the tablet.** **88There's just one thing I'd like to remind you of. This tablet requires regular updates.** Please don't ignore the update notifications.

mechanic n. 정비사, 수리공 diagnostic adj. 진단의
accurately adv. 정확하게 determine v. 판단하다, 결정하다
connect v. 연결하다 follow up with ~의 후속 조치를 취하다
remind v. 상기시키다 ignore v. 무시하다 notification n. 알림

해석
86-88번은 다음 담화에 관한 문제입니다.
86오늘부터 모든 정비사들은 Autocheck 진단 태블릿을 사용해야 합니다. 이 태블릿은 차량에 어떤 문제가 있는지 정확하게 판단하는 데 도움이 될 것입니다. 차량에 연결하고 "스캔" 옵션을 선택하기만 하면 됩니다. 그러면 태블릿에서 문제를 확인하기 위해 취할 수 있는 조치 목록을 제공할 것입니다. 87오늘 오후에, 저는 여러분 각자가 그 태블릿에 대해 어떻게 생각하는지 알아보기 위해서 후속 조치를 취할 것입니다. 88한 가지 상기시켜 드리고 싶은 것이 있습니다. 이 태블릿은 정기적인 업데이트가 필요합니다. 업데이트 알림을 무시하지 마세요.

86 장소 문제

해석 담화는 어디에서 일어나고 있는가?
(A) 자동차 정비소에서
(B) 피트니스 센터에서
(C) 전자제품 매장에서
(D) 장비 대여 회사에서

해설 담화가 이루어지는 장소를 묻는 문제이므로, 장소와 관련된 표현을 놓치지 않고 듣는다. "Starting today, all mechanics should use the Autocheck Diagnostic Tablet. This tablet will help you accurately determine what's wrong with a car."라며 정비사들에게 차량의 문제를 판단하는 데 도움이 되는 진단 태블릿을 사용해야 한다고 한 것을 통해 담화가 자동차 정비소에서 일어나고 있음을 알 수 있다. 따라서 (A)가 정답이다.

어휘 electronics n. 전자제품, 전자 기기 rental n. 대여

87 다음에 할 일 문제

해석 화자는 오늘 오후에 무엇을 할 것 같은가?
(A) 매뉴얼을 마무리한다.
(B) 제품 샘플을 가져온다.
(C) 의견을 수렴한다.
(D) 임시 노트북을 제공한다.

해설 질문의 핵심 어구(later today)가 언급된 주변을 주의 깊게 듣는다. "Later today, I'll follow up with each of you to find out what you think about the tablet."이라며 오늘 오후에 화자는 청자들 각자에게 그 태블릿을 어떻게 생각하는지 알아보기 위해 후속 조치를 취할 것이라고 하였다. 따라서 (C)가 정답이다.

어휘 finalize v. 마무리하다

Paraphrasing
find out what you think about 어떻게 생각하는지 확인하다
→ Gather some opinions 의견을 수렴하다

88 특정 세부 사항 문제

해석 청자들은 무엇을 하도록 상기되는가?
(A) 소프트웨어 업데이트하기
(B) 공급업체에 연락하기
(C) 공간을 치우기
(D) 설명서를 검토하기

해설 질문의 핵심 어구(reminded to do)와 관련된 내용이 언급된 주변을 주의 깊게 듣는다. "There's just one thing I'd like to remind you of. This tablet requires regular updates."라며 이 태블릿은 정기적인 업데이트가 필요하다고 상기시켜 주고 있다. 따라서 (A)가 정답이다.

어휘 supplier n. 공급업체, 공급자 instruction n. 설명서, 지시

[89-91] 🔊 미국식

Questions 89-91 refer to the following tour information.

I'm pleased to welcome you to the Lansbury Observatory. ⁸⁹This amazing research facility was built using funds ⟳ donated by Marion Clark, the president of Continental Bank. During today's tour, you will get to see almost every section of the observatory. ⁹⁰But before we begin, we will head to the conference room, where a group of astronomers will show you some pictures taken with the telescope and explain how it operates. ⁹¹Once the tour is complete, we will be stopping by the gift shop. There you can buy some items to remember your experience today.

observatory n. 천문대, 관측소 fund n. 자금, 기금
donate v. 기부하다 president n. 회장 astronomer n. 천문학자
telescope n. 망원경 operate v. 작동하다, 가동되다

해석
89-91번은 다음 관광 안내에 관한 문제입니다.
Lansbury 천문대에 오신 것을 환영합니다. ⁸⁹이 놀라운 연구 시설은 Continental 은행의 회장인 Marion Clark께서 기부하신 자금으로 지어졌습니다. 오늘 투어에서는 천문대의 거의 모든 구역을 보게 될 것입니다. ⁹⁰하지만 시작하기 전에, 우리는 회의실로 갈 것이고, 그곳에서 천문학자 그룹이 망원경으로 찍은 사진을 보여주고 그것의 작동 방식을 설명해 줄 것입니다. ⁹¹투어가 끝나면, 우리는 선물 가게에 들를 것입니다. 그곳에서 오늘 경험을 기억할 수 있는 몇몇 제품들을 구입할 수 있습니다.

89 언급 문제

해석 Lansbury 천문대에 대해 무엇이 언급되는가?
(A) 대중교통 역 근처에 있다.
(B) 한 달 동안 문을 닫을 것이다.
(C) 시설이 최근에 보수되었다.
(D) 기부된 자금을 사용하여 지어졌다.

해설 질문의 핵심 어구(Lansbury Observatory)가 언급된 주변을 주의 깊게 듣는다. "This amazing research facility was built using funds donated by Marion Clark"이라며 이 놀라운 연구 시설은 Marion Clark이 기부한 자금으로 지어졌다고 하였다. 따라서 (D)가 정답이다.

90 다음에 할 일 문제

해석 곧 무슨 일이 일어날 것인가?
(A) 실험이 시행될 것이다.
(B) 발표가 있을 것이다.
(C) 포스터가 보여질 것이다.
(D) 면접이 시작될 것이다.

해설 질문의 핵심 어구(take place momentarily)와 관련된 내용을 주의 깊게 듣는다. "But before we begin, we will head to the conference room, where a group of astronomers will show you some pictures taken with the telescope and explain how it operates."라며 투어를 시작하기 전에, 회의실로 갈 것이고, 그곳에서 천문학자들이 사진을 보여주고 현미경이 어떻게 작동하는지 보여줄 것이라고 한 것을 통해 곧 천문학자들의 발표가 있을 것임을 알 수 있다. 따라서 (B)가 정답이다.

어휘 experiment n. 실험

91 특정 세부 사항 문제

해석 화자에 따르면, 청자들은 투어 후에 무엇을 할 수 있는가?
(A) 기부한다.
(B) 사진을 본다.
(C) 기념품을 산다.
(D) 다른 투어를 신청한다.

해설 질문의 핵심 어구(after the tour)와 관련된 내용을 주의 깊게 듣는다. "Once the tour is complete, we will be stopping by the gift shop. There you can buy some items"라며 투어가 끝나면 선물 가게에 들를 것이고 그곳에서 몇몇 제품들을 살 수 있다고 하였다. 따라서 (C)가 정답이다.

어휘 donation n. 기부 souvenir n. 기념품

[92-94]

🎧 호주식

Questions 92-94 refer to the following news report.

> In business news, ⁹²**Western Medical Group held a press conference to respond to negative feedback about its dramatic decrease in profits last quarter**. Company spokesperson Judith Brown assured investors that this is a temporary problem. ⁹³**She blamed the situation on increased costs for equipment upgrades. But there are also new competitors.** ⁹³**This is a more likely explanation for the company's falling revenues.** We are now joined by economist Erik Stevens. ⁹⁴**He will discuss how the health-care market is changing and what companies like Western Medical Group must do to adapt.**

press conference 기자 회견 respond v. 대응하다, 반응하다
dramatic adj. 급격한, 극적인 profit n. 수익, 이윤
spokesperson n. 대변인 assure v. 확신시키다
temporary adj. 일시적인, 임시의 blame v. ~의 탓으로 돌리다
competitor n. 경쟁업체, 경쟁자 explanation n. 설명
revenue n. 매출, 수입 adapt v. 적응하다

해석
92-94번은 다음 뉴스 보도에 관한 문제입니다.

비즈니스 뉴스에서는, ⁹²Western 의료 그룹사가 지난 분기 수익의 급격한 감소에 대한 부정적인 피드백에 대응하기 위해 기자 회견을 열었습니다. 회사 대변인인 Judith Brown은 투자자들에게 이는 일시적인 문제라고 확신시켰습니다. ⁹³그녀는 장비 업그레이드 비용 증가를 상황 탓으로 돌렸습니다. 하지만 새로운 경쟁업체들도 있습니다. ⁹³이것은 회사의 매출 감소에 대한 더 그럴듯한 설명입니다. 이제 우리는 경제학자 Erik Stevens와 함께합니다. ⁹⁴그는 의료 시장이 어떻게 변화하고 있는지와 Western 의료 그룹사와 같은 기업들이 적응하기 위해 무엇을 해야 하는지에 대해 논의할 것입니다.

92 이유 문제

해석 Western 의료 그룹사는 왜 기자 회견을 열었는가?
(A) 대변인을 소개하기 위해
(B) 비판에 대처하기 위해
(C) 새로운 서비스를 알리기 위해
(D) 재정적 성과를 축하하기 위해

해설 질문의 핵심 어구(hold a press conference)가 언급된 주변을 주의 깊게 듣는다. "Western Medical Group held a press conference to respond to negative feedback about its dramatic decrease in profits last quarter"라며 Western 의료 그룹사가 지난 분기 수익의 급격한 감소에 대한 부정적인 피드백에 대응하기 위해 기자 회견을 열었다고 하였다. 따라서 (B)가 정답이다.

어휘 criticism n. 비판, 비난 accomplishment n. 성과, 업적

Paraphrasing

respond to negative feedback 부정적인 피드백에 대응하다
→ address a criticism 비판에 대처하다

93 의도 파악 문제

해석 화자는 "하지만 새로운 경쟁업체들도 있습니다"라고 말할 때 무엇을 의도하는가?
(A) 어려움은 감당할 수 있다.
(B) 비용은 아직 확정될 수 없다.
(C) 변화는 즉각적이지 않을 것이다.
(D) 이유가 불충분하다.

해설 질문의 인용어구(But there are also new competitors)가 언급된 주변을 주의 깊게 듣는다. "She blamed the situation on increased costs for equipment upgrades."라며 대변인은 장비 업그레이드 비용 증가를 상황 탓으로 돌렸다고 한 후, 하지만 새로운 경쟁업체들도 있다고 했다. "This is a more likely explanation for the company's falling revenues."라며 이것이 회사의 매출 감소에 대한 더 그럴듯한 설명이라고 한 것을 통해 이유를 보충하기 위해 한 말임을 알 수 있다. 따라서 (D)가 정답이다.

어휘 manageable adj. 감당할 수 있는, 관리할 수 있는
insufficient adj. 불충분한

94 특정 세부 사항 문제

해석 다음에 무엇이 논의될 것 같은가?
(A) 업계의 미래
(B) 투자 전략
(C) 의료 절차
(D) 회사의 확장

해설 질문의 핵심 어구(be discussed next)와 관련된 내용을 주의 깊게 듣는다. 지문 마지막에서 "He will discuss how the health-care market is changing and what companies like Western Medical Group must do to adapt."라며 의료 시장이 어떻게 변화하고 있는지와 Western 의료 그룹사와 같은 기업들이 적응하기 위해 무엇을 해야 하는지에 대해 논의할 것이라고 하였다. 따라서 (A)가 정답이다.

어휘 strategy n. 전략 procedure n. 절차, 수술
expansion n. 확장, 확대

[95-97]

🎧 캐나다식

Questions 95-97 refer to the following telephone message and wall arrangement.

> Hello, Maryanne. This is Jamarcus Flint. I was just reviewing our plans for the upcoming photo display for ⁹⁵**the exhibition on the evolution of clothing styles**. ⁹⁶**I feel that our**

main photo, the image of the dancer, should be in the upper-right section of the wall. Also, ⁹⁷I will need a little more time to finalize the brochures that we'll be handing out to visitors. Apparently, ⁹⁷our editors are still reviewing the captions that will accompany each image. Please give me a call back with your thoughts as soon as possible.

display n. 전시, 진열   exhibition n. 전시회   evolution n. 발전, 진화
finalize v. 마무리하다, 완결하다   brochure n. 책자
hand out ~을 나눠주다, 배포하다   editor n. 편집자
caption n. (사진·삽화의) 설명, 캡션   thought n. 생각, 사고

해석
95-97번은 다음 전화 메시지와 벽 배열 방식에 관한 문제입니다.
안녕하세요, Marayanne. 저는 Jamarcus Flint입니다. ⁹⁵의류 스타일의 발전에 관한 전시회에서 곧 공개될 사진 전시 계획을 검토하고 있었는데요. ⁹⁶저희의 메인 사진인 댄서의 이미지는 벽의 오른쪽 상단에 있어야 한다고 생각해요. 또한 저는 방문객들에게 나눠줄 ⁹⁷안내 책자를 마무리하는 데 시간이 조금 더 필요할 것입니다. ⁹⁷저희 편집자들이 각 이미지에 함께 들어갈 설명을 아직 검토 중인 것 같아요. 가능한 한 빨리 당신의 생각과 관련하여 제게 다시 전화해 주세요.

95 특정 세부 사항 문제

해석   전시회의 주제는 무엇인가?
(A) 현대 건축
(B) 패션 역사
(C) 지리적 형성
(D) 기술 혁신

해설   질문의 핵심 어구(the theme of the exhibition)와 관련된 내용을 주의 깊게 듣는다. "the exhibition on the evolution of clothing styles"라며 의류 스타일의 발전에 관한 전시회라고 하였다. 따라서 (B)가 정답이다.

어휘   architecture n. 건축   geological adj. 지리적인, 지질학의
formation n. 형성   innovation n. 혁신

Paraphrasing
evolution of clothing styles 의류 스타일의 발전 → Fashion history 패션 역사

96 시각 자료 문제

해석   시각 자료를 보아라. 화자는 어떤 위치에 메인 사진을 걸고 싶어 하는가?
(A) 위치 1
(B) 위치 2
(C) 위치 3
(D) 위치 4

해설   제시된 벽 배열 방식의 정보를 확인한 후 질문의 핵심 어구(place the main photo)와 관련된 내용을 주의 깊게 듣는다. "I feel that our main photo, the image of the dancer, should be in the upper-right section of the wall."이라며 메인 사진인 댄서의 이미지는 벽의 오른쪽 상단에 있어야 한다고 했고, 오른쪽 상단은 3임을 벽 배열 방식에서 알 수 있다. 따라서 (C)가 정답이다.

97 특정 세부 사항 문제

해석   화자에 따르면, 무엇이 지연을 발생시키고 있는가?
(A) 프린터가 제대로 작동하지 않고 있다.
(B) 몇몇 기구가 설치되고 있다.
(C) 글이 검토되고 있다.
(D) 사진 촬영이 일정보다 늦어졌다.

해설   질문의 핵심 어구(causing a delay)와 관련된 내용을 주의 깊게 듣는다. "I will need a little more time to finalize the brochures"라며 안내 책자를 마무리하는 데 시간이 더 필요할 것이라고 한 후, "our editors are still reviewing the captions that will accompany each image"라며 각 이미지와 함께 들어갈 설명을 검토 중이라고 하였다. 따라서 (C)가 정답이다.

어휘   malfunction v. 제대로 작동하지 않다   set up ~을 설치하다

Paraphrasing
caption 설명 → text 글

[98-100]   🎧 영국식

Questions 98-100 refer to the following excerpt from a meeting and workshop schedule.

⁹⁸As you know, the staff at our bank will be taking part in some cyber-security workshops next week. We originally planned to hold four sessions, but ⁹⁹the instructor we booked for Friday has an unexpected scheduling conflict. Therefore, there will only be three. I have asked our IT manager to put together some information on the topic we will be skipping for our staff to read through. ¹⁰⁰I'll call him in a few minutes to check on his progress.

take part in ~에 참여하다   instructor n. 강사
skip v. 건너뛰다, 생략하다   progress n. (일의) 진척, 진행

해석
98-100번은 다음 회의 발췌록과 워크숍 일정표에 관한 문제입니다.
⁹⁸아시다시피, 우리 은행의 직원들은 다음 주에 사이버 보안 워크숍에 참여할 것입니다. 원래 4개의 세션을 개최할 계획이었지만, ⁹⁹금요일로 예약해둔 강사가 예상치 못하게 일정이 겹쳤습니다. 따라서 3개 세션만 진행될 것입니다. 저는 우리의 IT 관리자에게 직원들이 읽을 수 있도록 건너뛸 주제에 대한 몇 가지 정보를 정리해 달라고 요청했습니다. ¹⁰⁰잠시 후 그에게 전화하여 진행 상황을 확인하겠습니다.

워크숍 주제	요일
이메일 피싱 사기	화요일
모바일 기기 보안	수요일
악성 소프트웨어와 바이러스	목요일
⁹⁹비밀번호 보호	금요일

98 화자 문제

해석 화자는 어디에서 일하는 것 같은가?
 (A) 금융 기관에서
 (B) 교육 시설에서
 (C) 보안 회사에서
 (D) 소프트웨어 개발 회사에서

해설 지문에서 신분 및 직업과 관련된 표현을 놓치지 않고 듣는다. "As you know, the staff at our bank will be taking part in some cyber-security workshops next week."이라며 우리 은행의 직원들은 다음 주에 사이버 보안 워크숍에 참석할 것이라고 한 것을 통해 화자가 금융 기관에서 일한다는 것을 알 수 있다. 따라서 (A)가 정답이다.

어휘 institution n. 기관 developer n. 개발회사, 개발자

Paraphrasing

bank 은행 → financial institution 금융 기관

99 시각 자료 문제

해석 시각 자료를 보아라. 어떤 워크숍이 취소되었는가?
 (A) 이메일 피싱 사기
 (B) 모바일 기기 보안
 (C) 악성 소프트웨어와 바이러스
 (D) 비밀번호 보호

해설 제시된 워크숍 일정표의 정보를 확인한 후 질문의 핵심 어구(canceled)와 관련된 내용을 주의 깊게 듣는다. "the instructor we booked for Friday has an unexpected scheduling conflict. Therefore, there will only be three."라며 금요일로 예약해 둔 강사가 예상치 못하게 일정이 겹쳐서 3개 세션만 진행될 것이라고 한 것을 통해 금요일 워크숍이 취소된 것임을 알 수 있고, 금요일로 예정되었던 워크숍은 '비밀번호 보호'임을 워크숍 일정표에서 알 수 있다. 따라서 (D)가 정답이다.

100 다음에 할 일 문제

해석 화자는 다음에 무엇을 할 것 같은가?
 (A) 강사를 만난다.
 (B) 보고서를 읽는다.
 (C) 애플리케이션을 다운로드한다.
 (D) 동료에게 연락한다.

해설 지문의 마지막 부분을 주의 깊게 듣는다. "I'll call him[our IT manager] in a few minutes to check on his progress."라며 잠시 후 우리의 IT 관리자에게 전화하여 진행 상황을 확인하겠다고 하였다. 따라서 (D)가 정답이다.

PART 5

101 형용사 자리 채우기

해설 빈칸 뒤의 명사(investors)를 꾸밀 수 있는 것은 형용사이므로 형용사 (C) satisfied(만족스러워하는)가 정답이다. 동사 (A)와 (B), 명사 (D)는 형용사 자리에 올 수 없다.

해석 성공적인 제품 출시 후에, 주주 총회는 만족스러워하는 투자자들로 가득 찼다.

어휘 shareholder n. 주주 investor n. 투자자

102 격에 맞는 인칭대명사 채우기

해설 빈칸은 주절의 주어 자리이므로, 주어 역할을 할 수 있는 주격 인칭대명사 (A)와 소유대명사 (C)가 정답의 후보이다. '그는 상세한 후기를 작성했다'라는 의미가 되어야 하므로 주격 인칭대명사 (A) he가 정답이다. 소유대명사 (C)를 쓸 경우 '그의 것이 후기를 작성했다'라는 어색한 의미를 만들기 때문에 답이 될 수 없다. 목적격 인칭대명사 (B)와 재귀대명사 (D)는 주어 자리에 올 수 없다. 참고로, (C) his는 소유격 인칭대명사로 쓰일 경우, 뒤에 명사가 온다.

해석 Mr. Kumar가 소설 *Eternal Spark*를 읽는 것을 끝냈을 때, 그는 상세한 후기를 작성했다.

어휘 detailed adj. 상세한, 세밀한

103 명사 자리 채우기

해설 부정관사(a) 다음에 올 수 있고 빈칸 뒤의 to 부정사구(to complete ~)의 꾸밈을 받을 수 있는 것은 명사이므로 명사 (C) reminder(상기시키는 것)가 정답이다. (B)는 동명사일 경우 부정관사(a) 다음에 올 수 없고, 현재분사일 경우 명사 자리에 올 수 없다. 동사 (A)와 동사 또는 과거분사 (D)는 명사 자리에 올 수 없다.

해석 그 알림 이메일은 의무적인 안전 교육을 완료할 것을 상기시키는 것으로의 역할을 한다.

어휘 notification n. 알림, 통지 mandatory adj. 의무적인, 법에 정해진 safety training 안전 교육

104 형용사 어휘 고르기

해설 '반품하려면 그것의 원래의 소포 상자에 보내주세요'라는 문맥이므로 (B) original(원래의)이 정답이다. (A) assorted는 '여러 가지의', (C) thin은 '얇은', (D) minimal은 '최소의'라는 의미이다.

해석 귀하의 제품을 저희에게 안전하게 반품하려면 그것의 원래의 소포 상자에, 가급적이면 상품 정보가 기재된 짐표와 함께 보내주세요.

어휘 package n. 소포 (상자), 포장
 preferably adv. 가급적이면, 되도록이면
 packing slip 상품 정보가 기재된 짐표

105 분사구문 채우기

해설 이 문장은 주어(Adams Law Firm), 동사(has provided), 목적어(legal services)를 갖춘 완전한 절이므로, ___ ~ law는 수식어 거품으로 보아야 한다. 이 수식어 거품은 동사가 없는 거품구이므로, 거품구를 이끌 수 있는 현재분사 (D) specializing이 정답이다. 형용사 (A), 동사 (B), 명사 (C)는 수식어 거품을 이끌 수 없다.

해석 Adams 법률 사무소는 가족법을 전문으로 하면서 20년 이상 법률 서비스를 제공해 왔다.

어휘 legal adj. 법률의, 법률과 관련된 specialize in ~을 전문으로 하다

106 부사 어휘 고르기

해설 '자동차 부품 비용이 상당히 더 높아질 것으로 예상되다'라는 문맥이므로 (A) considerably(상당히)가 정답이다. (B) adversely는 '불리하게', (C) generously는 '관대하게', (D) expertly는 '전문가답게'라는 의미이다.

해석 공급망 중단으로 인해 다음 분기에는 자동차 부품 비용이 상당히 더 높아질 것으로 예상된다.

어휘 automobile n. 자동차 component n. 부품, 요소
supply chain 공급망 disruption n. 중단, 붕괴

107 짝을 이루는 표현

해설 빈칸 앞의 동사 meet(지키다, 충족시키다)과 함께 '마감 기한에 맞추다'라는 의미의 어구 meet the deadline을 완성하는 명사 (B) deadline(마감 기한)이 정답이다. (A) performance는 '공연, 실적', (C) maintenance는 '유지, 보수 관리', (D) admission은 '입장, 승인'이라는 의미이다.

해석 편집팀은 마감 기한에 맞추기 위해 광고 문안 작성 작업의 일부를 프리랜서들에게 위탁했다.

어휘 editorial adj. 편집의, 사설의
outsource v. (외부에) 위탁하다, 외주를 주다
copywriting n. 광고 문안 작성

최신토익경향

'동사+명사' 형태의 짝 표현 문제는 꾸준히 출제되고 있다. 자주 나오는 짝 표현들을 덩어리로 암기해 두자.

<최근 출제된 '동사+명사' 짝 표현>
• host an event 행사를 주최하다
• conduct a survey 설문조사를 실시하다
• follow instructions 지시 사항을 따르다
• meet the demand 수요를 충족시키다
• exceed the weight limit 중량 제한을 초과하다

108 명사 어휘 고르기

해설 '연휴 시즌 동안 직원들은 그들의 정규 업무 외의 업무들을 수행하다'라는 문맥이므로 명사 duty(업무)의 복수형 (C) duties가 정답이다. (A)의 response는 '응답, 반응', (B)의 favor는 '호의, 부탁', (D)의 competitor는 '경쟁사'라는 의미이다.

해석 연말 연휴 시즌 동안 Sutton's 장난감사의 직원들은 그들의 정규 업무 외의 업무들을 수행해야 할 수도 있다.

어휘 year-end adj. 연말의, 연말에 일어나는 task n. 업무, 일
regular adj. 정규의, 규칙적인

109 명사 자리 채우기

해설 문장에 동사(will depend)만 있고 주어가 없으므로 주어 자리에 올 수 있는 동명사 (B)와 명사 (C)가 정답의 후보이다. 빈칸 뒤에 전치사(into)가 있으므로 명사 (C) Acceptance(수락, 받아들임)가 정답이다. 동사 accept(받아들이다)는 타동사이므로 동명사 (B) Accepting을 쓸 경우 전치사 없이 뒤에 목적어가 바로 나와야 한다. 동사 (A)와 형용사 (D)는 명사 자리에 올 수 없다.

해석 인턴십 프로그램에 대한 합격 여부는 학업 성과 및 관련된 업무 경험에 따라 달라질 것이다.

어휘 academic adj. 학업의, 학교의 performance n. 성과, 실적
relevant adj. 관련된, 관련 있는

110 부정대명사 채우기

해설 빈칸은 주절의 주어 자리이므로, 주어 자리에 올 수 있는 대명사 (B), (C), (D)가 정답의 후보이다. 'Mr. Patton과 Ms. Liu가 서로 다른 역량을 가졌지만, 둘 중 누구라도 관리 역할에 적합할 것이다'라는 의미가 되어야 하므로 (B) either(둘 중 누구라도)가 정답이다. 대명사로도 쓰이는 수량 표현 (C) more(더 많은 사람들, 더 많은 것들)는 어색한 문장을 만든다. 대명사 (D) anyone(누구나)은 불특정 다수 중 한 명을 가리키므로 이 문장의 문맥에는 적절하지 않다. 목적격 인칭대명사 (A) them은 주어 자리에 올 수 없다.

해석 비록 Mr. Patton과 Ms. Liu는 서로 다른 역량을 가졌지만, 둘 중 누구라도 프로젝트 관리 역할에 매우 적합할 것이다.

어휘 management n. 관리, 경영 role n. 역할

최신토익경향

부정대명사는 종류가 많기 때문에 의미와 쓰임을 정확하게 구별할 줄 알아야 한다. 자주 출제되는 부정대명사의 의미와 쓰임을 알아두자.

<부정대명사의 의미와 쓰임>

부정대명사	의미	쓰임
one	하나	불특정한 단수 가산 명사를 대신할 때
anyone	누구나, 어느 사람이든	불특정한 다수의 사람들을 대신할 때
another	또 다른 하나	이미 언급한 것 이외의 또 다른 하나를 대신할 때
neither	(둘 중) 어느 것도 아닌	이미 언급한 두 개의 대상이 모두 아닌 경우를 나타낼 때
either	(둘 중) 어느 하나	이미 언급한 두 개의 대상 중 하나를 나타낼 때

111 부사 자리 채우기

해설 형용사 역할을 하는 수 표현(three)을 꾸밀 수 있는 것은 부사이므로 부사 (C) roughly(대략)가 정답이다. 형용사 또는 동사 (A), 현재분사 (B), 명사 (D)는 형용사를 꾸밀 수 없다.

해석 Mr. Chapman은 회사 서버의 소프트웨어를 업데이트하는 데 대략 세 시간이 걸릴 것으로 예상한다.

어휘 take v. (시간이) 걸리다

112 명사 어휘 고르기

해설 '제품 카탈로그는 모든 의류 제품의 설명을 포함하다'라는 문맥이므로 명사 description(설명, 묘사)의 복수형 (D) descriptions가 정답이다. (A)의 statement는 '진술(서)', (B)의 procedure는 '절차', (C)의 uncertainty는 '불확실성'이라는 의미이다.

해석 Scout 의류사의 제품 카탈로그는 모든 의류 제품의 설명을 포함한다.

어휘 include v. 포함하다, 함유하다   clothing n. 의류, 옷

113 부사 자리 채우기

해설 빈칸 뒤의 동사(shot)를 꾸밀 수 있는 것은 부사이므로 부사 (B) intentionally(의도적으로)가 정답이다. 동사 (A), 명사 (C), 동명사 또는 현재분사 (D)는 동사를 꾸밀 수 없다.

해석 영화감독 Robert Duke는 긴장감을 조성하기 위해 영화 *Outcast*의 여러 장면들을 의도적으로 어둠 속에서 촬영했다.

어휘 shoot v. 촬영하다   several adj. 여럿의   scene n. 장면, 현장
suspense n. 긴장감, 불안

114 형용사 어휘 고르기

해설 '요리의 주된 재료는 신선한 바질이다'라는 문맥이므로 (B) primary (주된, 주요한)가 정답이다. (A) diverse는 '다양한', (C) prompt는 '즉각적인', (D) diligent는 '근면한'이라는 의미이다.

해석 Ms. Belano의 요리의 주된 재료는 신선한 바질인데, 이것이 그 요리가 그렇게 풍미 있는 이유이다.

어휘 ingredient n. 재료, 구성 요소   flavorful adj. 풍미 있는, 맛 좋은

115 동사 어휘 고르기

해설 '사업장 안전 문제는 회의에서 다룰 주제들 중 하나이다'라는 문맥이므로 (D) address(다루다)가 정답이다. (A) appear는 '나타나다', (B) activate는 '활성화하다', (C) complete는 '완료하다, 완성하다'라는 의미이다.

해석 사업장 안전 문제는 Mr. Lucas가 금요일에 회의에서 다룰 주제들 중 하나이다.

어휘 workplace n. 사업장, 업무 현장   issue n. 문제, 안건

최신토익경향

2024년 하반기에는 여러 의미를 갖는 다의어 동사를 정답으로 고르는 문제들이 출제되었다. 아래의 다의어 동사들과 그 의미를 모두 암기해 두자.

<다의어 동사와 의미>
- address (주제로) 다루다, 연설하다, 해결하다
- arrange 일정을 잡다, 정리하다
- extend 연장하다, 베풀다
- cover 씌우다, (주제로) 다루다, (돈을) 대다
- run 달리다, 운영하다, 작동하다, 계속되다

116 형용사 자리 채우기

해설 빈칸 뒤의 명사(feedback)를 수식할 수 있는 것은 형용사이므로 형용사 (A)와 형용사 역할을 하는 현재분사 (C)가 정답의 후보이다. '설문조사가 회사의 운영에 대한 건설적인 피드백을 제공하게 하다'라는 문맥이므로 형용사 (A) constructive(건설적인)가 정답이다. 현재분사 (C) constructing을 쓸 경우 '건설하는 피드백'이라는 어색한 문맥이 되고, 동명사로 본다 해도, 빈칸이 포함된 구조는 'offer + 간접 목적어(Rogers Furniture) + 직접 목적어(___ feedback)'의 구조이므로 'Rogers 가구사에 피드백을 건설하는 것을 제공하다'라는 어색한 문맥이 되어 답이 될 수 없다. 명사 (D) construction을 쓸 경우 '회사의 운영에 대한 건설 피드백'이라는 어색한 문맥이 되므로 답이 될 수 없다. 동사 (B)는 명사를 수식할 수 없다.

해석 연간 설문조사는 직원들이 Rogers 가구사에 그것의 운영에 대한 건설적인 피드백을 제공하게 한다.

어휘 annual adj. 연간의, 연례의   operation n. 운영, 사업

117 전치사 채우기

해설 '비록 최선이라고 생각하지 않지만, 계획에 동조하다'라는 문맥이므로 '~에 동조하다, 찬성하다'를 의미하는 어구 go along with를 완성하는 전치사 (D) along이 정답이다. (A) for는 '~를 위해', (B) to는 '~로, ~에게', (C) upon은 '~하자마자'라는 의미이다.

해석 Ms. Richardson은 비록 그것이 최선이라고 생각하지 않았지만, 회사의 계획에 동조했다.

118 to 부정사 채우기

해설 빈칸 앞의 be sure과 함께 '반드시 ~을 하다'라는 의미를 완성하는 to 부정사 (C) to submit이 정답이다. 참고로, be sure는 전치사 of 또는 about과 함께 'be sure of/about ~'(~에 대해 확신하다)으로, that절과 함께 'be sure that ~'(~라는 것을 확신하다)으로 쓰일 수 있음을 알아둔다.

해석 보증을 청구하려면 결함이 있는 제품의 일련번호와 영수증을 반드시 제출하세요.

어휘 warranty n. 보증(서)   claim n. 청구, 요구
defective adj. 결함이 있는   sales receipt 영수증

119 명사 어휘 고르기

해설 '모든 대표자들에게 3일간의 호텔 체류에 대한 비용을 댈 것이다'라는 문맥이므로 (B) stay(체류, 머무름)가 정답이다. (A) refund는 '환불', (C) amenity는 '생활 편의 시설', (D) status는 '상태'라는 의미이다.

해석 학회 동안, Bond 그룹은 참여하는 모든 대표자들에게 3일간의 호텔 체류에 대한 비용을 댈 것이다.

어휘 cover v. (비용 등을 충분히) 대다, 충당하다
representative n. 대표자, 대리인

120 부사 자리 채우기

해설 빈칸 뒤의 형용사(large)를 꾸밀 수 있는 것은 부사이므로 부사 (D) surprisingly(놀랄 만큼)가 정답이다. 동명사 또는 현재분사 (A), 명사 또는 동사 (B), 동사 또는 과거분사 (C)는 형용사를 꾸밀 수 없다.

해석 Haynesville 자연사 박물관은 나비 전시회를 방문하는 놀랄 만큼 많은 수의 사람들에 기뻐한다.

어휘 pleased adj. 기뻐하는, 기쁜   exhibition n. 전시회, 진열

121 to 부정사 채우기

해설 빈칸 앞의 수동태 동사(are asked)에 쓰인 동사 ask는 to 부정사를 취하는 동사이므로 (C) to provide가 정답이다. 참고로, 이 문장은 'At Adkins Consulting, they ask job applicants to provide ~.'의 능동태 문장이 수동태로 바뀌면서 목적어인 job applicants가

주어 자리로 오고 목적격 보어인 to provide가 수동태 동사 are asked 뒤에 남은 구조이다.

해석 Adkins 컨설팅사에서, 구직자들은 적어도 두 개의 전문가의 추천서를 제공할 것을 요구받는다.

어휘 job applicant 구직자, 취업 지원자
professional adj. 전문가의, 직업의   reference n. 추천서, 참조

122 동사 자리 채우기

해설 이 문장은 주어가 없는 명령문이므로, 명령문의 동사 자리에 올 수 있는 동사원형 (D) choose(선택하다)가 정답이다. 명사 (A), 과거 시제 동사 (B), 과거분사 (C)는 명령문의 동사 자리에 올 수 없다.

해석 태블릿을 설정하는 것을 끝내기 위해, 당신의 선호하는 언어와 표준 시간대를 선택하세요.

어휘 set up 설정하다, 준비하다   time zone 표준 시간대

123 형용사 어휘 고르기

해설 '이해관계자들에게 보낸 이메일은 설득력이 있어서, 자금을 확보할 수 있다'라는 문맥이므로 (B) persuasive(설득력 있는)가 정답이다. (A) vulnerable은 '취약한', (C) calculable은 '계산할 수 있는', (D) sequential은 '순차적인'이라는 의미이다.

해석 Ms. Collins가 Wrightwell 캐피털사의 이해관계자들에게 보낸 이메일은 설득력이 있어서, 이전을 위한 자금을 확보할 수 있었다.

어휘 stakeholder n. 이해관계자, 투자자   secure v. 확보하다, 보장하다
funding n. 자금, 투자   relocation n. 이전, 재배치

124 전치사 채우기

해설 '신생 기업에 투자하다'라는 문맥이므로 동사 invest와 함께 쓰여 '~에 투자하다'라는 의미를 완성하는 전치사 (A) in이 정답이다.

해석 Annika 금융사의 이사회는 인공 지능 주도의 금융 솔루션에 집중하는 신생 기업에 투자하기로 결정했다.

어휘 invest v. 투자하다   startup n. 신생 기업, 벤처 기업
AI-driven adj. 인공 지능 주도의

125 동사 어휘 고르기

해설 '강의가 매우 길어서 모든 정보를 받아들이기 어렵다'라는 문맥이므로 (A) absorb(받아들이다)가 정답이다. (B) withdraw는 '취소하다, 인출하다', (C) adapt는 '조정하다, 적응하다', (D) surpass는 '초과하다'라는 의미이다.

해석 경영 방식에 대한 강의는 매우 길어서, Mr. Lee는 모든 정보를 받아들이기 어려웠다.

어휘 lecture n. 강의, 강연

126 명사 자리 채우기

해설 빈칸은 동명사(making)의 목적어이면서 전치사구(to systems)의 꾸밈을 받는 명사 자리이므로 명사 (A)와 (D)가 정답의 후보이다. '시스템을 발전시키다'라는 의미가 되어야 하므로 명사 advancement(발전)의 복수형 (D) advancements가 정답이다. 명사 (A) advance(진보, 향상)는 관사(the)와 함께 쓰이거나 복수형 advances로 쓰여야 한다. 참고로, (A) advance는 '나아가다, 진보하다'라는 의미의 동사로도 자주 출제된다는 것을 알아둔다. 동명사 또는 현재분사 (B), 동사 또는 과거분사 (C)는 전치사구의 꾸밈을 받을 수 없다.

해석 Lowery 산업사의 사이버 보안 전문가들은 회사 데이터를 보호하기 위해 마련된 시스템을 발전시키는 일을 할 것이다.

어휘 cybersecurity n. 사이버 보안   expert n. 전문가

127 부사절 접속사 채우기

해설 '일단 수습 기간을 마치면 건강 보험 혜택을 받을 수 있다'라는 의미가 되어야 하므로 부사절 접속사 (C) once(일단 ~하면)가 정답이다. 부사절 접속사 (A) since(~ 이래로), (B) as if(마치 ~처럼), (D) unless(~하지 않는다면)를 쓸 경우 모두 어색한 문맥이 된다.

해석 직원 안내서에 따르면, 신입 직원들은 일단 90일의 수습 기간을 마치면 건강 보험 혜택을 받을 수 있다.

어휘 handbook n. 안내서, 편람
eligible adj. ~을 받을 수 있는, 자격이 있는
probationary period 수습 기간, 시험 채용 기간

128 전치사 채우기

해설 '최고의 지원자를 찾기 위해 지원서를 분류하다'라는 의미가 되어야 하므로 빈칸 앞의 동사 is sorting의 sort와 함께 쓰여 '~을 분류하다'라는 의미를 완성하는 (A) through가 정답이다. 'sort through(~을 분류하다)'를 덩어리로 암기해 두도록 하자. (B) except는 '~ 외에는', (C) between은 '~ 사이에', (D) within은 '~ 이내에'라는 의미이다.

해석 Solis 교육 그룹의 인사 부서는 최고의 지원자들을 찾기 위해 수백 장의 지원서를 분류하고 있다.

어휘 department n. 부서   application n. 지원(서), 신청

129 부사 어휘 고르기

해설 '어떠한 위험이라도 완화하기 위해 점진적으로 새로운 기술이 시행될 것이 권장되다'라는 문맥이므로 (B) gradually(점진적으로)가 정답이다. (A) randomly는 '무작위로', (C) reluctantly는 '마지못해', (D) interestingly는 '흥미롭게도'라는 의미이다.

해석 그것들(기술들)과 관련된 어떠한 위험이라도 완화하기 위해 점진적으로 새로운 기술들이 시행될 것이 권장된다.

어휘 implement v. 시행하다, 실시하다   mitigate v. 완화하다, 경감하다
associated with ~와 관련된

130 지시대명사 those 채우기

해설 빈칸은 동명사(including)의 목적어이면서 전치사구(for beginners)의 꾸밈을 받는 명사 자리이므로 지시대명사 (B)와 부정대명사 (C)가 정답의 후보이다. '초보자들을 위한 수업들을 포함한 다양한 수업들을 제공하다'라는 의미가 되어야 하므로 앞에 나온 복수 명사(classes)를 대신하는 지시대명사 (B) those가 정답이다. (C) one another는 '서로'라는 의미이므로 문맥상 적절하지 않다.

해설 (A) which는 관계대명사일 경우 앞에 선행사가 나와야 하고, 의문형용사일 경우 뒤에 명사가 나와야 한다. 목적격 인칭대명사 (D) them은 전치사구의 꾸밈을 받을 수 없다.

해석 FlexUp 피트니스는 서로 다른 레벨을 수용하기 위해 초보자들을 위한 수업들을 포함한 다양한 필라테스 수업들을 제공한다.

어휘 various adj. 다양한, 여러 가지의
accommodate v. 수용하다, 공간을 제공하다

PART 6

131-134번은 다음 설명에 관한 문제입니다.

> 131바나나 빵의 인기의 한 가지 이유는 그것이 만들기 쉽기 때문입니다. 시작하려면, 잘 익은 바나나 몇 개를 으깨주세요. 132당신은 이를 위해 포크를 사용할 수 있습니다. 133그다음에, 밀가루, 베이킹 소다, 그리고 소금을 추가하기 전에 버터, 설탕, 그리고 계란을 바나나와 섞으세요. 반죽을 빵틀에 붓고 그것을 섭씨 180도로 구워 주세요. 한 시간 후에 이쑤시개로 빵의 가운데를 찔러 보세요. 134만약 그것이 깨끗하게 나온다면, 빵을 오븐에서 꺼내세요.
>
> ripe adj. 잘 익은, 여문 flour n. 밀가루 batter n. 반죽
> stick v. 찌르다, 박다 toothpick n. 이쑤시개

131 명사 자리 채우기

해설 정관사(the)와 전치사(of) 사이에 올 수 있는 것은 명사이므로 명사 (B) popularity가 정답이다. 동사 (A), 형용사 (C), 부사 (D)는 명사 자리에 올 수 없다.

132 동사 어휘 고르기

해설 '당신은 이를 위해 포크를 사용할 수 있다'라는 문맥이므로 (A) use (사용하다)가 정답이다. (B) begin은 '시작하다', (C) remove는 '제거하다', (D) connect는 '연결하다'라는 의미이다.

133 접속부사 채우기 주변 문맥 파악

해설 빈칸이 콤마와 함께 문장의 맨 앞에 온 접속부사 자리이므로, 앞 문장과 빈칸이 있는 문장의 의미 관계를 파악하여 정답을 선택한다. 앞 문장에서 바나나를 으깨기 위해 포크를 사용할 수 있다고 했고, 빈칸이 있는 문장에서는 버터, 설탕, 그리고 계란을 바나나와 섞으라고 했으므로, 앞 문장의 내용에 이어질 다음 과정을 설명할 때 사용되는 (D) Then(그다음에)이 정답이다.

어휘 instead adv. 대신에 thus adv. 따라서, 그러므로

134 알맞은 문장 고르기

해설 (A) 많은 사람들은 빵 굽기가 그들의 스트레스를 줄여준다고 생각합니다.
(B) 만약 그것이 깨끗하게 나온다면, 빵을 오븐에서 꺼내세요.
(C) 베이킹 소다는 냄비와 팬을 세척하는 데 좋습니다.
(D) 잘 익은 과일 조각은 그것들이 오래 가게 하기 위해 냉장고에 보관하세요.

해설 앞 문장 'Stick a toothpick into the center of the loaf after an hour.'에서 한 시간 후에 이쑤시개로 빵의 가운데를 찔러 보라고 했으므로, 빈칸에는 이쑤시개로 반죽을 찌른 다음의 과정을 설명하는 내용이 들어가야 함을 알 수 있다. 따라서 (B)가 정답이다.

어휘 reduce v. 줄이다, 낮추다 pot n. 냄비 store v. 보관하다, 저장하다
fridge n. 냉장고

135-138번은 다음 정보에 관한 문제입니다.

> 전국적인 시 경연대회인 제5회 연례 Jabari 상의 시작을 알리게 되어 기쁩니다. 135올해 경연대회를 위한 출품은 3월 31일까지입니다. 그것들은 "소속감"이라는 주제를 탐구해야 합니다. 136시는 제목이 있어야 하며 40줄을 넘지 않아야 합니다. 그것들은 또한 이전에 출간된 적이 없어야 하고 작가의 원작이어야 합니다. 137또한, 참가자당 최대 세 편의 시라는 제한이 있으며 각각의 출품에는 5달러의 처리 비용이 적용될 것입니다. 138당선된 시를 출품한 사람들은 최대 1,000달러의 상금을 받을 것이며, 그들의 작품이 The Tinsley Review에 특별히 포함될 것입니다.
>
> nationwide adj. 전국적인 poetry n. 시
> competition n. 경연대회, 경쟁 explore v. 탐구하다, 답사하다
> theme n. 주제, 테마 previously adv. 이전에, 미리
> publish v. 출간하다, 출판하다 entrant n. 참가자, 출전자
> submission n. 출품, 제출 feature v. 특별히 포함하다, 특징을 이루다

135 올바른 시제의 동사 채우기 주변 문맥 파악

해설 '올해 경연대회를 위한 출품은 3월 31일까지이다'라는 문맥인데, 이 경우 빈칸이 있는 문장만으로는 올바른 시제의 동사를 고를 수 없으므로 주변 문맥이나 전체 문맥을 파악하여 정답을 고른다. 앞 문장에서 제5회 연례 Jabari 상의 시작을 알리게 되어 기쁘다고 하였고, 뒤 문장에서 출품작들은 "소속감"이라는 주제를 탐구해야 한다고 했으므로 이미 확정된 미래의 일을 나타낼 때 쓰는 현재 시제 (A) are가 정답이다.

136 알맞은 문장 고르기

해석 (A) 지난 우승자들은 그들 작품의 전체 모음집을 출간해 왔습니다.
(B) 참가자들은 이 날짜까지 대회 결과를 통지받을 것입니다.
(C) 아마추어와 전문 시인들 모두 축하받아야 합니다.
(D) 시는 제목이 있어야 하며 40줄을 넘지 않아야 합니다.

해설 뒤 문장 'They must also have not been previously published and be the original work of the author.'에서 그것들은 또한 이전에 출간된 적이 없어야 하고 작가의 원작이어야 한다고 했으므로, 빈칸에는 경연대회에 출품되는 시에 대한 요구사항과 관련된 내용이 들어가야 함을 알 수 있다. 따라서 (D)가 정답이다.

어휘 collection n. 모음집, 수집품 contestant n. 참가자

137 명사 어휘 고르기

해설 '참가자당 최대 세 편의 시라는 제한이 있다'라는 문맥이므로 (B) limit(제한)이 정답이다. (A) report는 '보도', (C) sign은 '징후', (D) program은 '프로그램'이라는 의미이다.

138 관계대명사 채우기

해설 이 문장은 주어(Those), 동사(will receive), 목적어(cash prizes)를 모두 갖춘 완전한 절이므로, ___ ~ poems는 수식어 거품으로 보아야 한다. 이 수식어 거품은 빈칸 앞의 대명사 Those를 선행사로 갖는 관계절이므로, (A)와 (B)가 정답의 후보이다. 관계절(~ poems) 내에 주어가 없고 선행사 Those가 사람이므로, 사람을 나타내는 주격 관계대명사 (B) who가 정답이다. (A) which는 선행사가 사물일 때 올 수 있다. (C) what은 선행사와 함께 쓰일 수 없고, (D) they는 접속사 없이 두 개의 절을 연결할 수 없으므로 답이 될 수 없다.

139-142번은 다음 웹페이지에 관한 문제입니다.

> Canton 운송사 요금 인상 예정
>
> 운송 서비스를 제공하는 비용은 연료와 노동의 단가 상승으로 인해 나라 전역에서 상승하고 있습니다. ¹³⁹그에 따라, Canton 운송사는 요금을 2.5퍼센트 인상할 것이고, 이는 1월 1일 자로 시행됩니다. ¹⁴⁰표준 편도 요금은 그 결과 3.75달러로 인상될 것입니다. ¹⁴¹저희는 가격을 인상함으로써, 저희가 몇몇 승객분들을 힘든 처지에 놓이게 한다는 것을 이해합니다. ¹⁴²따라서, 저희는 그 부담을 덜어 드리기 위한 조치들을 도입할 것인데, 자주 탑승하는 분들에게 보상하는 것을 포함합니다. 저희의 서비스를 정기적으로 이용하는 누구에게나 특별 월간 할인이 제공될 것입니다.
>
> transit n. 운송, 수송 fuel n. 연료 labor n. 노동, 근로
> fare n. 요금 effective adj. 시행되는, 효과적인
> passenger n. 승객, 여객 alleviate v. 덜다, 완화하다
> burden v. 부담, 짐 reward v. 보상하다, 보답하다
> on a regular basis 정기적으로

139 접속부사 채우기 주변 문맥 파악

해설 빈칸이 콤마와 함께 문장의 맨 앞에 온 접속부사 자리이므로, 앞 문장과 빈칸이 있는 문장의 의미 관계를 파악하여 정답을 선택한다. 앞 문장에서 운송 서비스를 제공하는 비용이 연료와 노동의 단가 상승으로 인해 나라 전역에서 상승하고 있다고 했고, 빈칸이 있는 문장에서는 Canton 운송사가 요금을 2.5퍼센트 인상할 것이라고 했으므로, 앞에서 말한 내용에 따른 결과를 언급할 때 사용되는 (D) Accordingly(그에 따라)가 정답이다.

어휘 nonetheless adv. 그럼에도 불구하고, 그렇기는 하지만
otherwise adv. 그렇지 않으면, 달리

140 알맞은 문장 고르기

해석 (A) 표준 편도 요금은 그 결과 3.75달러로 인상될 것입니다.
(B) 당신은 많은 편한 장소에서 당신의 카드에 돈을 넣을 수 있습니다.
(C) 환승은 당신이 여정 중에 차량을 여러 번 갈아탈 수 있게 합니다.
(D) 정류장에 몇 분 일찍 도착할 것이 권고됩니다.

해설 앞 문장 'Canton Transpo will be raising fares by 2.5 percent, effective January 1'에서 Canton 운송사가 요금을 2.5퍼센트 인상할 것이고, 이것이 1월 1일 자로 시행된다고 했으므로, 빈칸에는 요금 인상과 관련된 내용이 들어가야 함을 알 수 있다. 따라서 (A)가 정답이다.

어휘 standard adj. 표준의, 일반적인
convenient adj. 편한, 사용하기 좋은 transfer n. 환승, 이적
advisable adj. 권고되는, 권할 만한

141 전치사 채우기

해설 '가격을 인상함으로써'라는 의미가 되어야 하므로 빈칸 뒤의 동명사(increasing)와 함께 '~함으로써'라는 의미를 완성하는 전치사 (C) by가 정답이다. (A) plus는 '~을 더하여', (B) before는 '~ 전에', (D) for는 '~을 위한'이라는 의미이다.

142 형용사 어휘 고르기 주변 문맥 파악

해설 '그 부담을 덜기 위한 조치들을 도입할 것인데, ___ 탑승하는 분들에게 보상하는 것을 포함한다'라는 문맥이므로 모든 보기가 정답의 후보이다. 빈칸이 있는 문장만으로 정답을 고를 수 없으므로 주변 문맥이나 전체 문맥을 파악한다. 뒤 문장에서 '서비스를 정기적으로 이용하는 누구에게나 특별 월간 할인이 제공될 것입니다(Special monthly discounts will be given to anyone who uses our service on a regular basis.)'라고 했으므로 자주 탑승하는 사람들에게 보상해 줄 것임을 알 수 있다. 따라서 (B) frequent(자주 ~하는)가 정답이다. (A) previous는 '이전의', (C) elderly는 '연세가 드신', (D) first-time은 '첫 번째의, 처음의'라는 의미이다.

143-146번은 다음 이메일에 관한 문제입니다.

> 수신: Priscilla Murray <pmurray@SchmittCo.com>
> 발신: Damien Parsons <dparsons@SchmittCo.com>
> 날짜: 7월 7일
> 제목: 회신: 음식 공급
>
> 안녕하세요, Priscilla.
>
> ¹⁴³음식 공급 서비스에 있어 새로운 공급업체로 변경하는 것에 대한 우리의 이전 대화와 관련하여, 저는 여러 회사들의 장단점을 검토해 오고 있습니다. 지금까지, Lozano Kitchen이 그곳의 다양한 메뉴 선택지와 지속 가능성에 대한 전념 때문에 최고의 선택지인 것 같습니다. ¹⁴⁴또한, 그곳은 전문적인 요리사들에 의해 준비되는 음식치고 아주 저렴합니다. ¹⁴⁵저는 모두가 Lozano Kitchen이 제공하는 것을 시식하고 그것들이 마음에 드는지 판단할 기회를 갖기 위해 업체 대표에게 다음 주간 회의를 위한 샘플 음식을 준비해 달라고 연락했습니다. ¹⁴⁶만일 그렇다면, Lozano Kitchen은 우리의 새로운 공식 음식 공급 업체가 될 것입니다.
>
> Damien 드림
>
> catering n. 음식 공급 switch v. 변경하다, 바꾸다
> pros and cons 장단점, 찬반양론 commitment n. 전념, 헌신
> sustainability n. 지속 가능성, 유지 가능성 official adj. 공식의, 공적인

143 명사 어휘 고르기 주변 문맥 파악

해설 '음식 공급 서비스에 있어 새로운 ___로 변경하는 것'이라는 문맥이므로 모든 보기가 정답의 후보이다. 빈칸이 있는 문장만으로 정답을 고를 수 없으므로 주변 문맥이나 전체 문맥을 파악한다. 뒤 문장에서 'Lozano Kitchen이 그곳의 다양한 메뉴 선택지와 지속 가능성에 대한 전념 때문에 최고의 선택지인 것 같다(So far, Lozano

Kitchen seems like the best option due to its diverse menu options and commitment to sustainability).'라고 했으므로 새로운 음식 공급업체를 찾고 있는 상황임을 알 수 있다. 따라서 (C) provider(공급업체)가 정답이다. (A) facility는 '시설, 설비', (B) process는 '과정', (D) schedule은 '일정'이라는 의미이다.

144 알맞은 문장 고르기

해석 (A) 우리의 현재 음식 공급 회사는 다양한 채식 선택지를 가지고 있습니다.
(B) 다행히도, 그 회의는 다른 사람들의 일정과 겹치지 않을 것입니다.
(C) 또한, 그곳은 전문적인 요리사들에 의해 준비되는 음식치고 아주 저렴합니다.
(D) 직원들에게 사무실에서 점심을 제공하는 것은 생산성을 높입니다.

해설 앞 문장 'So far, Lozano Kitchen seems like the best option due to its diverse menu options and commitment to sustainability.'에서 Lozano Kitchen이 그곳의 다양한 메뉴 선택지와 지속 가능성에 대한 전념 때문에 최고의 선택지인 것 같다고 했고, 뒤 문장 'I contacted the owner ~'에서 업체 대표에게 샘플 음식을 준비해 달라고 연락했다고 했으므로, 빈칸에는 Lozano Kitchen의 또 다른 장점과 관련된 내용이 들어가야 함을 알 수 있다. 따라서 (C)가 정답이다.

어휘 current adj. 현재의 affordable adj. 저렴한, 입수 가능한
productivity n. 생산성

145 to 부정사 채우기

해설 빈칸이 있는 so that 이하의 절은 주어(everyone), 동사(can have), 목적어(the chance)를 갖춘 완전한 절이므로, ____ ~ offerings는 앞에 나온 명사(the chance)를 수식하는 거품구로 보아야 한다. 빈칸 앞에 명사 the chance는 부정사와 함께 쓰이므로 to 부정사 (B) to taste가 정답이다. 명사 또는 현재분사 (A) tasting을 명사를 수식하는 현재분사로 본다 해도, '~한 맛이 나는'이라는 의미로 어색한 문맥을 만들기 때문에 답이 될 수 없다. 동사 (C)와 (D)는 수식어 거품이 될 수 없다.

146 접속부사 채우기 주변 문맥 파악

해설 빈칸이 콤마와 함께 문장의 맨 앞에 온 접속부사 자리이므로, 앞 문장과 빈칸이 있는 문장의 의미 관계를 파악하여 정답을 선택한다. 앞 문장에서 모두가 Lozano Kitchen이 제공하는 것을 시식하고 마음에 드는지 확인할 기회를 갖기 위해 업체 대표에게 샘플 음식을 준비해 달라고 요청했다고 했고, 빈칸이 있는 문장에서는 Lozano Kitchen이 우리의 새로운 공식 음식 공급업체가 될 것이라고 했으므로, 앞에서 언급한 상황이 사실이라고 가정할 때 사용되는 (A) If so(만일 그렇다면)가 정답이다.

어휘 conversely adv. 정반대로, 역으로

PART 7

147-148번은 다음 정보에 관한 문제입니다.

> 안타깝게도, Melanie Weber는 [147]오늘밤 *Aeroplane*의 상연에서 연기하지 않을 것입니다. [148-(D)]Juliette Greer가 그녀를 대신할 것입니다. Juliette은 Kirkland 공연 예술 음악학교의 졸업생이며 큰 호평을 받은 뮤지컬 *Spilled Milk*에 출연했습니다. [148]이번이 *Aeroplane*에서 그녀의 첫 번째 출연일 것입니다.
>
> [147]우리는 여러분들이 이 쇼를 즐기길 바랍니다. 공연 동안 20분의 중간 휴식 시간이 있을 것이라는 점을 유념해 주십시오. 재입장에 표가 요구되므로 극장을 나가시는 경우 표를 지참할 것을 기억해 주십시오.

production n. 상연, 생산 replace v. 대신하다, 바꾸다
acclaimed adj. 호평을 받은, 칭찬을 받은 appearance n. 출연
interval n. 중간 휴식 시간 reentry n. 재입장, 다시 들어감

147 추론 문제

해석 안내문은 어디에서 발견될 것 같은가?
(A) 영화 벽보에서
(B) 잡지 논평에서
(C) 확정 이메일에서
(D) 극장 로비에서

해설 지문의 'tonight's production of *Aeroplane*'에서 이곳이 극장임을 알 수 있고, 'We hope you enjoy the show. Please note that there will be a 20-minute interval during the performance. Remember to take your ticket with you if you leave the theatre as it is required for reentry.'에서 공연 동안 20분의 중간 휴식 시간이 있을 것이고 재입장에 표가 요구된다고 알리고 있으므로, 극장 로비에 걸린 안내문일 것임을 추론할 수 있다. 따라서 (D)가 정답이다.

어휘 poster n. 벽보, 포스터 confirmation n. 확정, 확인

148 Not/True 문제

해석 Ms. Greer에 대해 명시된 것은?
(A) 공연 예술 학교에 다니고 있다.
(B) Ms. Weber를 영구히 대신할 것이다.
(C) *Spilled Milk*에서 주연을 맡았다.
(D) *Aeroplane*에서는 처음으로 연기할 것이다.

해설 지문의 'Juliette Greer will be replacing her[Melanie Weber].'에서 Juliette Greer가 Melanie Weber를 대신할 것이라고 했고, 'This will be her[Juliette Greer] first appearance in *Aeroplane*.'에서 이번이 *Aeroplane*에서 Juliette Greer의 첫 번째 출연일 것이라고 했으므로, Juliette Greer가 *Aeroplane*에서는 처음으로 연기할 것임을 알 수 있다. 따라서 (D)가 정답이다.

어휘 attend v. 다니다, 참석하다 permanently adv. 영구히, 영원히
lead role 주연, 주역

Paraphrasing

> her first appearance in ~ ~에서 그녀의 첫 번째 출연
> → is performing in ~ for the first time ~에서 처음으로 연기하다

149-150번은 다음 공지에 관한 문제입니다.

11월 12일 월요일 오전 6시부터 오후 2시까지 East Halifax가를 따라 있는 ¹⁴⁹가구들에 일시적인 단수가 영향을 미칠 것입니다. 이 단수는 작업자들이 그 지역의 수도관에 필요한 개선을 수행하게 할 것입니다. 대비를 위해, 주민들은 변기의 물을 내리고, 이를 닦기 위한 물을 확보하도록 권고됩니다. ¹⁵⁰또한, 그들은 상당한 물의 소비를 필요로 하는 모든 활동을 연기하도록 요청을 받게 되는데, 정원에 물을 주는 것, 개인 자동차를 세차하는 것, 혹은 세탁기를 가동하는 것과 같은 것들입니다.

문의를 위해서는, 555-3543으로 공공사업 유지 관리 수도 관리자인 Nancy Dutton에게 연락해 주십시오.

temporary adj. 일시적인, 임시의 outage n. 단수, 정전
household n. 가구, 가정 preparation n. 대비, 준비
resident n. 주민, 거주자 flush v. (변기의) 물을 내리다, ~을 씻어 내다
significant adj. 상당한, 중요한 consumption n. 소비
automobile n. 자동차 superintendent n. 관리자

149 목적 찾기 문제

해석 공지의 목적은 무엇인가?
(A) 주민들에게 회의에 대해 알리기 위해
(B) 가구들이 수도 고지서를 제때 납부하도록 상기시키기 위해
(C) 서비스 중단에 관한 정보를 제공하기 위해
(D) 프로젝트 시작의 지연을 보고하기 위해

해설 지문의 'A temporary water outage will affect households'에서 일시적인 단수가 가구들에 영향을 미칠 것이라고 알리고 있으므로 (C)가 정답이다.

어휘 remind v. 상기시키다, 생각나게 하다 interruption n. 중단

Paraphrasing
water outage 단수 → a service interruption 서비스 중단

150 육하원칙 문제

해석 주민들은 무엇을 하도록 요청받는가?
(A) 관리자와 만날 약속을 한다.
(B) 몇 가지 가정 활동의 일정을 변경한다.
(C) 작업자들이 그들의 집에 들어올 수 있도록 허락한다.
(D) 영향을 받는 지역에 주차된 차량들을 일시적으로 이동한다.

해설 지문의 'they[residents] are asked to delay any activities that may require significant water consumption, such as watering the garden, washing personal automobiles, or operating washing machines.'에서 주민들은 상당한 물의 소비를 필요로 하는 정원에 물을 주는 것, 개인 자동차를 세차하는 것, 혹은 세탁기를 가동하는 것과 같은 활동을 연기하도록 요청을 받게 된다고 했으므로, 주민들이 몇 가지 가정 활동의 일정을 변경하도록 요청받을 것임을 알 수 있다. 따라서 (B)가 정답이다.

어휘 appointment n. (만날) 약속, 예약 permit v. 허락하다

Paraphrasing
delay ~ activities 활동을 지연하다 → Reschedule ~ activities 활동의 일정을 변경하다

151-152번은 다음 브로슈어에 관한 문제입니다.

Marcus와 Elizabeth Sheppard의 가족 주택으로 19세기 후반에 지어진 Sheppard 호텔 & 티 하우스는 잊을 수 없는 휴가와 특별한 행사를 위한 이상적인 장소입니다. 로비로 들어서면, 크리스털 샹들리에, 스테인드글라스 창문, 그리고 ¹⁵¹본래의 상태로 복원된 목조부의 숨이 멎을 듯한 광경이 당신을 맞이할 것입니다. 하지만, 그 유서 깊은 외관에도 불구하고, ¹⁵¹각각의 객실은 고속 와이파이, 최신 오락 시스템, 그리고 소용돌이 욕조를 포함한 현대식 시설들을 갖추고 있습니다.

매일 오후 3시부터 5시까지 Serenity 호실에서 투숙객 전용 행사인 오후의 하이 티를 경험하세요. 그것은 다양한 풍미 있는 음식들을 특징으로 하는데, 모두 우리의 정원에서 나오는 재료들로 준비됩니다. ¹⁵²⁻⁽ᴮ⁾인도네시아에서 수입된 우리의 새로운 Wu Mei 차를 마셔볼 수 있는 이 기회를 잡으세요.

예약하시려면 646-555-4099로 전화주세요.

ideal adj. 이상적인 memorable adj. 잊을 수 없는, 기억할 만한
getaway n. 휴가 occasion n. 행사
breathtaking adj. 숨이 멎을 듯한 woodwork n. (문·계단 같은) 목조부
restore v. 복원하다, 복구하다 historic adj. 유서 깊은, 역사적인
state-of-the-art adj. 최신의 whirlpool n. 소용돌이
exclusive adj. 전용의, 독점적인 an array of 다양한
savory adj. 풍미 있는, 맛 좋은 ingredient n. 재료
import v. 수입하다

151 추론 문제

해석 Sheppard 호텔 & 티 하우스에 대해 암시되는 것은?
(A) 보수된 지 1년이 되지 않았다.
(B) 한 가족에 의해 소유되고 운영된다.
(C) 옛 요소와 새로운 요소의 조합을 특징으로 한다.
(D) 정원 경관이 보이는 방들이 있다.

해설 지문의 'woodwork restored to its original condition'에서 Sheppard 호텔 & 티 하우스에 본래의 상태로 복원된 목조부가 존재한다는 것을 알 수 있고, 'each of the guestrooms is equipped with modern facilities including high-speed Wi-Fi, a state-of-the-art entertainment system, and a whirlpool tub'에서 각각의 객실이 고속 와이파이, 최신 오락 시스템, 그리고 소용돌이 욕조를 포함한 현대식 시설들을 갖추고 있다는 것을 알 수 있으므로, Sheppard Inn & Tea House가 옛 요소와 새로운 요소의 조합을 특징으로 하고 있음을 추론할 수 있다. 따라서 (C)가 정답이다.

어휘 operate v. 운영하다, 작동하다 combination n. 조합, 결합
element n. 요소

152 Not/True 문제

해석 오후의 하이 티에 대해 명시된 것은?
(A) 투숙객들에게 무료로 제공된다.
(B) 다른 나라에서 온 차를 제공한다.

(C) 호텔 공터의 정원에서 제공된다.
(D) 호텔의 투숙객이 아닌 손님들에게도 열려 있다.

해설 지문의 'Take this opportunity to try our new Wu Mei tea, imported from Indonesia.'에서 인도네시아에서 수입된 Wu Mei 차를 마셔볼 수 있는 이 기회를 잡으라고 했으므로, 오후의 하이 티가 다른 나라에서 온 차를 제공한다는 것을 알 수 있다. 따라서 (B)가 정답이다.

어휘 at no charge 무료로   ground n. 공터, 땅바닥

Paraphrasing
Wu Mei tea, imported from Indonesia 인도네시아에서 수입된 Wu Mei 차 → tea from a different country 다른 나라에서 온 차

153-154번은 다음 문자 메시지 대화문에 관한 문제입니다.

> Kelly Thompson (오전 10시 14분)
> 안녕하세요, Michael. ¹⁵³저는 South Side 컴퓨터 수리점의 Kelly입니다. 저희는 당신의 컴퓨터가 멈추는 문제의 원인이 바이러스라는 점을 발견했고, 그것을 제거했어요.
>
> Michael Gage (오전 10시 15분)
> 감사해요! 저는 문제가 무엇이었는지 궁금해하고 있었어요.
>
> Kelly Thompson (오전 10시 16분)
> 저는 또한 저희가 당신의 하드 드라이브가 좋지 않은 상태라는 것을 발견했고 그것이 조만간 교체될 필요가 있을 것 같다는 점을 알려드려야 할 것 같아요.
>
> Michael Gage (오전 10시 17분)
> 아, 그것은 비용이 얼마나 들까요?
>
> Kelly Thompson (오전 10시 18분)
> 보통 100달러가 넘게 들지만, 저희는 500기가바이트의 새로운 것을 단 70달러에 설치해 드리고자 해요. ¹⁵⁴물론, 저희가 이곳으로 하드 드라이브를 배송받아야 할 필요가 있어서, 당신의 컴퓨터를 하루 더 가지고 있어야 해요.
>
> Michael Gage (오전 10시 20분)
> 저는 내일까지 하기로 예정된 보고서 작업을 해야 해요. ¹⁵⁴그 제안을 거절하고 나중에 새로운 하드 드라이브를 설치해야 할 것 같아요.
>
> Kelly Thompson (오전 10시 22분)
> 괜찮습니다. 그렇다면, 당신의 컴퓨터는 오늘 오후 12시 30분까지 찾아갈 준비가 되어있을 거예요.

discover v. 발견하다   source n. 원인, 원천
freeze v. (시스템이) 멈추다, 정지하다   condition n. 상태
install v. 설치하다

153 추론 문제

해석 Ms. Thompson은 누구일 것 같은가?
(A) 직업 상담가
(B) 배달 운전사
(C) 웹 개발자
(D) 수리공

해설 지문의 'This is Kelly from South Side Computer Repairs. We discovered that the source of your computer's freezing problem is a virus, which we've removed.'에서 Kelly Thompson이 South Side 컴퓨터 수리점에서 수리하는 일을 하고 있음을 추론할 수 있다. 따라서 (D)가 정답이다.

154 의도 파악 문제

해석 오전 10시 20분에, Mr. Gage가 "I need to work on a report that's due tomorrow"라고 썼을 때, 그가 의도한 것 같은 것은?
(A) 새로운 소프트웨어가 설치되기를 원한다.
(B) 밤사이에 컴퓨터를 가게에 놓아둘 수 없다.
(C) 새로운 업무를 완료하기 위해 일하느라 바쁘다.
(D) 오늘 오후에 Ms. Thompson을 만날 수 없다.

해설 지문의 'Of course, we would need to have the hard drive shipped here, so we'll have to keep your computer an extra day.'에서 하드 드라이브를 배송받아야 할 필요가 있어서 컴퓨터를 하루 더 가지고 있어야 한다고 하자, 'I need to work on a report that's due tomorrow'(저는 내일까지 하기로 예정된 보고서 작업을 해야 해요)라고 한 후, 'I think I'll pass on that offer and install a new hard drive later.'에서 제안을 거절하고 나중에 새로운 하드 드라이브를 설치해야 할 것 같다고 한 것을 통해, Mr. Gage가 밤사이에 컴퓨터를 가게에 놓아둘 수 없다는 것을 알 수 있다. 따라서 (B)가 정답이다.

어휘 overnight adv. 밤사이에   assignment n. 업무, 과제

155-157번은 다음 웹페이지에 관한 문제입니다.

> Howard 묘목장에 오신 것을 환영합니다—원예에 필요한 모든 것들을 한 곳에서 다 살 수 있는 상점!
>
> ¹⁵⁵아름다운 녹지 공간을 만들고 유지하기 위한 당신의 생각, 사진, 그리고 조언들을 공유해 보세요. 우리 웹사이트에서 동료 원예 애호가들과 함께하며 영감을 얻어보세요! [여기]를 클릭하세요]
>
> 자주 묻는 질문
>
> Q1. 어떤 종류의 실내 화분용 화초를 구할 수 있나요?
> 저희는 모든 크기와 종의 식물들을 보유하고 있습니다. 수백 가지의 다양한 다육 식물, 현화 식물, 허브, 그리고 더 많은 것들 중에서 골라보세요. 저희의 필터링 옵션을 사용하여 빠르게 당신의 기후에 맞는 식물을 찾아보세요.
>
> Q2. 야외 정원을 위한 식물들을 구입할 수 있나요?
> Howard 묘목장은 당신의 테라스, 발코니, 또는 정원을 단장하는 것에 적합한 ¹⁵⁶⁻⁽ᴮ⁾75개가 넘는 야외 식물들을 제공합니다. 관상용 식물과 식용 식물 모두를 구할 수 있습니다.
>
> Q3. 물품들은 어떻게 배송되나요?
> 저희의 배송 서비스는 배송 과정 동안 손상을 방지하기 위한 방법을 알고 있습니다. ¹⁵⁷⁻⁽ᴬ⁾대부분의 식물들은 영업일 기준 3에서 5일 이내에 배송됩니다. 식물을 곧장 받기를 원하는 고객들을 위해 야간 배송과 2일 배송도 이용 가능합니다. ¹⁵⁷⁻⁽ᴰ⁾안타깝게도, 저희는 미국 밖으로 식물들을 배송할 수 없습니다.

nursery n. 묘목장   enthusiast n. 애호가, 팬
houseplant n. 실내 화분용 화초   succulent n. 다육 식물
spruce up ~을 단장하다   patio n. 테라스, 베란다
ornamental adj. 관상용의, 장식용의   edible adj. 식용의, 먹을 수 있는
prevent v. 방지하다, 예방하다

155 육하원칙 문제

해석 웹페이지에 따르면, 웹사이트를 방문하는 사람들은 무엇을 할 수 있는가?
(A) 원예 사진 및 조언을 게시한다.
(B) 식물 관리 워크숍에 등록한다.
(C) 월간 소식지를 구독한다.
(D) 주택 조경 서비스의 일정을 잡는다.

해설 지문의 'Share your ideas, photos, and tips for creating and maintaining a beautiful green space. Join fellow gardening enthusiasts on our Web site and get inspired!'에서 아름다운 녹지 공간을 만들고 유지하기 위한 생각, 사진, 그리고 조언들을 공유해 보라고 한 후, 웹사이트에서 동료 원예 애호가들과 함께하며 영감을 얻어보라고 권유하고 있으므로 (A)가 정답이다.

어휘 register v. 등록하다 subscribe v. 구독하다
newsletter n. 소식지 landscaping n. 조경

156 Not/True 문제

해석 Howard 묘목장에서 제공되는 야외 식물들에 대해 언급된 것은?
(A) 그것들의 관리를 위한 상세한 설명이 함께 제공된다.
(B) 장식용과 식용 품종 모두를 포함한다.
(C) 평생 보증서와 함께 판매된다.
(D) 모두 미국 토종이다.

해설 지문의 'Howard Nursery offers more than 75 outdoor plants'에서 Howard 묘목장은 75개가 넘는 야외 식물들을 제공한다고 했고, 'Both ornamental plants and edible plants are available.'에서 관상용 식물과 식용 식물 모두를 구할 수 있다고 했으므로 (B)가 정답이다. (A), (C), (D)는 지문에 언급되지 않은 내용이다.

어휘 decorative adj. 장식용의 consumable adj. 식용의, 소비 가능한
guarantee n. 보증(서) native adj. 토종의

Paraphrasing

ornamental plants and edible plants 관상용 식물과 식용 식물
→ decorative and consumable varieties 장식용과 식용 품종

157 Not/True 문제

해석 Howard 묘목장의 배송 서비스에 대해 사실인 것은?
(A) 오직 야간 및 2일 배송만 제공한다.
(B) 앱을 통해 배송을 추적할 수 있도록 한다.
(C) 큰 식물의 배송을 수용할 수 없다.
(D) 오직 국내에서만 식물 배달이 가능하다.

해설 지문의 'Unfortunately, we are not able to ship plants outside the United States.'에서 안타깝게도 미국 밖으로 식물들을 배송할 수 없다고 했으므로 (D)는 지문의 내용과 일치한다. 따라서 (D)가 정답이다. (A)는 'Most plants are shipped within three to five business days'에서 대부분의 식물들이 영업일 기준 3일에서 5일 이내에 배송된다고 했으므로 지문의 내용과 일치하지 않는다. (B)와 (C)는 지문에서 언급되지 않은 내용이다.

어휘 track v. 추적하다 domestic adj. 국내의

Paraphrasing

not able to ship plants outside the United States 미국 밖으로 식물들을 배송할 수 없는 → only available for domestic plant delivery 오직 국내에서만 식물 배달이 가능한

158-160번은 다음 광고에 관한 문제입니다.

> **Sienna Plus 물 여과기, 버전 2**
>
> 가장 많이 팔리는 저희 기존 제품의 개선된 버전인, 새로운 Sienna Plus 물 여과기의 출시를 알리게 되어 기쁩니다. 기존 것과 마찬가지로, 새로운 버전은 여러분의 수도꼭지에 쉽게 부착될 수 있습니다. ¹⁵⁸그것은 최대 4년 동안 지속되는데, 이는 기존 제품보다 2배 더 긴 것입니다. 게다가, 그것은 원치 않는 화학 물질을 제거하는 데 있어 훨씬 더 효율적입니다. 일단 부착되면, 그 여과기는 영양 미네랄을 유지하면서도 수돗물에 포함되어 있는 해로운 화학 물질의 99퍼센트 이상을 제거할 것입니다.
>
> 고객들은 이미 그 필터에 대해 극찬하고 있으며, 그것이 "지금껏 맛본 가장 신선한 물"을 제공하고 "더 좋고 건강한 기분이 들게 한다"고 말하고 있습니다. ¹⁵⁹여과기가 작동하는 방식을 확인하기 위해서는, 그저 포장지의 QR 코드를 스캔하시면 영상이 여러분의 휴대전화에서 스트리밍될 것입니다. 그것을 시청하는 데 몇 분밖에 걸리지 않을 것입니다.
>
> ¹⁶⁰여과기는 저희 웹사이트에서 89.99달러에 판매됩니다. 그것은 현재 오프라인 매장에서는 구할 수 없습니다.
>
> filter n. 여과기 attach v. 부착하다 faucet n. (수도) 꼭지
> efficient adj. 효율적인 unwanted adj. 원치 않는
> eliminate v. 제거하다, 없애다 chemical n. 화학물질
> retain v. 유지하다, 함유하다 nutritional adj. 영양의, 영양상의
> mineral n. 미네랄, 광물 rave v. 극찬하다, 열변을 토하다
> brick-and-mortar adj. 오프라인 거래의, 소매의

158 육하원칙 문제

해석 새로운 Sienna Plus 물 여과기는 이전 모델보다 어떻게 더 나은가?
(A) 더 오랜 기간 동안 사용될 수 있다.
(B) 더 많은 유형의 수도꼭지에 맞출 수 있다.
(C) 수돗물에 화학 소독제를 추가한다.
(D) 물의 순도 수준을 보여주는 화면을 포함한다.

해설 지문의 'It lasts up to four years, twice as long as the original product.'에서 새로운 버전의 Sienna Plus 물 여과기가 최대 4년 동안 지속되는데, 이는 기존 제품보다 2배 더 긴 것이라고 하였다. 따라서 (A)가 정답이다.

어휘 predecessor n. 이전 모델, 이전 것 disinfectant n. 소독제
display n. 화면 purity n. 순도, 순수성

159 육하원칙 문제

해석 사람들은 QR 코드를 스캔하여 무엇을 할 수 있는가?
(A) 사용자 설명서를 다운로드한다.
(B) 할인 코드에 접근한다.
(C) 정보 영상을 시청한다.
(D) 고객 후기를 읽는다.

해설 지문의 'To see how our filter works, simply scan the QR code on the packaging and a video will be streamed to your phone.'에서 여과기가 작동하는 방식을 확인하기 위해서는, 포장지의 QR 코드를 스캔하면 영상이 휴대전화에서 스트리밍될 것이라고 했으므로, QR 코드를 스캔하면 기기에서 정보 영상을 시청할 수 있음을 알 수 있다. 따라서 (C)가 정답이다.

어휘 manual n. 설명서 informational adj. 정보의, 정보를 제공하는

160 육하원칙 문제

해설 사람들은 새로운 Sienna Plus 물 여과기를 어떻게 구입할 수 있는가?
(A) 고객 서비스 센터에 이메일을 보냄으로써
(B) 온라인으로 주문함으로써
(C) 지역 상점을 방문함으로써
(D) 전화를 함으로써

해설 지문의 'The filter sells for $89.99 on our Web site. It is not currently available in brick-and-mortar stores.'에서 여과기는 웹사이트에서 89.99달러에 판매되며, 현재 오프라인 매장에서는 구할 수 없다고 한 것을 통해, 사람들이 Sienna Plus 물 여과기를 온라인으로 주문하여 구입할 수 있음을 알 수 있다. 따라서 (B)가 정답이다.

Paraphrasing
on our Web site 우리 웹사이트에서 → online 온라인으로

161-164번은 다음 회람에 관한 문제입니다.

> 163-(B)수신: Durant 주식회사 생산부 직원들
> 발신: Jared Skinner
> 날짜: 9월 30일
> 제목: 새로운 장비
>
> 팀 여러분,
>
> 우리 산업 내 발전에 발맞추기 위해, 162Durant 주식회사는 최근 몇몇 로봇 바느질 기계들과 직물 절단기를 포함하여 많은 새로운 기계를 매입했습니다. 여러분 중 많은 분들이 앞으로 이 기계들을 매일의 작업에서 사용할 것이기에, 161우리는 여러분이 그것들 각각과 관련된 정확한 설치, 작동 및 기능 정지 절차에 익숙해질 수 있도록 고안된 포괄적인 교육 과정을 준비하고 있습니다. 163-(B)그것은 10월 10일에 2층 생산 시설 현장에서 열릴 것이고 전체 근무 시간에 걸쳐 이어질 것입니다.
>
> 교육 과정 동안, 새로운 장비가 우리의 지속 가능한 직물의 제품군의 생산에서 맡게 될 역할에 대해 특별히 초점을 맞출 것입니다. 이 직물이 회사의 전략적 목표에서 핵심이기 때문에, 기계를 숙달하는 것은 굉장히 중요합니다. 164만약 여러분이 어떠한 이유에서 10월 10일에 출근할 수 없다면, 여러분이 이 교육을 받을 수 있는 대안 시간을 마련할 수 있도록 가능한 한 빨리 저에게 알려주시기 바랍니다.
>
> Jared Skinner, 운영 담당자

keep pace with ~에 발맞추다 advancement n. 발전
acquire v. 매입하다, 얻다 sewing n. 바느질
going forward 앞으로, 장차 comprehensive adj. 포괄적인, 종합적인
familiarize v. 익숙하게 하다 setup n. 설치, 설정
operation n. 작동, 운영 shutdown n. 기능 정지, 폐쇄

span v. (기간에) 걸쳐 이어지다 sustainable adj. 지속 가능한
strategic adj. 전략적인 master v. 숙달하다
absolutely adv. 굉장히, 전적으로 vital adj. 중요한
alternate adj. 대안의

161 목적 찾기 문제

해설 회람의 목적은 무엇인가?
(A) 이전으로 인한 변경 사항들을 설명하기 위해
(B) 새로운 시설의 인수를 알리기 위해
(C) 장비의 정비에 관해 불평하기 위해
(D) 다가오는 교육에 대해 직원들에게 알리기 위해

해설 지문의 'we are organizing a comprehensive training session designed to familiarize you with the correct setup, operation, and shutdown processes associated with each of them[new machines]'에서 새로운 기계들의 정확한 설치, 작동 및 기능 정지 절차에 익숙해질 수 있도록 고안된 포괄적인 교육 과정을 준비하고 있다고 했으므로 (D)가 정답이다.

어휘 acquisition n. 인수, 습득 maintenance n. 정비, 유지

162 추론 문제

해설 Durant 주식회사에 대해 암시되는 것은?
(A) 업계에서 선두 주자이다.
(B) 새로운 지역으로 운영을 확장하고 있다.
(C) 직원 규모를 줄이고 있다.
(D) 직물 생산에 관여하고 있다.

해설 지문의 'Durant Ltd. has recently acquired a number of new machines, including some robotic sewing machines and fabric cutters'에서 Durant 주식회사가 최근 몇몇 로봇 바느질 기계와 직물 절단기를 포함하여 많은 새로운 기계를 매입했다고 했으므로, Durant 주식회사가 직물 생산에 관여하고 있는 회사임을 추론할 수 있다. 따라서 (D)가 정답이다.

어휘 expand v. 확장하다, 넓히다 workforce n. (모든) 직원
textile n. 직물

Paraphrasing
fabric 직물 → textile 직물

163 Not/True 문제

해설 생산부 직원들에 대해 사실인 것은?
(A) 인증 시험을 완수할 필요가 있을 것이다.
(B) 10월 10일에 2층에서 일할 것이다.
(C) 몇몇 장비들에 관한 동료들의 숙련도를 평가할 것이다.
(D) 교육을 받는 날에 연장 근무를 할 것이다.

해설 지문의 'To: Durant Ltd. Production Staff'에서 이 회람이 생산부 직원들을 대상으로 보내진 것이라는 것을 알 수 있고, 'It[training session] will take place on-site in our second-floor production facility on October 10 and will span the entire workday.'에서 교육 과정은 10월 10일에 2층 생산 시설 현장에서 열릴 것이라고 했으므로, 생산부 직원들이 10월 10일에는 2층에서

해설 일할 것임을 알 수 있다. 따라서 (B)가 정답이다. (A), (C), (D)는 지문에 언급되지 않은 내용이다.

어휘 certification n. 인증, 증명 evaluate v. 평가하다 peer n. 동료

164 동의어 찾기 문제

해석 2문단 네 번째 줄의 단어 "arrange"는 의미상 -와 가장 가깝다.
(A) 일정을 잡다
(B) 분류하다
(C) 영향을 주다
(D) 정리하다

해설 arrange를 포함하는 구절 'If you will not be at work on October 10 for any reason, please let me know as soon as possible so we can arrange an alternate time for you to receive this training.'에서 arrange는 '(시간을) 잡다, 예정을 세우다'라는 뜻으로 사용되었다. 따라서 (A)가 정답이다.

165-167번은 다음 이메일에 관한 문제입니다.

수신: Thelma Sanchez <t.sanchez@jmail.com>
발신: Carl Fontaine <c.fontaine@bigbuys.com>
날짜: 12월 2일
제목: 주문 번호 171009314

Ms. Sanchez께,

귀하께서 저희 웹사이트에서 하신 최근 주문에 관하여, 저희가 요청받은 물품 중 하나인 Tiny Town 게임 콘솔을 배송할 수 없게 된 점을 알리게 되어 유감입니다. — [1] —. ¹⁶⁵⁻⁽ᴬ⁾연휴 선물로서 그 제품의 인기 때문에, 저희의 모든 가게에서 재고가 떨어졌습니다. — [2] —. 저희는 이 불편에 대해 깊이 사과드립니다.

¹⁶⁶귀하께서 결제하신 300달러는 이미 환불해 드렸습니다. 해당 금액을 받았는지 확인하기 위해 귀하의 신용카드 명세서를 확인해주십시오. 또한, 재고가 있는 모든 품목에 대해 20퍼센트 할인을 제공해 드릴 것입니다. — [3] —. 이것을 이용하기 위해서는, 온라인 구매를 하실 때 프로모션 코드 827374를 입력하시거나 저희의 매장들 중 한 곳에서 계산원에게 이 코드를 제시하세요. ¹⁶⁷프로모션 코드는 12월 15일까지 사용되어야 하는 점을 명심하세요. — [4] —.

지속적인 거래에 감사드립니다.

Carl Fontaine 드림
고객 서비스 담당자
Big Buys

in reference to ~에 관하여 request v. 요청하다
out of stock 재고가 떨어진 inconvenience n. 불편
take advantage of ~을 이용하다

165 Not/True 문제

해석 Tiny Town 게임 콘솔에 대해 언급된 것은?
(A) 높은 수요 때문에 구할 수 없다.
(B) 제조업체가 제품을 회수했다.
(C) 어린아이들에게 추천되지 않는다.
(D) 공급 회사에 의해 도착이 지연되었다.

해설 지문의 'Due to the product[Tiny Town game console]'s popularity as a holiday gift item, we have run out of stock in all our stores.'에서 연휴 선물로서 Tiny Town 게임 콘솔의 인기 때문에 모든 가게에서 재고가 떨어졌다고 했으므로 (A)가 정답이다. (B), (C), (D)는 지문에 언급되지 않은 내용이다.

어휘 demand n. 수요 manufacturer n. 제조업체, 생산 회사
supplier n. 공급 회사, 공급자

Paraphrasing

the product's popularity 그 제품의 인기 → high demand 높은 수요

166 육하원칙 문제

해석 Mr. Fontaine은 Ms. Sanchez에게 무엇을 하기를 요청하는가?
(A) 실제 지점을 방문한다.
(B) 다른 결제 방법을 시도해 본다.
(C) 온라인 계정 비밀번호를 변경한다.
(D) 거래가 처리되었는지 확인한다.

해설 지문의 'We have already refunded the $300 payment you made. Please check your credit card statement to confirm that you have received that amount.'에서 결제한 300달러는 이미 환불해 줬으니, 해당 금액을 받았는지 확인하기 위해 신용카드 명세서를 확인하기를 바란다고 하였다. 따라서 (D)가 정답이다.

어휘 payment option 지불 방법 transaction n. 거래, 처리

167 문장 위치 찾기 문제

해석 [1], [2], [3], [4]로 표시된 위치 중, 다음 문장이 들어갈 곳으로 가장 적절한 것은?

"이 날짜 이후에는 더 이상 유효하지 않을 것이며, 귀하는 이 특별 제안을 놓치게 될 것입니다."

(A) [1]
(B) [2]
(C) [3]
(D) [4]

해설 주어진 문장은 유효 기간이 있는 특별 제안과 관련된 내용 주변에 나올 것임을 예상할 수 있다. [4]의 앞 문장인 'Note that the promotional code must be used by December 15.'에서 프로모션 코드는 12월 15일까지 사용되어야 한다고 했으므로 [4]에 주어진 문장이 들어가면 프로모션 코드는 12월 15일까지 사용되어야 하고, 이 날짜 이후에는 유효하지 않아 특별 제안을 놓치게 될 것이라는 자연스러운 문맥이 된다는 것을 알 수 있다. 따라서 (D)가 정답이다.

168-171번은 다음 기사에 관한 문제입니다.

리틀 록 (11월 19일) — ¹⁶⁸8월에 개점한 이후, Roll of the Dice는 성공을 거두고 있다. ¹⁶⁹고전적인 보드게임부터 최신의 탁상용 역할 연기 게임까지 모든 것을 제공함으로써, 이 보드게임 가게는 모든 연령대와 흥미의 **구미에 맞춘다**. — [1] —.

가게의 공동소유자인 Noah Lee와 Russel McClain은 몇 년 동안 그들의 지역 사회 내에 이와 같은 가게를 바라왔던 열렬한 보드게임 애호가이다. 시장에서 이러한 공백을 채울 기회가 생겼을 때, 두 사람은 그 기회를 잡았다. —[2]—. 그러나, 마을에 게임 가게가 있다는 소문이 퍼지자, 그 가게가 사람들로 가득 차는 것은 그렇게 오래 걸리지 않았다.

Mr. Lee와 Mr. McClain에 따르면, 사람들은 또한 그들이 좋아하는 게임들을 즐기기 위한 공간을 원한다. —[3]—. 그것이 바로 그들이 가게 뒤쪽에 사람들이 ¹⁷⁰가게의 일일 마감 시간인 오후 8시까지 사용할 수 있는 공간을 마련한 이유이다. —[4]—. ¹⁷⁰추후에는, 그들은 토너먼트를 개최하기 위해 더 늦게까지 영업할 계획이다.

tabletop adj. 탁상용의 role-playing game 역할 연기 게임, 역할놀이
avid adj. 열렬한, 열심인 enthusiast n. 애호가, 팬
opportunity n. 기회 gap n. 공백, 틈 pair n. 두 사람, 한 쌍

168 주제 찾기 문제

해석 기사는 주로 무엇에 대한 것인가?
(A) 최근에 설립된 한 사업체
(B) 가게 개업일의 변경
(C) 게임에 적용된 연령 제한
(D) 찾기 어려운 취미 용품을 위한 웹사이트

해설 지문의 'Since opening in August, Roll of the Dice has become a hit.'에서 8월에 개점한 이후 Roll of the Dice가 성공을 거두고 있다고 한 후 가게의 개점 배경, 소유자 등에 대해 설명하고 있으므로 (A)가 정답이다.

어휘 establish v. 설립하다 restriction n. 제한

169 동의어 찾기 문제

해석 1문단 다섯 번째 줄의 단어 "caters"는 의미상 -와 가장 가깝다.
(A) 받아들인다
(B) 공급한다
(C) 만족시킨다
(D) 적용한다

해설 caters를 포함한 구절 'Offering everything from classic board games to the latest tabletop role-playing games, this board game store caters to all ages and interests.'에서 caters는 '~의 구미에 맞추다'라는 뜻으로 사용되었다. 따라서 (C)가 정답이다.

170 추론 문제

해석 Roll of the Dice에 대해 무엇이 암시되는가?
(A) Mr. Lee와 Mr. McClain을 제외한 다른 직원이 없다.
(B) 유동 인구 규모가 많은 거리에 위치해 있다.
(C) 비슷한 사업체들과의 많은 경쟁에 직면해 있다.
(D) 특별한 행사를 위해 오후 8시 이후에도 영업할 것이다.

해설 지문의 'the store's daily closing time of 8 P.M.'에서 가게의 일일 마감 시간이 오후 8시라고 했고, 'In the future, they plan to stay open later to hold tournaments.'에서 추후에는 토너먼트를 개최하기 위해 더 늦게까지 영업할 계획이라고 했다. 따라서 (D)가

정답이다.

어휘 foot traffic 유동 인구 규모 competition n. 경쟁

171 문장 위치 찾기 문제

해석 [1], [2], [3], [4]로 표시된 위치 중, 다음 문장이 들어갈 곳으로 가장 적절한 것은?

"실제로, 두 사람은 사업의 첫 주 차에 한 건의 판매만을 이루었다."

(A) [1]
(B) [2]
(C) [3]
(D) [4]

해설 주어진 문장은 사업이 성공적이지 못했다는 것과 관련된 내용 주변에 나올 것임을 예상할 수 있다. [2]의 앞 문장인 'Business was slow at first.'에서 초기에는 사업이 부진했다고 했으므로, [2]에 주어진 문장이 들어가면 초기에는 사업이 부진했고, 실제로 두 사람은 사업의 첫 주 차에 한 건의 판매만을 이루었다는 자연스러운 문맥이 된다는 것을 알 수 있다. 따라서 (B)가 정답이다.

172-175번은 다음 온라인 채팅 대화문에 관한 문제입니다.

Ben Pollard (오전 9시 10분)
¹⁷²제가 급한 질문이 하나 있어요, Karen. Ms. Sadi의 항공편이 오늘 오전 9시 15분에 도착하죠, 그렇죠? 저는 모든 것이 예정대로 되고 있는지 확실히 하길 원해요.

Karen Chua (오전 9시 11분)
사실, 제가 방금 그녀에게 전화를 받았어요. 그녀의 항공편이 조금 일찍 착륙했고, 그녀는 이미 공항이래요.

Ben Pollard (오전 9시 12분)
반가운 소리네요. 공항에서 우리 사무실까지 택시로 대략 30분이 걸리니까, 그녀가 곧 이곳에 오겠네요.

Karen Chua (오전 9시 14분)
¹⁷³하지만 그녀는 택시를 타는 대신 셔틀버스를 탈 계획이에요. 9시 45분에 출발하는 것이 하나 있는데, 그것은 그녀를 40분 정도 후에 근처에 내려줄 거예요.

Ben Pollard (오전 9시 15분)
그럼 그녀가 여기에 10시 25분에 도착한다는 건가요? 회의는 10시 30분에 시작해요. 그건 너무 급박해요. ¹⁷³그녀에게 다시 생각해 달라고 물어봐 주실 수 있나요?

Karen Chua (오전 9시 16분)
알겠어요. ¹⁷⁴우리 최고 경영자가 그녀의 새로운 소설을 우리 회사에서 출간하는 것과 관련해서 그녀를 만나기 위해 출장을 연기했기 때문에, 그녀가 늦으면 좋지 않아 보일 것 같다고 말해볼게요.

Ben Pollard (오전 9시 18분)
좋은 생각이에요. 그나저나, 회의실에 모든 것이 다 준비되어 있나요?

Karen Chua (오전 9시 19분)
네. ¹⁷⁵그리고 제가 인턴들 중 한 명에게 길 건너 제과점에 가서 페이스트리와 커피를 사 오라고 이야기할게요.

catch v. 타다, 잡다 reconsider v. 다시 생각하다, 재고하다
postpone v. 연기하다, 미루다 publish v. 출간하다, 출판하다

172 육하원칙 문제

해석 Mr. Pollard는 왜 메시지를 보냈는가?
(A) 도착 시간을 확인하기 위해
(B) 여행 준비를 변경하기 위해
(C) 지연에 대한 설명을 요청하기 위해
(D) 여행 일정과 관련된 문제를 지적하기 위해

해설 지문의 'I have a quick question, Karen. Ms. Sadi's flight gets in at 9:15 this morning, right? I just want to make sure everything is on schedule.'에서 Ms. Sadi의 항공편이 9시 15분에 도착하는 것이 맞는지 물으며 모든 것이 예정대로 되고 있는지 확실히 하길 원한다고 했으므로, Mr. Pollard가 도착 시간을 확인하기 위해 메시지를 보냈음을 알 수 있다. 따라서 (A)가 정답이다.

어휘 arrangement n. 준비 explanation n. 설명, 해명
point out ~을 지적하다 itinerary n. 여행 일정

173 의도 파악 문제

해석 오전 9시 15분에, Mr. Pollard가 'That's too close for comfort'라고 썼을 때, 그가 의도한 것 같은 것은?
(A) Ms. Sadi가 더 이른 셔틀버스를 잡아야 한다.
(B) Ms. Sadi가 공항에서 택시를 타야 한다.
(C) Ms. Sadi가 회의 안건을 확인해야 한다.
(D) Ms. Sadi가 아침 항공편을 타야 한다.

해설 지문의 'But she[Ms. Sadi]'s planning to catch a shuttle bus instead of getting a taxi. There is one that leaves at 9:45, which will drop her off nearby about 40 minutes later.'에서 Ms. Sadi가 택시 대신 셔틀버스를 탈 계획이고 9시 45분에 출발하는 것이 그녀를 40분 정도 후에 근처에 내려줄 것이라고 하자, Mr. Pollard가 'That's too close for comfort'(그건 너무 급박해요)라고 한 후, 'Can you ask her to reconsider?'에서 그녀에게 다시 생각해 달라고 물어봐 줄 수 있는지 묻는 것을 통해, Mr. Pollard는 Ms. Sadi가 공항에서 택시를 타야 한다고 생각하는 것임을 알 수 있다. 따라서 (B)가 정답이다.

174 추론 문제

해석 Ms. Sadi에 대해 암시되는 것은?
(A) 최근에 새로운 책을 집필하는 것을 끝냈다.
(B) 이전 행사에서 Mr. Pollard와 만났다.
(C) 다가오는 출장을 연기할 계획이다.
(D) 현재 출판사에서 일한다.

해설 지문의 'I'll mention that our CEO postponed a business trip to meet with her about having her new novel published by our company'에서 최고 경영자가 그녀의 새로운 소설을 우리 회사에서 출간하는 것과 관련해서 그녀를 만나기 위해 출장을 연기했다고 한 것을 통해, Ms. Sadi가 최근에 새로운 책을 집필하는 것을 끝냈음을 추론할 수 있다. 따라서 (A)가 정답이다.

어휘 previous adj. 이전의 occasion n. 행사, 경우
publisher n. 출판사

175 육하원칙 문제

해석 Ms. Chua는 인턴에게 무엇을 하라고 요청할 것인가?
(A) 사무실의 다른 직원들에게 연락한다.
(B) 회의실에 가구를 배치한다.
(C) 회의에서 제공할 다과를 구입한다.
(D) 발표를 위한 시청각 장비를 설치한다.

해설 지문의 'And I'll tell one of the interns to go to the bakery across the street to pick up some pastries and coffee.'에서 Ms. Chua가 인턴들 중 한 명에게 길 건너 제과점에 가서 페이스트리와 커피를 사 오라고 이야기하겠다고 했으므로 (C)가 정답이다.

어휘 furniture n. 가구 refreshment n. 다과
audiovisual adj. 시청각의 equipment n. 장비

Paraphrasing

pick up some pastries and coffee 페이스트리와 커피를 사 오다
→ Buy some refreshments 다과를 구입하다

176-180번은 다음 공지와 이메일에 관한 문제입니다.

모든 직원들에게 알립니다.

[176]모든 컴퓨터와 모바일 기기가 보안 업그레이드를 받을 것이라는 점을 숙지해 주시기 바랍니다. [179]이 작업은 11월 22일 금요일, 오후 4시에 시작하는 것으로 일정이 잡혔습니다. Hallington 보험 그룹은 회사의 보안 시스템을 계속 평가하고 필요한 조정을 하는 것에 전념하고 있습니다. [177]우리는 애리조나에 기반을 둔 신생 기술회사인 Kellings 기술회사와 협력하기로 결정했습니다. 수석 기술자와의 논의에서, 우리는 소비자 계정과 근로자 정보를 위험에 처하게 하는 우리 시스템상의 몇 가지 약점들에 대해 전달받았습니다.

Kellings 기술회사의 직원들이 계획된 작업이 이뤄지는 날 하루 종일 현장에 있을 것입니다. 여러분이 원격 근무를 위해 사용하는 모든 기기들을 가져와 주시기 바랍니다. 11월 21일에 지급될 외장 하드 드라이브에 모든 파일들을 저장하세요. [178]질문이 있으시면 a.beckford@hallington.com으로 IT 부서 책임자인 Aaron Beckford에게 연락해 주세요.

undergo v. 받다, 겪다 insurance n. 보험
commit v. 전념하다, 헌신하다 continuously adv. 계속, 연달아
assess v. 평가하다 adjustment n. 조정
team up with ~와 협력하다, 협동하다 weakness n. 약점
remote adj. 원격의 external adj. 외장의, 외부의

발신: Martin Clarins <m.clarins@hallington.com>
수신: Aaron Beckford <a.beckford@hallington.com>
날짜: 11월 14일
제목: 보안 업그레이드

안녕하세요, Aaron.

저는 다가오는 보안 업그레이드에 대해 알게 되었습니다. [179]하지만, 아시다시피, 저는 현재 싱가포르에서 일을 하고 있으며 예정된 작업의 일주일 후에나 돌아갈 것입니다. 제 비서인 Consuelo Cortez가 제 사무실에 있는 컴퓨터에 접근할 수 있으니, 그 부분은 문제가 없을 것 같아요.

그러나, 저는 회사 스마트폰과 노트북 컴퓨터를 갖고 있습니다. 이 상황을 처리하기 위한 몇 가지 선택지가 있는 것 같습니다. 180-(A)저는 제가 돌아가자마자 기술자들에게 이 기기들을 넘겨줄 수 있습니다. 아니면 180-(B)제가 내려받아 직접 설치할 수 있는 소프트웨어 프로그램이 있을까요? 180-(C)저는 또한 당신이 제 업무용 노트북을 바로 우편으로 보내기를 바라는 경우 출장 중에 사용할 수 있는 또 다른 노트북에 접근할 수 있다는 점도 언급해야겠습니다. 180-(D)하지만 휴대폰은 제가 고객들과 연락하고 일정표를 조정하는 데 있어 필수적이기 때문에 제가 소지하고 있어야 합니다.

가능한 빨리 저에게 알려주세요.

Martin 드림

assistant n. 비서, 조수   hand ~ over ~을 넘겨주다
mail v. 우편으로 보내다   coordinate v. 조정하다

176 목적 찾기 문제

해석 공지의 목적은 무엇인가?
(A) 교육 세션에 초대하기 위해
(B) 회사 정책 변경을 설명하기 위해
(C) 일부 컴퓨터 작업을 알리기 위해
(D) 몇몇 장비 구매에 대해 설명하기 위해

해설 지문의 'Please be advised that all computers and mobile devices will undergo a security upgrade.'에서 모든 컴퓨터와 모바일 기기가 보안 업그레이드를 받을 것이라는 점을 숙지해 달라고 했으므로 (C)가 정답이다.

어휘 extend v. 보내다, 주다   policy n. 정책, 방침

177 추론 문제

해석 Hallington 보험 그룹에 대해 암시되는 것은?
(A) 대기업과 합병했다.
(B) 보안 업그레이드의 날짜를 확정하지 않았다.
(C) 새로운 데스크톱 컴퓨터에 투자했다.
(D) 이전에 Kellings 기술회사와 일한 적이 없다.

해설 지문의 'We have decided to team up with Kellings Tech, a new technology company based in Arizona.'에서 애리조나에 기반을 둔 신생 기술회사인 Kellings 기술회사와 협력하기로 결정했다고 했으므로, 이전에는 Kellings 기술회사와 함께 일한 적이 없다는 것을 추론할 수 있다. 따라서 (D)가 정답이다.

어휘 merge v. 합병하다   corporation n. 기업, 법인

178 추론 문제

해석 Mr. Beckford는 누구일 것 같은가?
(A) 기술 상담가
(B) 부서 관리자
(C) 회사 대표
(D) 개인 비서

해설 지문의 'Please contact the head of IT, Aaron Beckford, at a.beckford@hallington.com if you have any questions.'에서 질문이 있으면 IT 부서 책임자인 Aaron Beckford에게 연락해 달라고 한 것을 통해, Mr. Beckford가 부서 관리자임을 알 수 있다. 따라서 (B)가 정답이다.

어휘 consultant n. 상담가, 컨설턴트   personal adj. 개인의

179 추론 문제 연계

해석 Mr. Clarins가 그의 일에 대해 암시하는 것은?
(A) 11월 22일 이후에나 사무실에 있을 것이다.
(B) 싱가포르로 영구 전근되었다.
(C) 출장 환급 신청서를 제출했다.
(D) 1년 전에 새로운 지위로 승진했다.

해설 Mr. Clarins가 작성한 이메일을 먼저 확인한다.
단서 1 이메일의 'However, as you might know, I am currently working in Singapore and won't be back until the week after the scheduled work.'에서 Mr. Clarins가 현재 싱가포르에서 일을 하고 있으며 예정된 작업의 일주일 후에나 돌아갈 것이라고 했다. 그런데 예정된 작업 일정에 대해 제시되지 않았으므로 공지에서 관련 내용을 확인한다.
단서 2 공지의 'This work has been scheduled for Friday, November 22, starting at 4 P.M.'에서 보안 업그레이드가 11월 22일에 진행된다는 것을 확인할 수 있다.
두 단서를 종합할 때, Mr. Clarins가 11월 22일 이후에나 사무실에 있을 것이라는 점을 추론할 수 있다. 따라서 (A)가 정답이다.

어휘 transfer v. 전근시키다, 옮기다   permanently adv. 영구히
reimbursement n. 환급, 배상   promote v. 승진시키다

180 Not/True 문제

해석 Mr. Clarins에 의해 제안된 해결책이 아닌 것은?
(A) 출장이 끝날 때까지 기다렸다가 기기를 넘기는 것
(B) 도움 없이 소프트웨어 응용 프로그램을 설치하는 것
(C) 사무실 지점으로 컴퓨터를 배송되게 하는 것
(D) 휴대폰을 회사에 의해 지급된 것으로 교체하는 것

해설 이메일의 'The phone needs to remain with me though as it is essential for me to stay in touch with clients and coordinate my calendar.'에서 휴대폰은 고객들과 연락하고 일정표를 조정하는 데 있어 필수적이기 때문에 자신이 소지하고 있어야 한다고 했으므로 (D)는 제안된 해결책이 아니다. 따라서 (D)가 정답이다. (A)는 'I could just hand these devices over to the technicians once I get back.'에서 돌아오자마자 기술자들에게 기기들을 넘겨줄 수 있다고 했으므로 제안된 해결책이 맞다. (B)는 'is there a software program I could download and set up myself?'에서 직접 설치할 수 있는 소프트웨어 프로그램이 있을지 묻고 있으므로 제안된 해결책이 맞다. (C)는 'I should also mention that I have access to another laptop I can use during my trip in case you want me to mail my work one back right away.'에서 업무용 노트북을 바로 우편으로 보내기를 바라는 경우 출장 중에 사용할 수 있는 또 다른 노트북에 접근할 수 있다고 했으므로 제안된 해결책이 맞다.

어휘 turn over ~을 넘기다, 뒤집다   assistance n. 도움
issue v. 지급하다, 교부하다

181-185번은 다음 웹페이지와 이메일에 관한 문제입니다.

저희는 당신의 창문을 닦고 어떤 유리 수리 작업이든 할 수 있습니다. Windows Clear는 휴스턴에서 시작한 체인점입니다. ¹⁸¹⁻⁽ᶜ⁾다른 지점들이 뉴욕, 시카고, 그리고 다른 주요 도시들에 문을 열고 있습니다. 다음 서비스들이 이용 가능합니다.

• 서비스 1
매일의 창문 세척. 이것은 가게 앞에 딸린 공간이 있는 소매점들에 추천됩니다. 저희의 직원들은 당신의 업체에 최소한의 방해를 보장하기 위한 조치를 취할 것입니다. 현재, 저희는 휴스턴의 업체들을 위해 소개용 시범 주간을 99달러에 제공하고 있습니다.

• 서비스 2
주기적인 창문 세척. 저희는 또한 고층 건물들을 위한 장비를 보유하고 있습니다. 저희 근로자들의 매주 혹은 매월 방문을 신청하세요.

• 서비스 3
특정 행사나 일을 위한 일회성 작업. 저희는 당신의 사업장 혹은 주택의 창문을 빛나게 만들 것입니다.

• ¹⁸³서비스 4
¹⁸³창문 수리. 저희는 손상된 유리를 교체하고 다른 관련된 작업을 수행하면서 모든 종류의 창문을 수리할 수 있습니다. 이것은 사업장 및 주택에서 이용할 수 있습니다.

¹⁸²만약 당신이 어떤 서비스든 관심이 있다면, 저희 직원들 중 한 명이 당신의 사업장이나 주택을 점검하여 정확한 견적을 제공할 것입니다. 서비스 4를 위해서는, 피해 사진을 저희에게 보내주실 것을 권장합니다. 문의 사항이 있다면 info@windowsclear.com으로 이메일을 보내주세요.

franchise n. 체인점, 프랜차이즈   retail location 소매점
storefront n. 가게 앞에 딸린 공간   ensure v. 보장하다
minimal adj. 최소한의, 아주 적은   interruption n. 방해, 중단 기간
introductory adj. 소개용의   periodical adj. 주기적인
skyscraper n. 고층 건물   occurrence n. 일어난 일, 사건
accurate adj. 정확한   quote n. 견적

발신: Shion Yamada <s.yamada@shionopticalspace.com>
수신: Windows Clear <info@windowsclear.com>
날짜: 6월 25일
제목: 긴급

Windows Clear께,

¹⁸⁴/¹⁸⁵⁻⁽ᴬ⁾저는 Starset 피자 가게의 Harry Colton에게 귀사에 대해 듣게 되었는데, 그곳은 휴스턴 시내의 우리 매장에서 거리를 따라 내려가면 있습니다. 그는 귀사가 그의 업체를 매일 방문하며, 제 문제에 대해 도움을 줄 수 있을 것이라고 말했습니다.

¹⁸³제 안경점이 어젯밤에 침입당했고, 저는 제 가게 창문 중 두 개를 수리해야 합니다. 그것들은 매장의 정면 창문들이어서, ¹⁸⁵⁻⁽ᴮ⁾저는 그것들이 수리될 때까지 매장을 열 수 없습니다. 그러므로, 저는 귀사를 즉시 고용하길 원합니다. ¹⁸⁵⁻⁽ᴰ⁾제가 직접 비용을 지불하고 나서 추후에 보험 회사로부터 배상을 받을 것입니다. 시간을 정하기 위해 가능한 한 빨리 555-9493으로 저에게 전화주시기 바랍니다.

감사합니다.

Shion Yamada 드림

Shion Optical Space

optical shop 안경점   break into ~에 침입하다
reimburse v. 배상하다

181 Not/True 문제

해석 Windows Clear에 대해 명시된 것은?
(A) 시내 지역에만 서비스를 제공한다.
(B) 현지 신문에 광고를 하고 있다.
(C) 현재 다른 도시들로 확장하고 있다.
(D) 지난 분기에 매출액이 두 배가 되었다.

해설 웹페이지의 'Other locations are opening in New York, Chicago, and other major cities.'에서 다른 지점들이 뉴욕, 시카고, 그리고 다른 주요 도시들에 문을 열고 있다고 하였다. 따라서 (C)가 정답이다.

어휘 serve v. (서비스를) 제공하다   advertise v. 광고를 하다
quarter n. 분기

Paraphrasing

Other locations are opening in New York, Chicago, and other major cities. 다른 지점들이 뉴욕, 시카고, 그리고 다른 주요 도시들에 문을 열고 있다. → It is currently expanding into other cities. 현재 다른 도시들로 확장하고 있다.

182 육하원칙 문제

해석 웹페이지에 따르면, 고객이 비용 견적을 받기 전에 무슨 일이 일어날 것인가?
(A) 온라인 신청서가 검토될 것이다.
(B) 공간에 대한 점검이 수행될 것이다.
(C) 지불 방법이 확인될 것이다.
(D) 사진사가 파견될 것이다.

해설 웹페이지의 'If you are interested in any service, one of our representatives will inspect your business or home and provide you with an accurate quote.'에서 직원들 중 한 명이 사업장이나 주택을 점검하여 정확한 견적을 제공할 것이라고 했으므로, 비용 견적을 받기 전에 공간에 대한 점검이 수행될 것임을 알 수 있다. 따라서 (B)가 정답이다.

어휘 request form 신청서   inspection n. 점검, 검사
payment n. 지불, 지급   verify v. 확인하다
dispatch v. 파견하다, 보내다

Paraphrasing

one of our representatives ~ inspect your business or home 우리 직원들 중 한 명이 당신의 사업장이나 주택을 점검할 것이다 → An inspection of a space ~ be conducted 공간에 대한 점검이 수행될 것이다

183 추론 문제 연계

해석 Ms. Yamada는 어떤 서비스를 선택할 것 같은가?
(A) 서비스 1

(B) 서비스 2
(C) 서비스 3
(D) 서비스 4

해설 Ms. Yamada가 작성한 이메일을 먼저 확인한다.

단서 1 이메일의 'My optical shop was broken into last night, and I need to have two of the windows repaired.'에서 안경점이 어젯밤에 침입당해서 가게 창문 중 두 개를 수리해야 한다고 했다. 그런데 창문 수리 서비스에 대해 제시되지 않았으므로 웹페이지에서 관련 내용을 확인한다.

단서 2 웹페이지의 'Service 4'에서 'Window repair. We can repair all types of windows, replacing damaged glass and performing any other related work.'를 통해 서비스 4가 손상된 유리를 교체하고 다른 관련된 작업을 수행하면서 모든 종류의 창문을 수리할 수 있다고 했다.

두 단서를 종합할 때, Ms. Yamada가 선택할 서비스는 서비스 4임을 추론할 수 있다. 따라서 (D)가 정답이다.

184 육하원칙 문제

해설 Ms. Yamada는 어떻게 Windows Clear에 대해 듣게 되었는가?
(A) 업계 행사에서 직원을 만났다.
(B) 온라인에서 검색하다가 웹사이트를 방문했다.
(C) 한 업체 소유주로부터 추천을 받았다.
(D) 서비스에 대해 광고하는 벽보를 보았다.

해설 이메일의 'I was referred to you[Windows Clear] by Harry Colton from Starset Pizzeria'에서 Ms. Yamada가 Starset 피자 가게의 Harry Colton에게 Windows Clear에 대해 듣게 되었다고 했으므로 (C)가 정답이다.

어휘 search v. 검색하다, 찾아보다   referral n. 추천, 소개

185 Not/True 문제

해설 Shion Optical Space에 대해 언급되지 않은 것은?
(A) 휴스턴 시내에 위치해 있다.
(B) 수리가 될 때까지 문을 닫을 것이다.
(C) 같은 도시 내에 많은 지점이 있다.
(D) 보험 회사로부터 배상을 받을 것이다.

해설 (A)는 이메일의 'I was referred to you by Harry Colton from Starset Pizzeria, which is down the street from us in downtown Houston.'에서 Starset 피자 가게가 휴스턴 시내의 우리 매장에서 거리를 따라 내려가면 있다고 했으므로 지문의 내용과 일치한다. (B)는 'I cannot open my shop until they are fixed'에서 창문들이 수리될 때까지 매장을 열 수 없다고 했으므로 지문의 내용과 일치한다. (D)는 'I will pay myself and then get reimbursed by my insurance company later'에서 직접 비용을 지불하고 나서 추후에 보험 회사로부터 배상을 받을 것이라고 했으므로 지문의 내용과 일치한다. (C)는 지문에 언급되지 않은 내용이다. 따라서 (C)가 정답이다.

186-190번은 다음 회람, 광고, 후기에 관한 문제입니다.

회람

수신: 모든 Save Smart 직원들
발신: Tony Wilkins
제목: 재고 정리 판매
날짜: 9월 1일

여름이 거의 끝나가고 있으므로, 우리는 다음 주에 모든 여름 의류 및 용품들에 대한 재고 정리 판매를 진행할 것입니다. 여기에는 의류, 장난감 및 기타 품목들이 포함됩니다. 저는 판매될 제품들의 전체 목록을 내일 휴게실에 게시할 것입니다. 187운이 좋다면, 이러한 품목들은 첫 주에 25퍼센트 할인된 가격으로 다 팔릴 것입니다. 그러나 만약 상당한 수의 제품들이 선반에 여전히 남아 있다면, 우리는 그다음 주에 그것들의 가격을 50퍼센트 인하할 것입니다. 186오늘 저녁 언젠가, 저는 여러분들 중 몇몇이 앞 창문과 매장 주변에 할인 판매를 알리는 벽보들을 거는 것에 도움을 주기를 바랍니다. 그것은 공식적으로 9월 7일에 시작할 것입니다.

clearance sale 재고 정리 판매   substantial adj. 상당한
shelf n. 선반   officially adv. 공식적으로

Save Smart의 연례 여름 재고 정리 판매!

187/1899월 14일부터 9월 20일까지, 우리 매장 내 모든 여름 품목들은 50퍼센트 할인될 것입니다. 이것들이 포함됩니다:

- 티셔츠, 수영용 팬츠, 샌들, 그리고 반바지
- 잔디 깎는 기계와 스프링클러
- 물 미끄럼틀, 물총, 그리고 물 위에 뜨는 기구들
- 189석쇠 그리고 석쇠구이 부대용품

이번 할인 판매는 오직 일주일 동안만 진행되므로 서두르세요.
188-(C)Save Smart는 주 7일 오전 9시부터 오후 8시까지 문을 엽니다.

*189Save Smart 클럽의 회원들은 모든 품목에 10퍼센트 추가 할인을 받을 것입니다.

lawn mower 잔디 깎는 기계   flotation n. (물 위에) 뜸, 부유
additional adj. 추가의

Homeman 야외용 석쇠 후기
평가: 5/5

저는 미니애폴리스의 Save Smart 매장을 돌아다니다가 즉흥적으로 이 석쇠를 구입했습니다. 189저는 그것을 여름 재고 정리 판매 기간에 60퍼센트 할인된 가격으로 구매했기에, 거저나 마찬가지였습니다. 그것은 제가 지금까지 구입한 것들 중 최고의 석쇠인 것으로 드러났습니다.

제가 캘리포니아에서 보낸 겨울 달 동안, 저는 다양한 손님들을 위해 10차례 이상 이것을 요리하는 데 사용했습니다. 그것은 제가 소유해 왔던 다른 석쇠들보다 더 효율적으로 요리했습니다. 당신은 그저 고기 (혹은 야채)를 안에 넣고, 올바른 설정을 선택한 다음, 뚜껑을 닫고 기다리기만 하면 됩니다. 190그것과 관련된 유일한 문제는 처음으로 프로판 탱크를 교체할 때 발생했습니다. 새로운 것이 연결되지 않았습니다. 하지만 이 석쇠와 함께 제공된 설명서를 확인했을 때, 저는 제가 무엇을 잘못하고 있는지 빠르게 알아낼 수 있었습니다. 저는 이 제품을

매우 추천합니다.
Arthur Klepper

on a whim 즉흥적으로, 충동적으로　wander v. 돌아다니다, 거닐다
be a steal 거저나 마찬가지이다　efficiently adv. 효율적으로
lid n. 뚜껑　figure out ~을 알아내다, 이해하다

186 육하원칙 문제

해석　회람에 따르면, Save Smart의 몇몇 직원들은 9월 1일에 무엇을 했는가?
(A) 매장 선반의 제품들을 재편성했다.
(B) 재고로 있는 품목들의 상세한 목록을 받았다.
(C) 다가오는 판촉 행사에 관한 공고를 게시했다.
(D) 새로운 상품들을 위한 창가 진열을 설치했다.

해설　회람의 'Sometime this evening, I'd like some of you to help me hang up posters announcing the sale in our front windows and around the store.'에서 몇몇 직원들에게 앞 창문과 매장 주변에 할인 판매를 알리는 벽보들을 거는 것에 도움을 달라고 했으므로 (C)가 정답이다.

어휘　reorganize v. 재편성하다, 재조직하다　inventory n. 목록
promotion n. 판촉 (행사), 승진　merchandise n. 상품

Paraphrasing

hang up posters announcing the sale 할인 판매를 알리는 벽보들을 걸다 → posted notices about an upcoming promotion 다가오는 판촉 행사에 관한 공고를 게시했다

187 추론 문제 연계

해석　Save Smart의 여름 재고 정리 판매에 관해 결론지을 수 있는 것은?
(A) 초기의 할인 금액이 인하되었다.
(B) 많은 품목이 첫 주에 팔리지 않았다.
(C) 시작일이 하루 밀렸다.
(D) 몇몇 고객들이 구매를 할 수 없었다.

해설　Save Smart의 여름 재고 정리 판매에 대한 광고를 먼저 확인한다.
단서 1 광고의 'From September 14 until September 20, all summer items in our store will be 50 percent off.'에서 9월 14일부터 20일까지 모든 여름 품목들이 50퍼센트 할인될 것이라고 했다. 그런데 50퍼센트 할인된 품목에 대해 제시되지 않았으므로 공고에서 할인 관련 내용을 확인한다.
단서 2 공고의 'With luck, these items will sell out within the first week at a 25 percent discount. But if there are a substantial number of products still on the shelves, we'll reduce their prices by 50 percent the following week.'에서 운이 좋다면, 품목들은 첫 주에 25퍼센트 할인된 가격으로 다 팔릴 것이라고 했고, 만약 상당 수의 제품들이 선반에 여전히 남아 있다면, 그다음 주에 그것들의 가격을 50퍼센트 인하할 것이라고 하였다.
두 단서를 종합할 때, 많은 품목이 첫 주 차에 팔리지 않았음을 추론할 수 있다. 따라서 (B)가 정답이다.

어휘　initial adj. 초기의, 처음의　amount n. 금액, 양
unsold adj. 팔리지 않은

Paraphrasing

there are a substantial number of products still on the shelves 상당 수의 제품들이 선반에 여전히 남아 있다 → Many items were unsold 많은 품목이 팔리지 않았다

188 Not/True 문제

해석　광고에서 Save Smart에 대해 언급된 것은?
(A) 그들 자체의 제품들을 생산한다.
(B) 9월에 영업시간을 연장했다.
(C) 매일 영업한다.
(D) 최근 로열티 클럽의 명칭을 변경했다.

해설　광고의 'Save Smart is open from 9 A.M. to 8 P.M., seven days a week'에서 Save Smart가 주 7일 오전 9시부터 오후 8시까지 문을 연다고 했으므로 (C)가 정답이다. (A), (B), (D)는 지문에 언급되지 않은 내용이다.

어휘　extend v. 연장하다, 확대하다　operate v. 영업하다

Paraphrasing

is open 문을 연다 → operates 영업한다

189 추론 문제 연계

해석　Mr. Klepper에 대해 암시되는 것은?
(A) 지난달에 미니애폴리스로 이사했다.
(B) 제품을 환불하는 과정에 있다.
(C) 채식 요리만 요리한다.
(D) 9월에 Save Smart 클럽의 회원이었다.

해설　질문의 핵심 어구인 Mr. Klepper가 작성한 후기를 먼저 확인한다.
단서 1 후기의 'I[Mr. Klepper] got it[grill] for 60 percent off during the summer clearance sale'에서 Mr. Klepper가 석쇠를 60퍼센트 할인된 가격으로 구매했다고 했다. 그런데 60퍼센트 할인하여 구매한 물품에 대해 제시되지 않았으므로 광고에서 할인 관련 내용을 확인한다.
단서 2 광고의 'From September 14 until September 20, all summer items in our store will be 50 percent off.'에서 9월 14일부터 9월 20일까지 모든 여름 품목이 50퍼센트 할인될 것임을 알 수 있고, 'Grills and grilling accessories', 'Members of the Save Smart Club will receive an additional 10 percent discount on all of these items.'에서 석쇠가 50퍼센트 할인 품목에 포함되는 것과 Save Smart 클럽의 회원은 이 할인 품목에 10퍼센트 추가 할인을 받을 것임을 알 수 있다.
두 단서를 종합할 때, Mr. Klepper는 9월에 Save Smart 클럽의 회원이었음을 알 수 있다. 따라서 (D)가 정답이다.

어휘　vegetarian adj. 채식의, 채식주의자의

190 육하원칙 문제

해석　Mr. Klepper는 그가 석쇠에 대해 겪었던 문제를 어떻게 해결했는가?
(A) 웹사이트를 방문함으로써
(B) 사용자 설명서를 확인함으로써
(C) 매장 직원에게 이야기함으로써

(D) 서비스 센터에 전화함으로써

해설 후기의 'The only problem I had with it[grill] occurred when I first changed the propane tank. The new one would not connect. But when I checked the instructions that came with the grill, I was able to quickly figure out what I was doing wrong.'에서 석쇠에 있었던 유일한 문제는 프로판 탱크를 교체할 때 발생했고, 새로운 것이 연결되지 않는 문제였지만, 석쇠와 함께 제공된 설명서를 확인했을 때 무엇을 잘못하고 있는지 빠르게 알아낼 수 있었다고 했으므로 (B)가 정답이다.

어휘 resolve v. 해결하다

Paraphrasing

the instructions 설명서 → a user manual 사용자 설명서

191-195번은 다음 두 이메일과 문자 메시지에 관한 문제입니다.

수신: 전 직원 <group@leonfinancial.com>
발신: Brenda Carver <b.carver@leonfinancial.com>
제목: 워크숍
날짜: 1월 15일

안녕하세요 여러분,

지난주에 공지된 바와 같이 Core Tech사의 EZFile 소프트웨어 프로그램 사용이 우리의 대표 이사인 Logan Morales의 승인을 받았습니다. 이 애플리케이션은 우리 고객들의 소득세 신고서 제출과 관련된 많은 일상적인 작업을 자동화할 것입니다.

¹⁹¹저는 다음 달에 Core Tech사의 담당자가 우리의 사무실에서 워크숍을 진행할 수 있도록 준비했습니다. Tina Williams는 이 프로그램에 대해 매우 잘 알고 있으며 수석 설계자인 Brock Desai와 긴밀히 협력해 왔기 때문에 그녀에게서 많은 것을 배울 것이라고 확신합니다. ¹⁹⁵워크숍은 2월 17일에 201호실에서 열릴 것입니다. 오전 10시에 시작하여 오후 3시에 종료될 것이며 점심 식사를 위한 30분간의 휴식 시간이 있습니다. ¹⁹³EZFile 교육은 모든 회계사들에게 의무적입니다. 당사의 다른 직책에 있는 직원들은 참여하지 않아도 됩니다.

감사합니다.

Brenda Carver
인사팀, Leon 금융사

approve v. 승인하다   automate v. 자동화하다
knowledgeable adj. 잘 아는   mandatory adj. 의무적인, 필수의
accountant n. 회계사

Chad Ellis   [2월 17일, 오후 2시 10분]
부탁 하나 들어주시겠어요, Diya? 아시다시피 저는 사랑니를 뽑아야 해서 오후에 휴가를 냈어요. ¹⁹²치과에 가는 길에 제가 퇴근하기 전에 해야 할 일을 깜빡했다는 것을 깨달았어요.

Diya Patel   [2월 17일, 오후 2시 11분]
물론이죠. 제가 지금 시간이 좀 있어요. ¹⁹³사실 한가한 오후였어요. 여기의 다른 직원들의 기술 지원 요청이 많지 않았어요.

Chad Ellis   [2월 17일, 오후 2시 12분]
제 책상 위에 컴퓨터 부품 영수증이 들어 있는 ¹⁹⁴녹색 폴더가 있을 거예요. 회계사들의 몇몇 컴퓨터가 EZFile 소프트웨어를 설치하기

전에 업그레이드되어야 했어요. ¹⁹⁴오늘 퇴근하기 전에 부서장님께 그것을 전달해 주시겠어요?

Diya Patel   [2월 17일, 오후 2시 14분]
물론이죠. 제가 그것을 처리할게요.

favor n. 부탁   contain v. 들어 있다   department head 부서장

수신: 전 직원 <group@leonfinancial.com>
발신: Brenda Carver <b.carver@leonfinancial.com>
제목: 요청 사항
날짜: 2월 18일
첨부 파일: 설문지

안녕하세요,

¹⁹⁵저는 어제 아침 301호실에서 열린 EZFile 워크숍에 참석하신 분들의 의견을 모으고 싶습니다. 당신이 참여하셨다면 첨부된 설문지를 작성하여 2월 21일까지 제게 다시 보내주세요. 강사와 주제가 얼마나 잘 설명되었는지에 초점을 맞춘 몇 가지 질문이 있습니다. 또한 예정되었던 30분 휴식 시간이 충분했는지도 알고 싶습니다.

시간을 내어 작성해 주셔서 미리 감사드립니다.

Brenda Carver
인사팀, Leon 금융사

questionnaire n. 설문지, 질문지   gather v. 모으다
take part 참여하다   sufficient adj. 충분한   fill out ~을 작성하다

191 육하원칙 문제

해설 첫 번째 이메일에 따르면, 누가 교육 세션을 이끌 것인가?
(A) Brenda Carver
(B) Logan Morales
(C) Tina Williams
(D) Brock Desai

해설 첫 번째 이메일의 'I have arranged for a representative from Core Tech to conduct a workshop at our office next month. Tina Williams is highly knowledgeable about this program ~ so I am sure you will learn a lot from her.'에서 다음 달에 Core Tech사의 담당자가 우리의 사무실에서 워크숍을 진행할 수 있도록 준비했고, Tina Williams는 이 프로그램에 대해 잘 알고 있으므로 그녀에게서 많은 것을 배울 것이라고 했다. 따라서 (C)가 정답이다.

어휘 lead v. 이끌다

192 육하원칙 문제

해설 Mr. Ellis는 Ms. Patel에게 연락했을 때 무엇을 하고 있었는가?
(A) 병원에 가고 있었다.
(B) 그의 사무실을 청소하고 있었다.
(C) 기술자에게 전화하고 있었다.
(D) 그의 집으로 돌아가고 있었다.

해설 문자 메시지의 2시 10분 메시지인 'I was on the way to see my dentist when I realized I'd forgotten to do something before leaving the office.'에서 Mr. Ellis는 치과에 가는 길에 해

야 할 일을 깜박했다는 것을 깨달았다고 했으므로 (A)가 정답이다.

어휘 return v. 돌아가다

193 추론 문제 연계

해석 Ms. Patel에 대해 결론지을 수 있는 것은?
(A) 그녀는 Mr. Ellis의 일찍 퇴근하는 계획에 대해 알림을 받지 못했다.
(B) 그녀는 Leon 금융사 인사 부서의 일원이다.
(C) 그녀는 기기를 위한 몇몇 부품들을 살 것을 요청받았다.
(D) 그녀는 EZFile 소프트웨어를 사용하는 방법을 배우도록 요구되지 않는다.

해설 Ms. Patel이 주고받은 문자 메시지를 먼저 확인한다.

단서 1 [February 17, 2:11 P.M.]의 'It's been a slow afternoon, actually. There were not many tech support requests from the other staff here.'에서 Ms. Patel은 2월 17일 오후에 한가로운 업무 시간을 보내고 있고, 다른 직원들의 기술 지원 요청이 많지 않았다고 했다.

단서 2 첫 번째 이메일의 'The EZFile training is mandatory for all accountants. Staff members in other roles at our company do not have to participate.'에서 EZFile 교육은 회계사들에게는 의무적이지만 다른 직책의 사람들은 참여할 필요가 없다고 했다.

두 단서를 종합할 때 Ms. Patel은 기술 지원 부서 소속이라 워크숍에 참여할 필요가 없음을 유추할 수 있다. 따라서 (D)가 정답이다.

어휘 component n. 부품

194 육하원칙 문제

해석 Mr. Ellis는 Ms. Patel에게 무엇을 하도록 요청하는가?
(A) 부서 회의에 참석한다.
(B) 휴가 신청을 후속 처리한다.
(C) 금융 기록을 프린트한다.
(D) 관리자에게 물건을 가져다준다.

해설 문자 메시지의 2시 12분 메시지인 'There should be a green folder containing receipts', 'Could you give it to our department head before you go home today?'에서 책상 위에 있는 녹색 폴더를 퇴근하기 전에 부서장님께 전달해 달라고 요청하고 있다. 따라서 (D)가 정답이다.

어휘 departmental adj. 부서의 record n. 기록

Paraphrasing

department head 부서장 → manager 관리자

195 육하원칙 문제 연계

해석 Ms. Carver는 그녀의 원래 계획에 무엇을 변경했는가?
(A) 행사의 장소
(B) 휴식 시간의 길이
(C) 수업의 주제
(D) 워크숍의 날짜

해설 Ms. Carver의 원래 계획을 알 수 있는 첫 번째 이메일을 먼저 확인한다.

단서 1 첫 번째 이메일의 'The workshop will take place in Room 201 on February 17.'에서 워크숍은 2월 17일에 201호실에서 열릴 것이라고 했다. 그런데 변경된 계획에 대해 제시되지 않았으므로 두 번째 이메일에서 변경 관련 내용을 확인한다.

단서 2 두 번째 이메일의 'I'd like to gather some feedback from those of you who attended the EZFile workshop yesterday morning in Room 301.'에서 어제 아침 301호실에서 열린 EZFile 워크숍에 참석하신 분들의 의견을 모으고 싶다고 했다.

두 단서를 종합할 때, 원래 워크숍을 열기로 했던 201호실이 아니라 301호실에서 진행되었음을 알 수 있으므로 Ms. Carver가 워크숍 장소를 변경했음을 알 수 있다. 따라서 (A)가 정답이다.

어휘 location n. 장소 length n. 길이

Paraphrasing

workshop 워크숍 → event 행사

196-200번은 다음 웹페이지, 구인 공고, 온라인 후기에 관한 문제입니다.

Herman Solutions
귀사의 상품을 가야 하는 곳으로 배송해 드립니다!

고객에게 온라인 구매 옵션을 제공하는 것은 최소 규모의 오프라인 거래 매장에서도 필수적인 일이 되었지만, 빠른 배송을 제공하는 데 드는 비용이 엄두도 못 낼 정도로 비쌀 수 있습니다. 그것이 바로 Herman Solutions가 등장한 배경입니다. ¹⁹⁶저희는 귀사가 고객의 요구를 충족하는 데 집중할 수 있도록 모든 배송 물류를 처리합니다.

저희의 시스템은 아래와 같이 진행됩니다:

- ¹⁹⁷⁻⁽ᴬ⁾저희의 배송 처리 소프트웨어가 귀사의 웹사이트 및 모바일 애플리케이션에 통합됩니다.
- ¹⁹⁷⁻⁽ᴮ⁾고객이 배송 옵션을 선택하면, 주소가 자동으로 저희 시스템에 입력됩니다.
- ¹⁹⁷⁻⁽ᶜ⁾매주 금요일, 저희의 운전기사 중 한 명이 귀사의 매장을 방문하여 아직 처리되지 않은 주문품을 가져가서 배송해 드립니다.
- ¹⁹⁷⁻⁽ᴰ⁾완료된 배송 건은 매월 청구됩니다.

요금에 대한 자세한 내용은 여기를 클릭하세요. ¹⁹⁸그리고 11월 15일까지 가입하시면, 첫 10건에 대한 배송비는 청구되지 않을 것입니다.

brick-and-mortar adj. 오프라인 거래의, 소매의
prohibitive adj. 엄두도 못 낼 정도로 비싼, 금지하는 logistics n. 물류
integrate v. 통합시키다
outstanding adj. 아직 처리되지 않은, 미지불된, 뛰어난

Herman Solutions가 배송 기사를 고용합니다!

국내에서 가장 빠르게 성장하고 있는 배송 업체와 함께하세요. 당사는 건강 보험, 탄력적인 근무 시간, 넉넉한 연차 휴가를 포함한 다양한 혜택과 함께 경쟁력 있는 보수를 제공합니다.

¹⁹⁹자격 요건
- ¹⁹⁹⁻⁽ᴬ⁾최소 2년의 관련된 경력
- 유효한 상업용 운전면허증
- ¹⁹⁹⁻⁽ᶜ⁾무거운 물건을 들어 올릴 수 있는 능력 (최대 60킬로그램)
- ¹⁹⁹⁻⁽ᴰ⁾고등학교 졸업장

지원하시려면, www.herman.com/join을 방문하여 전자 지원서를 작성하세요. [200]모든 합격자는 정규 업무를 시작하기 전에 숙련된 기사와 함께 7일간 교육을 받아야 합니다.

competitive adj. 경쟁력 있는   compensation n. 보수, 보상
annual leave 연차 휴가   qualification n. 자격 요건
relevant adj. 관련 있는   valid adj. 유효한   diploma n. 졸업장, 수료증
undergo v. 받다, 겪다   instruction n. 교육   duty n. 업무, 의무

[198]David Wilkins의 후기

[198]11월 10일에 Herman Solutions에 등록했고, 전반적으로 깊은 인상을 받았습니다. 스포츠 기념품 및 수집품을 전문으로 하는 매장으로서, 저희는 전국에 고객이 있습니다. Herman Solutions는 그들에게 저희 제품을 빠르고 저렴하게 배송할 수 있게 했습니다. 게다가, Herman 직원들의 전문성에 매우 만족했습니다. 예를 들어, [200]저희 정규 운전기사인 Sharon은 항상 제시간에 도착하여 배송품이 손상되거나 분실되지 않도록 세심한 주의를 기울입니다. 배송 절차를 간소화하고자 하는 다른 소규모 기업 소유주들에게도 Herman Solutions를 강력히 추천합니다.

register v. 등록하다   specialize v. 전문으로 하다
memorabilia n. 기념품   collectible n. 수집품
affordably adv. 저렴하게, 감당할 수 있게   professionalism n. 전문성
simplify v. 간소화하다

196 목적 찾기 문제

해석 웹페이지의 목적은 무엇인가?
(A) 소매점의 기업과의 제휴를 발표하기 위해
(B) 최근의 배송비 증가를 설명하기 위해
(C) 기존 시스템의 개선 사항을 설명하기 위해
(D) 회사의 서비스에 대한 개요를 제공하기 위해

해설 웹페이지의 'We[Herman Solutions] handle all of the shipping logistics so that you can focus on meeting your customers' needs.'에서 Herman Solutions는 회사들이 고객의 요구를 충족하는 데 집중할 수 있도록 모든 배송 물류를 처리한다고 한 후, 업무 시스템에 대해 설명하고 있으므로 (D)가 정답이다.

어휘 retailer n. 소매점   existing adj. 기존의

197 Not/True 문제

해석 Herman Solutions에 대해 사실인 것은?
(A) 고객이 자체 모바일 애플리케이션을 사용할 것을 요구한다.
(B) 이메일을 통해 배송 주소를 요청한다.
(C) 일주일에 한 번 매장에서 배송품을 가져간다.
(D) 배송에 대한 선불을 요구한다.

해설 웹페이지의 'Every Friday, one of our drivers will visit your shop to pick up and deliver any outstanding orders.'에서 매주 금요일에 운전기사 중 한 명이 매장을 방문하여 아직 처리되지 않은 주문을 가져가서 배송해 준다고 했으므로 (C)는 지문의 내용과 일치한다. 따라서 (C)가 정답이다. (A)는 'Our shipment-processing software is integrated into your Web site and mobile application.'에서 배송 처리 소프트웨어는 고객의 회사의 웹사이트 및 모바일 애플리케이션에 통합된다고 했으므로 지문의 내용과 일치하지 않는다. (B)는 'When a customer selects the delivery option, the address is automatically entered into our system.'에서 고객이 배송 옵션을 선택하면 주소가 자동으로 시스템에 입력된다고 했으므로 지문의 내용과 일치하지 않는다. (D)는 'You will be billed monthly for completed deliveries.'에서 완료된 배송 건은 매월 청구된다고 했으므로 지문의 내용과 일치하지 않는다.

어휘 payment in advance 선불

Paraphrasing

Every Friday 매주 금요일에 → once a week 일주일에 한 번

198 육하원칙 문제 연계

해석 Mr. Wilkins는 무엇을 받을 자격이 있었는가?
(A) 고객 데이터베이스에 접근할 권리
(B) 무료 제품 업그레이드
(C) 빠른 배송에 대한 특별 요금
(D) 무료로 서비스 이용

해설 Mr. Wilkins가 작성한 온라인 후기를 먼저 확인한다.
단서 1 온라인 후기의 'Review by David Wilkins', 'I registered for Herman Solutions on November 10'에서 Mr. Wilkins가 11월 10일에 Herman Solutions에 등록했다고 했다. 그런데 Herman Solutions 가입 혜택이 무엇인지 제시되지 않았으므로 웹페이지에서 관련 내용을 확인한다.
단서 2 웹페이지의 'And if you sign up by November 15, you will not be charged for your first 10 deliveries.'에서 11월 15일까지 가입하면 첫 10건에 대한 배송비가 청구되지 않는다는 것을 알 수 있다.
두 단서를 종합할 때, Mr. Wilkins가 무료 배송 서비스를 이용할 자격이 있었음을 알 수 있다. 따라서 (D)가 정답이다.

어휘 access n. 접근, 입장

199 Not/True 문제

해석 배송 기사 직책의 자격 요건으로 언급된 것은 무엇인가?
(A) 유사한 임무로 일하며 보낸 1년
(B) 정부 안전 프로그램 수료
(C) 60킬로그램이 넘는 물건을 들어 올릴 수 있는 능력
(D) 고등학교 졸업 증명서

해설 구인 공고의 'Qualifications', 'High school diploma'에서 자격 요건이 고등학교 졸업장이라고 했으므로 (D)는 지문의 내용과 일치한다. 따라서 (D)가 정답이다. (A)는 'Minimum of two years' relevant experience'에서 최소 2년 이상의 관련된 경력이라고 했으므로 지문의 내용과 일치하지 않는다. (C)는 'Ability to lift heavy objects (up to 60 kilograms)'에서 자격 요건이 최대 60킬로그램의 무거운 물건을 들어 올릴 수 있는 능력이라고 했으므로 지문의 내용과 일치하지 않는다. (B)는 지문에 언급되지 않은 내용이다.

어휘 completion n. 수료, 완료   certificate n. 졸업 증명서, 증명서

Paraphrasing

High school diploma 고등학교 졸업장 → A certificate of graduation from high school 고등학교 졸업 증명서

200 추론 문제 연계

해석 Sharon에 대해 결론지을 수 있는 것은?
(A) 일주일 동안 교육을 받았다.
(B) 직접 지원서를 제출했다.
(C) 추가 연간 휴가를 요청할 것이다.
(D) 한 달 동안 다른 기사를 대신할 것이다.

해설 Sharon이 언급된 온라인 후기를 먼저 확인한다.

단서 1 온라인 후기의 'Our regular driver Sharon'에서 Sharon이 Herman Solutions의 정규 운전기사라는 것을 알 수 있다. 구인 공고에서 운전기사들에 대한 내용을 확인한다.

단서 2 구인 공고의 'All successful applicants will be required to undergo seven days of instruction with an experienced driver before beginning their regular duties.'에서 모든 합격자는 정규 업무를 시작하기 전에 숙련된 기사와 함께 7일간 교육을 받아야 한다는 것을 알 수 있다.

두 단서를 종합할 때, Sharon은 운전기사로 합격한 후 일주일 동안 교육을 받았음을 추론할 수 있다. 따라서 (A)가 정답이다.

어휘 replace v. 대신하다

TEST 3

LISTENING TEST
p.112

1 (C)	21 (B)	41 (D)	61 (C)	81 (D)
2 (A)	22 (C)	42 (D)	62 (D)	82 (C)
3 (C)	23 (C)	43 (A)	63 (C)	83 (A)
4 (D)	24 (A)	44 (C)	64 (D)	84 (D)
5 (C)	25 (C)	45 (C)	65 (A)	85 (A)
6 (A)	26 (B)	46 (C)	66 (B)	86 (B)
7 (B)	27 (A)	47 (A)	67 (D)	87 (C)
8 (C)	28 (A)	48 (B)	68 (B)	88 (A)
9 (B)	29 (B)	49 (D)	69 (D)	89 (C)
10 (A)	30 (C)	50 (B)	70 (B)	90 (D)
11 (C)	31 (B)	51 (D)	71 (B)	91 (D)
12 (A)	32 (A)	52 (C)	72 (A)	92 (B)
13 (C)	33 (C)	53 (B)	73 (A)	93 (C)
14 (C)	34 (C)	54 (C)	74 (D)	94 (D)
15 (C)	35 (B)	55 (B)	75 (C)	95 (A)
16 (B)	36 (D)	56 (A)	76 (D)	96 (B)
17 (A)	37 (B)	57 (C)	77 (C)	97 (C)
18 (C)	38 (B)	58 (A)	78 (C)	98 (A)
19 (C)	39 (D)	59 (B)	79 (B)	99 (D)
20 (A)	40 (C)	60 (C)	80 (B)	100 (B)

READING TEST
p.124

101 (B)	121 (B)	141 (C)	161 (D)	181 (D)
102 (C)	122 (A)	142 (A)	162 (B)	182 (A)
103 (C)	123 (C)	143 (B)	163 (C)	183 (A)
104 (B)	124 (B)	144 (C)	164 (D)	184 (D)
105 (A)	125 (C)	145 (D)	165 (A)	185 (C)
106 (D)	126 (D)	146 (A)	166 (B)	186 (C)
107 (D)	127 (A)	147 (D)	167 (D)	187 (C)
108 (C)	128 (B)	148 (C)	168 (A)	188 (B)
109 (B)	129 (B)	149 (A)	169 (D)	189 (C)
110 (A)	130 (B)	150 (B)	170 (D)	190 (C)
111 (B)	131 (D)	151 (A)	171 (B)	191 (A)
112 (D)	132 (D)	152 (C)	172 (B)	192 (C)
113 (D)	133 (B)	153 (C)	173 (A)	193 (C)
114 (C)	134 (B)	154 (D)	174 (C)	194 (B)
115 (C)	135 (C)	155 (B)	175 (B)	195 (C)
116 (B)	136 (B)	156 (A)	176 (B)	196 (D)
117 (B)	137 (A)	157 (B)	177 (D)	197 (B)
118 (C)	138 (D)	158 (D)	178 (C)	198 (A)
119 (A)	139 (A)	159 (C)	179 (D)	199 (B)
120 (C)	140 (C)	160 (D)	180 (B)	200 (C)

PART 1

1 2인 이상 사진
캐나다식

(A) The man is putting on his glasses.
(B) The woman is folding her jacket.
(C) The man is resting his elbows on his legs.
(D) The woman is taking a pen out of her bag.

fold v. 접다   rest v. 얹혀 있다, 받쳐져 있다   elbow n. 팔꿈치

해석 (A) 남자가 안경을 쓰고 있다.
(B) 여자가 재킷을 접고 있다.
(C) 남자가 팔꿈치를 다리에 얹혀 놓고 있다.
(D) 여자가 가방에서 펜을 꺼내고 있다.

해설 (A) [×] putting on his glasses(안경을 쓰고 있다)는 남자의 동작과 무관하므로 오답이다.
(B) [×] folding her jacket(재킷을 접고 있다)은 여자의 동작과 무관하므로 오답이다.
(C) [○] 남자가 팔꿈치를 다리에 얹히고 있는 모습을 가장 잘 묘사한 정답이다.
(D) [×] 사진에 있는 펜(pen)을 사용하여 혼동을 준 오답이다.

2 1인 사진
호주식

(A) He's opening a toolbox.
(B) He's setting up some tables for a party.
(C) He's repairing a microwave oven.
(D) He's painting some kitchen shelves with a brush.

toolbox n. 공구 상자   repair v. 수리하다
microwave oven 전자레인지

해석 (A) 그는 공구 상자를 열고 있다.
(B) 그는 파티를 위해 몇몇 탁자들을 준비하고 있다.
(C) 그는 전자레인지를 수리하고 있다.
(D) 그는 붓으로 몇몇 부엌용 선반을 칠하고 있다.

해설 (A) [○] 남자가 공구 상자를 열고 있는 모습을 가장 잘 묘사한 정답이다.
(B) [×] setting up some tables(몇몇 탁자들을 준비하고 있다)는 남자의 동작과 무관하므로 오답이다.
(C) [×] 남자가 전자레인지를 수리하고 있는(repairing a microwave oven) 모습이 아니므로 오답이다.
(D) [×] painting some kitchen shelves(몇몇 부엌용 선반을 칠하고 있다)는 남자의 동작과 무관하므로 오답이다. 사진에 있는 부엌용 선반(kitchen shelves)을 사용하여 혼동을 주었다.

3 2인 이상 사진　　　🔊 미국식

(A) People are waiting in line at a ticket kiosk.
(B) Travelers are putting their backpacks onto a rack.
(C) People are standing near a vehicle.
(D) Some tires are being replaced at a service center.

rack n. 선반, 받침대　vehicle n. 차량　replace v. 교체하다, 대신하다

해석　(A) 사람들이 티켓 키오스크에 줄을 서서 기다리고 있다.
　　　(B) 여행객들이 배낭을 선반 위에 올려 두고 있다.
　　　(C) 사람들이 차량 근처에 서 있다.
　　　(D) 몇몇 타이어들이 서비스 센터에서 교체되고 있다.

해설　(A) [×] 사진에 티켓 키오스크(a ticket kiosk)가 없으므로 오답이다. People are waiting in line(사람들이 줄을 서서 기다리고 있다)까지만 듣고 정답으로 선택하지 않도록 주의한다.
　　　(B) [×] putting their backpacks onto a rack(배낭을 선반 위에 올려 두고 있다)은 여행객들의 동작과 무관하므로 오답이다. 사진에 있는 배낭(backpacks)을 사용하여 혼동을 주었다.
　　　(C) [○] 사람들이 차량 근처에 서 있는 모습을 가장 잘 묘사한 정답이다.
　　　(D) [×] 타이어(tires)가 교체되고 있는(are being replaced) 모습이 아니므로 오답이다.

4 사물 및 풍경 사진　　　🔊 영국식

(A) A pile of leaves is being cleared away.
(B) Some large stones are blocking access to a park.
(C) Some wooden planter boxes have been placed outside.
(D) There's a shed built in a wooded area.

block v. 막다　planter box 화분　shed n. 헛간

해석　(A) 나뭇잎 더미가 치워지고 있다.
　　　(B) 몇몇 큰 돌들이 공원으로의 접근을 막고 있다.
　　　(C) 몇몇 나무로 된 화분들이 바깥에 놓여 있다.
　　　(D) 나무가 우거진 지역에 세워진 헛간이 있다.

해설　(A) [×] 나뭇잎 더미(A pile of leaves)가 치워지고 있는(being cleared away) 모습이 아니므로 오답이다.
　　　(B) [×] 큰 돌들(large stones)이 공원으로의 접근을 막고 있는(blocking access to a park) 모습이 아니므로 오답이다.
　　　(C) [×] 사진에 나무로 된 화분들(wooden planter boxes)이 없으므로 오답이다.
　　　(D) [○] 나무가 우거진 곳에 헛간이 세워져 있는 모습을 가장 잘 묘사한 정답이다.

최신토익경향

최근 PART 1에서는 RC에 나올 법한 어휘들이 등장해 체감 난도를 높이고 있다.

<최근 PART 1에 출제되었던 어려운 어휘>
　• shed 헛간, 오두막　　　• pallet 화물 운반대

· knob 손잡이
· log cabin 통나무집
· colleague 동료
· dip 담그다
· lane marking 차선 표시
· liquid 액체
· exit 나가다, 떠나다
· erase 지우다

5 1인 사진　　　🔊 호주식

(A) The woman is arranging some desks.
(B) Some chairs have been propped against the window.
(C) The woman is using a ladder to pick a book.
(D) Some books are being loaded onto a trolley.

arrange v. 정리하다　prop against 기대어 있다, ~에 받쳐 놓다
load v. 싣다　trolley n. 손수레, 카트

해석　(A) 여자가 몇몇 책상들을 정리하고 있다.
　　　(B) 몇몇 의자들이 창문에 기대어 있다.
　　　(C) 여자가 책을 꺼내기 위하여 사다리를 이용하고 있다.
　　　(D) 몇몇 책들이 손수레에 실리고 있다.

해설　(A) [×] arranging some desks(몇몇 책상들을 정리하고 있다)는 여자의 동작과 무관하므로 오답이다.
　　　(B) [×] 의자들(chairs)이 창문에 기대어 있는(have been propped against the window) 모습이 아니므로 오답이다.
　　　(C) [○] 여자가 책을 꺼내기 위하여 사다리를 이용하고 있는 모습을 가장 잘 묘사한 정답이다.
　　　(D) [×] 사진에 trolley(손수레)가 없으므로 오답이다. 사진에 있는 책들(books)을 사용하여 혼동을 주었다.

최신토익경향

PART 1 사진에서 도구를 이용하여 어떤 행동을 하는 모습일 때, 그 동작이 구체적으로 묘사되는 보기가 나오고 있다. 예를 들어, 사다리를 사용하여 책을 꺼내려는 위의 사진의 경우 단순히 '여자가 사다리에 올라가 있다(The woman is standing on a ladder)'가 아니라 책을 꺼내기 위해 사다리를 이용하고 있다고 묘사하는 방식이다.

<도구를 사용하는 목적을 포함하는 표현>
She's using a machine to move some items.
그녀는 몇몇 물건들을 옮기기 위해 기계를 사용하고 있다.
The man is using a shovel to remove snow from the road.
남자가 도로에서 눈을 치우기 위해 삽을 사용하고 있다.

6 사물 및 풍경 사진　　　🔊 미국식

(A) Some crates are stacked on the ground.
(B) The fruit market is full of shoppers.
(C) There are signs posted in a marketplace.
(D) A canopy has been put up over a dining area.

crate n. 상자　stack v. 쌓다　ground n. 땅바닥　canopy n. 덮개

해석　**(A) 몇몇 상자들이 땅바닥에 쌓여 있다.**

(B) 과일 가게가 손님들로 가득 차 있다.
(C) 시장에 게시된 표지판들이 있다.
(D) 덮개가 식사 공간 위에 달려 있다.

해설 (A) [o] 몇몇 상자들이 땅바닥에 쌓여 있는 모습을 가장 잘 묘사한 정답이다.
(B) [×] 사진에 손님들(shoppers)이 없으므로 오답이다.
(C) [×] 사진에 표지판들(signs)이 없으므로 오답이다.
(D) [×] 덮개(canopy)가 식사 공간 위에 달려 있는(has been put up over a dining area) 모습이 아니므로 오답이다.

PART 2

7 When 의문문  영국식 → 호주식

When is the board going to have a meeting?
(A) That's a good idea.
(B) This Thursday morning.
(C) On the second floor.

board n. 이사회   meeting n. 회의

해설 이사회는 언제 회의를 할 것인가요?
(A) 좋은 생각이네요.
(B) 이번 주 목요일 아침이요.
(C) 2층에서요.

해설 (A) [×] 이사회가 언제 회의를 할 것인지 물었는데, 이와 관련이 없는 좋은 생각이라고 응답했으므로 오답이다.
(B) [o] 이번 주 목요일 아침이라는 말로, 이사회가 회의를 하는 시점을 언급했으므로 정답이다.
(C) [×] 질문의 meeting(회의)에서 연상할 수 있는 장소와 관련된 second floor(2층)를 사용하여 혼동을 준 오답이다. 질문의 When을 Where로 혼동하여 이를 정답으로 선택하지 않도록 주의한다.

8 선택 의문문 캐나다식 → 미국식

Do we need to print the draft or e-mail it?
(A) To draft a list of supplies.
(B) What is your e-mail address?
(C) Let's get it printed.

draft n. 초안; v. 초안을 작성하다   supply n. 물품, 비품

해설 우리가 초안을 인쇄해야 하나요, 아니면 이메일로 보내야 하나요?
(A) 물품 목록의 초안을 작성하기 위해서요.
(B) 당신의 이메일 주소가 무엇인가요?
(C) 인쇄합시다.

해설 (A) [×] 질문의 draft(초안)를 '초안을 작성하다'라는 의미의 동사 draft로 반복 사용하여 혼동을 준 오답이다.
(B) [×] 질문의 e-mail을 반복 사용하여 혼동을 준 오답이다.
(C) [o] 인쇄하자는 말로, 초안을 인쇄하는 것을 선택했으므로 정답이다.

9 요청 의문문 미국식 → 캐나다식

Can I borrow your laptop computer?
(A) From a new electronics store.
(B) Sure. Here it is.
(C) Is this the correct order number?

borrow v. 빌리다   laptop computer 노트북
correct adj. 맞는, 정확한

해설 당신의 노트북을 빌릴 수 있을까요?
(A) 새로 생긴 전자제품 매장으로부터요.
(B) 그럼요. 여기 있어요.
(C) 이것은 맞는 주문 번호인가요?

해설 (A) [×] 질문의 laptop computer(노트북)와 관련 있는 electronics store(전자제품 매장)를 사용하여 혼동을 준 오답이다.
(B) [o] Sure로 노트북을 빌릴 수 있냐는 요청을 수락한 정답이다.
(C) [×] 노트북을 빌릴 수 있을지를 물었는데, 이와 관련이 없는 맞는 주문 번호냐고 물었으므로 오답이다.

10 평서문 미국식 → 호주식

You should call the warehouse supervisor tomorrow.
(A) You're right. Thanks for the reminder.
(B) The place is called Sunset Grill.
(C) No, it wasn't in storage.

warehouse n. 창고   supervisor n. 관리자
reminder n. 상기시키는 것   storage n. 보관소, 저장, 보관

해설 당신은 내일 창고 관리자에게 전화해야 해요.
(A) 맞아요. 상기시켜 주셔서 감사해요.
(B) 그 장소는 Sunset Grill이라 불러요.
(C) 아니요, 그것은 보관소에 없었어요.

해설 (A) [o] You're right으로 내일 창고 관리자에게 전화해야 하는 것이 맞다고 한 후, 상기시켜 주어서 감사하다고 했으므로 정답이다.
(B) [×] 질문의 call을 반복 사용하여 혼동을 준 오답이다.
(C) [×] 질문의 warehouse(창고)와 관련 있는 storage(보관소)를 사용하여 혼동을 준 오답이다.

11 Where 의문문 호주식 → 미국식

Where did you put the business trip expense report?
(A) Here is the revenue report.
(B) By Friday, I think.
(C) On Ms. Park's desk.

business trip 출장   expense n. 경비, 비용   revenue n. 수익

해설 출장 경비 보고서를 어디에 두었나요?
(A) 여기 수익 보고서요.
(B) 제 생각에는 금요일까지요.
(C) Ms. Park의 책상 위에요.

해설 (A) [×] 질문의 report를 반복 사용하여 혼동을 준 오답이다.

(B) [x] 출장 경비 보고서를 어디에 두었는지를 물었는데, 이와 관련이 없는 금요일까지라고 응답했으므로 오답이다. 질문의 Where를 When으로 혼동하여 이를 정답으로 선택하지 않도록 주의한다.
(C) [o] Ms. Park의 책상 위라는 말로, 출장 경비 보고서를 둔 위치를 언급했으므로 정답이다.

12 선택 의문문
영국식 → 캐나다식

Would you like to have pasta or pizza for dinner?
(A) I'm not that hungry.
(B) The most popular restaurant in town.
(C) Just another package delivery.

popular adj. 인기 있는   package n. 소포

해석 저녁 식사로 파스타를 먹고 싶나요, 아니면 피자를 먹고 싶나요?
(A) 저는 배가 그렇게 고프진 않아요.
(B) 시내에서 가장 인기 있는 식당이에요.
(C) 단지 또 다른 소포 배송이에요.

해설 (A) [o] 그렇게 배가 고프진 않다는 말로, 파스타와 피자 둘 다 간접적으로 선택하지 않은 정답이다.
(B) [x] 질문의 dinner(저녁 식사)에서 연상할 수 있는 restaurant(식당)을 사용하여 혼동을 준 오답이다.
(C) [x] 저녁 식사로 파스타를 먹을지 피자를 먹을지를 물었는데, 이와 관련이 없는 또 다른 소포 배송이라고 응답했으므로 오답이다.

13 부가 의문문
미국식 → 영국식

The special discount is still available at the department store, right?
(A) Because the rental fee is expensive.
(B) For the department meeting.
(C) Yes. I got my coat at half price yesterday.

available adj. 가능한, 이용할 수 있는   department store 백화점
rental fee 임대료   half adj. 반의, 절반의

해석 아직 백화점에서 특별 할인이 가능하죠, 그렇죠?
(A) 임대료가 비싸기 때문이에요.
(B) 부서 회의를 위해서요.
(C) 네. 어제 제 코트를 반값에 샀어요.

해설 (A) [x] 아직 백화점에서 특별 할인이 가능한지를 물었는데 이유로 답했으므로 오답이다.
(B) [x] 질문의 department를 반복 사용하여 혼동을 준 오답이다.
(C) [o] Yes로 아직 백화점에서 특별 할인이 가능하다고 전달한 후, 자신의 코트를 반값에 샀다는 부연 설명을 했으므로 정답이다.

14 Be동사 의문문
호주식 → 영국식

Are you planning to come to Patrisha's retirement luncheon?
(A) A party invitation.
(B) About the recent hiring decision.
(C) No. There's a schedule conflict.

retirement n. 은퇴   luncheon n. 오찬   invitation n. 초대장
recent adj. 최근의   schedule conflict 일정의 겹침

해석 Patrisha의 은퇴 기념 오찬에 올 계획인가요?
(A) 파티 초대장이에요.
(B) 최근 채용 결정에 관해서요.
(C) 아니요. 일정이 겹쳐요.

해설 (A) [x] 질문의 retirement luncheon(은퇴 기념 오찬)에서 연상할 수 있는 invitation(초대장)을 사용하여 혼동을 준 오답이다.
(B) [x] 질문의 retirement(은퇴)와 관련 있는 hiring decision(채용 결정)을 사용하여 혼동을 준 오답이다.
(C) [o] 일정이 겹친다는 말로, Patrisha의 은퇴 기념 오찬에 갈 수 없음을 간접적으로 전달했으므로 정답이다.

15 Who 의문문
미국식 → 호주식

Who can I talk to about registering for the gardening class?
(A) I can do that for you.
(B) Classroom 308.
(C) The flowers in the garden are beautiful.

register v. 등록하다

해석 원예 수업 등록에 대해 누구에게 문의하면 될까요?
(A) 제가 해드릴게요.
(B) 308호 교실이요.
(C) 정원에 있는 꽃들이 예쁘네요.

해설 (A) [o] 자신이 해주겠다는 말로, 원예 수업 등록에 대해 자신에게 문의하면 된다는 것을 전달했으므로 정답이다.
(B) [x] 질문의 class(수업)와 관련 있는 Classroom(교실)을 사용하여 혼동을 준 오답이다.
(C) [x] gardening - garden의 유사 발음 어휘를 사용하여 혼동을 준 오답이다.

16 평서문
호주식 → 영국식

The presentation for our new camera model is next Monday.
(A) We bought some camera accessories.
(B) I'll definitely complete the slides by then.
(C) Yes, it was a great speech.

accessory n. 액세서리, 부대용품   definitely adv. 반드시, 분명히
complete v. 완성하다, 완료하다   speech n. 연설

해석 우리의 새 카메라 모델의 발표가 다음 주 월요일이에요.
(A) 우리는 몇몇 카메라 액세서리들을 샀어요.
(B) 제가 그때까지 슬라이드들을 반드시 완성할게요.
(C) 네, 훌륭한 연설이었어요.

해설 (A) [x] 질문의 camera를 반복 사용하여 혼동을 준 오답이다.
(B) [o] 그때까지 슬라이드를 완성하겠다는 말로, 새 카메라 모델의 발표가 다음 주 월요일이라는 말에 대한 해결책을 제시했으므로 정답이다.
(C) [x] 질문의 presentation(발표)과 관련 있는 speech(연설)를 사

용하여 혼동을 준 오답이다.

17 평서문
캐나다식 → 미국식

Let's set up the stage before the rehearsal begins.
(A) I'm on-site right now.
(B) An equipment inventory.
(C) There are several stages in this project.

set up ~을 설치하다 on-site adj. 현장의
inventory n. (상품·물품) 목록

해석 예행연습이 시작되기 전에 무대를 설치합시다.
(A) 저는 지금 현장에 있어요.
(B) 장비 목록이요.
(C) 이 프로젝트는 여러 단계들이 있어요.

해설 (A) [o] 자신이 지금 현장에 있다는 말로, 예행연습이 시작되기 전에 무대를 설치하자는 제안을 간접적으로 수락했으므로 정답이다.
(B) [x] 질문의 set up(설치하다)에서 연상할 수 있는 equipment inventory(장비 목록)를 사용하여 혼동을 준 오답이다.
(C) [x] 질문의 stage(무대)를 '단계'라는 의미로 반복 사용하여 혼동을 준 오답이다.

최신토익경향
최근 PART 2에서 평서문에 대한 답변으로 나오는 간접 응답의 난이도가 높아지고 있다. 문제를 듣고 어떤 상황인지 바로 파악할 수 있어야 그 상황에서 할 수 있는 간접 응답을 고를 수 있다.

<평서문에 대한 간접 응답>
The company retreat has been postponed again.
회사 야유회가 또 연기되었어요.
[답변] Bad weather is predicted. 안 좋은 날씨가 예상돼요.
* 회사 야유회가 또 연기되었다는 말에 추후 계획이나 그 이유를 물어보는 직접적인 답변이 아닌, 안 좋은 날씨가 예상되어 또 연기된 것이 이해된다는 뉘앙스로 답한 응답

18 Why 의문문
영국식 → 캐나다식

Why hasn't the keynote speaker arrived yet?
(A) I'm sorry I was late.
(B) Because his flight was delayed.
(C) No, my seat is in the first row.

keynote speaker 기조연설자 delay v. 지연시키다 row n. 열, 줄

해석 기조연설자는 왜 아직 도착하지 않았나요?
(A) 제가 늦어서 죄송해요.
(B) 비행기가 지연되었기 때문이에요.
(C) 아니요, 제 좌석은 첫 번째 열에 있어요.

해설 (A) [x] 질문의 hasn't ~ arrived yet(아직 도착하지 않았다)과 관련 있는 late(늦은)을 사용하여 혼동을 준 오답이다.
(B) [o] 비행기가 지연되었기 때문이라는 말로, 기조연설자가 아직 도착하지 않은 이유를 언급했으므로 정답이다.
(C) [x] 의문사 의문문에 No로 응답했으므로 오답이다.

19 Which 의문문
캐나다식 → 미국식

Which clinic do you go to for regular checkups?
(A) Please wait in the waiting room.
(B) I've already checked the machinery.
(C) I moved here last week.

clinic n. 병원 checkup n. 건강 진단, 점검

해석 정기 건강 진단을 받으러 어느 병원에 가시나요?
(A) 대기실에서 기다려 주세요.
(B) 제가 이미 그 기계를 점검했어요.
(C) 저는 지난주에 여기로 이사 왔어요.

해설 (A) [x] 질문의 clinic(병원)에서 연상할 수 있는 waiting room(대기실)을 사용하여 혼동을 준 오답이다.
(B) [x] checkups - checked의 유사 발음 어휘를 사용하여 혼동을 준 오답이다.
(C) [o] 지난주에 여기로 이사 왔다는 말로, 정기 검진을 받으러 다니는 병원이 아직은 없음을 간접적으로 전달했으므로 정답이다.

20 What 의문문
영국식 → 호주식

What kind of room would you prefer to stay in?
(A) One with a mountain view.
(B) A hotel room renovation.
(C) Whenever I visit Paris.

prefer v. 선호하다 view n. 전망 renovation n. 개조, 보수

해석 어떤 종류의 방에서 묵기를 선호하시나요?
(A) 산 전망이 보이는 방이요.
(B) 호텔 방 개조요.
(C) 제가 파리에 방문할 때마다요.

해설 (A) [o] 산 전망이 보이는 방이라는 말로, 선호하는 방의 종류를 언급했으므로 정답이다.
(B) [x] 질문의 room을 반복 사용하여 혼동을 준 오답이다.
(C) [x] 어떤 종류의 방에서 묵고 싶은지 물었는데, 이와 관련이 없는 파리에 방문할 때마다라고 응답했으므로 오답이다.

21 How 의문문
호주식 → 영국식

How long should we keep the hard copy of the agreement with Volk Auto?
(A) One hundred dollars per day.
(B) Don't we also have an electronic version?
(C) We're in complete agreement on that.

agreement n. 계약서, 동의 per day 하루에 electronic adj. 전자의

해석 Volk 자동차사와의 서면 계약서를 얼마나 오래 보관해야 하나요?
(A) 하루에 백 달러요.
(B) 우리는 전자 버전도 가지고 있지 않나요?
(C) 우리는 그 점에 전적으로 동의해요.

해설 (A) [x] 기간을 나타내는 How long으로 물었는데 비용으로 응답했으므로 오답이다.

(B) [o] 전자 버전도 가지고 있지 않냐고 되물어, Volk 자동차사와의 계약서에 대한 추가 정보를 요구하는 정답이다.
(C) [x] 질문의 agreement(계약서)를 '동의'라는 의미의 명사로 반복 사용하여 혼동을 준 오답이다.

22 조동사 의문문
캐나다식 → 미국식

Do we have enough leather to make 10 more jackets?
(A) The leather shop on Mercer Street.
(B) You don't have an account with us.
(C) No. We'll have to order more.

leather n. 가죽 account n. 계좌, 계정

해석 우리가 재킷 10벌을 더 만들기 위한 충분한 가죽을 가지고 있나요?
(A) Mercer가에 있는 가죽 가게요.
(B) 당신은 저희 계좌를 갖고 있지 않습니다.
(C) 아니요. 우리는 더 주문해야 할 거예요.

해설 (A) [x] 질문의 leather를 반복 사용하여 혼동을 준 오답이다.
(B) [x] 질문의 have를 반복 사용하여 혼동을 준 오답이다.
(C) [o] No로 가죽이 충분하지 않음을 전달한 후, 더 주문해야 할 거라고 부연 설명을 했으므로 정답이다.

23 부정 의문문
영국식 → 캐나다식

Isn't the vending machine used frequently?
(A) By calling the mechanic.
(B) No, it wasn't difficult at all.
(C) There is a popular café downstairs.

vending machine 자판기 frequently adv. 자주
mechanic n. 정비공 downstairs adv. 아래층에

해석 자판기가 자주 사용되지 않나요?
(A) 정비공에게 전화함으로써요.
(B) 아니요, 전혀 어렵지 않았어요.
(C) 아래층에 인기 있는 카페가 있어요.

해설 (A) [x] 질문의 machine(기계)과 관련 있는 mechanic(정비공)을 사용하여 혼동을 준 오답이다.
(B) [x] 자판기가 자주 사용되지 않는지를 물었는데, 이와 관련 없는 어렵지 않았다고 응답했으므로 오답이다.
(C) [o] 아래층에 인기 있는 카페가 있다는 말로, 자판기가 자주 사용되지 않음을 간접적으로 전달했으므로 정답이다.

24 Who 의문문
캐나다식 → 영국식

Who will lead the group tour to Madrid in May?
(A) Didn't you hear from the manager?
(B) To enhance leadership skills.
(C) At the international boarding gate.

lead v. 이끌다, 안내하다 enhance v. 향상시키다

해석 5월에 마드리드로 가는 단체 여행을 누가 이끌 것인가요?
(A) 매니저에게 못 들으셨나요?
(B) 리더십 기술을 향상시키기 위해서요.
(C) 국제선 탑승구에서요.

해설 (A) [o] 매니저에게 못 들었냐고 되물어, 5월에 마드리드로 가는 단체 여행을 누가 이끄는지를 모른다는 것을 간접적으로 전달했으므로 정답이다.
(B) [x] 질문의 lead(이끌다)와 관련 있는 leadership(리더십)을 사용하여 혼동을 준 오답이다.
(C) [x] 질문의 group tour to Madrid(마드리드로 가는 단체 여행)에서 연상할 수 있는 international boarding gate(국제선 탑승구)를 사용하여 혼동을 준 오답이다.

최신 토익 경향
PART 2에서 담당자를 묻는 문제는 빈출 문제 중 하나이다. 특정 업무를 담당할 사람이 누구인지 묻는 질문에 대해 최근 등장하고 있는 여러 답변 유형들을 알아두자.

<담당자를 묻는 who 의문문에 대한 다양한 응답>
• Anna is doing it. Anna가 그걸 할 거예요.
• I can do that. 제가 할 수 있어요.
• Marcus may have assigned someone.
  Marcus가 누군가에게 맡겼을 거예요.
• It hasn't been announced yet. 아직 발표되지 않았어요.

25 How 의문문
호주식 → 캐나다식

How did the interview with the documentary filmmaker go?
(A) It was great to see you.
(B) About the filming techniques.
(C) It was rescheduled to next week.

filmmaker n. 영화 제작자 technique n. 기술, 기법
reschedule v. 일정을 변경하다

해석 다큐멘터리 영화 제작자와의 인터뷰는 어땠나요?
(A) 당신을 만나서 반가웠어요.
(B) 촬영 기술들에 대해서요.
(C) 그것은 다음 주로 일정이 변경되었어요.

해설 (A) [x] 다큐멘터리 영화 제작자와의 인터뷰가 어땠는지를 물었는데, 이와 관련이 없는 당신을 만나서 반가웠다고 응답했으므로 오답이다.
(B) [x] 질문의 filmmaker(영화 제작자)와 관련 있는 filming techniques(촬영 기술들)를 사용하여 혼동을 준 오답이다.
(C) [o] 그것은 다음 주로 일정이 변경되었다는 말로, 다큐멘터리 영화 제작자와의 인터뷰가 진행되지 않았음을 간접적으로 전달했으므로 정답이다.

26 조동사 의문문
영국식 → 미국식

Would you take charge of posting promotional content on our social media page?
(A) Some promotional photos.
(B) Hye-in is more suited for that job.
(C) No, for a social gathering.

take charge of ~을 담당하다 promotional adj. 홍보의
suit v. 어울리다

해석 우리 소셜 미디어 페이지의 홍보 콘텐츠를 게시하는 일을 담당하시겠어요?
(A) 몇몇 홍보 사진들이요.
(B) Hye-in이 그 일에 더 적합해요.
(C) 아니요, 사교 모임을 위해서요.

해설 (A) [×] 질문의 promotional content(홍보 콘텐츠)와 관련 있는 promotional photos(홍보 사진들)를 사용하여 혼동을 준 오답이다.
(B) [○] Hye-in이 그 일에 더 적합하다는 말로, 소셜 미디어 페이지의 홍보 콘텐츠를 담당하겠냐는 제안을 간접적으로 거절했으므로 정답이다.
(C) [×] 질문의 social을 반복 사용하여 혼동을 준 오답이다.

최신 토익 경향

Do, Have, Can/Will/Would/Should 등으로 시작하는 조동사 의문문은 PART 2에서 평균 2문제씩 출제되는 의문문으로, 사실이나 의견을 확인하는 것 외에도 제안하거나 가능성을 확인하는 질문으로 출제될 수 있다. 이때 Yes/No가 생략된 응답이 자주 나오므로 아래 예문을 통해 부정 또는 긍정의 답변을 전달하는 방식에 익숙해져 보자.

<조동사 의문문에 Yes/No를 생략한 응답>

Can you put these boxes in your office?
이 상자들을 당신의 사무실에 둘 수 있나요?

[답변] I have enough space.
저는 충분한 공간이 있어요.
* 상자들을 사무실에 둘 수 있는지 가능성을 확인하는 질문에 공간이 충분하다며 가능성을 전달한 답변

Would you like to see the sales data?
판매량 데이터를 보시겠어요?

[답변] I checked the report already.
저는 이미 보고서를 확인했어요.
* 판매량 데이터를 보겠냐는 제안에 이미 보고서를 확인했으니 볼 필요가 없다고 전달한 답변

27 부가 의문문
🎧 호주식 → 영국식

The ditch should be about eight meters long, shouldn't it?
(A) The engineer is going to confirm its measurements.
(B) It's about 45 minutes from here.
(C) Actually, we already bought a suitcase.

ditch n. 배수로 confirm v. 확인하다, 확정하다
measurement n. 치수, 측정

해석 배수로 길이가 약 8미터 정도여야 해요, 그렇지 않나요?
(A) 엔지니어가 그것의 치수를 확인할 거예요.
(B) 여기에서 45분 거리예요.
(C) 사실, 우리는 이미 여행 가방을 샀어요.

해설 (A) [○] 엔지니어가 그것의 치수를 확인할 것이라는 말로, 배수로 길이에 대해 자신은 잘 모른다는 것을 간접적으로 전달했으므로 정답이다.
(B) [×] 질문의 eight meters(8미터)에서 연상할 수 있는 거리와 관련된 45 minutes from here(여기에서 45분 거리)를 사용하여 혼동을 준 오답이다.
(C) [×] 배수로 길이가 약 8미터 정도여야 하는지를 물었는데, 이와 관련 없는 이미 여행 가방을 샀다고 응답했으므로 오답이다.

Actually까지만 듣고 정답으로 고르지 않도록 주의한다.

28 How 의문문
🎧 미국식 → 호주식

How would you feel about replacing the tiles on the lobby floor?
(A) Go straight, and turn right at the corner.
(B) In the cabinet behind the reception desk.
(C) I should check what the budget for this quarter is.

replace v. 교체하다 budget n. 예산 quarter n. 1분기, 4분의 1

해석 로비 바닥 타일들을 교체하는 것에 대해 어떻게 생각하나요?
(A) 직진 후에 모퉁이에서 우회전하세요.
(B) 접수처 뒤의 수납장 안에요.
(C) 이번 분기 예산이 얼마인지 확인해야 해요.

해설 (A) [×] 로비 바닥 타일들을 교체하는 것에 대해 어떻게 생각하는지를 물었는데, 이와 관련이 없는 직진 후에 모퉁이에서 우회전하라는 말로 응답했으므로 오답이다.
(B) [×] 질문의 lobby(로비)에서 연상할 수 있는 호텔과 관련된 reception desk(접수처)를 사용하여 혼동을 준 오답이다.
(C) [○] 로비 바닥 타일들을 교체하는 것에 대해 어떻게 생각하냐는 질문에, 이번 분기 예산이 얼마인지 확인해야 한다는 말로 예산 확인 후에 자신의 의견을 전달하겠다고 했으므로 정답이다.

29 Where 의문문
🎧 캐나다식 → 영국식

Where's the latest version of our employee manual?
(A) Which version of the software is installed?
(B) Mr. Choi is reading through my revisions.
(C) Some shipments have been late these days.

revision n. 수정본, 수정 사항 shipment n. 수송품

해석 직원 설명서의 최신 버전은 어디에 있나요?
(A) 어떤 버전의 소프트웨어가 설치되어 있나요?
(B) Mr. Choi가 제 수정본을 읽고 있어요.
(C) 요즘 몇몇 수송품들이 늦어지고 있어요.

해설 (A) [×] 질문의 version을 반복 사용하여 혼동을 준 오답이다.
(B) [○] Mr. Choi가 자신의 수정본을 읽고 있다는 말로, 직원 설명서의 최신 버전이 Mr. Choi에게 있음을 간접적으로 전달했으므로 정답이다.
(C) [×] latest - late의 유사 발음 어휘를 사용하여 혼동을 준 오답이다.

30 부정 의문문
🎧 호주식 → 미국식

Isn't our department's performance evaluation supposed to be submitted today?
(A) No, he performed yesterday.
(B) Express mail is more convenient.
(C) There's lots of information to be reviewed.

performance n. 실적, 성과, 공연 evaluation n. 평가
submit v. 제출하다 express mail 속달 우편 review v. 재검토하다

해석 우리 부서의 실적 평가를 오늘까지 제출하기로 되어 있지 않나요?
(A) 아니요, 그는 어제 공연했어요.
(B) 속달 우편이 더 편리해요.
(C) 재검토되어야 할 정보가 많아요.

해설 (A) [×] performance - performed의 유사 발음 어휘를 사용하여 혼동을 준 오답이다.
(B) [×] 우리 부서의 실적 평가를 오늘까지 제출하기로 되어 있지 않냐고 물었는데, 이와 관련이 없는 속달 우편이 더 편리하다고 응답했으므로 오답이다.
(C) [O] 재검토되어야 할 정보가 많다는 말로, 우리 부서의 실적 평가를 오늘까지 제출할 수 없음을 간접적으로 전달했으므로 정답이다.

31 평서문

🔊 미국식 → 캐나다식

It looks like I left my wallet at the office.
(A) To open a bank account.
(B) I'll buy you lunch this time.
(C) Sorry, he's left for the day.

leave v. 두고 오다, 남기다   bank account 은행 계좌

해석 제가 지갑을 사무실에 두고 왔나 봐요.
(A) 은행 계좌를 개설하기 위해서요.
(B) 이번에는 제가 점심을 살게요.
(C) 죄송해요, 그는 퇴근했어요.

해설 (A) [×] 질문의 wallet(지갑)에서 연상할 수 있는 bank account(은행 계좌)를 사용하여 혼동을 준 오답이다.
(B) [O] 지갑을 사무실에 두고 왔다는 말에, 이번에는 자신이 점심을 사겠다는 해결책을 전달했으므로 정답이다.
(C) [×] 질문의 left를 반복 사용하여 혼동을 준 오답이다.

PART 3

[32-34]

🔊 미국식 → 호주식

Questions 32-34 refer to the following conversation.

W: Joshua, ³²**could you look over this budget proposal? I have a meeting with our CEO tomorrow, but this is my first time**.
M: Sorry, but I have to complete this financial report by lunch today. By the way, what is the proposal about?
W: ³³**Next month, our company plans to expand its research laboratory**, which will require additional funding.
M: Why don't you ask Danielle? She has worked on the accounting team for over 15 years. ³⁴**Here is her e-mail address.**

look over 살펴보다, 훑어보다
budget proposal 예산안, 예산 제안서   financial adj. 재무의, 금융의
research laboratory 연구소   additional adj. 추가의, 가외의
accounting n. 회계

해석
32-34번은 다음 대화에 관한 문제입니다.
여: Joshua, ³²이 예산안을 검토해 주실 수 있나요? 내일 대표이사와 회의가 있는데, 제가 이번이 처음이에요.
남: 죄송하지만, 저는 오늘 점심까지 이 재무 보고서를 완성해야 해요. 그런데, 제안서는 무엇에 관한 것인가요?
여: ³³다음 달에 우리 회사가 연구소를 확장할 계획인데, 여기에 추가 자금이 필요해요.
남: Danielle에게 물어보는 게 어때요? 그녀는 회계팀에서 15년 넘게 근무했어요. ³⁴여기 그녀의 이메일 주소요.

32 이유 문제

해석 여자는 왜 도움을 요청하는가?
(A) 업무에 익숙하지 않다.
(B) 파일을 찾을 수 없다.
(C) 회의에 참석할 수 없다.
(D) 사업체 위치를 찾을 수 없다.

해설 질문의 핵심 어구(woman ask for help)와 관련된 내용을 주의 깊게 듣는다. 여자가 "could you look over this budget proposal? I have a meeting with our CEO tomorrow, but this is my first time"이라며 내일 대표이사와 회의가 있는데 이번이 처음이라서 예산안을 검토해 줄 수 있는지 물었다. 따라서 (A)가 정답이다.

어휘 unfamiliar adj. 익숙하지 않은, 잘 모르는   locate v. 위치를 찾다, 두다

Paraphrasing

first time 처음 → unfamiliar with ~에 익숙하지 않은

33 다음에 할 일 문제

해석 다음 달에 무슨 일이 일어날 것인가?
(A) 임원이 은퇴할 것이다.
(B) 몇몇 기술이 업데이트될 것이다.
(C) 회사가 시설을 확장할 것이다.
(D) 몇몇 신입사원들이 교육을 받을 것이다.

해설 질문의 핵심 어구(next month)가 언급된 주변을 주의 깊게 듣는다. 여자가 "Next month, our company plans to expand its research laboratory"라며 다음 달에 회사가 연구소를 확장할 계획이라고 하였다. 따라서 (C)가 정답이다.

어휘 executive n. 임원, 경영진   retire v. 은퇴하다
facility n. 시설, 기능

Paraphrasing

research laboratory 연구소 → facility 시설

34 특정 세부 사항 문제

해석 남자는 여자에게 무엇을 주는가?
(A) 수정된 도표
(B) 참석자 명단
(C) 연락처
(D) 고객 후기

해설 질문의 핵심 어구(man give ~ woman)와 관련된 내용을 주의 깊게 듣는다. 남자가 여자에게 "Here is her e-mail address."라며 이메일 주소가 여기 있다고 하였다. 따라서 (C)가 정답이다.

어휘 correct v. 수정하다, 바로잡다 attendance n. 참석자

Paraphrasing

e-mail address 이메일 주소 → Contact information 연락처

[35-37]

영국식 → 캐나다식

Questions 35-37 refer to the following conversation.

W: Look at the line in front of the entrance. ³⁵I've never seen so many people at this theater.
M: ³⁵Yeah, it's a popular musical play.
W: ³⁶I was really surprised when you said you got the tickets.
M: I was able to buy them online two months in advance. Anyway, ³⁷there are some booths over there with T-shirts, posters, and other merchandise. Let's get something to remember this performance.
W: Sounds great.

entrance n. 입구, 문 theater n. 극장 popular adj. 인기 있는
in advance 사전에 merchandise n. 상품, 물품

해석
35-37번은 다음 대화에 관한 문제입니다.
여: 입구 앞줄을 봐요. ³⁵이 극장에 이렇게 많은 사람들이 있는 것을 본 적이 없어요.
남: ³⁵그러네요, 그것은 인기 있는 뮤지컬이에요.
여: ³⁶당신이 티켓을 구했다고 했을 때 정말 놀랐다니까요.
남: 저는 두 달 앞서서 온라인으로 구매할 수 있었어요. 그나저나, ³⁷저기 저쪽에 티셔츠, 포스터, 그리고 다른 상품이 있는 부스가 몇 개 있네요. 이 공연을 기억할 만한 무언가를 사러 가요.
여: 좋아요.

35 장소 문제

해설 화자들은 어디에 있는 것 같은가?
(A) 동물원에
(B) 극장에
(C) 커뮤니티 센터에
(D) 역사박물관에

해설 대화에서 장소와 관련된 표현을 놓치지 않고 듣는다. 여자가 "I've never seen so many people at this theater."라며 이 극장에 이렇게 많은 사람들이 있는 것을 본 적이 없다고 하자, 남자가 "Yeah, it's a popular musical play."라며 그렇다고 하면서 그것은 인기 있는 뮤지컬이라고 한 것을 통해 화자들이 극장에 있음을 알 수 있다. 따라서 (B)가 정답이다.

36 특정 세부 사항 문제

해설 여자는 무엇에 대해 놀랐었는가?
(A) 행사의 일정
(B) 주차 비용
(C) 참석자들의 후기
(D) 티켓의 구매 가능함

해설 질문의 핵심 어구(woman surprised about)와 관련된 내용을 주의 깊게 듣는다. 여자가 "I was really surprised when you said you got the tickets."라며 티켓을 구했다고 했을 때 정말 놀랐다고 하였다. 따라서 (D)가 정답이다.

어휘 attendee n. 참석자 availability n. 구매 가능함, 입수 가능성

37 제안 문제

해설 남자는 무엇을 하라고 제안하는가?
(A) 자리 바꾸기
(B) 기념품 사기
(C) 사진 찍기
(D) 헤드폰 착용하기

해설 남자의 말에서 제안과 관련된 표현이 언급된 주변을 주의 깊게 듣는다. 남자가 "there are some booths over there with T-shirts, posters, and other merchandise. Let's get something to remember this performance."라며 여러 상품을 파는 부스가 있으니 가서 공연을 기억할 만한 무언가를 사자고 하였다. 따라서 (B)가 정답이다.

어휘 seat n. 자리, 좌석 souvenir n. 기념품

Paraphrasing

something to remember this performance 이 공연을 기억할 만한 무언가 → souvenirs 기념품

[38-40]

미국식 → 캐나다식 → 호주식

Questions 38-40 refer to the following conversation with three speakers.

W: ³⁸We're delighted to have you both in our supermarket to showcase your company's new line of organic fruit juice.
M1: Thank you for giving us the opportunity to promote our products here.
W: More people care about their health these days, so I'm confident that your natural fruit juices will attract many customers.
M1: Good to hear. ³⁹Sebastian, is everything ready?
M2: Hmm . . . ³⁹Is there a place where I can plug in our refrigerator?
W: Right over here. Also, ⁴⁰if you brought any samples, it'll be good to give those out to customers so they can taste your drinks.

delighted adj. 기쁜, 아주 기뻐하는 showcase v. 선보이다, 소개하다
organic adj. 유기농의 opportunity n. 기회
promote v. 홍보하다, 촉진하다 confident adj. 확신하는, 자신감 있는
refrigerator n. 냉장고

해석
38-40번은 다음 세 명의 대화에 관한 문제입니다.
여: 새로운 유기농 과일 주스 라인을 선보이기 위해 ³⁸두 분이 저희 슈퍼마켓에 와주셔서 기쁩니다.
남1: 이곳에서 제품을 홍보할 기회를 주셔서 감사합니다.
여: 요즘 더 많은 사람들이 건강에 신경을 쓰기 때문에, 귀사의 천연 과일 주스가 많은 고객을 끌어들일 것이라고 확신해요.
남1: 듣기 좋네요. ³⁹Sebastian, 모든 것이 준비되었나요?
남2: 흠... ³⁹저희 냉장고의 코드를 꽂을 수 있는 곳이 있나요?
여: 바로 여기요. 또한, ⁴⁰샘플을 가져오셨다면 음료를 맛볼 수 있도록 고객들에게 나눠주는 것도 좋을 거예요.

38 장소 문제

해석 대화는 어디에서 일어나는 것 같은가?
(A) 호텔에서
(B) 식료품점에서
(C) 유기농 농장에서
(D) 전자제품 매장에서

해설 대화에서 장소와 관련된 표현을 놓치지 않고 듣는다. 여자가 "We're delighted to have you both in our supermarket"이라며 우리 슈퍼마켓에 와줘서 기쁘다고 하였다. 따라서 (B)가 정답이다.

Paraphrasing
supermarket 슈퍼마켓 → grocery store 식료품점

39 특정 세부 사항 문제

해석 Sebastian은 무엇에 대해 물어보는가?
(A) 제품이 얼마인지
(B) 업무가 얼마나 오래 걸릴지
(C) 상점이 언제 문을 열지
(D) 전자제품 코드를 어디에 꽂을지

해설 질문의 핵심 어구(Sebastian ask about)와 관련된 내용을 주의 깊게 듣는다. 남자1이 "Sebastian, is everything ready?"라며 모든 것이 준비되었냐고 묻자, 남자2[Sebastian]가 "Is there a place where I can plug in our refrigerator?"라며 냉장고 코드를 꽂을 수 있는 곳이 있는지 물었다. 따라서 (D)가 정답이다.

어휘 plug in 플러그를 꽂다, 전원을 연결하다
appliance n. 전자제품, 기기

Paraphrasing
refrigerator 냉장고 → appliance 전자제품

40 제안 문제

해석 여자는 무엇을 제안하는가?
(A) 더 일찍 시작하기
(B) 새로운 맛 개발하기
(C) 샘플 제공하기
(D) 장비 주문하기

해설 여자의 말에서 제안과 관련된 표현이 언급된 주변을 주의 깊게 듣는다. 여자가 "if you brought any samples, it'll be good to give those out to customers so they can taste your drinks"라며 샘플을 가져왔으면 음료를 맛볼 수 있도록 고객들에게 나눠주는 것이 좋을 거라고 하였다. 따라서 (C)가 정답이다.

어휘 flavor n. 맛, 풍미   equipment n. 장비, 용품

[41-43]
[호주식 → 영국식]

Questions 41-43 refer to the following conversation.

M: ⁴¹**Have you looked over the latest visitor statistics of our museum? I reviewed them yesterday** and noticed last month's numbers showed a significant decline.
W: I recently saw in an article that ⁴²**a lot of museum visitors want more interactive displays with activities**.
M: Then, let's survey visitors this week to see what kind of interactive displays they want.
W: OK. ⁴³**I'll create a questionnaire and send it to you by e-mail.**

latest adj. 최신의, 최근의   statistics n. 통계
significant adj. 상당한, 중요한   decline n. 감소
interactive adj. 상호작용할 수 있는, 상호작용의   display n. 전시, 진열
survey v. 설문조사를 하다   questionnaire n. 설문지, 질문표

해석
41-43번은 다음 대화에 관한 문제입니다.
남: ⁴¹우리 박물관의 최신 방문객 통계를 검토했나요? 제가 어제 검토했는데, 지난달 수치에서 상당한 감소를 보이는 것을 확인했어요.
여: 제가 최근 기사에서 ⁴²많은 박물관 방문객들이 활동을 포함하는 상호작용 할 수 있는 전시를 원한다는 것을 봤어요.
남: 그렇다면, 이번 주에 방문객들에게 어떤 종류의 상호작용 전시를 원하는지 설문조사를 해봅시다.
여: 알겠어요. ⁴³설문지를 작성하여 이메일로 보내 드릴게요.

41 특정 세부 사항 문제

해석 남자는 어제 무엇을 검토했는가?
(A) 예산
(B) 물품 목록
(C) 직원 평가서
(D) 관객 수 보고서

해설 질문의 핵심 어구(review yesterday)와 관련된 내용을 주의 깊게 듣는다. 남자가 "Have you looked over the latest visitor statistics of our museum? I reviewed them yesterday"라며 박물관의 최신 방문객 통계를 어제 검토했다고 하였다. 따라서 (D)가 정답이다.

어휘 budget n. 예산   evaluation n. 평가서, 감정

Paraphrasing
visitor statistics 방문객 통계 → An attendance report 관객 수 보고서

42 특정 세부 사항 문제

해석 여자에 따르면, 몇몇 방문객들은 무엇을 하고 싶어 하는가?
(A) 기부하기
(B) 소식지 받기
(C) 다양한 그림 구매하기
(D) 전시품과 상호작용을 하기

해설 여자의 말에서 질문의 핵심 어구(visitors want to do)와 관련된 내용을 주의 깊게 듣는다. 여자가 "a lot of museum visitors want more interactive displays with activities"라며 많은 박물관 방문객들이 활동들을 포함하는 상호작용 하는 전시를 원한다고 하였다. 따라서 (D)가 정답이다.

어휘 donation n. 기부 newsletter n. 소식지
interact v. 상호작용을 하다, 교류하다

43 특정 세부 사항 문제

해석 여자는 이메일로 무엇을 보낼 것인가?
(A) 설문지 양식
(B) 선물 카탈로그
(C) 몇몇 영수증
(D) 몇몇 기사

해설 질문의 핵심 어구(send by e-mail)와 관련된 내용을 주의 깊게 듣는다. 여자가 "I'll create a questionnaire and send it to you by e-mail."이라며 설문지를 작성해서 이메일로 보내겠다고 하였다. 따라서 (A)가 정답이다.

[44-46]
캐나다식 → 미국식

Questions 44-46 refer to the following conversation.

> M: Sharon, the Springdale Flower Festival is coming up tomorrow. ⁴⁴**Do you think you can take some pictures of the event to feature in our newspaper?**
> W: ⁴⁴**Sure.** I'm not covering anything else tomorrow, so I can spend the entire day there.
> M: ⁴⁵**You'll need to apply for a press pass on the festival's official Web site. You can use it to get into all areas of the festival grounds.**
> W: Thank you. When do you need me to submit the images?
> M: By Friday at the latest. ⁴⁶**The story needs to be published next Monday.**

feature v. 특별히 포함하다, 특징으로 삼다 apply for ~을 신청하다
press pass 언론 통행증 at the latest 늦어도
publish v. 발행하다, 출판하다

해석
44-46번은 다음 대화에 관한 문제입니다.
남: Sharon, Springdale 꽃 축제가 내일로 다가와요. ⁴⁴**당신이 우리 신문에 특별히 포함할 사진들을 좀 찍어줄 수 있나요?**
여: ⁴⁴**물론이죠.** 저는 내일 다른 일은 다루지 않아서, 그곳에서 하루 종일 보낼 수 있어요.
남: ⁴⁵**당신은 축제 공식 웹사이트에서 언론 통행증을 신청해야 해요. 당신은 그것을 축제장의 모든 구역들에 들어가는 데 사용할 수 있어요.**
여: 감사합니다. 제가 당신에게 언제 사진을 제출하면 될까요?
남: 늦어도 금요일까지요. ⁴⁶**기사가 다음 주 월요일에 발행되어야 해요.**

44 화자 문제

해석 화자들은 어디에서 일하는 것 같은가?
(A) 국립 공원에서
(B) 광고 회사에서
(C) 언론사에서
(D) 사진 스튜디오에서

해설 대화에서 신분 및 직업과 관련된 표현을 놓치지 않고 듣는다. 남자가 "Do you think you can take some pictures of the event to feature in our newspaper?"라며 여자에게 우리 신문에 특별히 포함할 사진들을 찍어줄 수 있는지 묻자, 여자가 "Sure."라며 물론이라고 한 것을 통해 화자들이 언론사에서 일한다는 것을 알 수 있다. 따라서 (C)가 정답이다.

45 이유 문제

해석 남자에 따르면, 여자는 왜 통행증을 받을 필요가 있는가?
(A) 새로운 보안 규정을 따르기 위해서
(B) 행사 주최자를 만나기 위해서
(C) 현장의 모든 구역에 접근권을 얻기 위해서
(D) 입장료를 내지 않기 위해서

해설 질문의 핵심 어구(get a pass)와 관련된 내용을 주의 깊게 듣는다. 남자가 "You'll need to apply for a press pass on the festival's official Web site. You can use it to get into all areas of the festival grounds."라며 축제 공식 웹사이트에서 언론 통행증을 신청해야 한다고 말한 후, 그것을 축제장의 모든 구역들에 들어가는 데 사용할 수 있다고 하였다. 따라서 (C)가 정답이다.

어휘 security n. 보안, 안보 regulation n. 규정
organizer n. 주최자, 조직자 entrance fee 입장료

Paraphrasing

get into all areas 모든 구역에 들어가다 → gain access to all areas 모든 구역에 접근권을 얻다

46 다음에 할 일 문제

해석 다음 주 월요일에 무슨 일이 일어날 것인가?
(A) 축제가 끝날 것이다.
(B) 시설이 폐쇄될 것이다.
(C) 기사가 발표될 것이다.
(D) 공간이 다시 디자인될 것이다.

해설 질문의 핵심 어구(next Monday)가 언급된 주변을 주의 깊게 듣는다. 남자가 "The story needs to be published next Monday."라며 기사가 다음 주 월요일에 발행되어야 한다고 하였다. 따라서 (C)가 정답이다.

어휘 release v. 발표하다, 풀다 redesign v. 다시 디자인하다

Paraphrasing

be published 발행되다 → be released 발표되다

[47-49]

🔊 호주식 → 미국식 → 캐나다식

Questions 47-49 refer to the following conversation with three speakers.

> M1: Ms. Kim, welcome. ⁴⁷Thanks for taking the time for this meeting. We're eager to go over the results of our company's evaluation and your suggestions for our firm.
> W: Certainly. I went through your finances very carefully. ⁴⁸I noticed that the amount of money you spend on foreign investments has increased rapidly over the past three months. Why are you doing this?
> M2: We are expanding into overseas markets, like Singapore and Vietnam.
> W: I'm a bit concerned that this may cause you financial problems in the short-term. ⁴⁹Mr. Klein, may I take a look at what you have set aside for operating expenses?
> M1: ⁴⁹Sure. Let me get those figures for you.

suggestion n. 제안 사항, 제안   finance n. 재정 상황, 재무
foreign adj. 해외의   investment n. 투자   overseas adj. 해외의
set aside 마련하다, 확보하다   expense n. 비용   figure n. 수치, 숫자

해석 47-49번은 다음 세 명의 대화에 관한 문제입니다.

남1: Ms. Kim, 환영합니다. ⁴⁷이 회의에 시간을 내주셔서 감사해요. 우리는 우리 회사의 평가 결과와 회사에 대한 당신의 제안 사항들을 꼭 살펴보고 싶어요.
여: 물론입니다. 저는 귀사의 재정 상황을 매우 주의 깊게 살펴보았어요. ⁴⁸저는 지난 3개월간 귀사가 해외 투자에 지출하는 금액이 급격히 증가한 것을 확인했어요. 왜 이렇게 하고 계신 건가요?
남2: 우리는 싱가포르와 베트남과 같은 해외 시장들로 확장 중입니다.
여: 저는 이것이 귀사에 단기적으로 재정 문제를 야기할까 봐 조금 걱정돼요. ⁴⁹Mr. Klein, 귀사가 운영 비용으로 얼마를 마련했는지 제가 확인해도 될까요?
남1: ⁴⁹그럼요. 제가 그 수치들을 가져다드릴게요.

47 목적 문제

해석 여자는 왜 방문하고 있는가?
(A) 사업 조언을 제공하기 위해
(B) 계약을 협상하기 위해
(C) 협의회에 참석하기 위해
(D) 기업 행사에서 연설하기 위해

해설 여자가 방문한 목적을 묻는 문제이므로, 지문의 초반을 반드시 듣는다. 남자1이 "Thanks for taking the time for this meeting. We're eager to go over the results of our company's evaluation and your suggestions for our firm."이라며 회의에 시간을 내주셔서 감사하다고 한 후, 우리 회사의 평가 결과와 회사에 대한 제안 사항들을 꼭 살펴보고 싶다고 했으므로, 여자가 방문한 목적은 사업 조언을 제공하기 위함임을 알 수 있다. 따라서 (A)가 정답이다.

어휘 negotiate v. 협상하다   convention n. 협의회, 대회
corporate adj. 기업의, 법인의

48 특정 세부 사항 문제

해석 여자는 무엇에 대해 물어보는가?
(A) 부서장의 이름
(B) 늘어난 투자의 이유
(C) 해외 지사의 위치
(D) 사내 행사의 날짜

해설 질문의 핵심 어구(woman ask about)와 관련된 내용을 주의 깊게 듣는다. 여자가 "I noticed that the amount of money you spend on foreign investments has increased rapidly over the past three months. Why are you doing this?"라며 지난 3개월간 귀사가 해외 투자에 지출하는 금액이 급격히 증가한 것을 확인했다며 왜 이렇게 하고 있는지 물었다. 따라서 (B)가 정답이다.

어휘 cause n. 이유, 원인   branch n. 지사, 분점

49 다음에 할 일 문제

해석 Mr. Klein은 다음에 무엇을 할 것 같은가?
(A) 항공권을 예약한다.
(B) 다른 직원에게 연락한다.
(C) 새 사무용 가구를 주문한다.
(D) 재무 자료를 가져온다.

해설 질문의 핵심 어구(Mr. Klein ~ do next)와 관련된 내용을 주의 깊게 듣는다. 여자가 "Mr. Klein, may I take a look at what you have set aside for operating expenses?"라며 Mr. Klein에게 운영 비용으로 얼마를 마련했는지 확인해도 될지 묻자, 남자1[Mr. Klein]이 "Sure. Let me get those figures for you."라며 알겠다고 한 뒤 수치들을 가져다주겠다고 하였다. 따라서 (D)가 정답이다.

어휘 book v. 예약하다   furniture n. 가구

Paraphrasing

figures 수치들 → financial data 재무 자료

[50-52]

🔊 영국식 → 호주식

Questions 50-52 refer to the following conversation.

> W: Samuel, ⁵⁰this is the third complaint regarding ice on the walkway we've received this week. This is starting to become a serious safety issue.
> M: Yes, I agree. But the rock salt we are using doesn't work well when the weather gets this cold.
> W: ⁵¹I saw an advertisement for a new type of ice removal compound that is a lot more effective at low temperatures. We should try it. It's also better for the environment. The advertisement says it's noncorrosive to surfaces.
> M: ⁵²I'll check the product details and what the cost will be.

regarding prep. ~에 관한   serious adj. 심각한   issue n. 문제, 주제
compound n. 화합물   noncorrosive adj. 부식시키지 않는
surface n. 표면

해석
50-52번은 다음 대화에 관한 문제입니다.

여: Samuel, **50**이것이 이번 주에 우리가 접수한 보도 위 얼음에 관한 세 번째 항의예요. 이것이 심각한 안전 문제가 되기 시작하네요.
남: 네, 저도 동의해요. 하지만 우리가 사용하는 암염은 날씨가 이렇게 추워질 때는 효과가 잘 나타나지 않아요.
여: **51**저는 낮은 온도에서 훨씬 더 효과적인 새 종류의 얼음 제거용 화합물에 관한 광고를 봤어요. 그것을 한번 써봐야겠어요. 그것은 환경에도 더 좋아요. 그 광고에서 그것은 표면을 부식시키지 않는대요.
남: **52**제가 그 제품의 세부 정보들과 비용을 확인할게요.

50 주제 문제

해석 화자들이 주로 무엇에 대해 이야기하고 있는가?
(A) 의료 박람회 준비하기
(B) 안전 문제 해결하기
(C) 건물 투어 준비하기
(D) 더 많은 고객 유치하기

해설 대화의 주제를 묻는 문제이므로, 대화의 초반을 반드시 듣는다. 여자가 "this is the third complaint regarding ice on the walkway we've received this week. This is starting to become a serious safety issue."라며 이번 주에 보도 위 얼음에 관한 세 번째 항의를 접수했고, 이것이 심각한 안전 문제가 되기 시작한다고 한 후, 도로 위 얼음을 해결하는 것에 대한 내용으로 대화가 이어지고 있다. 따라서 (B)가 정답이다.

어휘 fair n. 박람회   address v. 해결하다, 다루다
arrange v. 준비하다, 정리하다

51 의도 파악 문제

해석 여자는 왜 "그것은 환경에도 더 좋아요"라고 말하는가?
(A) 방침을 설명하기 위해
(B) 오류를 확인하기 위해
(C) 동료를 칭찬하기 위해
(D) 제안을 뒷받침하기 위해

해설 질문의 인용어구(It's also better for the environment)가 언급된 주변을 주의 깊게 듣는다. 여자가 "I saw an advertisement for a new type of ice removal compound that is a lot more effective at low temperatures. We should try it."이라며 낮은 온도에서 훨씬 더 효과적인 새 종류의 얼음 제거용 화합물에 관한 광고를 봤다고 한 후, 그것을 써봐야겠다고 하였다. 따라서 (D)가 정답이다.

어휘 policy n. 방침, 정책   confirm v. 확인하다, 확정하다
compliment v. 칭찬하다

52 제안 문제

해석 남자는 무엇을 자원해서 할 것인가?
(A) 송장을 인쇄한다.
(B) 공장을 방문한다.
(C) 제품을 조사한다.
(D) 날씨를 확인한다.

해설 남자의 말에서 질문의 핵심 어구(volunteer to do)와 관련된 내용을 주의 깊게 듣는다. 남자가 "I'll check the product details and what the cost will be."라며 그 제품의 세부 정보들과 비용을 확인하겠다고 하였다. 따라서 (C)가 정답이다.

어휘 invoice n. 송장, 청구서   research v. 조사하다, 연구하다

Paraphrasing
check the product details and what the cost will be 제품의 세부 정보들과 비용을 확인하다 → Research a product 제품을 조사하다

[53-55] 캐나다식 → 미국식

Questions 53-55 refer to the following conversation.

M: **53**I think I've come up with a way to better serve our customers. How about setting up an information desk near the checkout area?
W: I like that idea. **54**We could assign an experienced staff member to answer questions from shoppers. Mike Williams would be perfect. He's been working here for several years.
M: But Mike recently reduced his hours. He's only working three days a week now.
W: Then, **55**I'll post a notice in the break room. It'll explain the new role.

come up with ~을 생각해 내다   serve v. 서비스를 제공하다
set up 설치하다   checkout n. 계산대   assign v. 배치하다, 맡기다
experienced adj. 경험 많은, 능숙한   shopper n. 쇼핑객

해석
53-55번은 다음 대화에 관한 문제입니다.

남: **53**제가 우리의 고객들에게 더 좋은 서비스를 제공할 수 있는 방법을 생각해 낸 것 같아요. 계산대 구역 근처에 안내 데스크를 설치하는 것은 어때요?
여: 그 생각 좋은걸요. **54**우리는 쇼핑객들의 질문들에 답하도록 경험 많은 직원을 배치할 수 있어요. Mike Williams가 완벽할 거예요. 그는 이곳에서 몇 년간 일하고 있잖아요.
남: 하지만 최근에 Mike는 근무 시간을 줄였어요. 그는 일주일에 3일만 일해요.
여: 그러면, **55**제가 휴게실에 공지문을 게시할게요. 그것이 새 역할에 관해 설명할 거예요.

53 특정 세부 사항 문제

해석 남자는 무엇을 개선하고 싶어 하는가?
(A) 직원 혜택
(B) 고객 서비스
(C) 팀원 협업
(D) 향후 매출액

해설 남자의 말에서 질문의 핵심 어구(want to improve)와 관련된 내용을 주의 깊게 듣는다. 남자가 "I think I've come up with a way to better serve our customers."라며 고객들에게 더 좋은 서비스를 제공할 수 있는 방법을 생각해 낸 것 같다고 한 것을 통해 남자

가 개선하고 싶은 것은 고객 서비스임을 알 수 있다. 따라서 (B)가 정답이다.

어휘 **benefit** n. 혜택, 이익   **collaboration** n. 협업, 협력
sales revenue 매출액, 매출 수입

54 이유 문제

해석 여자는 왜 Mike Williams를 추천하는가?
(A) 관련 분야를 전공했다.
(B) 직원상을 받았다.
(C) 많은 경험이 있다.
(D) 다른 부서에서 전근을 왔다.

해설 여자의 말에서 질문의 핵심 어구(recommend Mike Williams)와 관련된 내용을 주의 깊게 듣는다. 여자가 "We could assign an experienced staff member to answer questions from shoppers. Mike Williams would be perfect. He's been working here for several years."라며 쇼핑객들의 질문들에 답할 경험 많은 직원을 배치할 수 있다고 한 후, Mike Williams가 이곳에서 몇 년간 일하고 있기 때문에 적임자라고 하였다. 따라서 (C)가 정답이다.

어휘 **major in** ~을 전공하다   **related** adj. 관련된, 연관된
transfer v. 전근하다, 옮기다

Paraphrasing

has been working here for several years 여기서 몇 년간 일하고 있다 → has a lot of experience 많은 경험이 있다

55 다음에 할 일 문제

해석 여자는 나중에 무엇을 할 것이라고 말하는가?
(A) 문서를 복사한다.
(B) 직원에게 정보를 제공한다.
(C) 관리자와 만난다.
(D) 휴게실을 청소한다.

해설 대화의 마지막 부분을 주의 깊게 듣는다. 여자가 "I'll post a notice in the break room. It'll explain the new role."이라며 휴게실에 공지문을 게시하겠다고 한 후, 그것이 새 역할에 관해 설명할 거라고 한 것을 통해 직원에게 정보를 제공할 것임을 알 수 있다. 따라서 (B)가 정답이다.

어휘 **document** n. 문서, 서류   **supervisor** n. 관리자, 감독관

[56-58]   미국식 → 호주식

Questions 56-58 refer to the following conversation.

W: Hello. I want to get a job in the tourism industry, and ⁵⁶your company is the only travel agency at today's job fair.
M: That's right. ⁵⁷We're opening an overseas branch in Thailand next year, and we need new employees to work there. Are you interested?
W: Yes. I'd like to apply to your company. I've always wanted to work abroad.
M: ⁵⁸We plan to conduct interviews starting next Monday. What about the morning of that day?
W: I'll be working at my family's business then. Can I come in the afternoon?

tourism n. 관광, 관광업   **travel agency** 여행사
overseas adj. 해외의   **apply** v. 지원하다
abroad adv. 해외에서, 해외로

해석
56-58번은 다음 대화에 관한 문제입니다.
여: 안녕하세요. 저는 관광 산업에서 일자리를 구하고 싶고, ⁵⁶귀사가 오늘 채용 박람회에서 유일한 여행사예요.
남: 맞아요. ⁵⁷저희는 내년에 태국에 해외 지점을 열 예정이고, 그곳에서 일할 새로운 직원들이 필요해요. 관심이 있으신가요?
여: 네. 저는 귀사에 지원하고 싶어요. 저는 항상 해외에서 일하고 싶었어요.
남: ⁵⁸우리는 다음 주 월요일부터 면접을 볼 계획이에요. 그날 아침은 어떠신가요?
여: 저는 그때 가족 사업 일을 할 거예요. 오후에 가도 될까요?

56 특정 세부 사항 문제

해석 어떤 행사가 열리고 있는가?
(A) 취업 박람회
(B) 시상식
(C) 모금 만찬
(D) 학술 세미나

해설 질문의 핵심 어구(event)와 관련된 내용을 주의 깊게 듣는다. 여자가 "your company is the only travel agency at today's job fair"라며 귀사가 오늘 채용 박람회에서 유일한 여행사라고 한 것을 통해 취업 박람회가 진행 중임을 알 수 있다. 따라서 (A)가 정답이다.

어휘 **fundraising** n. 모금   **academic** adj. 학술의, 학업의

Paraphrasing

job fair 채용 박람회 → career fair 취업 박람회

57 언급 문제

해석 남자는 그의 회사에 관해 무엇이라 말하는가?
(A) 인턴십 프로그램을 기획하고 있다.
(B) 외국 기업과 합병했다.
(C) 다른 국가로 확장할 것이다.
(D) 무료 서비스를 제공할 것이다.

해설 남자의 말에서 질문의 핵심 어구(his company)와 관련된 내용을 주의 깊게 듣는다. 남자가 "We're opening an overseas branch in Thailand next year"라며 내년에 태국에 해외 지점을 열 예정이라고 하였다. 따라서 (C)가 정답이다.

어휘 **merge** v. 합병하다, 어우러지다

Paraphrasing

opening an overseas branch in Thailand 태국에 해외 지점을 열다 → expand to another country 다른 국가로 확장하다

58 의도 파악 문제

해석 여자는 "저는 그때 가족 사업 일을 할 거예요"라고 말할 때 무엇을 의도하는가?
(A) 시간이 나지 않을 것이다.
(B) 자신의 사업을 시작할 것이다.
(C) 프로젝트에 도움이 필요하다.
(D) 마감일이 연장되어야 한다고 생각한다.

해설 질문의 인용어구(I'll be working at my family's business then)가 언급된 주변을 주의 깊게 듣는다. 남자가 "We plan to conduct interviews starting next Monday. What about the morning of that day?"라며 다음 주 월요일부터 면접을 볼 계획이라고 한 후, 그날 아침은 어떠냐는 물음에 여자가 그때 가족 사업 일이 있다고 한 것을 통해 그때 시간이 나지 않을 것임을 알 수 있다. 따라서 (A)가 정답이다.

어휘 available adj. 시간이 있는, 이용할 수 있는
deadline n. 마감일, 기한 extend v. 연장하다, 늘리다

[59-61]

🎧 영국식 → 캐나다식

Questions 59-61 refer to the following conversation.

> W: Alex, ⁵⁹last Friday's meeting with Lucid Entertainment went well. I think we did our best.
> M: Yes. But they just sent me an e-mail. ⁶⁰Unfortunately, they're not satisfied with the first drafts of the blog posts we created. They want each of the blog posts to follow a specific template now.
> W: Do you have a copy of the template?
> M: Yes. I just forwarded it to you.
> W: OK. Let's have a meeting at 2 P.M. to discuss it.
> M: Actually, ⁶¹I'll be out of the office all afternoon. I scheduled a half-day to get some dental work done. Let's go over it first thing tomorrow.
>
> unfortunately adv. 아쉽게도, 안타깝게도 satisfied adj. 만족한, 충족된
> specific adj. 특정한, 구체적인 template n. 서식, 견본, 본보기
> forward v. 전달하다, 보내다 discuss v. 논의하다

해석
59-61번은 다음 대화에 관한 문제입니다.
여: Alex, ⁵⁹지난 금요일에 Lucid 엔터테인먼트사와의 회의는 잘 진행되었어요. 저는 우리가 최선을 다했다고 생각해요.
남: 네. 하지만 그들이 방금 제게 이메일을 보냈어요. ⁶⁰아쉽게도, 그들은 우리가 만든 블로그 게시물들의 초안들에 만족하지 못하네요. 그들은 이제 각 블로그 게시물들이 특정 서식을 따르길 원해요.
여: 그 서식의 사본이 있나요?
남: 네. 그것을 방금 전달해 드렸어요.
여: 좋아요. 오후 2시에 그것을 논의하기 위해 회의를 합시다.
남: 사실, ⁶¹저는 오후 내내 사무실에 없을 거예요. 저는 치과 진료를 받을 반나절 일정을 잡아뒀어요. 그것을 내일 아침에 제일 먼저 진행하죠.

59 특정 세부 사항 문제

해석 화자들은 최근에 무엇을 했는가?
(A) 몇 가지 물품들을 구매했다.
(B) 회의에 참석했다.
(C) 신입 직원을 교육했다.
(D) 함께 점심을 먹었다.

해설 질문의 핵심 어구(speakers recently do)와 관련된 내용을 주의 깊게 듣는다. 여자가 "last Friday's meeting with Lucid Entertainment went well. I think we did our best."라며 지난 금요일에 Lucid 엔터테인먼트사와의 회의는 잘 진행되었다고 한 후, 우리가 최선을 다했다고 생각한다고 한 것을 통해, 화자들이 최근에 회의에 참석했음을 알 수 있다. 따라서 (B)가 정답이다.

어휘 purchase v. 구매하다, 구입하다 attend v. 참석하다

60 문제점 문제

해석 남자는 무슨 문제를 언급하는가?
(A) 물품이 손상되었다.
(B) 웹사이트가 제대로 기능을 하지 않는다.
(C) 고객이 회사의 작업물에 만족하지 않는다.
(D) 중요한 문서가 분실되었다.

해설 남자의 말에서 부정적인 표현이 언급된 주변을 주의 깊게 듣는다. 남자가 "Unfortunately, they're not satisfied with the first drafts of the blog posts we created."라며 아쉽게도 엔터테인먼트사가 화자들이 만든 블로그 게시물들의 초안들에 만족하지 못한다고 하였다. 따라서 (C)가 정답이다.

어휘 damaged adj. 손상된, 하자가 생긴
function v. 기능을 하다, 작용하다 properly adv. 제대로

Paraphrasing

not satisfied with ~에 만족하지 못하는 → not happy with ~에 만족하지 않는

61 다음에 할 일 문제

해석 남자는 오후에 무엇을 할 것인가?
(A) 초안들을 수정한다.
(B) 전화를 건다.
(C) 치과에 간다.
(D) 웹사이트를 확인한다.

해설 질문의 핵심 어구(afternoon)가 언급된 주변을 주의 깊게 듣는다. 남자가 "I'll be out of the office all afternoon. I scheduled a half-day to get some dental work done."이라며 자신이 오후 내내 사무실에 없을 것이라 한 후, 치과 진료를 받을 반나절 일정을 잡아뒀다고 한 것을 통해 남자가 오후에 치과에 갈 것임을 알 수 있다. 따라서 (C)가 정답이다.

어휘 revise v. 수정하다 dentist n. 치과, 치과 의사

[62-64]

🎧 호주식 → 영국식

Questions 62-64 refer to the following conversation and list.

> M: ⁶²I've just finished placing the materials needed for the workshops in the conference rooms. Have you confirmed that each projector is working properly? All of the instructors said they will need one.

W: Yes. However, one projector keeps giving me trouble. The power comes on, but it doesn't display the images. ⁶³**Ms. Newson will be here in an hour to prepare for her workshop, so it should be replaced immediately.**
M: There is a spare projector in my office.
W: Thank you. ⁶⁴**When was the last time you used it?**
M: I used it yesterday, and there were no issues.

material n. 자료, 물질   conference n. 회의
instructor n. 강사, 전임 강사   display v. 보여주다, 진열하다
immediately adv. 즉시, 즉각적으로   spare adj. 예비의, 남는

해석
62-64번은 다음 대화와 목록에 관한 문제입니다.
남: ⁶²워크숍에 필요한 자료들을 회의실에 놓는 것을 제가 지금 막 마쳤어요. 각 영사기가 제대로 작동하는지 확인했나요? 모든 강사들은 그것이 필요할 것이라고 말했어요.
여: 네. 그런데, 한 영사기가 자꾸 문제를 일으켜요. 전원은 들어오지만, 이미지들을 보여주지 않아요. ⁶³Ms. Newson이 워크숍을 준비하기 위해 한 시간 내에 올 테니, 그것은 즉시 교체되어야 해요.
남: 제 사무실에 예비 영사기가 있어요.
여: 감사합니다. ⁶⁴마지막으로 그것을 사용한 것이 언제였죠?
남: 제가 그것을 어제 사용했는데, 문제가 없었어요.

강사	강의실
Sam Hurley	103
Mitch Marks	104
⁶³Claire Newson	105
Betty Walz	106

62 특정 세부 사항 문제

해석 남자가 방금 무슨 작업을 완료했는가?
(A) 주문하기
(B) 영상 편집하기
(C) 몇몇 장비를 대여하기
(D) 몇몇 자료들을 정리하기

해설 질문의 핵심 어구(task ~ just completed)와 관련된 내용을 주의 깊게 듣는다. 남자가 "I've just finished placing the materials needed for the workshops in the conference rooms."라며 워크숍에 필요한 자료들을 회의실에 놓는 것을 지금 막 마쳤다고 하였다. 따라서 (D)가 정답이다.

어휘 edit v. 편집하다, 수정하다   rent v. 대여하다, 빌리다

63 시각 자료 문제

해석 시각 자료를 보아라. 교체되어야 할 영사기가 있는 강의실은 어디인가?
(A) 103호
(B) 104호
(C) 105호
(D) 106호

해설 제시된 목록의 정보를 확인한 후 질문의 핵심 어구(projector ~ needs to be replaced)와 관련된 내용을 주의 깊게 듣는다. 여자가 "Ms. Newson will be here in an hour to prepare for her workshop, so it should be replaced immediately."라며 Ms. Newson이 워크숍을 준비하기 위해 한 시간 내에 올 테니, 그것이 즉시 교체되어야 한다고 하였고, Ms. Newson이 워크숍을 진행할 곳은 105호임을 목록에서 알 수 있다. 따라서 (C)가 정답이다.

64 특정 세부 사항 문제

해석 여자는 무엇에 관해 묻는가?
(A) 차를 어디에 주차할지
(B) 사무실이 열려 있는지
(C) 물품들이 얼마나 필요한지
(D) 장치를 언제 사용했는지

해설 여자의 말에서 질문의 핵심 어구(inquire about)와 관련된 내용을 주의 깊게 듣는다. 여자가 "When was the last time you used it?"이라며 마지막으로 그것을 사용한 때를 물었다. 따라서 (D)가 정답이다.

어휘 park v. 주차하다   device n. 장치, 기구

[65-67] 영국식 → 캐나다식

Questions 65-67 refer to the following conversation and order form.

W: Brad, ⁶⁵**have you placed the monthly office supply order for our medical clinic yet?**
M: I have the form open on my computer now. Do you want to add an item?
W: No. But ⁶⁶**please double the amount of paper**.
M: Got it. What about the other items, like ink cartridges and envelopes? Should I add more of those as well?
W: That won't be necessary. But before you submit the order, ⁶⁷**can you check in the storeroom to see if we are running low on anything?**
M: Sure. ⁶⁷**I'll take care of that now.**

monthly adj. 월별의, 매달의   office supply 사무용품
add v. 추가하다, 더하다   double v. 두 배로 늘리다, 두 배로 하다
envelop n. 봉투   necessary adj. 필요한, 필수적인
storeroom n. 창고, 저장실

해석
65-67번은 다음 대화와 주문서에 관한 문제입니다.
여: Brad, ⁶⁵우리 병원의 월별 사무용품 주문을 벌써 했나요?
남: 지금 제 컴퓨터에 서식이 열려 있어요. 품목을 추가하길 원하세요?
여: 아니요. ⁶⁶하지만 종이의 수량을 두 배로 늘려주세요.
남: 알겠습니다. 잉크 카트리지와 봉투 같은 다른 품목들은요? 제가 그것들도 더 추가해야 할까요?
여: 그럴 필요는 없어요. 하지만 주문을 제출하기 전에, ⁶⁷창고에 가서 우리가 부족한 것이 있는지 확인해 줄 수 있나요?
남: 그럼요. ⁶⁷제가 지금 처리할게요.

사무용품 주문서	
품목	수량
잉크 카트리지 (컬러)	4
⁶⁶프린터 용지 (팩)	8
마닐라 지 봉투 (박스)	2
스테이플러 (대형)	3

65 화자 문제

해석 화자들은 어느 산업에서 일하는 것 같은가?
(A) 의료 서비스
(B) 마케팅
(C) 회계
(D) 기술

해설 대화에서 신분 및 직업과 관련된 표현을 놓치지 않고 듣는다. 여자가 "have you placed the monthly office supply order for our medical clinic yet?"이라며 남자에게 병원의 월별 사무용품 주문을 벌써 했는지 묻는 것을 통해 화자들이 의료 서비스 산업에서 일한다는 것을 알 수 있다. 따라서 (A)가 정답이다.

66 시각 자료 문제

해석 시각 자료를 보아라. 여자가 늘려 달라고 요청한 수량은 무엇인가?
(A) 4
(B) 8
(C) 2
(D) 3

해설 제시된 주문서의 정보를 확인한 후 여자의 말에서 질문의 핵심 어구(quantity ~ to be increased)와 관련된 내용을 주의 깊게 듣는다. 여자가 "please double the amount of paper"라며 종이의 수량을 두 배로 늘려 달라고 했고, 종이의 수량이 8임을 주문서에서 알 수 있다. 따라서 (B)가 정답이다.

67 다음에 할 일 문제

해석 남자는 다음에 무엇을 할 것인가?
(A) 공급업체에 문의한다.
(B) 가격을 확인한다.
(C) 동료와 이야기한다.
(D) 보관 장소를 방문한다.

해설 대화의 마지막 부분을 주의 깊게 듣는다. 여자가 남자에게 "can you check in the storeroom to see if we are running low on anything?"이라며 창고에 가서 우리가 부족한 것이 있는지 확인해 줄 수 있냐고 묻자, 남자가 "I'll take care of that now."라며 지금 처리하겠다고 한 것을 통해 남자가 보관 장소를 방문할 것임을 알 수 있다. 따라서 (D)가 정답이다.

어휘 supplier n. 공급업체, 공급자 storage n. 보관, 저장

[68-70]

호주식 → 영국식

Questions 68-70 refer to the following conversation and map.

M: Ms. Reynolds, it's Simon LeBlanc from East End Studios. I received your voicemail, and ⁶⁸I can arrange a photo shoot for you. I have an opening tomorrow at 4 P.M.
W: That works for me. Also, ⁶⁹your Web site mentions a discount of 30 percent for first-time customers. Is it still available?
M: Yes. The offer is valid until the end of this month.
W: Excellent. And ⁷⁰your studio is located on Ridge Street, right?
M: ⁷⁰That's correct. The building is across from Devin Mall. There's a movie theater next door.

receive v. 받다 voicemail n. 음성 메시지, 음성 메일
arrange v. 준비하다, 배열하다 valid adj. 유효한

해석
68-70번은 다음 대화와 지도에 관한 문제입니다.
남: Ms. Reynolds, East End 스튜디오의 Simon LeBlanc입니다. 제가 당신의 음성 메시지를 받았는데, ⁶⁸저는 당신을 위해 사진 촬영을 준비할 수 있어요. 내일 오후 4시에 빈자리가 있어요.
여: 저는 좋아요. 또한, ⁶⁹당신의 웹사이트에서 신규 고객들에게 30퍼센트의 할인이 적용된다고 하네요. 여전히 가능한가요?
남: 네. 그 혜택은 이번 달 말까지 유효해요.
여: 훌륭해요. 그리고 ⁷⁰당신의 스튜디오는 Ridge가에 위치해 있죠, 그렇죠?
남: ⁷⁰맞아요. Devin 쇼핑몰 맞은편에 있는 건물이에요. 바로 옆에 영화관이 있어요.

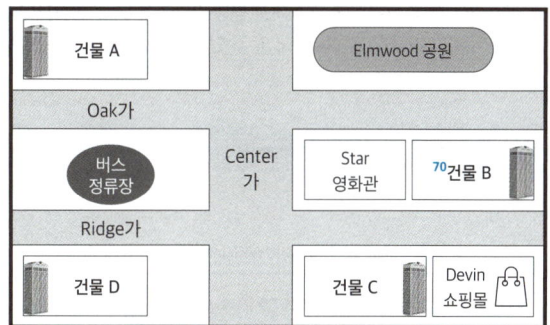

68 화자 문제

해석 남자는 누구인 것 같은가?
(A) 부동산 중개업자
(B) 사진작가
(C) 영화감독
(D) 회계사

해설 대화에서 신분 및 직업과 관련된 표현을 놓치지 않고 듣는다. 남자가 "I can arrange a photo shoot for you"라며 여자를 위해 사진 촬영을 준비할 수 있다고 한 것을 통해 남자는 사진작가라는 것을 알 수 있다. 따라서 (B)가 정답이다.

69 특정 세부 사항 문제

해석 여자는 웹사이트에서 무슨 정보를 확인했는가?
(A) 추적 번호
(B) 일정 변경
(C) 옵션 목록
(D) 할인 혜택

해설 여자의 말에서 질문의 핵심 어구(notice on the Web site)와 관련된 내용을 주의 깊게 듣는다. 여자가 "your Web site mentions a discount for 30 percent for first-time customers"라며 웹사이트에서 신규 고객들에게 30퍼센트의 할인을 적용한다고 하였다. 따라서 (D)가 정답이다.

어휘 tracking n. 추적 option n. 옵션, 선택권

70 시각 자료 문제

해석 시각 자료를 보아라. 화자들은 어디에서 만날 것인가?
(A) 건물 A에서
(B) 건물 B에서
(C) 건물 C에서
(D) 건물 D에서

해설 제시된 지도의 정보를 확인한 후 질문의 핵심 어구(the speakers meet)와 관련된 내용을 주의 깊게 듣는다. 여자가 남자에게 "your studio is located on Ridge Street, right?"이라며 남자의 스튜디오가 Ridge가에 위치해 있는 것이 맞냐고 묻자, 남자가 "That's correct. The building is across from Devin Mall. There's a movie theater next door."라며 Ridge가에 있는 것이 맞다고 한 후, Devin 쇼핑몰 맞은편에 있고 바로 옆에 영화관이 있다고 하였다. Devin 쇼핑몰 맞은편에 있고 바로 옆에 영화관인 Star 영화관이 있는 건물은 건물 B임을 지도에서 알 수 있다. 따라서 (B)가 정답이다.

PART 4

[71-73] 🔊 호주식

Questions 71-73 refer to the following advertisement.

> ⁷¹The most popular bookstore in our community, Terry's Books, finally reopened today. As always, ⁷¹you can get used books at low prices in almost new condition. And ⁷²now it will be much easier and more convenient to find books using our new mobile application. To celebrate our reopening, ⁷³we're giving away a free canvas bag with our logo to anyone who visits today.
>
> resident n. 주민, 거주자 community n. 지역, 주민, 공동체
> reopen v. 다시 문을 열다, 재개하다 used adj. 중고의, 익숙한
> condition n. 상태, 환경 convenient adj. 편리한, 간편한
> celebrate v. 기념하다, 축하하다 give away 주다, 나누어 주다

해석
71-73번은 다음 광고에 관한 문제입니다.
⁷¹저희 지역에서 가장 인기 있는 서점인 Terry's Books가 마침내 오늘 다시 문을 열었습니다. 언제나 그랬듯, 거의 새것의 상태인 ⁷¹중고 책들을 저렴한 값에 구매할 수 있습니다. 그리고 ⁷²이제 저희의 새로운 모바일 애플리케이션을 이용하여 책들을 찾는 것이 훨씬 더 쉽고 더 편리해졌습니다. 재개장을 기념하여, ⁷³저희의 로고가 박힌 무료 캔버스 가방을 오늘 방문하는 모두에게 드립니다.

71 주제 문제

해석 무엇이 광고되고 있는가?
(A) 지역 전문대학
(B) 중고 서점
(C) 문구점
(D) 출판사

해설 광고의 주제를 묻는 문제이므로, 지문의 초반을 반드시 듣는다. "The most popular bookstore in our community, Terry's Books, finally reopened today. ~ you can get used books at low prices"라며 지역에서 가장 인기 있는 서점인 Terry's Books가 마침내 오늘 다시 문을 열었다고 한 후, 중고 책들을 저렴한 값에 구매할 수 있다고 하였다. 따라서 (B)가 정답이다.

어휘 stationery n. 문구, 문방구 publishing n. 출판

72 특정 세부 사항 문제

해석 화자는 어떤 변화를 언급하는가?
(A) 앱이 개발되었다.
(B) 더 많은 직원들이 고용되었다.
(C) 영업시간이 연장되었다.
(D) 추가 지점이 문을 열었다.

해설 질문의 핵심 어구(change)와 관련된 내용을 주의 깊게 듣는다. "now it will be much easier and more convenient to find books using our new mobile application"이라며 이제 새로운 모바일 애플리케이션을 이용하여 책들을 찾는 것이 훨씬 더 쉽고 더 편리해졌다고 했으므로 서점 앱이 새로 개발되었음을 알 수 있다. 따라서 (A)가 정답이다.

어휘 hire v. 고용하다 operating hour 영업시간, 운영 시간
extend v. 연장하다, 늘리다 additional adj. 추가의, 가외의

73 특정 세부 사항 문제

해석 방문객들은 오늘 무엇을 무료로 받을 수 있는가?
(A) 천 가방
(B) 책꽂이
(C) 책상용 등
(D) 로고 티셔츠

해설 질문의 핵심 어구(visitors receive for free today)와 관련된 내용을 주의 깊게 듣는다. "we're is giving away a free canvas bag with our logo to anyone who visits today"라며 로고가 박힌 무료 캔버스 가방을 오늘 방문하는 모두에게 제공한다고 하였다. 따라서 (A)가 정답이다.

어휘 fabric n. 천, 직물 lamp n. 등, 램프

Paraphrasing

canvas bag 캔버스 가방 → fabric bag 천 가방

[74-76]

캐나다식

Questions 74-76 refer to the following excerpt from a meeting.

> [74]I'd like to give you an update on our ongoing clinical trials for the new allergy medication we're developing. Unfortunately, we have to put them on hold because of some minor side effects. So [75]your supervisors will assign you new tasks later this morning. One more thing. Building security has requested that you update your identification cards. [76]Please go to the security office to have a new photo taken for your badge by Friday.

ongoing adj. 진행 중인 clinical trial 임상 시험
medication n. 약, 약물 side effect 부작용
assign v. 할당하다, 지정하다 request v. 요청하다

해석
74-76은 다음 회의 발췌록에 관한 문제입니다.
[74]저는 여러분께 우리가 개발 중인 새로운 알레르기약에 관해 진행 중인 임상 시험들의 최신 정보를 전해드리고자 합니다. 안타깝게도, 몇몇 경미한 부작용들 때문에 우리는 그것들을 보류해야 합니다. 그래서 [75]여러분의 상사분들이 여러분께 오늘 오전 중으로 새 업무들을 할당할 것입니다. 한 가지 더 말씀드리겠습니다. 건물 보안팀에서 여러분의 사원증을 업데이트해 달라고 요청하였습니다. [76]금요일까지 보안 사무실로 가서서 사원증용 새 사진을 찍어주세요.

74 화자 문제

해석 화자는 어디에서 일하는 것 같은가?
(A) 마케팅 기관에서
(B) 컨설팅 회사에서
(C) 금융 기관에서
(D) 제약 회사에서

해설 지문에서 신분 및 직업과 관련된 표현을 놓치지 않고 듣는다. "I'd like to give you an update on our ongoing clinical trials for the new allergy medication we're developing."이라며 여러분에게 우리가 개발 중인 새로운 알레르기약에 관해 진행 중인 임상 시험의 최신 정보를 전해드리고자 한다고 하였다. 이를 통해 화자는 제약 회사에서 일하고 있음을 알 수 있다. 따라서 (D)가 정답이다.

어휘 financial adj. 금융의, 재무의 institution n. 기관
pharmaceutical adj. 제약의, 약학의

75 다음에 할 일 문제

해석 화자에 따르면, 오늘 오전 중으로 무슨 일이 일어날 것인가?
(A) 실험이 시작될 것이다.
(B) 고객이 방문할 것이다.
(C) 직원들이 새로 할당된 일을 받을 것이다.
(D) 주차장이 일시적으로 폐쇄될 것이다.

해설 질문의 핵심 어구(later this morning)가 언급된 주변을 주의 깊게 듣는다. "your supervisors will assign you new tasks later this morning"이라며 상사들이 오늘 오전 중으로 새 업무들을 할당할 것이라고 하였다. 따라서 (C)가 정답이다.

어휘 reassign v. 재배치하다, 다시 맡기다 temporarily adv. 일시적으로

Paraphrasing

tasks 업무 → assignment 할당된 일

76 특정 세부 사항 문제

해석 금요일까지 청자들은 무엇을 해야 하는가?
(A) 투표에 참여한다.
(B) 제품 아이디어를 제출한다.
(C) 사원증을 수령한다.
(D) 사진을 촬영한다.

해설 질문의 핵심 어구(by Friday)가 언급된 주변을 주의 깊게 듣는다. "Please go to the security office to have a new photo taken for your badge by Friday."라며 금요일까지 보안 사무실로 가서 사원증용 새 사진을 찍어달라고 하였다. 따라서 (D)가 정답이다.

어휘 participate in ~에 참여하다 poll n. 투표 submit v. 제출하다

[77-79]

미국식

Questions 77-79 refer to the following telephone message.

> Hello, Ms. Porter. This is Janet Crawford from Lucky Hairdressers. [77]I'm calling to let you know that your usual stylist, Miriam, will be out for a week on vacation. We've arranged for one of our most experienced stylists, Joshua, to take over your appointment scheduled for tomorrow at 11 o'clock. He has been with us for over 10 years. [78]He will take great care of you. But [79]please give us a call back if you still want to reschedule an appointment with your usual stylist. We apologize for any inconvenience.

usual adj. 평소의, 보통의 arrange v. 배정하다, 마련하다
experienced adj. 경험이 많은, 능숙한
take care of ~을 신경 써서 봐주다, 처리하다
apologize for ~을 사과하다 inconvenience n. 불편, 성가심

해석
77-79번은 다음 전화 메시지에 관한 문제입니다.
안녕하세요, Ms. Porter. 저는 Lucky 미용실의 Janet Crawford입니다. [77]저는 당신의 평소 스타일리스트인 Miriam이 일주일간 휴가를 간다는 사실을 알려드리고자 전화했습니다. 저희는 가장 경험이 많은 스타일리스트들 중 한 명인 Joshua를 내일 오전 11시에 예약된 당신의 시술 일정을 대신하도록 배정했습니다. 그는 저희와 10년 넘게 함께 하고 있습니다. [78]그가 당신을 정말 신경 써서 봐줄 것입니다. 하지만 당신이 여전히 평소 스타일리스트와 [79]예약을 다시 잡고 싶다면 저희에게 다시 전화 부탁드립니다. 불편을 끼쳐드려 죄송합니다.

77 목적 문제

해석 화자는 왜 전화하고 있는가?
(A) 주문을 확인하기 위해
(B) 예약을 취소하기 위해
(C) 직원의 휴가를 알리기 위해
(D) 선호하는 것을 확인하기 위해

해설 전화 메시지의 목적을 묻는 문제이므로, 지문의 초반을 반드시 듣

는다. "I'm calling to let you know that your usual stylist, Miriam, will be out for a week on vacation."이라며 평소 스타일리스트인 Miriam이 일주일간 휴가를 간다는 사실을 알려드리고자 전화했다고 하였다. 따라서 (C)가 정답이다.

어휘 cancel v. 취소하다 inform v. 알리다, 통지하다
preference n. 선호하는 것, 선호도

78 의도 파악 문제

해석 화자는 왜 "그는 저희와 10년 넘게 함께 하고 있습니다"라고 말하는가?
(A) 최신 정보를 전달하기 위해
(B) 비용을 정당화하기 위해
(C) 안심시키기 위해
(D) 책임을 부인하기 위해

해설 질문의 인용어구(He has been with us for over 10 years)가 언급된 주변을 주의 깊게 듣는다. "He will take great care of you."라며 그가 청자를 정말 신경 써서 봐줄 것이라고 한 것을 통해 화자가 청자를 안심시키고자 한다는 것을 알 수 있다. 따라서 (C)가 정답이다.

어휘 justify v. 정당화하다, 해명하다 reassurance n. 안심시키기, 안도감
deny v. 부인하다, 거부하다

79 방법 문제

해석 청자는 어떻게 일정 변경을 요청할 수 있는가?
(A) 링크를 클릭함으로써
(B) 전화로 회신함으로써
(C) 모바일 애플리케이션을 사용함으로써
(D) 직접 방문함으로써

해설 질문의 핵심 어구(request a schedule change)와 관련된 내용을 주의 깊게 듣는다. "please give us a call back if you still want to reschedule an appointment"라며 예약을 다시 잡기 위해서는 다시 전화 부탁드린다고 하였다. 따라서 (B)가 정답이다.

어휘 return a call 회신하다 in person 직접

Paraphrasing
give us a call back 다시 전화하다 → returning a phone call 전화를 회신하는 것

[80-82]

Questions 80-82 refer to the following excerpt from a meeting. 🎧 호주식

⁸⁰I asked you all to be here to discuss the product presentation for our new headsets—the ones we're launching next week. As you all know, Steven is in the hospital, so he might not be able to lead the presentation. ⁸¹Since we can't postpone the launch, we're looking for someone to replace him. I understand that most of you don't have much experience giving these presentations. However, our team has the most information on the headsets. ⁸²Please take a few minutes to decide which of you would be best suited for this role.

launch v. 출시하다, 착수하다 postpone v. 연기하다, 미루다
replace v. 대신하다, 교체하다 information n. 정보

decide v. 결정하다 suited adj. 적합한, 어울리는 role n. 역할, 기능

해석 80-82번은 다음 회의 발췌록에 관한 문제입니다.
⁸⁰저는 우리가 다음 주에 출시할 새 헤드셋의 제품 발표에 관해 논의하기 위해 여러분께 이곳에 와 달라고 요청했습니다. 아시다시피, Steven이 병원에 있어서, 그가 발표를 진행할 수 없을 겁니다. ⁸¹우리가 출시를 연기할 수 없기 때문에, 그를 대신할 사람을 찾고 있습니다. 제가 여러분 중 대부분이 이러한 발표를 경험해 본 적이 많이 없다는 것을 알고 있습니다. 그러나, 우리 팀은 헤드셋들에 관한 정보를 가장 많이 갖고 있습니다. ⁸²몇 분만 시간을 내어 여러분 중 누가 이 역할에 가장 적합할지 결정해 주세요.

80 주제 문제

해석 화자는 주로 무엇에 대해 이야기하고 있는가?
(A) 디자인 회의
(B) 제품 발표
(C) 지점 개점
(D) 교육 워크숍

해설 회의의 주제를 묻는 문제이므로 지문의 초반을 반드시 듣는다. "I asked you all to be here to discuss the product presentation for our new headsets—the one we're launching next week."이라며 다음 주에 출시할 새 헤드셋의 제품 발표에 관해 논의하기 위해 청자들에게 이곳에 와 달라고 요청했다고 한 후, 제품 발표에 대한 내용으로 지문이 이어지고 있다. 따라서 (B)가 정답이다.

어휘 conference n. 회의, 학회 opening n. 개점, 공석
training n. 교육, 연수

81 이유 문제

해석 화자에 따르면, Steven은 왜 교체될 것인가?
(A) 장소가 변경될 수 없다.
(B) 프로젝트가 취소되었다.
(C) 청중이 항의했다.
(D) 행사가 지연될 수 없다.

해설 질문의 핵심 어구(Steven be replaced)와 관련된 내용을 주의 깊게 듣는다. "Since we can't postpone the launch, we're looking for someone to replace him[Steven]."이라며 출시를 연기할 수 없기 때문에, Steven을 대신할 사람을 찾고 있다고 하였다. 따라서 (D)가 정답이다.

어휘 venue n. 장소 audience n. 청중, 시청자
complain v. 항의하다, 불평하다 delay v. 지연시키다, 미루다

Paraphrasing
postpone 연기하다 → be delayed 지연되다

82 특정 세부 사항 문제

해석 화자는 청자들이 무엇을 할 것이라고 기대하는가?
(A) 주문서를 작성한다.
(B) 의견을 제공한다.
(C) 후보자를 선택한다.
(D) 발표 슬라이드를 만든다.

해설 질문의 핵심 어구(speaker expect the listeners to do)와 관련된 내용을 주의 깊게 듣는다. "Please take a few minutes to decide which of you would be best suited for this role."이라며 몇 분만 시간을 내어 청자들 중 누가 이 역할에 가장 적합할지 결정해 달라고 한 것을 통해 화자는 청자들이 후보자를 선택하기를 기대하고 있음을 알 수 있다. 따라서 (C)가 정답이다.

어휘 complete v. 작성하다, 완료하다 feedback n. 의견
candidate n. 후보자, 지원자

[83-85]

🎧 영국식

Questions 83-85 refer to the following tour information.

Good morning, everyone. ⁸³**Welcome to our tour of the scenic Snowton area. I'm glad you could join me today.** Let me briefly explain today's schedule. First is a hike up Mt. Snowton. Everyone is wearing comfortable hiking clothes, right? Afterward, ⁸⁴**we will have lunch at a nearby restaurant**. It's always full of locals. ⁸⁴**They know where to get great food and service.** The last stop on our tour is one that I'm sure you'll enjoy . . . the hot springs. ⁸⁵**OK, then let's get on the bus.**

scenic adj. 경치 좋은, 무대 장치의   briefly adv. 간단히, 잠시
hike n. 하이킹, 도보 여행   comfortable adj. 편한, 쾌적한
afterward adv. 나중에, 후에   nearby adj. 인근의, 가까운 곳의
hot spring 온천

해석
83-85번은 다음 투어 정보에 관한 문제입니다.
좋은 아침입니다, 여러분. ⁸³경치 좋은 Snowton 지역 투어에 오신 것을 환영합니다. 오늘 저와 함께 해주셔서 기쁩니다. 오늘 일정을 간단히 설명하겠습니다. 첫 번째는 Snowton 산을 오르는 하이킹입니다. 모두 편한 등산복을 입고 계시죠, 그렇죠? 그 후에는 ⁸⁴인근의 식당에서 점심을 먹을 것입니다. 그곳은 항상 현지인들로 가득합니다. ⁸⁴그들은 훌륭한 음식과 서비스를 어디에서 받을 수 있는지 알죠. 우리 투어의 마지막 목적지는 여러분들이 좋아하실 거라 확신하는... 온천입니다. ⁸⁵좋아요, 그럼 버스에 탑시다.

83 화자 문제

해설 화자는 누구인 것 같은가?
(A) 여행 가이드
(B) 영업 사원
(C) 보안 요원
(D) 호텔 관리자

해설 지문에서 신분 및 직업과 관련된 표현을 놓치지 않고 듣는다. "Welcome to our tour of the scenic Snowton area. I'm glad you could join me today."라며 Snowton 지역 투어에 온 것을 환영하고 함께 해주셔서 기쁘다고 했으므로 화자는 여행 가이드임을 알 수 있다. 따라서 (A)가 정답이다.

어휘 security n. 보안, 경비

84 의도 파악 문제

해설 화자는 "그곳은 항상 현지인들로 가득합니다"라고 말할 때 무엇을 의도하는가?

(A) 지역사회는 한 장소로의 접근을 제한한다.
(B) 매장이 모두를 위해 충분히 크지 않다.
(C) 서비스는 주민들만 이용 가능하다.
(D) 사업장이 좋은 명성을 가지고 있다.

해설 질문의 인용어구(It's always full of locals)가 언급된 주변을 주의 깊게 듣는다. "we will have lunch at a nearby restaurant"이라며 인근의 식당에서 점심을 먹을 것이라고 한 후, "They know where to get great food and service."라며 현지인들은 훌륭한 음식과 서비스를 어디에서 받을 수 있는지 안다고 한 것을 통해 식당이 현지인들에게 좋은 명성을 가지고 있다는 것을 알 수 있다. 따라서 (D)가 정답이다.

어휘 restrict v. 제한하다, 통제하다, 방해하다   access n. 접근, 접촉 기회
resident n. 주민   reputation n. 명성

85 다음에 할 일 문제

해설 청자들은 다음에 무엇을 할 것 같은가?
(A) 버스에 탄다.
(B) 후기를 남긴다.
(C) 옷을 몇 벌 구매한다.
(D) 짐을 푼다.

해설 지문의 마지막 부분을 주의 깊게 듣는다. "OK, then let's get on the bus."라며 이제 버스에 타자고 하였다. 따라서 (A)가 정답이다.

어휘 purchase v. 구매하다   unpack v. (짐을) 풀다
luggage n. 짐, 수하물

Paraphrasing

get on 타다 → Board 타다

[86-88]

🎧 캐나다식

Questions 86-88 refer to the following broadcast.

You're listening to the KMC News traffic update. ⁸⁶**Expect significant delays for the evening commute. A water pipe burst under the surface of Highway 37.** As a result, the northbound lanes have been temporarily closed to allow for repairs. City workers are on their way to the scene, and ⁸⁷**the head of the transportation department, Paul Reeves**, said that the road should be reopened by 10 A.M. tomorrow morning. ⁸⁸**After the commercial break, I'll be back with the results of today's baseball games.**

significant adj. 상당한, 중요한   commute n. 통근, 출퇴근
burst v. 터지다, 파열하다   surface n. 지면, 표면
northbound adj. 북쪽 방향의   temporarily adv. 일시적으로
repair n. 수리   scene n. 현장, 장면   transportation n. 교통, 운송
commercial break 광고   result n. 결과

해설
86-88번은 다음 방송에 관한 문제입니다.
여러분은 KMC 뉴스의 교통 업데이트를 듣고 계십니다. ⁸⁶저녁 출퇴근이 상당히 지연될 것으로 예상하십시오. 37번 고속도로의 지면 아래 상수도관이 파열되었습니다. 그 결과, 북쪽 방향 차선이 수리를 위해 일시적으로 폐쇄되었습니다. 시 직원들이 현장으로 출동하고 있으며, ⁸⁷교통부 책임자인

Paul Reeves는 내일 아침 10시까지 도로를 재개통하겠다고 말했습니다. ⁸⁸광고 후에, 저는 오늘의 야구 경기 결과를 가지고 돌아오겠습니다.

86 이유 문제

해석 화자에 따르면, 왜 교통 지연이 예상되는가?
(A) 다리가 수리되고 있다.
(B) 파이프가 손상되었다.
(C) 퍼레이드가 개최될 것이다.
(D) 터널이 건설되고 있다.

해설 질문의 핵심 어구(traffic delays)와 관련된 내용을 주의 깊게 듣는다. "Expect significant delays for the evening commute. A water pipe burst under the surface of Highway 37."이라며 저녁 출퇴근이 상당히 지연될 것으로 예상되는데, 37번 고속도로의 지면 아래 상수도관이 파열되었다고 하였다. 따라서 (B)가 정답이다.

어휘 damage v. 손상을 주다, 훼손하다 take place 개최되다, 일어나다

87 특정 세부 사항 문제

해석 Paul Reeves는 누구인가?
(A) 사업체 소유주
(B) 건설 현장 근로자
(C) 공무원
(D) 회사 대변인

해설 질문의 대상(Paul Reeves)의 신분 및 직업과 관련된 표현을 놓치지 않고 듣는다. "the head of the transportation department, Paul Reeves"라며 교통부 책임자인 Paul Reeves라고 하였다. 따라서 (C)가 정답이다.

어휘 spokesperson n. 대변인

88 특정 세부 사항 문제

해석 청자들은 광고 후에 무엇을 들을 것인가?
(A) 스포츠 점수
(B) 선거 결과
(C) 새로 발매된 노래
(D) 유명 인사 인터뷰

해설 질문의 핵심어구(after a commercial break)가 언급된 주변을 주의 깊게 듣는다. "After the commercial break, I'll be back with the results of today's baseball games."라며 광고 후에 오늘의 야구 경기 결과를 가지고 돌아오겠다고 하였다. 따라서 (A)가 정답이다.

어휘 election n. 선거, 당선 celebrity n. 유명 인사

Paraphrasing
the results of today's baseball games 오늘의 야구 경기 결과
→ sports scores 스포츠 점수

[89-91] 🔊 미국식

Questions 89-91 refer to the following announcement.

⁸⁹Welcome, everyone, to this year's annual Culinary Arts Festival. ⁹⁰In a moment, special guest chef Nadine Wagner will be giving a cooking demonstration on our main stage. The demonstration will be shown on the large screen. And don't forget that the event's sponsor, Element Kitchen Supplies, is giving away items from its latest line of cookware throughout the day. So ⁹¹be sure to listen for the winning numbers to see if they match the ones written on your tickets.

annual adj. 연례의, 해마다의   culinary adj. 요리의, 음식의
demonstration n. 시연, 설명   sponsor n. 후원업체, 광고주; v. 후원하다
give away ~을 나누어 주다   cookware n. 취사도구
match v. 일치하다, 어울리다

해석
89-91번은 다음 공지에 관한 문제입니다.

⁸⁹여러분, 올해의 연례 요리법 축제에 오신 것을 환영합니다. ⁹⁰잠시 후, 특별 게스트 요리사인 Nadine Wagner가 메인 무대에서 요리 시연을 선보일 것입니다. 시연은 대형 스크린에서 상영될 예정입니다. 또한 행사의 후원업체인 Element 주방용품회사가 하루 종일 최신 조리 기구 라인 제품들을 증정한다는 점도 잊지 마세요. 그러니 ⁹¹여러분의 티켓에 적힌 것과 일치하는지 확인하기 위해 당첨 번호에 귀 기울이세요.

89 주제 문제

해석 어떤 종류의 행사가 열리고 있는 것 같은가?
(A) 은퇴 만찬
(B) 음식 축제
(C) 회사 야유회
(D) 요리 대회

해설 어떤 종류의 행사가 열리고 있는지 묻는 문제이므로, 지문의 초반을 반드시 듣는다. "Welcome, everyone, to this year's annual Culinary Arts Festival."이라며 올해의 연례 요리법 축제에 오신 것을 환영한다고 하였다. 따라서 (B)가 정답이다.

어휘 banquet n. 만찬, 연회

Paraphrasing
Culinary Arts Festival 요리법 축제 → food festival 음식 축제

90 특정 세부 사항 문제

해석 스크린에 무엇이 보일 것인가?
(A) 특별한 광고
(B) 후원업체의 메시지
(C) 다큐멘터리 영화
(D) 요리 발표회

해설 질문의 핵심 어구(shown on a screen)와 관련된 내용을 주의 깊게 듣는다. "In a moment, special guest chef Nadine Wagner will be giving a cooking demonstration on our main stage. The demonstration will be shown on the large screen."이라며 특별 게스트 요리사가 메인 무대에서 요리 시연을 선보일 것이고, 이것은 대형 스크린에서 상영될 예정이라고 하였다. 따라서 (D)가 정답이다.

Paraphrasing

cooking demonstration 요리 시연 → cooking presentation
요리 발표회

91 제안 문제

해석 화자는 청자들에게 무엇을 하라고 조언하는가?
(A) 일련의 지침을 읽는다.
(B) 메인 무대 가까이에 앉는다.
(C) 우승자에게 박수를 보낸다.
(D) 발표에 주의를 기울인다.

해설 지문의 중후반에서 제안과 관련된 표현이 언급된 다음을 주의 깊게 듣는다. "be sure to listen for the winning numbers to see if they match the ones written on your tickets"라며 여러분의 티켓에 적힌 것과 일치하는지 확인하기 위해 당첨 번호에 귀 기울이라고 하였다. 따라서 (D)가 정답이다.

어휘 applaud v. 박수를 보내다 announcement n. 발표, 소식

[92-94] 🔊 호주식

Questions 92-94 refer to the following excerpt from a meeting.

> ⁹²I know that many of you have experienced problems communicating with staff working from home. However, we need to adapt to the hybrid work model that the company has implemented. ⁹³Someone asked if we could have staff members come into the office more often, but we are just one of the departments. ⁹³We must follow company policy. Well . . . ⁹⁴I realize that regular, face-to-face interactions among workers influence job satisfaction the most, so I'll make sure to bring this issue up during my next meeting with the HR manager.

experience v. 겪다, 경험하다 communicate v. 소통하다, 전하다
adapt to ~에 적응하다 implement v. 시행하다, 실시하다
department n. 부서 realize v. 인식하다, 깨닫다
interaction n. 교류, 상호작용 influence v. 영향을 미치다; n. 영향력

해석
92-94번은 다음 회의 발췌록에 관한 문제입니다.
⁹²여러분 중 많은 분들이 재택근무를 하는 직원들과 소통하는 데 어려움을 겪었다는 것을 알고 있습니다. 하지만, 우리는 회사가 시행하는 하이브리드 업무 모델에 적응해야 합니다. ⁹³누군가 직원들을 사무실에 더 자주 출근시킬 수 있는지 물었지만, 우리는 부서들 중 하나일 뿐입니다. ⁹³우리는 회사 정책을 따라야 합니다. 음... ⁹⁴저는 직원들 간의 정기적인 대면 교류가 직무 만족도에 가장 큰 영향을 미친다는 것을 인식하고 있으므로 인사 담당자와의 다음 회의에서 이 문제를 반드시 제기하겠습니다.

92 주제 문제

해석 화자는 주로 무엇을 이야기하고 있는가?
(A) 직원들을 더 고용하는 것
(B) 집에서 일을 하는 것
(C) 신입사원을 교육하는 것
(D) 몇몇 도구를 구입하는 것

해설 회의의 주제를 묻는 문제이므로, 지문의 초반을 반드시 듣는다. "I know that many of you have experienced problems communicating with staff working from home."이라며 재택근무를 하는 직원들과 소통하는 데 어려움을 겪었다는 것을 알고 있다고 한 후, 재택근무 관련 이슈에 대한 내용으로 지문이 이어지고 있다. 따라서 (B)가 정답이다.

어휘 hire v. 고용하다 train v. 교육하다 tool n. 도구, 수단

93 의도 파악 문제

해석 화자는 "우리는 부서들 중 하나일 뿐입니다"라고 말할 때 무엇을 의도하는가?
(A) 결정이 곧 이루어져야 한다.
(B) 긴급한 회의가 잡힐 것이다.
(C) 요청이 이행될 수 없다.
(D) 해결책이 만족스럽지 않았다.

해설 질문의 인용어구(we are just one of the departments)가 언급된 주변을 주의 깊게 듣는다. "Someone asked if we could have staff members come into the office more often"이라며 누군가 직원들을 사무실에 더 자주 출근시킬 수 있는지 물었다고 한 후, "We must follow company policy."라며 우리는 회사 정책을 따라야 한다고 한 것을 통해 직원들을 사무실에 더 자주 출근시키라는 요청이 이행될 수 없다는 의도임을 알 수 있다. 따라서 (C)가 정답이다.

어휘 urgent adj. 긴급한, 시급한 fulfill v. 이행하다, 완료하다
solution n. 해결책

94 특정 세부 사항 문제

해석 화자에 따르면, 어떤 요인이 직무 만족도에 가장 큰 영향을 미치는가?
(A) 연간 보너스
(B) 휴가 정책
(C) 의료 보험
(D) 직원들 간의 유대감

해설 질문의 핵심 어구(job satisfaction the most)가 언급된 부분을 주의 깊게 듣는다. "I realize that regular, face-to-face interactions among workers influence job satisfaction the most"라며 직원들 간의 정기적인 대면 교류가 직무 만족도에 가장 큰 영향을 미친다는 것을 인식하고 있다고 하였다. 따라서 (D)가 정답이다.

[95-97] 🔊 영국식

Questions 95-97 refer to the following advertisement and price list.

> If you need a pair of hiking boots for the winter, Trek Master has you covered! ⁹⁵During the first week of November, many of our products will be up to 50 percent off to celebrate our 10th year of operation. You'll be able to pick from our most popular boots. ⁹⁶Included among these is our latest model made from recycled materials, which has been marked down to just 70 dollars. ⁹⁷Check how much our competitors charge, and you'll realize that you won't get a better deal anywhere else!

hiking boots 등산화 product n. 제품

celebrate v. 기념하다, 기리다   recycle v. 재활용하다, 재생하다
material n. 재료, 직물   competitor n. 경쟁업체, 참가자
charge v. 요금을 부과하다, 청구하다   deal n. 거래, 합의

해석
95-97번은 다음 광고와 가격 목록에 관한 문제입니다.

겨울을 대비한 하이킹 부츠가 필요하시다면 Trek Master가 도와드리겠습니다! ⁹⁵11월 첫째 주간 동안 운영 10주년을 기념하여 많은 제품들을 최대 50퍼센트 할인합니다. 저희의 가장 인기 있는 부츠 중에서 선택하실 수 있습니다. ⁹⁶이 중에는 재활용 재료로 만든 최신 모델이 포함되어 있으며, 가격은 단 70달러로 인하되었습니다. ⁹⁷저희의 경쟁업체들이 얼마로 값을 매겼는지 확인해 보시면, 다른 곳에서는 더 좋은 거래를 할 수 없다는 것을 알게 되실 것입니다!

| Trek Master 하이킹 부츠 ||
| *가격에 할인이 반영되어 있음 ||
제품	가격
Action Walk	90.70달러
Slope Ultra	65.00달러
Trail Runner	85.50달러
⁹⁶Route Plus	70.00달러

95 이유 문제

해설 할인의 이유는 무엇인가?
(A) 회사의 기념일을 기념하기 위해
(B) 여름의 시작을 축하하기 위해
(C) 새로운 매장 지점을 홍보하기 위해
(D) 새로운 재고를 위한 공간을 만들기 위해

해설 질문의 핵심 어구(reason for the sale)와 관련된 내용을 주의 깊게 듣는다. "During the first week of November, many of our products will be up to 50 percent off to celebrate our 10th year of operation."이라며 운영 10주년을 기념하기 위해 많은 제품들을 최대 50퍼센트 할인한다고 하였다. 따라서 (A)가 정답이다.

어휘 mark v. 기념하다, 표시하다   stock n. 재고

Paraphrasing

celebrate our 10th year of operation 운영 10주년을 기념하다
→ mark a company anniversary 회사 기념일을 기념하다

96 시각 자료 문제

해설 시각 자료를 보아라. 어떤 제품이 재활용된 재료로 만들어졌는가?
(A) Action Walk
(B) Slope Ultra
(C) Trail Runner
(D) Route Plus

해설 제시된 가격 목록의 정보를 확인한 후 질문의 핵심 어구(recycled materials)와 관련된 내용을 주의 깊게 듣는다. "Included among these is our latest model made from recycled materials, which has been marked down to just 70 dollars."라며 재활용된 재료들로 만든 최신 모델이 있는데, 이것들은 단돈 70달러까지 인하되었다고 하였고, 70달러인 제품은 Route Plus임을 가격 목록에서 알 수 있다. 따라서 (D)가 정답이다.

97 제안 문제

해설 화자는 청자들이 무엇을 하도록 권장하는가?
(A) 계정을 만든다.
(B) 쿠폰을 다운로드한다.
(C) 가격을 비교한다.
(D) 보증서를 확인한다.

해설 지문의 중후반에서 제안과 관련된 표현이 포함된 문장을 주의 깊게 듣는다. "Check how much our competitors charge"라며 다른 경쟁업체들이 얼마로 값을 매겼는지 확인하라고 하였다. 따라서 (C)가 정답이다.

어휘 account n. 계좌, 계정   compare v. 비교하다   warranty n. 보증서

[98-100] 🎧 미국식

Questions 98-100 refer to the following talk and map.

I'm happy to be working with all of you at the Cold Stream Campground. ⁹⁸**We increased the size of our facility last month**, so this will likely be our busiest summer. I'd like to start by showing you around since it's your first day. From here at the main entrance, we'll proceed to the campsites and then the pool. ⁹⁹**We'll end the tour at the playground, where you'll meet our assistant manager**, Beth Meyer. She's supervising the repairs to some equipment there. Before we begin, ¹⁰⁰**please make sure your name tags are properly attached to your uniforms**.

campground n. 캠핑장   increase v. 늘리다, 증가하다
facility n. 시설, 기능   entrance n. 입구
proceed to ~로 이동하다, ~에 이르다
assistant manager 부매니저, 대리   supervise v. 감독하다, 지도하다
equipment n. 장비, 용품   properly adv. 제대로, 적절히
attach v. 부착하다, 붙이다, 첨부하다

해석
98-100번은 다음 담화와 지도에 관한 문제입니다.

Cold Stream 캠핑장에서 여러분 모두와 함께 일할 수 있게 되어 기쁩니다. ⁹⁸저희는 지난달에 시설 규모를 늘렸기 때문에 이번 여름이 가장 바쁜 여름이 될 것 같습니다. 여러분들이 첫날이니 먼저 주변을 안내해 드리겠습니다. 우리는 이곳 정문에서 캠핑장으로 이동한 다음 수영장으로 이동할 것입니다. ⁹⁹놀이터에서 투어를 마칠 것인데, 그곳에서 저희의 부매니저인 Beth Meyer를 만날 것입니다. 그녀는 그곳에서 장비 수리를 감독하고 있습니다. 시작하기 전에 ¹⁰⁰유니폼에 명찰이 제대로 부착되어 있는지 확인하세요.

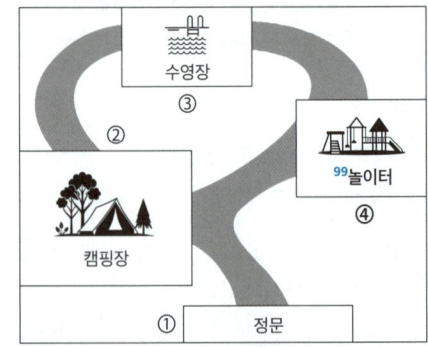

98 특정 세부 사항 문제

해석 화자에 따르면, 최근에 무엇이 완료되었는가?
(A) 직원 오리엔테이션
(B) 안전 점검
(C) 배달 주문
(D) 부지 확장

해설 질문의 핵심 어구(recently completed)와 관련된 내용을 주의 깊게 듣는다. "We increased the size of our facility last month"라며 지난달에 시설 규모를 늘렸다고 하였다. 따라서 (D)가 정답이다.

어휘 inspection n. 점검 expansion n. 확장

Paraphrasing

increased the size of ~ facility 시설 규모를 늘렸다 → site expansion 부지 확장

99 시각 자료 문제

해석 시각 자료를 보아라. 청자들은 어디에서 부매니저를 만날 것인가?
(A) 1번 위치에서
(B) 2번 위치에서
(C) 3번 위치에서
(D) 4번 위치에서

해설 제시된 지도의 정보를 확인한 후 질문의 핵심 어구(meet the assistant manager)와 관련된 내용을 주의 깊게 듣는다. "We'll end the tour at the playground, where you'll meet our assistant manager"라며 투어가 끝나는 놀이터에서 부매니저를 만날 것이라고 하였고, 놀이터는 4번 위치임을 지도에서 알 수 있다. 따라서 (D)가 정답이다.

100 요청 문제

해석 청자들은 무엇을 하도록 지시받는가?
(A) 평면도를 가지고 온다.
(B) 이름표를 착용한다.
(C) 기기를 수리한다.
(D) 다른 경로를 이용한다.

해설 지문의 중후반에서 요청과 관련된 표현이 포함된 문장을 주의 깊게 듣는다. "please make sure your name tags are properly attached to your uniforms"라며 유니폼에 명찰이 제대로 부착되어 있는지 확인하라고 하였다. 따라서 (B)가 정답이다.

어휘 floor plan 평면도 route n. 경로, 길

Paraphrasing

name tags ~ attached 명찰이 부착되어 있는 → Wear ~ name badge 이름표를 착용하다

PART 5

101 전치사 채우기

해설 '표지판은 카페 입구 옆에 놓여 있다'라는 의미가 되어야 하므로 위치를 나타내는 전치사 (B) beside(~ 옆에)가 정답이다. (A) down은 '아래쪽으로', (C) prior to는 '~에 앞서, 먼저', (D) aside from은 '~ 외에는'이라는 의미이다.

해석 표지판은 카페 입구 옆에 놓여 있어서 들어오는 모든 사람들은 그것을 볼 것이다.

어휘 position v. 놓다, 두다; n. 위치, 자리 entrance n. 입구

102 부사 자리 채우기

해설 조동사(will)와 동사(renew) 사이에 올 수 있는 것은 부사이므로 부사 (C) automatically(자동으로)가 정답이다. 형용사 (A), 명사 (B), 동사 (D)는 조동사와 동사 사이에 올 수 없다.

해석 귀하의 Mod 잡지에 대한 구독은 귀하가 그것을 취소하기 위해 저희에게 연락하지 않는 한 자동으로 갱신될 것입니다.

어휘 subscription n. 구독 renew v. 갱신되다, 재개하다

103 동사 어휘 고르기

해설 '박물관은 정기적으로 현대의 작품들을 전시하다'라는 문맥이므로 동사 showcase(전시하다)의 3인칭 단수형 (C) showcases가 정답이다. (A)의 tolerate는 '참다', (B)의 instruct는 '지시하다', (D)의 operate은 '운영하다'라는 의미이다.

해석 오래된 작품들에 더해, Sprockwell 박물관은 정기적으로 현대의 작품들을 전시한다.

어휘 regularly adv. 정기적으로 contemporary adj. 현대의, 동시대의

104 현재분사와 과거분사 구별하여 채우기

해설 빈칸 뒤의 명사(time)를 꾸밀 수 있는 것은 형용사이므로 형용사 역할을 하는 과거분사 (B)와 현재분사 (C)가 정답의 후보이다. 꾸밈을 받는 명사와 분사가 '시간이 지정되다'라는 수동의 의미이므로 과거분사 (B) designated(지정된)가 정답이다. 현재분사 (C) designating(지정하는)을 쓰면 '시간이 (무언가를) 지정하다'라는 어색한 의미가 되므로 답이 될 수 없다. 동사 (A)는 명사를 꾸밀 수 없고, 명사 (D)는 time과 복합 명사를 이루지 않으므로 답이 될 수 없다.

해석 고객들은 그들의 주문품을 가져가기 위해 지정된 시간에 도착할 것이 권장된다.

어휘 encourage v. 권장하다, 장려하다

105 부사 어휘 고르기

해설 '전화 회의는 정확히 오전 9시 30분에 시작할 것이다'라는 문맥이므로 (A) precisely(정확히)가 정답이다. (B) hourly는 '1시간마다', (C) spaciously는 '넓게', (D) simultaneously는 '동시에'라는 의미이다.

해석 Mr. Kline의 Henner 산업사 재정 고문과의 전화 회의는 정확히 오전

9시 30분에 시작할 것이다.

어휘 conference call 전화 회의 advisor n. 고문, 조언자

> **최신토익경향**
>
> 최근 부사 어휘 문제로 숫자를 수식하는 부사가 자주 출제되고 있다. 아래의 부사들을 알아두면 숫자 앞에 빈칸이 나왔을 때 빠르게 정답을 고를 수 있다.
>
> <시간이나 수량 표현 앞에 오는 부사>
> - approximately 대략, 거의
> - nearly 거의
> - promptly 정확히
> - roughly 대략
> - exactly 정확히
> - around 대략

106 최상급 표현 채우기

해설 빈칸 뒤의 명사(speakers)를 꾸밀 수 있는 것은 형용사이므로 형용사 persuasive(설득력 있는)의 최상급 형태인 (D) most persuasive가 정답이다. 참고로, 최상급 관련 표현 'one of the 최상급 + 복수 명사 (가장 -한 ~ 중 하나)'를 알아둔다.

해석 법무팀장은 그 사업 협상 내내 가장 설득력 있는 연사들 중 한 명이었다.

어휘 negotiation n. 협상

107 형용사 어휘 고르기

해설 '재고 정리 세일 동안 상당한 할인을 제공하다'라는 문맥이므로 (D) significant(상당한, 아주 큰)가 정답이다. (A) reputable은 '평판이 좋은', (B) disposable은 '일회용의, 처분할 수 있는', (C) redundant는 '불필요한, 쓸모없는'이라는 의미이다.

해석 Trett 전자제품사는 연례 재고 정리 세일 동안 모든 전자 기기에 대해 상당한 할인을 제공한다.

어휘 annual adj. 연례의, 매년의 clearance sale 재고 정리 세일

108 부사 자리 채우기

해설 동사(is based)를 꾸밀 수 있는 것은 부사이므로 부사 (C) loosely(막연하게, 느슨하게)가 정답이다. 형용사 또는 동사 (A), 동사 또는 과거분사 (B), 동사 (D)는 동사를 꾸밀 수 없다.

해석 공연 Gallegos Manor는 막연하게 역사적 사건을 기반으로 하며, 몇몇 등장인물과 사건들은 허구이다.

어휘 historical adj. 역사적인, 역사와 관련된
fictional adj. 허구의, 지어낸

109 전치사 채우기

해설 이 문장은 주어(the community), 동사(arranged), 목적어(a successful ~ event)를 갖춘 완전한 절이므로, ____ ~ group은 수식어 거품으로 보아야 한다. 이 수식어 거품은 동사가 없는 거품구이므로, 거품구를 이끌 수 있는 전치사 (A), (B), (D)가 정답의 후보이다. '자원봉사 단체의 도움으로 성공적인 동네 청소 행사를 준비했다'라는 의미가 되어야 하므로 '~로'의 의미를 갖는 전치사 (B) With가 정답이다. (A) In은 '~에, ~ 안에', (D) For는 '~을 위해, ~을 향하여'라는 의미이다. 형용사 또는 부사 (C) Only(유일한; 오직 ~만)는 수식어 거품구를 이끌 수 없다.

해석 지역 자원봉사 단체의 도움으로, 그 지역사회는 성공적인 동네 청소 행사를 준비했다.

어휘 cleanup n. (대)청소

110 형용사 자리 채우기

해설 2형식 동사 become은 주격 보어를 가지는 동사이고, 빈칸이 동사(became) 뒤에 왔으므로 주격 보어 자리에 올 수 있는 형용사 (A)와 명사 (D)가 정답의 후보이다. '디자인팀 내 압박이 극심해졌다'라는 의미로, 주격 보어가 주어(pressure)의 상태를 설명하고 있으므로 형용사 (A) intense(극심한, 강렬한)가 정답이다. 명사 (D)를 쓰면 주어와 동격이 되어 '압박이 극심함이 되다'라는 어색한 의미가 되므로 답이 될 수 없다. 동사 (B)와 부사 (C)는 주격 보어 자리에 올 수 없다.

해석 제출을 위한 마감 기한이 다가오자, 디자인팀 내의 압박이 극심해졌다.

어휘 submission n. 제출 approach v. 다가오다, 접근하다
pressure n. 압력

111 부사 어휘 고르기

해설 '다가오는 프로젝트들을 위해 숙련된 근로자들을 적극적으로 찾고 있다'라는 문맥이므로 (B) actively(적극적으로)가 정답이다. (A) deceptively는 '현혹될 정도로, 믿을 수 없게', (C) infinitely는 '무한히, 대단히', (D) loyally는 '충성스럽게'라는 의미이다.

해석 Milestone 건설사는 다가오는 프로젝트들을 위해 매우 다양한 숙련된 근로자들을 적극적으로 찾고 있다.

어휘 seek v. 찾다, 구하다 a wide variety of 매우 다양한

112 명사 자리 채우기

해설 문장에서 동사(has led to) 앞에 위치한 ____ in the housing market은 주어이고, 주어 자리에 오면서 전치사(in) 앞에 올 수 있는 것은 명사이므로 명사 (D) Weakness(약세, 약점)가 정답이다. 형용사 (A), 동사 (B)와 (C)는 주어 자리에 올 수 없다.

해석 주택 시장의 약세는 부동산 가치 하락으로 이어졌다.

어휘 decline n. 하락, 감소 property n. 부동산, 자산 value n. 가치

113 전치사 채우기

해설 '두 번째 면접을 위해 다시 오도록 선정된 지원자들 중 한 명이다'라는 의미가 되어야 하므로 전치사 (D) among(~ 중 한 명, ~ 중 하나)이 정답이다. 'be동사 + among + 복수 명사(~들 중 한 명/하나이다)'의 구조를 알아두자. (A) from은 '~로부터', (B) except는 '~을 제외하고', (C) onto는 '~ 위에, ~을 향하여'라는 의미이다.

해석 Joseph Tanner는 두 번째 면접을 위해 다시 오도록 선정된 지원자들 중 한 명이었다.

어휘 return v. 다시 (돌아)오다

114 사람명사와 사물/추상명사 구별하여 채우기

해설 부정관사(a)와 전치사(for) 사이에 올 수 있는 것은 명사이므로 명사 (A)와 (C)가 정답의 후보이다. '프린터들은 용지의 정렬을 조정하

는 기계 장치를 포함한다'라는 의미가 되어야 하므로 사물명사 (C) mechanism(기계 장치)이 정답이다. 사람명사 (A) mechanic(정비공)을 쓸 경우 '프린터가 정비공을 포함한다'라는 어색한 의미가 되므로 답이 될 수 없다. 동사 (B), 형용사 (D)는 명사 자리에 올 수 없다.

해석 프린터들은 용지 걸림을 방지하기 위해 용지의 정렬을 조정하는 기계 장치를 포함한다.

어휘 adjust v. 조정하다, 적응하다 alignment n. 정렬, 배열
jam n. (기계에 무엇이) 걸림, 막힘

115 동사 어휘 고르기

해설 '스타 선수가 벤치에 있는 상황에서, 승리할 것이라고 아무도 예상하지 못하다'라는 문맥이므로 expect(예상하다)의 과거형 (C) expected가 정답이다. (A)의 issue는 '발행하다', (B)의 approve는 '승인하다', (D)의 reveal은 '(비밀 등을) 밝히다'라는 의미이다.

해석 팀의 스타 선수가 벤치에 있는 상황에서, Paulsburg Pumas가 그렇게 압도적으로 승리할 것이라고는 아무도 예상하지 못했다.

어휘 decisively adv. 압도적으로, 결정적으로

116 격에 맞는 인칭대명사 채우기

해설 명사(staff) 앞에서 형용사처럼 명사를 꾸밀 수 있는 인칭대명사는 소유격이므로 소유격 인칭대명사 (B) its가 정답이다. 목적격 인칭대명사 (A), 재귀대명사 (C), 소유대명사 (D)는 명사를 꾸밀 수 없다.

해석 Harper 제조사는 자사의 직원들에게 다음 달에 있을 회사 워크숍의 주제를 제안하도록 권장하고 있다.

어휘 propose v. 제안하다 theme n. 주제, 테마

117 명사 어휘 고르기

해설 '임대차 계약에는 고려되어야 할 여러 조항들이 있다'라는 문맥이므로 명사 provision(조항)의 복수형 (B) provisions가 정답이다. (A)의 quality(품질, 특성)도 해석상 그럴듯해 보이지만 상품 또는 사람의 품질(자질)이나 특성을 나타내는 단어이므로 '계약'과는 어울리지 않는다. (C)의 appointment는 '약속', (D)의 capability는 '능력, 역량'이라는 의미이다.

해석 사무실 공간에 대한 임대차 계약에는 조기 해지에 관한 조항을 포함하여 고려되어야 할 여러 조항들이 있다.

어휘 lease n. 임대차 계약 consider v. 고려하다
premature adj. 조기의, 이른 termination n. 해지, 종료

최신 토익 경향

최근 PART 5에서는 어휘 문제의 오답률이 높은 편이다. 문맥상 빈칸에 들어갔을 때 그럴듯한 의미를 가진 어휘가 오답 보기로 나오기 때문에 어휘의 정확한 뜻과 쓰임을 알고 있어야 한다.

<최근 출제되었던 문맥상 혼동하기 쉬운 명사 어휘>
We invited [**feedback** / funding] on our new environmental protection policy.
우리는 새로운 환경 보호 정책에 대한 의견을 요청했다.

* 동사 invite가 '요청하다'라는 의미일 때는 무언가를 제안하거나 제출하는 것을 요청하는 경우에 쓰이므로 funding(자금)은 문맥상 어울리지 않는다.

Arin Travel Agency caters to various [guides / **interests**], from domestic to international travel.
Arin 여행사는 국내 여행부터 해외 여행까지 다양한 관심사를 충족시킨다.

* guide(가이드)는 서비스를 제공하는 주체로서 '(서비스를 제공하여) ~을 충족시키다'라는 의미의 cater to와 어울리지 않는다.

118 부사 자리 채우기

해설 빈칸 뒤의 동사(agreed)를 꾸밀 수 있는 것은 부사이므로 부사 (C) finally(마침내)가 정답이다. 형용사 (A), 동사 또는 과거분사 (B), 명사 (D)는 부사 자리에 올 수 없다.

해석 철저한 위험 평가를 실시한 후에, Connel 보험사는 마침내 그 기술 스타트업에 자금을 대기로 합의했다.

어휘 thorough adj. 철저한, 빈틈없는 assessment n. 평가
fund v. 자금을 대다

119 부사절 접속사 채우기

해설 이 문장은 필수 성분(Ms. Jin ~ her indoor cycling class)을 갖춘 완전한 절이므로 ____ ~ tried는 수식어 거품으로 보아야 한다. 이 수식어 거품은 동사(tried)가 있는 거품절이므로, 거품절을 이끌 수 있는 부사절 접속사 (A)와 (C)가 정답의 후보이다. 빈칸 뒤의 부사(hard)를 꾸미면서 '아무리 열심히 그녀가 시도해도, 따라잡을 수 없다'라는 의미가 되어야 하므로 복합관계부사 (A) However(아무리 ~해도)가 정답이다. (C) Even if(비록 ~이지만)는 부사를 꾸밀 수 없으므로 답이 될 수 없다. 참고로, 복합관계부사 however는 'however + 형용사/부사 + 주어 + 동사'의 형태로 자주 쓰임을 알아둔다. 부사 (B) Fairly(상당히, 꽤)와 (D) Somehow(어떻게든, 왠지)는 거품절을 이끌 수 없다.

해석 아무리 열심히 그녀가 시도해도, Ms. Jin은 나머지 실내 사이클링 수업을 따라잡을 수 없었다.

어휘 hard adv. 열심히, 세게; adj. 어려운, 굳은
keep up with ~를 따라잡다, ~에 뒤지지 않다

120 주어와 수일치하는 동사 채우기

해설 문장에 주어(sales associates)만 있고 동사가 없으므로 동사 (B)와 (C)가 정답의 후보이다. 주어가 복수 명사이므로 동사 (C) receive(받다)가 정답이다. 3인칭 단수형 (B)는 단수 주어와 함께 써야 한다. 동명사 또는 현재분사 (A)와 명사 (D)는 동사 자리에 올 수 없다.

해석 Acuo 의류사에서, 판매 직원들은 그들이 성사시키는 각 거래에 대해 15퍼센트의 수수료를 받는다.

어휘 sales associate 판매 직원, 영업 사원
commission n. 수수료, 커미션

121 형용사 어휘 고르기

해설 '많은 불만이 유입되기 시작한 후에 직원 교육 프로그램이 업데이트되다'라는 문맥이므로 (B) numerous(많은)가 정답이다. (A) responsible은 '책임이 있는', (C) average는 '평균의', (D) tolerant는 '관대한'이라는 의미이다.

해석 고객 서비스와 관련된 많은 불만이 유입되기 시작한 후에 직원 교육

프로그램이 업데이트되었다.

어휘 related to ~와 관련된

122 전치사 채우기

해설 빈칸 뒤의 and와 함께 쓰이면서 '마케팅팀과 연구 부서 간의 협업'이라는 의미가 되어야 하므로 (A) between(~ 간의, ~ 사이에)이 정답이다. (B) over는 '~ 동안, ~ 위에, ~이 넘는', (C) toward는 '~을 향하여', (D) behind는 '~ 뒤에'라는 의미이다.

해설 마케팅팀과 연구 부서 간의 협업의 결과로 성공적인 제품 출시가 이루어졌다.

어휘 collaboration n. 협업, 공동 작업   department n. 부서
launch n. 출시, 개시

123 형용사 어휘 고르기

해설 '오리엔테이션 세션은 신입 직원들이 정책에 대해 잘 알게 하다'라는 문맥이므로 (C) knowledgeable(잘 아는)이 정답이다. (A) acquainted(알고 있는, 접한 적이 있는)도 해석상 그럴듯해 보이지만 acquainted는 전치사 with와 함께 쓰이므로 답이 될 수 없다. (be acquainted with: ~을 알고 있다, ~와 아는 사이가 되다) (B) effective는 '효과적인, 유능한', (D) convenient는 '편리한'이라는 의미이다.

해설 오리엔테이션 세션은 반드시 모든 신입 직원들이 Pittman 금융사의 정책에 대해 잘 알게 한다.

어휘 ensure v. 반드시 ~하게 하다, 보장하다   policy n. 정책

124 부사절 접속사 채우기

해설 빈칸은 절(Additional staff members ~ hired)과 절(Murillo Department Store could extend ~ the holiday season)을 연결할 수 있는 접속사 자리이므로 부사절 접속사 (B)와 (D), 등위접속사 (C)가 정답의 후보이다. '영업시간을 연장할 수 있도록 하기 위해 추가 직원들이 고용되었다'라는 의미가 되어야 하므로 목적을 나타내는 부사절 접속사 (B) so that(~하도록 하기 위해서)이 정답이다. (C) or else는 '그렇지 않으면', (D) only if는 '~해야만'이라는 의미로 각각 어색한 문맥을 만들기 때문에 답이 될 수 없다. 형용사 또는 부사 (A) in effect(시행 중인; 사실상)는 절과 절을 연결할 수 없다.

해설 Murillo 백화점이 연휴 시즌 동안 영업시간을 연장할 수 있도록 하기 위해 추가 직원들이 고용되었다.

어휘 additional adj. 추가의   hire v. 고용하다
extend v. 연장하다, 확대하다   operating hours 영업시간

125 형용사 자리 채우기

해설 빈칸 앞에 be동사(are)가 있으므로 be동사의 보어 자리에 올 수 있는 명사 (A), (D)와 현재분사 (B), 형용사 (C)의 모든 보기가 정답의 후보이다. 주어(Tickets)와 보어가 '표는 양도할 수 없다'라는 의미가 되어야 하므로 형용사 (C) transferable(양도 가능한)이 정답이다. 명사 (A) transfer(이전, 옮김)를 쓸 경우 '표는 이전이 아니다'라는 어색한 의미가 되고, 명사 (D) transferability(이동성)를 쓸 경우 '표는 이동성이 아니다'라는 어색한 의미가 되므로 답이 될 수 없다. 현재분사

(B) transferring을 쓸 경우 '구독은 다른 사람에게 이동하지 않고 있다'라는 어색한 의미를 만들기 때문에 답이 될 수 없다.

해설 Western 항공사의 모든 항공편을 위해 구입된 표들은 다른 사람에게 양도할 수 없다.

어휘 purchase v. 구입하다

126 명사 자리 채우기

해설 빈칸 앞의 소유격(The CEO's)의 꾸밈을 받을 수 있는 것은 명사이므로 명사 (D) appearance(나타남, 출현)가 정답이다. 동사 (A)와 (B), to 부정사 (C)는 소유격의 꾸밈을 받을 수 없다.

해설 대표이사의 자선 갈라 행사 참석은 지역사회에 환원하고자 하는 Daugherty사의 헌신을 보여주었다.

어휘 charity n. 자선, 자선 단체   demonstrate v. 보여주다, 입증하다
dedication n. 헌신, 전념

127 동사 어휘 고르기

해설 '습지대와 숲을 보존하는 데 전념하다'라는 문맥이므로 동사 preserve(보존하다)의 동명사형 (A) preserving이 정답이다. (B)의 devote는 '헌신하다' (C)의 donate는 '기부하다', (D)의 enclose는 '둘러싸다'라는 의미이다.

해설 Meltonville은 지역 야생동물의 자연 서식지 역할을 하는 습지대와 숲을 보존하는 데 전념한다.

어휘 be committed to ~에 전념하다, 헌신하다   wetland n. 습지(대)
habitat n. 서식지

128 부정대명사 채우기

해설 빈칸 앞 동명사(reviewing)의 목적어 자리에 오면서 빈칸 뒤 전치사(of) 앞에 올 수 있는 것은 명사이므로 부정대명사 (A), (B), (C)가 정답의 후보이다. '다수의 제안들을 검토한 후 가장 비용 효율적인 옵션을 선택했다'라는 의미가 되어야 하므로 부정대명사 (B) many(다수)가 정답이다. 참고로, 'many + (of the) + 복수 명사'의 표현을 덩어리로 암기해 두자. (A) others는 '이미 언급한 것 이외의 것들 중 몇몇'을 나타내고, (C) anyone은 '누구나'라는 의미로 사람을 가리킬 때 쓰이므로 답이 될 수 없다. 목적격 관계대명사 또는 의문대명사 (D) whom은 전치사 앞에 올 수 없다.

해설 광고 캠페인에 대한 다수의 제안들을 검토한 후 위원회는 가장 비용 효율적인 옵션을 선택했다.

어휘 proposal n. 제안   advertising n. 광고   committee n. 위원회
cost-effective adj. 비용 효율적인, 비용 효율이 높은

129 올바른 시제의 동사 채우기

해설 주절에 주어(Ms. Buckley)만 있고 동사가 없으므로 동사 (A), (B), (D)가 정답의 후보이다. 주절(Ms. Buckley ~ supplier)에서 나타내는 사건, 즉 Ms. Buckley가 직물 공급업체를 만난 시점은 before가 이끄는 절(she confirmed ~ purchase)에서 나타내는 사건, 즉 Ms. Buckley가 대량 구매를 위한 계약 조건을 확정한 것보다 먼저 일어난 일이다. before가 이끄는 절에 과거 시제 동사(confirmed)가 쓰였으므로 과거의 특정 시점 이전에 발생한 일을 표현할 수 있는

과거완료 시제 (B) had met이 정답이다.

해석 Ms. Buckley는 대량 구매를 위한 계약 조건을 확정하기 전에 직물 공급업체와 만났다.

어휘 fabric n. 직물, 천 supplier n. 공급업체, 공급자
terms and conditions 계약 조건
bulk adj. 대량의; n. (큰) 규모, 대부분

130 형용사 어휘 고르기

해설 '융통성 있는 요리 스타일로 다양한 국제 손님들의 입맛에 맞는 요리를 만들어내다'라는 문맥이므로 (B) adaptable(융통성 있는, 적응할 수 있는)이 정답이다. (A) overall은 '전반적인', (C) incomplete는 '불완전한', (D) identical은 '동일한, 똑같은'이라는 의미이다.

해석 융통성 있는 요리 스타일로, 그 호텔의 요리사들은 다양한 국제 손님들의 입맛에 맞는 요리를 성공적으로 만들어냈다.

어휘 tailor v. (~에 맞춰서) 만들어내다, 조정하다; n. 재단사
suit v. 맞다, 적합하다 taste n. 입맛, 기호

PART 6

131-134번은 다음 공고에 관한 문제입니다.

> 모든 직원들에게 알림
>
> ¹³¹저는 Henderson 식품점이 셀프서비스 키오스크들을 설치할 것이라는 점을 알리게 되어 기쁩니다. 설치는 다음 주 월요일에 시작될 예정이고 동일한 주 이내에 완료될 것입니다. ¹³²이 키오스크들은 고객들이 그들의 구매를 자유롭게 계산할 수 있게 하기 위해 고안되었습니다. 이것은 향상된 고객 만족을 가져올 것입니다.
>
> ¹³³물론, 이 키오스크들의 도입이 우리 계산원들의 중요성을 감소시키는 것은 아닙니다. 모든 계산원들은 고객들이 필요로 할 때 도움을 줄 수 있도록 키오스크 사용 방법을 교육받을 것입니다. ¹³⁴교육 일정은 휴게실에 게시되어 있습니다.
>
> installation n. 설치 enhanced adj. 향상된 satisfaction n. 만족
> introduction n. 도입, 소개 diminish v. 감소하다, 줄어들다

131 올바른 시제의 동사 채우기 주변 문맥 파악

해설 'Henderson 식품점이 셀프서비스 키오스크들을 설치하다'라는 문맥인데, 이 경우 빈칸이 있는 문장만으로는 올바른 시제의 동사를 고를 수 없으므로 주변 문맥이나 전체 문맥을 파악하여 정답을 고른다. 뒤 문장에서 '설치는 다음 주 월요일에 시작될 예정이고 동일한 주 이내에 완료될 것이다(The installation is scheduled to begin next Monday and should be completed within the same week).'라고 했으므로, 설치가 이뤄지는 시점이 미래임을 알 수 있다. 따라서 미래 시제 (D) will install이 정답이다.

132 부사 자리 채우기

해설 빈칸 앞의 동사(check out)를 꾸밀 수 있는 것은 부사이므로, 부사 (D) independently(자유롭게, 독립적으로)가 정답이다. 형용사 (A), 명사 (B)와 (C)는 동사를 꾸밀 수 없다.

어휘 independent adj. 독립적인, 자유의 independence n. 독립, 자립
independency n. 독립, 자주

133 접속부사 채우기 전체 문맥 파악

해설 빈칸이 콤마와 함께 문장의 맨 앞에 온 접속부사 자리이므로, 앞부분과 빈칸이 있는 문장의 의미 관계를 파악하여 정답을 선택한다. 앞부분에서 Henderson 식품점이 셀프서비스 키오스크들을 설치할 것이고 이것이 향상된 고객 만족을 가져올 것이라고 했고, 빈칸이 있는 문장에서는 이 키오스크들의 도입이 우리 계산원들의 중요성을 감소시키는 것은 아니라고 했으므로, 이어질 내용의 당위성을 강조하기 위해 사용되는 (B) Of course(물론)가 정답이다.

어휘 alternatively adv. 그 대신에, 그렇지 않으면
on the other hand adv. 반면에, 다른 한편으로는
in that case adv. 그렇다면, 그런 경우에는

134 알맞은 문장 고르기

해석 (A) 키오스크 화면은 점내 할인에 대한 광고를 보여줄 것입니다.
(B) 교육 일정은 휴게실에 게시되어 있습니다.
(C) 고객들은 그들의 돈에 대해 좋은 가치를 제공하는 제품들을 선호합니다.
(D) 우리는 고객들에게 이 기계들과 관련된 의견을 전달해 줄 것을 권장합니다.

해설 앞 문장 'All cashiers will receive training on how to use the kiosks so they can assist customers when necessary.'에서 모든 계산원들이 고객들이 필요로 할 때 도움을 줄 수 있도록 키오스크 사용 방법을 교육받을 것이라고 했으므로, 빈칸에는 교육과 관련된 내용이 들어가야 함을 알 수 있다. 따라서 (B)가 정답이다.

어휘 favor v. 선호하다

135-138번은 다음 광고에 관한 문제입니다.

> 저희는 Quentin 가구 도매점의 개업을 알리게 되어 매우 기쁩니다! ¹³⁵기념하기 위해, 저희는 여러분이 놓치고 싶지 않을 할인 행사를 진행합니다. 4월 2일부터 16일까지, 독점적인 혜택들과 더 이상 좋을 수 없는 할인을 위해 저희와 함께하세요.
>
> ¹³⁶여러분의 집을 바꾸어 보세요! 여러분이 찾고 계시는 것이 무엇이든 상관없이, 저희는 여러분의 공간을 여러분이 원하는 집으로 바꾸는 데 도움을 드릴 것을 약속합니다. 이에 더해, 500달러 이상의 모든 구매에 대해 여러분은 무료 물품을 받으실 것입니다. ¹³⁷이 선물들은 저희의 광대한 범위의 집 장식 제품 중에서 선택될 수 있습니다. ¹³⁸만약 여러분이 집의 인테리어를 새롭게 하는 것을 생각하고 계신다면, 지금이 완벽한 시기입니다. 오늘 Hemlock로 437번지에서 저희를 방문하세요!
>
> exclusive adj. 독점적인, 단독의
> unbeatable adj. 더 이상 좋을 수 없는, 타의 추종을 불허하는
> complimentary adj. 무료의 refresh v. 새롭게 하다

135 알맞은 문장 고르기

해석 (A) 저희의 디자인 전문가 중 한 명과 상담을 예약하세요.
(B) 평생 보증이 모든 침대 프레임에 포함됩니다.
(C) 기념하기 위해, 저희는 여러분이 놓치고 싶지 않을 할인 행사를 진행합니다.
(D) 개장 행사는 눈에 띄게 성공적이었습니다.

해설 뒤 문장 'From April 2 to 16, join us for exclusive offers and unbeatable discounts.'에서 4월 2일부터 16일까지 독점적인 혜택들과 더 이상 좋을 수 없는 할인을 위해 자신들과 함께하라고 권하고 있으므로, 빈칸에는 할인 행사와 관련된 내용이 들어가야 함을 알 수 있다. 따라서 (C)가 정답이다.

어휘 consultation n. 상담 expert n. 전문가 warranty n. 보증
outstanding adj. 눈에 띄는

136 동사 어휘 고르기 주변 문맥 파악

해설 '여러분의 집을 ____ 보세요'라는 문맥이므로 모든 보기가 정답의 후보이다. 빈칸이 있는 문장만으로 정답을 고를 수 없으므로 주변 문맥이나 전체 문맥을 파악한다. 뒤 문장에서 '여러분이 찾고 계시는 것이 무엇이든 상관없이, 저희는 여러분의 공간을 여러분이 원하는 집으로 바꾸는 데 도움을 드릴 것을 약속한다(No matter what you're looking for, we promise we can help you turn your space into the home you want).'라고 했으므로, 집을 바꾸어 보라고 권하고 있음을 알 수 있다. 따라서 (B) Transform(바꾸다)이 정답이다. (A) Appreciate는 '가치를 인정하다', (C) Maintain은 '유지하다, 지속하다', (D) Rent는 '빌리다'라는 의미이다.

137 형용사 어휘 고르기

해설 '광대한 범위의 집 장식 제품 중에서 선택될 수 있다'라는 문맥이므로 (A) extensive(광대한)가 정답이다. (B) defective는 '결함이 있는', (C) compatible은 '호환이 되는', (D) dominant는 '지배적인, 우세한'이라는 의미이다.

138 부사절 접속사 채우기

해설 '만약 여러분이 집의 인테리어를 새롭게 하는 것을 생각하고 있다면, 지금이 완벽한 시기이다'라는 의미가 되어야 하므로, 조건을 나타내는 부사절 접속사 (D) If(만약 ~라면)가 정답이다. (A) When은 '~할 때', (B) Although는 '비록 ~일지라도', (C) While은 '~하는 동안'이라는 의미이다.

139-142번은 다음 보도 자료에 관한 문제입니다.

즉각 보도용

루이빌 (3월 14일)—139오늘 앞서 이뤄진 언론 보도에서, Archer Books의 소유주 Rob Foley는 그 유명한 가게가 올해 7월 렉싱턴에 새로운 지점을 개업할 예정이라고 말하면서 루이빌 서점의 확장 계획을 발표했다.

그의 발표에서, Mr. Foley는 "140우리는 Archer Books의 빠른 성장에 대해 들떠있습니다. 141우리는 여러 중요한 이유들로 인해 렉싱턴을 선택했습니다. 그 도시의 최근 경제 호황과 그곳의 혁신에 대한 명성이 그것을 명백한 선택으로 만들었습니다."라고 말했다.

독립된 서점으로서, Archer Books는 현지 지역사회의 흥미를 반영한 출판물 목록을 보유하고 있다. 142그곳은 고객들에게 귀를 기울이고 그들의 요청에 응하여 책들을 주문한다.

statement n. 보도, 발표 economic adj. 경제의 boom n. 호황
reputation n. 명성 obvious adj. 명백한 reflect v. 반영하다

139 다른 명사를 수식하는 명사 채우기

해설 빈칸은 동사(revealed)의 목적어 자리이므로 빈칸 뒤 명사(plans)와 복합 명사를 이룰 수 있는 명사 (A)와 명사를 꾸밀 수 있는 현재분사 (D)가 정답의 후보이다. '새로운 지점을 개업할 예정이라고 말하면서 확장 계획을 발표했다'라는 의미가 되어야 하므로 '확장 계획'이라는 의미의 복합 명사 expansion plan을 만드는 명사 (A) expansion(확장)이 정답이다. 현재분사 (D) expanding은 '확장하고 있는'이라는 의미로 어색한 문맥을 만들기 때문에 답이 될 수 없다. 동사 (B)와 to 부정사 (C)는 명사 앞에서 명사를 꾸밀 수 없다.

어휘 expand v. 확장하다

140 형용사 어휘 고르기

해설 'Archer Books의 빠른 성장에 대해 들떠있다'라는 문맥이므로 (C) rapid(빠른)가 정답이다. (A) loud는 '소리가 큰', (B) brief는 '잠시의, 간결한', (D) single은 '단일의'라는 의미이다.

141 알맞은 문장 고르기

해석 (A) 우리의 지점들은 각각 작은 커피 가게를 특별히 포함할 것입니다.
(B) 공상 과학 및 판타지 장르는 대유행을 경험하고 있습니다.
(C) 우리는 여러 중요한 이유들로 인해 렉싱턴을 선택했습니다.
(D) 고객들은 그들이 구매할 때마다 포인트를 획득할 수 있습니다.

해설 뒤 문장 'The city's recent economic boom and its reputation for innovation made it the obvious choice.'에서 그 도시의 최근 경제 호황과 그곳의 혁신에 대한 명성이 그것을 명백한 선택으로 만들었다고 했으므로, 빈칸에는 렉싱턴을 선택한 이유와 관련된 내용이 들어가야 함을 알 수 있다. 따라서 (C)가 정답이다.

어휘 feature v. 특별히 포함하다 earn v. 획득하다

142 동사 어휘 고르기 주변 문맥 파악

해설 '그곳은 고객들에게 귀를 기울이고 그들의 요청에 응하여 책들을 ____ 하다'라는 문맥이므로 (A), (B), (D)가 정답의 후보이다. 빈칸이 있는 문장만으로 정답을 고를 수 없으므로 주변 문맥이나 전체 문맥을 파악한다. 앞 문장에서 '독립된 서점으로서, Archer Books는 현지 지역사회의 흥미를 반영한 출판물 목록을 보유한다(Being an independent bookstore, Archer Books has an inventory of publications that reflects the interests of the local community).'라고 했으므로, Archer Books가 소비자들의 요청에 응하여 책들을 주문한다는 것을 알 수 있다. 따라서 order(주문하다)의 3인칭 단수형 (A) orders가 정답이다. (B)의 write는 '쓰다', (C)의 borrow는 '빌리다', (D)의 organize는 '정리하다'라는 의미이다.

143-146번은 다음 웹페이지 정보에 관한 문제입니다.

¹⁴³Stan Office Essentials에서, 저희는 단순히 고품질의 사무실 장비를 공급하는 것에만 전념하지 않고 지속 가능성에도 관심을 가집니다. 저희가 더 환경친화적인 미래를 위해 노력하기 때문에, 저희는 낡은 프린터, 컴퓨터 및 기타 기기들에 대한 재활용 서비스를 제공합니다. ¹⁴⁴저희가 이 프로그램을 시작한 이후, 저희의 매장들은 그렇게 하지 않았다면 결국 매립지에 버려졌을 백만 파운드 이상의 기기들을 재활용해 왔습니다. 참여하시려면, 여러분의 기기들을 Stan Office Essentials의 어느 매장으로라도 접수 데스크로 가져오시기만 하면 됩니다. ¹⁴⁵일단 여러분의 기기가 Stan Office Essentials의 직원에 의해 평가되면, 여러분은 저희의 재활용 보상 프로그램에 참여할 자격을 얻게 될 것입니다. 여러분이 재활용하는 각각의 기기들에 대해, 여러분은 포인트를 얻으실 것입니다. ¹⁴⁶이것들은 가게의 모든 것에 대한 할인으로 교환될 수 있습니다.

dedicate v. 전념하다, 헌신하다 equipment n. 장비
landfill n. 매립지 eligible adj. 자격이 있는 device n. 기기
assess v. 평가하다

143 명사 어휘 고르기 주변 문맥 파악

해설 '고품질의 사무실 장비 공급에만 전념하지 않고 ____에도 관심을 가지다'라는 문맥이므로 모든 보기가 정답의 후보이다. 빈칸이 있는 문장만으로 정답을 고를 수 없으므로 주변 문맥이나 전체 문맥을 파악한다. 뒤 문장에서 '저희가 더 환경친화적인 미래를 위해 노력하기 때문에, 저희는 낡은 프린터, 컴퓨터 및 기타 기기들에 대한 재활용 서비스를 제공합니다(Because we are striving for a greener future, we offer a recycling service for old printers, computers, and other devices).'라고 했으므로, 환경을 보존하는 것에 관심이 있음을 알 수 있다. 따라서 (B) sustainability(지속 가능성)가 정답이다. (A) affordability는 '감당할 수 있는 비용', (C) diversity는 '다양성', (D) profitability는 '수익성'이라는 의미이다.

144 올바른 시제의 동사 채우기

해설 주절에 주어(our stores)만 있고 동사가 없으므로 모든 보기가 정답의 후보이다. '~한 이후'라는 의미의 부사절 접속사 Since가 종속절을 이끌고 있고 종속절 동사(started)의 시제가 과거이므로, 과거에 시작된 일이 현재까지 계속되는 것을 나타내는 현재완료 시제 (C) have recycled가 정답이다.

145 부사절 접속사 채우기 주변 문맥 파악

해설 이 문장은 필수성분(You'll be eligible ~ Recycling Rewards Program)을 갖춘 완전한 절이므로 ____ ~ associate는 수식어 거품으로 보아야 한다. 이 수식어 거품은 주어(your devices)와 동사 (are assessed)를 갖춘 완전한 절이므로 부사절 접속사 (B), (C), (D)가 정답의 후보이다. 빈칸이 있는 문장만으로 정답을 고를 수 없으므로 주변 문맥이나 전체 문맥을 파악한다. 앞 문장에서 '참여하시려면, 여러분의 기기들을 Stan Office Essentials의 어느 매장으로라도 접수 데스크로 가져오시기만 하면 됩니다(To participate, simply bring your devices to the drop-off desk in any Stan Office Essentials).'라고 했으므로, '(접수 데스크로 가져온) 기기가 일단 직원에 의해 평가되면, 재활용 보상 프로그램에 참여할 자격을

얻게 된다'는 것임을 알 수 있다. 따라서 (D) once(일단 ~하면)가 정답이다. (B) whether는 '~이든 아니든', (C) unless는 '~하지 않는 한'이라는 의미이다. 형용사 또는 부사 (A) further(추가의; 더 나아가는)는 거품절을 이끌 수 없다.

146 알맞은 문장 고르기

해설 (A) 이것들은 가게의 모든 것에 대한 할인으로 교환될 수 있습니다.
(B) 종이 없는 청구서 발송으로 전환하는 것은 천연자원을 절약합니다.
(C) Stan Office Essentials는 이제 배송 및 인쇄 서비스를 제공합니다.
(D) 저희는 다양한 친환경 제품들을 판매합니다.

해설 앞 문장 'For each device you recycle, you'll earn points.'에서 재활용하는 각각의 기기들에 대해 포인트를 얻을 것이라고 했으므로, 빈칸에는 포인트와 관련된 내용이 들어가야 함을 알 수 있다. 따라서 (A)가 정답이다.

어휘 redeem v. 교환하다, 상쇄하다 conserve v. 절약하다, 보호하다

PART 7

147-148번은 다음 공고에 관한 문제입니다.

공고

7월 7일에, 해충을 퇴치하기 위한 노력의 일환으로, ¹⁴⁷각 호실을 포함한 건물의 모든 구역에 살충제를 뿌릴 것입니다. 다음 일정을 참조하세요:

1층-3층: 오전 8시에서 오전 10시까지
4층-6층: 오전 10시 30분에서 오후 12시 30분까지
¹⁴⁸7층-9층: 오후 1시에서 오후 3시까지
10층-12층: 오후 3시 30분에서 오후 5시 30분까지

귀하의 아파트에 스프레이가 뿌려질 때 반려동물을 안전하게 보호하거나 이동시켜 주세요.

eliminate v. 없애다, 제거하다 pest n. 해충 pesticide n. 살충제
individual adj. 각각의 secure v. 안전하게 보호하다

147 추론 문제

해설 공지는 누구를 대상으로 하는 것 같은가?
(A) 주택 조사관
(B) 건물 주민
(C) 전문 요리사
(D) 환경미화원

해설 지문의 'all areas of the building, including individual units'에서 각 호실을 포함한 건물의 모든 구역이라고 했으므로 건물 주민을 대상으로 한다는 것을 추론할 수 있다. 따라서 (B)가 정답이다.

어휘 inspector n. 조사관, 감독관 resident n. 주민, 거주자
professional adj. 전문적인 sanitation worker n. 환경미화원

148 육하원칙 문제

해석 8층에서 살충제 살포는 몇 시까지 끝날 것인가?
(A) 오후 12시 30분
(B) 오후 1시
(C) 오후 3시
(D) 오후 5시 30분

해설 지문의 'Floors 7–9: 1:00 P.M. to 3:00 P.M.'에서 7층부터 9층은 오후 1시에서 오후 3시까지 살충제를 살포한다고 했으므로 (C)가 정답이다.

149-150번은 다음 이메일에 관한 문제입니다.

수신: w_schaefer@sportsplaza.com
발신: d_conway@conwaysonslandscaping.com
제목: 조경 제안
날짜: 5월 14일

Ms. Schaefer께,

이 이메일이 잘 전달되기를 바랍니다. 제 이름은 Daniel Conway이고, 아름다운 야외 공간을 조성하는 데 10년 이상의 경험을 보유한 가족 소유 기업인 Conway & Sons 조경 회사를 대표합니다. [149]45번가에 있는 귀하의 스포츠 복합 시설에 서비스를 제공하기 위해 이 글을 쓰고 있으며 귀하의 요구 사항을 논의하기 위해 만날 수 있는 자리를 마련하고 싶습니다. 저는 화요일부터 금요일까지 오후 2시 이후에 가능합니다.

제 제안에 관심이 있으시다면, [150]예산의 대략적인 견적을 제게 제공해주실 수 있나요? 제가 검토하고 어떤 서비스를 저희가 제공할 수 있는지 알려드리겠습니다. 감사합니다. 답변을 기다리겠습니다.

Daniel Conway 드림
Conway & Sons

---
landscaping n. 조경 proposal n. 제안, 제의
represent v. 대표하다 decade n. 10년
rough adj. 대략적인, 대강의 estimate n. 견적, 추정치

149 목적 찾기 문제

해석 이메일의 목적은 무엇인가?
(A) 만남을 요청하기 위해
(B) 계약을 마무리하기 위해
(C) 결제를 요구하기 위해
(D) 의견을 수집하기 위해

해설 지문의 'I am writing to offer our services to your sports complex on 45th Street and would like to arrange a meeting to discuss your requirements.'에서 45번가에 있는 귀하의 스포츠 복합 시설에 서비스를 제공하기 위해 이 글을 쓰고 있으며 귀하의 요구 사항을 논의하기 위해 만날 수 있는 자리를 마련하고 싶다고 했으므로 (A)가 정답이다.

어휘 finalize v. 마무리하다 contract n. 계약 demand v. 요구하다
payment n. 결제 collect v. 수집하다, 모으다

150 육하원칙 문제

해석 Mr. Conway는 Ms. Schaefer에게 어떤 정보를 요청하는가?
(A) 번지수
(B) 대략의 예산
(C) 프로젝트 일정표
(D) 현장 청사진

해설 지문의 'could you please provide me with a rough estimate of your budget?'에서 예산의 대략적인 견적을 제공해 줄 수 있는지 묻고 있으므로 (B)가 정답이다.

어휘 approximate adj. 대략의 site n. 현장, 장소 blueprint n. 청사진

Paraphrasing

a rough estimate of your budget 예산의 대략적인 견적 → An approximate budget 대략의 예산

151-152번은 다음 광고에 관한 문제입니다.

Chenille 호텔: 당신의 기억에 남을 휴양지

데번포트 국제공항에서 불과 50킬로미터 떨어진 곳에 위치한 Chenille 호텔은 대도시의 분주함으로부터 벗어날 수 있는 이상적인 장소입니다. [151]아름다운 Mendi 호수에서 카약을 타는 것을 즐기는 것에서부터 35에이커에 달하는 호텔 부지에 걸쳐 펼쳐진 자전거 도로에서 자전거를 타는 것까지 다양한 활동을 즐겨보세요. 당신이 자연에서 시간을 보내는 것을 즐긴다면, 여기는 당신을 위한 곳입니다.

[152-(A)]저희의 모든 객실은 Mendi 호수를 내려다보는 발코니와 편한 침대를 포함합니다. 그리고 만약 당신이 특별한 무언가를 찾고 있다면, 월풀 욕조, [152-(B)]완비된 주방, 그리고 업무를 따라잡기 위한 [152-(D)]분리된 사무 공간을 특징으로 하는 저희의 [152-(C)]디럭스 객실 중 하나를 고려해 보세요. 지금 555-8245로 전화하여 예약하세요!

---
getaway n. (휴가의) 휴양지 hustle and bustle 분주함
overlook v. 내려다보다 separate adj. 분리된, 따로 떨어진
catch up on ~을 따라잡다

151 추론 문제

해석 광고는 누구를 대상으로 하는 것 같은가?
(A) 야외 활동을 즐기는 사람들
(B) 역사적인 명소를 찾는 관광객들
(C) 학회에 참석하는 비즈니스 여행객들
(D) 아동 친화적인 시설을 필요로 하는 가족들

해설 지문의 'Enjoy a variety of activities, from kayaking on beautiful Lake Mendi to cycling the bicycle paths that stretch across the 35-acre hotel grounds. If you enjoy spending time in nature, this is the place for you.'에서 호수에서 카약을 타는 것을 즐기는 것에서부터 자전거를 타는 것까지 다양한 활동을 즐겨보라고 했고, 자연에서 시간을 보내는 것을 즐긴다면 여기는 당신을 위한 곳이라고 했으므로 야외 활동을 즐기는 사람들을 대상으로 한다는 것을 추론할 수 있다. 따라서 (A)가 정답이다.

어휘 historic adj. 역사적인 attraction n. 명소
child-friendly adj. 아동 친화적인

152 Not/True 문제

해석 디럭스 객실에 대해 언급되지 않은 것은?
(A) 호수 경관을 제공한다.
(B) 음식을 준비할 공간이 있다.
(C) 분리된 침실을 특징으로 한다.
(D) 업무를 할 공간을 포함한다.

해설 (A)는 'All of our rooms include a balcony overlooking Lake Mendi'에서 모든 객실은 Mendi 호수를 내려다보는 발코니가 있다고 했으므로 지문에 언급된 내용이다. (B)는 'a full kitchen'에서 완비된 주방이 있다고 했으므로 지문에 언급된 내용이다. (D)는 'a separate office area'에서 분리된 사무 공간이 있다고 했으므로 지문에 언급된 내용이다. (C)는 지문에 언급되지 않은 내용이다. 따라서 (C)가 정답이다.

어휘 prepare v. 준비하다

Paraphrasing

a full kitchen 완비된 주방 → an area to prepare food 음식을 준비할 공간
office area 사무 공간 → space to do work 업무를 할 공간

153-154번은 다음 문자 메시지 대화문에 관한 문제입니다.

Bryan Taylor [오전 9시 22분]
우리의 공기 정화 필터의 첫 번째 테스트에서 긍정적인 결과가 나왔어요. ¹⁵³알레르기 유발 항원 수가 증가하는 두 번째 테스트를 당신이 진두지휘할 수 있나요?

Justine Kinney [오전 9시 23분]
물론이죠. ¹⁵⁴자금 조달은 어떻게 되고 있나요?

Bryan Taylor [오전 9시 24분]
지금으로서는 충분해요. ¹⁵⁴우리의 연구 자금이 다음 테스트를 위해 충분할 거예요. 저는 나중에 잠재적 투자자들과 만날 예정이에요. 이미 실험실에 계시나요?

Justine Kinney [오전 9시 25분]
네. 저는 시제품을 일부 수정하기 위해 기술자들과 협력하고 있어요. 언제든지 저와 함께하셔도 돼요.

Bryan Taylor [오전 9시 26분]
좋아요. 곧 봐요.

air filter 공기 정화 필터 spearhead v. 진두지휘하다
allergen n. 알레르기 유발 항원 tweak n. 수정, 변경
prototype n. 시제품, 견본

153 추론 문제

해석 공기 정화 필터에 대해 암시된 것은?
(A) 의료 종사자들에게 광고되고 있다.
(B) 매장들로 배송되기를 대기하고 있다.
(C) 또 다른 테스트 단계를 거칠 것이다.
(D) 공식 기관에서 검사되고 있다.

해설 지문의 'Can you spearhead a second run in which the number of allergens is increased?'에서 Mr. Taylor가 Ms. Kinney에게 알레르기 유발 항원 수가 증가하는 두 번째 테스트를 진두지휘할 수 있을지 묻고 있으므로 또 다른 테스트 단계를 거칠 것임을 추론할 수 있다. 따라서 (C)가 정답이다.

어휘 practitioner n. 종사자 phase n. 단계
inspect v. 검사하다, 점검하다

154 의도 파악 문제

해석 오전 9시 24분에, Mr. Taylor가 "We have enough for now"라고 썼을 때, 그가 의도한 것 같은 것은?
(A) 실험실 공간은 충분히 넓다.
(B) 비품들은 이미 주문되었다.
(C) 직원 수는 충분하다.
(D) 자금이 프로젝트를 충당할 것이다.

해설 지문의 'How are we doing on financing?'에서 Ms. Kinney가 자금 조달은 어떻게 되고 있는지 묻자, Mr. Taylor가 'We have enough for now'(지금으로서는 충분해요)라고 한 후, 'Our research funds should be enough for the next test.'에서 연구 자금이 다음 테스트를 위해 충분할 거라고 한 것을 통해, 자금이 프로젝트를 충당할 것이라는 의도임을 알 수 있다. 따라서 (D)가 정답이다.

어휘 laboratory n. 실험실 sufficient adj. 충분한 cover v. 충당하다

155-157번은 다음 기사에 관한 문제입니다.

밴쿠버 (10월 11일)— ¹⁵⁵에드먼턴에 본사를 둔 온라인 음식 배달 서비스 Doorbell Diners는 전국적으로 약 800명의 직원을 해고한다고 발표했다. 그 조치는 상승하는 인플레이션과 금리에 대응하여 비용을 절감하는 것을 목표로 한다.

Cartwright Foods가 비슷한 조치를 취한 지 불과 몇 달 만에 이번 발표가 나오면서, 업계에서 긱 이코노미로의 전환이 더욱 가속화될 것이라는 우려가 증가하고 있다. ¹⁵⁶9월에 Edward Reed의 사임 후에 CEO직을 맡은 Carolyn Hudson은 이번 해고가 긱 이코노미 근로자에 대한 선호를 반영한다는 것을 부인했다.

"¹⁵⁷이것은 쉬운 결정이 아니었으며, 저는 현재 직원들이 어려움을 겪고 있다는 점을 이해합니다."라고 Ms. Hudson은 말했다. "하지만, 저희가 취한 조치는 필요에 의해 취해진 것입니다. 앞으로 시장 상황이 개선되면 일부 일시 해고된 직원들을 재고용할 것으로 예상합니다."

layoff n. (일시) 해고 nationwide adv. 전국적으로 aim v. 목표로 하다
interest rate 금리, 이자율 mount v. 증가하다, 늘어나다
assume v. (책임을) 맡다 gig economy 긱 이코노미, 임시직 선호 경제
resignation n. 사임, 사직 deny v. 부인하다
gig worker 긱 이코노미 근로자(임시직으로 일하는 등 소속된 곳이 없는 근로자) struggle v. 어려움을 겪다 necessity n. 필요
rehire v. 재고용하다

155 목적 찾기 문제

해석 기사의 목적은 무엇인가?
(A) 회사의 새로운 서비스를 홍보하기 위해
(B) 조직 내 인사 변동을 발표하기 위해
(C) 회사 본사의 이전을 발표하기 위해

(D) 음식 배달 서비스 시장의 성장을 분석하기 위해

해설 지문의 'The online food delivery service Doorbell Diners, headquartered in Edmonton, has announced the layoff of approximately 800 employees nationwide.'에서 에드먼턴에 본사를 둔 온라인 음식 배달 서비스 Doorbell Diners가 전국적으로 약 800명의 직원을 해고한다고 발표했다고 했고, 이에 대한 배경과 상황 설명으로 지문이 이어지고 있으므로 (B)가 정답이다.

어휘 personnel adj. 인사의, 직원의 relocation n. 이전
corporate adj. 회사의, 기업의 analyze v. 분석하다

156 추론 문제

해설 Doorbell Diners에 대해 암시되는 것은?
(A) 최근에 경영진이 변경되었다.
(B) Cartwright Foods와 제휴를 맺었다.
(C) 배달 기사들을 더 고용할 것이다.
(D) 직원 교육에 대한 지출을 늘릴 계획이다.

해설 지문의 'Carolyn Hudson, who assumed the role of CEO following Edward Reed's resignation in September'에서 9월에 Edward Reed의 사임 후에 Carolyn Hudson이 CEO직을 맡았다고 했으므로 최근에 경영진이 변경되었다는 것을 추론할 수 있다. 따라서 (A)가 정답이다.

어휘 spending n. 지출

157 동의어 찾기 문제

해설 3문단 첫 번째 줄의 "appreciate"은 의미상 -와 가장 가깝다.
(A) 소중하게 여기다
(B) 이해하다
(C) 존경하다
(D) 대표하다

해설 appreciate를 포함한 구절 'This was not a simple decision, and I appreciate that people are struggling right now'에서 appreciate은 '이해하다'라는 뜻으로 사용되었다. 따라서 (B)가 정답이다.

158-160번은 다음 웹페이지에 관한 문제입니다.

| 홈 | 소개 | 서비스 | 소식 | 연락처 |

¹⁵⁸Pia는 국제 송금을 더 쉽게 만들겠다는 목표로 13년 전 말레이시아에서 설립되었습니다. 처음 시작했을 때, 저희는 5개 국가에서 서비스를 제공했습니다. 현재는 전 세계에서 가장 널리 사용되는 송금 플랫폼 중 하나이며, 클릭 몇 번으로 150개국에 100개 통화를 송금할 수 있게 합니다. ¹⁵⁹고객이 즉시 송금과 더 저렴한 가격으로 며칠이 걸리는 송금 중에서 선택할 수 있게 하는 것이 저희를 경쟁사들로부터 돋보이게 하는 하나의 방식입니다. 어느 쪽이든, 모든 거래가 안전하다는 것을 보장합니다.

저희의 본사는 쿠알라룸푸르에 있습니다. ¹⁶⁰⁻⁽ᴬ⁾마닐라, 뉴욕, 그리고 암스테르담에도 지사가 있습니다. ¹⁶⁰⁻⁽ᴮ⁾약 2,200명의 직원들이 근무하고 있으며, 각 직원은 뛰어난 고객 서비스를 제공합니다. ¹⁶⁰⁻⁽ᶜ⁾현재, 작년의 두 배인 420만 명의 이용자를 보유하고 있으며, 연간

81억 달러의 송금을 처리하고 있습니다.

money transfer 송금 currency n. 통화 instant adj. 즉시의, 즉각의
transaction n. 거래 exceptional adj. 뛰어난, 예외적인
process v. 처리하다 annually adv. 연간, 매년

158 육하원칙 문제

해설 웹페이지에는 어떤 정보가 포함되어 있는가?
(A) 만족한 고객들이 작성한 추천의 글
(B) 다가오는 변경에 대한 세부 사항
(C) 서비스 가입 방법에 대한 설명
(D) 회사의 초창기에 대한 정보

해설 지문의 'Pia was founded 13 years ago in Malaysia, with the goal of making international money transfers easier. When we first launched, we offered services in five countries.'에서 Pia가 13년 전에 설립되었고, 처음 시작했을 때 5개 국가에서 서비스를 제공했다고 했으므로 (D)가 정답이다. (A), (B), (C)는 지문에 없는 정보이다.

어휘 testimonial n. 추천의 글 instruction n. 설명

159 육하원칙 문제

해설 웹페이지에 따르면, Pia는 경쟁사와 구별 짓는 무엇을 제공하는가?
(A) 무료 거래를 할 수 있는 기능
(B) 24시간 고객 서비스
(C) 송금 속도에 대한 여러 옵션
(D) 빈번한 이용에 대한 보상

해설 지문의 'One way we stand out from our competitors is by allowing customers to choose between an instant transfer and one that will take a few days for a lower price.'에서 고객이 즉시 송금과 더 저렴한 가격으로 며칠이 걸리는 송금 중에서 선택할 수 있게 하는 것이 경쟁사들로부터 돋보이게 하는 하나의 방식이라고 했으므로 (C)가 정답이다.

어휘 distinguish v. 구별 짓다, 차이를 보이다
around-the-clock adj. 24시간 내내 reward n. 보상
frequent adj. 빈번한, 자주 일어나는

Paraphrasing

stand out from our competitors 경쟁사들로부터 돋보이다
→ distinguishes it from its rivals 경쟁사들과 구별 짓다

160 Not/True 문제

해설 Pia에 대해 언급되지 않은 것은?
(A) 여러 도시들에 사무실이 있다.
(B) 2,000명이 넘는 직원들이 고용되어 있다.
(C) 이용자들의 총수가 두 배가 되었다.
(D) 다른 회사와 합병했다.

해설 (A)는 'We also have offices in Manila, New York, and Amsterdam.'에서 마닐라, 뉴욕, 그리고 암스테르담에도 지사가 있다고 했으므로 지문에 언급된 내용이다. (B)는 'We have approximately 2,200 employees'에서 약 2,200명의 직원들이 있다고 했으므로 지문에 언급된 내용이다. (C)는 'We currently have 4.2 million users, twice as many as last year'에서 이용자들이 작년의 두 배라고 했으므로 지문에 언급된 내용이다. (D)는 지문에 언급되지 않은 내용이다. 따라서 (D)가 정답이다.

어휘 merge v. 합병하다

Paraphrasing

> have approximately 2,200 employees 약 2,200명의 직원들이 있다 → employs over 2,000 people 2,000명이 넘는 직원들이 고용되어 있다
> twice as many as last year 작년의 두 배인 → doubled 두 배가 되었다

161-163번은 다음 기사에 관한 문제입니다.

> 시카고는 준비가 되었다
> 2월 14일—¹⁶¹시카고 국제공항은 제빙 시설 세 곳을 추가했다. 그 시설들은 활주로와 가깝고 각각 두 대의 비행기를 한 번에 정비할 수 있다. 캘거리 공항에서 실시한 테스트에서 드러났듯이, 이 시스템은 매우 효율적이며, 유사한 시설들이 추운 달 동안 지연 시간을 80퍼센트 줄인 것으로 나타났다.
> ¹⁶²⁻⁽ᴮ⁾시카고에서는, 항공사들이 그 1억 달러 규모의 프로젝트 비용을 지불했고 유지보수 비용을 지불할 것이다. 이전에는, 항공사가 게이트에서 장비에 제빙액을 뿌려 개별적으로 해빙해야 했는데, 이 과정은 종종 시간이 많이 드는 작업이었다. 그 시설들은 또한 비행기가 제빙된 직후 이륙할 수 있기 때문에 안전을 향상시켜, 주요한 표면에 얼음이 다시 형성될 가능성을 최소화한다.
> ¹⁶³시카고 국제공항에서 가장 많은 항공기 대수를 보유하기 때문에, Virviana 항공사는 새로운 제빙 시설에 대한 우선적 접근권을 부여받아 이미 그것들을 사용하고 있다. 지금까지 95퍼센트의 성공률을 기록해 온 것으로 알려졌다.

de-ice v. 얼음을 제거하다 at once 한 번에, 동시에
evidence v. 드러내다, 입증하다 maintenance fee 유지보수 비용
defrost v. 해빙하다, 녹이다 time-consuming adj. 시간이 많이 드는
re-form v. 다시 만들다, 재결성하다 grant v. 부여하다, 주다

161 주제 찾기 문제

해석 기사는 주로 무엇에 관한 것인가?
(A) 터미널 리모델링 사업
(B) 항공사 주주총회
(C) 비행경로의 변경
(D) 공항의 새로운 특징

해설 지문의 'The Chicago International Airport has added three de-icing facilities.'에서 시카고 국제공항은 제빙 시설 세 곳을 추가했다고 한 후, 공항에 추가되어 겨울철 항공기 운항에 도움을 주는 그 시설들의 특징에 대해 설명하고 있으므로 (D)가 정답이다.

어휘 shareholders' meeting 주주총회 feature n. 특징, 기능

162 Not/True 문제

해석 시카고에 있는 항공사들에 대해 명시된 것은?
(A) 많은 겨울철 항공편을 취소해야 했다.
(B) 시설 유지에 자금을 댈 것이다.
(C) 제빙액을 계속 사용할 것이다.
(D) 프로젝트에 대한 정부 보조금을 받았다.

해설 지문의 'In Chicago, airlines paid for the $100 million project and will pay maintenance fees.'에서 시카고에서는 항공사들이 그 1억 달러 규모의 프로젝트(제빙 시설을 추가한 것) 비용을 지불했고 유지보수 비용을 지불할 것이라고 하였다. 따라서 (B)가 정답이다. (A), (C), (D)는 지문에 언급되지 않은 내용이다.

어휘 numerous adj. 많은 upkeep n. 유지, 관리
subsidy n. 보조금, 지원금

Paraphrasing

> pay maintenance fees 유지보수 비용을 지불하다 → fund the upkeep 유지에 자금을 대다

163 육하원칙 문제

해석 기사에 따르면, 왜 Virviana 항공사가 우선적 접근권을 갖는가?
(A) 선금을 냈다.
(B) 새로운 기술을 개발하는 것을 도왔다.
(C) 공항에서 가장 많은 항공기 대수를 보유하고 있다.
(D) 겨울철에 더 많은 항공편을 추가했다.

해설 기사의 'Having the largest plane fleet at the Chicago International Airport, Virviana Airlines has been granted priority access to the new de-icing facilities'에서 Virviana 항공사가 가장 많은 항공기 대수를 보유했기 때문에 새로운 제빙 시설에 대한 우선적 접근권을 부여받았다고 했으므로 (C)가 정답이다.

어휘 advanced payment 선금, 선지급

Paraphrasing

> largest plane fleet 가장 많은 항공기 대수 → largest number of aircraft 가장 많은 항공기 대수

164-167번은 다음 이메일에 관한 문제입니다.

> 수신: Beth Hong <b.hong@speedymail.com>
> 발신: Jeffrey Anderson <j.anderson@fenn.com>
> 날짜: 3월 10일
> 제목: Fenn 마트
>
> Ms. Hong께,
>
> 축하합니다. ¹⁶⁴귀하는 면접을 잘 보셨고 저희는 귀하에게 직위를 제의드리기로 결정했습니다. Clark가 249번지에 있는 저희 지점에서 열리는 교육 세션에 참석해 주셨으면 합니다. — [1] —. ¹⁶⁵⁻⁽ᴬ⁾그곳이 저희의 가장 큰 지점이므로, 저희는 모든 저희 신입사원을 거기서 교육합니다. 귀하께서는 저희의 경험 많은 직원 여럿과 긴밀히 협력하게 될 것입니다. 완벽을 기대하지는 않지만, 저희는 나서서 할 의지가 있는 사람을 찾습니다. — [2] —.

165-(A)귀하의 교육이 완료된 후에, 귀하께서는 다른 지점으로 배치될 것입니다. — [3] —. 어떤 특정한 요청 사항이 있으시다면 말씀해 주세요. 저희는 직원들이 집에서 가까운 지점에서 근무하는 것을 선호합니다.

166교육은 3월 17일 오전 8시부터 오후 12시까지로 예정되어 있으며, 귀하에게 유니폼이 지급될 것입니다. 166교육이 끝난 직후 점심식사가 제공될 것입니다. 167귀하의 참석 여부를 확정해 주시기를 바랍니다. — [4] —.

Jeffrey Anderson 드림
Fenn 마트

experienced adj. 경험이 많은, 노련한 willingness n. 의지
take the initiative 나서서 하다, 솔선수범을 보이다
assign v. 배치하다, 배정하다 conclude v. 끝나다

164 목적 찾기 문제

해석 이메일의 목적은 무엇인가?
(A) 회사의 채용 절차를 설명하기 위해
(B) 금융 정보를 요청하기 위해
(C) 일정 변경을 확인하기 위해
(D) 지원에 대한 최신 정보를 제공하기 위해

해설 지문의 'You did well during the interview, and we have decided to offer you a position.'에서 면접을 잘 봤고 직위를 제의하기로 결정했다고 하면서, 이후 예정된 신입사원 교육 관련 내용에 대해 안내하고 있으므로 (D)가 정답이다.

165 Not/True 문제

해석 Fenn 마트에 대해 사실인 것은?
(A) 한 곳이 넘는 지점이 있다.
(B) 지역 관리자를 교체하려고 한다.
(C) 매달 교육 세션을 연다.
(D) 일회용 플라스틱 음식 용기를 금지했다.

해설 지문의 'It is our biggest location'에서 그곳(Clark가에 있는 지점)이 가장 큰 지점이라고 했고, 'After your training is complete, you will be assigned to a different location.'에서 교육이 완료된 후에 다른 지점으로 배치될 것이라고 했으므로 (A)는 지문의 내용과 일치한다. 따라서 (A)가 정답이다. (B), (C), (D)는 지문에 언급되지 않은 내용이다.

어휘 ban v. 금지하다 single-use adj. 일회용의

166 육하원칙 문제

해석 3월 17일 오후에 무슨 일이 일어날 것인가?
(A) 면접이 실시될 것이다.
(B) 교육생들에게 식사가 제공될 것이다.
(C) 매장 지점들의 목록이 온라인에 게시될 것이다.
(D) 직원들의 사진이 촬영될 것이다.

해설 지문의 'The training session is scheduled for March 17, from 8 A.M. until 12 P.M. ~ Lunch will be provided immediately after the training concludes'에서 교육은 3월 17일 오전 8시부터 오후 12시까지로 예정되어 있으며, 교육이 끝난 직후 점심식사가 제공될 것이라고 했으므로 (B)가 정답이다.

어휘 serve v. 제공하다, 역할을 하다 trainee n. 교육을 받는 사람

Paraphrasing
Lunch will be provided 점심식사가 제공될 것이다 → A meal will be served 식사가 제공될 것이다

167 문장 위치 찾기 문제

해석 [1], [2], [3], [4]로 표시된 위치 중, 다음 문장이 들어갈 곳으로 가장 적절한 것은?

"늦어도 3월 15일까지 이것을 해 주시면 감사하겠습니다."

(A) [1]
(B) [2]
(C) [3]
(D) [4]

해설 주어진 문장은 요청과 관련된 내용 주변에 나올 것임을 예상할 수 있다. [4]의 앞 문장인 'Please confirm your attendance.'에서 참석 여부를 확정해 달라고 했으므로, [4]에 주어진 문장이 들어가면 참석 여부를 늦어도 3월 15일까지 확정해 달라는 자연스러운 문맥이 된다는 것을 알 수 있다. 따라서 (D)가 정답이다.

168-171번은 다음 기사에 관한 문제입니다.

조지타운 (1705월 17일)—최근 몇 달 동안, 조지타운에는 새로운 사업체들이 도시 곳곳에 잇따라 들어왔다. 그중에는 168동업자인 Natasha Baker와 Eric Pope가 운영하는 추리 소설 전문점인 The Whodunit이 있다. — [1] —. 169The Whodunit은 처음에 고객을 유치하는 데 어려움을 겪긴 했지만, 171Ms. Baker와 Mr. Pope는 지난 2월부터 매주 미스터리를 주제로 한 파티 이벤트를 개최하기 시작했다. — [2] —. 그 이후로, 사업체는 상당히 회복되었다. "지금 상황이 이보다 더 만족스러울 수 없습니다."라고 Ms. Baker가 말했다. 이 미스터리 이벤트를 시작한 이후 매장의 월 매출은 세 배로 증가했으며, 매주 모임에 평균 45명의 참가자들이 참석했다.

조지타운의 비즈니스 환경에 최근에 추가된 또 다른 사업체는 지역 사업가인 Norman Nash가 소유한 드라이클리닝 업체인 Suds이다. — [3] —. 점포 밖에 주차된 차량들의 수로 판단하자면 169불과 몇 달 전만 해도 Mr. Nash가 어려움에 처해 있었다고 상상하기 어렵다. "처음에는 거의 수익을 내지 못했습니다. 제가 영업을 하고 있다는 사실조차 아는 사람이 많지 않았어요."라고 Mr. Nash가 말했다. — [4] —. 하지만, 소셜 미디어에서 Suds의 존재감을 높이자, 주민들이 주목하기 시작했다. 이제 단골 고객층과 꾸준한 수익을 바탕으로, 170Mr. Nash는 당일 드라이클리닝 옵션을 포함하도록 다음 달에 서비스를 확장할 계획이다. 그 확장은 고객들이 비접촉식 픽업 및 배송 서비스를 예약할 수 있는 모바일 앱을 특징으로 할 것이다.

influx n. (잇따라) 들어오기, 유입 initially adv. 처음에
struggle v. 힘겹게 해 나가다 pick up 회복되다, 개선되다
considerably adv. 상당히 entrepreneur n. 사업가, 기업가
establishment n. 점포, 시설 barely adv. 거의 ~않다
presence n. 존재감 steady adj. 꾸준한 revenue n. 수익, 수입

168 육하원칙 문제

해석 Ms. Baker와 Mr. Pope는 어떤 사업체를 운영하는가?
(A) 서점
(B) 파티용품점
(C) 드라이클리닝점
(D) 세차장

해설 지문의 'a specialty shop dedicated to mystery novels, run by business partners Natasha Baker and Eric Pope'에서 동업자인 Natasha Baker와 Eric Pope가 추리 소설 전문점을 운영한다고 했으므로 (A)가 정답이다.

어휘 run v. 운영하다

Paraphrasing

a specialty shop dedicated to mystery novels 추리 소설 전문점 → A bookstore 서점

169 육하원칙 문제

해설 The Whodunit과 Suds의 공통점은 무엇인가?
(A) 그들은 둘 다 매주 고객을 위한 이벤트를 개최한다.
(B) 그들은 둘 다 자체 주차장이 있다.
(C) 그들은 둘 다 온라인에서 강력한 존재감을 가지고 있다.
(D) 그들은 둘 다 처음 오픈했을 때 어려움을 겪었다.

해설 지문의 'The Whodunit initially struggled to attract customers'에서 The Whodunit이 처음에 고객을 유치하는 데 어려움을 겪었다고 했고, 'Mr. Nash was in trouble just a few months ago. "I could barely turn a profit at first.'에서 Mr. Nash는 불과 몇 달 전만 해도 어려움에 처해 있었다며, 처음에는 거의 수익을 내지 못했다고 하였다. 따라서 (D)가 정답이다.

Paraphrasing

initially struggled to attract customers 처음에 고객을 유치하는 데 어려움을 겪었다 / could barely turn a profit at first 처음에는 거의 수익을 내지 못했다 → struggled when they were first opened 처음 오픈했을 때 어려움을 겪었다

170 추론 문제

해설 Mr. Nash는 6월에 무엇을 할 것 같은가?
(A) 광고 캠페인을 시작한다.
(B) 특별 홍보 활동을 한다.
(C) 상업용 건물을 개조한다.
(D) 새로운 서비스 옵션을 도입한다.

해설 지문의 'May 17', 'Mr. Nash is planning to expand his services next month to include same-day dry cleaning options.'에서 Mr. Nash는 당일 드라이클리닝 옵션을 포함하도록 다음 달에 서비스를 확장할 계획이라고 했으므로 Mr. Nash가 6월에 새로운 서비스 옵션을 도입할 것이라는 점을 추론할 수 있다. 따라서 (D)가 정답이다.

어휘 introduce v. 도입하다

171 문장 위치 찾기 문제

해석 [1], [2], [3], [4]로 표시된 위치 중, 다음 문장이 들어갈 곳으로 가장 적절한 것은?

"사람들은 매주 토요일 밤에 최신 출간작을 둘러보면서 허구의 범죄를 해결하는 데 참여할 수 있다."

(A) [1]
(B) [2]
(C) [3]
(D) [4]

해설 주어진 문장은 매주 진행되는 이벤트와 관련된 내용 주변에 나와야 함을 예상할 수 있다. [2]의 앞 문장인 'Ms. Baker and Mr. Pope began hosting weekly mystery-themed party events back in February'에서 Ms. Baker와 Mr. Pope는 지난 2월부터 매주 미스터리를 주제로 한 파티 이벤트를 개최하기 시작했다고 했으므로, [2]에 주어진 문장이 들어가면 Ms. Baker와 Mr. Pope는 지난 2월부터 매주 미스터리를 주제로 한 파티 이벤트를 개최하기 시작했고, 사람들은 매주 토요일 밤에 최신 출간작을 둘러보면서 가상의 범죄를 해결하는 데 참여할 수 있다는 자연스러운 문맥이 된다는 것을 알 수 있다. 따라서 (B)가 정답이다.

어휘 fictional adj. 허구의, 지어낸   browse v. 둘러보다

172-175번은 다음 온라인 채팅 대화문에 관한 문제입니다.

Jordan Mitchell (오후 2시 38분)
오늘로서, *Hidden Jungle: Escape*가 출시된 지 두 달이 지났네요. 매출은 어땠나요?

Alice Turner (오후 2시 39분)
172첫 번째 게임만큼 좋지 않아요. 지금까지, 약 50만 개 정도만 판매되었어요.

Jordan Mitchell (오후 2시 40분)
같은 기간 동안 첫 번째 게임보다 20만 개 정도 적네요. 우리가 이 이면에 있는 핵심 요인을 파악해야 할 것 같네요.

George Parker (오후 2시 41분)
좋지도 나쁘지도 않은 후기를 받은 것과 아마도 관련이 있을 거예요. 173대부분의 게임 평론가들이 단 10시간 만에 레벨을 끝낼 수 있다는 사실에 반감을 가졌어요.

Jordan Mitchell (오후 2시 42분)
게이머들의 반응은 어떤가요?

Alice Turner (오후 2시 43분)
음, 판매 페이지의 고객 후기를 보면, 반응은 대체로 긍정적이었어요. 174하지만, 몇 가지 기술적 결함을 지적하기도 해요.

Jordan Mitchell (오후 2시 44분)
그것들은 해결되고 있어요. 175George, 패치 진행 상황에 대해 업데이트해 주세요.

George Parker (오후 2시 45분)
175레벨 3에서 가끔 멈추는 현상과 일부 그래픽 해상도 문제를 고쳤어요. 패치는 9월 1일까지 다운로드할 수 있게 될 거예요.

Jordan Mitchell (오후 2시 46분)
훌륭해요. 그것이 더 많은 사람들을 게임으로 끌어들이면 좋겠어요.

mediocre adj. 좋지도 나쁘지도 않은, 평범한　critic n. 평론가, 비평가
object v. 반감을 가지다, 싫어하다　response n. 반응
reception n. 반응　point out 지적하다, 주목하다
technical adj. 기술적인　flaw n. 결함, 흠　address v. 해결하다
occasional adj. 가끔의　resolution n. 해상도, 해결

172 추론 문제

해석　Hidden Jungle: Escape에 대해 암시되는 것은?
(A) 새로운 게임 디자인 소프트웨어를 사용하여 제작되었다.
(B) 이전 게임의 속편이다.
(C) 출시 전 몇 달 동안 지연되었다.
(D) 10가지 도전적인 레벨을 특징으로 한다.

해설　지문의 'They're not quite as good as the first game.'에서 첫 번째 게임만큼 판매량이 좋지 않다고 했으므로 Hidden Jungle: Escape가 이전 게임의 속편임을 추론할 수 있다. 따라서 (B)가 정답이다.

어휘　sequel n. 속편

173 육하원칙 문제

해석　평론가들은 Hidden Jungle: Escape에 대해 어떤 불만이 있는가?
(A) 비교적 빠르게 완료할 수 있다.
(B) 시각적 기대를 충족시키지 못한다.
(C) 조종 장치와 잘 작동하지 않는다.
(D) 따라가기 어려운 줄거리를 가지고 있다.

해설　지문의 'Most game critics objected to the fact that you can finish the levels within just 10 hours.'에서 대부분의 게임 평론가들이 단 10시간 만에 레벨을 끝낼 수 있다는 사실에 반감을 가졌다고 했으므로 (A)가 정답이다.

어휘　complete v. 완료하다　relatively adv. 비교적
expectation n. 기대　storyline n. 줄거리

174 의도 파악 문제

해석　오후 2시 44분에, Mr. Mitchell이 "Those are being addressed"라고 썼을 때, 그가 의도한 것은?
(A) 새로운 레벨이 개발되고 있다.
(B) 예산 문제가 해결되고 있다.
(C) 몇몇 기술적인 사소한 결함이 고쳐지고 있다.
(D) 직원이 부족한 것이 해결될 것이다.

해설　지문의 'They do point out some technical flaws, though.'에서 Ms. Turner가 고객 후기들이 몇 가지 기술적 결함을 지적한다고 하자, Mr. Mitchell이 'Those are being addressed'(그것들은 해결되고 있어요)라고 한 것을 통해, Mr. Mitchell이 몇몇 기술적인 사소한 결함이 고쳐지고 있다는 것을 의도했음을 알 수 있다. 따라서 (C)가 정답이다.

어휘　resolve v. 해결하다　glitch n. 사소한 결함

175 추론 문제

해석　9월에 어떤 일이 일어날 것 같은가?
(A) 새로운 게임 제작이 시작될 것이다.
(B) 업데이트가 공개될 것이다.
(C) 회사 야유회가 열릴 것이다.
(D) 게임 대회가 열릴 것이다.

해설　지문의 'George, please provide an update on the progress of the patch.'에서 Mr. Mitchell이 패치 진행 상황에 대해 업데이트해 달라고 하자, Mr. Parker가 We've fixed the occasional freezes on level three, as well as some of the graphics resolution issues. The patch should be available for download by September 1.'에서 레벨 3에서 가끔 멈추는 현상과 일부 그래픽 해상도 문제를 고쳤으며, 패치는 9월 1일까지 다운로드할 수 있게 될 거라고 했으므로 9월에 업데이트가 공개될 것임을 추론할 수 있다. 따라서 (B)가 정답이다.

어휘　production n. 제작, 생산　competition n. 대회, 경쟁

176-180번은 다음 초대장과 일정에 관한 문제입니다.

> 7월 28일 금요일
> 오후 8시부터 자정까지
> 그랜드 센터, 더블린
>
> **176-(B)**더블린 재즈 쇼케이스는 매해 여름 인기 있는 볼거리가 되었으며, 올해 행사는 실망시키지 않을 것입니다. 이번에는 더 큰 장소로 옮겼고, 몇몇 사항을 조금 바꿨습니다. **177**일반적인 콘서트 방식 대신 한 번에 여러 콘서트를 열기로 결정했습니다. 센터에는, 여러 공연 공간들이 예약되어 있습니다. 한곳에 머무르시거나 그곳들 모두 방문하셔도 됩니다. 각 장소에서는, 독특한 요리가 제공될 것입니다. 맛있는 음식과 멋진 음악이 함께 어우러져 당신의 감각을 분명 즐겁게 할 것입니다.
>
> **178**티켓은 6월 24일 오전 10시에 매표소나 온라인 www.dublinjazzshowcase.ie에서 판매될 것입니다. 티켓은 프로그램당 50유로입니다. 할인은 어르신들과 학생이 이용 가능합니다. 입장 시 유효한 신분증을 제시해야 합니다. 티켓 가격은 대부분의 경우에는 제공되는 음식 비용을 포함합니다. 하지만, **179**테라스에서 제공되는 음식은 별도로 지불되어야 합니다.
>
> **178**더블린 재즈 협회 회원은 6월 22일 오전 10시부터 티켓을 구매할 수 있습니다. 예약하시기 전에 회원 식별 번호를 준비해 두세요.

attraction n. 볼거리, 명소　sizeable adj. 꽤 큰, 상당한 크기의
switch v. 바꾸다, 전환하다　venue n. 장소　valid adj. 유효한, 타당한
separately adv. 별도로, 따로따로

더블린 재즈 쇼케이스

장소	프로그램	식사 및 음료
210호실	재즈 3중창단 Tre가 전통 재즈로 즐겁게 해줄 것입니다.	트러플 오일과 다른 양념들로 맛을 낸 고급 팝콘을 드셔 보세요. Finglas 포도주 양조장에서 만든 스파클링 와인과 함께 즐기세요.
180105호 강당	**180**현대 재즈 4중창단인 Lubion에 더해, 가수 Roberta Woods의 노래를 감상해 보세요	**180**신선한 해산물과 Gilmore 양조장에서 만든 다양한 현지 맥주를 즐기세요.

¹⁷⁹테라스	그룹 CTjazz는 라틴 재즈를 전문으로 합니다. 라운지에서 편히 쉬시거나 무도장에서 즐겨보세요.	칵테일을 마시고, ¹⁷⁹Burnside 식당의 수석 셰프 Mary Mallet이 준비한 전통 아일랜드 요리 중에서 선택해 보세요.
310호실	James Danton과 그의 밴드가 보조 보컬인 Marvin Hammer와 함께 스무스 재즈를 연주합니다.	Harborview 카페의 커피를 마시고, Coleman 베이커리의 맛있는 페이스트리도 드셔 보세요.

contemporary adj. 현대의 quartet n. 4중창단, 4인조
specialize in ~을 전문으로 하다

176 추론 문제

해석 초대장이 행사에 대해 암시하는 것은?
(A) 이틀 동안 진행될 것이다.
(B) 지난 몇 년 동안 개최되어 왔다.
(C) 오후에 종료될 예정이다.
(D) 정부 프로그램의 자금 지원을 받았다.

해설 초대장의 'The Dublin Jazz Showcase has become a popular attraction each summer, and this year's event won't disappoint.'에서 더블린 재즈 쇼케이스가 매해 여름 인기 있는 볼거리가 되었다고 했으므로 행사가 지난 몇 년 동안 개최되어 왔다는 것을 추론할 수 있다. 따라서 (B)가 정답이다.

177 동의어 찾기 문제

해석 초대장에서, 1문단 세 번째 줄의 단어 "regular"는 의미상 -와 가장 가깝다.
(A) 품위 있는
(B) 정돈된
(C) 변함없는
(D) 종래의

해설 regular를 포함한 구절 'Instead of a regular concert format, we have decided to hold several concerts at once.'에서 regular는 '일반적인, 통상적인'이라는 뜻으로 사용되었다. 따라서 (D)가 정답이다.

178 육하원칙 문제

해석 왜 몇몇 사람들은 조기 티켓 예약을 할 수 있는가?
(A) 몇몇 이벤트 상품을 구매했다.
(B) 더블린 재즈 쇼케이스의 직원이다.
(C) 지역 단체의 회원 자격을 보유하고 있다.
(D) 단체에 후한 기부를 했다.

해설 초대장의 'Tickets will go on sale on 24 June at 10 A.M.'과, 'Members of the Dublin Jazz Association will have access to tickets starting on 22 June at 10 A.M.'에서 티켓은 6월 24일 오전 10시에 판매되지만, 더블린 재즈 협회 회원은 6월 22일 오전 10시부터 티켓을 구매할 수 있다고 했으므로 (C)가 정답이다.

어휘 eligible adj. ~할 수 있는

Paraphrasing

Members of the Dublin Jazz Association 더블린 재즈 협회 회원
→ membership with a local organization 지역 단체의 회원 자격

179 추론 문제 연계

해석 Mary Mallet에 대해 결론지을 수 있는 것은?
(A) 그녀는 유명한 음악 그룹과 함께 노래할 것이다.
(B) 그녀의 식당은 장소와 가까운 곳에 위치해 있다.
(C) 그녀는 이전에 더블린 재즈 협회에 음식을 제공한 적이 있다.
(D) 그녀의 요리는 별도로 구매해야 한다.

해설 질문의 핵심 어구인 Mary Mallet이 언급된 일정을 먼저 확인한다.
단서 1 일정의 'Terrace', 'choose from several traditional Irish dishes prepared by master chef Mary Mallet'에서 Mary Mallet의 요리는 테라스에서 제공될 것임을 알 수 있다.
단서 2 초대장의 'the dishes available on the terrace must be paid for separately'에서 테라스에서 제공되는 음식은 별도로 지불되어야 한다고 했다.
두 단서를 종합할 때, Mary Mallet의 요리는 테라스에서 제공되므로 별도로 돈을 지불하여 음식을 구매해야 함을 추론할 수 있다. 따라서 (D)가 정답이다.

어휘 cater v. 음식을 제공하다

180 육하원칙 문제

해석 참석자들은 어떤 종류의 음악을 Gilmore 양조장에서 만든 음료를 마시며 즐길 수 있을 것인가?
(A) 전통 재즈
(B) 현대 재즈
(C) 라틴 재즈
(D) 스무스 재즈

해설 일정의 'Auditorium 105', 그리고 'Listen to singer Roberta Woods, along with the contemporary jazz quartet Lubion.'과 'Enjoy ~ and a wide assortment of local beers from the Gilmore Brewery.'에서 105호 강당에서 Gilmore 양조장에서 만든 다양한 현지 맥주를 즐기고, 현대 재즈 4중창단의 노래를 감상해보라고 했다. 따라서 (B)가 정답이다.

Paraphrasing

beers 맥주 → beverage 음료

181-185번은 다음 두 이메일에 관한 문제입니다.

수신: Cathy Wang <cathy.w@wmail.com>
발신: Jim Ricci <jim28@clarksonpublishing.com>
제목: 삽화
날짜: 10월 29일
첨부 파일: 챕터 1

Ms. Wang께,

제 이름은 Jim Ricci이고, Clarkson 출판사 소속입니다. 저희가 직접적으로 함께 일한 적은 없지만, ¹⁸¹⁻⁽ᴰ⁾저희가 작년에 출간한 *Marine Line* 책의 일부 편집을 제가 했었는데, 그 책에 삽화를 넣는 것을 당신이 도와주셨어요. 당신의 삽화들이 정말 인상적이었고, 저희의 신간 도서인 *Dinosaurs: A Prehistoric Journey*에 당신이 저희와 다시 함께 작업할 예정임을 듣게 되어 기쁩니다.

¹⁸²이 책의 저자는 *Science Weekly* 잡지의 유명 기자인, Mike Hernandez입니다. 그는 첫 번째 챕터를 완성했고, 그것은 이 이메일에 첨부되어 있습니다. 저는 다음과 같은 그림을 포함할 생각입니다:

- ¹⁸³3페이지: 선사 시대 풍경 삽화 (컬러)
- 7페이지: 티라노사우루스 렉스 그림 (흑백)
- 12페이지: 선사 시대에 발견된 식물 그림 (흑백)
- 14페이지: 스테고사우루스 그림 (흑백)

이러한 삽화 계획에 대해 어떻게 생각하시는지 알려주세요. ¹⁸³그것들이 괜찮은 것 같으시면, 11월 10일까지 그림을 보내주세요.

Jim Ricci 드림
Clarkson 출판

어휘 edit n. 편집 illustrate v. 삽화를 넣다 prehistoric adj. 선사 시대의 landscape n. 풍경

수신: Jim Ricci <jim28@clarksonpublishing.com>
발신: Cathy Wang <cathy.w@wmail.com>
제목: Re: 삽화
¹⁸³날짜: 11월 10일
첨부 파일: 삽화_챕터 1

Mr. Ricci께

첨부된 것은 첫 번째 챕터의 삽화입니다. ¹⁸³컬러 삽화는 완성하는 데 시간이 조금 더 걸리겠지만 이틀 이내에 제출할 예정이라는 점을 알아두시기 바랍니다. ¹⁸⁴당신의 의견으로 이것들에 어떤 문제가 있다면, 즉시 제게 알려주시기 바랍니다.

원고 자체와 일부 외부 자료를 이용하여 이 삽화들을 완성할 수 있었지만, 저는 이 그림들을 만드는 데 필요한 모든 정보를 찾는 데 약간의 어려움을 겪었습니다. ¹⁸⁵공룡에 대해 배울 수 있는 가장 좋은 외부 자료는 무엇인가요? 저는 전문가가 아니기 때문에 정확한 이미지를 만들기 위해 조사를 좀 해야 할 것 같습니다.

지금까지 주신 모든 도움에 감사드립니다. 당신에게 연락받기를 기다리겠습니다.

Cathy Wang 드림

어휘 promptly adv. 즉시 source n. 자료, 출처 expert n. 전문가 accurate adj. 정확한

181 Not/True 문제

해석 첫 번째 이메일이 Mr. Ricci에 대해 명시하는 것은?
(A) 매우 성공적인 출판사를 설립했다.
(B) 선사 시대 생물에 관한 출판물을 저술했다.
(C) Ms. Wang에게 몇몇 샘플 삽화를 제공했다.
(D) 작년에 출간된 책에 일부 수정을 했다.

해설 첫 번째 이메일의 'I made some edits to the *Marine Line* book we put out last year'에서 Mr. Ricci가 다니는 직장에서 작년에 출간한 *Marine Line* 책의 일부 편집을 했다고 했으므로, 작년에 출간된 책에 일부 수정을 했다는 것을 알 수 있다. 따라서 (D)가 정답이다.

어휘 author v. 저술하다, 쓰다 release v. 출간하다, 발매하다

Paraphrasing

made some edits 일부 편집을 했다 → made some changes 일부 수정을 했다

put out 출간했다 → released 출간된

182 추론 문제

해석 Mike Hernandez는 누구인 것 같은가?
(A) 잡지 기자
(B) 도서 편집자
(C) 연구 과학자
(D) 잡지 삽화가

해설 지문의 'Our writer for the book is Mike Hernandez, a well-known reporter for *Science Weekly* magazine.'에서 이 책의 저자는 *Science Weekly* 잡지의 유명 기자인, Mike Hernandez라고 했으므로 (A)가 정답이다.

Paraphrasing

reporter for ~ magazine ~ 잡지의 기자 → A print journalist 잡지 기자

183 육하원칙 문제 연계

해석 Ms. Wang은 어떤 삽화를 제시간에 제출하지 않았는가?
(A) 3페이지 삽화
(B) 7페이지 삽화
(C) 12페이지 삽화
(D) 14페이지 삽화

해설 Ms. Wang이 작성한 두 번째 이메일을 먼저 확인한다.
단서 1 두 번째 이메일의 'November 10'과 'Note that the color illustration is going to take a little more time to complete, but I will submit that within two days'에서 Ms. Wang은 이메일을 11월 10일에 작성하였고, 컬러 삽화는 완성하는 데 시간이 조금 더 걸리겠지만 이틀 이내에 제출할 예정이라고 했다. 그런데 언제까지 삽화를 보내 달라고 했는지와, 컬러 삽화가 몇 페이지 삽화인지 제시되지 않았으므로 첫 번째 이메일에서 관련 내용을 확인한다.
단서 2 첫 번째 이메일의 'Page 3: An illustration of a prehistoric landscape (color)'와 'If they sound good to you, please send in your drawings by November 10.'에서 컬러 삽화는 3페이지에 들어가는 삽화이며, 그것들(삽화 계획)이 괜찮은 것 같다면, 11월 10일까지 그림을 보내줄 것을 요청했음을 확인할 수 있다.
두 단서를 종합할 때, Ms. Wang이 제시간인 11월 10일까지 제출하지 않은 삽화는 3페이지 삽화임을 알 수 있다. 따라서 (A)가 정답이다.

Paraphrasing

send in 보내다 → submit 제출하다

184 동의어 찾기 문제

해석 두 번째 이메일에서, 1문단 세 번째 줄의 단어 "estimation"은 의미상 -와 가장 가깝다.
(A) 사안
(B) 능력
(C) 방법
(D) 의견

해설 estimation을 포함한 구절 'If there's anything wrong with these in your estimation, please notify me promptly.'에서 estimation은 '의견'이라는 뜻으로 사용되었다. 따라서 (D)가 정답이다.

185 육하원칙 문제

해석 Ms. Wang은 Mr. Ricci로부터 어떤 정보를 요청하였는가?
(A) 일부 그림의 마감 기한
(B) 원고의 배치
(C) 주제에 가장 적합한 참고 자료
(D) Mr. Ricci의 연락처

해설 Ms. Wang이 작성한 두 번째 이메일의 'What are the best outside sources I can use to learn about dinosaurs?'에서 공룡에 대해 배울 수 있는 가장 좋은 외부 자료는 무엇인지 물어봤으므로, Ms. Wang이 요청한 정보가 공룡에 대해 배우기 적합한 참고 자료임을 알 수 있다. 따라서 (C)가 정답이다.

어휘 layout n. 배치, 배열

Paraphrasing

sources 자료 → references 참고 자료

186-190번은 다음 기사, 이메일, 회람에 관한 문제입니다.

싱가포르(7월 11일)— **186-(C)**25년 전에 사업을 시작한 가전제품 제조업체 Soltano가 올해 5월 1일 이전에 판매된 전기 그릴 약 1만 대를 회수할 것이다. **188**미국에서는 Firelight EZ1로, 캐나다에서는 Fireside Grill이라는 이름으로 판매되는 그 제품은 장시간 사용할 경우 과열되도록 유발하는 결함이 있다. Soltano의 제품 안전 책임자인 Tom Morgan에 따르면, 어떠한 심각한 사고도 보고되지 않았지만 고객 안전에 대한 우려로 회수가 실시될 것이라고 밝혔다.

186-(A) Morgan은 제품 결함이 회사에 의해 발견되었으며, **187**회사 공장 중 한 곳에서 있었던 품질 보증 절차에서의 과실로 인해 발생했다고 밝혔다. 그 제품의 추후 판매는 모두 중단되었으며, 이미 제품을 구매한 고객은 환불을 위해 그것을 반품하거나 추가 비용 없이 결함 있는 부품을 교체 받을 선택권을 갖는다.

recall v. 회수하다   defect n. 결함   incident n. 사고, 사건
specify v. 밝히다, 명시하다   lapse n. 과실, 실수
assurance n. 보장, 보증   halt v. 중단시키다, 멈추다
faulty adj. 결함이 있는, 불완전한

수신: Lauren Galloway <l.galloway@megatronic.com>
발신: Justin Hammond <j.hammond@megatronic.com>
제목: Soltano 회수
날짜: 7월 15일

안녕하세요 Lauren,

188우리 매장들에 제품을 공급하는 회사 중 하나인 Soltano에서 최근 Fireside Grill에 대한 회수를 실시했습니다. **190**아래는 우리 지역의 매장 목록과 그 그릴들의 재고 수입니다. 당신 매장 재고량이 우리의 집계와 일치하는지 확인해 주시고 얼마나 많이 고객들에게 팔렸는지 파악해 주시겠습니까? 당신은 또한 고객들이 적절히 정보를 제공받는 것을 보장하기 위해 회수에 대한 우리의 표준 절차를 준수해야 할 것입니다. 반품 배송을 위해 물품들을 준비시켜 주세요.

매장 이름	재고 총계
Bergland	237
Harrison	844
190 McGinnis	**190**911
Stratton	612

감사합니다.

Justin Hammond
188지역 관리자
Megatronic 가전제품사

inventory n. 재고(품), 재고 목록   verify v. 확인하다, 입증하다
match v. 일치하다   procedure n. 과정, 절차
adequately adv. 적절히, 충분히

회람

수신: 전 직원
발신: Lauren Galloway, 매장 관리자
날짜: **189**7월 16일
제목: 제품 회수

지역 매니저로부터 Soltano 제품 회수에 대한 통보를 받았습니다. **189**표준 방침에 따라, 저는 오늘 아침에 매장 정문 옆에 회수에 대한 정보를 게시했습니다. 여러분이 고객들로부터 제품 또는 회수에 대한 문의를 받으면 그것들을 고객 서비스 부서로 보내시기를 바랍니다. 또한 Megatronic이 웹사이트와 모바일 앱에 회수에 대한 정보를 게시했다는 것을 그들에게 알려주세요.

190우리 매장이 Megatronic의 모든 매장 중 Soltano에 반송해야 하는 가장 많은 수의 제품을 보유하고 있기 때문에, 물품들을 배송 준비시키는 것을 자원해서 도와줄 몇몇 사람들을 찾고 있습니다. 일정을 짤 수 있도록 여러분의 가능 여부를 알려주세요.

in line with ~에 따라, ~의 방침에 의거하여   policy n. 방침, 정책
direct v. 보내다   notify v. 알리다, 통지하다

186 Not/True 문제

해석 Soltano에 대해 명시된 것은?
(A) 고객에 의해 문제에 대해 통보받았다.
(B) 공장 중 한 곳에서 작은 화재가 발생했다.
(C) 20년 이상 사업을 해왔다.

(D) 자사 전기 그릴의 최신 모델을 계속 판매할 예정이다.

해설 기사의 'Appliance maker Soltano, which began operations 25 years ago'에서 25년 전에 사업을 시작한 가전제품 제조업체 Soltano라고 했으므로 Soltano가 20년 이상 사업을 해왔음을 알 수 있다. 따라서 (C)가 정답이다. (A)는 'Mr. Morgan specified that the product defect was discovered by the company'에서 Morgan은 제품 결함이 회사에 의해 발견되었음을 밝혔다고 했으므로, 지문의 내용과 일치하지 않는다. (B)와 (D)는 지문에 언급되지 않은 내용이다.

Paraphrasing

began operations 25 years ago 25년 전에 사업을 시작했다
→ has been in business for over two decades 20년 이상 사업을 해왔다

187 육하원칙 문제

해석 기사에서 무슨 문제가 언급되는가?
(A) 실제 제품의 가짜 복제품이 판매되었다.
(B) 한 공급업체가 잘못된 부품을 납품했다.
(C) 공장이 절차를 올바르게 따르지 않았다.
(D) 일부 공장 장비가 고장 났다.

해설 기사의 'it occurred due to lapses in the quality assurance procedures at one of the company's factories'에서 그것(제품 결함)이 회사 공장 중 한 곳에서 있었던 품질 보증 절차에서의 과실로 인해 발생했다고 하였다. 따라서 (C)가 정답이다.

어휘 fake adj. 가짜의, 모조의   break down 고장 나다

Paraphrasing

procedure 절차 → process 절차

188 추론 문제 연계

해석 Mr. Hammond에 대해 암시되는 것은?
(A) 최근에 관리자로 임명되었다.
(B) 캐나다의 매장 지점들을 관리한다.
(C) 가장 많은 수의 Soltano 그릴을 판매했다.
(D) 개인적으로 Soltano 그릴을 구매했다.

해설 질문의 핵심 어구인 Mr. Hammond가 작성한 이메일을 먼저 확인한다.
단서 1 이메일의 'Soltano, one of the companies that supply our stores with products, recently issued a recall of the Fireside Grill'과 'Regional Manager'에서, Mr. Hammond가 지역 관리자이며, 그가 관리하는 매장들에 Soltano가 Fireside Grill을 공급했고 최근 회수를 실시했음을 확인할 수 있다.
단서 2 기사의 'The product, which sells as the Firelight EZ1 in the United States and as the Fireside Grill in Canada'에서 그 제품(회수할 예정인 전기 그릴)이 미국에서는 Firelight EZ1로, 캐나다에서는 Fireside Grill이라는 이름으로 판매되는 것을 알 수 있다.
두 단서를 종합할 때, Mr. Hammond는 지역 관리자이며, 캐나다 매장을 관리한다는 점을 추론할 수 있다. 따라서 (B)가 정답이다.

어휘 appoint v. 임명하다   supervise v. 관리하다, 감독하다
personally adv. 개인적으로

189 육하원칙 문제

해석 Ms. Galloway는 7월 16일에 무엇을 했는가?
(A) 온라인에 정보를 게시했다.
(B) 쇼핑객이 양식을 작성하도록 도왔다.
(C) 고객 서비스 직원과 만났다.
(D) 입구 근처에 안내문을 게시했다.

해설 회람의 'July 16', 'I posted information about the recall next to the store's main door this morning'에서 7월 16일 아침에 Ms. Galloway가 정문 옆에 회수에 대한 정보를 게시했다고 했으므로 (D)가 정답이다.

어휘 shopper n. 쇼핑객   put up ~을 게시하다   entrance n. 입구

Paraphrasing

posted 게시했다 → put up 게시했다
next to the store's main door 매장의 정문 옆에 → near an entrance 입구 근처에

190 추론 문제 연계

해석 Ms. Galloway는 어느 매장에서 일하는 것 같은가?
(A) Bergland
(B) Harrison
(C) McGinnis
(D) Stratton

해설 질문의 핵심 어구인 Ms. Galloway가 작성한 회람을 먼저 확인한다.
단서 1 회람의 'we have the highest number of products that need to be returned to Soltano out of all Megatronic's stores'에서, Ms. Galloway가 일하는 매장이 Megatronic의 모든 매장 중 Soltano에 반송해야 하는 가장 많은 수의 제품을 보유하고 있음을 확인할 수 있다. 그런데 반송해야 하는 제품이 가장 많은 매장이 어느 매장인지에 대해 제시되지 않았으므로 이메일에서 관련 내용을 확인한다.
단서 2 이메일의 'Below is a list of the stores in our region and the inventory count of those grills.'와 'McGinnis', '911'에서 아래 표가 Megatronic의 지역 매장 목록이며, 회수 그릴들의 재고 수라는 점과, McGinnis 매장이 재고수가 911로 회수 대상 재고수가 가장 많음을 확인할 수 있다.
두 단서를 종합할 때, Mr. Galloway는 McGinnis에서 일한다는 점을 추론할 수 있다. 따라서 (C)가 정답이다.

191-195번은 다음 이메일, 송장, 쿠폰에 관한 문제입니다.

수신: Rossy 음료 회사 <sales@rossybeverages.net>
발신: Patricia Reyes <patricia@sipplecoffeshops.com>
제목: 문의
날짜: 6월 15일

관계자분께:

저는 Patricia Reyes이며, [191-(A)]샌프란시스코 대도시권에 10곳의

지점이 있는 Sipple 커피의 소유주입니다. ¹⁹¹⁻⁽ᶜ⁾저희는 에티오피아로부터 받는 자체 원두를 볶아 그것들을 다른 카페에 판매합니다. 또한 Organico 건강식품 체인을 포함한 여러 매장에 공급합니다. 저희는 저희의 커피를 병에 담아 식료품점에서 판매하고 싶습니다. ¹⁹⁵저희의 콜드브루 커피가 대단히 인기 있기 때문에, 할인이나 다른 특가 판매에 의지하지 않고도 성공할 수 있다고 확신합니다. 그것이 제가 귀사에 연락한 이유입니다. ¹⁹²귀사가 다른 소규모 사업체와 협업을 해 왔으므로, 저희가 그 사업을 실행에 옮기는 데 도움을 주실 수 있을 거라고 생각합니다. ¹⁹³저는 전반적으로 5,000달러의 예산을 염두에 두고 있습니다. 귀사로부터 연락받기를 기다리겠습니다.

Patricia Reyes
소유주, Sipple 커피

roast v. 볶다, 굽다 bottle v. 병에 담다 widely adv. 대단히, 널리
resort to ~에 의지하다, 기대다 reach out to ~에게 연락하다
operation n. 사업체, 운영

Rossy 음료 회사 송장

청구서 수신자: Patricia Reyes
회사: ¹⁹³Sipple 커피
계정: 5285
발송 날짜: 7월 2일

주문 세부 정보

항목	항목 설명	가격
항목 1	새로운 음료 개발	2,000달러
항목 2	조리법 소유권 및 상표	500달러
항목 3	디자인 및 포장	2,000달러
항목 4	200개의 유리병	400달러
항목 5	보관	200달러
항목 6	배송	100달러
항목 7	소매 운영 관리	500달러
소계		5,700달러
세금		570달러
¹⁹³총계		¹⁹³6,270달러

¹⁹⁴이 송장을 받고 10일 이내에 지불해주십시오. 이후에 지불이 되면 10퍼센트의 과태료가 부과될 것입니다. 귀하의 거래에 감사드립니다.

description n. 설명, 묘사 ownership n. 소유(권)
storage n. 보관, 저장 payment n. 지불, 납입

Cawston 식료품점 쿠폰

여러분이 가장 좋아하는 현지 커피숍인 Sipple 커피에서 특별한 음료를 만들었습니다. 그것은 오리지널 콜드브루 커피와 아가베즙에 우유와 바닐라 향을 더해 만든 것입니다. 맛있고 활력을 주는 음료를 위해 이것을 만들었습니다. 그리고 ¹⁹⁵Sipple 커피와의 독점 계약 덕분에 하나를 구매하면 두 번째 것을 무료로 받으실 수 있습니다. 이 제공은 샌프란시스코에 있는 Cawston 식료품점 지점에서만 유효합니다.

nectar n. 즙, 꿀 flavoring n. 향료, 양념
energize v. 활력을 주다, 기운을 북돋우다

191 Not/True 문제

해석 Sipple 커피에 대해 언급된 것은?
(A) 한 도시에서 여러 지점을 운영한다.
(B) 다른 나라들에서 음료 제품을 판매한다.
(C) 다른 카페 체인으로부터 원두를 구매한다.
(D) 고객들에게 건강식품을 제공한다.

해설 이메일의 'Sipple Coffee, which includes 10 locations in the greater San Francisco area'에서 Sipple 커피가 샌프란시스코 대도시권에 10곳의 지점이 있다고 했으므로 (A)가 정답이다. (B)와 (D)는 지문에 언급되지 않은 내용이다. 이메일의 'We roast our own beans that we get from Ethiopia and sell them to other cafés.'에서 Sipple Coffee가 에티오피아로부터 받는 자체 원두를 볶아 그것들을 다른 카페에 판매하고 있다고 했으므로, (C)는 지문의 내용과 일치하지 않는다.

어휘 sell v. 팔다

Paraphrasing

10 locations 10곳의 지점 → multiple branches 여러 지점

192 육하원칙 문제

해석 이메일에 따르면, Ms. Reyes는 왜 Rossy 음료 회사를 선택했는가?
(A) 경쟁사보다 낮은 수수료를 부과한다.
(B) 카페가 위치한 곳의 인근에 있다.
(C) 소규모 회사들과 협업해 왔다.
(D) 대규모 유통망을 담당하고 있다.

해설 이메일의 'Your company has worked with other small-scale operations, so I believe you can help us get the project off the ground.'에서 Rossy 음료 회사가 다른 소규모 사업체와 협업을 해 왔으므로, Sipple 커피가 사업을 실행에 옮기는 데에 도움을 줄 수 있다고 생각한다고 했다. 따라서 (C)가 정답이다.

어휘 fee n. 수수료, 요금 proximity n. 부근, 근접, 가까움
be in charge of ~을 담당하다

Paraphrasing

small-scale operations 소규모 사업체 → small companies 소규모 회사들

193 추론 문제 연계

해석 주문에 대해 암시되는 것은?
(A) 10 영업일 이내에 배송할 것이다.
(B) 여러 가지 음료 맛으로 구성되어 있다.
(C) 원래의 예산을 초과했다.
(D) 광고 비용이 포함되어 있다.

해설 주문 정보가 담긴 송장을 먼저 확인한다.
단서 1 송장의 'Sipple Coffee'와 'Total', '$6,270'에서 Sipple 커피가 주문한 항목의 총비용이 6,270달러임을 알 수 있다.
단서 2 이메일의 'I have a budget of $5,000 in mind overall'에서 Sipple 커피의 소유주인 Patricia Reyes가 5,000달러의 전체 예산을 염두에 두고 있었음을 알 수 있다.

두 단서를 종합할 때, Sipple 커피에서 주문한 금액이 원래의 예산인 5,000달러를 초과했음을 알 수 있다. 따라서 (C)가 정답이다.

어휘 consist of ~으로 구성되다 flavor n. 맛, 풍미

194 육하원칙 문제

해석 Ms. Reyes가 송장을 지불하기 위해 10일보다 더 오래 기다리면 무슨 일이 생길 것인가?
(A) 주문이 취소될 것이다.
(B) 요금이 적용될 것이다.
(C) 불만이 제시될 것이다.
(D) 계정이 폐쇄될 것이다.

해설 송장의 'Please send payment within 10 days of receiving this invoice. A 10 percent penalty fee will be charged if payment is made after this.'에서 송장을 받고 10일 이내에 지불하지 않으면 10퍼센트의 과태료가 부과될 것이라고 하였다. 따라서 (B)가 정답이다.

어휘 apply v. 적용하다

195 추론 문제 연계

해석 Ms. Reyes는 Cawston 식료품점을 위해 무엇을 변경했을 것 같은가?
(A) 마케팅 예산
(B) 주문 수량
(C) 판촉 전략
(D) 배송 주소

해설 질문의 핵심 어구인 Ms. Reyes가 작성한 이메일을 먼저 확인한다.
단서 1 이메일의 'Since our cold-brew coffee is widely popular, we feel confident that we can achieve success without resorting to discounts or other special offers.'에서 Sipple 커피의 콜드브루 커피가 대단히 인기 있기 때문에, 할인이나 다른 특가 판매에 의지하지 않고도 성공할 수 있다고 확신한다고 하였다.
단서 2 쿠폰의 'And thanks to an exclusive deal with Sipple Coffee, if you buy one, you will get a second one for free'에서 Sipple 커피와 독점 계약을 해서 음료 하나를 사면 하나를 무료로 받을 수 있는 행사 중임을 확인할 수 있다.
두 단서를 종합할 때, Ms. Reyes가 Cawston 식료품점을 위해 판촉 전략을 변경했다는 것을 추론할 수 있다. 따라서 (C)가 정답이다.

어휘 promotion n. 판촉, 홍보

196-200번은 다음 기사, 광고, 이메일에 관한 문제입니다.

시애틀(4월 18일)—¹⁹⁶시애틀 정부가 자전거를 무료로 이용할 수 있는 계획을 발표했다. ¹⁹⁹그 프로그램은 인기 관광 명소가 많은 Coleridge 지역에만 한정될 예정이다. 자전거 거치대들은 현재 설치 중이며 그것들은 5월 1일까지 사용할 준비가 갖춰질 것이다. 현재로서는, 인기 관광 명소에 30개의 거치대들이 계획되어 있다.

그 자전거 프로그램은 Seattle Path라고 불리며, 시애틀 관광청에 의해 설계되고 운영되는 온라인 애플리케이션을 이용한다. 정부 관계자에 따르면 자전거 대여 업계의 선두 주자인 Tapco와의 계약이 이루어질 수 없었다고 한다. Tapco는 통근용 대여에 초점을 맞춘 반면,

Seattle Path는 관광객을 대상으로 한다. Seattle Path 자전거의 1회 탑승 시간은 2시간으로 제한될 것이다. 그렇지 않으면, 요금이 발생할 것이다.

exclusive adj. 한정된, 독점적인 as of now 현재로서는
design v. 설계하다 insider n. 관계자, 내부자
target v. 초점을 맞추다, 목표로 삼다 occur v. 발생하다

Tapco
자전거를 선택하고, 탭하고, 이동하세요.
Tapco는 자전거 대여 업계의 선두 주자입니다. 시애틀 전역에서 이용할 수 있는 수백 대의 자전거로, 저희는 교통 체증을 피하고, 국내에서 가장 자전거 친화적인 도시 중 한 곳을 자전거를 타고 돌아다니는 것을 가능하게 합니다. Tapco 애플리케이션은 사용하기 쉬우며, 5월에는 많은 특별 프로모션을 진행합니다.

- ¹⁹⁸신규 회원에게는 최초 20달러 공제가 제공됩니다. 저희 자전거를 타보시고, 직접 확인해 보세요.
- 회원은 모든 탑승에서 20퍼센트 할인을 누리실 수 있습니다.
- 최소 12시간 자전거를 예약하는 회원은 50퍼센트 할인을 받을 수 있습니다.
- 20분 이내에 탭하여 타고 내리는 모든 탑승은 완전 무료이기에, 짧은 거리에 대한 무료 통근이 가능합니다.

¹⁹⁷저희는 사고 발생 시 부상 위험을 줄이기 위해 모든 탑승자가 헬멧을 착용할 것을 요구합니다.

see for oneself 스스로 확인하다 distance n. 거리
injury n. 부상, 피해

수신: Lucy Kimpton <l.kimpton@tapcobikes.com>
발신: Jackson Hoover <j.hoover@tapcobikes.com>
제목: 업데이트
날짜: 5월 21일
첨부: 성과 검토

Lucy,

첨부된, 시애틀 시장에 대한 우리의 성과 수치를 확인해 주시기 바랍니다. 우리는 자전거 이용면에서 전반적으로 5퍼센트 상승을 확인했습니다. 이는 프레즈노와 새크라멘토 등 서부 해안의 다른 시장과 비슷합니다.

하지만, 아시다시피, 우리는 시애틀에서 우리의 서비스를 아주 많이 할인했습니다. ¹⁹⁸등록한 신규 사용자는 거의 없었습니다. 우리 조사에 따르면, 불과 몇 주 만에 ¹⁹⁹Seattle Path가 저희 이용자 수의 15퍼센트를 가져갔습니다. 특히 Queen Ann과 Ballard 지역에 있는 거치대들이 인기가 높습니다.

²⁰⁰우리는 향후 다른 도시들과의 제휴를 고려해야 할 수도 있습니다. 오늘이나 내일 만나서 고객을 되찾기 위한 전략을 논의해 봅시다. 당신의 일정이 어떻게 되나요?

Jackson Hoover 드림

performance n. 성과, 실적, 수행 heavily adv. 아주 많이, 몹시
strategy n. 전략 regain v. 되찾다

196 주제 찾기 문제

해석 기사의 주로 무엇에 대한 것인가?
(A) 정치 선거 활동
(B) 곧 있을 도시 전역의 축하 행사
(C) 새로운 기술 장치에 대한 후기
(D) 공공 프로그램에 대한 알림

해설 기사의 'The Seattle government has announced a plan to provide free access to bicycles.'에서 시애틀 정부가 자전거를 무료로 이용할 수 있는 계획을 발표했다고 한 후, 계획의 세부 정보에 대해 설명하고 있으므로 (D)가 정답이다.

어휘 election n. 선거 gadget n. 장치, 도구

197 육하원칙 문제

해석 Tapco가 고객들에게 하라고 요청하는 것은 무엇인가?
(A) 애플리케이션을 사용하여 그들의 위치를 업데이트한다.
(B) 탑승하기 전에 안전 장비를 착용한다.
(C) 각 자전거 탑승 시간을 20분으로 제한한다.
(D) 어떠한 사고도 관계 당국에 알린다.

해설 광고의 'We require that each rider wear a helmet to reduce the risk of injury if an accident occurs'에서 Tapco는 사고 발생 시 부상 위험을 줄이기 위해 모든 탑승자가 헬멧을 착용할 것을 요구한다고 하였다. 따라서 (B)가 정답이다.

어휘 cycling n. 자전거 타기 authority n. (관계) 당국, 권한, 권위

Paraphrasing

wear a helmet 헬멧을 착용한다 → Put on safety equipment 안전 장비를 착용한다

198 육하원칙 문제 연계

해석 어떤 Tapco 프로모션이 성공적이지 못했는가?
(A) 20달러 공제
(B) 20퍼센트 할인
(C) 50퍼센트 할인
(D) 무료 통근

해설 Tapco에 대한 광고를 먼저 확인한다.
단서 1 광고의 'New members get a first-time $20 credit'에서 신규 회원에게는 최초 20달러 공제가 제공된다고 했다. 그런데 해당 프로모션이 성공적이었는지가 제시되지 않았으므로 이메일에서 관련 내용을 확인한다.
단서 2 이메일의 'There were almost no new users that registered'에서 등록한 신규 사용자는 거의 없었다는 점을 확인할 수 있다.
두 단서를 종합할 때, 신규 회원을 대상으로 한 최초 20달러 공제 프로모션이 성공적이지 못하여 등록한 신규 사용자가 거의 없었음을 알 수 있다. 따라서 (A)가 정답이다.

199 추론 문제 연계

해석 Seattle Path에 대해 암시되는 것은?
(A) 지역의 판매세 인상에 의한 자금을 제공받는다.
(B) 원래의 목표 지역에서 확장했다.
(C) 지역 주민들로부터 많은 불만을 받았다.
(D) 지역 기술 회사에 애플리케이션을 제작해 달라고 의뢰했다.

해설 질문의 핵심 어구인 Seattle Path에 대해 소개하는 기사를 먼저 확인한다.
단서 1 기사의 'The program will be exclusive to the Coleridge neighborhood,'에서 Seattle Path가 인기 관광 명소가 많은 Coleridge 지역에만 한정될 예정이라고 했다. Seattle Path가 언급된 이메일에서 추가적인 내용을 확인한다.
단서 2 이메일의 '~ Seattle Path has taken 15 percent of our ridership. Their stations in the Queen Ann and Ballard neighborhoods are particularly popular.'에서 Seattle Path의 거치대가 Queen Ann과 Ballard 지역에도 있다는 것을 확인할 수 있다.
두 단서를 종합할 때, Seattle Path가 원래 목표했던 Coleridge 지역에서 더 확장했음을 추론할 수 있다. 따라서 (B)가 정답이다.

어휘 finance v. 자금을 제공하다 commission v. 의뢰하다, 위임하다

200 육하원칙 문제

해석 Mr. Hoover는 회사가 무엇을 해야 할 수도 있다고 생각하는가?
(A) 더 많은 기술 인력을 고용한다.
(B) 시간당 요금을 영구적으로 낮춘다.
(C) 다른 도시들과 제휴를 맺는다.
(D) 일부 오래된 장비를 교체한다.

해설 이메일의 'We might have to consider partnering with other cities in the future.'에서 Mr. Hoover는 자신의 회사가 향후 다른 도시들과의 제휴를 고려해야 할 수도 있다고 했으므로 (C)가 정답이다.

어휘 lower v. 낮추다 permanently adv. 영구적으로, 영원히

TEST 4

LISTENING TEST
p.154

1 (A)	21 (B)	41 (D)	61 (B)	81 (B)
2 (C)	22 (A)	42 (B)	62 (A)	82 (D)
3 (B)	23 (C)	43 (D)	63 (C)	83 (B)
4 (B)	24 (A)	44 (C)	64 (D)	84 (D)
5 (D)	25 (C)	45 (B)	65 (C)	85 (C)
6 (A)	26 (A)	46 (A)	66 (A)	86 (D)
7 (C)	27 (B)	47 (D)	67 (C)	87 (A)
8 (B)	28 (C)	48 (B)	68 (C)	88 (C)
9 (B)	29 (B)	49 (D)	69 (A)	89 (C)
10 (A)	30 (A)	50 (C)	70 (D)	90 (A)
11 (C)	31 (C)	51 (D)	71 (B)	91 (B)
12 (C)	32 (B)	52 (B)	72 (A)	92 (C)
13 (B)	33 (A)	53 (D)	73 (D)	93 (D)
14 (A)	34 (D)	54 (B)	74 (B)	94 (B)
15 (A)	35 (B)	55 (C)	75 (D)	95 (A)
16 (C)	36 (C)	56 (A)	76 (D)	96 (D)
17 (A)	37 (D)	57 (B)	77 (B)	97 (B)
18 (B)	38 (A)	58 (C)	78 (B)	98 (B)
19 (C)	39 (D)	59 (B)	79 (A)	99 (D)
20 (A)	40 (A)	60 (C)	80 (B)	100 (B)

READING TEST
p.166

101 (D)	121 (C)	141 (A)	161 (B)	181 (B)
102 (D)	122 (D)	142 (D)	162 (A)	182 (B)
103 (B)	123 (B)	143 (C)	163 (C)	183 (C)
104 (A)	124 (A)	144 (D)	164 (B)	184 (A)
105 (B)	125 (D)	145 (A)	165 (C)	185 (B)
106 (B)	126 (C)	146 (B)	166 (C)	186 (B)
107 (D)	127 (C)	147 (B)	167 (A)	187 (D)
108 (A)	128 (B)	148 (B)	168 (C)	188 (D)
109 (C)	129 (B)	149 (C)	169 (D)	189 (B)
110 (C)	130 (A)	150 (C)	170 (C)	190 (B)
111 (C)	131 (A)	151 (C)	171 (B)	191 (C)
112 (A)	132 (D)	152 (D)	172 (B)	192 (D)
113 (D)	133 (A)	153 (D)	173 (C)	193 (D)
114 (A)	134 (C)	154 (C)	174 (B)	194 (B)
115 (D)	135 (C)	155 (B)	175 (D)	195 (D)
116 (C)	136 (B)	156 (D)	176 (B)	196 (C)
117 (C)	137 (C)	157 (D)	177 (A)	197 (A)
118 (A)	138 (C)	158 (C)	178 (C)	198 (C)
119 (B)	139 (D)	159 (A)	179 (B)	199 (B)
120 (C)	140 (B)	160 (C)	180 (D)	200 (D)

PART 1

1 1인 사진
 영국식

(A) He's crouching down in a yard.
(B) He's gripping a pump sprayer.
(C) He's pushing a wheelbarrow.
(D) He's picking up some tools.

crouch v. 웅크리다, 쭈그리다　yard n. 마당　grip v. 꽉 잡다
wheelbarrow n. 외바퀴 손수레

해석 (A) 그는 마당에서 웅크리고 있다.
(B) 그는 펌프 분무기를 꽉 잡고 있다.
(C) 그는 외바퀴 손수레를 밀고 있다.
(D) 그는 도구를 줍고 있다.

해설 (A) [O] 남자가 마당에서 웅크리고 있는 모습을 가장 잘 묘사한 정답이다.
(B) [X] 사진에 펌프 분무기(pump sprayer)가 없으므로 오답이다.
(C) [X] pushing a wheelbarrow(손수레를 밀고 있다)는 남자의 동작과 무관하므로 오답이다. 사진에 있는 외바퀴 손수레(wheelbarrow)를 사용하여 혼동을 주었다.
(D) [X] picking up some tools(도구를 줍고 있다)는 남자의 동작과 무관하므로 오답이다.

최신토익경향
사람이 등장하는 사진에서 허리를 구부리고 있거나 쭈그려 앉아 있는 모습을 묘사할 때 다양한 표현이 출제된다.

<몸이 굽혀진 모습을 묘사하는 빈출 표현>
• be crouching down 쭈그려 앉아 있다
• be bending over 몸을 앞으로 숙이고 있다
• be kneeling down 무릎을 꿇고 있다
• be leaning over 몸을 굽히고 있다

2 2인 이상 사진
 캐나다식

(A) One of the workers is carrying a ladder.
(B) One of the workers is replacing some flooring.
(C) The workers are installing a door.
(D) The workers are fixing a fence near a house.

replace v. 교체하다, 대신하다　flooring n. 바닥재　install v. 설치하다

해석 (A) 작업자들 중 한 명이 사다리를 나르고 있다.
(B) 작업자들 중 한 명이 몇몇 바닥재를 교체하고 있다.
(C) 작업자들이 문을 설치하고 있다.
(D) 작업자들이 집 근처에서 울타리를 수리하고 있다.

해설 (A) [×] carrying a ladder(사다리를 나르고 있다)는 작업자들의 동작과 무관하므로 오답이다.
(B) [×] 사진에 바닥재(flooring)가 없으므로 오답이다.
(C) [○] 작업자들이 문을 설치하고 있는 모습을 가장 잘 묘사한 정답이다.
(D) [×] 사진에 울타리(fence)가 없으므로 오답이다. The workers are fixing(작업자들이 수리하고 있다)까지만 듣고 정답으로 선택하지 않도록 주의한다.

3 사물 및 풍경 사진 영국식

(A) Some trees are shading a picnic area.
(B) There's a paved walkway next to a road.
(C) There are bushes surrounding a pond.
(D) Some trucks are passing each other on a country road.

paved adj. (도로가) 포장된 walkway n. 보도, 산책길
surround v. 둘러싸다

해설 (A) 몇몇 나무들이 피크닉 구역에 그림자를 드리우고 있다.
(B) 도로 옆에 포장된 보도가 있다.
(C) 연못을 둘러싸고 있는 덤불이 있다.
(D) 몇몇 트럭들이 시골길에서 서로 지나쳐 가고 있다.

해설 (A) [×] 사진에 피크닉 구역(picnic area)이 없으므로 오답이다.
(B) [○] 도로 옆에 포장된 보도가 있는 모습을 가장 잘 묘사한 정답이다.
(C) [×] 덤불(bushes)이 연못을 둘러싸고 있는(surrounding a pond) 모습이 아니므로 오답이다.
(D) [×] 사진에 트럭들(trucks)이 없으므로 오답이다. 사진에 있는 도로(road)를 사용하여 혼동을 주었다.

최신토익경향

PART 1에서 There is/are(~가 있다)로 사물을 묘사하는 표현이 정답으로 자주 출제되고 있다. 사물 뒤에 수식어구가 나올 경우 난도가 높아진다.

<'There is/are + 사물 + 수식어구' 표현>

• There is a waste bin blocking a path.
  길을 막고 있는 쓰레기통이 있다.
• There are signs posted in a parking area.
  주차 구역에 게시된 표지판들이 있다.
• There are crates stacked alongside a fence.
  울타리를 따라 쌓여 있는 상자들이 있다.

4 2인 이상 사진 호주식

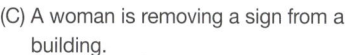

(A) Some people are gathered around a lighthouse.
(B) Some people are boarding a boat.
(C) One of the people is rowing a boat under a bridge.
(D) One of the people is paying for a ticket.

lighthouse n. 등대 row v. 노를 젓다 pay for ~의 값을 지불하다

해설 (A) 몇몇 사람들이 등대 주변에 모여 있다.
(B) 몇몇 사람들이 배에 탑승하고 있다.
(C) 사람들 중 한 명이 다리 아래에서 배의 노를 젓고 있다.
(D) 사람들 중 한 명이 푯값을 지불하고 있다.

해설 (A) [×] 사진에 등대(lighthouse)가 없으므로 오답이다.
(B) [○] 사람들이 배에 탑승하고 있는 모습을 가장 잘 묘사한 정답이다.
(C) [×] 사진에 노를 젓고 있는(rowing a boat) 사람이 없으므로 오답이다.
(D) [×] 사진에 푯값을 지불하고 있는(paying for a ticket) 사람이 없으므로 오답이다.

5 1인 사진 미국식

(A) Some folding chairs are leaning against a stone wall.
(B) A pile of bricks has been unloaded near a building.
(C) A woman is removing a sign from a building.
(D) A woman is holding up her cell phone.

lean against ~에 기대다 pile n. 더미 brick n. 벽돌
unload v. (짐을) 내리다 hold up ~을 들어 올리다

해설 (A) 몇몇 접이식 의자들이 돌벽 옆면에 기대어 있다.
(B) 벽돌 더미가 건물 근처에 내려져있다.
(C) 여자가 건물에서 표지판을 떼어내고 있다.
(D) 여자가 그녀의 휴대폰을 들어 올리고 있다.

해설 (A) [×] 사진에 접이식 의자들(folding chairs)이 없으므로 오답이다.
(B) [×] 사진에 벽돌 더미(a pile of bricks)가 없으므로 오답이다.
(C) [×] removing a sign from a building(건물에서 표지판을 떼어내고 있다)은 여자의 동작과 무관하므로 오답이다.
(D) [○] 여자가 휴대폰을 들어 올리고 있는 모습을 가장 잘 묘사한 정답이다.

6 사물 및 풍경 사진 호주식

(A) Some frames have been secured to a wall.
(B) A carpet has been rolled up in the hall.
(C) Some decorations are being taken down from a column.
(D) There are some cushions stacked on the floor.

secure v. 고정시키다 decoration n. 장식품 column n. 기둥

해설 (A) 몇몇 액자들이 벽에 고정되어 있다.
(B) 카펫이 복도에 말려져 있다.
(C) 몇몇 장식품들이 기둥에서 끌어내려지고 있다.
(D) 바닥에 쌓여 있는 몇몇 쿠션들이 있다.

해설 (A) [○] 몇몇 액자들이 벽에 고정된 모습을 가장 잘 묘사한 정답이다.
(B) [×] 사진에 카펫(carpet)이 없으므로 오답이다. 사진에 보이는 복도(hall)를 사용하여 혼동을 주었다.

(C) [×] 사진에 장식품들(decorations)이 없으므로 오답이다.
(D) [×] 사진에 쿠션들(cushions)은 보이지만 바닥(floor)이 아닌 소파 위에 있으므로 오답이다. There are some cushions (몇몇 쿠션들이 있다)까지만 듣고 정답으로 고르지 않도록 주의한다.

최신토익경향

사물이 벽이나 천장 등에 고정되어 있는 모습을 묘사하는 정답은 PART 1에서 다양한 표현으로 자주 출제된다.

<사물이 고정되어 있는 모습을 묘사하는 표현>
- be secured to ~에 고정되어 있다
- be attached to ~에 붙어 있다
- be pinned to ~에 (핀으로) 고정되어 있다

PART 2

7 Where 의문문 영국식 → 캐나다식

Where's the survey form going to be posted?
(A) Because I'm free that day.
(B) Twice a week.
(C) On our Web site.

survey n. 설문조사   twice adv. 두 번

해석 설문조사 양식은 어디에 게시될 것인가요?
(A) 제가 그날 한가하기 때문이에요.
(B) 일주일에 두 번요.
(C) 우리 웹사이트에요.

해설 (A) [×] 설문조사 양식이 게시되는 장소를 물었는데, 이와 관련 없는 자신이 그날 한가하기 때문이라는 내용으로 응답했으므로 오답이다.
(B) [×] 설문조사 양식이 게시되는 장소를 물었는데, 빈도로 응답했으므로 오답이다.
(C) [○] 우리 웹사이트라며, 설문조사 양식이 게시되는 장소를 언급했으므로 정답이다.

8 When 의문문 호주식 → 미국식

When can you send me the draft of the article?
(A) To my bank account.
(B) As soon as it's completed.
(C) About the opening of the shopping center.

draft n. 초안   account n. 계좌, 계정

해석 기사 초안을 언제 저에게 보내주실 수 있나요?
(A) 제 은행 계좌로요.
(B) 그것이 완성되는 대로요.
(C) 쇼핑센터 개장에 관해서요.

해설 (A) [×] 기사 초안을 언제 보내줄 수 있는지 물었는데, 이와 관련 없는 은행 계좌로라고 응답했으므로 오답이다. 질문의 When을 Where로 혼동하여 이를 정답으로 선택하지 않도록 주의한다.
(B) [○] 그것이 완성되는 대로라는 말로, 기사 초안을 보낼 시점을 언급했으므로 정답이다.
(C) [×] 기사 초안을 언제 보내줄 수 있는지 물었는데, 이와 관련이 없는 쇼핑센터 개장에 관해서라고 응답했으므로 오답이다.

9 부정 의문문 캐나다식 → 영국식

Isn't Ms. Wright organizing the annual company picnic?
(A) Usually for an annual checkup.
(B) Yes, she's planning it.
(C) Well, maybe a sandwich.

organize v. 준비하다, 조직하다   annual adj. 연례의, 매년의

해석 Ms. Wright이 연례 회사 야유회를 준비하고 있지 않나요?
(A) 보통 연례 검진을 위해서요.
(B) 네, 그녀가 그것을 계획하고 있어요.
(C) 글쎄요, 아마도 샌드위치요.

해설 (A) [×] 질문의 annual을 반복 사용하여 혼동을 준 오답이다.
(B) [○] Yes로 Ms. Wright이 회사 야유회를 준비하고 있다고 전달했으므로 정답이다.
(C) [×] 질문의 company picnic(회사 야유회)에서 연상할 수 있는 음식과 관련된 sandwich(샌드위치)를 사용하여 혼동을 준 오답이다.

10 Who 의문문 미국식 → 캐나다식

Who should I talk to about replacing my security card?
(A) There's a security team just upstairs.
(B) Within a month, I think.
(C) I lost my credit card.

replace v. 교체하다   upstairs adv. 위층에

해석 제 보안 카드를 교체하는 것에 대해 누구에게 이야기해야 하나요?
(A) 바로 위층에 보안팀이 있어요.
(B) 한 달 이내일 것 같아요.
(C) 저는 제 신용 카드를 잃어버렸어요.

해설 (A) [○] 바로 위층에 보안팀이 있다는 말로, 보안 카드를 교체하는 것에 대해 누구에게 이야기해야 하는지에 대한 정보를 간접적으로 전달했으므로 정답이다.
(B) [×] 보안 카드를 교체하는 것에 대해 누구에게 이야기해야 하는지 물었는데, 기간으로 응답했으므로 오답이다.
(C) [×] 질문의 card를 반복 사용하여 혼동을 준 오답이다.

11 요청 의문문 영국식 → 호주식

Could you ask Mr. Chung to finalize the travel arrangements?
(A) About the final offer.
(B) It's already sold out.
(C) He leaves early on Fridays.

finalize v. 끝내다, 완성하다   arrangement n. 준비, 계획
offer n. 제안

해석 Mr. Chung에게 출장 준비를 마무리해 달라고 요청해 주시겠어요?
(A) 최종 제안에 관해서요.
(B) 그것은 이미 매진되었어요.
(C) 그는 금요일마다 일찍 퇴근해요.

해설 (A) [×] finalize - final의 유사 발음 어휘를 사용하여 혼동을 준 오답이다.
(B) [×] 질문의 travel arrangements(출장 준비)에서 연상할 수 있는 티켓과 관련된 sold out(매진된)을 사용하여 혼동을 준 오답이다.
(C) [○] 그는 금요일마다 일찍 퇴근한다는 말로, Mr. Chung에게 출장 준비를 마무리해 달라고 요청할 수 없음을 간접적으로 전달했으므로 정답이다.

12 Why 의문문   호주식 → 캐나다식

Why is the road blocked for vehicles?
(A) No, I took a taxi.
(B) For about three hours.
(C) Because there's a street festival.

block v. 막다, 차단하다   vehicle n. 차량, 운송 수단

해설 그 도로는 왜 차량들을 막고 있나요?
(A) 아뇨, 저는 택시를 탔어요.
(B) 대략 3시간 동안이요.
(C) 거리 축제가 있기 때문이에요.

해설 (A) [×] 의문사 의문문에 No로 응답했으므로 오답이다. 질문의 vehicles(차량들)와 관련 있는 taxi(택시)를 사용하여 혼동을 주었다.
(B) [×] 도로가 차량들을 막고 있는 이유를 물었는데, 기간으로 응답했으므로 오답이다.
(C) [○] 거리 축제가 있기 때문이라는 말로, 차량들을 막고 있는 이유를 언급했으므로 정답이다.

13 Which 의문문   영국식 → 미국식

Which file should I download for the convention?
(A) At the convention center tomorrow.
(B) The one with today's date in the file name.
(C) He is a software developer.

convention n. 협의회   date n. 날짜   developer n. 개발자

해설 그 협의회를 위해 제가 어느 파일을 다운로드해야 하나요?
(A) 내일 컨벤션 센터에서요.
(B) 파일명에 오늘 날짜가 들어간 것이요.
(C) 그는 소프트웨어 개발자예요.

해설 (A) [×] 질문의 convention을 반복 사용하여 혼동을 준 오답이다.
(B) [○] 파일명에 오늘 날짜가 들어간 것이라는 말로, 다운로드해야 하는 파일이 무엇인지 언급했으므로 정답이다.
(C) [×] 질문의 file에서 연상할 수 있는 software(소프트웨어)를 사용하여 혼동을 준 오답이다.

14 선택 의문문   미국식 → 호주식

Will the meeting with our client be this week or next week?
(A) She hasn't replied yet.
(B) No, the agenda is already full.
(C) From the next issue of the magazine.

reply v. 답장을 보내다, 대답하다   agenda n. 안건

해설 우리 고객과의 회의가 이번 주인가요, 다음 주인가요?
(A) 그녀가 아직 답장을 보내지 않았어요.
(B) 아뇨, 안건이 이미 가득 찼어요.
(C) 잡지의 다음 호부터요.

해설 (A) [○] 그녀가 아직 답장을 보내지 않았다는 말로, 고객과의 회의 일정이 아직 정해지지 않아서 이번 주와 다음 주 둘 다 간접적으로 선택하지 않은 정답이다.
(B) [×] 선택 의문문에 No로 응답했으므로 오답이다. 질문의 meeting(회의)에서 연상할 수 있는 agenda(안건)를 사용하여 혼동을 주었다.
(C) [×] 질문의 next를 반복 사용하여 혼동을 준 오답이다.

15 조동사 의문문   캐나다식 → 미국식

Does the company pay for online training courses?
(A) Only half the cost.
(B) An interior design course.
(C) Please sign on the line.

cost n. 비용, 값

해설 그 회사는 온라인 교육 과정에 비용을 지불하나요?
(A) 비용의 절반만요.
(B) 인테리어 디자인 과정이요.
(C) 선 위에 서명해 주세요.

해설 (A) [○] 비용의 절반만이라는 말로 교육 과정에 비용을 절반만 지불한다고 응답한 정답이다.
(B) [×] 질문의 courses의 course를 반복 사용하여 혼동을 준 오답이다.
(C) [×] online - line의 유사 발음 어휘를 사용하여 혼동을 준 오답이다.

16 Who 의문문   미국식 → 영국식

Who has the keys to the warehouse?
(A) It's such a tall building.
(B) You can hang your keys here.
(C) I left the door open.

warehouse n. 창고   hang v. 걸다

해설 누가 창고의 열쇠를 가지고 있나요?
(A) 그것은 정말 높은 건물이네요.
(B) 당신의 열쇠를 이곳에 걸어도 돼요.
(C) 제가 문을 열어 뒀어요.

해설 (A) [×] 질문의 warehouse(창고)에서 연상할 수 있는 building(건

물)을 사용하여 혼동을 준 오답이다.
(B) [x] 질문의 keys(열쇠)를 반복 사용하여 혼동을 준 오답이다.
(C) [o] 자신이 문을 열어 두었다는 말로, 자신이 창고 열쇠를 가지고 있음을 간접적으로 전달했으므로 정답이다.

17 요청 의문문
🎧 미국식 → 캐나다식

Could you help Mr. Choi collect the sales performance data?
(A) I'll have time after lunch.
(B) For our summer collection.
(C) I applied for the sales position.

collect v. 수집하다   apply for ~에 지원하다

해석 Mr. Choi가 영업 실적 자료들을 수집하는 것을 도와주실 수 있나요?
(A) 저는 점심 이후에 시간이 있을 거예요.
(B) 우리의 여름 상품들을 위해서요.
(C) 저는 판매직에 지원했어요.

해설 (A) [o] 점심 이후에 시간이 있을 거라는 말로, Mr. Choi가 판매 성과 자료를 수집하는 것을 도와달라는 요청을 간접적으로 수락한 정답이다.
(B) [x] collect - collection의 유사 발음 어휘를 사용하여 혼동을 준 오답이다.
(C) [x] 질문의 sales를 반복 사용하여 혼동을 준 오답이다.

최신토익경향

최근 PART 2에서는 요청 의문문에 거절인지 수락인지 헷갈리게 답변하여 정답을 고르기 까다로운 문제들이 출제되고 있다. 따라서 답변을 듣고 빠르게 그 의도를 파악해야 한다.

<요청 의문문에 대한 간접 응답>
Could you drop me off at the furniture store?
가구점에 저를 내려주시겠어요?
[답변] I do need to buy a desk lamp.
저도 책상용 등을 구매해야 해요.
* 자신도 책상용 등을 구매해야 한다는 말로 가구점에 내려달라는 요청을 간접적으로 수락한 응답

Could you please pick up some salad from the café?
카페에서 샐러드를 좀 사다 줄 수 있나요?
[답변] I have to leave for the seminar soon.
저는 세미나를 위해 곧 떠나야 해요.
* 자신은 세미나를 위해 곧 떠나야 한다는 말로 샐러드를 사다 달라는 요청을 거절한 응답

18 부가 의문문
🎧 호주식 → 미국식

All the product brochures for the attendees are printed, right?
(A) Attendance is mandatory.
(B) Didn't you check the message from Mr. Lee?
(C) No, it's a reusable ink cartridge.

attendee n. 참석자   mandatory adj. 의무적인
reusable adj. 재사용할 수 있는

해석 참석자들을 위한 모든 제품 설명서들은 인쇄되어 있어요, 그렇죠?
(A) 참석은 의무예요.
(B) Mr. Lee가 보낸 메시지를 확인 안 하셨나요?
(C) 아니요, 그것은 재사용할 수 있는 잉크 카트리지예요.

해설 (A) [x] attendees - Attendance의 유사 발음 어휘를 사용하여 혼동을 준 오답이다.
(B) [o] Mr. Lee가 보낸 메시지를 확인 안 했는지 되물어 메시지에 제품 설명서가 출력되어 있는지 아닌지 써 있을 거라는 답변을 간접적으로 전달했으므로 정답이다.
(C) [x] 질문의 are printed(인쇄되다)에서 연상할 수 있는 ink cartridge(잉크 카트리지)를 사용하여 혼동을 준 오답이다.

19 조동사 의문문
🎧 호주식 → 캐나다식

Have you scheduled the charity event for the community center yet?
(A) Actually, I don't have a preference.
(B) A calendar for next year.
(C) Yes. I dealt with it yesterday.

charity n. 자선, 자선 단체   preference n. 선호하는 것, 선호
deal with ~을 처리하다, 다루다

해석 벌써 시민 문화 회관의 자선 행사 일정을 잡으셨나요?
(A) 사실, 저는 선호하는 것이 없어요.
(B) 내년 달력이요.
(C) 네, 저는 그것을 어제 처리했어요.

해설 (A) [x] 시민 문화 회관의 자선 행사 일정을 잡았는지 물었는데, 이와 관련이 없는 선호하는 것이 없다는 내용으로 응답했으므로 오답이다.
(B) [x] 질문의 scheduled(일정을 잡다)에서 연상할 수 있는 calendar(달력)를 사용하여 혼동을 준 오답이다.
(C) [o] Yes로 시민 문화 회관의 자선 행사 일정을 잡았다고 전달한 후, 그것을 어제 처리했다는 부연 설명을 했으므로 정답이다.

20 How 의문문
🎧 영국식 → 미국식

How did you like the presentation about the new car?
(A) It was as good as I expected.
(B) What's the speed limit?
(C) With one of our sales representatives.

speed limit 제한 속도   expect v. 예상하다, 기대하다

해석 신형 자동차에 대한 발표는 어떠셨나요?
(A) 그것은 제가 예상했던 것만큼 좋았어요.
(B) 제한 속도는 어떻게 되나요?
(C) 우리의 영업사원들 중 한 명과요.

해설 (A) [o] 그것이 예상했던 것만큼 좋았다는 말로, 발표에 대한 의견을 전달했으므로 정답이다.
(B) [x] 질문의 car(자동차)에서 연상할 수 있는 speed limit(제한 속도)을 사용하여 혼동을 준 오답이다.
(C) [x] presentation - representatives의 유사 발음 어휘를 사용하여 혼동을 준 오답이다.

21 평서문
캐나다식 → 영국식

I received an invitation to a professional development workshop.
(A) From the wrapping paper makers.
(B) I highly recommend attending it.
(C) Right. He's always so professional.

invitation n. 초대장   wrap v. 포장하다   highly adv. 매우, 대단히

해석   제가 전문성 개발 워크숍의 초대장을 받았어요.
(A) 포장용지 제조사로부터요.
(B) 저는 그것에 참석하는 것을 매우 추천해요.
(C) 맞아요. 그는 언제나 전문적이에요.

해설 (A) [×] 전문성 개발 워크숍의 초대장을 받았다고 말했는데, 이와 관련이 없는 포장용지 제조사로부터라는 내용으로 응답했으므로 오답이다.
(B) [○] 그것에 참석하는 것을 매우 추천한다는 말로, 전문성 개발 워크숍에 초대장을 받았다는 말에 추가 의견을 전달했으므로 정답이다.
(C) [×] 질문의 professional을 반복 사용하여 혼동을 준 오답이다.

22 Be동사 의문문
호주식 → 미국식

Are you having trouble using the copy machine?
(A) I'm not sure how to make double-sided copies.
(B) No, do you have a plan?
(C) A five-year warranty.

copy machine 복사기   double-sided adj. 양면의
warranty n. (품질) 보증

해석   복사기를 사용하는 데 문제를 겪고 있나요?
(A) 저는 양면 복사를 하는 방법을 모르겠어요.
(B) 아니요, 당신은 계획이 있나요?
(C) 5년 보증이요.

해설 (A) [○] 양면 복사를 하는 방법을 모르겠다는 말로, 복사기를 사용하는 데 문제를 겪고 있음을 간접적으로 전달했으므로 정답이다.
(B) [×] 질문의 have를 반복 사용하여 혼동을 준 오답이다. No까지만 듣고 정답으로 고르지 않도록 주의한다.
(C) [×] 질문의 copy machine(복사기)에서 연상할 수 있는 warranty(보증)를 사용하여 혼동을 준 오답이다.

23 선택 의문문
미국식 → 캐나다식

Would you like me to order steak or pizza for the business lunch?
(A) The table by the window.
(B) Sorry, but refunds are not allowed.
(C) Some staff are vegetarians.

refund n. 환불   vegetarian n. 채식주의자

해석   제가 업무상 점심을 위해 스테이크를 주문할까요, 아니면 피자를 주문할까요?
(A) 창문 옆 테이블이요.
(B) 죄송하지만, 환불은 허용되지 않습니다.
(C) 몇몇 직원들은 채식주의자예요.

해설 (A) [×] 질문의 business lunch(업무상 점심)에서 연상할 수 있는 식당과 관련된 table(테이블)을 사용하여 혼동을 준 오답이다.
(B) [×] 질문의 order(주문하다)에서 연상할 수 있는 refunds(환불)를 사용하여 혼동을 준 오답이다.
(C) [○] 몇몇 직원들이 채식주의자라는 말로, 스테이크는 선택 사항에서 제외할 것을 간접적으로 전달했으므로 정답이다.

24 부정 의문문
호주식 → 영국식

Won't it take a long time to set up the showroom floor?
(A) Yes. At least four days.
(B) For a trade show.
(C) Let's take a walk.

showroom n. 전시실   at least 적어도, 최소한
trade show 무역 박람회

해석   전시실 바닥을 설치하는 데 시간이 오래 걸리지 않을까요?
(A) 네. 적어도 4일이요.
(B) 무역 박람회를 위해서요.
(C) 산책하러 갑시다.

해설 (A) [○] Yes로 전시실 바닥을 설치하는 데 시간이 오래 걸릴 거라고 전달한 후, 적어도 4일이라는 말로 부연 설명을 했으므로 정답이다.
(B) [×] showroom - show의 유사 발음 어휘를 사용하여 혼동을 준 오답이다.
(C) [×] 질문의 take를 반복 사용하여 혼동을 준 오답이다.

25 What 의문문
캐나다식 → 영국식

What do you think about updating document security software?
(A) It turned out well.
(B) I think we can modify the design.
(C) This is the latest version.

modify v. 변경하다   latest adj. 최신의

해석   문서 보안 소프트웨어를 업데이트하는 것에 대해 어떻게 생각하세요?
(A) 그것은 잘 되었어요.
(B) 저는 우리가 디자인을 변경할 수 있을 것 같아요.
(C) 이것이 최신 버전이에요.

해설 (A) [×] 문서 보안 소프트웨어를 업데이트하는 것에 대해 어떻게 생각하는지 물었는데, 이와 관련이 없는 그것이 잘 되었다는 내용으로 응답했으므로 오답이다.
(B) [×] 질문의 think를 반복 사용하여 혼동을 준 오답이다. I think까지만 듣고 정답으로 고르지 않도록 주의한다.
(C) [○] 이것이 최신 버전이라는 말로, 문서 보안 소프트웨어를 업데이트할 필요가 없음을 간접적으로 전달했으므로 정답이다.

최신토익 경향

상대방의 생각이나 의견을 묻는 질문은 다양한 형태로 출제된다. 질문을 끝까지 들어야 정확한 답변을 고를 수 있으니 최근 자주 출제된 표현을 알아둔다.

<생각/의견을 묻는 빈출 표현>
· What do you think ~? ~을 어떻게 생각하세요?
· How would you feel about ~? ~에 대해 어떻게 생각하세요?
· Do you think ~? ~라고 생각하시나요?

How would you feel about replacing the desks in the office?
사무실의 책상을 교체하는 것에 대해 어떻게 생각하시나요?
[답변] I need to check next year's budget.
내년 예산을 확인해 봐야 해요.
* 사무실의 책상을 교체하는 것에 대해 어떻게 생각하는지 묻는 질문에 내년 예산을 확인해 봐야 한다고 긍정도 부정도 하지 않은 응답

26 평서문 🔊 영국식 → 호주식

The executives and employees really appreciated the lecture we gave.
(A) I'm glad they found it useful.
(B) No, but it can be offered online.
(C) The new employees are doing a great job.

appreciate v. 높이 평가하다, 고마워하다   useful adj. 유용한

해석 임직원분들이 저희가 제공한 강의를 정말 높이 평가했습니다.
(A) 저는 그들이 그것을 유용하다고 여겨줘서 기쁘네요.
(B) 아뇨, 하지만 그것은 온라인으로 제공될 수 있어요.
(C) 신입 직원들은 정말 잘하고 있어요.

해설 (A) [o] 그들이 그것을 유용하다고 여겨줘서 기쁘다는 말로, 임직원들이 강의를 높이 평가했다는 말에 대한 추가 의견을 전달했으므로 정답이다.
(B) [x] 질문의 lecture(강의)에서 연상할 수 있는 강의 제공 방식과 관련된 online(온라인)을 사용하여 혼동을 준 오답이다.
(C) [x] 질문의 employees를 반복 사용하여 혼동을 준 오답이다.

27 부가 의문문 🔊 미국식 → 호주식

This air conditioner needs to be fixed, doesn't it?
(A) In the storage facility.
(B) I called a technician this morning.
(C) Please open the window.

air conditioner 에어컨   fix v. 수리하다, 고치다
storage facility 저장 시설   technician n. 기술자

해석 이 에어컨은 수리될 필요가 있어요, 그렇지 않나요?
(A) 저장 시설 안에요.
(B) 제가 오늘 아침에 기술자를 불렀어요.
(C) 창문을 열어주세요.

해설 (A) [x] 에어컨이 수리될 필요가 있는지 물었는데, 이와 관련이 없는 저장 시설 안이라는 내용으로 응답했으므로 오답이다.
(B) [o] 오늘 아침에 기술자를 불렀다는 말로, 에어컨이 수리될 필요가 있다는 말에 간접적으로 동의했으므로 정답이다.
(C) [x] 에어컨이 수리될 필요가 있는지 물었는데, 이와 관련이 없는 창문을 열어달라는 내용으로 응답했으므로 오답이다.

28 Why 의문문 🔊 캐나다식 → 미국식

Why weren't we invited to our company's annual awards ceremony?
(A) Through social media.
(B) Sure. Let me know what you think.
(C) It's limited to senior staff.

invite v. 초대하다   through prep. ~을 통해
senior staff 고급 간부, 상급 직원

해석 저희는 왜 회사 연례 시상식에 초대되지 않았나요?
(A) 소셜미디어를 통해서요.
(B) 물론이죠. 어떻게 생각하시는지 제게 알려주세요.
(C) 고급 간부로 제한되었어요.

해설 (A) [x] 회사의 연례 시상식에 초대되지 않은 이유를 물었는데, 이와 관련이 없는 소셜미디어를 통해서라는 말로 응답했으므로 오답이다.
(B) [x] 이유를 묻는 질문에 Sure로 응답했으므로 오답이다.
(C) [o] 고급 간부로 제한되었다는 말로, 회사의 연례 시상식에 초대되지 않은 이유를 전달했으므로 정답이다.

29 How 의문문 🔊 호주식 → 영국식

How long should the podcast episode I'm creating be?
(A) With many favorable reviews.
(B) There's a lot to cover.
(C) About 11 kilometers.

episode n. 1회 방송분, 에피소드   favorable adj. 우호적인
cover v. 다루다, 덮다

해석 제가 제작하고 있는 팟캐스트 1회 방송분은 얼마나 길어야 하나요?
(A) 많은 우호적인 평가들과 함께요.
(B) 다뤄야 할 것들이 많아요.
(C) 11킬로미터 정도요.

해설 (A) [x] 질문의 podcast(팟캐스트)에서 연상할 수 있는 청취 후기와 관련된 reviews(평가들)를 사용하여 혼동을 준 오답이다.
(B) [o] 다뤄야 할 것들이 많다는 말로, 팟캐스트의 길이가 길어질 것임을 간접적으로 전달했으므로 정답이다.
(C) [x] 질문의 How long과 관련된 kilometers(킬로미터)를 사용하여 혼동을 준 오답이다.

30 Who 의문문 🔊 영국식 → 캐나다식

Who knows the final number of interns hired for the accounting department?
(A) The application deadline is tomorrow.
(B) Because she is on vacation.
(C) It was a winter internship program.

accounting n. 회계   application n. 지원

해석 누가 회계 부서에 채용된 인턴들의 최종 숫자를 알고 있나요?
(A) 지원 마감일은 내일이에요.
(B) 그녀가 휴가 중이기 때문이에요.
(C) 그것은 겨울 인턴십 프로그램이었어요.

해설 (A) [○] 지원 마감일이 내일이라는 말로, 아직 채용 절차가 마무리되지 않아 채용된 인턴들의 최종 숫자를 아는 사람이 없을 거라고 간접 응답을 한 정답이다.
(B) [×] 누가 회계 부서에 채용된 인턴들의 최종 숫자를 알고 있는지 물었는데, 이와 관련이 없는 그녀가 휴가 중이기 때문이라는 말로 응답했으므로 오답이다.
(C) [×] 질문의 interns(인턴들)와 관련 있는 internship program(인턴십 프로그램)을 사용하여 혼동을 준 오답이다.

31 평서문

3) 호주식 → 영국식

The Blue Line Subway will be adding stations next year.
(A) To commute to work.
(B) Morning trains are usually cheaper.
(C) I'll be able to use public transportation more often.

add v. 추가하다 commute v. 통근하다

해석 지하철의 파란색 노선이 내년에 새로운 역들을 추가할 거예요.
(A) 직장에 통근하기 위해서요.
(B) 오전 열차들이 대체로 더 저렴해요.
(C) 제가 대중교통을 더 자주 이용할 수 있겠네요.

해설 (A) [×] 질문의 Subway(지하철)에서 연상할 수 있는 commute(통근하다)를 사용하여 혼동을 준 오답이다.
(B) [×] 질문의 Subway(지하철)와 관련 있는 train(열차)을 사용하여 혼동을 준 오답이다.
(C) [○] 대중교통을 더 자주 이용할 수 있겠다는 말로, 지하철의 파란색 노선이 내년에 새로운 역들을 추가하는 것에 대한 추가 의견을 전달했으므로 정답이다.

PART 3

[32-34]

3) 캐나다식 → 미국식

Questions 32-34 refer to the following conversation.

M: Hi. ³²I want to make a reservation for my mother's birthday party this Saturday. Do you have a table available for 7 P.M.? There will be five of us in total.
W: Let me check . . . Oh, you're in luck. ³³We're usually fully booked on weekends, but a group with a table for 7:30 canceled this morning.
M: 7:30 is fine for us. I'll take that table.
W: OK. ³⁴Can I have your name and phone number, please?

reservation n. 예약 fully adv. 완전히

해석
32-34번은 다음 대화에 관한 문제입니다.

남: 안녕하세요. ³²저는 이번 주 토요일에 어머니의 생신 잔치를 위해 예약하고 싶습니다. 저녁 7시에 이용할 수 있는 테이블이 있을까요? 저희는 총 5명일 거예요.
여: 확인해 볼게요... 오, 운이 좋으시네요. ³³저희는 보통 주말에 예약이 완전히 차는데, 7시 30분 테이블을 예약하신 분들이 오늘 오전에 취소했어요.
남: 7시 30분은 저희에게 좋아요. 그 테이블로 하겠습니다.
여: 알겠습니다. ³⁴당신의 이름과 전화번호를 알려주시겠어요?

32 이유 문제

해석 남자는 왜 예약하길 원하는가?
(A) 동료들과 시간을 보내기 위해
(B) 생일을 축하하기 위해
(C) 고객과 만나기 위해
(D) 은퇴 파티를 주최하기 위해

해설 질문의 핵심 어구(make a reservation)가 언급된 주변을 주의 깊게 듣는다. 남자가 "I want to make a reservation for my mother's birthday party this Saturday."라며 이번 주 토요일에 어머니의 생신 잔치를 위해 예약하고 싶다고 하였다. 따라서 (B)가 정답이다.

어휘 colleague n. 동료

33 언급 문제

해석 여자는 식당에 대해 무엇을 말하는가?
(A) 보통 주말에 바쁘다.
(B) 모임을 위한 개인적인 공간을 제공한다.
(C) 이메일로 하는 예약을 받아들인다.
(D) 새로운 메뉴 항목을 내놓고 있다.

해설 여자의 말에서 질문의 핵심 어구(the restaurant)와 관련된 내용을 주의 깊게 듣는다. 여자가 "We're usually fully booked on weekends"라며 보통 주말에 예약이 완전히 찬다고 한 것을 통해, 식당이 보통 주말에 바쁘다는 것을 알 수 있다. 따라서 (A)가 정답이다.

어휘 typically adv. 보통, 일반적으로 accept v. 받아들이다

34 특정 세부 사항 문제

해석 남자는 다음에 어떤 정보를 제공할 것 같은가?
(A) 배달 주소
(B) 지불 방법
(C) 소셜미디어 링크
(D) 연락처

해설 질문의 핵심 어구(information ~ provide next)와 관련된 내용을 주의 깊게 듣는다. 여자가 남자에게 "Can I have your name and phone number, please?"라며 이름과 전화번호를 알려줄 수 있는지 물었으므로, 남자가 여자에게 자신의 연락처를 제공할 것임을 알 수 있다. 따라서 (D)가 정답이다.

어휘 method n. 방법

Paraphrasing

name and phone number 이름과 전화번호 → contact information 연락처

[35-37]
🔊 호주식 → 영국식

Questions 35-37 refer to the following conversation.

> M: ³⁵We should hire programmers to help with the video-editing application we are designing. How about attending the upcoming job fair? It's hosted by Tech Hire Solutions. And they are partnered with the Software Developers Association.
> W: Good idea. But hasn't the registration deadline for companies already passed?
> M: No. ³⁶I checked the event's Web page this morning, and we still have a few days to sign up for a booth.
> W: Then, let's register now. ³⁷I'll draft our recruitment notice.

partner with ~와 협력하다 registration n. 등록
register v. 등록하다 draft v. 초안을 작성하다 recruitment n. 채용

해석
35-37번은 다음 대화에 관한 문제입니다.
남: ³⁵우리는 우리가 설계하고 있는 영상 편집 응용 프로그램에 관해 도움을 줄 수 있는 프로그래머를 고용해야 해요. 곧 있을 직업 박람회에 참석해 보는 것은 어떨까요? 그것은 Tech Hire 솔루션스에 의해 주최돼요. 그리고 그들은 소프트웨어 개발자 협회와 협력하고 있어요.
여: 좋은 생각이네요. 하지만 기업들을 위한 등록 마감일이 이미 지나지 않았나요?
남: 아뇨. ³⁶제가 오늘 아침에 행사의 웹페이지를 확인해 봤고, 부스를 신청할 수 있는 날이 아직 며칠 남았어요.
여: 그럼 지금 등록합시다. ³⁷제가 채용 공고의 초안을 작성할게요.

35 화자 문제

해석 화자들은 어떤 산업에서 일하는 것 같은가?
(A) 회계
(B) 소프트웨어
(C) 운송
(D) 연예

해설 대화에서 신분 및 직업과 관련된 표현을 놓치지 않고 듣는다. 남자가 "We should hire programmers to help with the video-editing application we are designing."이라며 화자들이 설계하고 있는 영상 편집 응용 프로그램에 관해 도움을 줄 수 있는 프로그래머를 고용해야 한다고 했으므로, 화자들이 소프트웨어 업계에서 일하고 있음을 알 수 있다. 따라서 (B)가 정답이다.

36 특정 세부 사항 문제

해석 남자는 오늘 아침에 무엇을 했는가?
(A) 응용 프로그램을 다운로드했다.
(B) 면접에 참석했다.
(C) 웹사이트를 방문했다.
(D) 점검을 실시했다.

해설 질문의 핵심 어구(this morning)가 언급된 주변을 주의 깊게 듣는다. 남자가 "I checked the event's Web page this morning"이라며 오늘 아침에 행사의 웹페이지를 확인해 봤다고 하였다. 따라서 (C)가 정답이다.

37 제안 문제

해석 여자는 무엇을 해주겠다고 제안하는가?
(A) 안전 공지를 게시한다.
(B) 이메일을 보낸다.
(C) 영상 통화를 주선한다.
(D) 구인 광고를 제작한다.

해설 여자의 말에서 제안과 관련된 표현이 언급된 다음을 주의 깊게 듣는다. 여자가 "I'll draft our recruitment notice."라며 채용 공고의 초안을 작성하겠다고 하였다. 따라서 (D)가 정답이다.

어휘 video call 영상 통화

Paraphrasing
draft ~ recruitment notice 채용 공고의 초안을 작성하다 → Create a job advertisement 구인 광고 제작하기

[38-40]
🔊 미국식 → 호주식

Questions 38-40 refer to the following conversation.

> W: Devon, I just got off the phone with ³⁸Mr. Jennings. He completed an inspection of the drainage in our building and discovered that all the pipes should be replaced.
> M: That sounds like a big project. But I guess we don't have a choice.
> W: ³⁹He asked if we would prefer plastic or steel pipes. The steel ones are more durable, but they are quite costly.
> M: Well, we're on a tight budget.
> W: Then I will ask him to use plastic. ⁴⁰He has just e-mailed me several pictures of the current pipes. Do you want to take a look?

drainage n. 배수 (시설) steel n. 강철 costly adj. 많은 비용이 드는
tight adj. 빠듯한, 빡빡한 current adj. 현재의

해석
38-40번은 다음 대화에 관한 문제입니다.
여: Devon, 저는 방금 막 ³⁸Mr. Jennings와의 전화를 끊었어요. ³⁸그는 우리 건물의 배수 시설 점검을 완료했고, 모든 배관이 교체되어야 한다는 것을 발견했어요.
남: 그것은 큰 프로젝트로 들리네요. 하지만 우리에겐 선택지가 없는 것 같아요.
여: ³⁹그는 우리가 플라스틱 배관과 강철 배관 중 어떤 것을 선호하는지 물어봤어요. 강철로 된 것이 더 내구성이 좋지만, 그것들은 꽤 비싸요.
남: 글쎄요, 우리는 예산이 빠듯해요.
여: 그럼 그에게 플라스틱을 사용해 달라고 요청할게요. ⁴⁰그가 방금 현 배관의 여러 사진들을 이메일로 보냈어요. 보시겠어요?

38 특정 세부 사항 문제

해석 Mr. Jennings는 어떤 종류의 일을 하는가?
(A) 배관 작업
(B) 목공
(C) 원예

(D) 자동차 수리

해설 질문의 핵심 어구(Mr. Jennings)가 언급된 주변을 주의 깊게 듣는다. 여자가 "He[Mr. Jennings] completed an inspection of the drainage in our building and discovered that all the pipes should be replaced."라며 Mr. Jennings가 건물의 배수 시설 점검을 완료했고, 모든 배관이 교체되어야 한다는 것을 발견했다고 하였다. 따라서 (A)가 정답이다.

어휘 plumbing n. 배관 작업 carpentry n. 목공, 목수 일

39 의도 파악 문제

해설 남자는 "우리는 예산이 빠듯해요"라고 말할 때 무엇을 의도하는가?
(A) 예산안이 검토되어야 한다고 생각한다.
(B) 비싼 주문을 취소하기를 원한다.
(C) 할인을 요청할 것을 계획하고 있다.
(D) 비싸지 않은 자재를 선호한다.

해설 질문의 인용어구(we're on a tight budget)가 언급된 주변을 주의 깊게 듣는다. 여자가 "He[Mr. Jennings] asked if we would prefer plastic or steel pipes. The steel ones are more durable, but they are quite costly."라며 Mr. Jennings가 플라스틱 배관과 강철 배관 중 어떤 것을 선호하는지 물어봤다고 한 후, 강철로 된 것이 더 내구성이 좋지만 꽤 비싸다고 한 것을 통해 남자가 비싸지 않은 자재를 선호한다는 것을 알 수 있다. 따라서 (D)가 정답이다.

어휘 inexpensive adj. 비싸지 않은

40 특정 세부 사항 문제

해설 여자는 남자에게 무엇을 보여줄 것인가?
(A) 몇몇 사진
(B) 몇몇 도구
(C) 제품 샘플
(D) 건물 허가증

해설 질문의 핵심 어구(show to the man)와 관련된 내용을 주의 깊게 듣는다. 여자가 "He[Mr. Jennings] has just e-mailed me several pictures of the current pipes. Do you want to take a look?"이라며 Mr. Jennings가 방금 현 배관의 여러 사진들을 이메일로 보냈다고 한 후, 보겠느냐고 묻는 것을 통해 여자가 남자에게 몇몇 사진을 보여줄 것임을 알 수 있다. 따라서 (A)가 정답이다.

어휘 permit n. 허가(증)

[41-43]
🔊 영국식 → 미국식 → 캐나다식

Questions 41-43 refer to the following conversation with three speakers.

W1: Thank you for agreeing to be interviewed for our documentary film.
W2: Of course. **⁴¹As the director of the Toledo Museum, I know a lot about our city's past. And I'm happy to share this information with you.**
M: **⁴²Could you tell us how the city of Toledo was founded, Ms. Reyes?** I heard it was originally a small farming community.
W2: Actually, it started as just a single farm. Our records show that a family moved here in 1846. **⁴²In fact, a letter written by one of the members was discovered last month.**
W1: Interesting. Maybe we should include it in our documentary.
M: That's a good idea. **⁴³I could photograph it now.**

director n. 책임자, 관리자 past n. 과거 found v. 설립하다
record n. 기록 photograph v. 사진을 찍다

해석
41-43번은 다음 세 명의 대화에 관한 문제입니다.
여1: 저희의 다큐멘터리 영화 인터뷰에 동의해 주셔서 감사합니다.
여2: 물론입니다. ⁴¹톨레도 박물관의 관장으로서 저는 우리 도시의 과거에 대해 많이 알고 있습니다. 그리고 이 정보를 여러분과 공유하게 되어 기쁩니다.
남: ⁴²톨레도시가 어떻게 설립되었는지 말씀해 주실 수 있나요, Ms. Reyes? 원래는 작은 농업 공동체였다고 들었습니다.
여2: 사실, 이 도시는 하나의 농장으로 시작되었습니다. 저희 기록에 따르면 한 가족이 1846년에 이곳으로 이주한 것으로 나타납니다. ⁴²실제로, 한 가족 구성원이 쓴 편지가 지난달에 발견되었습니다.
여1: 흥미롭네요. 저희가 다큐멘터리에 그것을 포함해야 할 수도 있겠어요.
남: 좋은 생각입니다. ⁴³제가 지금 그것을 사진 찍어도 되겠어요.

41 주제 문제

해설 대화의 주제는 무엇인가?
(A) 시의 유명 인사
(B) 지역의 문화
(C) 지역의 요리
(D) 지역사회의 역사

해설 대화의 주제를 묻는 문제이므로, 대화의 초반을 반드시 듣는다. 여자2가 "As the director of the Toledo Museum, I know a lot about our city's past. And I'm happy to share this information with you."라며 톨레도 박물관의 관장으로서 우리 도시의 과거에 대해 많이 알고 있고 이것을 공유하게 되어 기쁘다고 했다. 따라서 (D)가 정답이다.

어휘 region n. 지역 cuisine n. 요리(법)

42 언급 문제

해설 Ms. Reyes는 최근에 무슨 일이 있었다고 말하는가?
(A) 조직이 형성되었다.
(B) 문서가 발견되었다.
(C) 기관이 문을 열었다.
(D) 인쇄물이 출판되었다.

해설 Ms. Reyes의 말에서 질문의 핵심 어구(recently happened)와 관련된 내용을 주의 깊게 듣는다. 남자2가 여자2에게 "Could you tell us how the city of Toledo was founded, Ms. Reyes?"라며 톨레도시가 어떻게 설립되었는지 말해줄 수 있냐고 물었다. 이에 대해 여자2[Ms. Reyes]가 간략히 역사를 설명한 뒤 "In fact, a letter written by one of the members was discovered last month."라며 한 가족 구성원이 쓴 편지가 지난달에 발견되었다고 하였다. 따라서 (B)가 정답이다.

어휘 form v. 형성되다

Paraphrasing

letter 편지 → document 문서
discovered 발견되었다 → found 발견되었다

43 다음에 할 일 문제

해석 남자는 다음에 무엇을 할 것인가?
(A) 편지를 쓴다.
(B) 기록을 확인한다.
(C) 날짜를 확정한다.
(D) 사진을 찍는다.

해설 대화의 후반부를 주의 깊게 듣는다. 남자가 "I could photograph it[a letter] now"라며 지난달에 발견된 편지의 사진을 지금 찍어도 되겠다고 하였다. 따라서 (D)가 정답이다.

어휘 record n. 기록

[44-46]

[호주식 → 미국식]

Questions 44-46 refer to the following conversation.

M: Good morning. This is Patrick Calhoun from Compu Zone.
W: Hi. Is this about my laptop order?
M: Yes. ⁴⁴**I'm sorry to say that the laptop you ordered yesterday is currently out of stock.** We won't get another shipment until May 15.
W: I ordered this model two weeks ago, and your Web site didn't show that it was sold out.
M: ⁴⁵**We've had some technical issues with our stock tracking system.** What about getting the Pro-5 laptop instead? It is the latest model and can be shipped today.
W: But ⁴⁶**isn't it more expensive?**
M: To make up for our mistake, the price will be the same.

out of stock 품절된, 재고가 떨어진   shipment n. 수송(품)
technical adj. 기술적인, 기술의   stock n. 재고
make up for ~에 대해 보상하다

해석
44-46번은 다음 대화에 관한 문제입니다.
남: 안녕하세요. 저는 Compu Zone의 Patrick Calhoun입니다.
여: 안녕하세요. 이것은 저의 노트북 컴퓨터 주문에 관한 것일까요?
남: 네. ⁴⁴말씀드리기에 죄송하지만 고객님께서 어제 주문하신 노트북 컴퓨터가 현재 품절되었습니다. 저희는 5월 15일이 되어야 또 다른 수송품을 받을 거예요.
여: 제가 2주 전에 이 모델을 주문했고, 당신의 웹사이트는 그것이 품절되었다는 것을 보여주지 않았어요.
남: ⁴⁵저희의 재고 추적 시스템에 약간의 기술적 문제가 있었습니다. 대신 Pro-5 노트북 컴퓨터를 구매하시는 것은 어떨까요? 그것은 최신 모델이고 오늘 발송될 수 있습니다.

여: 그렇지만 ⁴⁶그것이 더 비싸지 않나요?
남: 저희의 실수에 대해 보상하기 위해, 가격은 같을 것입니다.

44 목적 문제

해석 남자는 왜 전화를 하고 있는가?
(A) 가게의 판촉 활동을 설명하기 위해
(B) 취소 건에 대해 사과하기 위해
(C) 주문 문제에 대해 논의하기 위해
(D) 온라인 지불을 요청하기 위해

해설 전화의 목적을 묻는 문제이므로, 대화의 초반을 반드시 듣는다. 남자가 "I'm sorry to say that the laptop you ordered yesterday is currently out of stock."이라며 여자가 어제 주문한 노트북 컴퓨터가 현재 품절되었다고 한 것을 통해, 남자가 주문 문제에 대해 논의하기 위해 전화하고 있음을 알 수 있다. 따라서 (C)가 정답이다.

어휘 cancellation n. 취소

45 문제점 문제

해석 남자는 무슨 문제를 언급하는가?
(A) 몇몇 장비가 손상되었다.
(B) 기술적 오류가 있었다.
(C) 사업체는 인력이 부족하다.
(D) 몇몇 지침들이 명확하지 않았다.

해설 남자의 말에서 부정적인 표현이 언급된 주변을 주의 깊게 듣는다. 남자가 "We've had some technical issues with our stock tracking system."이라며 재고 추적 시스템에 약간의 기술적 문제가 있었다고 하였다. 따라서 (B)가 정답이다.

어휘 damage v. 손상을 입히다

46 특정 세부 사항 문제

해석 여자는 무엇에 대해 문의하는가?
(A) 제품의 가격
(B) 물품의 색
(C) 배송일자
(D) 환불 정책

해설 대화에서 여자의 말을 주의 깊게 듣는다. 여자가 "isn't it[Pro-5 laptop] more expensive?"라며 Pro-5 노트북 컴퓨터가 더 비싸지 않은지 묻고 있다. 따라서 (A)가 정답이다.

[47-49]

[영국식 → 캐나다식]

Questions 47-49 refer to the following conversation.

W: Alberno, ⁴⁷**did you select a candidate for the sales representative position yet?** I heard that there are several qualified applicants for the role.
M: Yes. ⁴⁸**Ms. Weston impressed me during the interview, but she won't be available until the end of December.**
W: We have a busy schedule this winter. ⁴⁸**It's essential that the new staff member is fully trained by the third week of October.**

M: Then, there's only one option. ⁴⁹**Mr. Connel has a lot of relevant work experience and is available to start next week. I'll call him tomorrow to discuss the offer.**

select v. 선정하다, 선발하다 **qualified** adj. 자격이 있는
train v. 교육시키다 **relevant** adj. 관련 있는

해석
47-49번은 다음 대화에 관한 문제입니다.
여: Alberno, ⁴⁷영업 사원 자리에 지원자를 선정했나요? 저는 그 직무에 있어 자격이 있는 여러 지원자들이 있다고 들었어요.
남: 네. ⁴⁸Ms. Weston이 면접 중에 저에게 깊은 인상을 주었는데, 12월 말까지는 입사할 수 없다고 해서요.
여: 우리는 이번 겨울에 바쁜 일정이 있어요. ⁴⁸새로운 직원이 10월 3주 차까지 완전히 교육을 받아야 해요.
남: 그렇다면, 한 가지 선택지만이 남았네요. ⁴⁹Mr. Connel은 많은 업무 관련 경험을 가지고 있고 다음 주에 일을 시작할 수 있어요. 제가 내일 그에게 전화해서 제안에 대해 논의해 볼게요.

47 주제 문제

해석 화자들이 주로 논의하고 있는 것은 무엇인가?
(A) 다른 위치에 사무실 열기
(B) 숙련된 직원 승진시키기
(C) 영업 전략 개발하기
(D) 공석 채우기

해설 대화의 주제를 묻는 문제이므로 대화의 초반을 반드시 듣는다. 여자가 "did you select a candidate for the sales representative position yet?"이라며 영업 사원 자리에 지원자를 선정했는지 묻고 난 후, 지원자 선정에 대한 내용으로 대화가 이어지고 있다. 따라서 (D)가 정답이다.

어휘 **fill** v. 채우다

48 의도 파악 문제

해석 여자는 왜 "우리는 이번 겨울에 바쁜 일정이 있어요"라고 말하는가?
(A) 지연을 설명하기 위해
(B) 한 선택지를 거부하기 위해
(C) 결정을 정당화하기 위해
(D) 몇몇 오류를 바로잡기 위해

해설 질문의 인용어구(We have a busy schedule this winter)가 언급된 주변을 주의 깊게 듣는다. 남자가 "Ms. Weston impressed me during the interview, but she won't be available until the end of December."라며 Ms. Weston이 면접 중 가장 인상 깊었는데 그녀는 12월 말까지는 입사할 수 없다고 하자, 여자가 "It's essential that the new staff member is fully trained by the third week of October."라며 새로운 직원이 10월 3주 차까지 완전히 교육을 받아야 한다고 한 것을 통해 여자가 지원자 Ms. Weston을 선택하는 것을 거부하고 있음을 알 수 있다. 따라서 (B)가 정답이다.

어휘 **reject** v. 거부하다, 거절하다 **justify** v. 정당화하다

49 다음에 할 일 문제

해석 남자는 다음에 무엇을 할 것인가?
(A) 의견 제공하기
(B) 고객 설문조사 만들기
(C) 회의 일정 변경하기
(D) 지원자에게 연락하기

해설 대화의 마지막 부분을 주의 깊게 듣는다. 남자가 "Mr. Connel has a lot of relevant work experience and is available to start next week. I'll call him tomorrow to discuss the offer."라며 Mr. Connel이 많은 업무 관련 경험을 가지고 있고 다음 주에 일을 시작할 수 있다고 한 후, 내일 그에게 전화해 제안에 대해 논의해 보겠다고 한 것을 통해 남자가 지원자에게 연락할 것임을 알 수 있다. 따라서 (D)가 정답이다.

[50-52]   영국식 → 호주식 → 캐나다식

Questions 50-52 refer to the following conversation with three speakers.

W: Timothy and Ivan, I have an update from the production strategy team. ⁵⁰**We have decided to no longer produce Taffy Candy due to its weak sales.**
M1: Then we should stop the advertisements for it, right?
W: Yes. Instead, ⁵⁰**we need to refocus on our chocolate bars**. I want you both to plan a promotion for these products.
M2: No problem. Ivan, ⁵¹**I can come up with some ideas. What about talking about them tomorrow?**
M1: ⁵¹**OK. Let's do that in my office.**
W: Great. And ⁵²**I'll be handling all future advertising decisions**, so you can discuss everything with me.

production n. 생산, 제조 **weak** adj. (능력이) 약한, 못하는
refocus v. 다시 집중하다 **come up with** ~을 생각해 내다
handle v. 처리하다, 다루다

해석
50-52번은 다음 세 명의 대화에 관한 문제입니다.
여: Timothy 그리고 Ivan, 저는 제품 전략팀에서 최신 정보를 가지고 왔어요. ⁵⁰우리는 저조한 판매로 인해 Taffy 사탕을 더 이상 생산하지 않기로 결정했어요.
남1: 그렇다면, 우리는 그것에 대한 광고를 중단해야 해요, 맞죠?
여: 네. 대신, ⁵⁰우리는 초콜릿 바에 다시 집중해야 돼요. 저는 여러분 둘 다 이 제품들에 대한 홍보 방안을 계획해 줬으면 해요.
남2: 문제없어요. Ivan, ⁵¹제가 몇몇 아이디어들을 생각해 낼 수 있어요. 내일 그것들에 대해 이야기해 보는 게 어때요?
남1: ⁵¹알겠습니다. 제 사무실에서 그렇게 하시죠.
여: 좋아요. 그리고 ⁵²제가 앞으로 모든 광고 결정을 처리할 것이니, 저와 모든 것에 대해 논의해도 돼요.

50 화자 문제

해석 화자들은 어느 산업에서 일하는 것 같은가?
(A) 관광
(B) 의학 연구

(C) 식품 생산
(D) 정보 기술

해설 대화에서 신분 및 직업과 관련된 표현을 놓치지 않고 듣는다. 여자가 "We have decided to no longer produce Taffy Candy due to its weak sales."라며 저조한 판매로 인해 Taffy 사탕을 더 이상 생산하지 않기로 결정했다고 한 후, "we need to refocus on our chocolate bars"라며 초콜릿 바에 다시 집중해야 된다고 한 것을 통해, 화자들이 식품 생산업에서 일하고 있음을 알 수 있다. 따라서 (C)가 정답이다.

어휘 research n. 연구

51 특정 세부 사항 문제

해설 남자들은 무엇을 하려고 계획하고 있는가?
(A) 계약서 검토하기
(B) 진열품 이동하기
(C) 행사 일정 수정하기
(D) 몇 가지 아이디어 공유하기

해설 질문의 핵심 어구(planning to do)와 관련된 내용을 주의 깊게 듣는다. 남자1이 "I can come up with some ideas. What about talking about them tomorrow?"라며 자신이 몇몇 아이디어들을 생각해 낼 수 있으니 내일 그것들에 대해 이야기해 보는 게 어떨지 제안하자, 남자2가 "OK. Let's do that in my office."라며 자신의 사무실에서 그렇게 하자고 한 것을 통해, 남자들이 몇 가지 아이디어들을 공유할 것임을 알 수 있다. 따라서 (D)가 정답이다.

어휘 display n. 진열(품)

52 특정 세부 사항 문제

해설 여자는 무엇을 책임질 것이라고 말하는가?
(A) 대체 날짜를 정하는 것
(B) 광고 전략을 관리하는 것
(C) 온라인 활동을 조사하는 것
(D) 새로운 판매 업체를 구하는 것

해설 여자의 말에서 질문의 핵심 어구(take care of)와 관련된 내용을 주의 깊게 듣는다. 여자가 "I'll be handling all future advertising decisions"라며 자신이 앞으로 모든 광고 결정을 처리할 것이라고 하였다. 따라서 (B)가 정답이다.

어휘 alternative adj. 대체의, 대안이 되는   obtain v. 구하다, 얻다

Paraphrasing

handling ~ advertising decisions 광고 결정을 처리하는 것
→ managing advertising strategies 광고 전략을 관리하는 것

[53-55]
캐나다식 → 미국식
Questions 53-55 refer to the following conversation.

M: [53]**Welcome to the** *World Cuisine* **podcast. My name is Mitch Austin, and my guest is Gong Chou.** She's a restaurant critic for *The Singapore Chronicle*, and today she's going to tell us about her favorite dish. Welcome, Ms. Chou.

W: Thank you. My job lets me try many amazing foods. But my all-time favorite is an Indonesian fish stew. [54]**It's a really distinctive dish because it's so spicy and sour.**

M: Is it easy to find in Singapore?

W: Yes. It's very popular with the locals. [55]**In fact, this dish will be featured in the Singapore Food Fair next month.**

critic n. 평론가   dish n. 요리   all-time adj. 불변의, 영원한
distinctive adj. 독특한   feature v. 특별히 포함하다, 특별히 다루다

해설
53-55번은 다음 대화에 관한 문제입니다.
남: [53]*세계 요리* 팟캐스트에 오신 것을 환영합니다. 제 이름은 Mitch Austin이고 게스트는 Gong Chou입니다. 그녀는 *싱가포르 크로니클*의 레스토랑 평론가이며, 오늘은 그녀가 가장 좋아하는 요리에 대해 말해주실 예정입니다. 어서 오세요, Ms. Chou.
여: 감사합니다. 제 직업은 멋진 음식을 많이 맛볼 수 있게 해줍니다. 하지만 저의 변하지 않는 가장 좋아하는 음식은 인도네시아 생선 스튜입니다. [54]아주 매콤하고 시기 때문에 정말 독특한 요리입니다.
남: 싱가포르에서 쉽게 찾을 수 있나요?
여: 네. 현지인들에게 매우 인기가 많습니다. [55]사실, 이 요리는 다음 달 싱가포르 식품 박람회에서 특별히 다루어질 예정입니다.

53 화자 문제

해설 남자는 누구일 것 같은가?
(A) 신문 기자
(B) 팟캐스트 진행자
(C) 레스토랑 주인
(D) 음식 평론가

해설 대화에서 신분 및 직업과 관련된 표현을 놓치지 않고 듣는다. 남자가 "Welcome to the *World Cuisine* podcast. My name is Mitch Austin, and my guest is Gong Chou."라며 *세계 요리* 팟캐스트에 오신 것을 환영하면서 자신과 게스트의 이름을 소개했다. 따라서 남자는 팟캐스트 진행자임을 알 수 있으므로 (B)가 정답이다.

어휘 host n. 진행자

54 언급 문제

해설 여자는 한 요리에 대해 무엇이 특별하다고 말하는가?
(A) 희귀한 재료를 포함한다.
(B) 맛있는 냄새를 풍긴다.
(C) 강한 맛을 가지고 있다.
(D) 긴 역사를 가지고 있다.

해설 여자의 말에서 질문의 핵심 어구(special about a dish)와 관련된 내용을 주의 깊게 듣는다. 여자가 "It's a really distinctive dish because it's so spicy and sour."라며 아주 맵고 시기 때문에 정말 특별한 요리라고 하였다. 따라서 (C)가 정답이다.

어휘 rare adj. 희귀한   possess v. 가지다

55 다음에 할 일 문제

해설 다음 달에 무슨 일이 있을 것인가?

(A) 사업체가 문을 열 것이다.
(B) 대회가 열릴 것이다.
(C) 축제가 개최될 것이다.
(D) 투어가 실시될 것이다.

해설 질문의 핵심 어구(next month)가 언급된 주변을 주의 깊게 듣는다. 여자가 "In fact, this dish will be featured in the Singapore Food Fair next month."라며 사실 이 요리는 다음 달 싱가포르 식품 박람회에서 특별히 다루어질 예정이라고 하였다. 따라서 (C)가 정답이다.

어휘 conduct v. 실시하다

Paraphrasing

Food Fair 식품 박람회 → festival 축제

[56-58] 영국식 → 호주식

Questions 56-58 refer to the following conversation.

W: Mr. Choi, ⁵⁶I heard you are planning a field trip for May 25. Have you decided where to go?
M: ⁵⁷I was thinking of the Marlow Aquarium. But I just found out ⁵⁷it'll be closed for a private event.
W: What about going to the Eastside Mountain Park? It offers nature walks led by park rangers. I took my students there last year, and they loved it.
M: But maybe it would be too tiring for my students.
W: Well, ⁵⁸you need to make a decision soon. That park is a popular tourist destination these days.

field trip n. 현장 학습   park ranger n. 공원 경비원
tiring adj. 피곤하게 만드는

해석
56-58번은 다음 대화에 관한 문제입니다.
여: Mr. Choi, ⁵⁶저는 당신이 5월 25일에 현장 학습을 계획하고 있다는 것을 들었어요. 어디로 갈지 결정하셨나요?
남: ⁵⁷Marlow 수족관을 생각하고 있었어요. 하지만 방금 전에 ⁵⁷그곳이 사적인 행사 때문에 문을 닫을 것이라는 점을 알게 됐어요.
여: Eastside 산 공원에 가는 것은 어때요? 그곳은 공원 경비원분들이 이끄는 자연 관찰 산책을 제공해요. 제가 작년에 제 학생들을 그곳에 데려갔었는데, 그들이 정말 좋아했어요.
남: 하지만 제 학생들에게는 너무 힘들지도 몰라요.
여: 음, ⁵⁸당신은 곧 결정을 내려야 해요. 그 공원은 요즘 인기 있는 관광지거든요.

56 주제 문제

해설 대화는 주로 무엇에 대한 것인가?
(A) 활동을 준비하는 것
(B) 수업을 연장하는 것
(C) 웹사이트를 재설계하는 것
(D) 발표하는 것

해설 대화의 주제를 묻는 문제이므로, 대화의 초반을 반드시 듣는다. 여자가 "I heard you are planning a field trip for May 25. Have you decided where to go?"라며 남자에게 5월 25일에 현장 학습을 계획하고 있다는 것을 들었는데, 어디로 갈지 결정했는지를 물은 후, 현장 학습 준비에 대한 내용으로 대화가 이어지고 있다. 따라서 (A)가 정답이다.

어휘 extend v. 연장하다   redesign v. 재설계하다, 디자인을 고치다

57 언급 문제

해설 남자는 Marlow 수족관에 대해 무엇을 말하는가?
(A) 이전될 것이다.
(B) 사적인 행사를 주최할 것이다.
(C) 예약이 필요하다.
(D) 입장료를 올릴 것이다.

해설 남자의 말에서 질문의 핵심 어구(Marlow Aquarium)가 언급된 주변을 주의 깊게 듣는다. 남자가 "I was thinking of the Marlow Aquarium."이라며 현장 학습 장소로 Marlow 수족관을 생각하고 있었다고 한 후, "it[Marlow Aquarium]'ll be closed for a private event"라며 Marlow 수족관이 사적인 행사 때문에 문을 닫을 것이라고 한 것을 통해, Marlow 수족관이 사적인 행사를 주최할 것임을 알 수 있다. 따라서 (B)가 정답이다.

어휘 relocate v. 이전하다   raise v. 올리다, 인상하다

58 이유 문제

해설 여자는 왜 곧 결정할 것을 제안하는가?
(A) 특별 요금이 제공된다.
(B) 예약은 환불되지 않는다.
(C) 장소가 변경될 것이다.
(D) 장소에 많은 방문객들이 온다.

해설 질문의 핵심 어구(deciding soon)와 관련된 내용을 주의 깊게 듣는다. 여자가 "you need to make a decision soon. That park is a popular tourist destination these days."라며 곧 결정을 내려야 한다고 한 후, 그 공원은 요즘 인기 있는 관광지라고 하였다. 따라서 (D)가 정답이다.

어휘 site n. 장소, 현장

[59-61] 미국식 → 캐나다식

Questions 59-61 refer to the following conversation.

W: ⁵⁹There have been widespread complaints regarding the changes to our orange-flavored soft drink. Many people say it tastes too bitter now.
M: ⁶⁰The bitterness of the drink is due to the new sweetener we recently switched to. Our initial tests were very favorable, though.
W: We need to let people know about the advantages of the sweetener we changed to.
M: I agree. ⁶¹I would highlight the fact that it is a natural ingredient with fewer calories when responding to customers.

widespread adj. 광범위한, 일반적인, 널리 퍼진   bitter adj. 맛이 쓴
sweetener n. 감미료   switch v. 바꾸다   initial adj. 처음의, 초기의
favorable adj. 호의적인   highlight v. 강조하다   ingredient n. 재료

해석
59-61번은 다음 대화에 관한 문제입니다.
여: [59]우리 오렌지 맛 청량음료의 변경에 대한 광범위한 항의가 있어요. 많은 사람들이 현재 그것이 너무 쓰다고 말해요.
남: [60]그 음료의 쓴맛은 우리가 최근에 바꾼 새로운 감미료 때문이에요. 하지만 처음 실험에서는 매우 호의적이었어요.
여: 우리는 사람들에게 우리가 바꾼 감미료의 이점에 대해 알려야 할 필요가 있어요.
남: 저도 동의해요. 고객들에게 응대할 때 [61]그것이 더 낮은 열량을 가지고 있는 천연 재료라는 사실을 강조할게요.

59 문제점 문제

해석 여자는 무슨 문제를 언급하는가?
(A) 몇몇 고객이 가격 책정에 대해 불평했다.
(B) 제품에 대한 반응이 부정적이다.
(C) 시설이 점검에서 불합격했다.
(D) 물품이 특정 가게에서 잘 팔리지 않는다.

해설 여자의 말에서 부정적인 표현이 언급된 주변을 주의 깊게 듣는다. 여자가 "There have been widespread complaints regarding the changes to our orange-flavored soft drink."라며 오렌지 맛 청량음료의 변경에 대한 많은 항의가 있다고 하였다. 따라서 (B)가 정답이다.

어휘 pricing n. 가격 책정 reaction n. 반응

Paraphrasing
widespread complaints 많은 항의 → Some reactions ~ are negative 반응이 부정적이다

60 특정 세부 사항 문제

해석 화자들의 회사는 최근에 무엇을 했는가?
(A) 창고를 지었다.
(B) 매장 홍보를 시작했다.
(C) 다른 재료를 사용했다.
(D) 새로운 공장에 투자했다.

해설 질문의 핵심 어구(the speakers' company recently do)와 관련된 내용을 주의 깊게 듣는다. 남자가 "The bitterness of the drink is due to the new sweetener we recently switched to."라며 음료의 쓴맛은 우리가 최근에 바꾼 새로운 감미료 때문이라고 한 것을 통해 화자들의 회사가 최근에 다른 재료를 사용했음을 알 수 있다. 따라서 (C)가 정답이다.

어휘 warehouse n. 창고

Paraphrasing
the new sweetener we recently switched to 최근에 바꾼 새로운 감미료 → Used a different ingredient 다른 재료를 사용했다

61 특정 세부 사항 문제

해석 남자는 무슨 정보를 강조할 것 같은가?
(A) 많은 양

(B) 건강상의 이점
(C) 구조적 개선
(D) 적절한 가격

해설 질문의 핵심 어구(man ~ emphasize)와 관련된 내용을 주의 깊게 듣는다. 남자가 "I would highlight the fact that it is a natural ingredient with fewer calories"라며 새로운 감미료가 더 낮은 열량을 가지고 있는 천연 재료라는 사실을 강조하겠다고 하였다. 따라서 (B)가 정답이다.

어휘 emphasize v. 강조하다 portion n. 1인분, 몫
structural adj. 구조상의, 구조적인

Paraphrasing
highlight 강조하다 → emphasize 강조하다

[62-64]

호주식 → 미국식

Questions 62-64 refer to the following conversation and map.

M: Hi, Ms. Takeda. [62]**Sorry I'm late.** The meeting with our hotel receptionists took longer than expected.
W: Oh, that's fine. I've just been reviewing our annual sales figures. [63]**I'm worried that we're losing business to the new hotel that went up across the road last year. You know, the one next to Meyer Park.**
M: Yeah, the number of reservations has definitely decreased. It will be peak season soon, so [64]**why don't we run a special promotion?** Since our hotel is famous for its spa, [64]**we could offer a free spa service** to anyone who makes a reservation during this period.

figure n. 수치 definitely adv. 확실히 run v. 하다, 진행하다

해석
62-64번은 다음 대화와 지도에 관한 문제입니다.
남: 안녕하세요, Ms. Takeda. [62]늦어서 죄송합니다. 우리의 호텔 접수원들과의 회의가 예상보다 오래 걸렸어요.
여: 오, 괜찮아요. 저는 지금 우리의 연례 매출 수치를 검토하고 있었어요. [63]저는 작년에 도로 건너에 들어선 새로운 호텔 때문에 실적을 잃고 있는 것 같아서 걱정이에요. 아시겠지만, Meyer 공원 옆에 있는 곳이요.
남: 네, 예약 건수가 확실히 감소했어요. 곧 성수기가 올 것이니, [64]특별 판촉 활동을 진행하는 것이 어떨까요? 우리 호텔은 스파가 유명하니까, 이 기간에 예약한 모두에게 [64]무료 스파 서비스를 제공할 수 있어요.

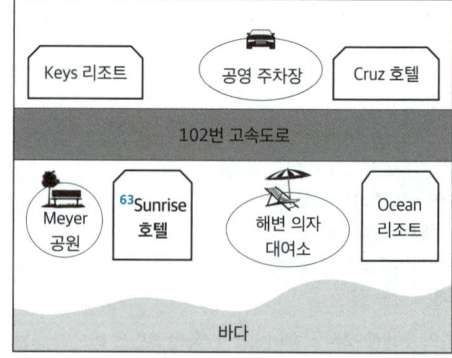

62 이유 문제

해석 남자는 왜 사과하는가?
(A) 늦게 도착했다.
(B) 회의를 빼먹었다.
(C) 메시지를 삭제했다.
(D) 티켓을 잊어버렸다.

해설 남자의 말에서 질문의 핵심 어구(apologize)와 관련된 내용을 주의 깊게 듣는다. 남자가 "Sorry I'm late."이라며 늦어서 죄송하다고 하였다. 따라서 (A)가 정답이다.

63 시각 자료 문제

해석 시각 자료를 보아라. 어느 숙박 시설이 작년에 지어졌는가?
(A) Keys 리조트
(B) Cruz 호텔
(C) Sunrise 호텔
(D) Ocean 리조트

해설 제시된 지도의 정보를 확인한 후 질문의 핵심 어구(built last year)와 관련된 내용을 주의 깊게 듣는다. 여자가 "I'm worried that we're losing business to the new hotel that went up across the road last year. You know, the one next to Meyer Park."라며 작년에 도로 건너에 들어선 새로운 호텔 때문에 실적을 잃는 것 같아 걱정이라고 한 후, Meyer 공원 옆에 있는 곳이라고 하였고 Meyer 공원 옆에 있는 호텔은 Sunrise 호텔임을 지도에서 알 수 있다. 따라서 (C)가 정답이다.

64 제안 문제

해석 남자는 어떤 해결책을 제안하는가?
(A) 더 많은 직원들을 고용하기
(B) 사업체를 이전하기
(C) 객실 요금을 인하하기
(D) 무료 서비스를 제공하기

해설 남자의 말에서 제안과 관련된 표현이 언급된 다음을 주의 깊게 듣는다. 남자가 "why don't we run a special promotion?"이라며 특별 판촉 활동을 진행하는 것이 어떠냐고 한 후, "we could offer a free spa service"라며 무료 스파 서비스를 제공할 수 있다고 하였다. 따라서 (D)가 정답이다.

어휘 reduce v. 인하하다, 낮추다

[65-67]

캐나다식 → 영국식

Questions 65-67 refer to the following conversation and product list.

M: Welcome to the Bridgetown Souvenir Shop. How can I help you today?
W: Hi. ⁶⁵I'm planning to give a gift to one of my business clients.
M: Do you have something specific in mind?
W: ⁶⁶I want to give him something he can use on a daily basis. I'm thinking of a travel mug. Do you carry anything like that?

M: We have some in stock. As you can see, there are a few options to choose from.
W: ⁶⁷The one with the handle and the logo of our town seems best. I'll take that one, please.

specific adj. 특정한   on a daily basis 매일
carry v. 취급하다, 지니다   in stock 재고가 있는   handle n. 손잡이

해석
65-67번은 다음 대화와 제품 목록에 관한 문제입니다.
남: Bridgetown 기념품 가게에 오신 것을 환영합니다. 오늘 제가 무엇을 도와드릴까요?
여: 안녕하세요. ⁶⁵저는 제 사업 고객들 중 한 명에게 선물을 드릴 계획을 하고 있어요.
남: 염두에 두고 계신 특정한 무언가가 있으실까요?
여: ⁶⁶저는 그에게 매일 사용할 수 있는 것을 드리고 싶어요. 저는 여행용 머그를 생각하고 있어요. 그런 것을 취급하시나요?
남: 몇 개 재고가 있어요. 보시듯이, 고르실 수 있는 몇 가지 옵션이 있어요.
여: ⁶⁷손잡이가 있고 우리 마을의 로고가 있는 것이 가장 좋은 것 같아요. 저는 그것을 살게요.

65 특정 세부 사항 문제

해석 여자는 누구에게 선물을 주려 하는가?
(A) 동료
(B) 친구
(C) 고객
(D) 가족 구성원

해설 질문의 핵심 어구(give a gift to)가 언급된 주변을 주의 깊게 듣는다. 여자가 "I'm planning to give a gift to one of my business clients."라며 사업 고객들 중 한 명에게 선물을 줄 계획이라고 하였다. 따라서 (C)가 정답이다.

66 특정 세부 사항 문제

해석 여자는 어떤 종류의 물품을 원하는가?
(A) 유용한 것
(B) 재미있는 것
(C) 가격이 적당한 것

(D) 독특한 것

해설 질문의 핵심 어구(item ~ the woman want)와 관련된 내용을 주의 깊게 듣는다. 여자가 "I want to give him something he can use on a daily basis."라며 매일 사용할 수 있는 것을 주고 싶다고 하였다. 따라서 (A)가 정답이다.

어휘 useful adj. 유용한 unique adj. 독특한

Paraphrasing
something he can use on a daily basis 매일 사용할 수 있는 것
→ Something useful 유용한 것

67 시각 자료 문제

해설 시각 자료를 보아라. 여자는 어떤 물품을 살 것 같은가?
(A) 물품 1
(B) 물품 2
(C) 물품 3
(D) 물품 4

해설 제시된 제품 목록의 정보를 확인한 후 질문의 핵심 어구(item ~ buy)와 관련된 내용을 주의 깊게 듣는다. 여자가 "The one with the handle and the logo of our town seems best. I'll take that one, please."라며 손잡이가 있고 우리 마을의 로고가 있는 것을 사겠다고 하였으므로 여자가 구입할 물품이 물품 3임을 제품 목록에서 알 수 있다. 따라서 (C)가 정답이다.

[68-70]
영국식 → 호주식

Questions 68-70 refer to the following conversation and seating chart.

> W: Carl, ⁶⁸how are the finishing touches coming along for tonight's charity banquet?
> M: Overall, things are going well. But ⁶⁹I'm worried about the appetizers. Apparently, one of the ovens isn't working properly, so everything is a little behind schedule.
> W: Well, make sure the chefs know that the guests will be arriving soon. Oh, that reminds me . . . ⁷⁰Which table is Olivia Stein sitting at? She's the guest of honor, so I want to make sure she has a good seat.
> M: ⁷⁰A back-row table—the one situated right in front of the food bar.

properly adv. 제대로, 적절히 guest of honor n. 귀빈, 주빈
situate v. 위치시키다

해설
68-70번은 다음 대화와 좌석표에 관한 문제입니다.

여: Carl, ⁶⁸오늘 저녁의 자선 연회를 위한 마무리 작업은 어떻게 되어가고 있어요?
남: 전반적으로, 잘 되어가고 있어요. 하지만 ⁶⁹전채 음식이 걱정이에요. 보아하니, 오븐 중 하나가 제대로 작동하지 않고 있어서 모든 것이 일정보다 조금 지연되고 있어요.
여: 음, 요리사들에게 손님들이 곧 도착할 것이라고 꼭 알려주세요. 오, 그러고 보니... ⁷⁰Olivia Stein이 어떤 테이블에 앉을 예정이죠? 그녀는 귀빈이라, 저는 그녀가 꼭 좋은 좌석에 앉길 원해요.

남: ⁷⁰뒤쪽 열의 테이블인데, 푸드 바 바로 앞에 위치한 곳이에요.

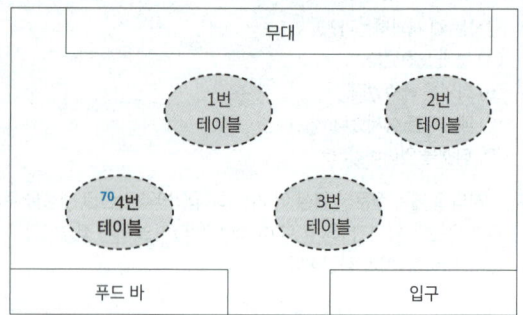

68 특정 세부 사항 문제

해설 어떤 유형의 행사가 열릴 것인가?
(A) 시상식
(B) 모금 행사
(C) 음악 축제
(D) 요리 시연

해설 질문의 핵심 어구(event)와 관련된 내용을 주의 깊게 듣는다. 여자가 "how are the finishing touches coming along for tonight's charity banquet?"이라며 오늘 저녁의 자선 연회를 위한 마무리 작업이 어떻게 되어 가고 있는지 묻고 있는 것을 통해, 모금 행사가 열릴 것임을 알 수 있다. 따라서 (B)가 정답이다.

어휘 fundraising n. 모금

69 문제점 문제

해설 남자는 무슨 문제를 언급하는가?
(A) 장비가 제대로 작동하지 않았다.
(B) 몇 개의 의자를 찾을 수 없다.
(C) 배달이 지연되고 있다.
(D) 기술자가 아직 도착하지 않았다.

해설 남자의 말에서 부정적인 표현이 언급된 주변을 주의 깊게 듣는다. 남자가 "I'm worried about the appetizers. Apparently, one of the ovens isn't working properly, so everything is a little behind schedule."이라며 전채 음식이 걱정이라고 한 후, 오븐 중 하나가 제대로 작동하지 않고 있어서 모든 것이 일정보다 지연되고 있다고 하였다. 따라서 (A)가 정답이다.

어휘 malfunction v. 제대로 작동하지 않다

Paraphrasing
the ovens 오븐 → some equipment 장비
isn't working properly 제대로 작동하지 않고 있다
→ has malfunctioned 제대로 작동하지 않았다

70 시각 자료 문제

해설 시각 자료를 보아라. Ms. Stein은 어디에 앉을 것인가?
(A) 1번 테이블에
(B) 2번 테이블에
(C) 3번 테이블에
(D) 4번 테이블에

해설 제시된 좌석표의 정보를 확인한 후 질문의 핵심 어구(Ms. Stein)가 언급된 주변을 주의 깊게 듣는다. 여자가 "Which table is Olivia Stein sitting at?"이라며 Olivia Stein이 앉은 테이블이 어디인지 묻자, 남자가 "A back-row table—the one situated right in front of the food bar."라며 뒤쪽 열의 테이블 중 푸드 바 바로 앞에 위치한 곳이라고 하였으므로, Ms. Stein이 앉을 테이블이 4번 테이블임을 좌석표에서 알 수 있다. 따라서 (D)가 정답이다.

PART 4

[71-73]

3) 미국식

Questions 71-73 refer to the following tour information.

> Welcome! We will start today's tour by hiking up a nearby trail to the top of Jade Mountain and down to Azure Bay. The hike is quite easy, and ⁷¹**snacks will be provided**. During the hike, I will share interesting facts about this island while you enjoy the incredible views. ⁷²**The journey will take five hours and end back here at the Coastal East Subway Station.** You are highly encouraged to take photographs, but ⁷³**please remember to stick with the group to avoid getting lost.**

trail n. 산길, 오솔길 share v. 공유하다 incredible adj. 놀라운, 굉장한
journey n. 여정 stick with ~와 함께 있다, ~의 곁에 머물다

해설
71-73번은 다음 투어 정보에 관한 문제입니다.
환영합니다! 오늘 투어는 인근 산길을 Jade 산 정상까지 오르고 Azure 해변으로 내려올 것입니다. 하이킹은 꽤 쉬우며 ⁷¹간식이 제공될 것입니다. 하이킹 동안 여러분들이 놀라운 전망을 즐기시는 동안 저는 이 섬의 흥미로운 사실들을 공유하겠습니다. ⁷²여정은 5시간이 걸릴 것이고 이곳 Coastal East 지하철역에서 끝날 것입니다. 사진을 찍는 것은 매우 권장되지만 ⁷³길을 잃지 않도록 그룹과 함께 있는 것을 잊지 마세요.

71 특정 세부 사항 문제

해설 청자들은 무엇을 받을 것인가?
(A) 식사 쿠폰
(B) 가벼운 다과
(C) 정보 안내 책자
(D) 입장권

해설 질문의 핵심 어구(listeners receive)와 관련된 내용을 주의 깊게 듣는다. "snacks will be provided"라며 간식이 제공될 것이라고 했다. 따라서 (B)가 정답이다.

어휘 light adj. 가벼운, 약간의

Paraphrasing
snacks 간식 → light refreshments 가벼운 다과

72 특정 세부 사항 문제

해설 투어는 어디에서 끝날 것인가?

(A) 대중교통 역에서
(B) 국립 박물관에서
(C) 레스토랑에서
(D) 근처 공원에서

해설 질문의 핵심 어구(tour end)와 관련된 내용을 주의 깊게 듣는다. "The journey will take five hours and end back here at the Coastal East Subway Station."이라며 여정은 Coastal East 지하철역에서 끝날 것이라고 했다. 따라서 (A)가 정답이다.

어휘 transit n. 수송기관

73 특정 세부 사항 문제

해설 청자들은 무엇을 하도록 상기되는가?
(A) 소지품을 신경 쓴다.
(B) 야생동물을 조심한다.
(C) 플래시 사진을 피한다.
(D) 항상 붙어 다닌다.

해설 질문의 핵심 어구(reminded to do)와 관련된 내용을 주의 깊게 듣는다. "please remember to stick with the group to avoid getting lost"라며 길을 잃지 않도록 그룹과 함께 있는 것을 잊지 말라고 했다. 따라서 (D)가 정답이다.

어휘 mind v. 신경 쓰다, 유의하다

Paraphrasing
stick with the group 그룹과 함께 있다 → stay close 붙어 다닌다

[74-76]

3) 캐나다식

Questions 74-76 refer to the following announcement.

> Attention, everyone. Management is aware of ⁷⁴**an issue that cashiers have been experiencing**. Several of our customers have been unable to pay for their groceries using their mobile wallets. After some investigating, ⁷⁵**this appears to be a network issue with the mobile wallet provider.** ⁷⁶**Please inform our customers that we will not be able to accept mobile payments.** For now, only cash and credit cards will be accepted.

management n. 경영진, 경영 be aware of ~을 알고 있다
unable adj. 할 수 없는 investigate v. 조사하다
provider n. 제공업체 inform v. 알리다

해설
74-76번은 다음 공지에 관한 문제입니다.
모두, 주목해 주세요. 경영진은 ⁷⁴계산원들이 겪고 있는 문제에 대해 알고 있습니다. 우리 고객들 중 몇몇 분들은 그들의 모바일 지갑을 이용하여 식료품을 계산할 수 없었습니다. 몇 차례 조사해 본 결과, ⁷⁵이것은 모바일 지갑 제공업체의 연결망 문제인 것 같습니다. ⁷⁶고객분들께 우리가 모바일 지불을 받을 수 없다는 것을 알려주시기 바랍니다. 현재로서는, 오직 현금과 신용카드만 받을 것입니다.

74 장소 문제

해설 공지는 어디에서 이뤄지고 있는 것 같은가?

(A) 아파트 단지에서
(B) 슈퍼마켓에서
(C) 은행에서
(D) 휴대폰 수리점에서

해설 지문에서 장소와 관련된 표현을 놓치지 않고 듣는다. "an issue that cashiers have been experiencing"이라며 계산원들이 겪고 있는 문제라고 한 것을 통해, 공지가 이루어지고 있는 장소가 슈퍼마켓임을 알 수 있다. 따라서 (B)가 정답이다.

75 특정 세부 사항 문제

해설 무엇이 문제를 야기했는가?
(A) 기한이 지난 납입
(B) 인력 문제
(C) 방침 변화
(D) 인터넷 연결

해설 질문의 핵심 어구(caused a problem)와 관련된 내용을 주의 깊게 듣는다. "this appears to be a network issue with the mobile wallet provider"라며 이 문제가 모바일 지갑 제공업체의 연결망 문제인 것 같다고 하였다. 따라서 (D)가 정답이다.

어휘 **overdue** adj. (지불) 기한이 지난
personnel n. 사람들, (총) 인원, (전) 직원

76 요청 문제

해설 화자는 청자들에게 무엇을 하라고 요청하는가?
(A) 개장을 미룬다.
(B) 설문조사를 실시한다.
(C) 업무 배치표를 확인한다.
(D) 고객들에게 통지한다.

해설 지문의 중후반에서 요청과 관련된 표현이 포함된 문장을 주의 깊게 듣는다. "Please inform our customers that we will not be able to accept mobile payments."라며 고객들에게 모바일 지불을 받을 수 없다는 것을 알려주길 바란다고 하였다. 따라서 (D)가 정답이다.

어휘 **assignment** n. 업무 **notify** v. 통지하다, 알리다

Paraphrasing

inform 알리다 → notify 통지하다

[77-79] 호주식

Questions 77-79 refer to the following excerpt from a meeting.

As you can see from this report, our rooms are expecting to be fully booked for the summer. So ⁷⁷we will need to hire staff to help out with carrying guests' bags, providing room service, and cleaning. As for our water sports equipment, they've been checked by the maintenance team and are in good working order. Later this week, we'll be getting a shipment of new pillows. I want to say it's about time. ⁷⁸The ones we are currently using are quite worn. Now, ⁷⁹I'd like to talk about each department's specific responsibilities.

in good working order 정상적으로 작동하는 상태인

pillow n. 베개 **worn** adj. 낡은, 닳은 **responsibility** n. 맡은 일, 책무

해설
77-79번은 다음 회의 발췌록에 관한 문제입니다.
여러분들이 이 보고서에서 확인할 수 있듯이, 우리 객실이 이번 여름에 모두 예약될 것으로 예상됩니다. 따라서 ⁷⁷우리는 손님들의 가방을 나르고, 룸서비스를 제공하고, 청소하는 것을 도울 직원들을 고용할 필요가 있습니다. 우리 수상 스포츠 장비들의 경우, 정비팀의 점검을 받았고 정상적으로 작동하고 있습니다. 이번 주 후반에, 우리는 새로운 베개들을 배송받을 것입니다. 저는 이제 때가 되었다고 말하고 싶습니다. ⁷⁸우리가 현재 사용하고 있는 것들은 다소 낡았습니다. 이제, ⁷⁹저는 각 부서의 특정한 책무들에 대해 이야기하고 싶습니다.

77 장소 문제

해설 회의는 어디에서 일어나고 있는가?
(A) 병원에서
(B) 호텔에서
(C) 부동산에서
(D) 철물점에서

해설 지문에서 장소와 관련된 표현을 놓치지 않고 듣는다. "we will need to hire staff to help out with carrying guests' bags, providing room service, and cleaning"이라며 손님들의 가방을 나르고, 룸서비스를 제공하고, 청소하는 것을 도울 직원들을 고용할 필요가 있다고 한 것을 통해 회의가 호텔에서 일어나고 있음을 알 수 있다. 따라서 (B)가 정답이다.

78 의도 파악 문제

해설 화자는 "저는 이제 때가 되었다고 말하고 싶습니다"라고 말할 때 무엇을 의도하는가?
(A) 몇몇 결과들은 뜻밖이었다.
(B) 몇몇 품목들은 교체될 필요가 있었다.
(C) 몇몇 직원들은 일찍 와야 한다.
(D) 몇몇 업무들은 긴급하게 처리되어야 한다.

해설 질문의 인용어구(I want to say it's about time)가 언급된 주변을 주의 깊게 듣는다. "The ones[pillows] we are currently using are quite worn."이라며 우리가 현재 사용하고 있는 베개들이 다소 낡았다고 한 것을 통해 몇몇 품목들이 교체될 필요가 있었음을 알 수 있다. 따라서 (B)가 정답이다.

어휘 **unexpected** adj. 뜻밖의, 예기치 않은 **urgently** adv. 긴급하게

79 특정 세부 사항 문제

해설 다음에 무엇이 논의될 것 같은가?
(A) 부서별 업무
(B) 음식 서비스 메뉴
(C) 정비 비용
(D) 재무 보고

해설 지문의 마지막 부분을 주의 깊게 듣는다. "I'd like to talk about each department's specific responsibilities."라며 각 부서의 특정한 책무들에 대해 이야기하고 싶다고 하였다. 따라서 (A)가 정답이다.

어휘 departmental adj. 부서별의 duty n. 업무

Paraphrasing

each department's specific responsibilities 각 부서의 특정한 책무 → departmental duties 부서별 업무

[80-82]   영국식

Questions 80-82 refer to the following broadcast.

This is Jamie Walsh with local information for Sunnyvale residents. ⁸⁰**Today, I'll talk about the highly anticipated Marina Towers project.** Recently, Tom Rosen was asked to join the team supervising the construction of the complex. ⁸¹**Mr. Rosen is an experienced engineer**, so his input should be valuable. The final plan now includes a shopping center, a metro stop, and two residential buildings. Despite the scale of the project, it will not take that long to complete. In fact, ⁸²**the shopping center will be welcoming its first visitors early next year**.

resident n. 주민 anticipate v. 기대하다, 고대하다
supervise v. 감독하다, 지휘하다 complex n. 복합 건물
input v. 조언, 투입 valuable adj. 가치가 큰, 귀중한
residential adj. 주거의 scale n. 규모

해석 80-82번은 다음 방송에 관한 문제입니다.
저는 Sunnyvale 주민들을 위한 지역 정보를 가지고 온 Jamie Walsh입니다. ⁸⁰오늘 저는 큰 기대를 모으고 있는 Marina 타워 프로젝트에 관해 이야기할 것입니다. 최근에, Tom Rosen은 그 복합 건물의 건설을 감독하기 위해 팀에 합류할 것을 요청받았습니다. ⁸¹Mr. Rosen은 경험이 많은 기술자이므로, 그의 투입은 가치가 클 것입니다. 현재 최종 계획은 쇼핑센터, 지하철역, 그리고 두 개의 주거 건물을 포함하고 있습니다. 그 프로젝트의 규모에도 불구하고, 완성되는 데는 그다지 오래 걸리지 않을 것입니다. 실제로, ⁸²쇼핑센터는 내년 초에 첫 방문객들을 맞이할 예정입니다.

80 주제 문제

해석 방송은 주로 무엇에 관한 것인가?
(A) 정치 행사
(B) 건설 프로젝트
(C) 교통 문제
(D) 주택 문제

해설 방송의 주제를 묻는 문제이므로 지문의 초반을 주의 깊게 듣는다. "Today, I'll talk about the highly anticipated Marina Towers project."라며 오늘은 큰 기대를 모으고 있는 Marina 타워 프로젝트에 관한 것이라고 하였다. 따라서 (B)가 정답이다.

어휘 political adj. 정치의

81 언급 문제

해석 화자는 Mr. Rosen에 대해 무엇을 말하는가?
(A) 계획을 거부했다.
(B) 기술자이다.
(C) 계약에 서명할 것이다.
(D) 내년에 은퇴할 것이다.

해설 질문의 핵심 어구(Mr. Rosen)와 관련된 내용을 주의 깊게 듣는다. "Mr. Rosen is an experienced engineer"라며 Mr. Rosen이 경험이 많은 기술자라고 하였다. 따라서 (B)가 정답이다.

82 특정 세부 사항 문제

해석 화자에 따르면, 내년에 무엇이 개장할 것인가?
(A) 경기장
(B) 지하철역
(C) 과학 박물관
(D) 소매 상업시설

해설 질문의 핵심 어구(next year)와 관련된 내용을 주의 깊게 듣는다. "the shopping center will be welcoming its first visitors early next year"라며 쇼핑센터는 내년 초에 첫 방문객들을 맞이할 것이라고 한 것을 통해, 내년에 소매 상업시설이 개장할 것임을 알 수 있다. 따라서 (D)가 정답이다.

어휘 retail adj. 소매상의

Paraphrasing

the shopping center 쇼핑센터 → retail facility 소매 상업시설

[83-85]   캐나다식

Questions 83-85 refer to the following talk.

Good morning, everyone. ⁸³**Your regular instructor is sick today, so I will be covering for her.** Although I do not have much experience teaching, ⁸⁴**I'm sure you will learn a lot from me.** I've spent over 20 years working in the advertising industry. For today's class, we are going to talk about market segmentation. You need to fully understand this if you ever hope to develop a successful advertising strategy. Are any of you familiar with this term? ⁸⁵**If so, raise your hand, and then provide a brief overview of the idea.**

cover v. 대신하다 segmentation n. 분할
successful adj. 성공적인 familiar with ~에 익숙한, ~을 아주 잘 아는
term n. 용어 raise v. 들어 올리다 brief adj. 간략한
idea n. 개념, 관념

해석 83-85번은 다음 담화에 관한 문제입니다.
여러분, 좋은 아침입니다. ⁸³기존 강사가 오늘 아프셔서, 제가 그녀를 대신할 것입니다. 저는 가르친 경험은 많지 않지만, ⁸⁴여러분은 저에게서 많은 것을 배울 것이라고 확신합니다. 저는 광고 업계에서 20년 넘게 일해 왔습니다. 오늘 수업에서는, 시장 세분화에 대해 이야기할 것입니다. 성공적인 광고 전략을 개발하려면 이것을 완전히 이해해야 합니다. 이 용어에 대해 알고 계신 분이 있으신가요? ⁸⁵그렇다면 손을 들어 주시고, 그런 다음 그 개념에 대해 간략한 설명을 해주세요.

83 청자 문제

해석 청자들은 누구인가?
(A) 지원자들
(B) 학생들

(C) 강사들
(D) 인턴들

해설 지문에서 신분 및 직업과 관련된 표현을 놓치지 않고 듣는다. "Your regular instructor is sick today, so I will be covering for her."라며 여러분의 기존 강사님이 오늘 아프셔서 본인이 대신할 것이라고 한 것을 통해 청자들이 학생들임을 알 수 있다. 따라서 (B)가 정답이다.

84 의도 파악 문제

해설 화자는 "저는 광고 업계에서 20년 넘게 일해 왔습니다"라고 말할 때 무엇을 의도하는가?
(A) 그는 은퇴를 고려하고 있다.
(B) 그는 좋은 조언을 받았다.
(C) 그는 직업을 바꾸기를 희망한다.
(D) 그는 유용한 정보를 제공할 것이다.

해설 질문의 인용어구(I've spent over 20 years working in the advertising industry)가 언급된 주변을 주의 깊게 듣는다. "I'm sure you will learn a lot from me."라며 본인에게 많은 것을 배울 것이라고 확신한다고 한 것을 통해 그가 유용한 정보를 제공하기 위해 자신의 경력을 말한 것임을 알 수 있다. 따라서 (D)가 정답이다.

어휘 consider v. 고려하다 career n. 직업

85 이유 문제

해설 청자들은 왜 손을 들어야 하는가?
(A) 예시를 제공하기 위해
(B) 질문하기 위해
(C) 개념을 설명하기 위해
(D) 실수를 정정하기 위해

해설 질문의 핵심 어구(raise their hand)와 관련된 내용을 주의 깊게 듣는다. "If so, raise your hand, and then provide a brief overview of the idea."라며 용어에 대해 아는 사람은 손을 들고 나서 그 개념에 대해 간략한 설명을 하라고 했다. 따라서 (C)가 정답이다.

어휘 concept n. 개념

Paraphrasing
provide a brief overview of the idea 개념에 대해 간략한 설명을 하다 → explain a concept 개념을 설명하다

[86-88]
🔊 미국식

Questions 86-88 refer to the following telephone message.

Hello, this is Marcia Jeffery. I'm the maintenance supervisor at Medford Medical School. ⁸⁶I'm interested in obtaining some of your air purifiers for our classrooms. Our city council recently passed a new law that requires all educational institutions to have them. ⁸⁷We require a model that doesn't make a lot of noise. We don't want the students to be disturbed. We plan on purchasing 40 units in total. ⁸⁸Do you offer a bulk discount to local schools? Please call me back at 555-9259.

air purifier 공기 청정기 law n. 법률, 법 institution n. 기관, 단체
disturb v. 방해하다 bulk discount 대량 구입 시의 할인

해석 86-88번은 다음 전화 메시지에 관한 문제입니다.
안녕하세요, 저는 Marcia Jeffery입니다. 저는 Medford 의과 대학의 정비 감독관입니다. ⁸⁶저는 저희 교실을 위한 귀사의 공기 청정기 몇 대를 구하는 것에 관심이 있습니다. 최근 시의회는 모든 교육 시설들이 그것들을 갖추도록 요구하는 새로운 법률을 통과시켰습니다. ⁸⁷저희는 소음을 많이 내지 않는 모델을 필요로 합니다. 저희는 학생들이 방해받는 것을 원치 않습니다. 저희는 총 40대를 구매할 계획입니다. ⁸⁸그리고, 지역 학교에 대량 구입 할인을 제공하시나요? 555-9295로 저에게 다시 전화 주십시오.

86 이유 문제

해설 화자는 왜 공기 청정기를 구매하고 싶어 하는가?
(A) 병원에 기부하기 위해
(B) 동생에게 선물로 주기 위해
(C) 직원 불만을 해결하기 위해
(D) 새로운 규정을 준수하기 위해

해설 질문의 핵심 어구(purchase air purifiers)와 관련된 내용을 주의 깊게 듣는다. "I'm interested in obtaining some of your air purifiers for our classrooms. Our city council recently passed a new law that requires all educational institutions to have them[air purifiers]."이라며 교실을 위한 공기 청정기 몇 대를 구하는 것에 관심이 있다고 한 후, 시의회가 모든 교육 시설들이 그것들을 갖추도록 요구하는 법률을 통과시켰다고 하였다. 따라서 (D)가 정답이다.

어휘 donate v. 기부하다 comply with ~을 준수하다

87 특정 세부 사항 문제

해설 화자는 공기 청정기를 위한 필요조건이 무엇이라고 말하는가?
(A) 조용해야 한다.
(B) 비싸지 않아야 한다.
(C) 품질 보증서가 있어야 한다.
(D) 소형이어야 한다.

해설 질문의 핵심 어구(requirement)와 관련된 내용을 주의 깊게 듣는다. "We require a model that doesn't make a lot of noises"라며 소음을 많이 내지 않는 모델이어야 한다고 하였다. 따라서 (A)가 정답이다.

어휘 requirement n. 필요조건, 요건 compact adj. 소형의, 간편한

Paraphrasing
doesn't make a lot of noises 소음을 많이 내지 않는다 → quiet 조용한

88 특정 세부 사항 문제

해설 화자는 무엇에 대해 묻는가?
(A) 청구서 오류
(B) 최소 주문 수량
(C) 할인 가능성

(D) 배송 서비스 유형

해설 질문의 핵심 어구(ask about)와 관련된 내용을 주의 깊게 듣는다. "Do you offer a bulk discount to local schools?"라며 지역 학교에 대량 구입 할인을 제공하는지 묻고 있다. 따라서 (C)가 정답이다.

[89-91]

🔊 영국식

Questions 89-91 refer to the following talk.

> Good morning. ⁸⁹As part of your training today, ⁹⁰you will learn the proper way to clean and organize cooking supplies so the chefs can use them. The pans on the top shelf should never be put in the dishwasher, and the utensils should be cleaned with this special cleaning solution. Now, let's move to the storage room. You will be assisting with receiving all of the restaurant's supply orders there. ⁹¹I'm going to share a list of items scheduled to be delivered today.
>
> proper adj. 올바른, 적한, 제대로 된 dishwasher n. 식기세척기
> utensil n. 기구, 도구 solution n. 용액 assist v. 돕다
> supply n. 용품, 비품

해석
89-91번은 다음 담화에 관한 문제입니다.

좋은 아침입니다. ⁸⁹여러분의 금일 교육의 일환으로, ⁹⁰여러분은 요리사들이 조리 기구들을 사용할 수 있도록 그것들을 세척하고 정리하는 올바른 방법을 배울 것입니다. 맨 위 선반의 팬은 절대 식기세척기 안에 들어가서는 안 되고, 기구들은 이 특수한 세척 용액으로 세척되어야 합니다. 이제, 보관실로 이동합시다. 여러분은 그곳에서 모든 식당의 물품 주문을 받는 것을 도울 것입니다. 제가 오늘 배송될 예정인 ⁹¹품목들의 목록을 공유해드리겠습니다.

89 목적 문제

해설 담화의 목적은 무엇인가?
(A) 일정을 논의하기 위해
(B) 공급자를 변경하는 것을 제안하기 위해
(C) 직원들을 교육하기 위해
(D) 재고 시스템을 개발하기 위해

해설 담화의 목적을 묻는 문제이므로, 지문의 초반을 반드시 듣는다. "As part of your training today"라며 금일 교육의 일환이라고 한 후, 조리 기구들을 세척하는 방법과 물품 관리에 대한 내용으로 지문이 이어지고 있다. 따라서 (C)가 정답이다.

어휘 inventory n. 재고, 물품 목록

90 장소 문제

해설 청자들은 어디에 있는가?
(A) 식당에
(B) 자전거 가게에
(C) 제조업체에
(D) 출판사에

해설 지문에서 장소와 관련된 표현을 놓치지 않고 듣는다. "you will learn the proper way to clean and organize cooking supplies so the chefs can use them"이라며 요리사들이 사용할 수 있도록 조리 기구들을 세척하고 정리하는 올바른 방법을 배울 것이라고 한 것을 통해 청자들이 식당에 있음을 알 수 있다. 따라서 (A)가 정답이다.

91 다음에 할 일 문제

해설 화자는 무엇을 할 것이라고 말하는가?
(A) 웹페이지 제작하기
(B) 제품 목록 제공하기
(C) 몇몇 직원들을 평가하기
(D) 설명서 업데이트하기

해설 지문의 마지막 부분을 주의 깊게 듣는다. "I'm going to share a list of items"라며 품목들의 목록을 공유해주겠다고 하였다. 따라서 (B)가 정답이다.

어휘 evaluate v. 평가하다

[92-94]

🔊 호주식

Questions 92-94 refer to the following podcast.

> Hello, everyone. For today's episode of the *Screentime* podcast, I'm sitting down with ⁹²Dora Lockwood, the acclaimed Australian director whose most recent accomplishment, *Countdown*, was nominated for the Best Environmental Documentary Film. Aside from her work, we will talk about Ms. Lockwood's professional history as well as her plans for the future. And stick around. ⁹³At the end of the interview, Ms. Lockwood will share useful tips that you won't want to miss. ⁹⁴As always, a video version of this podcast will be published online. Look for it at 6 P.M. Please like and follow our social media channel for access to all of our episodes.
>
> acclaimed adj. 호평을 받고 있는 accomplishment n. 업적
> nominate v. 지명하다, 추천하다 aside from ~외에도
> stick around (어떤 곳에서) 가지 않고 있다, 머무르다

해석
92-94번은 다음 팟캐스트에 관한 문제입니다.

안녕하세요, 여러분. *Screentime* 팟캐스트의 오늘 에피소드에서는 ⁹²가장 최근의 업적인 *Countdown*이 베스트 환경 다큐멘터리 영화상 후보에 올라 호평을 받고 있는 호주 감독 Dora Lockwood와 함께합니다. 그녀의 작품 외에도 추후 계획뿐 아니라, Ms. Lockwood의 직업적 이력에 대해 이야기하겠습니다. 그리고 채널 고정해 주세요. ⁹³인터뷰의 마지막에서 Ms. Lockwood가 당신이 놓치고 싶지 않을 유용한 팁을 공유할 예정입니다. ⁹⁴언제나 그렇듯이, 이 팟캐스트의 비디오 버전이 온라인에 게시될 예정입니다. 오후 6시에 그것을 찾아보세요. 저희의 소셜 미디어 채널에 좋아요를 누르시고 팔로우하여 모든 에피소드를 들어보세요.

92 특정 세부 사항 문제

해설 Ms. Lockwood는 어떤 산업에 종사할 것 같은가?
(A) 과학
(B) 교육
(C) 영화
(D) 출판

해설 질문 대상(Ms. Lockwood)의 신분 및 직업과 관련된 표현을 놓치

지 않고 듣는다. "Dora Lockwood, the acclaimed Australian director whose most recent accomplishment, Countdown, was nominated for the Best Environmental Documentary Film"이라며 가장 최근의 업적인 Countdown이 베스트 환경 다큐멘터리 영화상 후보에 올라 호평을 받고 있는 호주 감독 Dora Lockwood와 함께할 것이라고 했다. 따라서 (C)가 정답이다.

93 의도 파악 문제

해석 화자는 "그리고 채널 고정해 주세요"라고 말할 때 무엇을 의도하는가?
(A) 인기 있는 프로그램이 광고 후에 시작할 것이다.
(B) Ms. Lockwood가 특별한 요청을 했다.
(C) 청자들은 질문을 하기 위해 전화할 수 있다.
(D) 청자들은 게스트의 말을 듣고 싶어 할 것이다.

해설 질문의 인용어구(And stick around)가 언급된 주변을 주의 깊게 듣는다. "At the end of the interview, Ms. Lockwood will share useful tips that you won't want to miss."라며 인터뷰의 마지막에서 Ms. Lockwood가 당신이 놓치고 싶지 않을 유용한 팁을 공유할 예정이라고 했다. 따라서 (D)가 정답이다.

어휘 remark n. 말, 발언

94 다음에 할 일 문제

해석 오후 6시에 무슨 일이 일어날 것인가?
(A) 영화 예고편이 보여질 것이다.
(B) 소셜 미디어 페이지가 업데이트될 것이다.
(C) 일정이 공지될 것이다.
(D) 홍보를 위한 할인이 드러날 것이다.

해설 질문의 핵심 어구(6 P.M.)가 언급된 주변을 주의 깊게 듣는다. "As always, a video version of this podcast will be published online. Look for it at 6 P.M."이라며 언제나 그렇듯이 이 팟캐스트의 비디오 버전이 온라인에 게시될 예정이고, 오후 6시에 그것을 찾아보라고 했다. 따라서 (B)가 정답이다.

어휘 reveal v. 드러내다, 밝히다

[95-97] 미국식

Questions 95-97 refer to the following excerpt from a meeting and sales report.

As you're all aware, ⁹⁵we're launching a new commercial for our meal kits. But we've decided to make some last-minute changes to the advertisement content. ⁹⁶The focus will now be on the use of eco-friendly packaging materials. Research shows that this approach is sure to make these products best sellers. ⁹⁷In particular, it will appeal to our fastest growing group of customers. People in this age range purchased eight million dollars worth of these products last quarter, and we are very confident they will buy even more in the future.

last-minute adj. 막바지의, 마지막 순간의   content n. 내용
approach n. 접근(법)   appeal v. 관심을 끌다, 흥미를 끌다
age range 연령대

해석 95-97번은 다음 회의 발췌록과 매출 보고서에 관한 문제입니다.

여러분 모두가 알고 있듯이, ⁹⁵우리의 밀키트에 대한 새로운 광고를 시작할 예정입니다. 하지만 우리는 광고 내용에 몇 가지 마지막 수정을 하기로 결정했습니다. ⁹⁶이제 주안점은 친환경적인 포장 물질의 사용이 될 것입니다. 연구는 이러한 접근법이 틀림없이 이 제품들을 잘 나가는 상품으로 만들어 줄 것이라는 점을 보여줍니다. ⁹⁷특히, 그것은 우리의 가장 빠르게 성장한 고객 집단의 관심을 끌 것입니다. 이 연령대의 사람들은 지난 분기에 8백만 달러 어치의 이 제품들을 구입했고, 우리는 그들이 향후에 훨씬 더 많이 구매할 것이라고 매우 확신합니다.

분기별 매출 보고	
연령대	매출액 (백만 달러)
18세-25세	10
⁹⁷26세-35세	8
36세-45세	8.5
46세-55세	6

95 주제 문제

해석 어떤 종류의 제품이 논의되고 있는가?
(A) 간편식
(B) 통밀빵
(C) 즉석 수프
(D) 병에 담긴 소스

해설 지문의 주제를 묻는 문제이므로, 지문의 초반을 반드시 듣는다. "we're launching a new commercial for our meal kits"라며 밀키트에 대한 새로운 광고를 시작할 예정이라고 하였다. 따라서 (A)가 정답이다.

Paraphrasing

meal kits 밀키트 → Convenience food 간편식

96 특정 세부 사항 문제

해석 화자에 따르면, 무엇이 광고의 주안점이 될 것인가?
(A) 사용자 친화적인 웹사이트
(B) 가격의 인하
(C) 재료의 신선도
(D) 지속 가능한 포장재

해설 질문의 핵심 어구(the focus of the advertisement)와 관련된 내용을 주의 깊게 듣는다. "The focus will now be on the use of eco-friendly packaging materials."라며 이제 주안점은 친환경적인 포장 물질의 사용이 될 것이라고 하였으므로, 지속 가능한 포장재가 광고의 주안점이 될 것임을 알 수 있다. 따라서 (D)가 정답이다.

어휘 sustainable adj. 지속 가능한

Paraphrasing

eco-friendly 친환경적인 → Sustainable 지속 가능한

97 시각 자료 문제

해석 시각 자료를 보아라. 가장 빠르게 성장한 고객 집단의 연령대는 무엇인가?
(A) 18세-25세
(B) 26세-35세
(C) 36세-45세
(D) 46세-55세

해설 제시된 분기별 매출 보고서의 정보를 확인한 후 질문의 핵심 어구(the fastest growing customer group)가 언급된 주변을 주의 깊게 듣는다. "In particular, it will appeal to our fastest growing group of customers. People in this age range purchased eight million dollars worth of these products"이라며, 특히 그것이 우리의 가장 빠르게 성장한 고객 집단의 관심을 끌 것이라고 한 후, 이 연령대의 사람들이 지난 분기에 8백만 달러치의 이 제품들을 구입했다고 하였으므로, 가장 빠르게 성장한 고객 집단의 연령대가 26세-35세임을 분기별 매출 보고서에서 알 수 있다. 따라서 (B)가 정답이다.

[98-100]

🎧 캐나다식

Questions 98-100 refer to the following talk and building directory.

> Thank you all for coming to the grand opening of the Berkshire Office Tower. [98]**As the designer of this building**, I take great pride in its innovative features. Specifically, I feel that [99]**the inclusion of the large rooftop garden will be greatly appreciated by all of you working here**. I should also mention that all units in this building have been rented out. [100]**Macro Technologies signed a contract for the final available floor.** This neighborhood will definitely benefit from having great companies based here.
>
> feature n. 특징 inclusion n. 포함
> appreciate v. 환영하다, 고마워하다 final adj. 마지막의
> neighborhood n. 이웃 benefit v. 이득을 보다, 혜택을 입다

해석
98-100번은 다음 담화와 건물 안내판에 관한 문제입니다.

모두 Berkshire 오피스 타워의 개장식에 와 주신 것에 감사드립니다. [98]이 건물의 설계자로서, 저는 이곳의 혁신적인 특징들에 자부심을 가지고 있습니다. 구체적으로 말씀드리자면, 저는 [99]큰 옥상 정원의 포함이 이곳에서 일하시는 여러분 모두에게 큰 환영을 받을 것이라고 생각합니다. 저는 또한 이 건물의 모든 방이 임대되었다는 것을 언급해야겠습니다. [100]Macro 기술회사가 마지막으로 이용 가능한 층의 계약에 서명했습니다. 이웃들은 이곳에 입주한 훌륭한 기업들이 있다는 점에서 분명 이득을 볼 것입니다.

Berkshire 오피스 타워	
4층	Western 법률서비스
3층	Coleman 출판사
[100]2층	Macro 기술회사
1층	Larsen 소프트웨어사

98 화자 문제

해석 화자는 누구인 것 같은가?
(A) 작가
(B) 건축가
(C) 변호사
(D) 정원사

해설 지문에서 신분 및 직업과 관련된 표현을 놓치지 않고 듣는다. 화자가 "As the designer of this building"이라며 자신을 이 건물의 설계자라고 하였다. 따라서 (B)가 정답이다.

Paraphrasing

designer of ~ building 건물의 설계자 → architect 건축가

99 특정 세부 사항 문제

해석 화자에 따르면, 몇몇 근로자들이 즐기게 될 것은 무엇인가?
(A) 무료 조식
(B) 넓은 주차 공간
(C) 최신식 시설들
(D) 야외 공간 이용

해설 질문의 핵심 어구(some workers enjoy)와 관련된 내용을 주의 깊게 듣는다. "the inclusion of the large rooftop garden will be greatly appreciated by all of you working here"라며 큰 옥상 정원의 포함이 이곳에서 일하는 모두에게 큰 환영을 받을 것이라고 한 것을 통해, 몇몇 근로자들이 야외 공간 이용을 즐기게 될 것임을 알 수 있다. 따라서 (D)가 정답이다.

어휘 ample adj. 넓은, 충분한 state-of-the-art 최신식의

Paraphrasing

rooftop garden 옥상 정원 → outdoor area 야외 공간

100 시각 자료 문제

해석 시각 자료를 보아라. 어떤 층이 마지막으로 임대되었는가?
(A) 1층
(B) 2층
(C) 3층
(D) 4층

해설 건물 안내판의 정보를 확인한 후 질문의 핵심 어구(the last to be rented out)와 관련된 내용을 주의 깊게 듣는다. "Macro Technologies signed a contract for the final available floor."라며 Macro 기술회사가 마지막으로 이용 가능한 층의 계약에 서명했다고 했으므로, 마지막으로 임대된 층이 2층임을 건물 안내판에서 알 수 있다. 따라서 (B)가 정답이다.

PART 5

101 사람명사와 사물/추상명사 구별하여 채우기

해설 소유격(Calhoun Design's)의 꾸밈을 받을 수 있는 것은 명사이므로 명사 (A)와 (D)가 정답의 후보이다. '고객들과의 관계를 관리하기 위해 고용되다'라는 의미가 되어야 하므로 추상명사 (D) relationship(관계)이 정답이다. 사람명사 (A) relative(친척)는 가산 명사이므로 앞에 부정관사 a(n)이 오거나 복수 명사로 써야 하므로 답이 될 수 없다. 참고로, relative는 형용사로 '상대적인, 관계있는'의 의미로도 자주 쓰임을 알아둔다. 동사 또는 과거분사 (B)와 동사 (C)는 명사 자리에 올 수 없다.

해석 Joseph Sykes는 Calhoun 디자인사의 상하이 내 중요한 고객들과의 관계를 관리하기 위해 고용되었다.

어휘 hire v. 고용하다, 빌리다   manage v. 관리하다

102 명사 어휘 고르기

해설 '대회가 아마추어 사진가들에게 재능을 입증할 기회를 주다'라는 문맥이므로 (D) opportunity(기회)가 정답이다. (A) reservation은 '예약', (B) preference는 '선호', (C) expression은 '표현'이라는 의미이다.

해석 그 대회는 아마추어 사진가들에게 그들의 재능을 입증할 기회를 줄 것이다.

어휘 demonstrate v. 입증하다, 보여주다   talent n. 재능, 재주

103 다른 명사를 수식하는 명사 채우기

해설 빈칸은 동사(must follow)의 목적어 자리이므로 빈칸 앞 명사 safety와 함께 복합 명사를 이루는 명사 (B), 명사를 뒤에서 수식할 수 있는 현재분사 (C)와 to 부정사 (D)가 정답의 후보이다. '사고를 방지하기 위해 안전 규정을 따라야 한다'라는 문맥이므로 regulation(규정)의 복수형 (B) regulations가 정답이다. (safety regulation: 안전 규정) 현재분사 (C)를 쓸 경우 '규제하는 안전'이라는 어색한 문맥이 되고, to 부정사 (D)를 쓸 경우 '규제하기 위한 안전'이라는 어색한 문맥이 되므로 답이 될 수 없다. 동사 (A)는 명사를 뒤에서 수식할 수 없다.

해석 사고를 방지하기 위해, 모든 직원들은 중장비를 조작할 때 안전 규정을 반드시 따라야 한다.

어휘 prevent v. 방지하다, 막다   accident n. 사고, 우연
heavy machinery 중장비

104 형용사 어휘 고르기

해설 '인기 있는 팟캐스트를 제작하다'라는 문맥이므로 (A) popular(인기 있는)가 정답이다. (B) expandable은 '확장할 수 있는', (C) immediate은 '즉각적인', (D) equivalent는 '동등한'이라는 의미이다.

해석 Hannah Stevens는 인기 있는 개인 금융 팟캐스트를 2년간 제작해오고 있다.

어휘 produce v. 제작하다, 생산하다   personal adj. 개인의, 개인적인

105 부사절 접속사 채우기

해설 이 문장은 필수성분(Westover Road will not be ~ vehicles)을 갖춘 완전한 절이므로 ____ ~ overnight은 수식어 거품으로 보아야 한다. 이 수식어 거품은 주어(workers), 동사(clear), 목적어(all the snow)를 갖춘 완전한 절이므로 부사절 접속사 (B) until(~할 때까지)이 정답이다. 전치사 (A), 관계대명사 또는 의문사 (C), 전치사 (D)는 완전한 절을 이끌 수 없다.

해석 Westover 도로는 작업자들이 밤새 내린 모든 눈을 치울 때까지 차량이 통행할 수 없다.

어휘 passable adj. 통행할 수 있는   overnight adv. 밤새, 하룻밤 동안

> **최신토익경향**
>
> until(~할 때까지, ~까지)은 접속사 또는 전치사 문제로 꾸준히 출제되고 있다. until은 행위가 계속되는 의미를 지니고 있어서 주로 아래의 동사들과 출제된다.
>
> <until과 함께 쓰이는 동사>
> · wait 기다리다   · be open 영업하다
> · continue 계속되다   · remain ~한 상태를 유지하다
> · last 지속되다   · stay 머무르다

106 격에 맞는 인칭대명사 채우기

해설 명사(phone charger) 앞에서 형용사처럼 쓰일 수 있는 인칭대명사는 소유격이므로 (B) his가 정답이다. 목적격 인칭대명사 (A), 주격 인칭대명사 (C), 재귀대명사 (D)는 명사를 꾸밀 수 없다. 동사 bring을 4형식 동사로 보고 빈칸을 간접 목적어 자리로 본다 해도, phone charger는 가산 명사이므로 직접 목적어 자리에 쓰일 경우 앞에 부정관사 a(n)가 오거나 복수 명사로 써야 하므로 (A)와 (D)는 답이 될 수 없다.

해석 Mr. Cavendish는 그가 휴가로 칸쿤에 갔을 때 그의 휴대전화 충전기를 가지고 가는 것을 잊었다.

어휘 bring v. 가지고 가다, 가져오다   charger n. 충전기

107 태에 맞는 동사 채우기

해설 문장에 동사가 없고, 빈칸 앞에 조동사(can)가 있으므로 조동사 뒤에 올 수 있는 동사원형 (A)와 (D)가 정답의 후보이다. 주어(Updates)와 동사(view)가 '최신 정보는 확인되다'라는 수동의 의미가 되어야 하므로 수동태 동사 (D) be viewed가 정답이다.

해석 회사 정책에 대한 최신 정보는 우리의 인트라넷 페이지에서 언제든지 확인될 수 있다.

어휘 policy n. 정책   intranet n. 인트라넷, 내부 전산망

108 명사 어휘 고르기

해설 '다음 개발 단계로 넘어가면서 초점이 바뀌다'라는 문맥이므로 (A) phase(단계)가 정답이다. (B) root는 '(문제의) 근원, 뿌리', (C) certainty는 '확실성', (D) statement는 '진술, 서술'이라는 의미이다.

해석 우리가 다음 개발 단계로 넘어가면서, 우리의 주안점은 제품 기능과 사용자 경험을 개선하는 것으로 바뀔 것이다.

어휘 development n. 개발, 발달 focus n. 주안점, 초점
shift v. 바뀌다, 달라지다 functionality n. 기능, 기능성

109 동사 어휘 고르기

해설 '온라인 입지를 강화하기 위해 소셜 미디어 마케팅 관리자를 모집하다'라는 문맥이므로 동사 recruit(모집하다)의 현재분사형 (C) recruiting이 정답이다. (A)의 compose는 '구성하다', (B) service는 '(서비스를) 제공하다', (D)의 analyze는 '분석하다'라는 의미이다.

해석 Baxter 그룹은 자사의 온라인 입지를 강화하기 위해 숙련된 소셜 미디어 마케팅 관리자들을 현재 모집하고 있다.

어휘 enhance v. 강화하다, 높이다 presence n. 입지, 존재(함)

110 분사구문 채우기

해설 이 문장은 필수성분(The Witwave ~ this year)을 갖춘 완전한 절이므로, ___ ~ from around the world는 수식어 거품으로 보아야 한다. 이 수식어 거품은 동사가 없는 거품구이므로 거품구를 이끌면서 '코미디 팬들을 끌어모으면서 개최될 것이다'라는 의미를 나타내는 현재분사 (C) attracting이 정답이다. 명사 (A), 동사 (B), 형용사 (D)는 수식어 거품을 이끌 수 없다.

해석 Witwave 코미디 축제는 전 세계의 코미디 팬들을 끌어모으면서 올해 에드먼턴시에서 개최될 것이다.

어휘 hold v. 개최하다, 열다 attract v. 끌어모으다, 마음을 끌다

111 to 부정사 채우기

해설 빈칸 앞의 명사(company)를 꾸밀 수 있는 것은 형용사이므로 형용사 역할을 하는 현재분사 (A)와 to 부정사 (C)가 정답의 후보이다. '어느 회사와 계약할지를 결정하다'라는 의미가 되어야 하므로 to 부정사 (C) to contract가 정답이다. 현재분사 (A) contracting을 쓰면 '계약을 맺는 어느 회사를 결정하다'라는 어색한 문맥을 만들기 때문에 답이 될 수 없다. 참고로, 이 문장은 동사(decided) 뒤 목적어 자리에 명사절을 이끄는 '의문형용사(which) + 명사(company) + to 부정사'의 형태가 쓰였음을 알아둔다.

해석 모든 온라인 후기들을 읽은 후, 우리는 우리 식당을 홍보하기 위해 어느 회사와 계약할지를 결정했다.

어휘 promote v. 홍보하다, 촉진하다

112 부사 어휘 고르기

해설 '박람회에 대한 기대가 매우 높아서 근처의 호텔 객실들은 예약이 완전히 찼다'라는 문맥이므로 (A) completely(완전히)가 정답이다. (B) occasionally는 '가끔', (C) instinctively는 '본능적으로, 무의식적으로', (D) structurally는 '구조적으로'라는 의미이다.

해석 그 비즈니스 박람회에 대한 기대가 매우 높아서 근처의 호텔 객실들은 몇 주 동안 예약이 완전히 찼다.

어휘 anticipate v. 기대하다, 고대하다 nearby adj. 근처의, 가까이의

113 관계대명사 채우기

해설 이 문장은 주어(The logo)와 동사(will be revealed)를 갖춘 완전한 절이므로, ___ ~ subsidiary는 수식어 거품으로 보아야 한다. 이 수식어 거품은 빈칸 앞의 명사(The logo)를 선행사로 갖는 관계절이므로 관계대명사 (C)와 (D)가 정답의 후보이다. 관계절 내에 동사(was selected)가 있고 주어가 없으므로 주격 관계대명사 (D) that이 정답이다. 목적격 관계대명사 (C) whom은 목적어가 생략된 불완전한 절을 이끌기 때문에 답이 될 수 없다. 의문사 또는 관계대명사 (A) what은 앞에 선행사를 가질 수 없고, 지시대명사 또는 지시형용사 (B) those는 수식어 거품을 이끌 수 없다.

해석 Air 테크사의 해외 자회사를 대표하기 위해서 선택된 로고는 다음 주에 공개될 예정이다.

어휘 represent v. 대표하다, 대변하다 overseas adj. 해외의
subsidiary n. 자회사; adj. 부수적인

114 동사 어휘 고르기

해설 '기사가 주택 담보 대출 금리가 곧 안정화될 것이라고 예측하다'라는 문맥이므로 predict(예측하다)의 3인칭 단수형 (C) predicts가 정답이다. (A)의 write는 '작성하다', (B)의 issue는 '발행하다', (D)의 comply는 '준수하다, 따르다'라는 의미이다.

해석 Economic Eye 잡지의 최근 기사는 주택 담보 대출 금리가 곧 안정화될 것이라고 예측한다.

어휘 mortgage n. 주택 담보 대출, 저당
stabilize v. 안정화되다, 안정시키다

115 형용사 자리 채우기

해설 빈칸 뒤의 명사(paintings)를 꾸밀 수 있는 것은 형용사이므로 형용사 (D) past(과거의, 지난)가 정답이다. 부사 (A)와 (C), 전치사 또는 부사 (B)는 형용사 자리에 들어갈 수 없다.

해석 예술가의 뛰어난 과거의 그림들은 미래의 작품들도 그만큼 대단히 평가될 것이라고 보장하지는 않는다.

어휘 brilliant adj. 뛰어난, 훌륭한 guarantee v. 보장하다, 약속하다
widely adv. 대단히, 널리 praise v. (높이) 평가하다, 칭찬하다

116 전치사 채우기

해설 '30일 이내에 매장으로 가지고 오세요'라는 문맥이므로 기간을 나타내는 전치사 (C) within(~ 이내에)이 정답이다. (A) upon은 '~하자마자, ~하는 즉시'라는 의미로 시점을, (B) toward는 '~ 쪽으로, ~을 향하여'라는 의미로 방향을 나타낸다. (D) during은 '~ 동안'이라는 의미이다.

해석 환불을 받기 위해서는, 당신의 구매품을 영수증 날짜의 30일 이내에 매장으로 가지고 오세요.

어휘 receipt n. 영수증

117 조동사 다음에 동사원형 채우기

해설 조동사(will) 다음에는 동사원형이 와야 하므로 동사원형 (C) educate(교육하다)이 정답이다. 동명사 또는 현재분사 (A), 과거 시제 동사 또는 과거분사 (B), 과거완료 시제 동사 (D)는 조동사 뒤에 올 수 없다.

해석 Estes Valley 커뮤니티 센터의 교육 프로그램은 참가자들에게 응급 처치를 실시하는 방법을 교육할 것이다.

어휘 administer v. 실시하다, 관리하다   first aid 응급처치

118 부사 어휘 고르기

해설 '지속적으로 고객 만족도를 향상시키다'라는 문맥이므로 (A) consistently(지속적으로)가 정답이다. (B) emotionally는 '감정적으로, 정서적으로', (C) commonly는 '보통, 흔히', (D) resistantly는 '저항하여'라는 의미이다.

해설 그 고객 설문조사 결과는 East 항공사가 지속적으로 고객 만족도를 향상시켜 왔다는 것을 보여 준다.

어휘 indicate v. 보여 주다, 나타내다   improve v. 향상시키다, 개선하다
satisfaction n. 만족(도), 충족

119 현재분사와 과거분사 구별하여 채우기

해설 빈칸 뒤의 명사(insurance specialists)를 꾸밀 수 있는 것은 형용사이므로 형용사 역할을 하는 과거분사 (B)와 현재분사 (C)가 정답의 후보이다. '숙련된 보험 전문가들'이라는 의미가 되어야 하므로 과거분사 (B) experienced(숙련된)가 정답이다. 현재분사 (C) experiencing은 '(특정 상황)을 경험하는'이라는 의미로 어색한 문맥을 만들기 때문에 답이 될 수 없다. 명사 또는 동사 (A)와 (D)는 명사일 경우 빈칸 뒤의 명사(insurance specialists)와 복합 명사를 이루지 않고, 동사일 경우 형용사 자리에 올 수 없으므로 답이 될 수 없다.

해설 우리의 숙련된 보험 전문가 팀은 당신의 필요에 가장 적합한 플랜을 선택하는 데 도움을 줄 수 있도록 준비되어 있다.

어휘 insurance n. 보험   specialist n. 전문가, 전공자
suitable adj. 적합한, 적절한

120 동사 어휘 고르기

해설 '고객 커뮤니케이션의 주요 접점 역할을 하다'라는 문맥이므로 serve(역할을 하다)의 3인칭 단수형 (C) serves가 정답이다. (A)의 drive는 '추진시키다', (B)의 hold는 '수용하다, 잡고 있다', (D)의 employ는 '고용하다, (수단을) 쓰다'라는 의미이다.

해설 계정 관리자로서, Ms. Abara는 모든 고객 커뮤니케이션의 주요 접점 역할을 한다.

어휘 account n. 계정, 계좌   point of contact 접점, 접촉하는 사람

121 부사 자리 채우기

해설 빈칸 앞의 동사(are distributed)를 꾸밀 수 있는 것은 부사이므로 부사 (C) domestically(국내에서)가 정답이다. 동사 (A), 형용사 (B), 명사 (D)는 동사를 꾸밀 수 없다.

해설 Barron 보석상에서 만든 보석 제품들은 단단히 보안 장치가 되어 있는 차량을 통해 국내에서 유통된다.

어휘 jewelry n. 보석, 장신구   distribute v. 유통시키다, 나누어 주다
secure v. 단단히 보안 장치를 하다
domesticate v. 길들이다, 가축화하다

122 형용사 어휘 고르기

해설 '두 회사가 합병 실패의 원인에 대한 상반되는 이야기를 제시하다'라는 문맥이므로 (D) conflicting(상반되는)이 정답이다. (A) restful은 '편안한, 평화로운', (B) premature는 '시기상조의', (C) payable은 '지불할 수 있는'이라는 의미이다.

해설 기자회견에서, 두 회사는 합병 실패의 원인에 대한 상반되는 이야기를 제시했다.

어휘 cause n. 원인, 이유   merger n. 합병   failure n. 실패

최신토익경향

conflicting(상반되는, 상충하는)은 토익에서 자주 출제되는 형용사 중 하나이다. conflicting과 자주 쓰이는 명사와 함께 덩어리로 암기해 두자.

<'conflicting + 명사' 빈출 표현>
• conflicting opinions 상반되는 의견
• conflicting results 상반되는 결과
• conflicting interests 상충하는 이해관계
• conflicting schedule 상충하는 일정

123 수량 표현 채우기

해설 빈칸 뒤의 단수 가산 명사(Tuesday evening)를 꾸밀 수 있는 수량 표현 (B) every(매 ~, 모든)가 정답이다. (A) other(다른)와 (D) some은 뒤에 복수 가산 명사가 와야 한다. 한정사 또는 대명사 (C) either(둘 중 하나의; 둘 중 하나)는 두 가지 대상 중 하나를 가리킬 때 쓰이므로 답이 될 수 없다.

해설 Archway 영화관은 매주 화요일 저녁 모든 성인 티켓에 15퍼센트 할인을 제공한다.

124 전치사 채우기

해설 이 문장은 접속사 but 앞뒤로 완전한 절(Ms. Knapp intended ~ this year, she postponed her purchase)이 있는 구조이므로, ____ ~ prices는 수식어 거품으로 보아야 한다. 이 수식어 거품은 동사가 없는 거품구이므로 거품구를 이끌 수 있는 전치사 (A), (B), (C)가 정답의 후보이다. '인상된 가격 때문에 새 차 구입을 미뤘다'라는 의미가 되어야 하므로 (A) because of(~ 때문에)가 정답이다. (B) in spite of는 '~에도 불구하고', (C) such as는 '~과 같은'이라는 의미이다. (D) provided that은 '만일 ~이라면'이라는 의미의 부사절 접속사로 거품구가 아닌 거품절을 이끈다.

해설 Ms. Knapp은 올해 새 차를 사려고 했지만, 인상된 가격 때문에 그녀의 구매를 미뤘다.

어휘 intend v. (~하려고) 하다, 의도하다   postpone v. 미루다, 지연시키다

125 명사 어휘 고르기

해설 '이전 공급업체가 폐업한 후 새로운 자재 공급처를 찾다'라는 문맥이므로 (D) source(공급처, 원천)가 정답이다. (A) license는 '면허, 허가', (B) host는 '주최 측'이라는 의미이다. (C)의 format(형식, 형태)도 해석상 그럴듯해 보이지만 format은 '어떤 것이 배열되거나 제시되는 형식이나 형태'를 의미하므로 material(자재, 재료)과 함께 쓰이기에는 어색하다.

해설 Burch 가구사는 이전 공급업체가 폐업한 후 새로운 자재 공급처를 찾아야 했다.

어휘 previous adj. 이전의 supplier n. 공급업체, 공급자
go out of business 폐업하다

126 형용사 자리 채우기

해설 빈칸 뒤의 명사(skills)를 수식할 수 있는 것은 형용사이므로 형용사 역할을 하는 과거분사 (A)와 형용사 (C)가 정답의 후보이다. '새로운 팀 리더는 강력한 관리 역량을 필요로 할 것이다'라는 의미가 되어야 하므로 형용사 (C) supervisory(관리의, 감독의)가 정답이다. 과거분사 (A)는 '감독된 기량'이라는 어색한 문맥을 만들기 때문에 답이 될 수 없다. 동사 (B)와 (D)는 명사를 수식할 수 없다.

해설 새로운 팀 리더는 효과적으로 프로젝트를 관리하고 팀의 생산성을 보장하기 위해 강력한 관리 역량을 필요로 할 것이다.

어휘 effectively adv. 효과적으로, 실질적으로
ensure v. 보장하다, 확실히 하다 productivity n. 생산성
supervise v. 감독하다, 관리하다

127 명사 자리 채우기

해설 전치사(of)와 전치사(for) 사이에 올 수 있는 것은 명사이므로 명사 (C) debate(논의, 논쟁)가 정답이다. 부사 (A)와 동사 또는 과거분사 (B), 형용사 (D)는 명사 자리에 올 수 없다.

해설 직원들이 집에서 근무할 수 있게 하는 것은 계속해서 Winn사의 경영팀의 논의 주제가 되고 있다.

어휘 debatably adv. 논란의 여지가 있게

128 상관접속사 채우기

해설 빈칸 뒤의 and와 함께 상관접속사 both A and B(A와 B 둘 다)를 만드는 (B) both(둘 다)가 정답이다. 참고로, 이 문장에서 both가 수동태 동사(was signed)의 행위자를 나타내는 Mr. Lim과 Mast Telecom을 연결하고 있음을 알아둔다. (C) neither는 nor와 함께 neither A nor B(A도 B도 아닌)의 형태로 쓰인다.

해설 그 서비스 계약은 어제 회의에서 Mr. Lim과 Mast 텔레콤사 둘 다에 의해 서명되었다.

어휘 contract n. 계약(서), 약정 sign v. 서명하다

129 부사 자리 채우기

해설 빈칸 뒤의 형용사(more)를 수식할 수 있는 것은 부사이므로 부사 (B) considerably(상당히)가 정답이다. 명사 (A), 동명사 또는 현재분사 (C), 형용사 (D)는 형용사를 수식할 수 없다.

해설 Zimmerman 음료사는 자사의 모바일 애플리케이션을 재설계한 이후로 상당히 더 많은 온라인 주문을 받고 있다.

어휘 receive v. 받다 redesign v. 재설계하다, 다시 디자인하다

130 부사 어휘 고르기

해설 '메인 서버가 간헐적으로 멈추는데, 이는 문서에 접근하는 것을 일시적으로 막는다'라는 문맥이므로 (A) intermittently(간헐적으

로)가 정답이다. (B) hesitantly는 '머뭇거리며', (C) correctly는 '정확히, 똑바로', (D) indirectly는 '간접적으로'라는 의미이다.

해설 Belton 투어사의 메인 서버는 간헐적으로 멈추는데, 이는 중요한 사업 문서들에 접근하는 것을 일시적으로 막는다.

어휘 freeze v. 멈추다, 얼다 temporary adj. 일시적인
crucial adj. 중요한

PART 6

131-134번은 다음 이메일에 관한 문제입니다.

수신: wesley_j_moore@kruegerinc.ca
발신: contact@gilmorefamilydental.ca
제목: 자동 회신: 문의
날짜: 9월 7일

Gilmore Family 치과에 연락해 주신 것에 감사드립니다. ¹³¹저희 사무실은 현재 닫혀 있지만, 귀하의 문의는 저희 직원 중 한 명에게 전달되었습니다. ¹³²직원이 저희의 정규 근무 시간인 월요일부터 토요일까지 오전 9시에서 오후 5시 사이에 회신할 것입니다. ¹³³만약 상황이 긴급하다면, 저희의 근무 시간 외 상담 전화인 555-9283으로 연락해 주시기를 바랍니다. 치과 전문의가 언제든 귀하의 전화를 받을 수 있을 것입니다. ¹³⁴그 어떠한 시급한 문제에 대해서라도 즉각적인 도움을 받을 것입니다.

The Gilmore Family 치과 팀 드림

inquiry n. 문의 forward v. 전달하다, 보내다
professional n. 전문가; adj. 전문적인

131 전치사 채우기

해설 '문의가 직원 중 한 명에게 전달되다'라는 의미가 되어야 하므로 (A) to(~에게)가 정답이다. (B) as는 '~로서', (C) at은 '~에서', (D) on은 '~ 위에'라는 의미이다.

132 동사 어휘 고르기 주변 문맥 파악하기

해설 '직원이 정규 근무 시간인 월요일부터 토요일까지 오전 9시에서 오후 5시 사이에 ___ 것이다'라는 문맥이므로 (A), (C), (D)가 정답의 후보이다. 빈칸이 있는 문장만으로 정답을 고를 수 없으므로 주변 문맥이나 전체 문맥을 파악한다. 앞 문장에서 '사무실은 현재 닫혀 있지만, 귀하의 문의는 저희 직원 중 한 명에게 전달되었다(Our office is currently closed, but your inquiry has been forwarded to a member of our staff)'라고 했으므로, 직원이 정규 근무 시간에 회신할 것임을 알 수 있다. 따라서 (D) reply(회신하다)가 정답이다. (A) move는 '이동하다', (B) agree는 '승낙하다, 동의하다', (C) participate는 '참가하다'라는 의미이다.

133 형용사 자리 채우기

해설 빈칸은 be동사 is의 주격 보어 자리이므로 형용사 (A)와 명사 (C)가 정답의 후보이다. '상황이 긴급하다'라는 의미가 되어야 하므로 형용사 (A) urgent(긴급한)가 정답이다. 명사 (C)가 쓰이는 경우 '상황이

긴급성이다'라는 어색한 문맥이 된다. 부사 (B)와 동사 (D)는 주격 보어 자리에 올 수 없다. (D)는 명사로도 쓰이는데, 빈칸에 명사 urge가 들어가면 '상황이 충동이다'라는 어색한 문맥이 된다.

어휘 urgency n. 긴급성, 위급함 urge v. 충고하다, 촉구하다; n. 충동, 욕구

134 알맞은 문장 고르기

해석 (A) 저희 병원은 다음 주말까지 완전히 예약되어 있습니다.
(B) 저희는 최근 밴쿠버에 새로운 지점을 열었습니다.
(C) 그 어떠한 시급한 문제에 대해서라도 즉각적인 도움을 받을 것입니다.
(D) 매년 2회의 정기 치과 검진이 권장됩니다.

해설 앞 문장 'A dental professional will always be available to take your call.'에서 치과 전문가가 언제든 귀하의 전화를 받을 수 있을 거라고 했으므로, 빈칸에는 근무 외 상담 전화를 받는 치과 전문의들이 도움을 줄 수 있는 것과 관련된 내용이 들어가야 함을 알 수 있다. 따라서 (C)가 정답이다.

어휘 immediate adj. 즉각적인 assistance n. 도움
pressing adj. 시급한, 긴급한

135-138번은 다음 웹페이지에 관한 문제입니다.

> **135**Cadabra 스펀지는 Spencer & Sutton에서 10년 이상 가장 높은 성과를 얻은 제품으로, 가장 힘든 주방과 욕실 청소일을 처리하기 위해 고안되었습니다. **136**그것은 당신이 최소한의 노력으로 없애기 힘든 자국들을 지울 수 있게 해줍니다. 가볍게 밀어내는 것만으로도 가장 더러운 얼룩을 처리하는 데 충분합니다. 측면의 홈들은 당신의 손가락 위치와 일치합니다. **137**그러므로 그것은 완벽하게 당신의 손바닥에 맞을 것입니다. 그 안전한 그립 디자인이 미끄러짐을 방지하여 과도한 힘의 필요를 없애면서 손의 피로도를 줄여줍니다. **138**무엇보다도, 화학 물질의 필요 없이 제 기능을 하는데, 이는 그것을 아이들과 반려동물 주변에서 사용하는 것을 안전하게 해줍니다.
>
> decade n. 10년 tough adj. 힘든
> stubborn adj. 없애기 힘든, 완고한 stain n. 자국
> tackle v. 처리하다, 다루다 grimy adj. 더러운 groove n. 홈, 패인 곳
> match v. 일치하다, 어울리다 slip v. 미끄러지다
> eliminate v. 없애다, 제거하다 excessive adj. 과도한, 지나친
> force n. 힘, 물리력 fatigue n. 피로, 피곤

135 태에 맞는 동사 채우기

해설 문장에 동사가 없으므로 모든 보기가 정답의 후보이다. 주어(The Cadabra Sponge)와 동사(design)가 'Cadabra 스펀지가 고안되다'라는 수동의 의미가 되어야 하므로 수동태 동사 (D) has been designed가 정답이다.

136 형용사 어휘 고르기 주변 문맥 파악

해설 '그것은 당신이 ___ 노력으로 없애기 힘든 자국들을 지울 수 있게 해준다'라는 문맥이므로 모든 보기가 정답의 후보이다. 빈칸이 있는 문장만으로 정답을 고를 수 없으므로 주변 문맥이나 전체 문맥을 파악한다. 뒤 문장에서 '가볍게 밀어내는 것만으로도 가장 더러운 얼룩을 처리하는 데 충분하다(Just a light swipe is enough to tackle

even the grimiest spots).'라고 했으므로, 최소한의 노력으로 없애기 힘든 자국들을 지울 수 있게 해준다는 문맥이 되어야 한다. 따라서 (B) minimal(최소한의)이 정답이다. (A) mutual은 '상호 간의, 공동의', (C) continuous는 '계속되는, 지속적인', (D) extra는 '추가의'라는 의미이다.

137 알맞은 문장 고르기

해석 (A) 당신의 주방 스펀지를 2주마다 교체하는 것이 바람직합니다.
(B) Cadabra 스펀지는 일반적으로 5개짜리 팩으로 판매됩니다.
(C) 그러므로 그것은 완벽하게 당신의 손바닥에 맞을 것입니다.
(D) 특정 세제와 함께 그것을 사용하는 것은 효과를 두 배로 만들었습니다.

해설 앞 문장 'The grooves on the sides match your finger placement.'에서 측면의 홈들은 손가락 위치와 일치한다고 했으므로, 빈칸에는 손가락 위치와 일치해서 좋은 점과 관련된 내용이 들어가야 함을 알 수 있다. 따라서 (C)가 정답이다.

어휘 advisable adj. 바람직한, 권할 만한
typically adv. 일반적으로, 전형적으로
specific adj. 특정한, 구체적인 detergent n. 세제
effectiveness n. 효과

138 접속부사 채우기 주변 문맥 파악

해설 빈칸이 콤마와 함께 문장의 맨 앞에 온 접속부사 자리이므로, 앞 문장과 빈칸이 있는 문장의 의미 관계를 파악하여 정답을 선택한다. 앞 문장에서 안전한 그립 디자인이 미끄러짐을 방지하여 과도한 힘의 필요를 없애면서 손의 피로도를 줄여준다고 했고, 빈칸이 있는 문장에서는 Cadabra 스펀지가 화학 물질의 필요 없이 제 기능을 하는데, 이는 그것을 아이들과 반려동물 주변에서 사용하는 것을 안전하게 해준다고 했으므로, 여러 가지 장점 중 가장 뛰어난 점을 강조하기 위해 사용되는 (C) Best of all(무엇보다도)이 정답이다.

어휘 in comparison ~와 비교하여 in other words 다시 말해서

139-142번은 다음 공지에 관한 문제입니다.

> Rockford 아파트 주민분들께 알립니다
> **139**5월 1일부터, 평일 오전 8시부터 오후 7시까지 Robson가에 주차하는 것을 금지하는 시 조례가 시행될 것입니다. 이 시간 동안 그 도로의 어떤 구역이든 주차한 사람들은 벌금의 대상이 될 것입니다. **140**그들의 차량이 심지어 견인될 수도 있습니다.
> **141**Robson가는 우리 아파트 건물의 바로 앞에 있기 때문에, 사람들은 보통 입주자들을 방문하는 동안 그곳에 차를 놓아둡니다. 여러분께서는 그들이 이 위치에 주차하지 않도록 손님들에게 확실히 그 새로운 규칙을 알려야 합니다. **142**대신에, 그들은 우리 건물 뒤편의 2번가를 이용할 수 있습니다. 그곳은 주차하는 것이 온종일 허용됩니다.
>
> 질문이 있으시면, 건물 관리 사무소로 편하게 연락해 주세요.
>
> ordinance n. 조례, 법령 individual n. 사람, 개인
> be subject to ~의 대상이다 fine n. 벌금 commonly adv. 보통
> permit v. 허용하다 management n. 관리

139 동사 어휘 고르기 주변 문맥 파악

해설 '오전 8시부터 오후 7시까지 Robson가에 주차하는 것을 ___ 하는 시 조례가 시행될 것이다'라는 문장이므로 보기 (A), (B), (D)가 정답의 후보이다. 빈칸이 있는 문장만으로 정답을 고를 수 없으므로 주변 문맥이나 전체 문맥을 파악한다. 뒤 문장에서 '이 시간 동안 그 도로의 어떤 구역이든 주차한 사람들은 벌금의 대상이 될 것이다(Individuals who park on any part of the street during these hours will be subject to fines).'라고 했으므로, Robson가에 주차하는 것을 금지하는 시 조례가 시행될 것임을 알 수 있다. 따라서 prohibit(금지하다)의 현재분사형 (D) prohibiting이 정답이다. (A)의 introduce는 '도입하다', (B)의 guarantee는 '보장하다', (C)의 schedule은 '일정을 잡다'라는 의미이다.

140 알맞은 문장 고르기

해석 (A) 시의 웹사이트에서 일정을 확인하세요.
(B) 그들의 차량이 심지어 견인될 수도 있습니다.
(C) 이것들은 늦어도 5월 10일까지 지불되어야 합니다.
(D) 그 도로는 오전에 폐쇄될 것입니다.

해설 앞 문장 'Individuals who park on any part of the street during these hours will be subject to fines.'에서 이 시간 동안 그 도로의 어떤 구역이든 주차한 사람들은 벌금의 대상이 될 것이라고 했으므로, 빈칸에는 도로에 주차한 사람들이 받게 될 처벌과 관련된 내용이 들어가야 함을 알 수 있다. 따라서 (B)가 정답이다.

어휘 tow away 견인하다   block off 폐쇄하다, 막다

141 명사 어휘 고르기

해설 'Robson가는 아파트 건물의 바로 앞에 있기 때문에, 사람들은 보통 입주자들을 방문하는 동안 그곳에 차를 놓아둔다'라는 문장이므로, occupant(입주자)의 복수형 (A) occupants가 정답이다. (B)의 pedestrian은 '보행자', (C)의 employee는 '직원', (D)의 driver는 '운전사'라는 의미이다.

142 접속부사 채우기 주변 문맥 파악

해설 빈칸이 콤마와 함께 문장의 맨 앞에 온 접속부사 자리이므로, 앞 문장과 빈칸이 있는 문장의 의미 관계를 파악하여 정답을 선택한다. 앞 문장에서 이 위치에 주차하지 않도록 손님들에게 확실히 그 새로운 규칙을 알려야 한다고 했고, 빈칸이 있는 문장에서는 손님들이 건물 뒤편의 2번가를 이용할 수 있다고 했으므로, 앞에 언급된 내용을 대체하는 내용을 언급할 때 사용되는 (D) Instead(대신에)가 정답이다.

어휘 furthermore adv. 뿐만 아니라, 더욱이

143-146번은 다음 광고에 관한 문제입니다.

Crystal Clear 수영장 정비
121번지 Carter로, 서니베일, 오하이오주

여름이 다가오고 있으니, 수영장이 준비되게 할 시간입니다! ¹⁴³저희와의 계약에 서명하세요, 그러면 저희는 당신의 수영장의 청결과 제대로 된 기능을 보장하기 위해 매주 전문가를 당신의 주택으로 파견할 것입니다. 저희는 모든 쓰레기들을 치우고 물의 화학적 균형에 있어 필요한 조정을 할 것입니다. ¹⁴⁴게다가, 저희는 펌프와 다른 장비들에 그것들의 작동에 부정적으로 영향을 미칠 기술적인 문제가 있는지를 점검할 것입니다.

¹⁴⁵모든 저희 직원들은 광범위한 경험을 가지고 있습니다. 각각은 이 분야에서 최소 5년의 기간 동안 고용되어 왔습니다. ¹⁴⁶무료 상담을 잡기 위해, 오늘 555-0292로 저희에게 전화해 주세요. 당신은 최종 결정을 내리기 전에 검토할 상세한 비용 견적을 제공받게 될 것입니다.

cleanliness n. 청결   debris n. 쓰레기   adjustment n. 조정
chemical adj. 화학적인   negatively adv. 부정적으로
estimate n. 견적

143 명사 자리 채우기

해설 형용사(proper)와 전치사(of) 사이에 올 수 있는 것은 명사이므로 명사 (C) function(기능)이 정답이다. 부사 (A), 형용사 (B), 동사 또는 과거분사 (D)는 명사 자리에 올 수 없다.

144 접속부사 채우기 주변 문맥 파악

해설 빈칸이 콤마와 함께 문장의 맨 앞에 온 접속부사 자리이므로, 앞 문장과 빈칸이 있는 문장의 의미 관계를 파악하여 정답을 선택한다. 앞 문장에서 모든 쓰레기들을 치우고 물의 화학적 균형에 있어 필요한 조정을 할 것이라고 했고, 빈칸이 있는 문장에서는 펌프와 다른 장비들에 기술적인 문제가 있는지를 점검할 것이라고 했으므로, 앞에서 언급된 내용에 추가 정보를 덧붙일 때 사용되는 접속부사 (D) Moreover (게다가)가 정답이다.

어휘 in contrast 그에 반해서
nevertheless adv. 그럼에도 불구하고, 그렇기는 하지만

145 알맞은 문장 고르기

해석 (A) 모든 저희 직원들은 광범위한 경험을 가지고 있습니다.
(B) 저희는 구매할 수 있는 다양한 수영장 부대용품들을 보유하고 있습니다.
(C) 수영장을 사용하지 않을 때는 덮개를 덮어두어야 한다는 것을 기억하세요.
(D) 당신의 수영장은 만약 손상을 입었을 경우 교체될 필요가 있을 것입니다.

해설 뒤 문장 'Each has been employed in the field for a period of at least five years.'에서 각각은 이 분야에서 최소 5년의 기간 동안 고용되어 왔다고 했으므로, 빈칸에는 직원들의 경력과 관련된 내용이 들어가야 함을 알 수 있다. 따라서 (A)가 정답이다.

어휘 extensive adj. 광범위한, 아주 넓은
accessory n. 부대용품, 액세서리

146 to 부정사 채우기

해설 이 문장은 주어가 없는 명령문(call us at 555-0292 today)이므로, ___ a free consultation은 수식어 거품으로 보아야 한다. 이 수식어 거품은 동사가 없는 거품구이므로, 거품구를 이끌 수 있는 to 부정사구 (B), 분사구 (C)와 (D)가 정답의 후보이다. '무료 상담을 잡기 위해, 오늘 555-0292로 전화하세요'라는 의미가 되어야 하므로 목

적을 나타내는 to 부정사구 (B) To arrange가 정답이다. 3형식 동사로 쓰이는 arrange는 수동태로 쓰일 경우 뒤에 목적어를 취할 수 없으므로 수동형 (C)와 (D)는 답이 될 수 없다. 동사 (A)는 거품구를 이끌 수 없다.

PART 7

147-148번은 다음 광고에 관한 문제입니다.

> Spark의 파티 창고
> 89번지 Hamilton가, 워터타운, 코네티컷주 06795
> www.sparkspartydepot.com
>
> 행사를 계획하고 계십니까? 다른 곳 말고 Spark의 파티 창고를 찾아보세요. [147]이번 달에, 우리는 회원분들에게 다양한 제품에 대한 할인을 제공하고 있습니다. 아직 회원이 아니신가요? 다음과 같은 제품에서 할인 혜택을 누리기 위해 지금 가입하세요:
>
> - 풍선과 장식품
> - 식탁용 식기 및 기구
> - 파티 선물
> - 맞춤 제작한 현수막
> - 테마가 있는 파티용품 세트
>
> 반품은 구입 후 30일 이내에 전액 환불로 수락됩니다. 물품들은 사용되지 않은 상태이고 손상되지 않았어야 합니다. [148-(D)]그것들을 반품하시려는 이유를 명시하는 양식을 작성하도록 요구될 것입니다.

depot n. 창고 decoration n. 장식품, 장식
tableware n. 식탁용 식기 utensil n. (가정용) 기구
party favor 파티 선물 custom adj. 맞춤 제작한, 주문 제작한
banner n. 현수막, 플래카드 themed adj. 테마가 있는

147 목적 찾기 문제

해석 광고의 목적은 무엇인가?
(A) 파티 계획 서비스를 제공하기 위해
(B) 고객들이 회원이 되도록 장려하기 위해
(C) 행사 장소를 홍보하기 위해
(D) 새로운 지점의 개점을 알리기 위해

해설 지문의 'This month, we're offering our members deals on a variety of products! Not a member yet? Sign up now to enjoy discounts on'에서 회원들에게 다양한 제품에 대한 할인을 제공하고 있으니 아직 회원이 아니라면 할인 혜택을 누리기 위해 지금 가입하라고 장려하고 있으므로 (B)가 정답이다.

어휘 encourage v. 장려하다, 권장하다 venue n. 장소

148 Not/True 문제

해석 반품된 물품들에 대해 명시된 것은?
(A) 매장 관리자에 의해 점검될 것이다.
(B) 발신자 부담으로 보내져야 한다.
(C) 매장 크레딧으로 교환만 된다.
(D) 양식과 함께 제출되어야 한다.

해설 지문의 'You will be asked to fill out a form that specifies why you are returning them.'에서 반품하려는 이유를 명시하는 양식을 작성하도록 요구될 것이라고 했으므로 (D)가 정답이다. (A), (B), (C)는 지문에 언급되지 않은 내용이다.

어휘 ship v. 보내다 sender n. 발신자, 발송인

149-150번은 다음 편지에 관한 문제입니다.

> 편집자님께,
>
> 저는 귀사의 최신 호에서 "사라지는 북아메리카의 야생동물"이라는 제목의 기사를 읽었습니다. 그것은 대부분 유익했지만, [149]저는 아메리카담비에 대해 작성된 오류를 바로잡아야 할 것 같습니다. 기사는 이 동물종이 현재 뉴펀들랜드에서 멸종됐다고 언급하고 있습니다. 그것이 여기에서 수십 년 동안 위험에 처해있고 멸종되기 직전이라는 것은 사실입니다. [150]하지만, 제가 전문적으로 관여하고 있는 보존 노력으로 아메리카담비는 이 지방 내에서 의미 있는 회복을 이루고 있습니다. 만약 당신이 기사를 수정하기 위해 더 많은 정보가 필요하다면, 언제든 편하게 저에게 연락해 주세요.
>
> Sonya Lee 드림

vanish v. 사라지다 issue n. (발행물의) 호, 발행 부수
informative adj. 유익한 marten n. 담비(족제비과 동물)
state v. 언급하다, 말하다 extinct adj. 멸종된, 사라진
endangered adj. 위험에 처한 on the verge of ~하기 직전의
conservation n. 보존 involve v. 개입하다
professionally adv. 전문적으로 significant adj. 의미 있는, 중요한
province n. 지방, 주(州)

149 목적 찾기 문제

해석 Ms. Lee는 왜 편지를 썼는가?
(A) 구독을 취소하기 위해
(B) 해명을 요청하기 위해
(C) 잘못을 바로잡기 위해
(D) 출처에 관해 문의하기 위해

해설 지문의 'I must correct an error that was made about the American marten'에서 아메리카담비에 대해 작성된 오류를 바로잡아야 한다고 했으므로 (C)가 정답이다.

어휘 subscription n. 구독 clarification n. 해명, 설명
source n. 출처, 근원

Paraphrasing

an error 오류 → a mistake 잘못

150 추론 문제

해석 Ms. Lee에 대해 사실일 것 같은 것은?
(A) 잡지에 기사들을 기고해 왔다.
(B) 출판물의 오랜 독자이다.
(C) 지역의 야생동물을 보호하는 일을 한다.
(D) 대학에서 환경 과학을 연구한다.

해설 지문의 'However, conservation efforts that I have been involved in professionally have resulted in the American marten making a significant comeback within the province[Newfoundland].'에서 자신이 전문적으로 관여하고 있는 보존 노력으로 아메리카담비가 뉴펀들랜드에서 의미 있는 회복을 이루었다고 한 것을 통해, Ms. Lee가 뉴펀들랜드의 야생동물을 보호하는 일을 하고 있음을 추론할 수 있다. 따라서 (C)가 정답이다.

어휘 contribute v. 기고하다, 기여하다   publication n. 출판물, 출판
environmental adj. 환경의, 환경과 관련된

151-152번은 다음 온라인 채팅 대화문에 관한 문제입니다.

> Amy Hong [오전 8시 41분]
> Takeshi가 방금 제게 전화해서 그가 아파서 오늘 올 수 없다고 알렸어요. 그의 오후 12시 보트 투어는 예약이 꽉 차 있어요. ¹⁵¹그것을 이끌 시간이 되는 다른 누군가가 있을까요?
>
> Connor Morris [오전 8시 41분]
> ¹⁵¹안타깝게도, 다른 가이드들 전부 오후 12시에 그들에게 예정된 투어가 있어요.
>
> Amy Hong [오전 8시 43분]
> 그거 좋지 않네요. 우리가 그 투어를 취소해야 할지도 몰라요.
>
> Connor Morris [오전 8시 44분]
> 그러지 않기를 바라요. ¹⁵²제가 Duncan River 여행사에 전화해서 그들의 가이드들 중 한 명을 보내줄 수 있을지 확인해 볼게요.
>
> Amy Hong [오전 8시 45분]
> 그래요, 좋네요. 알아본 것을 제게 알려주세요.
>
> Connor Morris [오전 8시 46분]
> 몇 분 안에 연락할게요.

book v. 예약하다   lead v. 안내하다, 이끌다   cancel v. 취소하다
get back 연락하다, 돌아가다

151 의도 파악 문제

해석 오전 8시 43분에, Ms. Hong이 "That's too bad"라고 썼을 때, 그녀가 의도한 것 같은 것은?
(A) 새로운 직원들을 고용해야 할 수도 있다.
(B) 고객이 불합리하게 행동했다고 생각한다.
(C) 시간이 있는 직원이 없다는 것에 낙담했다.
(D) 고객들에게 전액 환불을 제공할 계획이다.

해설 지문의 'Is anyone else available to lead it[boat tour]?'에서 Ms. Hong이 보트 투어를 이끌 시간이 되는 사람이 있을지 묻자, 'Unfortunately, the other guides all have tours of their own scheduled for 12 P.M.'에서 Mr. Morris가 안타깝게도 다른 가이드들 전부 오후 12시에 예정된 투어가 있다고 대답한 후, Ms. Hong이 'That's too bad'(그거 좋지 않네요)라고 한 것을 통해, Ms. Hong이 시간이 있는 직원이 없다는 것에 낙담했음을 알 수 있다. 따라서 (C)가 정답이다.

어휘 unreasonably adv. 불합리하게, 비이성적으로
disappointed adj. 낙담한, 실망한

152 육하원칙 문제

해석 Mr. Morris는 다음에 무엇을 할 것인가?
(A) 고객들에게 이메일을 보낸다.
(B) 새로운 강 투어를 예약한다.
(C) 게시된 일정을 변경한다.
(D) 전화를 한다.

해설 지문의 'Let me call Duncan River Tours and see if they can send over one of their guides.'에서 Duncan River 여행사에 전화해 그들의 가이드들 중 한 명을 보내줄 수 있는지 확인해 보겠다고 했으므로 (D)가 정답이다.

어휘 alter v. 변경하다, 바꾸다

153-154번은 다음 공지에 관한 문제입니다.

> 데이턴 커뮤니티 센터 방문자분들께 알립니다
>
> ¹⁵³매년 12월 31일에, 우리는 새로운 한 해의 도래를 축하하기 위해 커뮤니티 센터를 조명으로 장식합니다. 올해의 행사에는, 목도리와 니트 모자뿐만 아니라 ¹⁵⁴⁻⁽ᴬ⁾쿠키와 핫초코를 판매하는 노점상들도 있을 것입니다. 오후 11시 59분에, 우리는 강당에서 카운트다운을 거행한 다음, 새해가 도래하는 그 순간에 색종이 조각을 날려 보낼 것입니다. 그다음에는, ¹⁵⁴⁻⁽ᴮ⁾지역 밴드인 Lake Lovers의 공연이 있을 것입니다. ¹⁵⁴⁻⁽ᶜ⁾사진기사들이 방문객들의 사진을 찍을 것이고 그것들을 우리 웹사이트 www.daytoncenter.com에 게시할 것입니다.

decorate v. 장식하다   celebrate v. 축하하다, 기념하다
advent n. 도래, 출현   vendor n. 노점상, 행상인   auditorium n. 강당
countdown n. 카운트다운, 초읽기   release v. 날려 보내다, 방출하다
confetti n. 색종이 조각

153 주제 찾기 문제

해석 축하 행사의 이유는 무엇인가?
(A) 센터의 설립 기념일
(B) 새로운 시설의 완공
(C) 새로운 한 해로의 변화
(D) 지역 활동의 성공

해설 지문의 'Every year on December 31, we decorate the community center with lights to celebrate the advent of the new year.'에서 매년 12월 31일에 새로운 한 해의 도래를 축하하기 위해 커뮤니티 센터를 조명으로 장식한다고 했으므로 (C)가 정답이다.

어휘 occasion n. 이유, 경우   anniversary n. 기념일
founding n. 설립, 창립   completion n. 완공, 완료

Paraphrasing

the advent of the new year 새로운 한 해의 도래 → The change to a new year 새로운 한 해로의 변화

154 Not/True 문제

해석 축하 행사의 특징으로 열거되지 않은 것은?
(A) 단것들의 판매

(B) 음악 공연
(C) 전문가에 의한 사진
(D) 상금이 딸린 추첨

해설 (A)는 'there will be vendors selling cookies and hot chocolate'에서 쿠키와 핫초코를 판매하는 노점상이 있을 것이라고 했으므로 지문에 언급된 내용이다. (B)는 'a concert by local band Lake Lovers will take place'에서 지역 밴드인 Lake Lovers의 공연이 있을 것이라고 했으므로 지문에 언급된 내용이다. (C)는 'Photographers will take pictures of visitors'에서 사진사들이 방문객들의 사진을 찍을 것이라고 했으므로 지문에 언급된 내용이다. (D)는 지문에 언급되지 않은 내용이다. 따라서 (D)가 정답이다.

어휘 sweet n. 단것, 단맛 lottery n. 추첨, 복권

Paraphrasing

selling cookies and hot chocolate 쿠키와 핫초코를 판매하는
→ sales of sweets 단것들의 판매

a concert by local band 지역 밴드의 공연
→ musical performance 음악 공연

photographers will take pictures 사진사들이 사진을 찍을 것이다
→ professional photographs 전문가에 의한 사진

155-157번은 다음 기사에 관한 문제입니다.

VDF 산업이 변화하다

미시간(6월 5일) — 지속 가능한 이동 수단에 대한 전 세계적 수요가 계속 증가함에 따라, 자동차 제조업체들은 그들의 주안점을 환경친화적인 제품들로 옮겨가고 있다. — [1] —. 많은 자동차 제조사들은 이미 휘발유 동력의 자동차를 단계적으로 폐지하기 시작했는데, 이는 이 자동차들의 부품을 특정적으로 제조하는 회사들에 난제를 야기했다. — [2] —.

¹⁵⁵VDF 산업은 휘발유 동력의 자동차를 위한 부품의 선두적인 공급업체 중 하나로, 이러한 변화의 영향을 받는 기업들 중 하나이다. — [3] —. ¹⁵⁷경쟁력 있는 상태를 유지하기 위해, 그곳은 전기 자동차 부품을 생산하기 시작했다는 결정을 발표했다. — [4] —.

¹⁵⁶VDF 산업의 최고 경영자인 Drew Soto에 따르면, 전기 자동차 부품을 제조하는 것은 그 회사가 고객들의 진화하는 욕구를 충족시키는 것에 도움이 될 것이다. "저는 강력한 하이브리드 시장 때문에 휘발유 동력의 자동차 부품이 완전히 사라질 것이라고는 생각하지 않습니다. 우리는 여전히 그것들을 만들 것이지만, 다각화하는 것은 우리가 다재다능한 상태를 유지하도록 도울 것입니다."

sustainable adj. 지속 가능한 transportation n. 이동 수단, 수송
shift v. 옮기다; n. 변화 automobile n. 자동차
phase out 단계적으로 폐지하다 manufacture v. 제조하다
competitive adj. 경쟁력 있는, 경쟁의 evolve v. 진화하다, 발달하다
disappear v. 사라지다 entirely adv. 완전히, 전부
hybrid adj. (자동차가) 하이브리드의 diversify v. 다각화하다
versatile adj. 다재다능한, 다방면의

---

155 추론 문제

해설 VDF 산업은 무엇을 파는 것 같은가?
(A) 전기 자동차
(B) 자동차 부품
(C) 조종 장치
(D) 제조 장비

해설 지문의 'VDF Industries, one of the leading suppliers of parts for gasoline-powered vehicles'에서 VDF 산업이 휘발유 동력의 자동차를 위한 부품의 선두적인 공급업체 중 하나라고 했으므로 VDF 산업이 자동차 부품을 파는 회사임을 추론할 수 있다. 따라서 (B)가 정답이다.

어휘 navigation n. 조종, 운항, 항해 equipment n. 장비

156 육하원칙 문제

해설 VDF 산업은 왜 제품 제공을 다각화하기를 원하는가?
(A) 새로운 기술의 이점을 이용하기 위해
(B) 브랜드 평판을 높이기 위해
(C) 해외에서 제품들을 판매하기 위해
(D) 변화하는 소비자 수요를 충족시키기 위해

해설 지문의 'According to VDF Industries CEO Drew Soto, manufacturing electric vehicle parts should help the company meet the evolving needs of customers.'에서 VDF 산업의 최고 경영자인 Drew Soto가 전기 자동차 부품을 제조하는 것이 고객들의 진화하는 욕구를 충족시키는 것에 도움이 될 것이라 했다고 했으므로 (D)가 정답이다.

어휘 take advantage of ~을 이용하다 enhance v. 높이다
reputation n. 평판, 명성

Paraphrasing

evolving needs of customers 고객들의 진화하는 욕구
→ changing consumer demand 변화하는 소비자 수요

157 문장 위치 찾기 문제

해설 [1], [2], [3], [4]로 표시된 위치 중, 다음 문장이 들어갈 곳으로 가장 적절한 것은?

"그 새로운 부품들은 내년 초부터 구입할 수 있을 것이다."

(A) [1]
(B) [2]
(C) [3]
(D) [4]

해설 주어진 문장은 새로운 부품들과 관련된 내용이 나오는 부분에 들어가야 함을 알 수 있다. [4]의 앞 문장인 'To remain competitive, it[VDF Industries] has announced its decision to begin producing electric vehicle parts.'에서 VDF 산업이 전기 자동차 부품을 생산하기 시작했다는 결정을 발표했다고 했으므로, [4]에 주어진 문장이 들어가면 VDF 산업이 생산하기 시작한 전기 자동차 부품을 내년 초부터 구입할 수 있을 것이라는 자연스러운 문맥이 된다는 것을 알 수 있다. 따라서 (D)가 정답이다.

어휘 component n. 부품

158-160번은 다음 이메일에 관한 문제입니다.

수신: 신시내티 지점 전 직원 <cincinnati.staff@mixologystores.com>
발신: Brandon Flannigan <b.flannigan@mixologystores.com>
제목: 캐나다
¹⁵⁹날짜: 9월 4일

직원분들께,

¹⁵⁸저는 특별한 임무를 수행할 수 있는 팀을 구성하는 것을 고려하고 있습니다. 이미 아시겠지만, ¹⁵⁹우리 회사는 다음 달 캐나다에 첫 번째 지점을 열 예정입니다. 우리 지점이 토론토의 새로운 Mixology 매장을 개시하는 것에 도움을 주도록 선정되었습니다. 이것은 10월 3일부터 10월 18일까지 매장 직원들을 교육하는 것을 포함할 것입니다.

만약 이 흥미진진한 도전에 관심이 있다면, 이메일을 통해 저에게 직접 연락해 주시기 바랍니다. 저는 전체 기간 동안 풀타임 일정에 전념할 수 있는 사람들만 찾고 있습니다. 모든 비용이 지불될 것입니다. 당사는 항공편, ¹⁶⁰⁻⁽ᴬ⁾토론토 Mirage 호텔의 객실, 현지 교통 비용, 그리고 일일 식사 비용을 제공할 것입니다. 게다가, ¹⁶⁰⁻⁽ᴮ⁾현재의 시간당 임금이 일시적으로 20퍼센트 인상될 것입니다. ¹⁶⁰⁻⁽ᴰ⁾5일의 추가 휴가일도 받게 될 것입니다.

Brandon Flannigan 드림
지점 관리자, Mixology

capable adj. ~을 할 수 있는 **assignment** n. 임무, 과제
be set to ~할 예정이다 **select** v. 선정하다, 고르다
commit v. 전념하다, 헌신하다 **entire** adj. 전체의, 온
expense n. 비용 **transportation** n. 교통, 운송
allowance n. 비용, 수당 **hourly wage** 시간당 임금
temporarily adv. 일시적으로 **additional** adj. 추가의

158 목적 찾기 문제

해석 이메일의 목적은 무엇인가?
(A) 직원들에게 확장에 대해 알리기 위해
(B) 복지 프로그램을 알리기 위해
(C) 몇몇 직원들을 모집하기 위해
(D) 새로운 매장 정책을 소개하기 위해

해설 지문의 'I am looking to form a team capable of taking on a special assignment.'에서 특별한 임무를 수행할 수 있는 팀을 구성하는 것을 고려하고 있다고 했으므로 (C)가 정답이다.

어휘 **expansion** n. 확장 **benefit** n. 복지, 혜택
recruit v. 모집하다, 선발하다 **policy** n. 정책

159 육하원칙 문제

해석 이메일에 따르면, 10월에 무슨 일이 일어날 것인가?
(A) 새로운 매장 지점이 문을 열 것이다.
(B) 한정판 제품군이 출시될 것이다.
(C) 전사적인 축하 행사가 열릴 것이다.
(D) 자금 요청이 승인될 것이다.

해설 지문의 'DATE: September 4'에서 이메일이 작성된 일자가 9월 4일임을 알 수 있고, 'our company is set to open its very first location in Canada next month'에서 다음 달에 캐나다에 첫 번째 지점을 열 것이라고 했으므로 (A)가 정답이다.

어휘 **company-wide** adj. 전사적인 **celebration** n. 축하 행사, 축하

160 Not/True 문제

해석 토론토에서 일하는 것의 혜택으로 언급되지 않은 것은?
(A) 무료 호텔 숙박
(B) 일시적인 임금 인상
(C) 프로젝트 완료 상여금
(D) 추가 휴가일

해설 (A)는 'a room at the Toronto Mirage Hotel'에서 토론토 Mirage 호텔의 객실 사용이 혜택으로 언급되었다. (B)는 'your current hourly wage will be temporarily increased by 20 percent'에서 현재의 시간당 임금이 일시적으로 20퍼센트 인상될 것이라고 했으므로 혜택으로 언급되었다. (D)는 'You will also receive an additional five vacation days.'에서 5일의 추가 휴가일을 받게 될 것이라고 했으므로 혜택으로 언급되었다. (C)는 지문에 언급되지 않은 내용이다. 따라서 (C)가 정답이다.

어휘 **accommodation** n. 숙박, 숙소

Paraphrasing

a room at the ~ Hotel ~ 호텔의 객실 → hotel accommodations 호텔 숙박

161-164번은 다음 기사에 관한 문제입니다.

베드퍼드(5월 15일) — ¹⁶¹베드퍼드시는 지역 예술 그룹인 Up Studios와 제휴하여 야심 찬 공공 예술 프로젝트에 착수했다. 3개월 동안 지속될 것으로 예상되고 ¹⁶²⁻⁽ᴬ⁾시에 의해 25만 달러의 예산을 할당받은 그 프로젝트는 많은 대규모 벽화를 그리는 것을 포함할 것인데, 주민들은 5월 31일까지 이에 대한 그들의 아이디어를 제출할 수 있다.

예술위원인 Loretta Weiss에 따르면, 몇몇 부지들이 이미 벽화를 위해 선정되었는데, 여기에는 Bautisa 역의 지하도뿐만 아니라 상업 지구의 많은 빈 벽이 포함된다. ¹⁶⁴벽화를 위해 선정된 모든 부지들은 대중의 접근이 가능하도록 유지될 것이다.

"우리가 도시의 역사 및 문화를 반영하는 벽화의 구상을 추구하고 있다는 점을 명심하세요"라고 Ms. Weiss가 말했다. "¹⁶³우리는 기준을 온라인에 게시해 두었으니, 여러분의 아이디어를 제출하기 전에 정보를 반드시 확인해 주세요." 벽화 그리기에 도움을 주기 위해 자원하기를 바라는 주민들은 www.upstudios.org에서 Up Studios로 연락할 수 있다. 이 계획에 대한 더 많은 정보를 원하거나 아이디어를 기여하기 위해서는, 도시의 공식 웹사이트를 방문하면 된다.

embark on ~에 착수하다 **ambitious** adj. 야심 찬
allocate v. 할당하다 **budget** n. 예산 **resource** n. 재원, 자원
involve v. 포함하다 **mural** n. 벽화 **resident** n. 주민, 거주민
contribute v. 기여하다, 기고하다 **commissioner** n. 위원
blank adj. 빈 **commercial** adj. 상업의 **district** n. 지구, 지역
underpass n. 지하도 **reflect** v. 반영하다 **criteria** n. 기준
initiative n. 계획

161 목적 찾기 문제

해석 기사의 목적은 무엇인가?

(A) 미술관을 홍보하기 위해
(B) 시의 계획을 설명하기 위해
(C) 그리기 대회를 알리기 위해
(D) 최근의 몇몇 개선을 칭찬하기 위해

해설 지문의 'The City of Bedford is embarking on an ambitious public art project in partnership with the local art group Up Studios.'에서 베드퍼드시가 지역 예술 그룹인 Up Studios와 제휴하여 야심 찬 공공 예술 프로젝트에 착수했다고 한 것을 통해, 기사의 목적이 시의 계획을 설명하기 위함임을 알 수 있다. 따라서 (B)가 정답이다.

어휘 promote v. 홍보하다, 촉진하다 praise v. 칭찬하다
improvement n. 개선

162 Not/True 문제

해석 프로젝트에 대해 언급된 것은?
(A) 시의 자금으로 지불된다.
(B) 결국 몇몇 도로의 폐쇄로 이어질 것이다.
(C) 지역의 관광을 촉진하기 위해 의도된 것이다.
(D) 이전에 한 번 넘게 연기되었다.

해설 지문의 'The project, which ~ has been allocated a budget of $250,000 by the city'에서 이 프로젝트가 시에 의해 25만 달러의 예산을 할당받았다고 했으므로 (A)는 지문의 내용과 일치한다. 따라서 (A)가 정답이다. (B), (C), (D)는 지문에 언급되지 않은 내용이다.

어휘 municipal adj. 시의, 지방 자치제의 fund n. 자금, 기금
closure n. 폐쇄 intend v. 의도하다, 의미하다

Paraphrasing

a budget ~ by the city 시에 의한 예산 → municipal funds 시의 자금

163 육하원칙 문제

해석 Ms. Weiss는 사람들에게 무엇을 하라고 조언하는가?
(A) Up Studios의 회원이 된다.
(B) 벽화 디자인에 대한 투표에 참여한다.
(C) 온라인에서 몇몇 지침들을 확인한다.
(D) 몇몇 장소의 사진을 찍는다.

해설 지문의 'We've posted the criteria online, so be sure to check that information before submitting your ideas.'에서 Ms. Weiss가 기준을 온라인에 게시해 두었으니, 아이디어를 기여하기 전에 정보를 반드시 확인해 달라고 하였다. 따라서 (C)가 정답이다.

어휘 participate v. 참여하다 vote n. 투표 guideline n. 지침
site n. 장소, 현장

164 동의어 찾기 문제

해설 2문단 일곱 번째 줄의 단어 "accessible"은 의미상 -와 가장 가깝다.
(A) 만족스러운
(B) 열려 있는
(C) 실현 가능한
(D) 분명한

해설 accessible을 포함한 구절 'All sites chosen for the murals will remain accessible to the public.'에서 accessible은 '접근이 가능한'이라는 뜻으로 사용되었다. 따라서 (B)가 정답이다.

165-168번은 다음 직무 기술서에 관한 문제입니다.

¹⁶⁵Citadel 건설사는 잭슨 카운티에서 진행 중인 많은 주거용 주택 개발 프로젝트를 감독할 경험 있는 건설 현장 감독관을 찾고 있습니다. ¹⁶⁶여러 현장에 접근할 필요가 있을 것이기에, 업무용 차량이 경쟁력 있는 급여와 포괄적인 의료 보험에 더해 제공될 것입니다. — [1] —.

¹⁶⁷⁻⁽ᴮ⁾이 직위의 책무는 건설 현장의 정기적인 점검을 수행하는 것과 ¹⁶⁷⁻⁽ᶜ⁾건설 인력에 업무를 위임하는 것, 그리고 사용되는 자재들이 적절한지 책임지는 것을 포함합니다. ¹⁶⁷⁻⁽ᴰ⁾건설 현장 감독관은 또한 잠재적 안전 위험 요소를 확인하고 대처할 책임이 있는데, 이것은 반드시 모든 인력이 필요한 보호 장비를 착용하고 장비를 제대로 사용하도록 하는 것을 수반합니다. — [2] —.

또한, ¹⁶⁸합격한 후보자는 프로젝트 관리자들과 긴밀히 협력해야 할 것입니다. — [3] —. 지원자들은 야외 근무가 빈번하기 때문에 연속적으로 바뀌는 기상 환경에 적응할 준비가 되어 있어야 합니다. 때때로 주말 근무가 프로젝트의 시간표에 따라 요구될 수 있습니다. —[4] —. 지원하시려면, 이력서와 자기소개서를 5월 7일까지 careers@citadelconstruction.com으로 보내주시기를 바랍니다.

experienced adj. 경험 있는, 능숙한 supervisor n. 감독관, 관리자
residential adj. 주거용의, 주택의 competitive adj. 경쟁력 있는
comprehensive adj. 포괄적인, 종합적인 health benefits 의료 보험
responsibility n. 책무, 책임 delegate v. 위임하다
personnel n. 인력, 직원 appropriate adj. 적절한
identify v. 확인하다, 찾다 address v. 대처하다, 해결하다
hazard n. 위험 (요소) protective gear 보호 장비
candidate n. 후보자, 지원자 applicant n. 지원자
varying adj. 연속적으로 바뀌는 frequent adj. 빈번한, 잦은
occasional adj. 때때로의, 가끔의

165 추론 문제

해설 잭슨 카운티에 대해 암시되는 것은?
(A) 새로운 건설 프로젝트에 세금 혜택을 제공한다.
(B) 다른 지역들보다 더 적당한 가격의 주택을 보유하고 있다.
(C) 주택 분야에서 성장을 경험하고 있다.
(D) 관광객들에게 인기 있는 목적지이다.

해설 지문의 'Citadel Construction is seeking an experienced construction site supervisor to oversee a number of ongoing residential housing development projects in Jackson County.'에서 Citadel 건설사가 잭슨 카운티에서 진행 중인 많은 주거용 주택 개발 프로젝트를 감독할 경험 있는 건설 현장 감독관을 찾고 있다고 한 것을 통해, 잭슨 카운티가 주택 분야에서 성장을 경험하고 있음을 추론할 수 있다. 따라서 (C)가 정답이다.

어휘 tax incentive 세금 혜택, 감세 조치
affordable adj. (가격이) 적당한, 알맞은 housing n. 주택 (공급)
undergo v. 경험하다, 겪다 destination n. 목적지

166 추론 문제

해석 건설 현장 감독관에게 제공되는 업무용 차량은 무엇에 사용될 것 같은가?
(A) 회사 본사로 통근하는 것
(B) 건설 자재를 운반하는 것
(C) 여러 작업장들 간에 이동하는 것
(D) 투자자들을 위한 현장 견학을 하는 것

해설 지문의 'As multiple sites will need to be accessed, a work vehicle will be provided'에서 여러 현장에 접근할 필요가 있을 것이기에 업무용 차량이 제공될 것이라고 했으므로 업무용 차량이 여러 작업장들 간에 이동하는 것에 사용될 것임을 추론할 수 있다. 따라서 (C)가 정답이다.

어휘 commute v. 통근하다   headquarters n. 본사
conduct v. (특정 활동을) 하다

Paraphrasing

multiple sites 여러 현장 → various worksites 여러 작업장

167 Not/True 문제

해석 건설 현장 감독관의 책무로 언급되지 않은 것은?
(A) 건물 자재를 조달하는 것
(B) 작업 현장을 주기적으로 점검하는 것
(C) 작업자들에게 업무를 배정하는 것
(D) 안전 문제를 처리하는 것

해설 (A)는 지문에서 언급되지 않은 내용이다. 따라서 (A)가 정답이다. (B)는 'Responsibilities for this position include performing regular inspections of construction sites'에서 건설 현장의 정기적인 점검을 수행하는 것이 건설 현장 감독관의 책무로 언급되었다. (C)는 'delegating tasks to construction personnel'에서 건설 인력에 업무를 위임하는 것이 건설 현장 감독관의 책무로 언급되었다. (D)는 'The construction site supervisor will also be responsible for identifying and addressing potential safety hazards'에서 건설 현장 감독관은 또한 잠재적 안전 위험 요소를 확인하고 대처하는 것이 건설 현장 감독관의 책무로 언급되었다.

어휘 source v. 조달하다, 공급하다   periodically adv. 주기적으로
assign v. 배정하다, 맡기다

Paraphrasing

performing regular inspections of construction sites 건설 현장의 정기적인 점검을 수행하는 것 → Inspecting worksites periodically 작업 현장을 주기적으로 점검하는 것
delegating tasks to construction personnel 건설 인력에 업무를 위임하는 것 → Assigning tasks to workers 작업자들에게 업무를 배정하는 것
addressing potential safety hazards 잠재적 안전 위험 요소에 대처하는 것 → Handling safety concerns 안전 문제를 처리하는 것

168 문장 위치 찾기 문제

해석 [1], [2], [3], [4]로 표시된 위치 중, 다음 문장이 들어갈 곳으로 가장 적절한 것은?

"이것은 진행 상황 업데이트를 제공하는 것과 발생할 수 있는 모든 변경 사항에 대해 논의하는 것을 포함할 것입니다."

(A) [1]
(B) [2]
(C) [3]
(D) [4]

해설 주어진 문장은 다른 사람과의 협업과 관련된 내용이 나오는 부분에 들어가야 함을 예상할 수 있다. [3]의 앞 문장인 'the successful candidate will work closely with project managers'에서 합격한 후보는 프로젝트 관리자들과 긴밀히 협력해야 할 것이라고 했으므로, [3]에 주어진 문장이 들어가면 합격한 후보는 프로젝트 관리자들과 협력해야 하는데, 진행 상황 업데이트를 제공하고 발생할 수 있는 모든 변경 사항에 대해 논의할 것을 포함한다는 자연스러운 문맥이 된다는 것을 알 수 있다. 따라서 (C)가 정답이다.

어휘 arise v. 발생하다, 생기다

169-171번은 다음 회람에 관한 문제입니다.

회람

수신: 모든 부서장
발신: Elina Poole, 인사 담당자
주제: 원격 근무 시험
날짜: 8월 20일

여러분들이 알고 계시듯, ¹⁶⁹⁻⁽ᴰ⁾**Wellington 주식회사는 우리의 현재 공간을 임대하는 비용의 최근 인상으로 인해 내년에 더 작은 사무실로 이사할 계획을 하고 있습니다.** 우리가 직원들의 규모를 줄이는 것이 아니기 때문에, 우리는 대체 가능한 근무 제도를 살펴볼 필요가 있습니다. 이를 위해, 저는 직원들이 주의 일부 동안 사무실 밖에서 일하는 것이 얼마나 실용적인지를 평가하기 위한 시험용 프로그램을 시작해 보고자 합니다. ¹⁷⁰**그러므로 저는 여러분 각자 여러분의 팀에서 이 시험에 참여할 두 명의 팀원을 선정해 주실 것을 요청드립니다.**

참가자들은 두 달이라는 기간 동안 월요일, 수요일, 그리고 금요일에 원격으로 근무를 할 것이며, 이 기간 동안 그들은 가상 회의 소프트웨어 같은 재택근무 기술을 활용할 것입니다. 여러분은 그들이 수행한 작업의 질과 규칙성을 평가할 책임이 있을 것입니다. 적절한 직원들의 이름을 이번 주가 끝날 때까지 저에게 이메일로 보내주시기 바랍니다. 승인되면, ¹⁷¹**참가자들은 시작하기 전에 프로그램의 기술적 측면에 대해 간단히 듣게 될 것입니다.**

감사합니다.

Elina Poole

---

rent v. 임대하다, 빌리다   current adj. 현재의
explore v. 살피다, 탐구하다   alternative adj. 대체 가능한, 대안이 되는
arrangement n. 제도, 준비   initiate v. 시작하다, 착수하다
pilot n. 시험적으로 하는 것   assess v. 평가하다
viable adj. 실용적인, 실행 가능한   virtual adj. 가상의, 사실상의
suitable adj. 적절한, 적합한   approve v. 승인하다, 찬성하다

169 Not/True 문제

해석 Wellington 주식회사에 대해 언급된 것은?
(A) 최근 새로운 사무실 공간으로 이사했다.
(B) 낮은 의욕으로 인해 생산성이 악화되고 있다.
(C) 내년 초에 직원들을 해고하기 시작할 것이다.
(D) 근무 공간의 임대 비용이 상승했다.

해설 지문의 'Wellington Ltd. is planning to move to a smaller office next year due to the recent increase in the cost of renting our current space'에서 Wellington 주식회사는 공간을 임대하는 비용의 최근 인상으로 인해 내년에 더 작은 사무실로 이사할 계획을 하고 있다고 했으므로 (D)가 정답이다. (A), (B), (C)는 지문에 언급되지 않은 내용이다.

어휘 productivity n. 생산성 suffer v. 악화되다, 겪다
morale n. 의욕, 사기 lay off ~를 해고하다

Paraphrasing
the cost of renting 임대하는 비용 → rental costs 임대 비용

170 육하원칙 문제

해석 각 부서장은 무엇을 하라고 요청받는가?
(A) 재택근무 기술을 추천한다.
(B) 주의 3일을 원격으로 근무한다.
(C) 시험에 참가할 팀원을 선정한다.
(D) 가상 회의 소프트웨어를 사용하기 위해 직원들을 교육한다.

해설 지문의 'I therefore ask that you[department heads] each select two members of your team to take part in this trial.'에서 팀에서 이 시험에 참여할 두 명의 팀원을 선정해달라고 요청했으므로 (C)가 정답이다.

어휘 remotely adv. 원격으로, 멀리서

Paraphrasing
take part in ~에 참여하다 → participate in ~에 참가하다

171 동의어 찾기 문제

해석 2문단 다섯 번째 줄의 단어 "aspects"는 의미상 -와 가장 가깝다.
(A) 어려움
(B) 요소
(C) 견해
(D) 요건

해설 aspects를 포함한 문장 'participants will be briefed on the technical aspects of the programme before beginning'에서 aspects는 '측면'이라는 뜻으로 사용되었다. 따라서 (B)가 정답이다.

172-175번은 다음 온라인 채팅 대화문에 관한 문제입니다.

Jeffrey Kwon [오전 10시 59분]
안녕하세요, Eric. ¹⁷²저는 제가 간행물에 제출했던 기사에 대한 보수를 언제 받을 수 있을지 궁금해요.

Eric Michaels [오전 11시]
어떤 것이었나요? 죄송하지만, 이곳이 지난 며칠 동안 꽤 바빠요.

Jeffrey Kwon [오전 11시 2분]
아, 사람들의 휴가를 계획하는 데 인공지능을 사용하는 온라인 여행사에 관한 것이에요.

Eric Michaels [오전 11시 2분]
아, 그래요. 제 생각에는 저희 콘텐츠 편집자인 Ms. Beecham이 그것을 읽었던 것 같고, 그녀에게 의견이 좀 있을 거예요. 제가 그녀에게 확인해 볼게요.

Jeffrey Kwon [오전 11시 4분]
¹⁷³감사해요, 그리고 이것으로 귀찮게 해서 죄송해요. 당신이 바쁘다는 것을 알지만, 저는 누구에게 보수에 대해 이야기해야 할지 몰랐어요.

Eric Michaels [오전 11시 5분]
걱정 말아요! 우리는 Ms. Beecham을 몇 분 기다려야 해요. 그녀는 고객과 이야기 중이에요.

Sandy Beecham [오전 11시 10분]
¹⁷⁵Mr. Kwon, 저는 당신이 작성한 것을 봤어요. 그것은 정말 좋은 것 같아요! 이번 호에 그것을 그대로 사용하고 싶어요. Eric, 가서 Mr. Kwon의 지급을 처리해 주세요. 제가 바로 컴퓨터 시스템에 승인을 기록할게요.

Jeffrey Kwon [오전 11시 11분]
다행이네요. 감사합니다, Ms. Beecham.

Eric Michaels [오전 11시 12분]
¹⁷⁴수표도 괜찮으실까요, Mr. Kwon? 수령하실 수 있도록 Ms. Summers가 지금 준비할 수 있어요.

Jeffrey Kwon [오전 11시 13분]
좋습니다. 도와주셔서 감사해요.

payment n. 보수, 지급 publication n. 발행물, 출판물
feedback n. 의견 bother v. 귀찮게 하다, 신경 쓰이게 하다
upcoming adj. 이번의, 곧 있을 approval n. 승인

172 추론 문제

해석 Mr. Kwon은 누구일 것 같은가?
(A) 잡지 구독자
(B) 콘텐츠 개발자
(C) 최근의 직무 지원자
(D) 컴퓨터 프로그래머

해설 지문의 'I was wondering when I would receive my payment for the article I submitted for publication.'에서 간행물에 제출했던 기사에 대한 자신의 보수를 언제 받을 수 있을지 궁금하다고 한 것을 통해, Mr. Kwon이 콘텐츠 개발자라는 것을 추론할 수 있다. 따라서 (B)가 정답이다.

어휘 subscriber n. 구독자

173 육하원칙 문제

해석 Mr. Kwon은 무엇에 대해 사과하는가?
(A) 과제를 늦게 제출한 것
(B) 중요한 회의를 놓친 것

(C) 직원의 근무 시간을 방해한 것
(D) 양식을 작성하는 것을 잊은 것

해설 지문의 'Thanks, and I'm sorry to bother you with this. I realize you're busy, but I wasn't sure who else to ask about payment.'에서 Mr. Michaels가 바쁘다는 것을 알지만 누구에게 보수에 대해 이야기해야 할지 몰랐다며, 이것으로 귀찮게 해서 미안하다고 하였다. 따라서 (C)가 정답이다.

어휘 assignment n. 과제 miss v. 놓치다 interrupt v. 방해하다

174 추론 문제

해설 Ms. Summers는 어느 부서에서 일할 것 같은가?
(A) 법무
(B) 회계
(C) 운송
(D) 정보 기술

해설 지문의 'Is a check OK with you, Mr. Kwon? Ms. Summers can prepare it now for you to pick up.'에서 Mr. Kwon에게 수표도 괜찮을지 물으며, Ms. Summers가 그것을 지금 준비할 수 있다고 한 것을 통해, Ms. Summers가 회계 부서에서 일하고 있음을 추론할 수 있다. 따라서 (B)가 정답이다.

175 의도 파악 문제

해설 오전 11시 11분에, Mr. Kwon이 "That's good to know"라고 썼을 때, 그가 의도한 것 같은 것은?
(A) 직위에 지원할 자격이 있다.
(B) 어떤 작업도 수정할 필요가 없다.
(C) 그가 예상했던 것보다 많은 돈을 받게 될 것이다.
(D) 찾고 있던 연락처를 발견했다.

해설 지문의 'Mr. Kwon, I saw what you wrote. I think it's great! I'd like to use it in our upcoming issue as is.'에서 Ms. Beecham이 Mr. Kwon이 작성한 것을 봤고 이번 호에 그것을 그대로 사용하고 싶다고 하자, Mr. Kwon이 'That's good to know' (다행이네요)라고 한 것을 통해, 그가 어떤 작업도 수정할 필요가 없음을 알 수 있다. 따라서 (B)가 정답이다.

어휘 eligible adj. 자격이 있는, 적격의 revise v. 수정하다

176-180번은 다음 두 웹페이지에 관한 문제입니다.

홈	소개	예약	후기	연락

Meyers 호텔에서, 우리는 웨스턴오스트레일리아주에서 가장 인기 있는 숙박 시설 중 하나라는 것에 자부심을 느낍니다. 176-(B)경이로운 Forest Grove 국립 공원에서 도보로 불과 20분 거리에 위치해 있기 때문에, 우리는 이 지역의 자연의 경이로움을 탐험한 후에 머리를 누일 수 있는 완벽한 장소를 제공합니다.

우리의 모든 객실은 청결하고, 편안하며, 아늑합니다. 176-(C)우리는 각각의 손님에게 우리의 식당에서 차려지는 무료 아침 식사를 제공합니다. 그리고 방문객들이 즐길 수 있는 현지 예술가들의 광범위한 그림 소장품뿐만 아니라 넓은 정원도 있습니다.

우리의 디럭스 객실은 하룻밤에 85달러를 청구하고 최고급 객실은 하룻밤에 105달러를 청구합니다. 당신은 여기에서 이용 가능성을 확인할 수 있습니다. 177여름은 일반적으로 가장 바쁜 계절이므로, 그 시기에 방문하기를 계획하고 있다면 적어도 8주 전에 반드시 예약해 주시기를 바랍니다.

178각 객실의 최대 수용 인원은 각각의 추가 손님에 대한 35달러의 비용이 지불되지 않는다면, 성인 2명과 아이 1명이라는 점에 주의해 주십시오.

inn n. (작은) 호텔, 여관 marvellous adj. 경이로운
wonder n. 경이로움, 불가사의 comfortable adj. 편안한, 쾌적한
cosy adj. 아늑한 extensive adj. 광범위한 maximum adj. 최대의
occupancy n. 수용 인원, 사용

홈	소개	예약	후기	연락

손님: Tim Blackwell
평점: 4/5

178저는 배우자와 아이 둘을 데리고 Meyers 호텔을 방문했습니다. 저는 이 공간이 너무 잘 관리되어 있었다는 점에 감명을 받았습니다. 투숙 수속 절차는 순조롭게 진행되었고 객실은 매우 널찍하고 현대적이었습니다. 우리는 또한 매일 아침에 제공된 무료 아침 식사를 정말로 즐겼습니다. 그리고 소유주인 Gunnar Meyers는 믿을 수 없을 정도로 친절했습니다. 179그는 심지어 제 아이 중 한 명이 독감에 걸렸을 때 인근 마을의 병원으로 태워 주기까지 했습니다. 180제가 이 장소에서 경험했던 유일한 문제는 제가 아무리 자주 온도 조절 장치를 조정하더라도, 객실이 너무 덥거나 너무 추웠다는 점인 것 같습니다. 그렇지만, 전반적으로 저는 이 호텔을 매우 추천합니다.

impressed adj. 감명을 받은 manage v. 관리하다
spacious adj. 널찍한 incredibly adv. 믿을 수 없을 정도로
flu n. 독감 adjust v. 조정하다 thermostat n. 온도 조절 장치

176 Not/True 문제

해설 첫 번째 웹페이지가 Meyers 호텔에 대해 명시하는 것은?
(A) 큰 실내 수영장을 갖추고 있다.
(B) 휴양 지역과 가까이 위치해 있다.
(C) 하루 세 번의 무료 식사를 제공한다.
(D) 가족에게 할인된 요금을 제공한다.

해설 첫 번째 웹페이지의 'Located just a 20-minute walk from the marvellous Forest Grove National Park'에서 Forest Grove 국립 공원에서 도보로 불과 20분 거리에 위치해 있다고 했으므로 (B)가 정답이다. (A)와 (D)는 지문에 언급되지 않은 내용이다. (C)는 'We offer each guest a complimentary breakfast served in our dining room.'에서 무료 아침 식사를 제공한다고 했으므로 지문의 내용과 일치하지 않는다.

어휘 indoor adj. 실내의 recreational adj. 휴양의, 오락의

Paraphrasing

Located just a 20-minute walk from the marvellous Forest Grove National Park 경이로운 Forest Grove 국립 공원에서 도보로 불과 20분 거리에 위치해 있다 → is located close to a recreational area 휴양 지역과 가까이 위치해 있다

177 육하원칙 문제

해석 여름 중에 방문하기를 계획하고 있다면 손님들은 무엇을 해야 하는가?
(A) 두 달 전에 예약한다.
(B) 근처 정원의 투어의 예정을 세운다.
(C) 객실 이용 가능성을 전화로 확인한다.
(D) 계절에 따른 가격 인상을 확인한다.

해설 첫 번째 웹페이지의 'Summer is usually our busiest season, so be sure to make a reservation at least eight weeks earlier if you plan to visit during that time.'에서 여름은 일반적으로 가장 바쁜 계절이므로, 그 시기에 방문하기를 계획하고 있다면 적어도 8주 전에 반드시 예약해야 한다고 하였다. 따라서 (A)가 정답이다.

어휘 booking n. 예약   arrange v. 예정을 세우다

Paraphrasing

make a reservation at least eight weeks earlier 적어도 8주 전에 예약하다 → Make a booking two months in advance 두 달 전에 예약하다

178 추론 문제 연계

해석 Mr. Blackwell에 대해 결론지을 수 있는 것은?
(A) 국립 공원에 관한 책을 구입했다.
(B) 가장 한산한 달에 그 호텔을 방문했다.
(C) 객실에 대한 추가 비용을 지불했다.
(D) 호주로 자주 여행한다.

해설 질문의 핵심 어구인 Mr. Blackwell이 작성한 후기가 있는 두 번째 웹페이지를 먼저 확인한다.
단서 1 두 번째 웹페이지의 'I visited the Meyers Inn with my wife and two children.'에서 Mr. Blackwell이 배우자와 아이 둘을 데리고 Meyers 호텔에 방문했다고 했다. 그런데 수용 인원에 대해 제시되지 않았으므로 첫 번째 웹페이지에서 관련 내용을 확인한다.
단서 2 첫 번째 웹페이지의 'Please note that each room has a maximum occupancy of two adults and one child unless a fee of $35 for each extra guest is paid.'에서 각 객실의 최대 수용 인원은 각각의 추가 손님에 대한 35달러의 비용이 지불되지 않는다면, 성인 2명과 아이 1명이라고 했다.
두 단서를 종합할 때, Mr. Blackwell이 객실에 대한 추가 비용을 지불했을 것임을 알 수 있다. 따라서 (C)가 정답이다.

어휘 quiet adj. 한산한, 조용한   additional adj. 추가의

179 육하원칙 문제

해석 Mr. Meyers가 Mr. Blackwell의 가족을 위해 해준 것은 무엇인가?
(A) 객실 업그레이드를 제공했다.
(B) 그들을 의료 시설로 수송했다.
(C) 평소보다 더 늦게 퇴실하도록 허용했다.
(D) 기상 환경에 대한 정보를 제공했다.

해설 두 번째 웹페이지의 'He[Mr. Meyers] even gave us a ride to a hospital in a neighbouring town when one of my children came down with the flu.'에서 Mr. Meyers가 심지어 Mr. Blackwell의 아이 중 한 명이 독감에 걸렸을 때 인근 마을의 병원으로 태워 주기까지 했다고 하였다. 따라서 (B)가 정답이다.

어휘 medical adj. 의료의, 의학의   facility n. 시설, 기관

Paraphrasing

a hospital 병원 → a medical facility 의료 시설

180 육하원칙 문제

해석 Mr. Blackwell은 그의 객실과 관련하여 무슨 문제가 있었는가?
(A) 욕실이 제대로 청소되지 않았다.
(B) 크기가 한 가족에게 충분하지 않았다.
(C) 가구가 좋지 않은 상태였다.
(D) 온도가 쾌적하지 않았다.

해설 두 번째 웹페이지의 'I suppose the only problem I had with this place was that the room was either too hot or too cold, no matter how often I adjusted the thermostat.'에서 Mr. Blackwell이 이 장소에서 경험했던 유일한 문제는 아무리 자주 온도 조절 장치를 조정하더라도, 객실이 너무 덥거나 너무 추웠다는 점이었다고 했으므로 (D)가 정답이다.

어휘 properly adv. 제대로, 적절하게   sufficient adj. 충분한
furniture n. 가구   temperature n. 온도

181-185번은 다음 통지서와 이메일에 관한 문제입니다.

통지

운전자분께,

차량 등록 번호가 X09123인 귀하의 차량이 제한 구역에 주차되어 있음을 이것을 통해 알려드립니다. Coleman가의 1800 구역은 주차 허가증을 소지하신 분들을 위해 따로 마련된 구역입니다. [183]오전 10시까지 차량을 이동하지 않으시면, 시에서 어쩔 수 없이 귀하의 비용으로 그것을 견인하게 될 것입니다.

귀하의 차량이 견인되는 경우, 시의 견인 차량 보관소 중 한 곳에서 그것을 돌려받으실 수 있습니다. [182]그것을 찾기 위해 www.sanjosecity.com/towedvehicles로 가셔서 귀하의 차량 등록 번호를 검색하세요. [181]견인 비용은 7,500파운드 미만 차량의 경우 150달러, 그 무게가 넘는 차량의 경우 250달러입니다.

질문이나 우려 사항이 있으시다면, towing@sanjosecity.com으로 저희에게 이메일 주세요.

감사합니다,

새너제이시

motorist n. 운전자   hereby adv. 이것을 통해, 이것에 의해
license plate number 차량 등록 번호   restricted adj. 제한된, 한정된
reserve v. 따로 마련하다, 예약하다   tow v. 견인하다

수신: towing@sanjosecity.com
발신: Alison Pierce <a.pierce@fastmail.com>
제목: 견인
날짜: 5월 8일

관계자분께:

제 이름은 Alison Pierce이고 차량 등록 번호가 X09123인 빨간색 세단 소유주입니다. ¹⁸³제가 오늘 일찍 고객과 커피를 마시고 있을 때, Coleman가에 1시간 정도 차를 주차했습니다. 제가 돌아왔을 때, 제 차는 견인되어 있었습니다.

문제는 제 차가 견인되어서는 안 되었다는 것입니다. ¹⁸⁵저는 이 거리에 자주 주차하고, 전면 유리 좌측 하단 모서리에 주차 허가증이 있습니다. 낙엽 등에 의해 가려졌을 가능성이 있습니다. 그래도 당신이 제 차를 살펴본다면, 그것을 찾게 될 겁니다. ¹⁸⁴이 거리에 주차하는 것이 허용된 사람들에 대한 데이터베이스가 있다면, 제 이름을 검색해 보시길 권합니다.

¹⁸⁵당신이 이러한 정보를 확인하실 수 있다면, 요금을 지불하지 않고 제 차를 찾아가고 싶습니다.

Alison Pierce 드림

frequently adv. 자주, 빈번하게 **windshield** n. 전면 유리, 바람막이 창
obscure v. 가리다, 덮어 감추다 **verify** v. 확인하다, 입증하다

181 육하원칙 문제

해석 어떤 정보가 통지서에 기재되어 있는가?
(A) 운전자 이름
(B) 차량 견인 요금
(C) 시설의 위치
(D) 거주민에 대한 주차 요금

해설 통지서의 'The costs of towing are $150 for vehicles under 7,500 pounds and $250 for vehicles over that weight.'에서 견인 비용은 7,500파운드 미만 차량의 경우 150달러, 그 무게가 넘는 차량의 경우 250달러라고 하였다. 따라서 (B)가 정답이다.

어휘 **rate** n. 요금, 비율, 속도 **resident** n. 거주민

Paraphrasing

costs of towing 견인 비용 → towing rates 견인 요금

182 육하원칙 문제

해석 사람들은 어떻게 그들의 차량이 어디로 견인되었는지 찾을 수 있는가?
(A) 수신자 부담 전용 번호로 전화함으로써
(B) 온라인 검색 엔진을 사용함으로써
(C) 시 공무원에게 이메일을 보냄으로써
(D) 관공서에 방문함으로써

해설 통지서의 'Go to www.sanjosecity.com/towedvehicles, and search for your license plate number to find it.'에서 명시된 웹사이트 주소로 가서 차량 등록 번호로 검색하여 차량을 찾으라고 하였다. 따라서 (B)가 정답이다.

어휘 **special** adj. 전용의, 특별한 **toll-free number** 수신자 부담 번호

183 추론 문제 연계

해석 Ms. Pierce에 대해 암시되는 것은?
(A) Coleman가에 있는 아파트 건물에 산다.
(B) 최근에 새 차량을 구입하기로 결정했다.
(C) 오전 10시 이후에 커피숍에서 떠났다.

(D) 이전에 시에 의해 자신의 차량이 견인되게 한 적이 있다.

해설 Ms. Pierce가 작성한 이메일을 먼저 확인한다.
단서 1 이메일의 'I parked my car on Coleman Street earlier today for about an hour, as I was having coffee with a client. When I returned, my car had been towed.'에서 Ms. Pierce가 아침에 고객과 커피를 마시고 있었고, 돌아왔을 때는 차가 견인되어 있었다고 했다. 그런데 커피숍을 언제 떠났는지에 대해 제시되지 않았으므로 통지서에서 관련 내용을 확인한다.
단서 2 통지서의 'If you do not move your car by 10 A.M., the city will be forced to tow it at your expense.'에서 오전 10시까지 차량을 이동하지 않으면 시에서 차량을 견인하게 될 것임을 알 수 있다.
두 단서를 종합할 때, Ms. Pierce는 그녀의 차량이 견인된 시간인 오전 10시 이후에 커피숍에서 떠났음을 알 수 있다. 따라서 (C)가 정답이다.

어휘 **depart** v. 떠나다, 출발하다

184 육하원칙 문제

해석 Ms. Pierce는 시에 무엇을 해 달라고 요청하는가?
(A) 디렉터리에서 그녀의 이름을 찾는다.
(B) 새 주차 허가증을 발급한다.
(C) 그녀의 차량을 어떤 장소로 되돌려 보낸다.
(D) 도시정책을 찾아본다.

해설 이메일의 'If there is a database of people permitted to park on this street, I encourage you to search for my name.'에서 이 거리, 즉 Coleman가에 주차하는 것이 허용된 사람들에 대한 데이터베이스가 있다면 자신의 이름을 검색해 볼 권한다고 하였다. 따라서 (A)가 정답이다.

어휘 **directory** n. 디렉터리(정보를 포함하는 레코드의 집합)
issue v. 발급하다, 발표하다 **municipal** adj. 도시의

Paraphrasing

search for ~을 검색하다 → Look for ~을 찾다
database 데이터베이스 → directory 디렉터리

185 육하원칙 문제

해석 Ms. Pierce는 왜 견인 요금이 면제되어야 한다고 생각하는가?
(A) 그녀는 그 지역 주민을 방문하고 있었다.
(B) 그녀는 유효한 주차 허가증을 가지고 있다.
(C) 견인 과정 동안 그녀의 차량이 손상되었다.
(D) 시 공무원이 그녀에게 견인이 실수로 이루어졌다고 말했다.

해설 이메일의 'I frequently park on this street and have a permit that's located on the bottom left corner of my windshield.'와, 'Provided that you're able to verify this information, I would like to pick up my car without paying the fee.'에서 Ms. Pierce는 자신의 차량 전면 유리 좌측 하단 모서리에 주차 허가증이 있고, 그러한 정보를 확인할 수 있다면, 요금을 지불하지 않고 차를 찾아가고 싶다고 하였다. 따라서 (B)가 정답이다.

어휘 **waive** v. 면제하다, 포기하다, 자제하다 **in error** 실수로, 잘못하여

Paraphrasing

without paying the fee 요금을 지불하지 않고 → fee should be waived 요금이 면제되어야 한다

186-190번은 다음 광고, 양식, 이메일에 관한 문제입니다.

사진 촬영 준비 완료 - Space Photoland

Space Photoland는 여러분의 사진 촬영에 필요한 모든 것을 충족시킬 수 있습니다. 186-(B)South Grand가 384번지에 위치한 저희 복합 건물에서 다음 스튜디오들을 대여하실 수 있습니다.

187스튜디오 1	소형 스튜디오(45제곱미터): 어두운 벽과 187자연광이 없는 이 스튜디오는 조명 조건을 더 잘 제어할 수 있습니다. 간단한 사진 촬영에 적합합니다.
187스튜디오 2	중형 스튜디오(75제곱미터): 밝은 벽이 있고 다양한 가구를 포함합니다. 187자연광은 차단되어 조명 장비로 특정 효과를 더 쉽게 만들 수 있습니다.
스튜디오 3	대형 스튜디오(100제곱미터): 고급 아파트처럼 보이도록 설계된 이 스튜디오에는 주방, 거실, 침실이 있습니다. 각 공간에는 자연광을 받을 수 있는 창문이 있습니다.
188스튜디오 4	초대형 스튜디오(150제곱미터): 188대형 스튜디오의 모든 아파트 시설을 갖추고 있으며, 도시가 내려다보이는 수영장이 있는 야외 공간도 갖추고 있습니다.

자세한 정보와 예약을 위해서 www.photoland.com을 방문하세요.

189필요하시면, ImageSource의 조명과 사진 장비가 합리적인 요금에 대여 가능합니다.

complex n. 복합 건물, (건물) 단지   operate v. 운영하다
absence n. 없음, 부재   equip v. (장비를) 갖추다
overlook v. 내려다보다

Space Photoland 예약 요청 양식

이름: Albert Compton
회사: Sanas 투자회사
주소: 3801번지 퀘벡가, 덴버, 콜로라도주 80207
전화: 555-4884
이메일: a.compton@sanasinvestments.com

이틀 동안 스튜디오 중 한 곳을 예약하고 싶습니다. 제 회사는 잡지에 게재할 광고 시리즈를 제작할 예정입니다. 6월 23일과 24일이 저희에게 가장 좋지만, 필요하다면 다른 날짜도 고려할 의향이 있습니다. 188수영장뿐만 아니라 고급스러운 생활 공간이 포함된 스튜디오를 선호합니다.

consider v. 고려하다   luxurious adj. 고급스러운

수신: Connie Orwell <connie@spacephotoland.com>
발신: Albert Compton <a.compton@sanasinvestments.com>
제목: 촬영
날짜: 6월 29일

Ms. Orwell께,

캠페인 촬영 중 도움을 주셔서 다시 한번 감사드리고 싶었습니다. 저희에게 필요했던 모든 콘텐츠를 하루와 저녁에 얻을 수 있었다는 사실에 놀랐습니다. 189모든 것이 잘 진행되었고, 귀사에 의해 제공된 ImageSource 카메라는 정확히 저희가 원했던 것이었습니다. 사내 사진작가가 이 점에 매우 깊은 인상을 받았습니다. 190그래서 곧 있을 마케팅 캠페인을 위해 귀사의 스튜디오 중 한 곳을 다시 예약하고 싶습니다. 현재 기획 단계에 있으며 다른 예약이 준비되면 연락드리겠습니다.

Albert Compton 드림
Sanas 투자회사

assistance n. 도움   in-house adj. 사내의, 내부의

186 Not/True 문제

해석 Space Photoland에 대해 명시된 것은?
(A) 사교 행사용으로도 대여될 수 있다.
(B) 한 주소에 여러 스튜디오가 있다.
(C) 최근 잡지 기사에 특집 기사로 다루어졌다.
(D) 보수를 위해 일시적으로 폐쇄될 수 있다.

해설 광고의 'The following studios are available to rent at our complex at 384 South Grand Avenue.'에서 South Grand가 384번지에 위치한 복합 건물에서 다음 스튜디오들을 대여할 수 있다고 했으므로 (B)는 지문에 명시되어 있다. 따라서 (B)가 정답이다. (A), (C), (D)는 지문에 명시되지 않은 내용이다.

어휘 feature v. 특집 기사로 다루다   temporarily adv. 일시적으로, 임시로

187 육하원칙 문제

해설 스튜디오 1과 스튜디오 2의 공통점은 무엇인가?
(A) 다양한 가구 품목으로 꾸며져 있다.
(B) 크기는 50제곱미터가 넘는다.
(C) 어두운색의 벽을 포함한다.
(D) 인공 광원 사용을 필요로 한다.

해설 광고의 'Studio 1', 'the absence of natural light', 'Studio 2', 'Natural light is blocked'에서 스튜디오 1, 2가 각각 자연광이 없고 차단되어 있다고 했으므로 (D)가 정답이다.

어휘 decorate v. 꾸미다, 장식하다   artificial adj. 인공의
light source 광원

188 육하원칙 문제 연계

해설 Mr. Compton이 가장 예약하고 싶어 하는 곳은 어느 스튜디오인가?
(A) 스튜디오 1
(B) 스튜디오 2
(C) 스튜디오 3
(D) 스튜디오 4

해설 Mr. Compton이 작성한 양식을 먼저 확인한다.
단서 1 양식의 'We would prefer to use the studio that includes a luxurious living space as well as a pool.'에서 수영장뿐만 아니라, 고급스러운 생활 공간이 포함된 스튜디오를 선호한다고 했다. 그런데 어떤 스튜디오가 고급스러운 생활 공간과 수영장

을 포함하는지 제시되지 않았으므로 광고에서 관련 내용을 확인한다.

단서 2 광고의 'Studio 4', 'Equipped with all of the apartment facilities of the large studio, it also features an outdoor area with a pool'에서 스튜디오 4가 대형 스튜디오의 모든 아파트 시설을 갖추고 있고, 수영장이 있는 야외 공간도 갖추고 있다는 것을 알 수 있다.

두 단서를 종합할 때, Mr. Compton이 가장 예약하고 싶어 하는 스튜디오는 스튜디오 4임을 알 수 있다. 따라서 (D)가 정답이다.

189 추론 문제 연계

해석 Mr. Compton에 대해 추론될 수 있는 것은?
(A) ImageSource의 장비를 온라인으로 구입했다.
(B) Space Photoland에 기기 대여 비용을 지불했다.
(C) 조명 문제 때문에 촬영 시간을 일찍 끝냈다.
(D) 사진 촬영 한 달 전에 예약했다.

해설 Mr. Compton이 작성한 이메일을 먼저 확인한다.

단서 1 이메일의 'Everything went well, and the ImageSource camera provided by your company was exactly what we needed.'에서 모든 것이 잘 진행되었고, 귀사에 의해 제공된 ImageSource 카메라는 정확히 우리가 원했던 것이라고 했다. 그런데 ImageSource에 대한 정보가 제시되지 않았으므로 광고에서 관련 내용을 확인한다.

단서 2 광고의 'If needed, lighting and photography equipment from ImageSource is available to rent at reasonable rates.'에서 ImageSource의 조명과 사진 장비가 합리적인 요금에 대여 가능하다고 하였다.

두 단서를 종합할 때, Mr. Compton이 Space Photoland에서 ImageSource의 조명과 사진 장비를 대여하여 사용했다는 것을 추론할 수 있다. 따라서 (B)가 정답이다.

어휘 issue n. 문제, 사안

190 육하원칙 문제

해석 이메일에 따르면, Mr. Compton의 회사는 현재 무엇을 하고 있는가?
(A) 결제 전 송장을 검토하는 것
(B) 광고 캠페인을 개념화하는 것
(C) 다양한 사진 중에서 선택하는 것
(D) 일부 카메라 부속품을 주문하는 것

해설 이메일의 'So I'd love to book one of your studios again for our upcoming marketing campaign. We are currently in the planning stages'에서 곧 있을 마케팅 캠페인을 위해 스튜디오 중 한 곳을 다시 예약하고 싶다며, 현재 기획 단계에 있다고 했으므로 (B)가 정답이다.

어휘 invoice n. 송장 conceptualize v. 개념화하다

Paraphrasing

in the planning stages 기획 단계에 있는 → Conceptualizing 개념화하는 것

191-195번은 다음 이메일, 일정표, 문자 메시지 대화문에 관한 문제입니다.

수신: Pam Headly <p.headly@brownhigh.com>,
   Nathan Michaels<n.michaels@brownhigh.com>
발신: Samantha Bowman <s.bowman@brownhigh.com>
제목: 학회
날짜: 3월 11일

Ms. Headly와 Mr. Michaels께,

Brown 고등학교에서 가장 경험이 풍부한 교사들로서, 여러분은 학생들이 양질의 교육을 받을 수 있도록 보장하는 데 중요한 역할을 합니다. 그렇기 때문에 [191]올랜도에서 곧 있을 플로리다 교육자 학회에 두 분을 초대하고 싶은데, 그것은 5월 1일에 열립니다.

이 학회에서는 플로리다 공립 고등학교의 교사와 관리자가 그들의 교육 전략을 공유하고 교육 분야의 최신 발전에 대해 논의할 예정입니다. [194]저는 교실에서의 태블릿 사용에 대해 한 시간 동안 이야기할 예정이며, 뒤이은 패널 토론에 두 분이 함께할 수 있기를 바라고 있었습니다. [192-(D)]우리 학교가 혁신적인 교육 프로그램으로 여러 차례 정부 상을 받았다는 것을 감안하면, 많은 참가자들이 여러분의 의견에 관심을 가질 것입니다. 참석하실 수 있으신지 제게 곧 알려주세요.

Samantha Bowman 드림
교장, Brown High School

vital adj. 중요한 quality adj. 양질의, 고급의
administrator n. 관리자, 행정가 strategy n. 전략
subsequent adj. 뒤이은, 그 후의 innovative adj. 혁신적인
participant n. 참가자 principal n. 교장

플로리다 교육자 학회

5월 1일
Cody 컨벤션 센터
올랜도, 플로리다주

플로리다에서 가장 큰 규모의 교사 및 관리자 연례 모임에 참여하세요. 참석자 등록 비용은 40달러이며 모든 연사들에게는 무료입니다. 아래는 올해의 일정표입니다.

오전 10시	Nick D'Annunzio: 효과적인 학습 게임
오전 11시 30분	[194]Samantha Bowman: 교육 기술 - 생성형 인공지능
오후 12시	점심
[195]오후 1시 30분	[195]Samantha Bowman, Pam Headly, Nathan Michaels: 패널 토론
오후 3시	Robert Sash: 완벽한 현장 학습 계획하기
오후 5시	Carmen Hernandez: 이중 언어 사용 교육 재고하기

[193]www.floridaeducators.com을 방문하여 등록하세요. 그러면 출입증이 발송될 것입니다.

educator n. 교육자 gathering n. 모임 registration n. 등록
attendee n. 참석자 effective adj. 효과적인
educational adj. 교육의 generative AI 생성형 인공지능(이용자의 요구에 맞춰 다른 결과물을 만들어 내는 인공지능) field trip 현장 학습
rethink v. 재고하다, 다시 생각하다 bilingual adj. 이중 언어를 사용하는

Pam Headly [5월 1일, 오후 12시 40분]
안녕하세요, Samantha. 제가 약간의 문제가 생겼어요. 저는 컨벤션 센터 입구에 있는데, 호텔에 출입증을 두고 온 걸 방금 알았어요.

Samantha Bowman [5월 1일, 오후 12시 42분]
아, 이런. 입구에 있는 사람에게 신분증만 보여주면 안 되나요? 등록되어 있으니 이름이 목록에 있을 거예요.

Pam Headly [5월 1일, 오후 12시 43분]
시도해 봤는데 건물에 들어가려면 출입증이 필요하대요. 그래서 지금 출입증을 가지러 호텔로 가려고 해요. 호텔이 여기서 택시로 약 30분 거리에 있다는 점을 감안하면, **195**1시 45분이 되어서야 돌아올 거예요.

Samantha Bowman [5월 1일, 오후 12시 44분]
안타깝네요. **195**서둘러 주시고 돌아오면 우리와 합류해 주세요.

entrance n. 입구   register v. 등록하다

191 목적 찾기 문제

해석 이메일은 왜 작성되었는가?
(A) 학회에서 강연을 계획하기 위해
(B) 두 교사의 능력을 칭찬하기 위해
(C) 수신자들을 협의회에 초대하기 위해
(D) 초대할 몇몇 교사들을 나열하기 위해

해설 이메일의 'I'd like to invite both of you to join me at the upcoming Florida Educators Conference in Orlando'에서 올랜도에서 곧 있을 플로리다 교육자 학회에 두 분을 초대하고 싶다고 했으므로 (C)가 정답이다.

어휘 praise v. 칭찬하다   recipient n. 수신자
convention n. 협의회, 협약   instructor n. 교사, 강사

192 Not/True 문제

해석 Brown 고등학교에 대해 언급된 것은?
(A) 재적자 수를 늘리기 위해 새로운 프로그램을 시작할 것이다.
(B) 학업 성적이 좋은 학생만 입학을 허락한다.
(C) 개인과 기업의 기부금으로 자금을 조달받는다.
(D) 정부로부터 공식적인 인정을 받았다.

해설 이메일의 'our school has won several government awards for its innovative education programs'에서 우리 학교가 혁신적인 교육 프로그램으로 여러 차례 정부 상을 받았다고 했으므로 (D)는 지문에 언급되어 있다. 따라서 (D)가 정답이다. (A), (B), (C)는 지문에 언급되지 않은 내용이다.

어휘 launch v. 시작하다   enrollment n. 재적자 수, 입학, 등록
admit v. 입학(가입)을 허락하다   academic adj. 학업의
donation n. 기부금   individual n. 개인   recognition n. 인정

Paraphrasing

has won several government awards 여러 차례 정부 상을 받았다
→ has received formal recognition from the government
정부로부터 공식적인 인정을 받았다

193 육하원칙 문제

해석 학회에 참석하기 위한 요건은 무엇인가?
(A) 우편으로 개인 정보를 보내는 것
(B) 학교 관계자의 초대를 받는 것
(C) 컨벤션 센터 직원에게 전화하는 것
(D) 온라인 등록 과정을 완료하는 것

해설 일정표의 'Visit www.floridaeducators.com to sign up. A pass will then be sent to you.'에서 www.floridaeducators.com을 방문하여 등록하면 출입증이 발송될 것이라고 했으므로 (D)가 정답이다.

어휘 personal adj. 개인의   invitation n. 초대   official n. 관계자, 직원

194 추론 문제 연계

해석 Ms. Bowman에 대해 암시되는 것은?
(A) 세 명의 교사와 함께 올랜도로 갔다.
(B) 강연의 주제를 바꾸기로 결정했다.
(C) 발표를 연기해 달라는 요청을 받았다.
(D) 행사 티켓을 구매할 것을 요구받았다.

해설 Ms. Bowman이 작성한 이메일을 먼저 확인한다.
단서 1 이메일의 'I[Ms. Bowman]'m going to be giving an hour-long talk about the use of tablets in the classroom'에서 Ms. Bowman이 교실에서의 태블릿 사용에 대해 한 시간 동안 이야기할 것이라고 했다. 그런데 실제 강연 주제에 대해 제시되지 않았으므로 일정표에서 관련 내용을 확인한다.
단서 2 일정표의 'Samantha Bowman: Educational Technology — Generative AI'에서 Ms. Bowman이 강연하기로 한 주제가 '교육 기술 — 생성형 인공지능'인 것을 알 수 있다.
두 단서를 종합할 때, Ms. Bowman이 강연의 주제를 바꾸기로 결정했음을 추론할 수 있다. 따라서 (B)가 정답이다.

195 추론 문제 연계

해석 Ms. Headly에 대해 추론될 수 있는 것은?
(A) 택시에 학회 출입증을 깜빡 잊고 두고 왔다.
(B) Ms. Bowman과 합류할 수 없을 것이다.
(C) 잘못된 입구로 갔다.
(D) 토론의 처음 부분을 놓칠 것이다.

해설 Ms. Headly가 등장한 문자 메시지 대화문을 먼저 확인한다.
단서 1 문자 메시지 대화문의 'I won't return until about 1:45.'에서 Ms. Headly가 1시 45분이 되어서야 돌아올 거라고 했고, 이에 대해 Ms. Bowman이 'Please hurry and join us when you get back.'에서 돌아오면 우리와 합류해 달라고 했다. 그런데 해당 시간에 진행되는 일정에 대해 제시되지 않았으므로 일정표에서 관련 내용을 확인한다.
단서 2 일정표의 '1:30 P.M.', 'Samantha Bowman, Pam Headly, and Nathan Michaels: Panel Discussion'에서 오후 1시 30분에 Samantha Bowman, Pam Headly, Nathan Michaels가 함께 패널 토론을 진행하는 것을 알 수 있다.
두 단서를 종합할 때, Ms. Headly가 토론의 처음 부분을 놓칠 것임을 추론할 수 있다. 따라서 (D)가 정답이다.

196-200번은 다음 두 이메일과 회람에 관한 문제입니다.

수신: Saul Samson <s.samson@pfg.com>
발신: Luanne Mendez <l.mendez@coral.com>
제목: 당신의 작업물
[197]날짜: 5월 25일

Mr. Samson께,

우리가 다음 달에 출간할 교과서의 보충 자료를 만드는 데 투입된 당신의 노고에 대해 감사드려요. 늘 그렇듯이, 당신의 작업물은 훌륭했어요. 실제로, [198]당신은 우리 회사와 협업하는 프리랜서들 중에서 가장 신뢰할 만한 사람 중 한 명이라는 것이 입증되었어요. [196/198]그것이 바로 제가 당신이 우리 회사에 합류하는 것을 고려해 주었으면 하는 이유예요. [196]우리는 전임 작가 자리에 공석이 있고, 제 생각에는 당신이 안성맞춤일 것 같아요.

[197]저는 내일 도서 박람회에 참석해야 해서 온종일 사무실 밖에 있을 예정이지만, 어떤 문의 사항이라도 있으시다면 그 다음 날 편하게 저에게 연락해 주세요.

Luanne Mendez 드림
Coral 출판사

supplementary adj. 보충의 textbook n. 교과서
reliable adj. 신뢰할 만한, 믿을 수 있는

수신: Anjay Khan <a.khan@coral.com>
발신: Luanne Mendez <l.mendez@coral.com>
제목: 후속 조치
날짜: 5월 28일

Mr. Khan께,

우리는 작가 자리를 위한 광고를 게시할 필요가 있을 거예요. [198]논의했던 대로, 저는 우리 프리랜서들 중 한 명에게 관심이 있는지를 물어봤어요. 하지만, 그는 런던의 한 대학에서 2년의 대학원 과정에 등록했고 이번 달 말에 영국으로 떠날 거예요.

광고는 이번 주 말까지 게시될 것이고, 제가 직접 면접을 진행할 거예요. [199]지원자들은 세 편의 학술적인 글의 견본을 제출하도록 요구될 것인데, 그것들은 우리의 수석 편집자인 Clara Dover에 의해 검토될 거예요. 저는 7월 10일까지 적절한 후보자를 찾을 것이라 예상하고 있고, 과정 내내 당신에게 계속해서 최신 정보를 전달해 드리도록 할게요.

감사합니다.

Luanne Mendez 드림

enroll v. 등록하다 graduate program 대학원 과정
conduct v. 진행하다, (특정 활동을) 하다
academic adj. 학술적인, 학업의 review v. 검토하다
suitable adj. 적절한 candidate n. 후보자

회람

수신: Coral 출판사 전 직원
발신: Luanne Mendez
제목: 다음 주
날짜: 7월 15일

우리는 마침내 집필팀의 새로운 사원을 고용했습니다. [199]Tanya Murray가 그녀의 지원서와 함께 제출했던 견본 글의 우수성에 근거하여, 저는 그녀가 이 역할을 매우 잘 해낼 것이라 예상합니다.

Ms. Murray는 월요일 오전 9시에 이곳에서 근무를 시작할 것이고, 저는 그녀에게 직원 안내서를 전달하고 그녀의 예비 교육을 처리할 것입니다. 하지만, [200]저는 그날 오전 10시까지 중요한 회의가 있어서, 여러분 중 한 명이 자원하여 Ms. Murray에게 먼저 사무실을 견학시켜 주기를 바랍니다. 이 일을 기꺼이 하고자 하신다면 저에게 알려주세요.

application n. 지원서 manual n. 안내서, 설명서
handle v. 처리하다

---

196 목적 찾기 문제

해석 첫 번째 이메일은 왜 쓰였는가?
(A) 출판물의 변경 사항을 논의하기 위해
(B) 채용 제안을 하기 위해
(C) 지불금 수령을 확인하기 위해
(D) 프리랜서 프로젝트를 기술하기 위해

해설 첫 번째 이메일의 'That's why I'd like you[Mr. Samson] to consider joining our firm.'에서 Mr. Samson에게 회사에 합류하는 것을 고려해 주었으면 한다고 한 후, 'We have an opening for a full-time writer, and I think you[Mr. Samson] would be perfect.'에서 전임 작가 자리에 공석이 있고 Mr. Samson이 안성맞춤일 것 같다고 했으므로 (B)가 정답이다.

어휘 employment n. 채용, 고용 receipt n. 수령, 영수증

197 육하원칙 문제

해석 Ms. Mendez는 5월 26일에 무엇을 할 것인가?
(A) 업계 행사에 참가한다.
(B) 리더십 워크숍에 참석한다.
(C) 후보자에 대한 면접을 진행한다.
(D) 작문 강의에 등록한다.

해설 첫 번째 이메일의 'Date: May 25'에서 이메일이 작성된 날짜가 5월 25일임을 알 수 있고, 'I'll be out of the office all day tomorrow attending a book fair'에서 내일 도서 박람회에 참석해야 해서 온종일 사무실 밖에 있을 것이라고 했으므로 (A)가 정답이다.

어휘 participate v. 참가하다 industry n. (특정 분야의) 업, 산업

Paraphrasing

attending a book fair 도서 박람회에 참석하다 → Participate in an industry event 업계 행사에 참가하다

198 Not/True 문제 연계

해석 Mr. Samson에 대해 명시된 것은?
(A) Ms. Mendez와 지역 도서 박람회에서 만났다.
(B) 현재 새로운 일자리를 찾고 있다.
(C) 최근에 대학 과정을 끝냈다.
(D) 다른 나라로 이주할 계획이다.

해설 Mr. Samson에게 발송된 첫 번째 이메일을 먼저 확인한다.
단서 1 첫 번째 이메일의 'you have proven to be one of the most reliable freelancers our company works with'에서 Mr. Samson이 Ms. Mendez의 회사와 협업하는 프리랜서들 중 한 명임을 알 수 있고, 'That's why I'd like you to consider joining our firm.'에서 Mr. Samson이 Ms. Mendez의 채용 제안을 받았음을 알 수 있다. 그런데 Mr. Samson의 채용 결과에 대한 내용이 제시되지 않았으므로 두 번째 이메일에서 관련 내용을 확인한다.
단서 2 두 번째 이메일의 'As we discussed, I asked one of our freelancers if he would be interested. However, he has enrolled in a two-year graduate program at a university in London and will be moving to the UK later this month.'에서 프리랜서들 중 한 명에게 관심이 있는지 물어보았지만, 그가 런던의 한 대학에서 2년의 대학원 과정에 등록하여 이번 달 말에 영국으로 떠날 것이라고 하였다.
두 단서를 종합할 때, Mr. Samson이 다른 나라로 이주할 계획을 하고 있음을 알 수 있다. 따라서 (D)가 정답이다.

어휘 relocate v. 이주하다

Paraphrasing

will be moving to the UK 영국으로 떠날 예정이다 → relocate to another country 다른 나라로 이주하다

199 추론 문제 연계

해설 Ms. Murray의 견본 글에 대해 암시되는 것은?
(A) 학술 분야가 아닌 내용을 포함했다.
(B) Ms. Dover에 의해 평가되었다.
(C) 마감일 이후에 제출되었다.
(D) Mr. Khan의 의견을 받았다.

해설 Ms. Murray가 언급된 회람을 먼저 확인한다.
단서 1 회람의 'Based on the quality of the writing samples Tanya Murray submitted with her application, I expect she will perform well in this role.'에서 Tanya Murray가 그녀의 지원서와 함께 견본 글들을 제출했음을 알 수 있다. 그런데 지원자들이 제출한 견본 글의 평가 과정에 대해 제시되지 않았으므로 두 번째 이메일에서 관련 내용을 확인한다.
단서 2 두 번째 이메일의 'Applicants will be required to submit three academic writing samples, which will be reviewed by our head editor, Clara Dover.'에서 지원자들은 세 편의 학술적인 글의 견본을 제출하도록 요구될 것이고 그것들이 수석 편집자인 Clara Dover에 의해 검토될 것이라고 하였다.
두 단서를 종합할 때, Ms. Murray가 지원할 때 제출한 글이 Ms. Dover에 의해 평가되었음을 추론할 수 있다. 따라서 (B)가 정답이다.

어휘 evaluate v. 평가하다

200 육하원칙 문제

해설 Ms. Mendez는 왜 자원자가 필요한가?
(A) 사무실 점검을 수행하기 위해
(B) 직원 안내서의 복사본을 출력하기 위해
(C) 프로젝트를 위해 새로운 직원을 교육하기 위해
(D) 최근의 신입 사원에게 사무 공간 주변을 보여주기 위해

해설 회람의 'I[Ms. Mendez] have an important meeting until 10 A.M. that morning, so I'd like one of you to volunteer to give Ms. Murray a tour of our office first'에서 Ms. Mendez가 오전 10시까지 중요한 회의가 있어서, 누군가 자원하여 Ms. Murray에게 먼저 사무실을 견학시켜 주기를 바란다고 하였다. 따라서 (D)가 정답이다.

어휘 hire n. 신입 사원; v. 고용하다

TEST 5

LISTENING TEST
p.196

1 (C)	21 (B)	41 (D)	61 (D)	81 (A)
2 (D)	22 (A)	42 (B)	62 (C)	82 (D)
3 (B)	23 (A)	43 (C)	63 (D)	83 (D)
4 (C)	24 (C)	44 (A)	64 (B)	84 (C)
5 (B)	25 (B)	45 (B)	65 (B)	85 (A)
6 (C)	26 (B)	46 (A)	66 (D)	86 (A)
7 (A)	27 (C)	47 (C)	67 (B)	87 (B)
8 (C)	28 (A)	48 (B)	68 (A)	88 (A)
9 (C)	29 (C)	49 (D)	69 (C)	89 (B)
10 (B)	30 (A)	50 (C)	70 (C)	90 (B)
11 (A)	31 (B)	51 (D)	71 (C)	91 (C)
12 (B)	32 (C)	52 (B)	72 (C)	92 (B)
13 (A)	33 (A)	53 (A)	73 (C)	93 (C)
14 (B)	34 (B)	54 (C)	74 (C)	94 (C)
15 (C)	35 (D)	55 (B)	75 (D)	95 (D)
16 (C)	36 (A)	56 (B)	76 (A)	96 (C)
17 (B)	37 (D)	57 (C)	77 (B)	97 (B)
18 (A)	38 (A)	58 (B)	78 (D)	98 (D)
19 (C)	39 (A)	59 (D)	79 (C)	99 (B)
20 (C)	40 (C)	60 (A)	80 (C)	100 (C)

READING TEST
p.208

101 (D)	121 (B)	141 (D)	161 (C)	181 (B)
102 (D)	122 (D)	142 (B)	162 (C)	182 (C)
103 (D)	123 (C)	143 (C)	163 (D)	183 (B)
104 (B)	124 (B)	144 (D)	164 (D)	184 (B)
105 (C)	125 (A)	145 (A)	165 (D)	185 (C)
106 (B)	126 (C)	146 (C)	166 (C)	186 (B)
107 (C)	127 (A)	147 (C)	167 (C)	187 (C)
108 (B)	128 (B)	148 (D)	168 (D)	188 (C)
109 (D)	129 (C)	149 (B)	169 (B)	189 (D)
110 (A)	130 (D)	150 (B)	170 (A)	190 (A)
111 (D)	131 (C)	151 (C)	171 (C)	191 (C)
112 (B)	132 (B)	152 (C)	172 (C)	192 (D)
113 (D)	133 (A)	153 (A)	173 (C)	193 (B)
114 (B)	134 (B)	154 (C)	174 (A)	194 (B)
115 (A)	135 (D)	155 (D)	175 (C)	195 (D)
116 (B)	136 (C)	156 (C)	176 (B)	196 (B)
117 (B)	137 (B)	157 (B)	177 (D)	197 (A)
118 (D)	138 (A)	158 (B)	178 (A)	198 (D)
119 (D)	139 (C)	159 (A)	179 (D)	199 (C)
120 (C)	140 (C)	160 (D)	180 (B)	200 (A)

PART 1

1 1인 사진
미국식

(A) She's plugging in a phone.
(B) She's reaching for a book.
(C) She's facing a machine.
(D) She's placing a card on a cabinet.

plug in ~의 플러그를 꽂다 reach for (~을 잡으려고) 손을 뻗다
face v. ~을 마주 보다

해석 (A) 그녀는 휴대폰의 플러그를 꽂고 있다.
(B) 그녀는 책을 향해 손을 뻗고 있다.
(C) 그녀는 기계를 마주 보고 있다.
(D) 그녀는 진열장 위에 카드를 놓고 있다.

해설 (A) [×] plugging in(플러그를 꽂고 있다)은 여자의 동작과 무관하므로 오답이다.
(B) [×] 사진에 책(book)이 없으므로 오답이다.
(C) [○] 여자가 ATM 기계를 마주 보고 있는 모습을 가장 잘 묘사한 정답이다.
(D) [×] 사진에 진열장(cabinet)이 없으므로 오답이다.

2 1인 사진
영국식

(A) He's pouring a beverage into a cup.
(B) He's emptying a waste basket.
(C) He's handing a plate to a server.
(D) He's checking his wristwatch.

pour v. 붓다 beverage n. 음료 empty v. 비우다
waste basket 휴지통 wristwatch n. 손목시계

해석 (A) 그는 컵에 음료를 붓고 있다.
(B) 그는 휴지통을 비우고 있다.
(C) 그는 종업원에게 접시를 건네고 있다.
(D) 그는 손목시계를 확인하고 있다.

해설 (A) [×] pouring a beverage(음료를 붓고 있다)는 남자의 동작과 무관하므로 오답이다. 사진에 있는 음료(beverage)와 컵(cup)을 사용하여 혼동을 주었다.
(B) [×] 사진에 휴지통(waste basket)이 없으므로 오답이다.
(C) [×] handing(건네고 있다)은 남자의 동작과 무관하므로 오답이다.
(D) [○] 남자가 손목시계를 확인하고 있는 모습을 가장 잘 묘사한 정답이다.

3 사물 및 풍경 사진 🎧 캐나다식

(A) Warning signs have been hung from the ceiling.
(B) **Vehicles have been parked on both sides.**
(C) Lane markings are being painted on the ground.
(D) There are some cars driving into a parking garage.

vehicle n. 차량   park v. 주차하다   paint v. (페인트를) 칠하다
parking garage 주차장

해석 (A) 경고 표지판들이 천장에 매달려 있다.
  (B) 차들이 양쪽에 주차되어 있다.
  (C) 바닥에 차선 표시가 칠해지고 있다.
  (D) 주차장 안으로 들어가는 몇몇 차들이 있다.

해설 (A) [×] 사진에 경고 표지판들(warning signs)이 없으므로 오답이다.
  (B) [○] 차들이 양쪽에 주차된 모습을 가장 잘 묘사한 정답이다.
  (C) [×] 사진에서 차선 표시는 보이지만, 칠해지고 있는(being painted) 모습은 아니므로 오답이다.
  (D) [×] 사진에서 주차장 안으로 들어가고 있는 몇몇 차들(some cars driving into)이 없으므로 오답이다.

최신 토익 경향

자전거, 버스, 배, 비행기 등의 교통수단이 등장하는 사진은 매회 평균 1문제씩 출제된다.

<교통수단 관련 빈출 표현>
• The bicycles are lined up in a row.
  자전거들이 일렬로 서있다.
• Some boxes have been loaded onto a truck.
  몇몇 상자들이 트럭에 실려 있다.
• Some boats are docked at the harbor.
  몇몇 배들이 항구에 정박되어 있다.
• Lanes have been painted on a runway.
  활주로 위에 선이 그려져 있다.

4 2인 이상 사진 🎧 호주식

(A) The man is adjusting his glasses.
(B) The man is tacking a notice on the wall.
(C) The woman is holding a device.
(D) The woman is zipping up her jacket.

tack v. 압정으로 고정하다   device n. 기기, 장치   zip up 지퍼를 올리다

해석 (A) 남자가 안경을 고쳐 쓰고 있다.
  (B) 남자가 벽에 안내문을 압정으로 고정하고 있다.
  (C) 여자가 기기를 들고 있다.
  (D) 여자가 재킷 지퍼를 올리고 있다.

해설 (A) [×] adjusting his glasses(안경을 고쳐 쓰고 있다)는 남자의 동작과 무관하므로 오답이다. 사진에 있는 안경(glasses)을 사용하여 혼동을 주었다.
  (B) [×] tacking a notice(안내문을 압정으로 고정하고 있다)는 남자의 동작과 무관하므로 오답이다.
  (C) [○] 여자가 기기를 들고 있는 모습을 가장 잘 묘사한 정답이다.
  (D) [×] 여자가 재킷 지퍼를 올리고 있는(zipping up her jacket) 모습이 아니므로 오답이다.

5 사물 및 풍경 사진 🎧 영국식

(A) Several buses are lined up in front of a building.
(B) A fountain has been erected in a city park.
(C) Some tables are being set up in a picnic area.
(D) A tree is surrounded by some benches.

erect v. 세우다, 건립하다

해석 (A) 여러 버스들이 건물 앞에 줄지어 서 있다.
  (B) 분수대가 도시공원에 세워져 있다.
  (C) 피크닉 공간에 몇몇 테이블들이 마련되어 있다.
  (D) 나무가 몇몇 의자들로 둘러싸여 있다.

해설 (A) [×] 사진에 버스들(buses)이 없으므로 오답이다. 사진에 있는 건물(building)을 사용하여 혼동을 주었다.
  (B) [○] 분수대가 공원에 세워져 있는 모습을 가장 잘 묘사한 정답이다.
  (C) [×] 사진에 테이블들(tables)이 없으므로 오답이다.
  (D) [×] 사진에 벤치들(benches)이 없으므로 오답이다. 사진에 있는 나무(trees)를 사용하여 혼동을 주었다.

6 2인 이상 사진 🎧 호주식

(A) Some bushes are being trimmed in a garden.
(B) Some carts have been left next to a stairway.
(C) People are taking some stairs to an upper level.
(D) People are walking past a pedestrian crosswalk.

trim v. 다듬다   pedestrian crosswalk 보행자 횡단보도

해석 (A) 몇몇 덤불들이 정원에서 다듬어지고 있다.
  (B) 몇몇 카트들이 계단 옆에 남겨져 있다.
  (C) 사람들이 계단으로 위층에 올라가고 있다.
  (D) 사람들이 보행자 횡단보도를 지나쳐 걷고 있다.

해설 (A) [×] 사진에 덤불(bushes)은 보이지만, 다듬어지고 있는(are being trimmed) 모습은 아니므로 오답이다.
  (B) [×] 사진에 카트들(carts)이 없으므로 오답이다. 사진에 있는 계단(stairway)을 사용하여 혼동을 주었다.
  (C) [○] 사람들이 계단으로 위층에 올라가고 있는 모습을 가장 잘 묘사한 정답이다.
  (D) [×] walking past a pedestrian crosswalk(보행자 횡단보도를 지나쳐 걷고 있다)는 사람들의 동작과 무관하므로 오답이다.

최신 토익 경향

최근 PART 1에서는 계단이 있는 사진이 자주 출제되고 있다. 계단이 있는 사진에서 정답으로 나올 수 있는 아래의 표현들을 알아두자.

<계단 관련 빈출 표현>
- 사람이 계단을 오르거나 내려가고 있는 동작
  - be climbing up some stairs 계단을 올라가고 있다
  - be walking down some stairs 계단을 걸어 내려가고 있다
  - be taking the stairs to the lower floor
    계단으로 아래층에 내려가고 있다
  - be going up/down the staircase
    계단을 올라가고/내려가고 있다
- 계단이 입구 쪽으로 연결되어 있는 모습
  - steps lead to the entrance 계단이 입구로 이어진다

PART 2

7 Why 의문문
캐나다식 → 미국식

Why did Mr. Cohen miss the staff meeting?
(A) **Because his car broke down.**
(B) From the company headquarters.
(C) Yes. He retired last month.

headquarters n. 본사   retire v. 은퇴하다, 퇴직하다

해석 왜 Mr. Cohen이 직원회의에 참석하지 않았나요?
(A) 그의 자동차가 고장 났기 때문이에요.
(B) 회사 본사로부터요.
(C) 네. 그는 지난달에 은퇴했어요.

해설 (A) [○] 그의 자동차가 고장 났기 때문이라는 말로, Mr. Cohen이 직원회의에 불참한 이유를 언급했으므로 정답이다.
(B) [×] 질문의 staff meeting(직원회의)에서 연상할 수 있는 headquarters(본사)를 사용하여 혼동을 준 오답이다.
(C) [×] 의문사 의문문에 Yes로 응답했으므로 오답이다.

8 Be동사 의문문
호주식 → 영국식

Is the photo exhibition open all year round?
(A) That date works for me.
(B) With my camera.
(C) **No. Only from May to July.**

exhibition n. 전시회, 전시

해석 그 사진 전시회는 일 년 내내 열리나요?
(A) 그 날짜가 저에게 괜찮아요.
(B) 제 사진기로요.
(C) 아니요. 5월에서 7월까지만요.

해설 (A) [×] 사진 전시회가 일 년 내내 열리는 것인지를 물었는데, 이와 관련이 없는 그 날짜가 자신에게 괜찮다는 내용으로 응답했으므로 오답이다.
(B) [×] 질문의 photo exhibition(사진 전시회)에서 연상할 수 있는 camera(사진기)를 사용하여 혼동을 준 오답이다.
(C) [○] No로 사진 전시회가 일 년 내내 열리지 않는다고 전달한 후, 5월에서 7월까지만이라는 말로 부연 설명을 했으므로 정답이다.

9 Where 의문문
영국식 → 캐나다식

Where should I send my résumé?
(A) Two pages long.
(B) By seven o'clock.
(C) **Let me text you the link.**

résumé n. 이력서

해석 제가 어디로 제 이력서를 보내야 할까요?
(A) 두 장 분량이요.
(B) 7시까지요.
(C) 제가 그 링크를 문자로 보내드릴게요.

해설 (A) [×] 질문의 résumé(이력서)에서 연상할 수 있는 Two pages long(두 장 분량)을 사용하여 혼동을 준 오답이다.
(B) [×] 어디로 이력서를 보내야 할지를 물었는데, 시간으로 응답했으므로 오답이다. 질문의 Where를 When으로 혼동하여 이를 정답으로 선택하지 않도록 주의한다.
(C) [○] 그 링크를 문자로 보내주겠다는 말로, 이력서를 어디로 보내야 하는지 문자로 알려주겠다고 전달했으므로 정답이다.

10 Who 의문문
미국식 → 영국식

Who's in charge of inventory management?
(A) On top of the shelves.
(B) **David and Shannon.**
(C) Twelve euros per hour.

in charge of ~을 담당하는   inventory n. 재고, 물품 목록

해석 누가 재고 관리를 담당하고 있나요?
(A) 선반 맨 위에요.
(B) David와 Shannon이요.
(C) 한 시간에 12유로예요.

해설 (A) [×] 질문의 inventory(재고)에서 연상할 수 있는 shelves(선반)를 사용하여 혼동을 준 오답이다.
(B) [○] David와 Shannon이라는 말로, 재고 관리를 담당하고 있는 사람을 언급했으므로 정답이다.
(C) [×] 질문의 charge(담당, 책임)를 '부과하다'라는 의미의 동사로 이해할 경우 연상할 수 있는 요금과 관련된 Twelve euros (12유로)를 사용하여 혼동을 준 오답이다.

11 부가 의문문
캐나다식 → 미국식

The trip to Bangkok is supposed to take a couple of hours, isn't it?
(A) **Yes. I'll take an express train.**
(B) A one-way ticket, please.
(C) Parking is not free.

express adj. 급행의, 신속한   one-way adj. 편도의, 일방통행의

해석 방콕으로의 이동에 두어 시간은 걸릴 거예요, 그렇지 않나요?
(A) 네. 저는 급행열차를 탈 거예요.
(B) 편도 승차권으로 주세요.
(C) 주차는 무료가 아닙니다.

해설 (A) [O] Yes로 방콕으로의 이동에 두어 시간이 걸릴 것이라고 전달한 후, 자신은 급행열차를 탈 것이라고 부연 설명을 했으므로 정답이다.
(B) [x] 질문의 trip(이동)에서 연상할 수 있는 교통수단과 관련된 one-way ticket(편도 승차권)을 사용하여 혼동을 준 오답이다.
(C) [x] 방콕으로의 이동에 두어 시간이 걸리는 것이 맞는지를 물었는데, 이와 관련이 없는 주차는 무료가 아니라는 내용으로 응답했으므로 오답이다.

12 How 의문문
🎧 호주식 → 영국식

How can I schedule an interview with Ms. Clark?
(A) We can reschedule the plumber's visit.
(B) Call her assistant.
(C) For the open position of bus driver.

assistant n. 조수, 보조원   open position 공석

해설 제가 어떻게 Ms. Clark와의 인터뷰 일정을 잡을 수 있을까요?
(A) 우리는 배관공의 방문 일정을 다시 잡을 수 있어요.
(B) 그녀의 보조원에게 전화하세요.
(C) 버스 운전자의 공석을 위해서요.

해설 (A) [x] schedule - reschedule의 유사 발음 어휘를 사용하여 혼동을 준 오답이다.
(B) [O] 그녀의 보조원에게 전화하라는 말로, Ms. Clark와의 인터뷰 일정을 잡을 수 있는 방법을 전달했으므로 정답이다.
(C) [x] 질문의 interview(인터뷰)에서 연상할 수 있는 채용과 관련된 open position(공석)을 사용하여 혼동을 준 오답이다.

13 Where 의문문
🎧 미국식 → 호주식

Where is the stationery kept?
(A) In the drawer by the printer.
(B) To a train station.
(C) Every Monday.

stationery n. 문구류   drawer n. 서랍

해설 문구류는 어디에 보관되나요?
(A) 프린터 옆 서랍 안에요.
(B) 기차역으로요.
(C) 매주 월요일마다요.

해설 (A) [O] 프린터 옆 서랍 안에라며, 문구류가 보관되어 있는 장소를 언급했으므로 정답이다.
(B) [x] stationery - station의 유사 발음 어휘를 사용하여 혼동을 준 오답이다.
(C) [x] 문구류가 어디에 보관되는지를 물었는데, 이와 관련이 없는 매주 월요일마다라는 말로 응답했으므로 오답이다. 질문의 Where를 When으로 혼동하여 이를 정답으로 선택하지 않도록 주의한다.

14 평서문
🎧 미국식 → 호주식

Let's use less electricity in the office starting this month.
(A) You can use mine instead.
(B) What's your plan?
(C) The electrician is coming soon.

electricity n. 전기   instead adv. 대신에   electrician n. 전기 기사

해설 이번 달부터 사무실에서 전기를 덜 사용하도록 합시다.
(A) 제 것을 대신 사용하셔도 돼요.
(B) 당신의 계획은 무엇인가요?
(C) 전기 기사가 곧 올 거예요.

해설 (A) [x] 질문의 use를 반복 사용하여 혼동을 준 오답이다.
(B) [O] 당신의 계획이 무엇인지 되물어, 사무실에서 전기를 덜 쓰는 것에 대한 추가 정보를 요구한 정답이다.
(C) [x] 질문의 electricity(전기)와 관련 있는 electrician(전기 기사)을 사용하여 혼동을 준 오답이다.

최신토익경향

최근 PART 2에서 제안·제공·요청하는 평서문에 대해 간접 응답이 정답으로 자주 출제되어 난도가 높아지고 있다.

<간접적으로 수락 또는 거절하는 응답>
Let's begin planning the company retreat.
회사 야유회를 계획하는 것을 시작합시다.
[답변] We've got some time this afternoon.
  우리는 오늘 오후에 시간이 좀 있어요.
* 회사 야유회를 계획하는 것을 시작하자는 제안 평서문에 오늘 오후에 시간이 좀 있다는 말로, 제안을 수락하는 의도를 간접적으로 전달하는 답변

I can give you a tour of the museum if you want.
당신이 원한다면 제가 박물관을 안내할게요.
[답변] My coworker will be here soon.
  제 동료가 여기로 곧 올 거예요.
* 박물관을 안내하겠다는 제공 평서문에 동료가 곧 올 것이라는 말로, 제공을 거절하는 의도를 간접적으로 전달하는 답변

15 제공 의문문
🎧 호주식 → 영국식

Would you like some help using the conference call system?
(A) You should call the manager.
(B) It was helpful, wasn't it?
(C) Thanks, but the manual is detailed.

conference call 전화 회의, 전화 회담   manual n. 설명서
detailed adj. 상세한

해설 전화 회의 시스템을 사용하는 데 도움이 필요하신가요?
(A) 당신은 관리자에게 전화해야 해요.
(B) 그건 도움이 되었어요, 그렇지 않나요?
(C) 감사해요, 하지만 설명서가 상세하네요.

해설 (A) [x] 질문의 call(전화)을 '전화하다'라는 의미의 동사로 반복 사용하여 혼동을 준 오답이다.
(B) [x] help - helpful의 유사 발음 어휘를 사용하여 혼동을 준 오답이다.
(C) [O] 감사하지만 설명서가 상세하다는 말로, 전화 회의 시스템을

사용하는 데 도움이 필요하지 않다고 간접적으로 전달했으므로 정답이다.

16 When 의문문
캐나다식 → 호주식

When will the caterers start setting up the tables for today's luncheon?
(A) Mostly local food.
(B) At a banquet hall on Bayview Avenue.
(C) Within a few hours from now.

caterer n. 연회 업자, 음식 공급자 luncheon n. 오찬
banquet hall 연회장

해석 언제 연회 업자가 오늘 오찬을 위한 테이블을 준비하기 시작할 것인가요?
(A) 대부분 현지 음식이에요.
(B) Bayview가의 연회장에서요.
(C) 지금부터 몇 시간 이내로요.

해설 (A) [×] 질문의 luncheon(오찬)과 관련 있는 food(음식)를 사용하여 혼동을 준 오답이다.
(B) [×] 질문의 luncheon(오찬)에서 연상할 수 있는 장소와 관련된 banquet hall(연회장)을 사용하여 혼동을 준 오답이다.
(C) [○] 지금부터 몇 시간 이내라는 말로, 연회 업자가 테이블을 준비하기 시작할 시점을 전달했으므로 정답이다.

17 Be동사 의문문
영국식 → 캐나다식

Is this building the only one with a poor Internet connection?
(A) There's a floor guide on the wall.
(B) No. The whole region is affected.
(C) It's a technology company.

connection n. 연결 floor guide 층별 안내도

해석 이 건물이 인터넷 연결이 좋지 않은 유일한 곳인가요?
(A) 벽에 층별 안내도가 있어요.
(B) 아니요. 전체 지역이 영향을 받고 있어요.
(C) 그것은 기술 회사예요.

해설 (A) [×] 질문의 building(건물)과 관련 있는 floor guide(층별 안내도)를 사용하여 혼동을 준 오답이다.
(B) [○] No로 이 건물이 인터넷 연결이 좋지 않은 유일한 곳은 아님을 전달한 후, 전체 지역이 영향을 받고 있다는 부연 설명을 했으므로 정답이다.
(C) [×] 질문의 Internet connection(인터넷 연결)과 관련 있는 technology(기술)를 사용하여 혼동을 준 오답이다.

18 선택 의문문
미국식 → 캐나다식

Should I bring the client to the reception room or to your office?
(A) He canceled the appointment.
(B) Don't forget to bring your receipt.
(C) I agree with you.

reception room 응접실 appointment n. 약속 receipt n. 영수증

해석 제가 그 고객을 응접실로 데리고 가야 할까요, 아니면 당신의 사무실로 데리고 가야 할까요?
(A) 그는 약속을 취소했어요.
(B) 당신의 영수증을 가져오는 것을 잊지 마세요.
(C) 저는 당신의 말에 동의해요.

해설 (A) [○] 그가 약속을 취소했다는 말로, 응접실과 사무실 둘 다 간접적으로 선택하지 않은 정답이다.
(B) [×] 질문의 bring을 반복 사용하여 혼동을 준 오답이다.
(C) [×] 고객을 응접실로 데리고 가야 할지, 사무실로 데리고 가야 할지를 물었는데, 이와 관련이 없는 동의한다고 응답했으므로 오답이다.

19 요청 의문문
캐나다식 → 호주식

Could you recommend the best restaurant in the neighborhood?
(A) The soup was delicious.
(B) We use lots of butter and sugar.
(C) Try the one with the green sign.

recommend v. 추천하다 neighborhood n. 근처, 주위

해설 이 근처에서 최고의 식당을 추천해 주시겠어요?
(A) 그 수프는 맛있었어요.
(B) 우리는 많은 버터와 설탕을 사용합니다.
(C) 초록색 간판이 있는 곳을 한번 가보세요.

해설 (A) [×] 질문의 restaurant(식당)에서 연상할 수 있는 수프(soup)를 사용하여 혼동을 준 오답이다.
(B) [×] 질문의 restaurant(식당)에서 연상할 수 있는 요리 재료와 관련된 butter and sugar(버터와 설탕)를 사용하여 혼동을 준 오답이다.
(C) [○] 초록색 간판이 있는 곳에 한번 가보라는 말로, 근처에서 최고의 식당을 추천했으므로 정답이다.

20 평서문
호주식 → 영국식

We can't check the status of our hotel reservation on the Web site now.
(A) Thanks for the reservation.
(B) A hotel in London.
(C) Then let's wait for the confirmation e-mail.

status n. 상태 reservation n. 예약 confirmation n. 확인

해설 우리는 지금 웹사이트에서 우리의 호텔 예약 상태를 확인할 수가 없어요.
(A) 예약해 주셔서 감사합니다.
(B) 런던의 한 호텔이요.
(C) 그럼 확인 메일을 기다려봅시다.

해설 (A) [×] 질문의 reservation(예약)을 반복 사용하여 혼동을 준 오답이다.
(B) [×] 질문의 hotel(호텔)을 반복 사용하여 혼동을 준 오답이다.
(C) [○] 확인 메일을 기다려보자는 말로, 문제점에 대한 해결책을 제시했으므로 정답이다.

21 When 의문문
캐나다식 → 호주식

When is the revised leave policy going into effect?
(A) Yes, for the first shift.
(B) At the end of this month, I believe.
(C) I live two blocks away from the station.

leave n. 휴가　go into effect 실시되다, 효력이 발생되다

해석 변경된 휴가 정책이 언제부터 실시될 것인가요?
(A) 네, 첫 번째 근무 시간대를 위해서요.
(B) 이번 달 말부터인 것 같아요.
(C) 저는 그 역에서 두 블록 떨어진 곳에 살아요.

해설 (A) [×] 의문사 의문문에 Yes로 응답했으므로 오답이다. 질문의 policy(정책)에서 연상할 수 있는 회사와 관련된 shift(근무 시간대)를 사용하여 혼동을 주었다.
(B) [○] 이번 달 말부터인 것 같다는 말로, 변경된 휴가 정책이 실시될 시점을 언급했으므로 정답이다.
(C) [×] leave - live의 유사 발음 어휘를 사용하여 혼동을 준 오답이다.

22 부정 의문문
영국식 → 미국식

Shouldn't Mr. Parker evaluate your research proposal?
(A) I'm seeing him at 4:30.
(B) No, it's down the hallway.
(C) Please do the research soon.

evaluate v. 평가하다　research n. 연구　proposal n. 제안, 제의
hallway n. 복도

해석 Mr. Parker가 당신의 연구 제안을 평가해야 하지 않나요?
(A) 저는 4시 30분에 그를 만날 거예요.
(B) 아니요, 그것은 복도를 따라 내려가면 있어요.
(C) 조사를 빨리 해주세요.

해설 (A) [○] 4시 30분에 그를 만날 거라는 말로, Mr. Parker와 만나서 연구 제안 평가 결과에 대해 논의할 것임을 간접적으로 전달했으므로 정답이다.
(B) [×] Mr. Parker가 당신의 연구 제안을 평가해야 하지 않냐고 물었는데, 이와 관련이 없는 그것은 복도를 따라 내려가면 있다고 응답했으므로 오답이다. No까지만 듣고 정답으로 고르지 않도록 주의한다.
(C) [×] 질문의 research를 반복 사용하여 혼동을 준 오답이다.

23 조동사 의문문
영국식 → 캐나다식

Do you mind if I lower the air conditioner temperature?
(A) It's a bit hot in here.
(B) I've just checked a room size.
(C) Are you sure it can be fixed?

air conditioner 에어컨　temperature n. 온도

해석 제가 에어컨 온도를 낮춰도 괜찮을까요?
(A) 여기 안이 조금 덥네요.
(B) 제가 방금 방 크기를 확인했어요.
(C) 그것이 고쳐질 수 있다고 확신하시나요?

해설 (A) [○] 여기 안이 조금 덥다는 말로, 에어컨 온도를 낮춰도 괜찮음을 간접적으로 전달했으므로 정답이다.
(B) [×] 에어컨 온도를 낮춰도 괜찮을지를 물었는데, 이와 관련이 없는 방금 자신의 방 크기를 확인했다는 내용으로 응답했으므로 오답이다.
(C) [×] 질문의 air conditioner(에어컨)에서 연상할 수 있는 be fixed(고쳐지다)를 사용하여 혼동을 준 오답이다.

24 선택 의문문
미국식 → 영국식

Would you prefer to handle this project alone or do you need assistance?
(A) I prefer an aisle seat.
(B) The projector isn't working, is it?
(C) I think I can do it myself.

prefer v. 선호하다　assistance n. 도움　aisle seat 통로 쪽 좌석
projector n. 영사기

해석 이 프로젝트를 혼자서 처리하는 것을 선호하시나요, 아니면 도움이 필요하신가요?
(A) 저는 통로 쪽 좌석을 선호해요.
(B) 그 영사기는 작동하지 않고 있어요, 그렇죠?
(C) 저는 혼자서 할 수 있을 것 같아요.

해설 (A) [×] 질문의 prefer를 반복 사용하여 혼동을 준 오답이다.
(B) [×] project - projector의 유사 발음 어휘를 사용하여 혼동을 준 오답이다.
(C) [○] 혼자서 할 수 있을 것 같다는 말로, 프로젝트를 혼자서 처리하는 것을 선택한 정답이다.

25 부정 의문문
호주식 → 캐나다식

Doesn't the travel agency provide free guide services for major tourist attractions?
(A) A 15-minute break.
(B) We've employed a private tour guide.
(C) Make sure to stick to your travel budget.

travel agency 여행사　stick to ~을 (굳게) 지키다, 고수하다
budget n. 예산

해석 여행사에서 주요 관광 명소에 대한 무료 가이드 서비스를 제공하지 않나요?
(A) 15분간의 휴식이요.
(B) 저희는 개인 여행 가이드를 고용했어요.
(C) 반드시 당신의 여행 예산을 지키세요.

해설 (A) [×] 여행사에서 주요 관광 명소에 대한 무료 가이드 서비스를 제공하지 않는지를 물었는데, 이와 관련이 없는 15분간의 휴식이라는 말로 응답했으므로 오답이다.
(B) [○] 개인 여행 가이드를 고용했다는 말로, 여행사에서 주요 관광 명소에 대한 무료 가이드 서비스를 제공하지 않는다는 것을 간접적으로 전달했으므로 정답이다.
(C) [×] 질문의 travel을 반복 사용하여 혼동을 준 오답이다.

26 Who 의문문
캐나다식 → 미국식

Who was appointed as the Tokyo branch manager?
(A) For a business trip.
(B) No decision has been made yet.
(C) That's a good point.

appoint v. 임명하다 branch n. 지점, 분점

해석 누가 도쿄 지점 관리자로 임명되었나요?
(A) 출장을 위해서요.
(B) 아직 어떠한 결정도 내려지지 않았어요.
(C) 좋은 지적이네요.

해설 (A) [x] 질문의 Tokyo branch(도쿄 지점)에서 연상할 수 있는 business trip(출장)을 사용하여 혼동을 준 오답이다.
(B) [o] 아직 어떠한 결정도 내려지지 않았다는 말로, 도쿄 지점의 관리자로 임명된 사람이 누구인지 모른다는 것을 간접적으로 전달했으므로 정답이다.
(C) [x] appointed - point의 유사 발음 어휘를 사용하여 혼동을 준 오답이다.

27 평서문
미국식 → 캐나다식

We didn't receive your feedback on the blueprint.
(A) I'll take the blue one.
(B) At the building across the street.
(C) I was assigned to the team yesterday.

blueprint n. 청사진, 계획 assign v. 배정하다, 맡기다

해석 우리는 그 청사진에 대한 당신의 의견을 받지 못했어요.
(A) 저는 파란색의 것을 살게요.
(B) 길 건너 건물에서요.
(C) 저는 어제 팀에 배정되었어요.

해설 (A) [x] blueprint - blue의 유사 발음 어휘를 사용하여 혼동을 준 오답이다.
(B) [x] 질문의 blueprint(청사진)와 관련 있는 building(건물)을 사용하여 혼동을 준 오답이다.
(C) [o] 어제 팀에 배정되었다는 말로, 청사진에 대한 의견을 전달할 수 없었던 이유를 언급했으므로 정답이다.

28 조동사 의문문
영국식 → 호주식

Has Mr. Norwood contacted you yet?
(A) He's on leave today.
(B) Here is my contact information.
(C) On the sales team.

contact information 연락처

해석 Mr. Norwood가 벌써 당신에게 연락했나요?
(A) 그는 오늘 휴가예요.
(B) 여기 제 연락처요.
(C) 영업팀에서요.

해설 (A) [o] 그는 오늘 휴가라는 말로, Mr. Norwood가 연락하지 않았음을 간접적으로 전달했으므로 정답이다.
(B) [x] 질문의 contact(연락하다)를 '연락'이라는 의미의 명사로 반복 사용하여 혼동을 준 오답이다.
(C) [x] Mr. Norwood가 연락했는지를 물었는데, 이와 관련이 없는 영업팀에서라는 말로 응답했으므로 오답이다.

29 부가 의문문
호주식 → 미국식

The new applications introduced at the fair were really creative, weren't they?
(A) Are there any products left?
(B) Please remove the crates.
(C) They were much better than expected.

fair n. 박람회 creative adj. 창의적인 crate n. 상자

해석 박람회에서 소개된 새로운 애플리케이션들은 정말 창의적이었어요, 그렇지 않나요?
(A) 남은 제품들이 있나요?
(B) 그 상자들을 치워주세요.
(C) 기대한 것보다 훨씬 더 좋았어요.

해설 (A) [x] 질문의 fair(박람회)에서 연상할 수 있는 products(제품들)를 사용하여 혼동을 준 오답이다.
(B) [x] creative - crates의 유사 발음 어휘를 사용하여 혼동을 준 오답이다.
(C) [o] 기대한 것보다 훨씬 더 좋았다는 말로, 박람회에서 소개된 새로운 애플리케이션들이 창의적이었다는 말에 간접적으로 동의했으므로 정답이다.

30 선택 의문문
영국식 → 호주식

Would you rather go to a jazz concert or a basketball game?
(A) I want to see a musical performance.
(B) Sure, I'll e-mail them in advance.
(C) It was a really intense match.

performance n. 공연 in advance 미리, 사전에
intense adj. 치열한, 극심한

해석 재즈 콘서트에 가고 싶나요, 아니면 농구 경기에 가고 싶나요?
(A) 저는 음악 공연을 보고 싶어요.
(B) 물론이죠, 제가 그것들을 미리 이메일로 보낼게요.
(C) 그것은 정말 치열한 경기였어요.

해설 (A) [o] 음악 공연을 보고 싶다는 말로, 재즈 콘서트를 간접적으로 선택했으므로 정답이다.
(B) [x] 재즈 콘서트에 가고 싶은지, 농구 경기에 가고 싶은지를 물었는데, 이와 관련이 없는 미리 그것들을 이메일로 보내겠다는 말로 응답했으므로 오답이다.
(C) [x] 질문의 basketball game(농구 경기)과 관련 있는 match(경기)를 사용하여 혼동을 준 오답이다.

31 Which 의문문
미국식 → 영국식

Which cereal advertisement did our focus group like best?
(A) By focusing on the experiment.

(B) We had some issues with the sound system.
(C) A cup of milk, please.

focus group 포커스 그룹(시장 조사 참가자들로 이뤄진 그룹)
focus on ~에 집중하다   experiment n. 실험

해석 우리의 포커스 그룹은 어떤 시리얼 광고를 가장 좋아했나요?
(A) 실험에 집중함으로써요.
(B) 음향 시스템에 약간의 문제가 있었어요.
(C) 우유 한 잔 부탁해요.

해설 (A) [×] focus - focusing의 유사 발음 어휘를 사용하여 혼동을 준 오답이다.
(B) [○] 음향 시스템에 약간의 문제가 있었다는 말로, 포커스 그룹이 시리얼 광고들을 확인하지 못해 어떤 광고를 가장 좋아하는지 모른다는 것을 간접적으로 전달했으므로 정답이다.
(C) [×] 질문의 cereal(시리얼)에서 연상할 수 있는 milk(우유)를 사용하여 혼동을 준 오답이다.

최신토익경향

그동안 Which 의문문은 Which 뒤에 나오는 명사만 정확하게 들으면 정답을 쉽게 고를 수 있었다. 하지만, 최근에는 Which 뒤에 나오는 명사 중 하나를 고르는 답변이 아닌 예측하기 어려운 답변이 나와 오답률이 높다.

<Which 의문문에 대한 간접 응답>
Which brand should I order?
어떤 브랜드를 주문해야 할까요?
[답변] The store catalog is over there.
상점 카탈로그가 저기에 있어요.
* 어떤 브랜드를 주문할지 묻는 질문에 저기에 카탈로그가 있으니 직접 보고 선택하라는 의도를 간접적으로 전달하는 답변

Which band is going to perform at the club tonight?
오늘 밤 클럽에서 어떤 밴드가 연주하나요?
[답변] We have a comedy show every Wednesday night.
매주 수요일 밤에는 코미디쇼를 해요.
* 어떤 밴드가 오늘 밤에 공연할지 묻는 질문에 수요일 밤마다 코미디 쇼가 있다며 오늘은 밴드 공연이 없음을 간접적으로 전달하는 답변

PART 3

[32-34] 캐나다식 → 미국식

Questions 32-34 refer to the following conversation.

M: Hello. ³²I need to change some light bulbs in my house. Which section of this store should I go to?
W: They're located in Section C. ³³I can help you find what you are looking for.
M: Oh, thank you. I want to buy ones that are energy efficient.
W: ³⁴Have you considered LED bulbs? They use 75 percent less power than traditional ones.
M: That's a big difference. ³⁴I'll give them a try.

light bulb 전구   section n. 구역   energy efficient 에너지 효율이 좋은
consider v. 고려하다, 생각하다   traditional adj. 기존의, 전통적인
difference n. 차이, 다름

해석 32-34번은 다음 대화에 관한 문제입니다.
남: 안녕하세요. ³²저희 집에 몇몇 전구를 바꿔야 하는데요. 이 매장의 어느 구역으로 가야 하나요?
여: 그것들은 C구역에 위치해 있습니다. ³³구하고 있는 것을 찾으시는 데 제가 도움을 드릴 수 있습니다.
남: 아, 감사합니다. 저는 에너지 효율이 좋은 것들을 사고 싶어요.
여: ³⁴LED 전구를 고려해 보셨나요? 기존 전구보다 75퍼센트 더 적은 전력을 사용해요.
남: 그거 큰 차이네요. ³⁴그것들을 한번 사용해 볼게요.

32 장소 문제

해석 대화는 어디에서 일어나고 있는 것 같은가?
(A) 옷 가게에서
(B) 약국에서
(C) 철물점에서
(D) 예술 용품점에서

해설 대화에서 장소와 관련된 표현을 놓치지 않고 듣는다. 남자가 "I need to change some light bulbs in my house. Which section of this store should I go to?"라며 집에 몇몇 전구를 바꿔야 하는데 이 매장의 어느 구역으로 가면 되냐고 물었으므로 전구를 파는 철물점에서 대화가 일어나고 있음을 알 수 있다. 따라서 (C)가 정답이다.

어휘 boutique n. 가게, 상점   hardware n. 철물, 하드웨어

33 제안 문제

해석 여자는 무엇을 도와주겠다고 제안하는가?
(A) 몇몇 제품들의 위치를 찾는 것
(B) 환불을 처리하는 것
(C) 몇몇 용품들을 나르는 것
(D) 몇몇 장비를 조립하는 것

해설 여자의 말에서 남자를 위해 해주겠다고 언급한 내용을 주의 깊게 듣는다. 여자가 "I can help you find what you are looking for."라며 구하고 있는 것을 찾는 데 도움을 줄 수 있다고 하였다. 따라서 (A)가 정답이다.

어휘 locate v. ~의 위치를 찾다, 두다   process v. 처리하다
assemble v. 조립하다   equipment n. 장비, 용품

Paraphrasing

find what you are looking for 구하고 있는 것을 찾다 → locating ~ items 제품들의 위치를 찾는 것

34 다음에 할 일 문제

해석 남자는 무엇을 하겠다고 말하는가?
(A) 나중에 사업장에 돌아온다.
(B) 다른 제품 유형으로 바꾼다.
(C) 사용자 매뉴얼을 읽는다.
(D) 온라인에서 정보를 확인한다.

해설 대화의 마지막 부분을 주의 깊게 듣는다. 여자가 "Have you considered LED bulbs? They use 75 percent less power than traditional ones."라며 기존 전구보다 더 적은 전력을 사용하

는 LED 전구를 고려해 봤냐고 묻자, 남자가 "I'll give them a try."라며 그것들을 사용해 보겠다고 하였다. 따라서 (B)가 정답이다.

[35-37]

3ω 미국식 → 호주식 → 캐나다식

Questions 35-37 refer to the following conversation with three speakers.

W: ³⁵My team leader mentioned that management is considering remodeling our office to create more open space. Have either of you heard anything about this?
M1: Yeah. The plan is to remove all the cubicles. I think it's a great idea because it'll promote teamwork.
W: ³⁶What about you, Erik?
M2: ³⁶I'm worried that I won't be able to focus on my work because people will be chatting more often.
W: ³⁷Well, there will be a meeting next week for staff to provide feedback on this proposal. You should bring up your concern then.

mention v. 말하다, 언급하다 management n. 경영진, 운영
remodel v. 개조하다 remove v. 제거하다
cubicle n. 칸막이, 작은 방 promote v. 촉진하다, 홍보하다
proposal n. 제안 bring up 제기하다, 말을 꺼내다
concern n. 우려 사항

해석
35-37번은 다음 세 명의 대화에 관한 문제입니다.
여: ³⁵저의 팀장님은 경영진이 더 많은 개방 공간을 만들기 위해 우리의 사무실을 개조하는 것을 고려하고 있다고 말했어요. 두 분 중 이에 대해 들은 분이 있나요?
남1: 네. 그 계획은 모든 칸막이를 제거하는 것이에요. 팀워크를 촉진할 것이기 때문에 저는 좋은 생각인 것 같아요.
여: ³⁶Erik, 당신은 어때요?
남2: ³⁶사람들이 더 자주 이야기를 할 것 같아서 제 일에 집중하지 못할까 봐 걱정돼요.
여: ³⁷음, 다음 주에 직원들이 이 제안에 대한 피드백을 제공하는 회의가 있을 거예요. 그때 당신의 우려 사항을 제기하셔야겠어요.

35 주제 문제

해석 대화는 주로 무엇에 대한 것인가?
(A) 팀워크 활동
(B) 사무실 이전
(C) 경영진 변화
(D) 작업 공간 구조 변경

해설 대화의 주제를 묻는 문제이므로, 대화의 초반을 반드시 듣는다. 여자가 "My team leader mentioned that management is considering remodeling our office to create more open space. Have either of you heard anything about this?"라며 경영진이 더 많은 개방 공간을 만들기 위해 사무실을 개조하는 것을 고려하고 있다는 것에 대해 들었는지 남자들에게 물은 후, 사무실 개조에 대한 내용으로 대화가 이어지고 있다. 따라서 (D)가 정답이다.

어휘 relocation n. 이전 transition n. 변화
reconfiguration n. 구조 변경

Paraphrasing

remodeling our office 우리 사무실을 개조하는 것 → a workspace reconfiguration 작업 공간 구조 변경

36 문제점 문제

해석 Erik은 무엇에 대해 걱정하는가?
(A) 방해 증가
(B) 추가 비용
(C) 감소된 혜택
(D) 부정적인 후기

해설 질문의 핵심 어구(Erik)가 언급된 주변을 주의 깊게 듣는다. 여자가 "What about you, Erik?"이라며 Erik의 생각을 묻자 남자2[Erik]가 "I'm worried that I won't be able to focus on my work because people will be chatting more often."이라며 사람들이 더 자주 이야기를 할 것 같아서 일에 집중하지 못할까 봐 걱정이라고 하였다. 따라서 (A)가 정답이다.

어휘 distraction n. 방해, 혼란 expense n. 비용
negative adj. 부정적인

37 제안 문제

해석 여자는 무엇을 하라고 제안하는가?
(A) 정보 확인하기
(B) 피드백 모으기
(C) 회의 준비하기
(D) 문제 제기하기

해설 여자의 말에서 제안과 관련된 표현이 언급된 주변을 주의 깊게 듣는다. 여자가 "Well, there will be a meeting next week for staff to provide feedback on this proposal. You should bring up your concern then."이라며 다음 주에 직원들이 이 제안에 대한 피드백을 제공하는 회의가 있을 테니 그때 우려 사항을 제기하라고 하였다. 따라서 (D)가 정답이다.

어휘 verify v. 확인하다 organize v. 준비하다, 정리하다
raise v. (문제 등을) 제기하다, 일으키다

Paraphrasing

bring up ~ concern 우려 사항을 제기하다 → Raising an issue 문제 제기하기

[38-40]

3ω 호주식 → 영국식

Questions 38-40 refer to the following conversation.

M: ³⁸I'm sorry I wasn't able to make it on time for our appointment. I got stuck in a traffic jam on my way here.
W: It's fine. ³⁹I caught up on some of my real estate agency's paperwork while I waited for you.
M: Thanks for understanding. The reason I contacted you is that I'm thinking about opening another branch of my coffee shop. Do you know of any rental properties available on Robson Street?

W: A grocery store in a building near Breton Park just completed its lease. The owner wants someone new right away. ⁴⁰You would be in a strong position to negotiate the monthly rental fee.

traffic jam 교통 체증 catch up on 밀린 ~을 하다, 따라잡다
real estate agency 부동산 중개소 property n. 부동산, 재산
grocery store 식료품점 lease n. 임대차 계약
negotiate v. 협상하다, 성사시키다 rental fee 임대료

해석
38-40번은 다음 대화에 관한 문제입니다.
남: ³⁸우리의 약속 시간을 지키지 못해서 죄송해요. 이곳으로 오는 길에 교통 체증으로 차가 막혔어요.
여: 괜찮아요. 당신을 기다리는 동안 ³⁹제 부동산 중개업소의 밀린 서류 작업을 하고 있었어요.
남: 이해해 주셔서 감사해요. 제가 연락드렸던 이유는 제 커피숍의 다른 분점을 열려고 생각 중이기 때문입니다. 혹시 Robson가에 임대 가능한 매물을 알고 계신가요?
여: Breton 공원 근처의 한 건물에 있는 식료품점이 방금 임대차 계약을 완료했어요. 주인이 당장 새 임차인을 원하고 있어요. ⁴⁰당신은 월 임대료를 협상할 수 있는 유리한 위치에 있을 것입니다.

38 이유 문제

해석 남자는 약속에 왜 늦었는가?
(A) 도로가 혼잡했다.
(B) 주차장이 꽉 찼다.
(C) 일정이 변경되었다.
(D) 건물에 접근할 수 없었다.

해설 질문의 핵심 어구(late for the appointment)와 관련된 내용을 주의 깊게 듣는다. 남자가 "I'm sorry I wasn't able to make it on time for our appointment. I got stuck in a traffic jam on my way here."라며 약속 시간을 지키지 못해서 죄송하다며, 오는 길에 차가 막혔다고 하였다. 따라서 (A)가 정답이다.

어휘 congested adj. 혼잡한, 붐비는 inaccessible adj. 접근할 수 없는

Paraphrasing
got stuck in a traffic jam 차가 막혔다 → road was congested 도로가 혼잡했다

39 화자 문제

해석 여자는 누구인 것 같은가?
(A) 부동산 중개인
(B) 여행 가이드
(C) 접수원
(D) 건축가

해설 대화에서 신분 및 직업과 관련된 표현을 놓치지 않고 듣는다. 여자가 "I caught up on some of my real estate agency's paperwork"라며 자신의 부동산 중개업소의 밀린 서류 작업을 하고 있었다고 했으므로 여자는 부동산 중개업소에서 일하는 부동산 중개인임을 알 수 있다. 따라서 (A)가 정답이다.

40 의도 파악 문제

해석 여자는 "주인이 당장 새 임차인을 원하고 있어요"라고 말할 때 무엇을 의도하는가?
(A) 남자는 어떠한 지연도 피해야 한다.
(B) 남자는 이전에 주인을 만났었다.
(C) 남자는 좋은 거래를 할 수 있다.
(D) 남자는 올바른 결정을 내렸다.

해설 질문의 인용어구(The owner wants someone new right away)가 언급된 주변을 주의 깊게 듣는다. 여자가 남자에게 "You would be in a strong position to negotiate the monthly rental fee."라며 월 임대료를 협상할 수 있는 유리한 위치에 있을 것이라고 했으므로 남자가 좋은 거래를 할 수 있음을 알 수 있다. 따라서 (C)가 정답이다.

어휘 deal n. 거래, 합의 decision n. 결정, 판단

[41-43] 캐나다식 → 영국식

Questions 41-43 refer to the following conversation.

M: Nancy, ⁴¹are you available to help me with the order system? I cannot seem to access the records.
W: Sure. What are you trying to find?
M: ⁴²My manager asked me to prepare a summary of the online orders at our company during the last quarter.
W: Oh, the program interface has changed a little. That information can be accessed by typing "order history" in the search bar.
M: That worked. One more thing . . . ⁴³do you know where I can find information about the delivery times for these orders?
W: I'm not sure. ⁴³Maybe you should ask the head of the shipping department.

access v. 접근하다, 이용하다, 접속하다 summary n. 요약
quarter n. 분기 interface n. 인터페이스, 접속기
department n. 부서

해석
41-43번은 다음 대화에 관한 문제입니다.
남: Nancy, ⁴¹주문 시스템에 대해 저를 도와주실 수 있나요? 제가 기록에 접근할 수 없는 것 같아요.
여: 물론이죠. 무엇을 찾으려고 하시나요?
남: ⁴²제 매니저가 지난 분기 동안 우리 회사의 온라인 주문 요약본을 준비해 달라고 요청하셨어요.
여: 아, 프로그램 인터페이스가 약간 변경되었어요. 그 정보는 검색창에 "주문 내역"을 입력하면 이용할 수 있어요.
남: 해결됐어요. 한 가지 더... ⁴³이 주문들의 배송 시간에 대한 정보를 어디에서 찾을 수 있는지 아세요?
여: 잘 모르겠어요. ⁴³아마도 배송 부서장에게 물어보셔야 할 것 같아요.

41 이유 문제

해석 남자는 왜 여자의 도움을 필요로 하는가?
(A) 음성 파일을 녹음하기 위해
(B) 문서 교정을 보기 위해

(C) 다운로드 링크에 접속하기 위해
(D) 기록을 얻기 위해

해설 질문의 핵심 어구(need the woman's help)와 관련된 내용을 주의 깊게 듣는다. 남자가 "are you available to help me with the order system? I cannot seem to access the records."라며 주문 시스템에 대해 도와줄 수 있는지 물은 후, 기록에 접근할 수 없다고 하였다. 따라서 (D)가 정답이다.

어휘 proofread v. 교정을 보다 obtain v. 얻다, 구하다

42 특정 세부 사항 문제

해설 남자는 어떤 업무를 배정받았는가?
(A) 시스템을 업데이트하는 것
(B) 보고서를 준비하는 것
(C) 발표를 하는 것
(D) 회의록을 요약하는 것

해설 질문의 핵심 어구(task ~ the man been assigned)와 관련된 내용을 주의 깊게 듣는다. 남자가 "My manager asked me to prepare a summary of the online orders at our company during the last quarter."라며 매니저가 지난 분기 동안 우리 회사의 온라인 주문 요약본을 준비해 달라고 요청했다고 하였다. 따라서 (B)가 정답이다.

43 다음에 할 일 문제

해설 남자는 다음에 무엇을 할 것 같은가?
(A) 고객과 이야기한다.
(B) 요약본을 인쇄한다.
(C) 관리자에게 연락한다.
(D) 배달 일정을 조정한다.

해설 대화의 마지막 부분을 주의 깊게 듣는다. 남자가 여자에게 "do you know where I can find information about the delivery times for these orders?"라며 주문들의 배송 시간에 대한 정보를 어디에서 찾을 수 있는지 묻자, 여자가 "Maybe you should ask the head of the shipping department."라며 배송 부서장에게 물어보라고 하였다. 따라서 (C)가 정답이다.

어휘 supervisor n. 관리자, 감독관 adjust v. 조정하다, 바로잡다

Paraphrasing

the head of the shipping department 배송 부서장
→ a supervisor 관리자

[44-46]
３ｍ 미국식 → 캐나다식

Questions 44-46 refer to the following conversation.

W: ⁴⁴Craig, a shipment from Martin Cornwall's studio just arrived at our gallery. Where do you want me to place the paintings?
M: They belong in the contemporary art section. Please inspect them carefully first. ⁴⁵The shipping company damaged a painting in a previous shipment. I have a meeting downtown this afternoon, so ⁴⁶could you take pictures of the works after unwrapping them?
W: ⁴⁶Sure. I'll text you the images so that you can confirm the works are all in good condition.

place v. 두다, 배치하다 belong in ~에 들어가다
contemporary adj. 현대의 inspect v. 검사하다, 점검하다
damage v. 손상시키다, 훼손하다 previous adj. 이전의
downtown n. 시내 unwrap v. (포장지 등을) 풀다
confirm v. 확인하다 condition n. 상태

해석
44-46번은 다음 대화에 관한 문제입니다.
여: ⁴⁴Craig, Martin Cornwall의 스튜디오에서 보낸 배송품이 방금 우리 갤러리에 도착했어요. 제가 그림을 어디에 두기 원하세요?
남: 그것들은 현대 미술 섹션에 들어가요. 먼저 그것들을 신중하게 검사해 주세요. ⁴⁵배송 회사가 이전 배송에서 그림을 손상시켰어요. 제가 오늘 오후에 시내에서 회의가 있으니, ⁴⁶당신이 작품 포장을 푼 후에 사진을 찍어주실 수 있나요?
여: ⁴⁶물론이죠. 작품들이 모두 양호한 상태인지 당신이 확인하실 수 있도록 이미지를 문자로 보낼게요.

44 화자 문제

해설 화자들은 어디에서 일하는 것 같은가?
(A) 미술관에서
(B) 가구 제조업체에서
(C) 우체국에서
(D) 인테리어 회사에서

해설 대화에서 신분 및 직업과 관련된 표현을 놓치지 않고 듣는다. 여자가 "Craig, a shipment from Martin Cornwall's studio just arrived at our gallery."라며 Martin Cornwall의 스튜디오에서 보낸 배송품이 방금 우리 갤러리에 도착했다고 하였다. 따라서 (A)가 정답이다.

어휘 manufacturer n. 제조업체, 생산 회사

45 언급 문제

해설 남자는 배송 회사에 대해 무엇을 말하는가?
(A) 좋은 명성을 가지고 있다.
(B) 전에 실수를 했다.
(C) 시내에 사무실이 있다.
(D) 새로운 서비스를 출시했다.

해설 남자의 말에서 질문의 핵심 어구(a shipping company)가 언급된 주변을 주의 깊게 듣는다. 남자가 "The shipping company damaged a painting in a previous shipment."라며 배송 회사가 이전 배송에서 그림을 손상시켰다고 하였다. 따라서 (B)가 정답이다.

어휘 reputation n. 명성, 평판 launch v. 출시하다, 시작하다; n. 출시

46 특정 세부 사항 문제

해설 여자는 남자에게 무엇을 보낼 것인가?
(A) 사진
(B) 송장

(C) 디자인 초안
(D) 잡지 기사

해설 질문의 핵심 어구(send)와 관련된 부분을 주의 깊게 듣는다. 남자가 "could you take pictures of the works after unwrapping them?"이라며 포장을 푼 후에 사진을 찍어달라고 요청하자, 여자가 "Sure. I'll text you the images so that you can confirm the works are all in good condition."이라며 물론이라고 답한 후, 작품들이 모두 양호한 상태인지 확인할 수 있도록 이미지를 문자로 보내겠다고 하였다. 따라서 (A)가 정답이다.

[47-49]

호주식 → 영국식

Questions 47-49 refer to the following conversation.

M: Hello. You've reached Stream Airline.
W: Hi. ⁴⁷I'm calling to inquire about a ticket I bought for a flight to Istanbul tomorrow evening. I just realized I qualify for 10 percent off because I'm a university student.
M: That's right. You need to select the student option when booking a ticket.
W: Got it. ⁴⁸Can you refund my ticket so I can purchase one at a reduced price?
M: Sorry, but tickets are nonrefundable within three days of departure. ⁴⁹I can give you a hundred-dollar voucher to use for a future flight, though.

inquire v. 문의하다   qualify for ~을 받을 수 있다, ~의 자격이 있다
nonrefundable adj. 환불되지 않는   departure n. 출발
voucher n. 쿠폰, 할인권

해석
47-49번은 다음 대화에 관한 문제입니다.
남: 안녕하세요. Stream 항공사입니다.
여: 안녕하세요. ⁴⁷제가 구입한 내일 저녁 이스탄불행 항공편 티켓에 대해 문의하려고 전화했습니다. 제가 대학생이기 때문에 10퍼센트 할인을 받을 수 있다는 것을 방금 알았어요.
남: 맞습니다. 티켓을 예약할 때 학생 옵션을 선택하셔야 해요.
여: 알겠습니다. ⁴⁸할인된 가격으로 티켓을 구매할 수 있도록 제 티켓을 환불해 주시겠어요?
남: 죄송하지만 티켓은 출발 3일 이내에는 환불되지 않습니다. 하지만 ⁴⁹향후 항공편에 사용할 수 있는 100달러 상당의 쿠폰을 드릴 수 있습니다.

47 목적 문제

해설 여자는 왜 전화를 걸고 있는가?
(A) 멤버십을 신청하기 위해
(B) 시간표를 확인하기 위해
(C) 구매한 것에 대해 문의하기 위해
(D) 예약을 취소하기 위해

해설 전화의 목적을 묻는 문제이므로, 대화의 초반을 반드시 듣는다. 여자가 "I'm calling to inquire about a ticket I bought for a flight to Istanbul tomorrow evening."이라며 본인이 구입한 내일 저녁 이스탄불행 항공편 티켓에 대해 문의하려고 전화했다고 하였다. 따라서 (C)가 정답이다.

어휘 timetable n. 시간표, 일정표   purchase n. 구매한 것, 구입
reservation n. 예약

48 요청 문제

해설 여자는 무엇을 요청하는가?
(A) 영수증
(B) 환불
(C) 안내 책자
(D) 업그레이드

해설 여자의 말에서 요청과 관련된 표현이 포함된 문장을 주의 깊게 듣는다. 여자가 "Can you refund my ticket so I can purchase one at a reduced price?"라며 할인된 가격으로 티켓을 구매할 수 있도록 티켓을 환불해 줄 수 있냐고 물었다. 따라서 (B)가 정답이다.

49 제안 문제

해설 남자는 무엇을 해주겠다고 제안하는가?
(A) 티켓을 이메일로 보낸다.
(B) 가격을 확정한다.
(C) 일정을 변경한다.
(D) 쿠폰을 제공한다.

해설 남자의 말에서 여자를 위해 해주겠다고 언급한 내용을 주의 깊게 듣는다. 남자가 "I can give you a hundred-dollar voucher to use for a future flight"이라며 향후 항공편에 사용할 수 있는 100달러 상당의 쿠폰을 줄 수 있다고 하였다. 따라서 (D)가 정답이다.

Paraphrasing

give you a hundred-dollar voucher 100달러 상당의 쿠폰을 주다
→ Provide a coupon 쿠폰을 제공한다

[50-52]

미국식 → 호주식

Questions 50-52 refer to the following conversation.

W: ⁵⁰Do you remember we asked the design team for feedback about the upcoming first issue of our new magazine? Well, I just had a lunch meeting with them.
M: What did they say?
W: ⁵⁰They suggested that we change the layout of the cover and include brighter colors.
M: But ⁵¹we spent months working on the current cover. It'll take a lot of effort to implement that feedback.
W: We still have a few weeks until the publication date. ⁵²Why don't we meet with the other project staff and come up with some ideas?
M: ⁵²OK. I'll call everyone into the conference room now.

first issue 창간호, 첫 호   current adj. 현재의
implement v. 구현하다, 시행하다   publication n. 발행, 출판물

해석
50-52번은 다음 대화에 관한 문제입니다.
여: ⁵⁰우리 새 잡지의 곧 발행될 창간호에 대해 디자인 팀에 피드백을 요청했던 것 기억하시나요? 음, 방금 그들과 점심 미팅을 했어요.
남: 그들이 뭐라고 했나요?

여: ⁵⁰그들은 우리가 표지 레이아웃을 변경하고 더 밝은 색상을 포함해야 된다고 제안했어요.
남: 하지만 ⁵¹우리는 현재 표지를 작업하는 데 몇 달을 보냈어요. 그 의견을 구현하려면 많은 노력이 필요할 거예요.
여: 발행일까지 아직 몇 주가 남아있어요. ⁵²다른 프로젝트 직원들과 만나서 아이디어를 내보는 건 어떨까요?
남: ⁵²알겠습니다. 지금 회의실로 모두 부를게요.

50 주제 문제

해석 화자들은 주로 무엇에 대해 논의하고 있는가?
(A) 금융 문제
(B) 생산 과정
(C) 디자인 변경
(D) 홍보 전략

해설 대화의 주제를 묻는 문제이므로, 대화의 초반을 반드시 듣는다. 여자가 "Do you remember we asked the design team for feedback about the upcoming first issue of our new magazine?"이라며 우리의 새 잡지의 곧 발행될 창간호에 대해 디자인 팀에 피드백을 요청했던 것을 기억하냐고 물은 후, "They suggested that we change the layout of the cover and include brighter colors."라며 그들이 표지 레이아웃을 변경하고 더 밝은 색상을 포함해야 된다고 제안했다고 하였다. 따라서 (C)가 정답이다.

어휘 financial adj. 금융의 production n. 생산 strategy n. 전략

51 의도 파악 문제

해석 남자는 왜 "그 의견을 구현하려면 많은 노력이 필요할 거예요"라고 말하는가?
(A) 다른 선택안을 요청하기 위해
(B) 오해를 바로잡기 위해
(C) 더 많은 세부 사항을 제공하기 위해
(D) 의구심을 표현하기 위해

해설 질문의 인용어구(It'll take a lot of effort to implement that feedback)가 언급된 주변을 주의 깊게 듣는다. 남자가 "we spent months working on the current cover"라며 현재 표지를 작업하는 데 몇 달 동안의 시간을 들였다고 한 것을 통해 의견을 구현하는 데 추가로 시간을 들이는 것에 대해 의구심을 표현하고 있음을 알 수 있다. 따라서 (D)가 정답이다.

어휘 misunderstanding n. 오해 express v. 표현하다
doubt n. 의구심, 의문

52 다음에 할 일 문제

해석 화자들은 다음에 무엇을 할 것 같은가?
(A) 문서에 서명한다.
(B) 예산을 수정한다.
(C) 출판물을 읽는다.
(D) 회의를 연다.

해설 대화의 마지막 부분을 주의 깊게 듣는다. 여자가 "Why don't we meet with the other project staff and come up with some ideas?"라며 다른 프로젝트 직원들과 만나서 아이디어를 내보자고 제안하자, 남자가 "OK. I'll call everyone into the conference room now."라며 지금 회의실로 모두 부르겠다고 하였다. 따라서 (D)가 정답이다.

어휘 revise v. 수정하다

[53-55] 호주식 → 영국식 → 캐나다식

Questions 53-55 refer to the following conversation with three speakers.

M1: Welcome to Tech Hub.
W: Hi. I bought this laptop here, and it hasn't worked properly since ⁵³the latest version of the operating system was automatically installed last week.
M1: We can take care of this right now. ⁵⁴Markus, could you help this customer with her laptop?
M2: ⁵⁴Sure. I'll only need about 15 minutes to fix it. Please have a seat while you wait.
W: ⁵⁵How much will I have to pay for the service?
M2: It's covered under your six-month warranty.

properly adv. 제대로, 적절히 operate v. 운영하다
automatically adv. 자동으로 install v. 설치하다

해석
53-55번은 다음 세 명의 대화에 관한 문제입니다.
남1: Tech Hub에 오신 것을 환영합니다.
여: 안녕하세요. 제가 이곳에서 이 노트북을 구입했는데, ⁵³지난주에 최신 버전의 운영 체제가 자동으로 설치된 이후 제대로 작동하지 않아요.
남1: 저희가 지금 바로 처리할 수 있습니다. ⁵⁴Markus, 이 고객님의 노트북을 봐주실 수 있나요?
남2: ⁵⁴물론이죠. 고치는 데 15분 정도만 필요합니다. 기다리는 동안 자리에 앉아계세요.
여: ⁵⁵서비스에 대한 비용은 얼마를 지불해야 하나요?
남2: 그것은 고객님의 6개월 보증이 적용됩니다.

53 특정 세부 사항 문제

해석 지난주에 무슨 일이 있었는가?
(A) 프로그램이 업데이트되었다.
(B) 배송품이 수령되었다.
(C) 노트북이 반품되었다.
(D) 주문이 취소되었다.

해설 질문의 핵심 어구(last week)가 언급된 주변을 주의 깊게 듣는다. 여자가 "the latest version of the operating system was automatically installed last week"이라며 지난주에 최신 버전의 운영 체제가 자동으로 설치되었다고 하였다. 따라서 (A)가 정답이다.

Paraphrasing

the latest version of the operating system was automatically installed 최신 버전의 운영 체제가 자동으로 설치되었다 → A program was updated 프로그램이 업데이트되었다

54 특정 세부 사항 문제

해석 Markus는 그가 무엇을 할 수 있다고 말하는가?
(A) 기계를 교체한다.
(B) 할인을 제공한다.
(C) 기기를 수리한다.
(D) 제품을 찾는다.

해설 질문의 핵심 어구(Markus ~ can do)와 관련된 내용을 주의 깊게 듣는다. 남자1이 "Markus, could you help this customer with her laptop?"이라며 Markus에게 여자의 노트북을 봐달라고 요청하자, 남자2[Markus]가 "Sure. I'll only need about 15 minutes to fix it."이라며 노트북을 고치는 데 15분이면 된다고 하였다. 따라서 (C)가 정답이다.

어휘 replace v. 교체하다

Paraphrasing

fix 고치다 → repair 수리하다
laptop 노트북 → device 기기

55 특정 세부 사항 문제

해석 여자는 무엇에 대해 문의하는가?
(A) 모델의 구입 가능 여부
(B) 서비스의 비용
(C) 직원의 이름
(D) 매장의 운영 시간

해설 대화에서 여자의 말을 주의 깊게 듣는다. 여자가 "How much will I have to pay for the service?"라며 서비스(노트북을 수리하는 것)에 대한 비용을 얼마를 지불해야 하는지 물었다. 따라서 (B)가 정답이다.

어휘 availability n. 구입 가능 여부, 이용 가능성   employee n. 직원

[56-58]
영국식 → 캐나다식

Questions 56-58 refer to the following conversation.

W: Tyler, I think the short videos we posted on our social media page have been really effective. [56]**I've already gotten several inquiries about our gym memberships.**

M: That's great news. Oh, I saw a large crate in our lobby. Do you need me to move it inside?

W: No. [57]**It's a rowing machine for the branch in Collingwood. The delivery person accidentally dropped it off here.**

M: Got it. Anyway, [58]**some customers have been complaining that our washrooms aren't being cleaned regularly. I'm going to tell our janitorial staff about this now.**

어휘 effective adj. 효과적인   inquiry n. 문의   crate n. 상자
accidentally adv. 실수로, 우연히   washroom n. 화장실
janitorial adj. 청소부의, 잡역부의

해석 56-58번은 다음 대화에 관한 문제입니다.

여: Tyler, 우리가 소셜 미디어 페이지에 올린 짧은 영상들이 정말 효과적이었던 것 같아요. [56]이미 우리의 헬스장 멤버십에 대한 여러 문의를 받았어요.

남: 좋은 소식이네요. 아, 제가 로비에서 큰 상자를 봤어요. 제가 그것을 안으로 옮길까요?

여: 아니요. [57]그것은 Collingwood 지점의 조정 기계예요. 배달원이 실수로 여기에 놔두었어요.

남: 알겠습니다. 그건 그렇고, [58]일부 고객들이 화장실 청소가 정기적으로 이루어지지 않는다고 불평하고 있어요. 제가 지금 청소부 직원에게 이것에 대해 말할게요.

56 화자 문제

해석 화자들은 어디에서 일하는 것 같은가?
(A) 광고 회사에서
(B) 피트니스 센터에서
(C) 언어 학교에서
(D) 병원에서

해설 대화에서 신분 및 직업과 관련된 표현을 놓치지 않고 듣는다. 여자가 "I've already gotten several inquiries about our gym memberships."라며 헬스장 멤버십에 대한 여러 문의를 받았다고 하였다. 따라서 (B)가 정답이다.

57 언급 문제

해석 여자는 기계에 대해 무엇을 말하는가?
(A) 곧 설치되어야 한다.
(B) 긍정적인 후기를 받았다.
(C) 실수로 배송되었다.
(D) 새로운 특징들을 포함한다.

해설 여자의 말에서 질문의 핵심 어구(machine)가 언급된 부분을 주의 깊게 듣는다. 여자가 "It's a rowing machine for the branch in Collingwood. The delivery person accidentally dropped it off here."라며 Collingwood 지점의 조정 기계인데 배달원이 실수로 여기에 두었다고 하였다. 따라서 (C)가 정답이다.

어휘 positive adj. 긍정적인   feature n. 특징

Paraphrasing

accidentally 실수로 → by mistake 실수로

58 다음에 할 일 문제

해석 남자는 다음에 무엇을 할 것 같은가?
(A) 몇몇 영상을 편집한다.
(B) 의견을 공유한다.
(C) 한 구역을 청소한다.
(D) 기기의 포장을 푼다.

해설 대화의 마지막 부분을 주의 깊게 듣는다. 남자가 "some customers have been complaining that our washrooms aren't being cleaned regularly. I'm going to tell our janitorial staff about this now."라며 일부 고객들이 화장실 청소가 정기적으로 이루어지지 않는다고 불평하고 있고, 지금 청소부 직원에게 이것에 대해 말할 거라고 하였다. 따라서 (B)가 정답이다.

어휘 edit v. 편집하다 unpack v. 포장을 풀다

[59-61]

영국식 → 호주식

Questions 59-61 refer to the following conversation.

> W: I just got off the phone with Mr. Roberts at our company headquarters. ⁵⁹He received the results of the recent government safety inspection of our factory.
> M: Are there any issues we should be aware of?
> W: We received high marks in every category except one. The fire sprinkler system needs to be modernized because it's quite old.
> M: ⁶⁰I'm a little worried because upgrading the system could cause some production delays.
> W: ⁶¹I'll contact Safe Sprinkler—the company that installed our current system, and schedule a time to discuss the issue. Hopefully, they can offer a solution to minimize disruptions.

headquarters n. 본사   inspection n. 점검
except prep. ~을 제외하고   modernize v. 현대화하다   delay n. 지연
solution n. 해결책   minimize v. 최소화하다
disruption n. 업무 지장, 방해, 중단

해석
59-61번은 다음 대화에 관한 문제입니다.
여: 저는 방금 본사에 있는 Mr. Roberts와 통화했어요. ⁵⁹그는 최근 우리 공장에 대한 정부 안전 점검 결과를 받았습니다.
남: 우리가 알아야 할 문제가 있나요?
여: 한 가지 항목을 제외한 모든 항목에서 높은 점수를 받았어요. 소방 스프링클러 시스템이 상당히 오래되었기 때문에 현대화되어야 해요.
남: ⁶⁰그 시스템을 업그레이드하는 것이 생산 지연을 야기할 수 있어서 조금 걱정되네요.
여: ⁶¹제가 현재의 시스템을 설치해 준 회사인 Safe Sprinkler에 연락해서 이 문제에 대해 논의할 시간을 잡을게요. 업무 지장을 최소화할 수 있는 해결책을 그들이 제공할 수 있기를 바랍니다.

59 특정 세부 사항 문제

해석 최근 회사에 무슨 일이 있었는가?
(A) 워크숍 일정이 변경되었다.
(B) 안전 정책이 변경되었다.
(C) 사업 합병이 마무리되었다.
(D) 점검이 수행되었다.

해설 질문의 핵심 어구(happened at the business)와 관련된 부분을 주의 깊게 듣는다. 여자가 "He received the results of the recent government safety inspection of our factory."라며 최근 우리 공장에 대한 정부 안전 점검 결과를 받았다고 하였다. 따라서 (D)가 정답이다.

어휘 merger n. 합병   finalize v. 마무리하다

60 문제점 문제

해석 남자는 무엇에 대해 걱정하는가?
(A) 생산 중단
(B) 자재 부족
(C) 건물 폐쇄
(D) 보안 위반

해설 남자의 말에서 부정적인 표현이 언급된 주변을 주의 깊게 듣는다. 남자가 "I'm a little worried because upgrading the system could cause some production delays."라며 소방 스프링클러 시스템을 업그레이드하는 것이 생산 지연을 야기할 수 있어서 조금 걱정된다고 하였다. 따라서 (A)가 정답이다.

어휘 shortage n. 부족, 결핍   closure n. 폐쇄   breach n. 위반, 파기

61 이유 문제

해석 여자는 왜 Safe Sprinkler에 연락할 것인가?
(A) 서비스에 대해 항의하기 위해
(B) 몇몇 수치를 수정하기 위해
(C) 예약을 변경하기 위해
(D) 약속을 잡기 위해

해설 질문의 핵심 어구(Safe Sprinkler)가 언급된 주변을 주의 깊게 듣는다. 여자가 "I'll contact Safe Sprinkler—the company that installed our current system, and schedule a time to discuss the issue."라며 현재의 시스템을 설치한 Safe Sprinkler에 연락하여 이 문제에 대해 논의할 시간을 잡겠다고 하였다. 따라서 (D)가 정답이다.

어휘 figure n. 수치, 숫자

Paraphrasing
schedule a time 시간을 잡다 → make an appointment 약속을 잡다

[62-64]

호주식 → 영국식

Questions 62-64 refer to the following conversation and weather forecast.

> M: Hey, Linda. ⁶²We should go to Hampton Park sometime after work this week. I heard they added new paths, benches, and even a café.
> W: Sounds great! When should we go?
> M: Well, ⁶³I'm meeting a client after work on Wednesday, but any other days should be fine.
> W: OK. ⁶³Since we'll be walking, we should go when there isn't any chance of rain.
> M: I'll check the weather report. And, ⁶⁴here's a map of the park in case you can't find the entrance.

add v. 추가하다, 더하다   chance n. 가능성, 기회   entrance n. 입구

해석
62-64번은 다음 대화와 일기 예보에 관한 문제입니다.
남: 안녕하세요, Linda. ⁶²우리 이번 주 퇴근 후에 시간 내서 Hampton 공원에 가요. 새로운 길과 벤치, 심지어 카페를 추가했다고 들었어요.

여: 좋아요! 언제 가면 될까요?
남: 음, ⁶³수요일에는 제가 퇴근 후에 고객을 만나기로 했지만, 나머지 다른 날은 괜찮을 것 같아요.
여: 좋아요. ⁶³우리는 걸을 것이기 때문에 비가 올 가능성이 없을 때 가죠.
남: 제가 일기 예보를 확인해 볼게요. 그리고, 당신이 입구를 못 찾을 경우를 대비해서, ⁶⁴여기 공원 지도가 있어요.

일기 예보			
	날씨	강수 확률	최고 기온
화요일	☁️///	80%	18도
수요일	⛅	0%	20도
목요일	☁️	20%	19도
⁶³금요일	☀️	0%	21도

62 제안 문제

해설 남자는 무엇을 할 것을 제안하는가?
(A) 업무를 마무리하는 것
(B) 새로운 레스토랑에 가 보는 것
(C) 도시공원을 방문하는 것
(D) 고객과 얘기하는 것

해설 남자의 말에서 제안과 관련된 표현이 언급된 다음을 주의 깊게 듣는다. 남자가 "We should go to Hampton Park sometime after work this week."이라며 이번 주 퇴근 후에 시간 내서 Hampton 공원에 가자고 제안하였다. 따라서 (C)가 정답이다.

63 시각 자료 문제

해설 시각 자료를 보아라. 화자들은 언제 만날 것 같은가?
(A) 화요일에
(B) 수요일에
(C) 목요일에
(D) 금요일에

해설 제시된 일기 예보의 정보를 확인한 후 질문의 핵심 어구(meet)와 관련된 내용을 주의 깊게 듣는다. 남자가 "I'm meeting a client after work on Wednesday, but any other days should be fine"이라며 수요일을 제외하고 나머지 다른 날은 괜찮다고 하자, 여자가 "Since we'll be walking, we should go when there isn't any chance of rain."이라며 걸어야 하니까 비가 올 가능성이 없을 때 가야 한다고 했다. 수요일을 제외하고 비가 올 확률이 없는 날은 금요일임을 일기 예보에서 알 수 있다. 따라서 (D)가 정답이다.

64 특정 세부 사항 문제

해설 남자는 여자에게 무엇을 주는가?
(A) 티켓
(B) 지도
(C) 보고서
(D) 메뉴

해설 질문의 핵심 어구(give to the woman)와 관련된 부분을 주의 깊게 듣는다. 남자가 "here's a map of the park"라며 공원 지도가 여기에 있다고 하였다. 따라서 (B)가 정답이다.

[65-67]
🔊 미국식 → 호주식

Questions 65-67 refer to the following conversation and store display.

W: Welcome to Luby Furniture. Are you looking for a particular item?
M: Hi. ⁶⁵I need a closet for the bedroom in my new apartment.
W: We actually just got a new model in. You can see it on display over there. ⁶⁶The piece is made of a special wood that keeps clothes smelling fresh and prevents mold.
M: Oh, I recognize the brand. In fact, I read some positive reviews of it online.
W: Good to hear. By the way, ⁶⁷how did you find out about our store?
M: ⁶⁷My colleague bought a table here last month and recommended your shop to me.

particular adj. 특정한 closet n. 옷장 prevent v. 방지하다, 막다
mold n. 곰팡이 recognize v. 알다 colleague n. 동료
recommend v. 추천하다

해설
65-67번은 다음 대화와 매장 전시에 관한 문제입니다.
여: Luby 가구에 오신 것을 환영합니다. 특정한 제품을 찾으시나요?
남: 안녕하세요. ⁶⁵저의 새 아파트에 침실을 위한 옷장이 필요해요.
여: 저희가 방금 새 모델을 들였습니다. 저기 전시되어 있는 것을 보실 수 있어요. ⁶⁶그 제품은 옷에서 신선한 냄새가 나게 유지하고 곰팡이를 방지하는 특수 목재로 만들어졌습니다.
남: 아, 그 브랜드를 알고 있어요. 사실, 온라인에서 긍정적인 후기를 읽었습니다.
여: 좋은 소식이네요. 그런데 ⁶⁷저희 매장은 어떻게 알게 되셨나요?
남: ⁶⁷제 동료가 지난달에 여기에서 탁자를 샀고 저에게 매장을 추천해 주었어요.

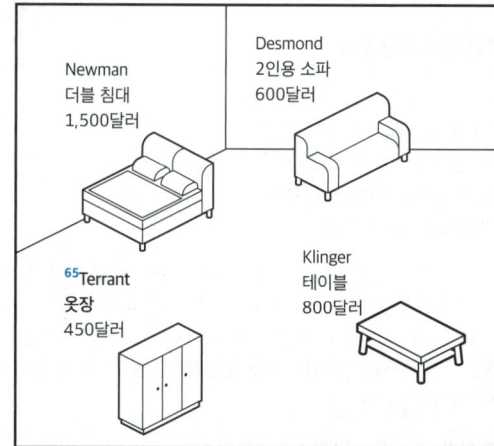

65 시각 자료 문제

해석 시각 자료를 보아라. 남자는 어떤 회사의 제품을 구입하는 것에 관심이 있는가?
(A) Newman
(B) Terrant
(C) Desmond
(D) Klinger

해설 제시된 매장 전시의 정보를 확인한 후 질문의 핵심 어구(man interested in buying)와 관련된 내용을 주의 깊게 듣는다. 남자가 "I need a closet for the bedroom in my new apartment."라며 새 아파트에 옷장이 필요하다고 했고, 옷장의 브랜드는 Terrant임을 매장 전시에서 알 수 있다. 따라서 (B)가 정답이다.

66 특정 세부 사항 문제

해석 여자는 남자와 어떤 정보를 공유하는가?
(A) 제품의 가격
(B) 브랜드의 기원
(C) 사업체의 정책
(D) 자재의 이점

해설 대화에서 여자의 말을 주의 깊게 듣는다. 여자가 "The piece is made of a special wood that keeps clothes smelling fresh and prevents mold."라며 그 제품은 옷에서 신선한 냄새가 나게 유지하고 곰팡이를 방지하는 특수 목재로 만들어졌다고 하였다. 따라서 (D)가 정답이다.

어휘 origin n. 기원, 출신   material n. 자재, 재료

Paraphrasing

wood 목재 → material 자재

67 방법 문제

해석 남자는 매장에 대해 어떻게 알게 되었는가?
(A) 웹사이트로부터
(B) 동료로부터
(C) TV 광고로부터
(D) 이웃으로부터

해설 질문의 핵심 어구(learn about the store)와 관련된 부분을 주의 깊게 듣는다. 여자가 "how did you find out about our store?"라며 매장에 대해 어떻게 알았는지 묻자, 남자가 "My colleague bought a table here last month and recommended your shop to me."라며 지난달에 자신의 동료가 이곳에서 탁자를 샀고 매장을 추천해 주었다고 하였다. 따라서 (B)가 정답이다.

어휘 commercial n. 광고   neighbor n. 이웃

Paraphrasing

colleague 동료 → coworker 동료

[68-70]

캐나다식 → 미국식

Questions 68-70 refer to the following conversation and menu.

M: Thanks for meeting me for lunch today, Claire. I want to talk to you about this afternoon's meeting. ⁶⁸A lot has been added to the agenda because of the new product we're launching. So your presentation will be pushed back to next week.
W: I understand. That will also give me extra time to prepare.
M: You're planning to talk about how to improve customer service, right? ⁶⁹The company recently completed an online survey that might be helpful.
W: That's good to know. ⁶⁹I'll look through it after lunch.
M: Great. Have you decided what to order?
W: I'll just order a Ceasar salad.
M: ⁷⁰I think I'll get a hamburger.

agenda n. 안건, 의제   launch v. 출시하다   presentation n. 발표
push back 미루다   improve v. 개선하다   complete v. 완료하다
helpful adj. 도움이 되는   order v. 주문하다

해석

68-70번은 다음 대화와 메뉴에 관한 문제입니다.

남: 오늘 점심 식사에 저를 만나줘서 고마워요, Claire. 오후 회의에 대해 이야기하고 싶어요. ⁶⁸저희가 출시할 신제품 때문에 안건에 많은 것이 추가되었어요. 그래서 당신의 발표는 다음 주로 미뤄질 예정이에요.
여: 이해합니다. 그렇게 하면 저에게 준비할 시간도 더 생길 거예요.
남: 고객 서비스를 개선하는 방법에 대해 이야기하실 계획이시죠, 그렇죠? ⁶⁹회사가 최근에 도움이 될 수 있는 온라인 설문조사를 완료했어요.
여: 좋은 소식이네요. ⁶⁹점심 식사 후에 살펴볼게요.
남: 좋아요. 무엇을 주문할지 결정하셨나요?
여: 저는 시저 샐러드를 주문할 거예요.
남: ⁷⁰저는 햄버거를 먹어야겠어요.

```
        Sandalwood 식당
          점심 특선 요리

1인 피자 ················· 6달러
시저 샐러드 ·············· 9달러
⁷⁰클래식 햄버거 ········· 10달러
치킨 파스타 ············· 12달러
```

68 이유 문제

해석 여자의 발표는 왜 미뤄졌는가?
(A) 회의 안건이 업데이트되었다.
(B) 기술적인 문제가 발생했다.
(C) 특별 게스트가 불참할 것이다.
(D) 회의실이 사용 중이다.

해설 질문의 핵심 어구(presentation ~ postponed)와 관련된 부분을 주의 깊게 듣는다. 남자가 "A lot has been added to the agenda because of the new product we're launching. So your presentation will be pushed back to next week."이라며 신제품 때문에 안건에 많은 것이 추가되어서 여자의 발표는 다음

주로 미뤄질 예정이라고 하였다. 따라서 (A)가 정답이다.

어휘 postpone v. 미루다   technical adj. 기술적인
absent adj. 불참한, 결근한   occupied adj. 사용 중인

69 다음에 할 일 문제

해석 여자는 점심 식사 후에 무엇을 할 것인가?
(A) 제품 가격을 비교한다.
(B) 마케팅 전략을 수정한다.
(C) 설문 결과를 검토한다.
(D) 후기를 남긴다.

해설 질문의 핵심 어구(after lunch)가 언급된 부분을 주의 깊게 듣는다. 남자가 "The company recently completed an online survey that might be helpful."이라며 회사가 최근에 도움이 될 수 있는 온라인 설문조사를 완료했다고 하자, 여자가 "I'll look through it after lunch."라며 점심 식사 후에 그것을 살펴보겠다고 하였다. 따라서 (C)가 정답이다.

어휘 compare v. 비교하다   result n. 결과

Paraphrasing

look through 살펴보다 → Go over 검토한다

70 시각 자료 문제

해석 시각 자료를 보아라. 남자의 점심 식사는 얼마일 것인가?
(A) 6달러
(B) 9달러
(C) 10달러
(D) 12달러

해설 제시된 메뉴의 정보를 확인한 후 질문의 핵심 어구(man's lunch cost)와 관련된 내용을 주의 깊게 듣는다. 남자가 "I think I'll get a hamburger."라며 햄버거를 먹어야겠다고 했고, 햄버거의 가격이 10달러임을 메뉴에서 확인할 수 있다. 따라서 (C)가 정답이다.

PART 4

[71-73]   영국식

Questions 71-73 refer to the following telephone message.

Hello. This is Michelle McGee from Voltex Technology. I'm calling with regard to order number 1198. ⁷¹**It seems that you tried to place an order for our high-resolution monitor.** ⁷²**However, the payment did not go through, so the order was never completed.** To complete the checkout process, you will need to log in to your account on our Web site and reenter your payment details. ⁷³**Once that is done, you will receive a number that allows you to track the delivery right on our Web site.** Our standard delivery time is three to five business days.

with regard to ~와 관련하여   resolution n. 해상도
checkout process 결제 절차   reenter v. 다시 입력하다
track v. 추적하다   standard adj. 표준의

해석
71-73번은 다음 전화 메시지에 관한 문제입니다.

안녕하세요. Voltex 기술사의 Michelle McGee입니다. 주문 번호 1198번과 관련하여 전화드렸습니다. ⁷¹당신이 고해상도 모니터를 주문하려고 한 것으로 보입니다. ⁷²하지만, 지불이 진행되지 않아 주문이 완료되지 않았습니다. 결제 절차를 완료하기 위해서는 저희의 웹사이트에서 계정에 로그인하시고 결제 세부 정보를 다시 입력해야 합니다. ⁷³그것이 완료되면 웹사이트에서 배송을 바로 추적할 수 있는 번호를 받으실 겁니다. 저희의 표준 배송 기간은 영업일 기준 3일에서 5일입니다.

71 화자 문제

해석 화자는 어떤 종류의 업체에서 일하는가?
(A) 조경 서비스
(B) 인터넷 서비스 제공업체
(C) 전자제품 상점
(D) 소셜 미디어 플랫폼

해설 지문에서 신분 및 직업과 관련된 표현을 놓치지 않고 듣는다. "It seems that you tried to place an order for our high-resolution monitor."라며 청자가 고해상도 모니터를 주문하려고 한 것으로 보인다고 했으므로 화자가 전자제품 상점에서 일하고 있음을 알 수 있다. 따라서 (C)가 정답이다.

72 특정 세부 사항 문제

해석 화자는 어떤 문제점을 언급하는가?
(A) 배송이 늦게 도착했다.
(B) 지불이 진행되지 않았다.
(C) 제품이 더 이상 재고가 없다.
(D) 구역이 대중에게 폐쇄되었다.

해설 질문의 핵심 어구(problem)와 관련된 내용을 주의 깊게 듣는다. "However, the payment did not go through, so the order was never completed."라며 지불이 진행되지 않아 주문이 완료되지 않았다고 하였다. 따라서 (B)가 정답이다.

어휘 shipment n. 배송   in stock 재고가 있는, 비축되어   public n. 대중

Paraphrasing

did not go through 진행되지 않았다 → was not processed 진행되지 않았다

73 특정 세부 사항 문제

해석 웹사이트에서 무엇이 이용 가능한가?
(A) 특별 할인
(B) 매장 안내도
(C) 추적 정보
(D) 영업시간

해설 질문의 핵심 어구(Web site)와 관련된 내용을 주의 깊게 듣는다. "Once that is done, you will receive a number that allows you to track the delivery right on our Web site."라며 결제가 완료되면 웹사이트에서 배송을 바로 추적할 수 있는 번호를 받을 거라고 하였다. 따라서 (C)가 정답이다.

어휘 directory n. 안내도, 안내 책자

Paraphrasing

a number that allows you to track the delivery 배송을 추적할 수 있는 번호 → Tracking information 추적 정보

[74-76]

🎧 캐나다식

Questions 74-76 refer to the following advertisement.

> ⁷⁴**If you are planning your next family vacation, consider the Grotto Campground.** Located right next to the Angel River National Park, our site provides easy access to winding forest paths, beautiful waterfront picnic areas, and much more. And ⁷⁵**unlike other campgrounds in the region, we operate a shuttle bus to take our guests to all of the local landmarks**. So what are you waiting for? ⁷⁶**Visit our official Web site today to learn more about what we offer and to book your campsite.**
>
> campground n. 캠핑장, 야영지 winding adj. 구불구불한
> path n. 길 waterfront n. 해안가 operate v. 운영하다
> landmark n. 명소, 랜드마크 official adj. 공식의 book v. 예약하다

해석

74-76번은 다음 광고에 관한 문제입니다.

⁷⁴다음 가족 휴가를 계획하고 계신다면 Grotto 캠핑장을 고려해 보세요. Angel River 국립공원 바로 옆에 위치한 저희 캠핑장에서는 구불구불한 숲길, 아름다운 해안가 피크닉 구역 등을 쉽게 이용하실 수 있습니다. 그리고 이 지역의 ⁷⁵다른 캠핑장들과 달리 저희는 셔틀버스를 운영하여 모든 지역 명소에 투숙객분들을 모셔다 드립니다. 그렇다면 무엇을 기다리고 계신가요? ⁷⁶오늘 저희의 공식 웹사이트를 방문하여 저희가 제공하는 것에 대해 자세히 알아보고 캠핑장을 예약하세요.

74 목적 문제

해석 광고의 목적은 무엇인가?
(A) 캠핑용품을 광고하기 위해
(B) 야외 행사를 위한 티켓을 판매하기 위해
(C) 휴양 시설을 홍보하기 위해
(D) 새로운 여행사를 소개하기 위해

해설 광고의 목적을 묻는 문제이므로 지문의 초반을 반드시 듣는다. "If you are planning your next family vacation, consider the Grotto Campground."라며 캠핑장을 홍보하고 있다. 따라서 (C)가 정답이다.

어휘 gear n. 용품, 장비 recreational adj. 휴양의, 오락의
travel agency 여행사

Paraphrasing

Campground 캠핑장 → recreational facility 휴양 시설

75 특정 세부 사항 문제

해석 화자의 회사는 경쟁사들과 어떻게 다른가?
(A) 장비를 무료로 제공한다.
(B) 전화 예약이 가능하다.
(C) 가족 할인을 제공한다.
(D) 교통편을 제공한다.

해설 질문의 핵심 어구(different from its competitors)와 관련된 부분을 주의 깊게 듣는다. "unlike other campgrounds in the region, we operate a shuttle bus to take our guests to all of the local landmarks"라며 다른 캠핑장들과 달리 셔틀버스를 운영하여 모든 지역 명소에 투숙객들을 데려다준다고 하였다. 따라서 (D)가 정답이다.

어휘 competitor n. 경쟁사 transportation n. 교통

Paraphrasing

operate a shuttle bus 셔틀버스를 운영한다 → provides transportation 교통편을 제공한다

76 이유 문제

해석 청자들은 왜 웹사이트를 방문해야 하는가?
(A) 예약하기 위해
(B) 후기를 게시하기 위해
(C) 티켓을 구입하기 위해
(D) 쿠폰을 다운로드하기 위해

해설 질문의 핵심 어구(visit a Web site)가 언급된 주변을 주의 깊게 듣는다. "Visit our official Web site today to learn more about what we offer and to book your campsite."라며 공식 웹사이트를 방문하여 제공하는 것에 대해 자세히 알아보고 캠핑장을 예약하라고 하였다. 따라서 (A)가 정답이다.

어휘 purchase v. 구입하다

Paraphrasing

book 예약하다 → make a reservation 예약하다

[77-79]

🎧 미국식

Questions 77-79 refer to the following instructions.

> Hello, I'm Marcia Gray from Arkane Software. ⁷⁷**I'm here to train you on using the latest version of Schedule Bee, your project management software.** Before we start training, let me talk about this version. ⁷⁸**It will help you analyze data and produce reports much faster compared to what you are used to.** Everyone's ready? Then, let's try it to become familiar with its features. ⁷⁹**Please turn on your laptop or tablet.**
>
> management n. 관리 analyze v. 분석하다 familiar adj. 익숙한
> feature n. 기능, 특징

해석

77-79번은 다음 설명에 관한 문제입니다.

안녕하세요, 저는 Arkane 소프트웨어사의 Marcia Gray입니다. ⁷⁷저는 프로젝트 관리 소프트웨어인 Schedule Bee의 최신 버전을 사용하는 방법을 교육하러 이곳에 왔습니다. 교육을 시작하기 전에 이 버전에 대해 말씀드릴게요. ⁷⁸그것은 여러분들이 기존에 사용하던 것과 비교해서 훨씬 더 빠르게 데이터를 분석하고 보고서를 작성하는 데 도움이 될 것입니다. 모두 준비되셨죠? 그러면, 그것의 기능에 익숙해지도록 한번 사용해 보죠. ⁷⁹여러분의 노트북이나 태블릿을 켜주세요.

77 특정 세부 사항 문제

해석 교육의 중점은 무엇인가?
(A) 광고 만들기
(B) 소프트웨어 사용하기
(C) 회사 정책 이해하기
(D) 고객 불만 처리하기

해설 질문의 핵심 어구(focus of the training)와 관련된 부분을 주의 깊게 듣는다. "I'm here to train you on using the latest version of Schedule Bee, your project management software."라며 프로젝트 관리 소프트웨어의 최신 버전을 사용하는 방법을 교육하러 이곳에 왔다고 하였다. 따라서 (B)가 정답이다.

어휘 process v. 처리하다 complaint n. 항의, 불만

78 특정 세부 사항 문제

해석 화자에 따르면, 새 버전의 특징은 무엇인가?
(A) 설치하는 것이 더 쉽다.
(B) 다양한 언어를 지원한다.
(C) 고품질의 그래픽을 만들어낸다.
(D) 업무 진행 속도를 높인다.

해설 질문의 핵심 어구(new version)와 관련된 내용을 주의 깊게 듣는다. "It will help you analyze data and produce reports much faster compared to what you are used to."라며 기존에 사용하던 것과 비교해서 훨씬 더 빠르게 데이터를 분석하고 보고서를 작성하는 데 도움이 될 거라고 하였다. 따라서 (D)가 정답이다.

어휘 install v. 설치하다 high-quality adj. 고품질의

79 요청 문제

해석 청자들은 무엇을 하도록 요청받는가?
(A) 비밀번호를 변경한다.
(B) 최신 소식을 제시한다.
(C) 기기를 활성화한다.
(D) 신분 확인 명찰을 단다.

해설 지문의 중후반에서 요청과 관련된 표현이 포함된 부분을 주의 깊게 듣는다. "Please turn on your laptop or tablet."이라며 노트북이나 태블릿을 켜 달라고 하였다. 따라서 (C)가 정답이다.

어휘 activate v. 활성화하다 identification n. 신분 확인, 신분증

Paraphrasing

turn on ~ laptop or tablet 노트북이나 태블릿을 켜다 → Activate devices 기기를 활성화한다

[80-82]

Questions 80-82 refer to the following talk.

Good morning, everyone. ⁸⁰This is Seaward Technology's main laboratory, where my colleagues and I perform tests and develop new materials. As you will be working here during your internship, I would like to show you around today. ⁸¹Please make sure to put on the coveralls and safety goggles that I gave you a few minutes ago. Additionally, remove all electronic devices because they can interfere with the equipment. ⁸²You may leave them on this tray, but we've also got some lockers. They are in the room just through that door behind you.

laboratory n. 연구소, 실험실 material n. 재료 coverall n. 작업복
safety goggle 보안경 equipment n. 장비 locker n. 사물함

해석 80-82번은 다음 담화에 관한 문제입니다.
좋은 아침입니다, 여러분. ⁸⁰이곳은 Seaward 기술사의 메인 연구소이며, 제 동료들과 함께 테스트를 수행하고 새로운 재료를 개발하는 곳입니다. 여러분의 인턴십 기간 동안 이곳에서 일하게 되셨으니, 오늘 주변을 안내해 드리고 싶습니다. ⁸¹몇 분 전에 제가 드린 전신 작업복과 보안경을 반드시 착용해 주세요. 또한, 모든 전자 기기는 장비에 지장을 줄 수 있으므로 풀어주세요. ⁸²그것들을 이 판 위에 두어도 되지만, 저희는 사물함도 몇 개 있습니다. 그것들은 여러분들의 뒤에 있는 문을 지나서 바로 있는 방에 있습니다.

80 화자 문제

해석 화자는 누구일 것 같은가?
(A) 공무원
(B) 상담가
(C) 연구원
(D) 판매 직원

해설 지문에서 신분 및 직업과 관련된 표현을 놓치지 않고 듣는다. "This is Seaward Technology's main laboratory, where my colleagues and I perform tests and develop new materials."라며 이곳은 Seaward 기술사의 메인 연구소로, 동료들과 함께 테스트를 수행하고 새로운 재료를 개발하는 곳이라고 했으므로 화자가 연구원임을 알 수 있다. 따라서 (C)가 정답이다.

81 특정 세부 사항 문제

해석 청자들은 앞서 무엇을 받았는가?
(A) 보호 장비
(B) 건물 지도
(C) 직원 매뉴얼
(D) 보안 카드

해설 질문의 핵심 어구(receive earlier)와 관련된 부분을 주의 깊게 듣는다. "Please make sure to put on the coveralls and safety goggles that I gave you a few minutes ago."라며 몇 분 전에 준 전신 작업복과 보안경을 반드시 착용해달라고 하였다. 따라서 (A)가 정답이다.

어휘 protective adj. 보호의 security n. 보안, 경비

Paraphrasing

coveralls and safety goggles 전신 작업복과 보안경 → Protective equipment 보호 장비

82 의도 파악 문제

해석 화자는 왜 "저희는 사물함도 몇 개 있습니다"라고 말하는가?

(A) 업무를 할당하기 위해
(B) 확신을 주기 위해
(C) 정책 변경을 설명하기 위해
(D) 대안을 제시하기 위해

해설 질문의 인용어구(we've also got some lockers)가 언급된 주변을 주의 깊게 듣는다. "You may leave them on this tray"라며 이 판 위에 그것들(전자 기기)을 두어도 된다고 했으므로 물건을 둘 수 있는 또 다른 장소를 제공하기 위함임을 알 수 있다. 따라서 (D)가 정답이다.

어휘 assign v. 할당하다 assurance n. 확신 alternative n. 대안

[83-85]
캐나다식

Questions 83-85 refer to the following announcement.

> [83]Attention, representatives of all participating companies. The home bathroom showcase will begin in an hour in Hall D of the convention center. Before the doors are opened to the public, everything must be prepared. [84]Therefore, we ask that you check your booth to ensure that your materials are set up properly. All booths are equipped with power outlets and lighting. If you experience any issues with these, [85]we have staff members throughout the hall. Simply speak with one of them to receive assistance.
>
> representative n. 대표 participate v. 참가하다
> ensure v. 확실하게 하다 outlet n. 콘센트
> experience v. 겪다, 경험하다 assistance n. 도움

해석
83-85번은 다음 공고에 관한 문제입니다.
[83]주목해 주세요, 모든 참가 기업 대표 여러분. 가정용 욕실 쇼케이스는 컨벤션 센터 D홀에서 한 시간 후에 시작될 것입니다. 대중에게 공개되기 전에 모든 것이 준비되어 있어야 합니다. [84]그러므로, 여러분들의 부스를 확인하여 자재가 제대로 설치되어 있는지 확인하시기 바랍니다. 모든 부스에는 콘센트와 조명이 구비되어 있습니다. 이것들에 대해 문제를 겪으신다면, [85]홀 전체에 직원들이 있습니다. 도움을 받으시기 위해서는 그들 중 한 명에게 이야기하시면 됩니다.

83 주제 문제

해설 어떤 종류의 행사가 열리고 있는 것 같은가?
(A) 음식 축제
(B) 시상식
(C) 기자회견
(D) 산업 박람회

해설 공고의 주제를 묻는 문제이므로 지문의 초반을 반드시 듣는다. "Attention, representatives of all participating companies. The home bathroom showcase will begin"이라며 참가 기업 대표자들에게 가정용 욕실 쇼케이스가 시작될 것이라고 하였다. 따라서 (D)가 정답이다.

84 요청 문제

해설 화자는 청자들에게 무엇을 하라고 요청하는가?

(A) 기기를 설치한다.
(B) 문을 연다.
(C) 부스를 점검한다.
(D) 콘센트를 점검한다.

해설 지문의 중후반에서 요청과 관련된 표현이 포함된 문장을 주의 깊게 듣는다. "Therefore, we ask that you check your booth to ensure that your materials are set up properly."라며 여러분들의 부스를 확인하여 자재가 제대로 설치되어 있는지 확인하라고 하였다. 따라서 (C)가 정답이다.

어휘 inspect v. 점검하다

85 방법 문제

해설 화자에 따르면, 청자들은 어떻게 도움을 요청할 수 있는가?
(A) 직원에게 이야기함으로써
(B) 안내소에 방문함으로써
(C) 양식을 작성함으로써
(D) 모바일 애플리케이션을 사용함으로써

해설 질문의 핵심 어구(request help)와 관련된 내용을 주의 깊게 듣는다. "we have staff members throughout the hall. Simply speak with one of them to receive assistance"라며 홀 전체에 직원들이 있으니 도움을 받기 위해서는 그들 중 한 명에게 이야기하면 된다고 하였다. 따라서 (A)가 정답이다.

어휘 complete v. 작성하다, 완료하다

[86-88]
영국식

Questions 86-88 refer to the following radio broadcast.

> This is Hannah Tanner with your evening news. [86]Organizers of the music festival in Kinley Park this weekend have decided to postpone the event due to unexpected heavy rains. They were planning to move all the performances indoors but have chosen to reschedule the festival instead. [87]The ticketholders were asked to share feedback about this plan on the festival's Web site. And nobody raised any issues. Full refunds will be issued to anyone unable to attend on the new dates. [88]Regarding the weather, please stay tuned. Our expert, Greg Harvey, will be here to provide the forecast for this weekend.
>
> postpone v. 연기하다 indoors adv. 실내로
> reschedule v. 일정을 변경하다 ticketholder n. 티켓 소지자
> refund n. 환불 unable adj. ~할 수 없는 forecast n. 예보

해석
86-88번은 다음 라디오 방송에 관한 문제입니다.
저녁 뉴스와 함께하는 저는 Hannah Tanner입니다. [86]이번 주말 Kinley 공원에서 열리는 음악 행사의 주최 측은 예상치 못한 폭우로 인해 행사를 연기하기로 결정했습니다. 모든 공연을 실내로 옮길 계획이었지만 대신 행사 일정을 변경하기로 결정했습니다. [87]티켓 소지자들은 행사 웹사이트에서 이 계획에 대한 피드백을 공유하도록 요청받았습니다. 그리고 아무도 문제를 제기하지 않았습니다. 새로운 날짜에 참석할 수 없는 분들께 전액 환불이 제공될 것입니다. [88]날씨와 관련해서는 채널 고정해 주세요. 우리의 전문가인 Greg Harvey가 이번 주말에 대한 예보를 알려드리기 위해 이곳에 계실 것입니다.

86 주제 문제

해석 방송은 주로 무엇에 대한 것인가?
(A) 행사 일정의 변경
(B) 라디오 진행자의 은퇴
(C) 음악 행사의 출연진
(D) 공연을 위한 리허설

해석 방송의 주제를 묻고 있으므로 지문의 초반을 반드시 듣는다. "Organizers of the music festival in Kinley Park this weekend have decided to postpone the event due to unexpected heavy rains."라며 이번 주말 Kinley 공원에서 열리는 음악 행사의 주최 측은 예상치 못한 폭우로 인해 행사를 연기하기로 결정했다고 한 후, 행사 일정의 변경에 대한 내용으로 지문이 이어지고 있다. 따라서 (A)가 정답이다.

어휘 retirement n. 은퇴 lineup n. 출연진, 인원

87 의도 파악 문제

해석 화자는 "아무도 문제를 제기하지 않았습니다"라고 말할 때 무엇을 의도하는가?
(A) 의견이 요청되지 않았다.
(B) 결정이 지지를 받았다.
(C) 회의 일정이 변경되었다.
(D) 정보를 얻을 수 없었다.

해석 질문의 인용어구(nobody raised any issues)가 언급된 주변을 주의 깊게 듣는다. "The ticketholders were asked to share feedback about this plan on the festival's Web site."라며 티켓 소지자들은 행사 웹사이트에서 일정 변경 계획에 대한 피드백을 공유하도록 요청받았다고 한 후, 아무도 문제를 제기하지 않았다고 했으므로 일정 변경 계획에 대해 모두 지지했음을 알 수 있다. 따라서 (B)가 정답이다.

어휘 request v. 요청하다 decision n. 결정

88 다음에 할 일 문제

해석 청자들은 다음에 무엇을 들을 것인가?
(A) 일기 예보
(B) 광고
(C) 최신 교통 정보
(D) 새로운 노래

해석 질문의 핵심 어구(hear next)와 관련된 내용을 주의 깊게 듣는다. "Regarding the weather, please stay tuned. Our expert, Greg Harvey, will be here to provide the forecast for this weekend."라며 날씨와 관련해서는 채널을 고정해 달라고 했고, Greg Harvey가 이번 주말에 대한 예보를 알려줄 것이라고 하였다. 따라서 (A)가 정답이다.

[89-91]   호주식

Questions 89-91 refer to the following excerpt from a meeting.

⁸⁹**Let's take a moment to welcome Mr. Jones to our team.** He has transferred from our Adelaide branch, where he's been for the last four years. ⁹⁰**He'll be reviewing customer applications for car loans and mortgages.** I'm sure he will do well in this role. ⁹¹**During his time at the Adelaide branch, Mr. Jones streamlined the loan-approval procedure, reducing wait times by up to 20 percent.** It is my hope that he will be able to make similar changes here.

transfer v. 전근 가다 application n. 신청, 지원 loan n. 대출
mortgage n. 융자, 대출 streamline v. 간소화하다
procedure n. 절차

해석
89-91번은 다음 회의 발췌록에 관한 문제입니다.
⁸⁹Mr. Jones를 우리 팀에 환영하는 시간을 가져봅시다. 그는 지난 4년간 근무했던 애들레이드 지점에서 전근을 왔습니다. ⁹⁰그는 자동차 대출과 융자에 대한 고객 신청을 검토할 것입니다. 저는 그가 이 역할을 잘 해낼 것이라 확신합니다. ⁹¹그가 애들레이드 지점에서 일하는 동안, Mr. Jones는 대출 승인 절차를 간소화하여 대기 시간을 최대 20퍼센트까지 단축했습니다. 그가 이곳에서 비슷한 변화를 가져올 수 있기를 바랍니다.

89 주제 문제

해석 화자는 주로 무엇에 대해 이야기하고 있는가?
(A) 유지 관리 보고
(B) 새로운 팀원
(C) 지점 폐쇄
(D) 고객 항의

해석 회의의 주제를 묻는 문제이므로, 지문의 초반을 반드시 듣는다. "Let's take a moment to welcome Mr. Jones to our team."이라며 Mr. Jones를 팀에 환영하는 시간을 가져보자고 하였다. 따라서 (B)가 정답이다.

어휘 maintenance n. 유지 관리 closure n. 폐쇄, 종료

90 청자 문제

해석 청자들은 어디에서 일하는 것 같은가?
(A) 자동차 대리점에서
(B) 금융 기관에서
(C) 건설 회사에서
(D) 부동산 중개소에서

해석 지문에서 신분 및 직업과 관련된 표현을 놓치지 않고 듣는다. "He'll be reviewing customer applications for car loans and mortgages."라며 그는 자동차 대출과 융자에 대한 고객 신청을 검토할 예정이라고 했으므로 청자들은 금융 기관에서 일하고 있음을 알 수 있다. 따라서 (B)가 정답이다.

91 특정 세부 사항 문제

해석 화자는 어떤 일이 일어나기를 바라는가?
(A) 금액이 훨씬 더 늘어날 것이다.
(B) 신청서가 주의 깊게 검토될 것이다.
(C) 절차가 더 효율적이게 될 것이다.
(D) 이체가 빨리 승인될 것이다.

해석 질문의 핵심 어구(hope will happen)와 관련된 내용을 주의 깊게

듣는다. "During his time at the Adelaide branch, Mr. Jones streamlined the loan-approval procedure, reducing wait times by up to 20 percent. It is my hope that he will be able to make similar changes here."라며 Mr. Jones가 애들레이드 지점에서 일하는 동안 대출 승인 절차를 간소화하여 대기 시간을 20퍼센트까지 단축했고 이곳에서 비슷한 변화를 가져오기를 바란다고 하였다. 따라서 (C)가 정답이다.

어휘 efficient adj. 효율적인 approve v. 승인하다

[92-94]

🎧 영국식

Questions 92-94 refer to the following excerpt from a meeting.

> Thank you for attending this presentation. ⁹²**I realize that as city council members, you all have busy schedules.** The time has come to replace the bus stop shelters in our community. ⁹³**Many are in bad condition, with cracked roofs and peeling paint.** Myron Engineering builds a model that is quite impressive. Although ⁹⁴**we would need to increase our budget to install these**, each includes a digital display for advertisements. So ⁹⁴**the city could charge companies fees to promote their products.**
>
> city council 시의회 replace v. 교체하다 shelter n. 쉼터, 보호소
> crack v. 금이 가다 impressive adj. 인상적인

해석
92-94번은 다음 회의 발췌록에 관한 문제입니다.
이 발표에 참석해 주셔서 감사합니다. ⁹²시 의원으로서 여러분 모두 바쁜 일정을 보내고 있다는 것을 알고 있습니다. 이제 우리 지역사회의 버스 정류장 쉼터를 교체할 때가 왔습니다. ⁹³많은 것들이 금이 간 지붕과 벗겨진 페인트가 있는 등 상태가 좋지 않습니다. Myron 엔지니어링사는 꽤 인상적인 모델을 구축합니다. ⁹⁴이것들을 설치하기 위해서는 예산을 늘려야 하지만, 각각은 광고를 할 수 있는 디지털 화면을 포함합니다. 따라서 시는 기업들에 그들의 제품 홍보를 위한 수수료를 부과할 수도 있습니다.

92 청자 문제

해설 화자는 누구에게 발표하고 있는가?
(A) 건설 근로자들
(B) 시 의원들
(C) 영업 직원들
(D) 지역 기자들

해설 지문에서 신분 및 직업과 관련된 표현을 놓치지 않고 듣는다. "I realize that as city council members, you all have busy schedules."라며 시의원으로서 여러분 모두 바쁜 일정을 보내고 있다는 것을 알고 있다고 했으므로 청자들이 시 의원들임을 알 수 있다. 따라서 (B)가 정답이다.

어휘 representative n. 직원, 대리인 journalist n. 기자

93 언급 문제

해설 화자는 몇몇 기존의 구조물에 대해 무엇을 말하는가?
(A) 건설 중이다.
(B) 자주 이용되지 않는다.
(C) 파손되어 있다.
(D) 유지하기에 비용이 많이 든다.

해설 질문의 핵심 어구(existing structures)와 관련된 내용을 주의 깊게 듣는다. "Many are in bad condition, with cracked roofs and peeling paint."라며 많은 것들이 금이 간 지붕과 벗겨진 페인트가 있는 등 상태가 좋지 않다고 하였다. 따라서 (C)가 정답이다.

어휘 existing adj. 기존의 disrepair n. 파손

Paraphrasing

in bad condition, with cracked roofs and peeling paint 금이 간 지붕과 벗겨진 페인트가 있는 등 상태가 좋지 않은 → in disrepair 파손되어 있는

94 의도 파악 문제

해설 화자는 왜 "각각은 광고를 할 수 있는 디지털 화면을 포함합니다"라고 말하는가?
(A) 정보를 정정하기 위해
(B) 비용을 정당화하기 위해
(C) 문제를 말하기 위해
(D) 서비스 지연을 설명하기 위해

해설 질문의 인용어구(each includes a digital display for advertisements)가 언급된 주변을 주의 깊게 듣는다. "we would need to increase our budget to install these"라며 버스 정류장 쉼터를 설치하기 위해서는 예산을 늘려야 한다고 한 후, "the city could charge companies fees to promote their products"라며 시는 기업들에 제품 홍보를 위한 수수료를 부과할 수 있을 것이라고 하였다. 따라서 예산을 늘려야 하기는 하지만 광고를 할 수 있는 디지털 화면이 있어서 나중에 기업들에 수수료를 받을 수 있다는 의미이므로 비용을 정당화하기 위해 한 말임을 알 수 있다. 따라서 (B)가 정답이다.

어휘 justify v. 정당화하다 state v. 말하다, 진술하다

[95-97]

🎧 미국식

Questions 95-97 refer to the following talk and pie chart.

> I'd like to thank everyone for helping the company achieve its growth targets for the year. You have done an incredible job improving our position. At the same time, as you can see from this chart, ⁹⁵**we only have 19 percent of the market share in our industry**. For that reason, ⁹⁶**I'd like us to win new customers**. To do that, we'll need to come up with some strategies we can implement next year. ⁹⁷**I asked Ms. Keith in market research to help us by doing a detailed survey of consumers. She will now share her findings with us.**
>
> growth n. 성장 incredible adj. 놀라운 industry n. 업계, 산업
> implement v. 실행하다 finding n. 결과

해설
95-97번은 다음 담화와 원 그래프에 관한 문제입니다.
회사가 올해 성장 목표를 달성할 수 있도록 도와준 모든 분들께 감사드립니다. 여러분은 우리의 입지를 향상시키는 데 놀라운 일을 해냈습니다. 동시에, 이 차트에서 볼 수 있듯이, ⁹⁵우리는 업계에서 19퍼센트의 시장 점유율

만 가지고 있습니다. 그렇기 때문에 ⁹⁶저는 우리가 새로운 고객을 확보했으면 좋겠습니다. 그러기 위해서는 내년에 실행할 수 있는 몇 가지 전략을 마련해야 합니다. ⁹⁷저는 시장 조사팀의 Ms. Keith에게 소비자에 대한 자세한 설문조사를 해서 저희를 도와줄 것을 요청했습니다. 그녀가 지금 결과를 우리와 공유할 것입니다.

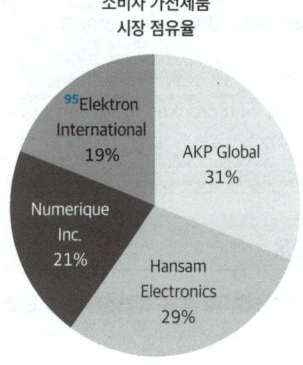

소비자 가전제품 시장 점유율
⁹⁵Elektron International 19%
AKP Global 31%
Hansam Electronics 29%
Numerique Inc. 21%

95 시각 자료 문제

해석 시각 자료를 보아라. 화자는 어떤 회사에서 일하는가?
(A) AKP Global
(B) Hansam Electronics
(C) Numerique Inc.
(D) Elektron International

해설 제시된 원 그래프의 정보를 확인한 후 질문의 핵심 어구(speaker work)와 관련된 내용을 주의 깊게 듣는다. "we only have 19 percent of the market share in our industry"라며 우리는 업계에서 19퍼센트의 시장 점유율만 가지고 있다고 했고, 시장 점유율이 19퍼센트인 회사는 Elektron International임을 원 그래프에서 알 수 있다. 따라서 (D)가 정답이다.

96 특정 세부 사항 문제

해석 화자는 무엇을 하기를 원하는가?
(A) 회사 광고를 늘린다.
(B) 새로운 직책을 추가한다.
(C) 새로운 고객을 확보한다.
(D) 마케팅 회사를 고용한다.

해설 질문의 핵심 어구(speaker want to do)와 관련된 내용을 주의 깊게 듣는다. "I'd like us to win new customers."라며 우리가 새로운 고객을 확보하면 좋겠다고 하였다. 따라서 (C)가 정답이다.

어휘 job position 직책 acquire v. 확보하다, 얻다

Paraphrasing
win new customers 새로운 고객 확보하기 → Acquire new clients 새로운 고객을 확보한다

97 특정 세부 사항 문제

해석 Ms. Keith는 다음에 무엇을 할 것인가?
(A) 제품을 시연한다.
(B) 설문조사 결과를 제시한다.
(C) 질문지를 나누어 준다.
(D) 금융 보고서를 준다.

해설 질문의 핵심 어구(Ms. Keith do next)와 관련된 내용을 주의 깊게 듣는다. "I asked Ms. Keith in market research to help us by doing a detailed survey of consumers. She will now share her findings with us."라며 시장 조사팀의 Ms. Keith에게 소비자에 대한 자세한 설문조사를 해서 우리를 도와줄 것을 요청했고, 그녀가 지금 결과를 우리와 공유할 것이라고 하였다. 따라서 (B)가 정답이다.

어휘 demonstrate v. 시연하다 present v. 제시하다
hand out ~을 나누어 주다 questionnaire n. 질문지, 설문지

[98-100] 호주식

Questions 98-100 refer to the following announcement and schedule.

> Attention, all passengers. ⁹⁸**Train 11, bound for Midland, has been canceled due to engine trouble.** We apologize for the inconvenience and assure you that we are doing our best to restore normal service as quickly as possible. ⁹⁹**Passengers holding tickets for this train may make use of shuttle buses.** These buses will depart from Terminal B. Alternatively, ¹⁰⁰**they may wait to board today's final train bound for Midland at 3:20 P.M.** For further inquiries, please approach your nearest information booth.
>
> passenger n. 승객 bound for ~행의 inconvenience n. 불편
> assure v. 보장하다, 확인하다 restore v. 복구하다
> make use of ~을 이용하다 depart v. 출발하다

해석 98-100번은 다음 공지와 일정표에 관한 문제입니다.

주목해 주세요, 승객 여러분. ⁹⁸Midland행 11번 열차가 엔진 문제로 인해 취소되었습니다. 불편을 끼쳐 죄송하며 가능한 한 빠르게 정상적인 서비스를 복구하기 위해 최선을 다하겠습니다. ⁹⁹이 열차의 티켓을 가지고 있는 승객들은 셔틀버스를 이용할 수 있습니다. 이 버스들은 B 터미널에서 출발할 것입니다. 또는 ¹⁰⁰오후 3시 20분에 오늘 Midland로 가는 마지막 열차에 탑승하기 위해 기다리셔도 됩니다. 자세한 문의는 가장 가까운 안내 부스를 방문해 주세요.

열차 번호	출발 시간
11	오후 1:10
81	오후 2:35
¹⁰⁰25	오후 3:20
20	오후 4:45

98 이유 문제

해석 일정은 왜 변경되었는가?
(A) 근로자 집단이 파업했다.
(B) 역에 정전이 발생했다.
(C) 선로에서 신호 장애가 발생했다.
(D) 열차에 수리가 필요하다.

해설 질문의 핵심 어구(schedule changed)와 관련된 내용을 주의 깊

게 듣는다. "Train 11, bound for Midland, has been canceled due to engine trouble."이라며 Midland행 11번 열차가 엔진 문제로 인해 취소되었다고 하였다. 따라서 (D)가 정답이다.

어휘 strike n. 파업 outage n. 정전, 단수 repair n. 수리

99 특정 세부 사항 문제

해석 몇몇 승객들에게 무엇이 제공될 것인가?
(A) 무료 한 달 정기권
(B) 셔틀 서비스
(C) 티켓 환불
(D) 무료 음료

해설 질문의 핵심 어구(offered to some passengers)와 관련된 내용을 주의 깊게 듣는다. "Passengers holding tickets for this train may make use of shuttle buses."라며 이 열차의 티켓을 가지고 있는 승객들은 셔틀버스를 이용할 수 있다고 하였다. 따라서 (B)가 정답이다.

어휘 monthly adj. 한 달의, 매월의 complimentary adj. 무료의

100 시각 자료 문제

해석 시각 자료를 보아라. 어떤 열차가 Midland로 가는 오늘의 마지막 기차인가?
(A) 11
(B) 81
(C) 25
(D) 20

해설 제시된 일정표의 정보를 확인한 후 질문의 핵심 어구(last train to Midland)와 관련된 내용을 주의 깊게 듣는다. "they may wait to board today's final train bound for Midland at 3:20 P.M."이라며 오후 3시 20분에 오늘 Midland로 가는 마지막 열차에 탑승하기 위해 기다려도 된다고 했고, 3시 20분에 출발하는 기차는 25번 열차임을 일정표에서 알 수 있다. 따라서 (C)가 정답이다.

PART 5

101 재귀대명사 채우기

해설 빈칸 앞에 4형식 동사 buy의 과거형(bought)이 쓰였고 빈칸 뒤에 직접 목적어(a comfortable chair)가 쓰였으므로 빈칸에는 간접 목적어 자리에 올 수 있는 목적격 인칭대명사 (B), 소유대명사 (C), 재귀대명사 (D)가 정답의 후보이다. 'Ms. Tate는 그녀의 홈 오피스 환경을 개선하기 위해 그녀 자신에게 편안한 의자를 사 주었다'라는 의미가 되어야 하므로 주어와 목적어가 같은 사람을 지칭할 때 목적어 자리에 올 수 있는 재귀대명사 (D) herself가 정답이다. 목적격 인칭대명사 (B) her를 쓸 경우 'Ms. Tate는 그녀의 홈 오피스 환경을 개선하기 위해 그녀에게(Ms. Tate가 아닌 다른 사람에게) 편안한 의자를 사 주다'라는 어색한 의미가 되고, 소유대명사 (C) hers를 쓸 경우 'Ms. Tate는 그녀의 홈 오피스 환경을 개선하기 위해 그녀의 것에게 편안한 의자를 사 주다'라는 어색한 의미를 만들기 때문에 답이 될 수 없다. 주격 인칭대명사 (A)는 목적어 자리에 올 수 없다.

해석 Ms. Tate는 그녀의 홈 오피스 환경을 개선하기 위해 그녀 자신에게 편안한 의자를 사 주었다.

어휘 improve v. 개선하다, 향상시키다

102 전치사 채우기

해설 이 문장은 주어가 생략된 명령문으로 필수성분(Please make sure ~ books)을 갖춘 완전한 절이므로, ___ the due date는 수식어 거품으로 보아야 한다. 이 수식어 거품은 동사가 없는 거품구이므로, 거품구를 이끌 수 있는 전치사 (A)와 (D)가 정답의 후보이다. '예정일까지 반드시 반납하다'라는 의미가 되어야 하므로 (D) by(~까지)가 정답이다. (A) for는 '~ 동안'이라는 의미로 어색한 의미를 만들기 때문에 답이 될 수 없다. 부사 또는 부사절 접속사 (B) once(한 번; ~할 때)와 형용사 또는 부사 (C) next(다음의; 그다음에)는 수식어 거품구를 이끌 수 없다.

해석 모든 도서관 책들을 예정일까지 반드시 반납하세요, 그렇게 하지 않으면 추가 대출이 제한될 것입니다.

어휘 borrowing n. 대출 restrict v. 제한하다

103 비교급 표현 채우기

해설 빈칸은 be동사(is)의 주격 보어 자리이고 빈칸 뒤에 than(~보다)이 왔으므로, 형용사 brief(간결한)의 비교급 (D) briefer가 정답이다.

해석 관리자의 이메일 요약본은 완전한 보고서보다 더 간결하지만, 여전히 모든 중요점을 다루고 있다.

어휘 summary n. 요약(본) full adj. 완전한 still adv. 여전히

104 다른 명사를 수식하는 명사 채우기

해설 빈칸은 동사(is introducing)의 목적어 자리이므로 빈칸 앞 명사 service와 함께 복합 명사를 이룰 수 있는 명사 (B)와 (C)가 정답의 후보이다. 빈칸 앞에 부정관사 a가 있으므로 단수 명사 (B) category(범주)가 정답이다. 동사 (A)와 형용사 (D)는 명사 자리에 올 수 없다.

해석 Innova 통신사는 더 큰 시장 점유율을 차지하기 위해 새로운 서비스 범주를 내놓을 것이다.

어휘 capture v. 차지하다, 붙잡다 market share 시장 점유율

105 형용사 어휘 고르기

해설 '긍정적인 평가를 받아서, 임금 인상을 받다'라는 문맥이므로 (C) positive(긍정적인)가 정답이다. (A) detailed는 '상세한', (B) convenient는 '편리한', (D) mandatory는 '의무적인'이라는 의미이다.

해석 Mr. Arnold는 그의 연례 성과 평가에 대해 긍정적인 평가를 받아서, 임금 인상을 받았다.

어휘 evaluation n. 평가 raise n. (물가·임금 등의) 인상

106 형용사 자리 채우기

해설 빈칸 뒤의 명사(story)를 꾸밀 수 있는 것은 형용사이므로 형용사 (B) moving(감동적인)이 정답이다. 부사 (A) movingly(감동적으

로)는 명사를 꾸밀 수 없다. 명사 (C) mover(움직이는 사람)와 (D) movement(움직임)는 story(이야기)와 복합 명사를 이루지 못한다.

해석 그 영화는 살아남기 위해 많은 도전들을 극복하는 19세기의 한 중국인 가족에 대한 감동적인 이야기를 표현한다.

어휘 overcome v. 극복하다

107 명사 자리 채우기

해설 빈칸은 소유격(his)의 꾸밈을 받는 명사 자리이므로 명사 (C) resignation(사임)이 정답이다. 동사 또는 과거분사 (A), 동사 (B), to 부정사 (D)는 소유격의 꾸밈을 받을 수 없다.

해석 Draper 식품회사의 주가는 최고 재무 경영자가 공개적으로 그의 사임을 발표한 후에 떨어졌다.

어휘 stock price 주가   publicly adv. 공개적으로

108 동사 어휘 고르기

해설 '독일에서 수입되는 부품의 수령 지연으로 인해 생산 일정이 조정되다'라는 문맥이므로 import(수입하다)의 과거분사 (B) imported가 정답이다. (A)의 maintain은 '유지하다', (C)의 reflect는 '반영하다', (D)의 preserve는 '보존하다'라는 의미이다.

해석 독일에서 수입되는 부품의 수령 지연으로 인해 생산 일정이 조정되었다.

어휘 adjust v. 조정하다   component n. 부품

109 태에 맞는 동사 채우기

해설 종속절(while ~ ____)에 주어(the main entrance)만 있고 동사가 없으므로 동사인 (A), (C), (D)가 정답의 후보이다. 주어(the main entrance)와 동사(paint)가 '정문이 페인트칠 되다'라는 수동의 의미가 되어야 하므로 현재진행 수동태 (D) is being painted가 정답이다.

해석 직원들은 정문이 페인트칠 되는 동안 지정된 출입 장소를 이용해야 한다.

어휘 designated adj. 지정된

110 부사 자리 채우기

해설 동사(be priced)를 꾸밀 수 있는 것은 부사이므로 부사 (A) competitively(경쟁력 있게)가 정답이다. 명사 (B)와 (D), 형용사 (C)는 동사를 꾸밀 수 없다.

해석 Barrera 의류사의 제품들은 베트남 시장을 위해 경쟁력 있게 값을 매겨져야 하는데, 그렇지 않으면 그것들은 팔리지 않을 것이다.

어휘 price v. 값을 매기다   sell v. 팔리다, 팔다

111 to 부정사의 in order to 채우기

해설 이 문장은 필수성분(The marketing team ~ extensive research)을 갖춘 완전한 절이므로 ____ better understand customers' needs는 수식어 거품으로 보아야 한다. 빈칸 뒤의 동사(understand)를 이끌면서 '고객들의 욕구를 더 잘 이해하기 위해'라는 목적을 나타내는 (D) in order to가 정답이다. 부사절 접속사 (A)와 (B)는 주어와 동사로 이루어진 거품절을 이끌고, 접속부사 (C)는 문장과 문장을 연결하므로 답이 될 수 없다.

해석 Baldwin 미디어사의 마케팅팀은 고객들의 욕구를 더 잘 이해하기 위해 광범위한 조사를 수행했다.

어휘 extensive adj. 광범위한, 대규모의

112 명사 자리 채우기

해설 부정관사(an)와 전치사(to) 사이에 올 수 있는 것은 명사이므로 명사 (B) exception(예외)이 정답이다. 전치사 또는 접속사 (A)와 형용사 (C), 부사 (D)는 명사 자리에 올 수 없다.

해석 Pollard 모바일사의 복장 규정은 캐주얼 업무 복장이지만, 금요일마다 이 규칙에 대한 예외가 적용된다.

어휘 rule n. 규칙   exceptional adj. 예외의, 특출한

113 등위접속사 채우기

해설 빈칸은 절(Hurst Designs made ~ to the building's interior)과 절(left the outside ~ unchanged)을 연결할 수 있는 접속사 자리이므로 등위접속사인 (B), (C), (D)가 정답의 후보이다. '건물의 내부에는 뚜렷한 변경을 주었지만 그것의 외부는 대부분 바뀌지 않은 채로 남겨두었다'라는 의미가 되어야 하므로 (D) but(하지만)이 정답이다. 참고로, 등위접속사로 연결된 절에서 등위접속사 뒤에 중복된 단어(Hurst Designs)가 생략되었음을 알아둔다. (B) or는 '또는', (C) so는 '그래서'라는 의미로, 모두 어색한 의미를 만들기 때문에 답이 될 수 없다. 부사 (A) not(~이 아니다)은 접속사 자리에 올 수 없다.

해석 Hurst 디자인사는 그 건물의 내부에는 뚜렷한 변경을 주었지만 그것의 외부는 대부분 바뀌지 않은 채로 남겨두었다.

어휘 noticeable adj. 뚜렷한, 눈에 띄는   modification n. 변경, 수정

최신 토익 경향

등위접속사는 한 시험에 두 문제가 나온 적도 있으므로 학습을 소홀히 하지 않도록 한다. 오답 보기에 접속사나 부사가 함께 나올 경우 문장의 정확한 의미를 해석해야 한다.

<등위접속사의 종류>
- and 그리고   • or 또는   • but 그러나
- yet 그러나   • so 그래서   • for 왜냐하면

114 사람명사와 사물/추상명사 구별하여 채우기

해설 빈칸은 동사(may have to work)의 주어 자리이므로 빈칸 앞 명사 machine과 함께 복합 명사를 이룰 수 있는 명사 (B)와 (C)가 정답의 후보이다. '기계 조작자들이 초과 근무를 하다'라는 의미가 되어야 하므로 명사 machine(기계)와 함께 '기계 조작자들'이라는 의미의 복합 명사 machine operators를 만드는 명사 (B) operators(조작자들)가 정답이다. 명사 (C) operations(작동)를 쓸 경우 '기계 작동이 초과 근무를 하다'라는 어색한 의미를 만들기 때문에 답이 될 수 없다. 동사 (A)는 명사 자리에 올 수 없다. 동명사 또는 현재분사 (D)는 동명사일 경우 명사 앞에 와야 하고, 현재분사일 경우 '작동하는 기계가 초과 근무를 하다'라는 어색한 의미가 된다.

해석 주문에 대한 높은 수요 때문에, Bowers 제조사의 기계 조작자들은 이번 달에 초과 근무를 해야 할지도 모른다.

어휘 demand n. 수요   work overtime 초과 근무를 하다

115 부사 어휘 고르기

해석 '책자를 봉투에 넣기 전에 깔끔하게 접다'라는 문맥이므로 (A) neatly (깔끔하게)가 정답이다. (B) honestly는 '정직하게', (C) deeply는 '깊게', (D) occasionally는 '가끔'이라는 의미이다.

해석 행사 봉사자들은 책자를 봉투에 넣기 전에 깔끔하게 접어달라는 요청을 받는다.

어휘 fold v. 접다   envelope n. 봉투

116 동사 어휘 고르기

해설 'Mr. Wilson은 혁신과 시스템 보안 사이에서 균형을 유지해야 한다'라는 문맥이므로 (B) balance(균형을 유지하다)가 정답이다. (A) overwhelm은 '압도하다', (C) gather는 '모으다', (D) deposit은 '(돈을) 맡기다, 예금하다'라는 의미이다.

해석 Garner 그룹의 기술 담당 최고 책임자로서 성공하기 위해, Mr. Wilson은 혁신과 시스템 보안 사이에서 균형을 유지해야 한다.

어휘 succeed v. 성공하다

117 전치사 채우기

해설 '텐트는 땅에 고정되어 있어야 한다'라는 의미가 되어야 하므로 빈칸 앞의 동사 be secured와 함께 '~에 고정되어 있다'라는 의미의 어구 be secured to를 만드는 전치사 (B) to가 정답이다. (A) beside는 '~ 옆에', (C) of는 '~의, ~에 대한', (D) down은 '~ 아래로'라는 의미이다.

해석 텐트는 그것이 날아가는 것을 방지하기 위해 말뚝으로 땅에 고정되어 있어야 한다.

어휘 secure v. 고정시키다   stake n. 말뚝   prevent v. 방지하다, 막다

최신토익 경향

빈칸 앞의 동사와 함께 쓰이는 전치사를 묻는 문제는 두 시험에 한 번꼴로 자주 출제되고 있다. '동사 + 전치사'를 덩어리째 암기해 두어야 헷갈리지 않는다.

<최근 출제된 '동사 + 전치사' 표현>
• be secured to ~에 고정되어 있다
• be listed on ~에 기재되어 있다
• sort through ~을 분류하다
• specialize in ~을 전문으로 하다
• belong to ~에 속하다

118 명사 어휘 고르기

해설 '브랜드 충성도 가치에 대한 분석이 고객 유지 전략의 중요성을 보여주다'라는 문맥이므로 (D) value(가치)가 정답이다. (A) reason은 '근거, 이유', (B) decision은 '결정', (C) project는 '과제, 프로젝트'라는 의미이다.

해석 Mr. Bain의 브랜드 충성도 가치에 대한 분석은 고객 유지 전략의 중요성을 보여준다.

어휘 analysis n. 분석   retention n. 유지, 보유

119 부사절 접속사 채우기

해설 이 문장은 필수성분(The bridge ~ to traffic)을 갖춘 완전한 절이므로 ____ ~ in the area는 수식어 거품으로 보아야 한다. 이 수식어 거품은 동사(caused)가 있는 거품절이므로, 거품절을 이끌 수 있는 부사절 접속사 (D) after(~한 후에)가 정답이다. 전치사 (A), 부사 또는 전치사 (B), 형용사 또는 전치사 (C)는 거품절을 이끌 수 없다.

해석 Coldwater 강을 가로지르는 다리는 폭우가 그 지역에 홍수를 야기한 후에 차량이 통제되었다.

어휘 cause v. ~을 야기하다; n. 원인   flooding n. 홍수, 범람

120 전치사 채우기

해설 이 문장은 필수성분(Mr. Choi ~ the local community center)을 갖춘 완전한 절이므로 ____ ~ at the library는 수식어 거품으로 보아야 한다. 이 수식어 거품은 동사가 없는 거품구이므로, 거품구를 이끌 수 있는 현재분사 (A)와 전치사 (C)가 정답의 후보이다. '도서관에서 일하는 것 외에도'라는 의미가 되어야 하므로 전치사 (C) Besides(~ 외에도)가 정답이다. 2형식 동사 become의 현재분사 (A) Becoming을 분사구문을 이끄는 것으로 본다 해도, become 뒤에 오는 주격 보어 자리에는 동작을 나타내는 분사가 아닌 상태를 나타내는 형용사가 와야 하므로 답이 될 수 없다. 부사 (B)와 (D)는 수식어 거품을 이끌 수 없다.

해석 도서관에서 일하는 것 외에도, Mr. Choi는 지역 주민 센터에서 아이들을 가르친다.

어휘 tutor v. 가르치다, 개인 교습을 하다

121 동사 어휘 고르기

해설 '리더십에 감사를 표하다'라는 문맥이므로 (B) express(표하다, 나타내다)가 정답이다. (A) revoke는 '폐지하다', (C) enlist는 '요청하다', (D) conclude는 '결론을 내리다, 체결하다'라는 의미이다.

해석 출시 과정에서의 귀하의 리더십에 감사를 표하기 위해, 우리는 귀하를 이달의 사원으로 지명할 것입니다.

어휘 nominate v. 지명하다, 추천하다

122 부사 어휘 고르기

해설 '확장 계획에 대해 열심히 일했을 뿐만 아니라, 수익성도 향상시켰다'라는 문맥이므로 (D) diligently(열심히)가 정답이다. (A) completely (전적으로, 완전히)도 해석상 그럴듯해 보이지만, completely는 동작의 정도나 완료 상태를 강조할 때 쓰이므로 어색한 문맥을 만든다. (B) accessibly는 '접근 가능하게', (C) functionally는 '기능적으로'이라는 의미이다. 참고로, 이 문장은 부정어구(Not only)가 문장 맨 앞으로 오면서 주어(Mr. Shin)와 조동사(has)가 도치된 도치 구문이다.

해석 Mr. Shin은 BeilCo사의 확장 계획에 대해 열심히 일했을 뿐만 아니라, 회사의 수익성도 향상시켰다.

어휘 profitability n. 수익성

123 형용사 자리 채우기

해설 빈칸 뒤의 명사(renewal option)를 꾸며줄 수 있는 것은 형용사이므로 형용사 (C) automatic(자동의)이 정답이다. 명사 (A) automation(자동화)은 renewal option(갱신 옵션)과 복합 명사를 이룰 수 없고, 동사 (B)와 부사 (D)는 명사를 꾸밀 수 없다.

해석 Streaming Sphere의 고객들은 그들의 계정에 접속하여 "나의 구독 관리"를 클릭함으로써 자동 갱신 옵션을 끌 수 있다.

어휘 account n. 계정, 계좌 renewal n. 갱신, (기한) 연장

124 명사 어휘 고르기

해설 'Amaryllis 호텔의 정책에 따르면, 손님들은 어떠한 피해에 대해서도 책임져야 한다'라는 문맥이므로 (B) policy(정책)가 정답이다. (A) addition은 '추가', (C) distribution은 '배포, 분배', (D) industry는 '산업'이라는 의미이다.

해석 Amaryllis 호텔의 정책에 따르면, 손님들은 호텔 자산에 야기한 어떠한 피해에 대해서도 책임져야 한다.

어휘 damage n. 피해, 손상 property n. 자산, 건물

125 형용사 어휘 고르기

해설 '재무 자료가 정확하다면, 회계 부서는 그것을 사용할 것이다'라는 문맥이므로 (A) accurate(정확한)이 정답이다. (B) intellectual은 '지적인', (C) deliberate은 '신중한, 고의의', (D) flexible은 '유연한'이라는 의미이다.

해석 재무 자료가 정확하다면, 회계 부서는 보고서를 준비하는 데 그것을 사용할 것이다.

어휘 financial adj. 금융의, 재정의 accounting n. 회계

126 전치사 채우기

해설 '일 년 내내 견고한 매출을 기록하다'라는 의미가 되어야 하므로 기간을 나타내는 전치사 (C) throughout(~ 내내)이 정답이다. (A) about은 '~에 대한', (B) near는 '~에 가까운', (D) among은 '~ 사이에'라는 의미이다.

해석 Manos 가구점은 일 년 내내 견고한 매출을 기록했으며, 마지막 분기가 가장 견고했다.

어휘 record v. 기록하다 quarter n. 분기, 4분의 1

127 부사절 접속사 채우기

해설 이 문장은 필수성분(many are raising ~ layoffs)을 갖춘 완전한 절이므로 ____ ~ the upcoming merger는 수식어 거품으로 보아야 한다. 이 수식어 거품은 동사(are)가 있는 거품절이므로, 부사절 접속사인 모든 보기가 정답의 후보이다. '직원들은 다가올 합병에 대해 알고 있기 때문에, 많은 이들이 해고에 대해 우려를 제기하고 있다'라는 의미가 되어야 하므로 (A) Now that(~이기 때문에)이 정답이다. (B) As long as는 '~하는 한', (C) In case는 '~에 대비하여', (D) In order that은 '~하기 위해'라는 의미이다.

해석 Koch 화장품사의 직원들은 다가올 합병에 대해 알고 있기 때문에, 많은 이들이 해고에 대해 우려를 제기하고 있다.

어휘 raise v. 제기하다, 들어 올리다 layoff n. (일시적) 해고

128 부정대명사 채우기

해설 빈칸은 동사(prefer)의 목적어 자리에 오면서 뒤에 전치사구(with nuts)의 꾸밈을 받는 명사 자리이므로 대명사 (B)와 (D)가 정답의 후보이다. '설문조사가 소비자들이 견과류가 들어간 무엇이든 선호한다는 것을 보여준다'라는 의미가 되어야 하므로 부정대명사 (B) anything(무엇이든)이 정답이다. (D) somebody는 '누군가, 어떤 사람'이라는 의미로 어색한 문맥을 만든다. 부사 (A) almost(거의)와 관계대명사 또는 의문사 (C) which(어느)는 전치사구의 꾸밈을 받을 수 없다.

해석 시리얼 제조사의 최근 설문조사는 소비자들이 견과류가 들어간 무엇이든 선호한다는 것을 보여준다.

어휘 manufacturer n. 제조사, 생산 회사
prefer v. 선호하다, ~을 더 좋아하다

129 부사절 접속사 채우기

해설 이 문장은 필수성분(they should ~ administrator)을 갖춘 완전한 절이므로 ____ ~ five days는 수식어 거품으로 보아야 한다. 이 수식어 거품은 동사(plan)가 있는 거품절이므로, 거품절을 이끌 수 있는 부사절 접속사 (B)와 (C)가 정답의 후보이다. '세입자들이 방을 5일 넘게 비울 때마다, 관리자에게 알려야 한다'라는 의미가 되어야 하므로 복합관계부사 (C) Whenever(~할 때마다)가 정답이다. (B) So that은 '~하기 위해서'라는 의미로 어색한 문맥을 만든다. 부사 (A) Simply(단순히, 그저)와 전치사 (D) Owing to(~ 때문에)는 거품절을 이끌 수 없다.

해석 세입자들이 그들의 방을 5일 넘게 비울 때마다, 그들은 건물 관리자에게 알려야 한다.

어휘 tenant n. 세입자 vacant adj. 비어 있는, 사람이 없는
administrator n. 관리자, 행정인

130 형용사 어휘 고르기

해설 '예측하지 못한 상황이 생산에 영향을 미쳤다는 것을 이해하면서도, 배송일을 맞춰 주기를 기대한다'라는 문맥이므로 (D) unforeseen(예측하지 못한)이 정답이다. (A) favorable은 '호의적인', (B) approximate는 '근사치인, 거의 정확한', (C) reputable은 '평판이 좋은'이라는 의미이다.

해석 우리는 예측하지 못한 상황이 생산에 영향을 미쳤다는 것을 이해하면서도, 여전히 공급업체가 배송일을 맞춰 주기를 기대한다.

어휘 circumstance n. 상황, 환경 affect v. 영향을 미치다

PART 6

131-134번은 다음 상품권에 관한 문제입니다.

> Gladstone 식당 상품권
>
> ¹³¹이 상품권은 소지자가 Gladstone 식당의 모든 지점에서 15달러 이상의 값이 매겨진 메인 요리 주문에 대해 무료 전채 요리 한 개 또는 후식을 받을 수 있게 합니다. ¹³²그것의 만료일까지, 그것은 평일이나 주말에 우리의 정규 영업시간 중에 사용될 수 있습니다. ¹³³모든 지점들은 오전 11시부터 오후 10시까지 영업합니다.
>
> 식사하는 일행당 하나의 상품권만 인정될 것이며, 그것은 다른 특별 할인과 결합되지 않을 수 있습니다. 주문하기 전에 당신이 이 상품권을 사용하고자 한다는 것을 종업원에게 알려주시기 바랍니다. 그러면 그 종업원이 그것이 만료되지 않았는지 확인할 것입니다. ¹³⁴일단 그것의 유효성이 확인되면, 당신은 선택을 하셔도 됩니다.
>
> 8월 15일 만료

voucher n. 상품권 holder n. 소지자, 보유자 appetizer n. 전채 요리
entrée n. 메인 요리, 주요리 expiration n. 만료 operation n. 영업
combine v. 결합하다 expire v. 만료되다 selection n. 선택

131 전치사 채우기
해설 '15달러 이상의 값이 매겨진 메인 요리 주문에 대해 무료 전채 요리 한 개 또는 후식을 받을 수 있다'라는 의미가 되어야 하므로 (C) with (~에 대해)가 정답이다. (A) over는 '~ 위에', (B) as는 '~로서', (D) at은 '~에서'라는 의미이다.

132 상관접속사 채우기
해설 빈칸 뒤의 or(또는)와 함께 상관접속사 either A or B(A 또는 B 중 하나)를 완성하는 (B) either(둘 중 하나의)가 정답이다. 참고로, 이 문장에서 either가 명사(weekdays)와 명사(weekends)를 연결하고 있음을 알아둔다.

133 알맞은 문장 고르기
해석 (A) 모든 지점들은 오전 11시부터 오후 10시까지 영업합니다.
(B) 상품권은 명시된 날에만 유효합니다.
(C) 저희는 10달러 이하의 다양한 메인 요리를 제공합니다.
(D) 저희의 일일 점심 특선에 대해 꼭 물어보세요.

해설 앞 문장 'Until its expiration date, it may be used ~ during our regular hours of operation.'에서 상품권이 정규 영업시간 중에 사용될 수 있다고 했으므로, 빈칸에는 정규 영업시간과 관련된 내용이 들어가야 함을 알 수 있다. 따라서 (A)가 정답이다.

어휘 specify v. 명시하다

134 명사 어휘 고르기 주변 문맥 파악
해설 '그것의 ___이 확인되다'라는 문맥이므로 모든 보기가 정답의 후보이다. 빈칸이 있는 문장만으로 정답을 고를 수 없으므로 주변 문맥이나 전체 문맥을 파악한다. 앞 문장 'The server will then check to ensure it[voucher] hasn't expired.'에서 종업원이 상품권

이 만료되지 않았는지 확인할 것이라고 했으므로, 그것의 유효성이 확인된다는 것임을 알 수 있다. 따라서 (B) validity(유효성)가 정답이다. (A) quality는 '품질, 우수함', (C) location은 '소재지, 장소', (D) ownership은 '소유권'이라는 의미이다.

135-138번은 다음 기사에 관한 문제입니다.

> Surge Solutions가 FT3을 출시하다
>
> 시애틀(6월 1일)—Surge Solutions는 이제 막 FT3의 출시를 발표했다. ¹³⁵이 스마트워치는 그것의 이전 모델인 FT2의 뒤를 잇는 것인데, 그것은 작년에 출시되었고 그것의 주요 기능은 기본적인 활동 추적이었다. ¹³⁶대조적으로, 더 새로워진 버전은 광범위한 건강 관찰 시스템을 갖추고 있는데, 이는 고급 심박동 수 감지기와 수면 분석 능력을 포함한다. ¹³⁷그것의 배터리 수명 또한 훨씬 더 길다. 그러므로 당신은 그것을 자주 충전하는 것에 대해 걱정할 필요가 없을 것이다. ¹³⁸만약 당신이 찾고 있는 것이 당신의 건강을 포괄적으로 모니터링하는 기능을 가진 기기라면, FT3이 이상적인 선택이다.

predecessor n. 이전 것 primary adj. 주요한
extensive adj. 광범위한, 폭넓은 capability n. 능력
comprehensively adv. 포괄적으로

135 동사 어휘 고르기
해설 '이 스마트워치의 주요 기능은 이전 모델인 FT2의 뒤를 잇는 것이다'라는 문맥이므로 동사 follow(~의 뒤를 잇다)의 3인칭 단수형 (D) follows가 정답이다. (A)의 interest는 '~의 관심을 끌다', (B)의 benefit은 '~에 이롭다, 이익을 주다', (C)의 enhance는 '(가치를) 높이다, 향상시키다'라는 의미이다.

136 접속부사 채우기 주변 문맥 파악
해설 빈칸이 콤마와 함께 문장 맨 앞에 온 접속부사 자리이므로, 앞 문장과 빈칸이 있는 문장의 의미 관계를 파악하여 정답을 선택한다. 앞 문장에서 FT2의 주요 기능이 기본적인 활동 추적이었다고 했고, 빈칸이 있는 문장에서는 더 새로워진 버전이 광범위한 건강 관찰 시스템을 갖추고 있다고 했으므로, 빈칸에는 앞 내용과 상반되는 내용을 언급할 때 사용되는 (C) In contrast(대조적으로, 그에 반해서)가 정답이다.

어휘 in other words 다시 말해서, 즉 otherwise adv. 그렇지 않으면

137 알맞은 문장 고르기
해석 (A) 그 기기는 2년의 보증이 딸려 온다.
(B) 그것의 배터리 수명 또한 훨씬 더 길다.
(C) 이것은 그것을 알맞은 가격의 대안으로 만든다.
(D) 기기가 가열되는 문제들이 보고되어 왔다.

해설 뒤 문장 'So you won't have to worry about charging it often.'에서 자주 충전하는 것에 대해 걱정할 필요가 없을 것이라고 했으므로 빈칸에는 배터리 수명에 관한 장점이 들어가야 함을 알 수 있다. 따라서 (B)가 정답이다.

어휘 alternative n. 대안; adj. 대체 가능한, 대안이 되는 issue n. 문제

138 명사절 접속사 채우기

해설 빈칸 이하(___ you are looking for)는 If절의 주어 역할을 하고 있고 동사(are looking for)가 있으므로 명사절을 이끌 수 있는 명사절 접속사 (A)와 (C)가 정답의 후보이다. 빈칸 뒤에 목적어가 생략된 불완전한 절이 왔으므로 (A) what이 정답이다. 명사절 접속사 (C) that은 뒤에 완전한 절이 와야 하므로 답이 될 수 없다. 부정대명사 또는 부정형용사 (B) some과 (D) most는 명사절을 이끌 수 없다.

139-142번은 다음 이메일에 관한 문제입니다.

> 수신: Laura Buchanan <l_buchanan@tierra.com>
> 발신: Dominic Hubert <domhubert@homebasics.com>
> 제목: 귀하의 수제 양초
> 날짜: 11월 3일
>
> Ms. Buchanan께,
>
> ¹³⁹저는 귀하의 수제 양초에 대한 저희 고객들의 반응에 관해 씁니다. 대부분의 경우에, 의견은 매우 긍정적이었습니다. ¹⁴⁰많은 이들이 그것들이 얼마나 좋은 냄새가 나는지에 대해 언급했습니다.
>
> 그것들은 수요가 높기 때문에, 저는 저희가 이전에 주문했던 양초 수의 두 배를 주문하고 싶습니다. ¹⁴¹귀하께서 그렇게 대량의 주문을 이행하실 수 있으신가요?
>
> 저는 귀하의 제품 품질을 훼손하는 것을 원치 않아서, 생산을 늘리는 것이 지금 당장 문제가 된다면 우리는 대신 장기 계약으로 들어가는 것에 대해 논의할 수도 있을 것 같습니다. ¹⁴²저는 그러한 조정이 우리 모두에게 확실히 도움이 될 것이라 생각합니다. 이에 대한 귀하의 생각을 저에게 알려주시기를 바랍니다.
>
> Dominic Hubert 드림
> Home Basics

어휘 handcrafted adj. 수제의 candle n. 양초 demand n. 수요
compromise v. 훼손하다, 타협하다 arrangement n. 조정

139 명사 어휘 고르기 주변 문맥 파악

해설 '고객들의 ___ 에 관해 쓰다'라는 문맥이므로 모든 보기가 정답의 후보이다. 빈칸이 있는 문장만으로 정답을 고를 수 없으므로 주변 문맥이나 전체 문맥을 파악한다. 뒤 문장 'For the most part, the feedback has been very positive.'에서 대부분의 경우에 의견은 매우 긍정적이었다고 했으므로, 소비자들의 반응에 관해 쓰고 있음을 알 수 있다. 따라서 (C) response(반응)가 정답이다. (A) access는 '접근', (B) sensitivity는 '민감함, 감수성', (D) objection은 '이의, 반대'라는 의미이다.

140 알맞은 문장 고르기

해석 (A) 귀하의 제품을 다른 구매자들에게 판매하는 것은 계약 위반입니다.
(B) 저희는 고객 로열티 프로그램을 시작하는 것을 고려하고 있습니다.
(C) 많은 이들이 그것들이 얼마나 좋은 냄새가 나는지에 대해 언급했습니다.
(D) 저희는 저희의 매장 내에서 그것들을 더 잘 보이게 하기 위해 이것을 했습니다.

해설 앞 문장 'For the most part, the feedback has been very positive.'에서 의견이 매우 긍정적이었다고 했으므로, 빈칸에는 고객들의 긍정적인 의견과 관련된 내용이 들어가야 함을 알 수 있다. 따라서 (C)가 정답이다.

어휘 goods n. 제품, 상품 breach n. 위반

141 동사 어휘 고르기 전체 문맥 파악

해설 '그렇게 대량의 주문을 ___ 할 수 있는가'라는 문맥이므로 모든 보기가 정답의 후보이다. 빈칸이 있는 문장만으로 정답을 고를 수 없으므로 주변 문맥이나 전체 문맥을 파악한다. 앞 문장에서 '그것들이 수요가 높기 때문에, 저는 저희가 이전에 주문했던 개수의 두 배를 주문하고 싶습니다(Because they are in high demand, I would like to order twice the number of candles as we did last time).'라고 했고, 뒤 문장에서 '저는 귀하의 제품 품질을 훼손하는 것을 원치 않아서, 생산을 늘리는 것이 지금 당장 문제가 된다면 우리는 대신 장기 계약으로 들어가는 것에 대해 논의할 수도 있을 것 같습니다(I do not want to compromise the quality of your product, so if increasing production is a challenge right now, perhaps we could discuss entering into a longer-term contract instead).'라고 했으므로, 대량의 주문을 이행할 수 있는지 묻고 있다는 것을 알 수 있다. 따라서 (D) fulfill(이행하다, 수행하다)이 정답이다. (A) modify는 '변경하다, 수정하다', (B) purchase는 '구입하다', (C) delay는 '지연시키다'라는 의미이다.

142 인칭대명사 채우기 주변 문맥 파악

해설 '그러한 조정이 ___ 모두에게 확실히 도움이 될 것이라 생각하다'라는 문맥이므로, 모든 보기가 정답의 후보이다. 빈칸이 있는 문장만으로 정답을 고를 수 없으므로 주변 문맥이나 전체 문맥을 파악한다. 앞 문장에서 '저는 귀하의 제품 품질을 훼손하는 것을 원치 않아서, 생산을 늘리는 것이 지금 당장 문제가 된다면 우리는 대신 장기 계약으로 들어가는 것에 대해 논의할 수도 있을 것 같습니다(I do not want to compromise the quality of your product, so if increasing production is a challenge right now, perhaps we could discuss entering into a longer-term contract instead).'라고 했으므로, 그러한 조정이 우리 모두에게 확실히 도움이 될 것이라는 문맥이 되어야 한다. 따라서 (B) us(우리)가 정답이다.

143-146번은 다음 이메일에 관한 문제입니다.

> 수신: 전 직원, 연구 부서
> 발신: mina_vo@armstronginc.com
> 제목: 사무실 프린터 오작동
> 날짜: 10월 17일
>
> 안녕하세요, 여러분.
>
> ¹⁴³사무실 프린터가 오작동하고 있어 즉시 교체되어야 합니다. ¹⁴⁴저는 몇몇 직원들은 가동되는 프린터 없이는 그들의 업무를 수행하는 것이 어렵다는 점을 이해하고 있습니다. 따라서, 저는 새로운 것을 주문했고, 그것은 다음 주 초까지 도착할 것입니다.
>
> ¹⁴⁵그동안에, 여러분이 어떤 문서들을 출력해야 한다면, 마케팅팀의 사무실에 있는 프린터를 이용해주시기 바랍니다. 그것은 네 자리의 접근 코드(1928)가 필요하다는 점을 유념하세요. ¹⁴⁶저는 이것이

우리 사무실에 프린터가 있는 것보다 덜 편리하다는 점을 인식하고 있습니다. 이해해 주셔서 감사합니다.

Mina Vo, 사무실 관리자

malfunction v. 오작동하다   replace v. 교체하다
functional adj. 가동되는, 기능을 하는   document n. 문서

143 부사 자리 채우기

해설 빈칸 앞의 to 부정사구(to be replaced)를 꾸밀 수 있는 것은 부사이므로 부사 (C) promptly(즉시)가 정답이다. 형용사 또는 동사 (A), 동사 (B), 명사 (D)는 to 부정사구를 꾸밀 수 없다.

144 전치사 채우기

해설 '몇몇 직원들은 가동되는 프린터 없이는 그들의 업무를 수행하는 것이 어렵다'라는 문맥이므로 (D) without(~ 없이)이 정답이다. (A) outside는 '밖에, ~ 외에', (B) against는 '~에 반대하여', (C) beyond는 '~ 너머, ~을 지나'라는 의미이다.

145 접속부사 채우기 주변 문맥 파악

해설 빈칸이 콤마와 함께 문장의 맨 앞에 온 접속부사 자리이므로, 앞 문장과 빈칸이 있는 문장의 의미 관계를 파악하여 정답을 선택한다. 앞 문장에서 자신이 주문한 새로운 프린터가 다음 주 초까지 도착할 예정이라고 했고, 빈칸이 있는 문장에서는 문서들을 출력해야 한다면, 마케팅팀의 사무실에 있는 프린터를 이용해 달라고 했으므로, 두 가지 일 사이의 기간을 언급할 때 사용되는 (A) In the meantime (그동안에)이 정답이다.

어휘 to this end 이를 위하여   in particular 특히, 특별히

146 알맞은 문장 고르기

해설 (A) 회사 소식지가 오늘 이메일로 배부될 것입니다.
(B) 우리는 다음 주 목요일 오후에 팀워크 행사를 열 것입니다.
(C) 저는 이것이 우리 사무실에 프린터가 있는 것보다 덜 편리하다는 점을 인식하고 있습니다.
(D) 새로운 프린터는 무선 인쇄를 포함한 여러 새로운 기능들을 가지고 있습니다.

해설 앞 문장 'if you need to print out any documents, please use the one in the marketing team's office. Note that it requires a four-digit access code (1928).'에서 문서들을 출력해야 하는 경우 마케팅팀의 사무실에 있는 것을 이용해야 하고 그 프린터는 접근 코드가 필요하다고 했으므로, 빈칸에는 다른 팀의 프린터를 이용하는 것과 관련된 내용이 들어가야 함을 알 수 있다. 따라서 (C)가 정답이다.

어휘 wireless adj. 무선의

PART 7

147-148번은 다음 보고서에 관한 문제입니다.

Verona 가전제품사
2월 [147]기업 서비스 전화 보고서

항목	수치
총 [147]수신 통화 수	811
[148-(A)]평균 통화 대기 시간(분)	[148-(A)]7
평균 통화 길이(분)	4
[148-(D)]해결된 통화 수	[148-(D)]349
[148-(D)]미해결 통화 수	[148-(D)]462
[147/148-(C)]5점 만점의 고객 만족도 평균 점수	[148-(C)]2
[147]내부 전용	

hotline n. 서비스 전화, 직통 전화   average adj. 평균의
resolve v. 해결하다   satisfaction n. 만족   internal adj. 내부의

147 추론 문제

해설 어떤 부서의 활동이 보고서에 의해 다루어지는 것 같은가?
(A) 마케팅
(B) 회계
(C) 고객 서비스
(D) 인사

해설 지문의 'Company Hotline Report', 'received calls', 'Average customer satisfaction score out of 5', 'For Internal Use Only'에서 기업 서비스 전화 보고서, 수신 통화, 5점 만점의 고객 만족도 평균 점수, 내부 전용이라고 했으므로 회사의 고객 서비스 부서의 활동을 다루고 있다는 것을 추론할 수 있다. 따라서 (C)가 정답이다.

어휘 cover v. 다루다

148 Not/True 문제

해설 보고서에 명시된 것은?
(A) 전화를 받는 데 평균 5분 미만이 걸렸다.
(B) 몇몇 고객은 한 번 이상 다시 전화를 걸었다.
(C) 대부분의 고객이 서비스에 만족했다.
(D) 해결된 통화보다 미해결 통화가 더 많았다.

해설 지문의 'Number of resolved calls', '349', 'Number of unresolved calls', '462'에서 해결된 통화 수가 349통, 미해결 통화 수가 462통이라고 했으므로 (D)는 지문에 명시되어 있다. 따라서 (D)가 정답이다. (A)는 'Average call waiting time (in minutes)', '7'에서 평균 통화 대기 시간이 7분이라고 했으므로 지문의 내용과 일치하지 않는다. (B)는 지문에 명시되지 않은 내용이다. (C)는 'Average customer satisfaction score out of 5', '2'에서 5점 만점의 고객 만족도 평균 점수가 2점이라고 했으므로 지문의 내용과 일치하지 않는다.

어휘 once adv. 한 번

149-150번은 다음 공고에 관한 문제입니다.

올해 클리블랜드 레스토랑 주간은 8월 24일부터 8월 30일까지 진행될 것이며, ¹⁴⁹⁻⁽ᴮ⁾아늑한 카페부터 고급 스테이크 레스토랑까지 50곳의 멋진 레스토랑들이 참여합니다. 엄선된 점심 및 저녁 메뉴가 최대 25퍼센트 할인된 가격으로 제공될 것입니다. 일주일 내내, ¹⁵⁰⁻⁽ᴬ⁾Main가를 따라 주차가 무료로 제공될 것이며, 이는 음식 애호가들이 도시의 다양한 요리 옵션을 더 쉽게 둘러볼 수 있도록 해줄 것입니다. 또한 ¹⁵⁰⁻⁽ᶜ⁾거리 공연자들이 제공하는 야외 공연을 무료로 즐기고 행사를 기념하기 위한 ¹⁵⁰⁻⁽ᴰ⁾무료 티셔츠와 모자를 받을 것입니다.

참여 레스토랑 목록을 위해서는 클리블랜드 시청의 공식 웹사이트를 방문하세요.

cozy adj. 아늑한 enthusiast n. 애호가, 팬 culinary adj. 요리의
open-air adj. 야외의 performer n. 공연자 mark v. 기념하다

149 Not/True 문제

해석 클리블랜드 레스토랑 주간에 대해 언급된 것은?
(A) 일 년 중 보통과 다른 시기에 개최될 것이다.
(B) 많은 수의 참여 사업장들을 특징으로 할 것이다.
(C) Main가에서 열리는 행사로 끝날 것이다.
(D) 국경일을 기념하기 위해 조직되었다.

해설 지문의 'with 50 amazing dining establishments ranging from cozy cafés to upscale steak houses participating'에서 아늑한 카페부터 고급 스테이크 레스토랑까지 50곳의 멋진 레스토랑들이 참여한다고 했으므로 (B)는 지문에 언급되어 있다. 따라서 (B)가 정답이다. (A), (C), (D)는 지문에 언급되지 않은 내용이다.

어휘 conclude v. 끝나다

150 Not/Ture 문제

해석 클리블랜드 레스토랑 주간 동안 무료로 제공되지 않을 것은 무엇인가?
(A) 주차
(B) 식사
(C) 공연
(D) 기념품

해설 (A)는 지문의 'parking along Main Street will be free of charge'에서 주차가 무료로 제공된다고 했으므로 지문에 언급된 내용이다. (C)는 'enjoy the open-air entertainment provided by street performers at no cost'에서 거리 공연자들이 제공하는 야외 공연을 무료로 즐길 수 있다고 했으므로 지문에 언급된 내용이다. (D)는 'will receive complimentary T-shirts and hats'에서 무료 티셔츠와 모자를 받을 것이라고 했으므로 지문에 언급된 내용이다. (B)는 지문에 언급되지 않은 내용이다. 따라서 (B)가 정답이다.

151-152번은 다음 안내문에 관한 문제입니다.

Lanai 식물원에 오신 것을 환영합니다!

여러분의 안전과 편안함을 보장하기 위해, 다음 규칙을 준수하세요:

• 모든 쓰레기는 시설 곳곳에 있는 파란색 쓰레기통에 넣으세요. 쓰레기를 버리지 마세요.
• 어떠한 꽃도 따지 마세요. ¹⁵¹⁻⁽ᴰ⁾방문객들은 사진을 찍어도 좋지만, 어떠한 식물도 만지지 마세요.
• 대규모 그룹에 있는 경우, 통로를 막지 않도록 해주세요.
• Lanai 식물원 내에서는 반려동물이 허용되지 않습니다. ¹⁵²피크닉장 옆에 지정된 반려동물 놀이 공간에 반려동물을 맡겨 주세요.

botanical garden 식물원 comfort n. 편안함 observe v. 준수하다
garbage n. 쓰레기 litter v. (쓰레기 등을) 버리다

151 Not/True 문제

해석 Lanai 식물원에 대해 명시된 것은?
(A) 주 7일 영업한다.
(B) 셀프 가이드 투어를 제공한다.
(C) 식물의 사진이 촬영되는 것을 허용한다.
(D) 고령자들에게는 인하된 입장료를 받는다.

해설 지문의 'Visitors are welcome to take photographs'에서 방문객들이 사진을 찍어도 좋다고 했으므로 (C)는 지문에 명시되어 있다. 따라서 (C)가 정답이다. (A), (B), (D)는 지문에 명시되지 않은 내용이다.

어휘 admission fee 입장료

Paraphrasing

are welcome to take photographs 사진을 찍어도 좋다
→ allows ~ to be photographed 사진이 촬영되는 것을 허용한다

152 육하원칙 문제

해석 안내문에 따르면, 반려동물을 동반한 모든 방문객들은 무엇을 해야 하는가?
(A) 반려동물이 예방 접종을 받았다는 증명서를 제공한다.
(B) 반려동물을 항상 줄에 매어 둔다.
(C) 명시된 곳에 반려동물을 데려다 놓는다.
(D) 반려동물의 쓰레기를 파란색 쓰레기통에 버린다.

해설 지문의 'Please leave your pet within the designated pet play area next to the picnic grounds.'에서 피크닉장 옆에 지정된 반려동물 놀이 공간에 반려동물을 맡겨 달라고 했으므로 (C)가 정답이다.

어휘 proof n. 증명(서), 증거 vaccinate v. ~에게 예방 접종을 하다
leash v. 줄에 매어 두다 specified adj. 명시된
dispose v. 버리다, 처분하다

Paraphrasing

leave your pet within the designated pet play area 지정된 반려동물 놀이 공간에 반려동물을 맡기다 → Drop their pet off at a specified location 명시된 곳에 반려동물을 데려다 놓다

153-154번은 다음 문자 메시지 대화문에 관한 문제입니다.

Carolina Rojas (오후 1시 36분)
Noah, 아직 문구점에 계세요? ¹⁵³몇 가지 추가 물품이 필요해서요.

Noah Filler (오후 1시 37분)
방금 나오기는 했는데, 다시 들어갈 수 있어요. 무엇이 필요하세요?

Carolina Rojas (오후 1시 39분)
우리의 커피숍 앞에 놓을 홍보 간판을 만들면 좋을 것 같아요. 그래서, 칠판과 다양한 색상의 분필이 필요해요.

Noah Filler (오후 1시 41분)
154아, 그런 제품이 있는지는 잘 모르겠지만, 관리자에게 물어볼게요.

Carolina Rojas (오후 1시 42분)
있을 거 같아요. 154그런 매장에서 그 물품들을 취급하는 것이 매우 흔하잖아요. 저는 그동안 디자인에 대해 생각해 보고 돌아오시면 시작할 수 있게 할게요.

Noah Filler (오후 1시 43분)
알겠어요. 저도 몇 가지 아이디어를 생각해 볼게요.

stationery n. 문구류 promotional adj. 홍보의, 판촉의
chalk n. 분필 common adj. 흔한
come up with ~을 생각하다, 제안하다

153 목적 찾기 문제

해석 Ms. Rojas는 왜 Mr. Filler에게 연락했는가?
(A) 더 많은 물품을 구매해 달라고 요청하기 위해
(B) 디자인에 대한 도움을 요청하기 위해
(C) 커피숍에서 발생한 문제를 알리기 위해
(D) 너무 오래 나가 있었다고 불평하기 위해

해설 지문의 'I need some additional items.'에서 Ms. Rojas가 몇 가지 추가 물품이 필요하다고 했으므로 (A)가 정답이다.

어휘 assistance n. 도움, 지원 inform v. 알리다

Paraphrasing
some additional items 몇 가지 추가 물품 → more items 더 많은 물품

154 의도 파악 문제

해석 오후 1시 42분에, Ms. Rojas가 "I think they will"이라고 썼을 때, 그녀가 의도한 것 같은 것은?
(A) 관리자가 요청 사항을 알고 있을 거라고 믿는다.
(B) 손님들이 홍보 활동을 인식할 거라고 생각한다.
(C) 매장이 몇 가지 물품을 보유하고 있을 거라고 확신한다.
(D) 할인이 가능할 것으로 예상한다.

해설 지문의 'Oh, I am not sure if they have anything like that, but I will ask the manager.'에서 Mr. Filler가 그런 제품이 있는지는 잘 모르겠지만 관리자에게 물어보겠다고 하자, Ms. Rojas가 'I think they will'(있을 거 같아요)이라고 한 후, 'It's very common for a store like that to carry those items.'에서 그런 매장에서 그 물품들을 취급하는 것은 매우 흔하다고 한 것을 통해, 매장이 몇 가지 물품을 보유하고 있을 거라고 확신하는 것을 알 수 있다. 따라서 (C)가 정답이다.

어휘 appreciate v. 인식하다, 알아차리다

155-157번은 다음 편지에 관한 문제입니다.

6월 5일

Calista Parker
769번지 River Place로, 321호
디트로이트, 미시간주 48207

Ms. Parker께,

이로써 디트로이트 푸드 센터에서의 귀하의 자원봉사 신청을 수락합니다. 155/156귀하와 같은 자원봉사자는 수백 명의 사람들에게 다른 방법으로는 제공될 수 없을지도 모르는 매일의 건강한 식사를 제공하려는 저희의 목표에 매우 중요합니다. 155귀하께서는 요리사이시므로, 주방에서 일하시도록 할 것입니다. 대체로, 저희는 간단한 미국식 클래식 요리를 제공하지만, 항상 새로운 아이디어에 대해 열린 마음을 가지고 있습니다.

귀하께서는 일주일에 6시간씩 자원봉사를 하실 예정입니다. 주말을 선호한다고 하셔서, 토요일 1교대 근무를 배정해 드리고자 합니다. 오전 7시에 시작해서 오후 1시에 끝납니다. 157이 시간이 괜찮으시다면 555-4985로 저에게 직접 전화해 주세요.

도움을 주셔서 다시 한번 감사드립니다.

Jonathan Dempsey 드림
디트로이트 푸드 센터
프로그램 책임자

hereby adv. 이로써, 이에 의하여
otherwise adv. 다른 방법으로는, 그렇지 않으면
assign v. 배정하다, 할당하다 suit v. 괜찮다, 맞다

155 추론 문제

해석 Ms. Parker에 대해 암시되는 것은?
(A) 최근에 셰프 직에서 은퇴했다.
(B) 토요일 오후에는 일할 수 없다.
(C) 새로운 메뉴를 만들 것으로 기대된다.
(D) 자원봉사로 식사를 준비할 것이다.

해설 지문의 'Volunteers like you[Ms. Parker] are critical to our goal of serving hundreds of people a daily healthy meal that might not be available to them otherwise.'에서 Ms. Parker와 같은 자원봉사자는 수백 명의 사람들에게 매일의 건강한 식사를 제공하려는 목표에 매우 중요하다고 했고, 'As you are a chef, we will have you work in the kitchen.'에서 요리사이기 때문에 주방에서 일할 거라고 했으므로 Ms. Parker는 자원봉사로 식사를 준비할 것임을 추론할 수 있다. 따라서 (D)가 정답이다.

어휘 voluntary adj. 자원봉사로 하는, 자발적인

156 동의어 찾기 문제

해설 1문단 두 번째 줄의 단어 "critical"은 의미상 -와 가장 가깝다.
(A) 우수한
(B) 비판적인
(C) 필수적인
(D) 꾸준한

해설 critical을 포함한 구절 'Volunteers like you are critical to our goal of serving hundreds of people a daily healthy meal that might not be available to them otherwise.'에서 critical은 '매우 중요한'이라는 뜻으로 사용되었다. 따라서 (C)가 정답이다.

157 추론 문제

해석 Ms. Parker는 왜 Mr. Dempsey에게 전화할 것 같은가?
(A) 자원봉사 장소를 변경하기 위해
(B) 근무 일정을 확정하기 위해
(C) 기부금 지급을 마무리하기 위해
(D) 그녀의 자격에 대해 논의하기 위해

해설 지문의 'Please call me[Mr. Dempsey] directly at 555-4985 to let me know if this time suits you.'에서 시간이 괜찮으면 555-4985로 자신에게 직접 전화해 달라고 했으므로 Ms. Parker가 근무 일정을 확정하기 위해 Mr. Dempsey에게 전화할 것임을 추론할 수 있다. 따라서 (B)가 정답이다.

어휘 finalize v. 마무리하다 qualification n. 자격, 능력

158-160번은 다음 초대장에 관한 문제입니다.

> 에든버러 오페라 극장에서 주최하는 Three Colours 단독 공연에 귀하를 정중하게 초대합니다. ¹⁵⁸행사는 10월 25일 그 작품의 공식 데뷔 3일 전인 10월 22일에 열릴 것입니다. 호평을 받고 있는 테너 Sandra Walker와 알토 Patrick Fern을 비롯한 전체 출연자들이 공연을 펼칠 것입니다.
>
> ¹⁵⁹⁻⁽ᴬ⁾에든버러 오페라 극장의 회원인 사람들만이 이 행사에 대한 티켓을 이용할 수 있으며, 각 참석자에게는 처음 12열의 무대 앞쪽에 가까운 좌석이 주어질 것입니다. ¹⁶⁰이 특별한 기회를 이용하고 싶으시다면, Claire Keith에게 tickets@edinburghopera.scot으로 연락해 주세요. 손님 한 명을 데리고 오셔도 됩니다.
>
> 에든버러 오페라 극장

cordially adv. 정중하게, 진심으로 exclusive adj. 단독적인, 독점적인
production n. 작품, 제작(물) acclaimed adj. 호평을 받고 있는

158 육하원칙 문제

해석 초대장은 어떤 행사를 위한 것인가?
(A) 오페라 기금 모금 행사
(B) 공연의 시사회
(C) 극장의 기념일 축하 행사
(D) 출연진 및 제작진과의 사진 촬영

해설 지문의 'The event will take place on 22 October, three nights before the production's official debut on 25 October.'에서 이 행사는 10월 25일 그 작품의 공식 데뷔 3일 전인 10월 22일에 열린다고 했으므로 시사회임을 알 수 있다. 따라서 (B)가 정답이다.

어휘 fundraiser n. (기금) 모금 행사 celebration n. 축하 행사

159 Not/True 문제

해석 에든버러 오페라 극장의 회원들에 대해 명시된 것은?
(A) 공연 공간에 가까이 앉을 것이다.
(B) 복장 규정을 충실히 지킬 것으로 기대받을 것이다.
(C) 사인회에 우선권을 얻게 될 것이다.
(D) 그들의 손님의 티켓에 대한 할인을 받을 것이다.

해설 지문의 'Only those who are members of the Edinburg Opera Theatre can access tickets to this event, and each attendee will be given a seat close to the front of the stage'에서 에든버러 오페라 극장의 회원인 사람들만이 이 행사에 대한 티켓을 이용할 수 있으며 각 참석자에게는 무대 앞쪽에 가까운 좌석이 주어질 것이라고 했으므로 회원들이 공연 공간에 가까이 앉을 것임을 알 수 있다. 따라서 (A)가 정답이다.

어휘 adhere to ~을 충실히 지키다, 고수하다

160 추론 문제

해석 Ms. Keith는 누구일 것 같은가?
(A) 예술 평론가
(B) 오페라 가수
(C) 공연 감독
(D) 극장 직원

해설 지문의 'If you are interested in taking advantage of this unique opportunity, please contact Claire Keith at tickets@edinburghopera.scot.'에서 이 특별한 기회를 이용하고 싶으면 Claire Keith에게 tickets@edinburghopera.scot으로 연락해 달라고 했으므로 Ms. Keith가 극장 직원임을 추론할 수 있다. 따라서 (D)가 정답이다.

어휘 critic n. 평론가

161-163번은 다음 공고에 관한 문제입니다.

> Jefferson 금융사는 ¹⁶¹우리의 직원들에게 자원봉사 기회를 제공하기 위해 Abrams 재단과 제휴했습니다. ― [1] ―. Jefferson 금융사에서는 적극적인 지역 사회 참여와 우리가 신뢰하는 단체에 환원하는 것을 권장합니다. ¹⁶²Abrams 재단은 에번스턴에 본사를 둔 비정부 기구로, 과외 서비스를 위해 자원봉사자와 어린아이들을 매칭합니다. ― [2] ―. 공립학교는 보통 과외 서비스를 위한 자금이 부족하고 학부모는 적합한 사람을 찾는 데 어려움을 겪기 때문에 그것은 중요한 역할을 합니다. ¹⁶¹저희는 여러분이 다양한 과목에서 아이들을 도와주시기를 바랍니다. ― [3] ―.
>
> 여러분 각자는 재정적 전문 지식을 넘어서는 가치 있는 기술을 가지고 있다고 확신합니다. 관심 있으신 분은 누구든지 Kathy Winfrey에게 k.winfrey@jeffersonfinancial.com으로 이메일을 보내주세요. 지식 분야와 선호하는 시간 약속을 포함해 주세요. ¹⁶³매주 같은 아이와 함께하는 자원봉사 세션을 권장합니다. ― [4] ―. 참여하는 모든 사람은 과외 일정이 잡히면 반차 휴무를 받을 것입니다.

volunteer v. 자원봉사 하다; n. 자원봉사자
encourage v. 권장하다, 장려하다 engagement n. 참여, 관여
nongovernmental adj. 비정부의 lack v. 부족하다
expertise n. 전문 지식 commitment n. 약속, 전념

161 목적 찾기 문제

해석 공고의 목적은 무엇인가?
(A) 기업 합병을 발표하기 위해
(B) 시간제 근로자를 채용하기 위해
(C) 직원들에게 사회적 참여 기회에 대해 알리기 위해
(D) 예산 산정을 공유하기 위해

해설 지문의 'to provide volunteering opportunities for our staff'에서 직원들에게 자원봉사 기회를 제공하고 있다고 했고, 'We would like to have you help children in a variety of subjects.'에서 다양한 과목에서 아이들을 도와주기를 바란다며 과외 봉사에 참여할 직원을 모집하고 있으므로 (C)가 정답이다.

어휘 merger n. 합병 recruit v. 채용하다 calculation n. 산정, 계산

Paraphrasing
> volunteering opportunities 자원봉사 기회 → a social engagement opportunity 사회적 참여 기회

162 추론 문제

해석 Abrams 재단에 대해 암시되는 것은?
(A) 분기별 기부금 목표에 도달하지 못했다.
(B) 어학원을 열 것이다.
(C) 정부 공무원들에 의해 경영되지 않는다.
(D) 사립학교에 재정적 도움을 제공한다.

해설 지문의 'Abrams Foundation is an Evanston-based nongovernmental organization'에서 Abrams 재단이 에번스턴에 본사를 둔 비정부기구라고 했으므로 정부 공무원들에 의해 경영되지 않는다는 것을 추론할 수 있다. 따라서 (C)가 정답이다.

어휘 quarterly adj. 분기별의 official n. 공무원

Paraphrasing
> nongovernmental organization 비정부기구 → not managed by government officials 정부 공무원들에 의해 경영되지 않는

163 문장 위치 찾기 문제

해석 [1], [2], [3], [4]로 표시된 위치 중, 다음 문장이 들어갈 곳으로 가장 적절한 것은?
"이는 일관성이 더 단단한 관계를 형성하는 데 도움이 되기 때문입니다."
(A) [1]
(B) [2]
(C) [3]
(D) [4]

해설 주어진 문장은 일관성과 관련된 내용 주변에 나올 것임을 예상할 수 있다. [4]의 앞 문장인 'We encourage weekly volunteering sessions with the same child.'에서 매주 같은 아이와 함께하는 자원봉사 세션을 권장한다고 했으므로, [4]에 주어진 문장이 들어가면 매주 같은 아이와 함께하는 자원봉사 세션을 권장하며, 이는 일관성이 더 단단한 관계를 형성하는 데 도움이 되기 때문이라는 자연스러운 문맥이 된다는 것을 알 수 있다. 따라서 (D)가 정답이다.

어휘 consistency n. 일관성, 한결같음 relationship n. 관계

164-167번은 다음 문자 메시지 대화문에 관한 문제입니다.

> **Beth Lawrence** [오후 1시 25분]
> 오늘 몇 시에 웨스트버러 회계 사무실에 갈 예정이죠, Chuck? ¹⁶⁴우리 회사가 그들을 위해 만든 인쇄 광고에 대해 그들이 어떻게 생각하는지 알고 싶어요.
>
> **Chuck Jancovik** [오후 1시 26분]
> 제가 원래는 2시에 그곳에 가기로 했는데 ¹⁶⁵그 회사의 CEO가 회의를 4시로 미뤘어요. 그가 오늘 이른 오후에 해외 전화 회의가 있어서, 그때까지 시간이 안 될 거예요.
>
> **Beth Lawrence** [오후 1시 27분]
> 알겠어요. 어떻게 되어 가는지 제게 알려주세요. 그나저나, 다음 주에 우리 건물 주차장이 폐쇄될 것이라는 소식 들으셨나요? 벽이 다시 칠해질 것 같아요. 다른 곳에 주차하는 데 제가 돈을 내야 한다는 뜻이라 조금 짜증 나네요.
>
> **Chuck Jancovik** [오후 1시 28분]
> 실은, ¹⁶⁶직원들이 Oakley가에 있는 유료 주차장을 무료로 이용할 수 있다는 내용의 경영진의 회람이 오늘 아침에 있었어요. 저희가 그저 인사과에서 임시 주차권을 신청하기만 하면 돼요.
>
> **Beth Lawrence** [오후 1시 29분]
> ¹⁶⁷제가 그걸 못 봤다니 믿을 수가 없네요. 지금 거기로 가고 있어요.
>
> **Chuck Jancovik** [오후 1시 32분]
> 좋은 생각이에요. ¹⁶⁷주차권 요청 절차는 꽤 간단해요. 그리고 제 것을 이번 주 안에 받을 수 있을 것이라고 저는 들었어요.

originally adv. 원래, 본래 **conference call** 전화 회의
pay lot 유료 주차장, 유료 부지 **temporary** adj. 임시의, 일시적인
process n. 절차, 과정 **receive** v. 받다, 수령하다

164 추론 문제

해석 글쓴이들은 어떤 유형의 회사에서 일하는 것 같은가?
(A) 출판사
(B) 회계 회사
(C) 법률 사무소
(D) 마케팅 대행사

해설 지문의 'I'm curious to find out what they think of the print advertisement our firm created for them.'에서 Ms. Lawrence는 우리 회사가 웨스트버러 회계 사무실을 위해 만든 인쇄 광고를 그들이 어떻게 생각하는지 알고 싶다고 했으므로, 메시지를 쓴 사람들은 마케팅을 대신 해주는 회사에서 일한다는 것을 추론할 수 있다. 따라서 (D)가 정답이다.

어휘 firm n. 회사

165 육하원칙 문제

해석 고객과의 미팅이 왜 미뤄졌는가?
(A) 사무실 건물이 일시적으로 폐쇄될 것이다.
(B) 해외 지점이 제시간에 문을 열지 않을 것이다.
(C) 비즈니스 회의가 계획된 것보다 늦게 시작될 것이다.

(D) 회사 임원이 시간이 안 될 것이다.

해설 지문의 'the CEO of that company pushed the meeting back to 4. He has an overseas conference call to make earlier this afternoon, so he won't be free until then.'에서 Mr. Jancovik은 그 회사(고객의 회사)의 CEO가 회의를 4시로 미뤘는데, 오후에 그가 전화 회의가 있어서 그때까지 시간이 안 될 것이라고 하였다. 따라서 (D)가 정답이다.

어휘 executive n. 임원, 간부

Paraphrasing
won't be free 시간이 안 될 것이다 → will not be available 시간이 안 될 것이다

166 의도 파악 문제

해설 오후 1시 29분에, Ms. Lawrence가 "I'm heading there now"라고 썼을 때, 그녀가 의도한 것은?
(A) 주차 위반 딱지 요금을 납부해야 한다.
(B) 회의에 참석할 것이다.
(C) 그녀가 알게 된 것을 적용할 것이다.
(D) 불만을 제기할 것이다.

해설 지문의 'there was a memo from management this morning saying that staff can use the pay lot on Oakley Street for free. We just need to apply for a temporary parking pass at the HR office.'에서 Mr. Jancovik이 Oakley가에 있는 유료 주차장을 직원들이 무료로 이용할 수 있다는 회람이 아침에 있었고, 인사과에서 임시 주차권을 신청하기만 하면 된다고 하자, Ms. Lawrence가 'I can't believe I missed that.'에서 회람을 못 본 것을 믿을 수 없다고 한 후, 'I'm heading there now'(지금 거기로 가고 있어요)라고 한 것을 통해, Mr. Jancovik이 알려준 대로 인사과로 가서 임시 주차권을 신청할 것임을 알 수 있다. 따라서 (C)가 정답이다.

어휘 parking ticket 주차 위반 딱지 apply v. 적용하다, 신청하다

167 추론 문제

해설 Mr. Jancovik에 대해 추론될 수 있는 것은?
(A) 오후 2시에 Ms. Lawrence와 만날 것이다.
(B) 온라인 광고를 전문으로 한다.
(C) 임시 주차권을 요청했다.
(D) 인사팀의 일원이다.

해설 지문의 'The process for requesting one is pretty simple. And I was told that I'd receive mine before the end of the week.'에서 요청 절차가 꽤 간단하다고 말하며, 자신의 것(임시 주차권)을 이번 주 안에 받을 수 있다고 들었다고 했으므로 그가 이미 임시 주차권을 요청했다는 것을 추론할 수 있다. 따라서 (C)가 정답이다.

어휘 specialize in ~을 전문으로 하다

168-171번은 다음 이메일에 관한 문제입니다.

수신: Sophia Bauer<s.bauer@myconnectbox.net>
발신: Justin Duval<justin@freeyostores.ca>

날짜: 7월 28일
제목: 회신: 문의

Ms. Bauer께,

가맹점을 여는 것에 대해 문의해 주셔서 감사합니다. 약 10년 전에 설립된 이래로, [168]Freeyo는 토론토에서 가장 인기 있는 냉동 요거트 체인점이 되었습니다. 저희는 현재 다른 지역들로 확장할 계획을 하고 있습니다. 귀하의 문의로 미루어 보면, 제 생각에 귀하는 위니펙에 계신 것 같습니다. 저희는 그곳에 가맹점을 여는 것에 매우 관심이 있습니다. [169]저희가 작년에 실시한 그 도시의 여건에 대한 분석은 우리 제품에 대한 소비자들 사이의 큰 수요를 보여주었습니다. 게다가, [170]저희는 Freeyo 분점에 안성맞춤일, 많은 유동 인구를 보유한 여러 곳들이 있다는 것을 알게 되었습니다.

저희의 선임 직원 중 한 명인 [171]Jessica Rodriguez가 가맹점을 내는 절차의 초기 단계를 담당하고 있습니다. 제가 귀하의 문의를 그녀에게 전달했으며, 그녀가 곧 귀하께 연락드려 회의 일정을 잡을 것입니다. [171]기밀 유지 서약에 서명하도록 요청받으실 예정이라는 점에 유념해 주시기를 바랍니다. 귀하가 그녀와 만날 때, 그녀가 그것을 확인해 줄 것입니다.

Justin Duval 드림, Freeyo

franchise n. 가맹점, 프랜차이즈   analysis n. 분석
condition n. 여건, 상황, 조건   foot traffic 유동 인구(수)
senior adj. 선임의, 연장자인   handle v. 담당하다, 다루다, 처리하다
stage n. 단계   shortly adv. 곧
confidentiality agreement 기밀 유지 서약
go over ~을 확인하다, 살펴보다

168 추론 문제

해설 Freeyo에 대해 암시되는 것은?
(A) 15년 이상 전에 설립되었다.
(B) 이제 토론토 지역으로 확장할 계획을 하고 있다.
(C) 다른 체인점과 제휴를 맺었다.
(D) 현재 한 도시에서만 지점들을 운영하고 있다.

해설 지문의 'Freeyo has become the most popular frozen yoghurt chain in Toronto. We are now planning to expand into other communities.'에서 Freeyo는 토론토에서 가장 인기 있는 냉동 요거트 체인점이며, 현재 다른 지역들로 확장할 계획 중에 있다고 했으므로 지금은 한 도시에서만 지점들을 운영하고 있다는 것을 추론할 수 있다. 따라서 (D)가 정답이다.

어휘 found v. 설립하다

169 육하원칙 문제

해설 Mr. Duval에 따르면, 작년에 무슨 일이 있었는가?
(A) 영업 컨설턴트가 고용되었다.
(B) 시장 상황에 대한 조사가 실시되었다.
(C) 신제품이 개발되었다.
(D) 지점의 실적에 대한 자료가 입수되었다.

해설 지문의 'An analysis of conditions in the city[Winnipeg] that we performed last year'에서 Freeyo가 작년에 위니펙의 여건 분석을 실시했다고 하였다. 따라서 (B)가 정답이다.

어휘 obtain v. 입수하다, 얻다

Paraphrasing

an analysis of conditions in the city 그 도시의 여건에 대한 분석
→ Research on market conditions 시장 상황에 대한 조사

170 동의어 찾기 문제

해석 1문단 여섯 번째 줄의 단어 "determined"는 의미상 -와 가장 가깝다.
(A) 알아냈다
(B) 확정했다
(C) 예측했다
(D) 영향을 주었다

해설 determined를 포함한 구절 'we determined that there are a number of sites with high foot traffic that would be perfect for a Freeyo branch'에서 determined는 '알게 되었다'라는 뜻으로 사용되었다. 따라서 (A)가 정답이다.

171 추론 문제

해석 Ms. Rodriguez에 대해 결론지을 수 있는 것은?
(A) 법적 분쟁에서 Freeyo를 대변했다.
(B) Ms. Bauer와 연락할 수 없었다.
(C) 계약 조건을 설명할 것이다.
(D) 가맹점에 투자했다.

해설 지문의 'Jessica Rodriguez, is handling the initial stages of the franchising process'와, 'Please note that you will be asked to sign a confidentiality agreement. She will go over it when you meet with her.'에서 Jessica Rodriguez가 가맹점을 내는 절차의 초기 단계를 담당하고 있고, 그녀가 기밀 유지 서약에 대해 확인해 줄 것이라고 했으므로 해당 계약에 관한 조건을 설명해 줄 것임을 추론할 수 있다. 따라서 (C)가 정답이다.

어휘 dispute n. 분쟁, 논쟁 term n. 조건, 기간, 용어

172-175번은 다음 기사에 관한 문제입니다.

시카고 (4월 10일)- **172오래전에 약속된 주거 단위와 상업 단위를 둘 다 포함할 Miller Yard 개발을 맡은 회사가 마침내 공사를 시작했다. — [1] —. 173-(D)시카고 강 남부 지류 옆에 위치한 그 건축물은** Roosevelt로에서 Monroe가까지 전체 도시 블록에 뻗어 있을 것이며, 건설하는 데 어림잡아 8천 5백만 달러가 들 것이다.

Marlene Carter 시장의 열정적인 프로젝트 중 하나인 173-(A)그것은 계획 단계에서 많은 난관에 직면했다. — [2] —. 173-(A)/(B)시의 세수를 통해 개발에 부분적으로 자금을 대기로 한 Carter 시장의 결정에 대한 비판과 강에 미치는 환경 영향에 대한 우려도 있었다. 그러나 프로젝트는 현재 진행 중이며 새로운 영화관과 도서관을 포함할 예정이다. 175건물에는 여러 개의 주요 소매점들도 있을 것이다. — [3] —.

공사는 이번 주에 시작되었고 내년 중반까지 계속될 예정이며, 7월 1일에 임시 오픈이 예정되어 있다. "이 프로젝트는 시카고에 있어서 중요한 진전이며, 도시의 그 지역을 재활성화할 뿐만 아니라 가격이 적당한 주거에 대한 시급한 수요를 다룬다는 측면에서 그러합니다."라고 Carter 시장은 말했다. "174우리는 이 개발에 포함된 주거

단위의 20퍼센트가 시세보다 상당히 저렴한 가격으로 주택이 필요한 사람들에게 제공되게 하는 규정을 포함시켰습니다. — [4] —. 게다가, Miller Yard는 수백 개의 일자리를 창출할 것이고, 이는 지역 경제를 강화할 것입니다."

long-promised adj. 오래전에 약속된 residential adj. 주거의
unit n. 단위, 1개 break ground 공사를 시작하다, 착공하다
branch n. 지류, 지점 structure n. 건축물, 구조물
hurdle n. 난관, 장애물 underway adj. 진행 중인
tentative adj. 임시의, 잠정적인
revitalize v. 재활성화하다, 새로운 활력을 불어넣다
address v. 다루다, 처리하다 remark v. 말하다; n. 발언
provision n. 규정, 대비, 공급

172 주제 찾기 문제

해석 기사는 주로 무엇에 대한 것인가?
(A) 시의 선거
(B) 정부 정책
(C) 다용도 건축물
(D) 기금 모금 행사

해설 지문의 'The company behind the long-promised Miller Yard development, which will include both residential and commercial units, has finally broken ground.'에서 주거 단위와 상업 단위를 둘 다 포함할 Miller Yard 개발을 맡은 회사가 마침내 공사를 시작했다고 한 후, 부지 개발에 대해 설명하고 있으므로 (C)가 정답이다.

어휘 municipal adj. (도)시의, 지방 자치의 multi-use adj. 다용도의

Paraphrasing

include both residential and commercial units 주거 단위와 상업 단위를 둘 다 포함하다 → A multi-use structure 다용도 건축물

173 Not/True 문제

해석 Miller Yard에 대해 언급되지 않은 것은?
(A) 계획 중에 어려움에 맞닥뜨렸다.
(B) 부분적으로 지방세로 자금을 조달한다.
(C) 대중교통 역과 연결될 것이다.
(D) 물가 옆에 위치할 것이다.

해설 지문의 'it faced many hurdles in the planning phase'에서 계획 단계에서 많은 난관에 직면했다고 했으므로 (A)는 지문의 내용과 일치한다. 'There was criticism of Mayor Carter's decision to partially fund the development through city tax revenues, as well as concern about the environmental impact on the river.'에서 시의 세수를 통해 개발에 부분적으로 자금을 대기로 한 시장의 결정에 비판이 있었고 강에 미치는 환경 영향에 대한 우려가 있었다고 했으므로 (B)는 지문의 내용과 일치한다. 'Located alongside the Chicago River's southern branch, the structure'에서 시카고 강 남부 지류 옆에 위치한 그 건축물이라고 했으므로 (D)는 지문의 내용과 일치한다. (C)는 지문에 언급되지 않은 내용이다. 따라서 (C)가 정답이다.

어휘 encounter v. 맞닥뜨리다, 부닥치다

Paraphrasing

faced many hurdles in the planning phase 계획 단계에서 많은 난관에 직면했다 → encountered difficulties during planning 계획 중에 어려움에 맞닥뜨렸다

city tax revenues 시의 세수 → local taxes 지방세

alongside the ~ River's southern branch 강의 남부 지류 옆에 → next to a water body 물가 옆에

174 육하원칙 문제

해석 Ms. Carter가 Miller Yard의 주거 단위에 대해 명시한 것은?
(A) 몇몇은 낮춘 가격에 구할 수 있을 것이다.
(B) 전체 공간의 20퍼센트를 차지할 것이다.
(C) 몇몇은 시에 의해 직접 관리될 것이다.
(D) 가구가 완비된 인테리어가 제공될 것이다.

해설 지문의 'We've included provisions for 20 percent of the residential units within this development to be offered to individuals in need of housing at significantly lower than market rates.'에서 개발에 포함된 주거 단위의 20퍼센트가 시세보다 상당히 저렴한 가격으로 주택이 필요한 사람들에게 제공하게 하는 규정을 포함시켰다고 했으므로 (A)가 정답이다.

어휘 take up 차지하다 furnished adj. 가구가 갖춰진

Paraphrasing

at significantly lower than market rates 시세보다 상당히 저렴한 가격에 → at reduced prices 낮춘 가격에

175 문장 위치 찾기 문제

해석 [1], [2], [3], [4]로 표시된 위치 중, 다음 문장이 들어갈 곳으로 가장 적절한 것은?

"예를 들어, 슈퍼마켓 체인점인 Wellmax는 이미 지점을 열 계획을 발표했다."

(A) [1]
(B) [2]
(C) [3]
(D) [4]

해설 주어진 문장은 지점을 열 예정인 슈퍼마켓과 관련된 내용 주변에 나와야 함을 알 수 있다. [3]의 앞 문장인 "There will be several major retail outlets in the building as well."에서 건물에는 몇몇 주요 소매점들도 있을 것이라고 했으므로, [3]에 주어진 문장이 들어가면 주요 소매점들도 있을 것이고, 그 예로 소매점인 Wellmax 슈퍼마켓 체인점은 이미 지점을 열 것이라고 발표했다는 자연스러운 문맥이 된다는 것을 알 수 있다. 따라서 (C)가 정답이다.

176-180번은 다음 이메일과 예약 확인서에 관한 문제입니다.

수신: Allen Sanders <a.sanders@spluravisions.uk>
발신: Carol Mason <c.mason@spluravisions.uk>
날짜: 4월 19일
제목: 요청

안녕하세요 Allen,

들으셨겠지만, [176]우리 생산팀 대표단이 베이징에서 디자인을 발표해 줄 것을 요청받았습니다. 제가 그곳에 가야 할 사람들의 예비 명단을 만들었습니다. [177]그 그룹을 위해 호텔과 항공편 둘 다 예약해 주세요. 회의는 5월 2일에 열리므로, 5월 1일에 도착하고 5월 3일에 떠나는 것을 제안하고 싶습니다. 2박 동안, [178]저는 대표단이 Bravo 인터내셔널 호텔에 머물면 좋을 것 같은데 우리가 그 호텔 체인의 로열티 프로그램에 기업 회원권을 보유하고 있기 때문입니다. [179]다음의 사람들이 잠정적으로 출장을 가기로 예정되어 있습니다:

- Benjamin Aiden
- Ken Izaki
- [179]Tyler Lowe
- Paulina Jansen
- Su-min Chung

예약하기 전에, 막판에 곤란한 상황이 없도록 각자에게 출장을 갈 수 있는지 다시 한번 확인해 주시기 바랍니다. [179]문제가 발생하면, 제게 알려주시면 대표단에 합류할 다른 누군가를 찾아보겠습니다.

예약을 처리해 주셔서 감사합니다.

Carol Mason 드림

delegation n. 대표(단), 위임 invite v. 요청하다, 초대하다
preliminary adj. 예비의 tentatively adv. 잠정적으로, 임시적으로
last-minute adj. 막판의, 막바지의 complication n. 곤란한 상황, 문제
arise v. 발생하다, 생기다 take care of ~을 처리하다

예약 확인서

예약 일자: 4월 22일 예약 번호: 5YUT32
회사명: Splura Visions 계정 번호: 233-9112-2345
총 청구 금액: 2,530파운드 [180-(A)]신용카드 번호: 300-994-XXX-XXX

항공편 요약

출발지	도착지	출발	항공편
런던	베이징	[180-(D)]4월 30일, 오전 10시	B323

예약 세부사항

[179]여행객 이름	티켓 번호	[180-(C)]좌석 번호	등급	[180-(B)]저녁 식사 선호
[180-(B)]Su-min Chung	440231	[180-(C)]5F	비즈니스	[180-(B)]닭고기
Benjamin Aiden	440232	[180-(C)]5E	비즈니스	해산물
[179/180-(B)]Sandra Morton	440233	[180-(C)]23B	이코노미	[180-(B)]닭고기
[180-(B)]Ken Izaki	440234	[180-(C)]25C	이코노미	[180-(B)]닭고기
Paulina Jansen	440245	[180-(C)]36B	이코노미	소고기

모든 예약은 환불이 불가합니다. 모든 예약 변경에 대해 50파운드의 서비스 요금이 부과될 것입니다.

preference n. 선호(도) charge v. 부과하다, 청구하다

176 동의어 찾기 문제

해설 이메일에서, 1문단 첫 번째 줄의 단어 "present"는 의미상 -와 가장 가깝다.
(A) 제공하다
(B) 지정하다

(C) 보여 주다
(D) 준비하다

해설 present를 포함한 구절 'a delegation from our production team has been invited to present some designs in Beijing'에서 present는 '발표하다'라는 뜻으로 사용되었다. 따라서 (C)가 정답이다.

177 목적 찾기 문제

해설 Ms. Mason은 왜 Mr. Sanders에게 이메일을 썼는가?
(A) 배송을 확정하기 위해
(B) 고객과의 약속을 잡기 위해
(C) 프로젝트에 대한 정보를 요청하기 위해
(D) 출장과 관련된 업무를 주기 위해

해설 이메일의 'Please book both the hotel and flights for the group.'에서 그 그룹(베이징에 출장을 갈 사람들)을 위해 호텔과 항공편 둘 다 예약해 달라고 하였다. 따라서 (D)가 정답이다.

어휘 assignment n. 업무, 과제

178 추론 문제

해설 Bravo 인터내셔널 호텔 체인에 대해 암시되는 것은?
(A) 이전에 Splura Visions사의 직원들을 응대한 적이 있다.
(B) 편리한 위치로 유명하다.
(C) 베이징에서 스파 브랜드를 출시했다.
(D) 일부 건물들을 보수할 계획이다.

해설 이메일의 'I would like the delegation to stay at the Bravo International Hotel as we have a corporate membership in that chain's loyalty programme'에서 Ms. Mason은 대표단이 Bravo 인터내셔널 호텔에 머물면 좋을 것 같은데 자신의 회사(Splura Visions)가 그 호텔 체인의 로열티 프로그램에 기업 회원권을 보유하고 있기 때문이라고 했으므로, Bravo 인터내셔널 호텔 체인이 Splura Visions사의 직원들을 이전에 응대한 적이 있음을 추론할 수 있다. 따라서 (A)가 정답이다.

어휘 host v. 응대하다, 주최하다   property n. 건물, 부동산

179 추론 문제 연계

해설 Ms. Mason에 대해 결론지을 수 있는 것은?
(A) 회의 전에 다양한 디자인을 평가할 것이다.
(B) 문의를 위해 항공사에 연락했다.
(C) 베이징으로 직원들과 동행하기로 결정했다.
(D) 대표단 구성을 변경해야 했다.

해설 Ms. Mason이 작성한 이메일을 먼저 확인한다.
단서 1 이메일의 'The following people are tentatively planned for the trip'과 사람들의 명단, 그리고 'If a problem does arise, let me know and I will find someone else to join the delegation.'에서 출장이 예정된 인원이 있고, 문제가 발생하는 경우 자신에게 알려주면 대표단에 합류할 다른 누군가를 찾아보겠다고 한 것을 알 수 있다. 그런데 최종 대표단 인원이 제시되지 않았으므로 예약 확인서에서 관련 내용을 확인한다.
단서 2 예약 확인서의 'Traveller Name', 'Sandra Morton'에서 기존 명단에 있던 Tyler Lowe가 없고 대신 Sandra Morton이 포함되어 있는 것을 알 수 있다.
두 단서를 종합할 때, 문제가 발생하여 Ms. Mason이 대표단 구성을 변경해야 했음을 추론할 수 있다. 따라서 (D)가 정답이다.

어휘 appraise v. 평가하다   accompany v. 동행하다, 동반되다
composition n. 구성

180 Not/True 문제

해설 예약 확인서에서 몇몇 여행객들에 대해 명시된 것은?
(A) 그들은 전부 서로 다른 신용카드로 결제했다.
(B) 몇몇은 동일한 식사 옵션을 요청했다.
(C) 그들은 전부 서로 가까이 앉지 않을 것이다.
(D) 몇몇은 다른 이들보다 더 늦은 날짜에 출발할 것이다.

해설 예약 확인서의 'Dinner Preference', 'Su-min Chung: Chicken', 'Sandra Morton: Chicken', 'Ken Izaki: Chicken'에서 저녁 식사 선호 항목에서 여러 사람들이 닭고기를 선택했음을 알 수 있다. 따라서 (B)가 정답이다. (A)는 'Credit Card Number: ~'에서 신용카드 번호가 하나만 제시되어 있으므로 하나의 신용카드로 결제했다는 것을 알 수 있다. 따라서 지문의 내용과 일치하지 않는다. (C)는 'Seat Number'에서 좌석 번호가 다양하게 예약되어 있으므로 지문의 내용과 일치하지 않는다. (D)는 'Departure, 30 April, 10 A.M.'에서 출발 날짜가 하나만 제시되어 있으므로 모두 함께 출발할 것임을 알 수 있다. 따라서 지문의 내용과 일치하지 않는다.

어휘 separate adj. 서로 다른, 별개의

181-185번은 다음 구인 광고와 이메일에 관한 문제입니다.

> ### VegLite에서의 취업 기회
>
> VegLite는 빠르게 성장하고 있는 채식주의 식당 체인점으로 로스앤젤레스 지역을 장악해 나갈 것입니다. 샌프란시스코에서 처음으로 설립되어, [181-(B)]VegLite는 워싱턴과 뉴욕 같은 주들에 지점들을 추가해 오고 있습니다. VegLite는 건강한 식물 기반의 식단의 가치를 믿습니다. 그러나, [181-(C)]저희는 저희 팀원들이 채식주의자가 될 것을 요구하지는 않습니다. 현재 저희가 채우고자 하는 자리들입니다:
>
> - [184]요리사: 최소 2년의 관련 경험이 요구됩니다. 채식주의 요리에 정통해야 합니다. [184]상근직만 가능합니다.
> - 식당 지배인: 최소 3년의 관련 경험과 경영학 학위가 요구됩니다. 상근직만 가능합니다.
> - [182]부지배인: 최소 5년의 관련 경험이 요구됩니다. 경영학 학위가 선호되지만 필수는 아닙니다. 상근직과 비상근직 모두 가능합니다.
> - 종업원: 최소 1년의 관련 경험이 요구됩니다. 훌륭한 고객 서비스 역량을 가지고 있어야 합니다. 상근직과 비상근직 모두 가능합니다.
>
> 오늘 www.veglite.com/careers에서 지원하세요. [183]관심 있는 일자리를 선택한 다음, 당신의 이력서와 이전 고용주로부터 받은 추천서를 업로드하세요.

take over ~을 장악하다   establish v. 설립하다, 확립하다
relevant adj. 관련된, 적절한   be familiar with ~에 정통하다, 친숙하다
degree n. 학위   business administration 경영학

수신: Martin Cunningham <m.cunningham@veglite.com>
발신: Fumiko Yamamoto <f.yamamoto@veglite.com>
제목: 시내 지점
날짜: 4월 29일

Mr. Cunningham께,

¹⁸⁴저는 시내 지점에 요리사 한 명을 개인적으로 추천하고자 합니다. Brandon Soloway는 보증된 요리사로 비슷한 업체들에서 일을 해왔습니다. 사실 저희는 몇 년 전에 같은 요리 학교를 함께 다녔습니다. 이 자리가 아직 채워지지 않은 유일한 자리이기 때문에 우리는 빠르게 직원을 배치할 필요가 있습니다.

다른 이야기인데, ¹⁸⁵저는 그 지점에 작은 야외 테라스를 추가하는 것이 좋은 아이디어일 것 같다고 생각합니다. 하지만, ¹⁸⁵저는 시의 인가 규정에 대해 잘 모릅니다. 이것에 대해 알고 계신 것이 있을까요?

Fumiko Yamamoto 드림

personally adv. 개인적으로 **certified** adj. 보증된
establishment n. 업체, 점포 **staff** v. 직원을 배치하다; n. 직원
patio n. (옥외) 테라스 **permit** n. 인가, 허가

181 Not/True 문제

해석 VegLite에 대해 언급된 것은?
(A) 로스앤젤레스의 한 주민에 의해 설립되었다.
(B) 여러 지역에 지점들을 열어 오고 있다.
(C) 모든 직원들에게 채식주의자가 될 것을 요구한다.
(D) 다른 나라로 확장할 것이다.

해설 구인 광고의 'VegLite has been adding branches in states like Washington and New York'에서 VegLite는 워싱턴과 뉴욕 같은 주들에 지점을 추가해 오고 있다고 하였다. 따라서 (B)가 정답이다. (A)와 (D)는 지문에 언급되지 않은 내용이다. (C)는 'we do not require our team members to be vegetarian'에서 팀원들이 채식주의자가 될 것을 요구하지는 않는다고 했으므로 지문의 내용과 일치하지 않는다.

어휘 **found** v. 설립하다 **resident** n. 주민, 거주자 **region** n. 지역

182 육하원칙 문제

해석 부지배인 자리의 요건은 무엇인가?
(A) 고기가 없는 요리가 준비되는 방법에 대한 익숙함
(B) 사업체를 관리하는 것과 관련된 대학 학위
(C) 비슷한 직무에서의 최소 5년의 경험
(D) 고객들에게 좋은 서비스를 제공하는 능력

해설 구인 광고의 'Assistant Managers: A minimum of five years of relevant experience is required.'에서 부지배인은 최소 5년의 관련 경험이 요구된다고 하였다. 따라서 (C)가 정답이다.

어휘 **familiarity** n. 익숙함 **meatless** adj. 고기가 없는
manage v. 관리하다

Paraphrasing

A minimum of five years of relevant experience 최소 5년의 관련 경험 → At least five years of experience in a similar role 비슷한 직무에서의 최소 5년의 경험

183 육하원칙 문제

해석 모든 지원자들이 지원서와 함께 포함해야 하는 것은 무엇인가?
(A) 교육 기록
(B) 전문가 추천서
(C) 자기소개서
(D) 정부 증명서

해설 구인 광고의 'Pick the position you are interested in, and then upload your résumé and a letter of recommendation from a former employer.'에서 관심 있는 일자리를 선택한 다음, 이력서와 이전 고용주로부터 받은 추천서를 업로드하라고 하였다. 따라서 (B)가 정답이다.

어휘 **reference** n. 추천서, 참조 **cover letter** 자기소개서
certificate n. 증명서

Paraphrasing

a letter of recommendation 추천서 → reference 추천서

184 추론 문제 연계

해석 Mr. Soloway에 대해 추론될 수 있는 것은?
(A) Mr. Cunningham의 이전 동료이다.
(B) 상근 직무에 추천되었다.
(C) 패스트푸드 식당을 관리했었다.
(D) 유럽 요리를 전문으로 한다.

해설 Mr. Soloway가 언급된 이메일을 먼저 확인한다.
단서 1 이메일의 'I would like to personally recommend a cook for the downtown location. Brandon Soloway is a certified chef who has worked in similar establishments.'에서 Ms. Yamamoto가 시내 지점을 위해 요리사 한 명을 개인적으로 추천하고자 한다며, Brandon Soloway가 비슷한 업체들에서 일한 보증된 요리사라고 하였다. 그런데 요리사 직무에 대해 제시되지 않았으므로 구인 광고에서 관련 내용을 확인한다.
단서 2 구인 광고의 'Cooks', 'Only full-time positions are available.'에서 요리사는 상근직만 가능하다고 하였다.
두 단서를 종합할 때, Mr. Soloway는 상근 직무에 추천되었음을 추론할 수 있다. 따라서 (B)가 정답이다.

185 육하원칙 문제

해석 Ms. Yamamoto는 왜 시의 규정에 대해 질문하는가?
(A) 다른 나라에서 온 직원들을 고용하는 것에 관심이 있다.
(B) 정부의 점검 일정을 잡을 수 없었다.
(C) 야외 좌석 구역을 만들고 싶어 한다.
(D) 식당을 하루 24시간 동안 영업하기를 바란다.

해설 이메일의 'I think it would be a great idea to add a small outdoor patio at that branch'에서 작은 야외 테라스를 설치하는 것이 좋은 아이디어일 것 같다고 생각한다고 한 후, 'I am not familiar with the city permit regulations'에서 시의 인가 규정에 대해 잘 모른다고 한 것을 통해, Ms. Yamamoto가 야외 좌석 구역을 만들고 싶어 한다는 것을 알 수 있다. 따라서 (C)가 정답이다.

어휘 **hire** v. 고용하다 **inspection** n. 점검

Paraphrasing

a small outdoor patio 작은 야외 테라스 → outdoor seating area 야외 좌석 구역

186-190번은 다음 주문 양식, 이메일, 그리고 온라인 후기에 관한 문제입니다.

Bright 전자제품사

| 홈 | 주문 | 제품 후기 | 연락처 |

주문 번호: LK8272   고객: Alita Adams
주문 일자: 5월 15일
[189]배달 주소: 456번지 Oak길, 포틀랜드, 오리건주, 97035

품목	수량	개당 가격	총가격
[189]Delta Tech 43인치 스마트 TV 모델 번호: 72736009	1	850.00달러	850.00달러
Westgate 무선 헤드셋 모델 번호: 94857847	2	120.00달러	240.00달러
	할인		-
	소계		1,090.00달러
	세금		144.00달러
	배송비		25.00달러
	합계		1,259.00달러

- [186-(A)]반품은 구매 일자로부터 최대 한 달까지 인정됩니다.
- 일반 배송은 영업일로 4일에서 7일 소요되고, [186-(B)]빠른 배송은 영업일로 2일에서 3일 소요됩니다. (추가 비용 15달러)
- [186-(C)]Bright 전자제품사의 모든 제품은 2년의 보증이 포함됩니다.
- [186-(D)]500달러 이상의 구매 건은 무료 설치를 받을 자격이 있습니다. 오래된 기기들은 재활용을 위해 매장으로 보내질 수 있습니다.

[188]Bright 회원 카드를 발급하여 모든 구매에 대해 10퍼센트 할인을 받으세요.

quantity n. 수량   shipping n. 배송   warranty n. 보증
qualify v. 자격이 있다   installation n. 설치

수신: Bright 전자제품사 <cs@brightelectronics.com>
발신: Alita Adams <a.adams@starmail.com>
제목: 주문 LK8272
날짜: 5월 16일

관계자분께:

온라인 주문을 넣은 이후, 저는 의도했던 한 개가 아닌 두 개의 헤드셋을 실수로 요청했다는 것을 알게 되었습니다. 그러나, 저는 귀사의 웹사이트에서 처리된 주문을 변경하는 방법을 못 찾겠습니다. [187]필요한 변경을 해주시고 헤드셋 한 개의 가격을 환불해 주시기 바랍니다. 이것을 처리하시는 동안, [188]제가 Bright 회원 카드(계정 번호: 4448373)를 가지고 있다는 점을 참고해 주셨으면 합니다. 이것은 제 주문에도 반영되어야 합니다.

저와 이야기하실 필요가 있다면, 저는 555-3938로 연락될 수 있습니다.

감사합니다.

Alita Adams

mistakenly adv. 실수로, 잘못하여   intend v. 의도하다
adjustment n. 변경, 조정   reflect v. 반영하다

Bright 전자제품사

| 홈 | 주문 | 제품 후기 | 연락처 |

[189]제품: Delta Tech 43인치 스마트 TV
고객: Alita Adams
6월 2일에 게시됨

[189]저는 Data Solutions라는 작은 회사의 소유주이고, 최근 사무실의 접수처 구역을 다시 꾸미기로 결정하였습니다. 이 세련되고 현대적인 TV가 배달되었을 때, 저는 그것이 제가 구매했던 가구들과 잘 어울릴 것임을 바로 알아차릴 수 있었습니다. 또한, 화면과 음향의 품질은 아주 훌륭합니다. [190]제가 지적할 필요를 느끼는 유일한 문제는 리모컨의 버튼이 너무 작아서, 채널을 변경하거나 설정 메뉴에 접근하는 것이 조금 어렵다는 것입니다. 실제로, 제가 제 와이파이에 접속하는 것에만 거의 15분이 걸렸습니다.

제품 평가: 4/5

redecorate v. 다시 꾸미다, 새로 장식하다   reception n. 접수처
sleek adj. 세련된, 매끄러운   furnishing n. 가구, 비품

186 Not/True 문제

해석   Bright 전자제품사에 대해 명시된 것은?
(A) 8주의 기간 동안 반품을 허용한다.
(B) 추가 요금으로 신속 배송을 제공한다.
(C) 품목에 1년 기간의 보증을 포함시킨다.
(D) 모든 고객들에게 설치 비용을 청구한다.

해설   주문 양식의 'express shipping takes two to three business days (additional $15 fee)'에서 빠른 배송은 영업일로 2일에서 3일 소요되고, 추가 비용이 15달러라고 했으므로 지문의 내용과 일치한다. 따라서 (B)가 정답이다. (A)는 'Returns are accepted up to one month from the date of purchase.'에서 반품은 구매 일자로부터 최대 한 달까지 인정된다고 했으므로 지문의 내용과 일치하지 않는다. (C)는 'All Bright Electronics products come with a two-year warranty.'에서 모든 Bright 전자제품사 제품은 2년의 보증이 포함된다고 했으므로 지문의 내용과 일치하지 않는다. (D)는 'Purchases over $500 qualify for free installation.'에서 500달러 이상의 구매 건은 무료 설치를 받을 자격이 있다고 했으므로 지문의 내용과 일치하지 않는다.

어휘   permit v. 허용하다, 허가하다   expedite v. 신속히 처리하다
charge v. (비용을) 청구하다

Paraphrasing

express shipping 빠른 배송 → expedited shipping 신속 배송

187 목적 찾기 문제

해석   이메일의 목적은 무엇인가?
(A) 온라인 서비스에 대한 접근을 요청하기 위해

(B) 제품 결함에 대해 불평하기 위해
(C) 주문에서 품목 한 개를 없애기 위해
(D) 지불 방법을 변경하기 위해

해설 이메일의 'Please make the necessary adjustment and refund the cost of one headset.'에서 필요한 변경을 해주고 헤드셋 한 개의 가격을 환불해 달라고 했으므로 (C)가 정답이다.

어휘 defect n. 결함 method n. 방법

188 추론 문제 연계

해설 Ms. Adams에 대해 암시되는 것은?
(A) 주문하는 동안 잘못된 제품을 골랐다.
(B) 장치가 설치되기 위해 비용을 지불해야 한다.
(C) 구매에 대한 할인을 받을 자격이 있다.
(D) 배달용으로 부정확한 주소를 제공했다.

해설 질문의 핵심 어구인 Ms. Adams가 작성한 이메일을 먼저 확인한다.
단서 1 이메일의 'please also note that I have a Bright Membership Card (account number: 4448373)'에서 Ms. Adams가 Bright 회원 카드를 가지고 있음을 알 수 있다. 그런데 회원 카드의 혜택에 대해 제시되지 않았으므로 주문 양식에서 회원 카드 관련 내용을 확인한다.
단서 2 주문 양식의 'Get a Bright Membership Card to receive 10 percent off on all purchases.'에서 Bright 회원 카드를 발급하여 모든 구매에 대해 10퍼센트 할인을 받으라고 하였다. 두 단서를 종합할 때, Ms. Adams는 구매에 대해 10퍼센트 할인을 받을 자격이 있음을 알 수 있다. 따라서 (C)가 정답이다.

어휘 eligible adj. ~할 자격이 있는 incorrect adj. 부정확한, 맞지 않는

189 추론 문제 연계

해설 Data Solutions에 대해 결론지을 수 있는 것은?
(A) 6월에 보수 공사를 위해 문을 닫을 예정이다.
(B) 소유권이 최근 변화를 겪었다.
(C) 재활용을 위해 TV 한 대를 Bright 전자제품사로 보냈다.
(D) 사무실이 포틀랜드시에 위치해 있다.

해설 질문의 핵심 어구인 Data Solutions가 언급된 온라인 후기를 먼저 확인한다.
단서 1 후기의 'Product: Delta Tech 43-inch Smart TV', 'I am the owner of a small company called Data Solutions, and I recently decided to redecorate the reception area of my office. When this sleek, modern TV was delivered'에서 회사(Data Solutions)의 접수처 구역을 다시 꾸미기 위해 Delta Tech 43인치 스마트 TV를 주문했고 사무실로 배달되었다고 하였다. 배달 정보에 관한 추가적인 내용을 주문 양식에서 확인한다.
단서 2 주문 양식의 'Delivery Address: 456 Oak Lane, Portland OR, 97035', 'Delta Tech 43-inch Smart TV'에서 스마트 TV가 배달된 주소가 456번지 Oak길, 포틀랜드, 오리건주, 97035라고 하였다. 두 단서를 종합할 때, TV가 배달된 주소인 Data Solutions의 사무실이 포틀랜드시에 위치해 있음을 추론할 수 있다. 따라서 (D)가 정답이다.

어휘 ownership n. 소유(권) undergo v. 겪다

190 육하원칙 문제

해설 온라인 후기에 따르면, Delta Tech 스마트 TV의 결점은 무엇인가?
(A) 부속품이 사용하기 어렵다.
(B) 영상 품질이 부적절하다.
(C) 메뉴가 이해하기 어렵다.
(D) 다른 기기들과 호환이 되지 않는다.

해설 온라인 후기의 'The only issue I feel the need to point out is that the remote-control buttons are too small, so it is kind of hard to change the channels or access the settings menus.'에서 Ms. Adams가 지적할 필요를 느끼는 유일한 문제는 리모컨의 버튼이 너무 작아서 채널을 변경하거나 설정 메뉴에 접근하는 것이 조금 어려운 것이라고 하였다. 따라서 (A)가 정답이다.

어휘 drawback n. 결점, 문제점 accessory n. 부속품, 부대용품
inadequate adj. 부적절한
incompatible adj. 호환이 되지 않는, 호환성이 없는

191-195번은 다음 웹페이지, 목록, 그리고 이메일에 관한 문제입니다.

191-(C) 50년 이상, Desmond 부동산은 시애틀의 소규모 업체 소유주들이 그들의 사업을 위한 완벽한 장소를 찾을 수 있도록 도왔습니다. 우리의 중개인들은 이 도시에 대해 매우 아는 것이 많고 우리 고객들이 그들이 지불할 수 있는 금액으로 그들에게 필요한 것을 반드시 찾게 해준다는 평판을 가지고 있습니다.

우리의 많은 경쟁업체들과는 달리, 우리는 건물 소유주가 아닌 세입자들을 우리의 고객으로 간주합니다. 이것은 우리 중개인들이 제공하는 추가 서비스에 반영되어 있습니다. 192일단 여러분이 사양에 맞는 공간을 발견하시면, 중개인은 소유주와 여러분의 중개자 역할을 하여 필요로 하는 임대 계약의 모든 변경 사항을 요청할 것입니다.

시애틀 북부의 건물들은 Peter Walker에 의해 처리되고, 193시애틀 중부의 것들은 Judith Harris에 의해 관리됩니다. 모든 다른 지역들은 William Lee와 Deanna Lewis가 이끌 것입니다.

real estate 부동산 enterprise n. 사업, 기업
reputation n. 평판, 명성 knowledgeable adj. 아는 것이 많은
competitor n. 경쟁업체, 경쟁자 tenant n. 세입자, 임차인
property n. 건물, 부동산 specification n. 사양, 명세 (사항)
go-between n. 중개자 lease n. 임대 agreement n. 계약, 합의
handle v. 처리하다 district n. 지역, 구역

Desmond 부동산
이용 가능한 건물 목록

위치	이용 가능일	크기	가격
101호, 234번지 Bailey가 (시애틀 북부)	7월 1일	220 제곱미터	월 1,800달러
4736번지 Center가 (시애틀 동부)	6월 1일	410 제곱미터	월 2,400달러

¹⁹³202호, 324번지 Pine가 (시애틀 중부)	8월 1일	260 제곱미터	월 1,950달러
3445번지 Harborview가 (시애틀 서부)	7월 1일	520 제곱미터	월 2,900달러

¹⁹⁵구경은 평일 오전 9시부터 오후 7시까지, 그리고 주말 오전 9시부터 정오까지 일정을 잡으실 수 있습니다.

availability n. 이용할 수 있음 weekday n. 평일 weekend n. 주말

수신: Desmond 부동산 <information@desmondrealestate.com>
발신: Liam Morris <l.morris@seattleflowers.com>
제목: 문의
날짜: 5월 17일

관계자분께,

¹⁹⁴제가 현재 꽃 가게를 운영하고 있는 건물이 최근 매각되었고, 새로운 소유주는 그 공간을 자기 소유의 사업에 사용할 계획입니다. 그래서 저는 7월 1일까지 새로운 장소를 찾아야 합니다. 저는 최근 귀사에 대한 광고를 보게 되어, 서비스를 이용해 보기로 결정했습니다.

이용할 수 있는 건물들의 목록을 살펴본 결과, 제 기한에 맞는 것이 두 곳 있다는 점을 확인했습니다. ¹⁹⁵이번 주 일요일에 그것들 각각을 구경할 시간을 잡을 수 있을까요? 제가 가게에서 너무 바빠서 다른 날은 시간을 낼 수 없습니다. 감사합니다.

Liam Morris 드림
시애틀 꽃 가게

inquiry n. 문의, 질문 operate v. 운영하다, 작동하다

191 Not/True 문제

해석 Desmond 부동산에 대해 사실인 것은?
(A) 12명이 넘는 부동산 중개인을 고용하고 있다.
(B) 다양한 도시에서 서비스를 제공한다.
(C) 주로 상업적 공간에 집중한다.
(D) 현지 주민들에게 할인된 요금을 제공한다.

해설 웹페이지의 'Desmond Real Estate has helped small business owners in Seattle find the perfect locations for their enterprises'에서 Desmond 부동산은 시애틀의 소규모 업체 소유주들이 그들의 사업을 위한 완벽한 장소를 찾을 수 있도록 도왔다고 한 것을 통해, Desmond 부동산이 상업적 공간에 집중한다는 것을 알 수 있다. 따라서 (C)가 정답이다.

어휘 dozen adj. 12의 primarily adv. 주로
commercial adj. 상업적인, 통상의

192 육하원칙 문제

해석 웹페이지에 따르면, 중개인은 고객을 위해 무엇을 할 것인가?
(A) 소유주의 재무 이력을 확인한다.
(B) 건물의 점검을 실시한다.
(C) 임대 요금의 비교를 제공한다.
(D) 계약의 조건을 협상한다.

해설 웹페이지의 'Once you have found a space that meets your specifications, the agent will act as your go-between with the owner to request any changes to the lease agreement that you require.'에서 사양에 맞는 공간을 발견하면, 중개인이 소유주와의 중개자 역할을 하여 고객이 필요로 하는 임대 계약의 모든 변경 사항을 요청할 것이라고 하였다. 따라서 (D)가 정답이다.

어휘 comparison n. 비교 negotiate v. 협상하다

Paraphrasing

request any changes to the lease agreement 임대 계약의 모든 변경 사항을 요청하다 → Negotiate the terms of a contract 계약의 조건을 협상하다

193 육하원칙 문제 연계

해석 Pine가에 있는 건물을 임대하는 것은 누가 담당하는가?
(A) Peter Walker
(B) Judith Harris
(C) William Lee
(D) Deanna Lewis

해설 질문의 핵심 어구인 Pine Street가 등장한 목록을 먼저 확인한다.
단서 1 목록의 'Unit 202, 324 Pine Street (Central Seattle)'에서 Pine가가 시애틀 중부에 있음을 알 수 있다. 그런데 시애틀 중부를 담당하고 있는 사람에 대해 제시되지 않았으므로 웹페이지에서 관련 내용을 확인한다.
단서 2 웹페이지의 'Properties ~ while those in Central Seattle are managed by Judith Harris.'에서 시애틀 중부의 건물들은 Judith Harris에 의해 관리된다고 하였다.
두 단서를 종합할 때, Judith Harris가 Pine가에 있는 건물을 임대하는 것을 담당한다는 점을 알 수 있다. 따라서 (B)가 정답이다.

194 추론 문제

해석 Mr. Morris에 대해 암시되는 것은?
(A) 시애틀에 있는 건물을 구매하려고 계획하고 있다.
(B) 그의 업체를 이전하도록 강요받았다.
(C) 그의 꽃 가게의 두 번째 지점을 열 것이다.
(D) 이전에 Desmond 부동산의 서비스를 이용한 적이 있다.

해설 이메일의 'The building in which I[Mr. Morris] currently operate my flower shop was recently sold, and the new owner plans to use the space for her own business. So I need to find a new location by July 1.'에서 Mr. Morris가 현재 꽃 가게를 운영하고 있는 건물이 최근 매각되었고, 새로운 소유주가 그 공간을 자기 소유의 사업에 사용할 계획이라 7월 1일까지 새로운 장소를 찾아야 한다고 하였으므로 그의 업체(꽃 가게)를 이전하도록 강요받았음을 추론할 수 있다. 따라서 (B)가 정답이다.

어휘 force v. 강요하다, 억지로 하다 relocate v. 이전하다

195 추론 문제 연계

해석 Mr. Morris가 시간을 잡고 싶어 하는 구경에 대해 결론지을 수 있는 것은?

(A) 완료하는 데 하루보다 더 걸릴 것이다.
(B) 7월 초에 일어나도록 예정될 것이다.
(C) 같은 지역의 건물들을 포함할 것이다.
(D) 오전에 실시되어야 할 것이다.

해설 질문의 핵심 어구인 Mr. Morris가 작성한 이메일을 먼저 확인한다.

단서 1 이메일의 'Could I arrange viewings of each of them this Sunday? I am not available on any other day because I am too busy at my shop.'에서 Mr. Morris는 이번 주 일요일에 그 건물들 각각을 구경할 시간을 잡을 수 있을지 물으며, 자신이 너무 바빠서 다른 날은 시간을 낼 수 없다고 하였다. 그런데 주말에 구경이 가능한 시간에 대해 제시되지 않았으므로 목록에서 관련 내용을 확인한다.

단서 2 목록의 'Viewings can be scheduled on weekdays from 9 A.M. to 7 P.M. and on weekends from 9 A.M. to noon.'에서 구경은 평일 오전 9시부터 오후 7시까지, 그리고 주말 오전 9시부터 정오까지 일정을 잡을 수 있다고 하였다.

두 단서를 종합할 때, Mr. Morris는 오전에 구경하도록 시간을 잡아야 할 것임을 추론할 수 있다. 따라서 (D)가 정답이다.

어휘 occur v. 일어나다, 발생하다 involve v. 포함하다, 수반하다

Paraphrasing

from 9 A.M. to noon 오전 9시부터 정오까지 → in the morning 오전에

196-200번은 다음 전단지, 이메일, 그리고 일정에 관한 문제입니다.

^{196/200}Dearborn 마을 축제
^{196/200}8월 4일, 토요일 - 8월 5일, 일요일
오전 9시부터 오후 11시 30분까지
무료 입장

Dearborn 마을 축제가 세 번째 해를 맞이했고, 저희는 확장했습니다. 축제 행사는 Pollock가와 Indiana가가 교차하는 Dearborn 거리에서 열릴 것입니다. 도로는 일반 차량 운행이 금지될 것입니다. 공예품 천막을 방문하고 현지 노점에서 서로 다른 수백 가지의 음식 선택지를 즐겨보세요. Pollock가 인근의 주 무대에서는 슈퍼스타 그룹인 The Callers, 찬사를 받고 있는 바이올리니스트인 Jessica Diaz, 가수인 Justin Woo, 그리고 ²⁰⁰재즈 사중주단인 Midnight Clue와 그 밖의 다른 사람들을 포함하여 다양한 음악 게스트들이 출연할 예정입니다. 우리는 아직 자원봉사자를 찾고 있습니다. 도움을 주실 수 있으면 brianna@dearbornblockparty.com으로 연락해 주세요.

block party 마을 축제, 블록 파티 entry n. 입장, 등장
festivity n. 축제 행사 intersect v. 교차하다, 가로지르다
traffic n. (차량) 운행, 교통량 craft n. 공예품 vendor n. 노점, 행상
acclaimed adj. 찬사를 받고 있는 quartet n. 사중주단, 사중창단

수신: Stanis Hemsworth <stanis.hemsworth@dearbornblockparty.com>
발신: Carissa Walder <c.walder@upstartmusicagency.com>
날짜: 7월 19일
제목: Justin Woo

Mr. Hemsworth께,

제 고객인 Justin Woo에게 겹치는 일정이 있다는 점을 알려드리고자 합니다. 안타깝게도, 그는 8월 4일 행사에서 공연할 수 없을 것입니다. 토요일에는 그에게 이미 다른 장소에서의 공연 일정이 있어서, 저는 마을 축제에서의 그의 무대를 다음 날로 미루고 싶습니다.

¹⁹⁸이 불편에 대해 보상하기 위해, 저는 저의 떠오르는 스타 중 한 명이 특별 게스트로서 Justin과 함께 공연하도록 할 것입니다. 그러나, 이 공연을 위한 충분한 시간을 확보하기 위해 추가 30분을 따로 떼어 두셔야 할 것입니다.

Mr. Woo는 음향 점검을 위한 시간이 없을 것이기에, 반드시 모든 것이 그의 요구에 맞게 설정되도록 해주시기를 바랍니다. 원하신다면, 저는 Justin이 그 후에 몇 장의 사진을 위해 자세를 취하게 할 수도 있습니다. ¹⁹⁷이와 관련하여, 행사를 보도할 뉴스 기관이 있는지를 저에게 알려주실 수 있으신가요?

Carissa Walder 드림
Upstart Music 대행사

make up for ~에 대해 보상하다 inconvenience n. 불편
aspiring adj. 상승하는, 높이 솟은 set aside 따로 떼어 두다, 확보하다
requirement n. 요구 cover v. 보도하다, 다루다

Dearborn 마을 축제

8월 5일, 일요일
Pollock 무대

오전 9시 30분 - 오전 10시 30분	지역 강사 Patrick Yellen이 이끄는 에어로빅 강좌
오전 11시 - 오후 12시 30분	다음 식당 요리사들에 의한 요리 시연: The Light Duck, Pizzeria Quatro, Loop Dumplings, 그리고 The Taco Bowl.
오후 2시 - 오후 3시 30분	¹⁹⁹The River North 극단에 의해 제공되는 아이들을 위한 오락
오후 4시 - 오후 5시	현지 주민들이 노래하고, 춤을 추고, 낭송 등을 할 수 있는 마이크 개방 시간
오후 6시 - 오후 7시	Jessica Diaz
오후 8시 - 오후 9시 30분	¹⁹⁸Justin Woo(특별 게스트 Celeste Perry와 함께)
²⁰⁰오후 10시 - 폐막	²⁰⁰Midnight Clue

최신 정보를 받기 위해 소셜미디어에서 Dearborn 마을 축제를 팔로우하세요.

instructor n. 강사 demonstration n. 시연

196 육하원칙 문제

해석 전단지에는 무슨 정보가 포함되어 있는가?
(A) 자원봉사자의 수
(B) 행사의 기간
(C) 주차 가능 여부
(D) 음식 노점의 이름

해설 전단지의 'Saturday, August 4 - Sunday, August 5'에서 행사의 기간이 8월 4일 토요일에서 8월 5일 일요일까지임을 알 수 있다. 따

라서 (B)가 정답이다.

어휘 duration n. 기간, 지속

197 육하원칙 문제

해석 Ms. Walder는 무엇에 대해 질문했는가?
(A) 행사가 언론의 보도를 받을 것인지
(B) 예행연습 공간을 어디에서 예약할 수 있는지
(C) 일부 임대 장비의 비용이 얼마가 드는지
(D) 음향 점검은 언제 시작할 수 있는지

해설 이메일의 'could you let me know if any news organizations will be covering the event?'에서 행사를 보도할 뉴스 기관이 있는지를 알려줄 수 있는지 묻고 있으므로 (A)가 정답이다.

어휘 coverage n. 보도   rehearsal n. 예행연습, 리허설
commence v. 시작하다

198 추론 문제 연계

해석 Ms. Walder에 대해 암시되는 것은?
(A) 잘 알려진 사진사의 조수이다.
(B) 음악 행사를 위한 예약 책임자이다.
(C) 이틀 모두 마을 축제에 참석할 것이다.
(D) 그녀의 대행사에서 Celeste Perry를 대리한다.

해설 질문의 핵심 어구인 Ms. Walder가 작성한 이메일을 먼저 확인한다.
단서 1 이메일의 'To make up for the inconvenience, I will have one of my aspiring stars perform with Justin as a special guest.'에서 불편을 보상하기 위해 Ms. Walder는 그녀의 떠오르는 스타 중 한 명이 특별 게스트로서 Justin과 함께 공연하게 할 것이라고 하였다. 그런데 특별 게스트에 대해 제시되지 않았으므로 일정에서 관련 내용을 확인한다.
단서 2 일정의 'Justin Woo (with special guest Celeste Perry)'에서 특별 게스트가 Celeste Perry임을 알 수 있다.
두 단서를 종합할 때, Ms. Walder는 그녀의 대행사에서 Celeste Perry를 대리하고 있음을 추론할 수 있다. 따라서 (D)가 정답이다.

어휘 assistant n. 조수, 보조원   coordinator n. 책임자, 조정자
represent v. 대리하다, 대변하다

199 육하원칙 문제

해석 일정에 따르면, 무슨 유형의 행사가 어린이들을 위해 특별히 준비되었는가?
(A) 운동 강좌
(B) 요리 시연
(C) 연극 공연
(D) 마이크 개방 시간

해설 일정의 'Entertainment for kids provided by The River North Theater Group'에서 오후 2시부터 오후 3시 30분까지 The River North 극단에 의해 제공되는 아이들을 위한 오락이 예정되어 있음을 알 수 있다. 따라서 (C)가 정답이다.

200 Not/True 문제 연계

해석 재즈 그룹에 대해 명시된 것은?
(A) 이틀 간의 행사를 마무리할 것이다.
(B) 다른 음악가의 노래를 연주할 것이다.
(C) Justin Woo와 함께 순회공연 중이다.
(D) 녹음 계약을 체결했다.

해설 질문의 핵심 어구인 jazz가 등장한 전단지를 먼저 확인한다.
단서 1 전단지의 'Dearborn Block Party', Saturday, August 4 - Sunday, August 5', 'will host a variety of musical guests including ~ and the jazz quartet Midnight Clue'에서 이틀간 진행되는 Dearborn 마을 축제는 재즈 사중주단인 Midnight Clue를 포함한 다양한 음악 게스트들이 출연할 것이라고 하였다. 그런데 Midnight Clue에 대해 제시되지 않았으므로 일정에서 관련 내용을 확인한다.
단서 2 일정의 '10:00 P.M. - closing : Midnight Clue'에서 오후 10시부터 폐막까지 Midnight Clue의 공연이 있을 예정임을 알 수 있다.
두 단서를 종합할 때, Midnight Clue라는 이름의 재즈 그룹이 이틀 간의 행사를 마무리할 것임을 알 수 있다. 따라서 (A)가 정답이다.

어휘 on tour 순회공연 중인   recording n. 녹음, 녹화   contract n. 계약

MEMO

MEMO